What Do We Know about Civil Wars?

What Do We Know about Civil Wars?

Edited by T. David Mason and
Sara McLaughlin Mitchell

ROWMAN & LITTLEFIELD
Lanham • Boulder • New York • London

Published by Rowman & Littlefield
A wholly owned subsidiary of The Rowman & Littlefield Publishing Group, Inc.
4501 Forbes Boulevard, Suite 200, Lanham, Maryland 20706
www.rowman.com

Unit A, Whitacre Mews, 26-34 Stannary Street, London SE11 4AB, United Kingdom

Copyright © 2016 by Rowman & Littlefield

British Library Cataloguing in Publication Information Available

Library of Congress Cataloging-in-Publication Data Available
ISBN 978-1-4422-4224-1 (cloth : alk. paper)
ISBN 978-1-4422-4225-8 (pbk. : alk. paper)
ISBN 978-1-4422-4226-5 (electronic)

™
∞ The paper used in this publication meets the minimum requirements of American National Standard for Information Sciences—Permanence of Paper for Printed Library Materials, ANSI/NISO Z39.48-1992.

Printed in the United States of America

Contents

List of Figures   vii

Acknowledgments   ix

List of Acronyms   xi

What Do We Know about Civil Wars?: Introduction and Overview   1
   T. David Mason, Sara McLaughlin Mitchell, and Alyssa K. Prorok

PART I: FACTORS THAT BRING ABOUT CIVIL WAR

1   Introduction—Patterns of Armed Conflict since 1945   15
   Nils Petter Gleditsch, Erik Melander, and Henrik Urdal

2   Antecedents of Civil War Onset: Greed, Grievance, and
   State Repression   33
   Joseph K. Young

3   Identity Issues and Civil War: Ethnic and Religious Divisions   43
   Lee J. M. Seymour and Kathleen Gallagher Cunningham

4   State Capacity, Regime Type, and Civil War   59
   Karl DeRouen Jr. and David Sobek

5   Transnational Dimensions of Civil Wars: Clustering, Contagion,
   and Connectedness   75
   Erika Forsberg

PART II: FACTORS THAT END CIVIL WARS AND PROMOTE PEACE

6 Third Party Intervention and the Duration and Outcomes of
Civil Wars   93
Christopher Linebarger and Andrew Enterline

7 Ripe for Resolution: Third Party Mediation and Negotiating
Peace Agreements   109
Jacob D. Kathman and Megan Shannon

8 Negotiated Peace: Power Sharing in Peace Agreements   121
Caroline A. Hartzell

9 Breaking the Conflict Trap: The Impact of Peacekeeping on
Violence and Democratization in the Post-Conflict Context   139
Paul F. Diehl

10 The Legacies of Civil War: Health, Education, and
Economic Development   157
Clayton L. Thyne

PART III: EMERGING TRENDS IN CIVIL WAR RESEARCH

11 Transitional Justice: Prospects for Postwar Peace and Human Rights   179
Jacqueline H. R. DeMeritt

12 Gender and Civil Wars   197
Erik Melander

13 Exploring the Resource–Civil War Nexus   215
Benjamin Smith

14 Environment and Conflict   231
Cullen Hendrix, Scott Gates, and Halvard Buhaug

15 Trends in Civil War Data: Geography, Organizations, and Events   247
David E. Cunningham, Kristian Skrede Gleditsch, and Idean Salehyan

Notes   261

References   271

Index   327

About the Contributors   347

Figures

Figure 1.1.   The Number of Ongoing Armed Conflicts by Type and Year,
              1945–2014   17

Figure 1.2.   Share of Countries with Intrastate Armed Conflict on Their
              Territory, 1946–2014   18

Figure 1.3.   Share of Countries Participating in Armed Conflict,
              1946–2014   19

Figure 1.4.   The Number of Annual Battle Deaths, 1946–2014   21

Figure 1.5.   Conflict Zones, 2006–2008   24

Figure 1.6.   Battle Deaths per 1,000 Population by Region, 1946–2014   25

Figure 1.7.   Global Trends of Religious Dimensions in Wars, 1975–2013   26

Figure 1.8.   Armed Conflicts by Incompatibility, 1946–2014   27

Figure 1.9.   Civil Conflict Onset and Terminations (Five-Year Averages),
              1950–2014   28

Figure 1.10. Deaths in Intrastate Conflict, Non-State Conflict, and
              One-Sided Violence, 1989–2014   30

Figure 1.11. Average Magnitude of Genocide in Civil Conflict,
              1955–2014   31

Figure 5.1.   Clustering   77

Figure 5.2.   Contagion   78

Figure 5.3.   Connectedness   83

Figure 10.1.   Civil Wars and Health   159

Figure 10.2.   Civil Wars and Education   164

Figure 10.3.   Civil Wars and Economies   168

Figure 12.1.   Theoretical Scheme   198

TABLE

Table 8.1.   Trends in the Use of Power Sharing in Civil War Termination,
              1945–2006   130

Acknowledgments

As noted by the Uppsala Conflict Data Program (UCDP), over one hundred thousand people were killed in armed conflicts in 2014, especially in civil wars in Syria and Iraq. We have not seen death rates from civil wars reach this level since the Rwandan genocide, although civil wars have been an ongoing feature of global politics for the past few centuries. As scholars who teach classes on civil wars, we want to provide our students with a comprehensive review of what we know about the causes and consequences of civil wars. We are grateful to the scholars who have contributed chapters to this book, as their insightful reviews help students understand what prior research teaches us about civil wars and identify new paths for future research.

The Department of Political Science Benjamin F. Shambaugh Memorial Fund at the University of Iowa provided generous financial support to host a conference in September 2014 where contributors presented drafts of their chapters. We are grateful to our co-organizer for the conference, Alyssa Prorok, who provided excellent feedback to the participants and took notes on all discussions. We also acknowledge the support provided by our conference assistants, Ruoxi Du, Dongkyu Kim, Sojeong Lee, Samantha Lange, and Desmond Wallace. Several of our colleagues also served as discussants at the conference, including Kelly Kadera, Brian Lai, Tyler Pack, Jason Renn, Bryce Reeder, Jessie Rumsey, Kieun Sung, Ashly Townsen, and John Vasquez. Will Moore, Pat Regan, and Reed Wood presented chapters for authors who were unable to attend and also provided useful feedback on several chapters as discussants. Shuai Jin provided copyediting assistance for the final manuscript. We are also thankful to the Castleberry Peace Institute at the University of North Texas for providing financial support for the project.

We thank John Vasquez for bringing us together to coedit this book. We were both inspired by his edited volumes, *What Do We Know About War*, and we thought that civil war scholars would benefit from a similar compilation of what we know about civil wars. We are also grateful to Susan McEachern at Rowman & Littlefield for her support of this book manuscript and guidance throughout the publication process. We hope that scholars and students will find the volume useful for teaching and conducting research on civil wars.

Acronyms

ACD	Armed Conflict Dataset
AFDL	Alliance of Democratic Forces for the Liberation of Congo-Zaire
BE	best estimates
CAVR	Commission for Reception, Truth, and Reconciliation
CIM	contract-intensive money
CINC	Composite Index of National Capability
CIRI	Cingranelli-Richards Physical Integrity Index
COW	Correlates of War
CTF	Commission for Truth and Friendship
CWM	Civil War Mediation
DALE	disability-adjusted life expectancy
DALY	disability-adjusted life year
DCJ	During-Conflict Justice
DDR	demobilization, disarmament, and reintegration
DES	demographic-environmental stress
DRC	Democratic Republic of Congo
ELF	ethno-linguistic fractionalization
EPR	Ethnic Power Relations
FARC	Fuerzas Armadas Revolucionarias de Colombia
FMLN	Farabundo Martí National Liberation Front
FRELIMO	Mozambique Liberation Front
FSA	Free Syrian Army
GAM	Free Aceh Movement (*Gerakan Aceh Merdeka*)
GDP	gross domestic product
GED	Geo-referenced Events Dataset
GED	Geocoded Event Data

GG   good governance
GoSS   Government of South Sudan
HE   high estimates
ICOW   Issues Correlates of War
ICT   international criminal tribunal
ICTR   International Criminal Tribunal for Rwanda
ICTY   International Criminal Tribunal for the Former Yugoslavia
IGO   intergovernmental organization
IPCC   Intergovernmental Panel on Climate Change
IS   Islamic State
ISIL   Islamic State of Iraq and the Levant
IV   instrumental variable
KLA   Kosovo Liberation Army
KNUFNS   Kampuchean National United Front for National Salvation
LE   low estimates
LRA   Lord's Resistance Army
MAR   Minorities at Risk
MAUP   Modifiable Areal Unit Problem
MDG   Millennium Development Goal
MILC   Managing Intrastate Low-Intensity Conflict
MNLF   Moro National Liberation Front
NSA   Non-State Actor
PCJ   Post-Conflict Justice
PREG   politically relevant ethnic groups
PRIO   Peace Research Institute Oslo
PTS   Political Terror Scale
R2P   Responsibility to Protect
RCD   Congolese Rally for Democracy
RENAMO   Mozambican National Resistance
RPC   relative political capacity
SCAD   Social Conflict in Africa Database
SDO   social dominance orientation
TJ   transitional justice
TRC   truth and reconciliation commission
UCDP   Uppsala Conflict Data Program
UNFICYP   United Nations Peacekeeping Force in Cyprus
UNSF   UN Security Force
UNTAC   United Nations Transitional Authority in Cambodia
URNG   Guatemalan National Revolutionary Unity

What Do We Know about Civil Wars?

Introduction and Overview

T. David Mason, Sara McLaughlin Mitchell, and Alyssa K. Prorok

It is now widely recognized that since the end of World War II, civil wars (wars *within* nations) have replaced interstate wars (wars *between* nations) as the most frequent and deadly form of armed conflict in the world. This simple observation highlights several other dramatic shifts in the patterns of armed conflict in the world since 1945. First, armed conflict in the post–World War II era has been predominantly a matter of civil war: there have been four to five times as many civil wars as interstate wars during this time period (see, for instance, Sarkees and Wayman 2010; Gleditsch et al. 2002: 620; chapter 1 in this volume). Second, since 1945, armed conflict has been largely a Third World phenomenon: the predominant form and location of wars has shifted from interstate wars among the major powers of Europe, North America, China, and Japan (prior to 1945) to civil wars in the Third World nations of Asia, Africa, and Latin America (Mason 2004: 3–4). Third, for a subset of nations in the world, civil war has become a chronic condition: almost half of the nations that had one civil war during this period later experienced a relapse into renewed war within a few years after the initial conflict ended (Collier, Hoeffler, and Söderbom 2004; Collier et al. 2003). Finally, on a more encouraging note, while the number of civil wars ongoing in the world at any given time increased steadily from the late 1950s through the mid-1990s, that number began to decline in the mid-1990s following the end of the Cold War, leveling off at a relatively steady count of about thirty conflicts ongoing per year since about the year 2000. Yet the death tolls in the ongoing Syrian civil war (estimated between 100,000 and 350,000) remind us of the serious risks that citizens face from intrastate violence in today's world.

Besides these observable patterns in armed conflict, what do we know about civil wars? How do we explain these shifting patterns in armed conflict? More specifically, how do we account for where and when civil wars are likely to occur, when and how they are likely to end, and whether or not they will recur? In this book, we have enlisted some of the leading scholars in the field of civil conflict research to guide us through what the latest research has to tell us about these big questions in civil war research. Perhaps more importantly, as each author delves into one of these streams of civil war research, they highlight the most important questions and puzzles that have emerged in the field over the last two decades. In mapping out what the current state of our knowledge indicates about what we know about civil wars, these authors also locate in that intellectual map the puzzles that define what we do *not* know about civil wars. These research questions provide us with a new research agenda going forward.

The book is divided into three sections. The first five chapters (Part I) focus on issues of civil war onset: what do we know about the factors that make a nation-state more or less susceptible to the outbreak of civil war? The second set of chapters (Part II) is concerned with the dynamics and outcome of civil wars, once they are underway. What factors explain the duration and outcome of civil wars (i.e., whether they end in rebel victory, government victory, or a peace agreement of some sort)? Once a civil war has been brought to an end, what factors make a postwar country more or less susceptible to a relapse into renewed conflict? The third set of chapters (Part III) presents essays that address new directions in civil war research on phenomena that may not be implicated exclusively in either the onset, outcome, or duration of civil wars and that, therefore, have implications beyond any one phase of the conflict process. These topics include the emergence of transitional justice institutions in post-conflict environments, the "resource curse," the impact of the status of women in a society on the civil conflict process, and the relationship between the environment and civil conflicts. Finally, the concluding chapter in this section highlights new trends in civil war data collection that have enabled scholars to examine the geographic and temporal patterns of conflict *within* a given civil war.

The remainder of this introduction presents some background on the different forms of civil conflict that can occur: ethnic versus ideological conflicts, and revolutionary versus secessionist wars. These distinctions can be important in sorting out different possible causal pathways to civil war onset, duration, and outcome as well as post-conflict peace duration. Following this discussion, we delineate the broad framework within which individual chapters will address what we know about specific dimensions of civil war.

TYPES OF CIVIL WARS

In order to gain some understanding of why, where, and when civil wars are likely to occur, it is important to distinguish among types of civil war (e.g., ethnic versus ideological or revolutionary versus secessionist) because the causal processes that lead to these different types of civil war are likely to differ from each other in several critical ways. The dynamics of the conflict—especially the duration and the outcome—are also likely to vary across these types of conflict. Finally, the prospects for the durability of post-conflict peace will vary according to whether the now-ended conflict involved ethnic divisions and whether the goals of the rebels were revolutionary or secessionist.

Generally, civil wars can be categorized according to the goals of the rebels, the issues that motivate the rebellion, and the population base that the rebels mobilize to support their movement. Regarding the goals of the rebellion, we can distinguish between revolutionary and secessionist civil wars. This dichotomy corresponds to the Uppsala Conflict Data Project's (UCDP) distinction between the type of "incompatibility" over which government and rebels are fighting. UCDP codes two types of incompatibility: "government" and "territory" (some conflicts are coded as involving both). In a revolutionary civil war, the incompatibility between government and rebels is over control of the government. The goal of the rebels is to overthrow the incumbent regime and establish themselves as the new government of that nation-state. In a secessionist conflict, the conflict is over territory. The goal of the rebels is not to take over the existing government but to gain independence from it for the population of a particular ethno-regional enclave. In short, their goal is to carve out a second nation from a portion of an existing nation-state's territory.

With respect to the issues that motivate the rebellion and the mobilization strategy of the rebels, we can draw a broad distinction between conflicts that are based in ethnic divisions and those that are not (sometimes referred to as "ideological" conflicts; see Licklider 1995a). In ethnically based conflicts, rebels appeal to a particular ethnic group as their support base and use issues of ethnic discrimination as a means to mobilize supporters from that ethnic group. In an ideological conflict, the rebels appeal to a particular social class (e.g., peasants) by highlighting issues of economic inequality, exploitation, and poverty.

Combining the two dimensions, we can identify ideological revolutions, ethnic revolutions, and ethnic secessionist movements. Most secessionist conflicts of the last half century have been ethnically based.

In an *ethnic secessionist* revolt, the incompatibility between rebels and government is over territory. The rebels seek not to replace the incumbent regime but to secede from it and create a new sovereign nation-state out of a portion of the territory of the existing one. A series of secessionist rebellions in southern Sudan eventually resulted in the Comprehensive Peace Agreement signed in 2005. The key provision in the agreement was that the people of South Sudan would vote in a referendum on whether to become an independent nation. In January of 2011, that referendum passed overwhelmingly, and South Sudan became an independent nation-state. The Eritrean civil war in Ethiopia (1974–1991) resulted in the establishment of the new sovereign nation of Eritrea out of a portion of the territory of Ethiopia. In 1971, East Pakistan seceded from Pakistan to form the new nation of Bangladesh. The Biafran civil war in Nigeria (1967–1970) was an attempt by the Igbo ethnic minority to secede from Nigeria and establish their homeland in the southeastern region of that nation as the new nation-state of Biafra. That rebellion failed after more than three years of fighting and a million deaths, most of them civilians.

The distinction between ideological and ethnic civil wars revolves around the issues that motivated the rebellion and the identity basis of the rebel movement. In an *ideological civil war*, the issues that divide rebels from government usually concern matters of governance and extreme inequality in the distribution of land, wealth, income, and political power. Many Third World conflicts of this sort are peasant based and revolve around issues of access to land. Peasant-based insurgencies escalated to civil war in El Salvador, Nicaragua, Guatemala, Peru, Cambodia, the Philippines, and Nepal, to name but a few. Popular support for the revolutionary movement is mobilized around shared class identity and community ties among landless and land-poor peasants.

Ethnic revolutions have a similar dynamic, and the goal is the same as that of ideological revolutions: to overthrow the existing regime and replace it with a new one. However, what distinguishes ethnic revolutions is the role of ethnicity as a source of identity for the rebels. Often, ethnicity and class coincide in ethnic revolutions. One ethnic group dominates the government and monopolizes high status positions in the economy while other ethnic groups are relegated to subordinate status in the economy and the political arena. Under these circumstances, rebel leaders can mobilize support for an armed challenge by framing grievances as not just a matter of deprivation but of ethnic discrimination. The civil war in Rwanda that ended in 1994 with the overthrow of the Habyaramina regime by the Rwandan Patriotic Front (RPF) was a revolutionary war between a rebel group based in the ethnic Tutsi minority fighting against a government based largely in the majority Hutu ethnic group. That war was marked by one of the most deadly episodes of genocidal violence since the Holocaust.

PHASES OF CIVIL WAR

From an initial concern with the causal antecedents of civil war, streams of research on civil war duration, outcome, and recurrence have emerged over the last two decades. Accordingly, we have organized the chapters in this book around the three phases of the civil conflict process: (1) the initiation or onset of civil war, (2) the duration and outcome of civil wars, and (3) the stability or duration of the peace that follows the end of a civil war.

PART I: FACTORS THAT BRING ABOUT CIVIL WAR

The first section of the book presents several chapters that address questions of civil war onset: what explains the occurrence of civil war? What nation-states are most susceptible to civil war? Among those nations, what conditions explain when civil war is likely to erupt? In chapter 1, Nils Petter Gleditsch, Erik Melander, and Henrik Urdal spell out in more detail the changing patterns of armed conflict generally and

civil war specifically since 1945. We noted in the opening paragraph of this introduction some of the broad shifts in the patterns of armed conflict since the end of
World War II: civil wars becoming more frequent than interstate wars; the location
of conflict shifting from the major power system to Third World regions of Asia,
Africa, and Latin America; and civil war becoming a chronic condition for a small
subset of countries in those regions. Gleditsch, Melander, and Urdal document more
recent shifts in the patterns of armed conflict following the end of the Cold War.
In particular, since the mid-1990s, we have witnessed a decline in the number of
conflicts ongoing in any given year. Their chapter offers some explanations for this
decline and for why this trend leveled off at about thirty conflicts in the middle of
the last decade. One reason for the decline in armed conflicts has been the proactive
role that the international community has begun to play, largely through the United
Nations (UN), in brokering peace agreements to bring protracted civil wars to an
earlier and less destructive conclusion. Kreutz (2010: 246) reports that between
1946 and 1989, only 12 civil wars ended in a peace agreement while 82 ended in a
military victory; between 1990 and 2005, 27 ended in a peace agreement while only
20 ended in a military victory. The evidence, then, makes it clear that since the end
of the Cold War, more civil wars have been brought to a conclusion by negotiated
settlement than by military victory.

In chapter 2, Joe Young takes on the question of what we know about civil war
onset: what makes a nation-state more or less susceptible to civil war? Over the last
two decades, civil war research has centered around a series of empirical studies on
the causal antecedents of civil war. These studies employ cross-sectional time-series
datasets to identify the characteristics of a nation-state that make it more or less
susceptible to the onset of civil war. These attributes identify the risk set of nation-
states that are more likely than others to experience a civil war. Onset studies have
pointed to several syndromes of conditions that are implicated in the onset of civil
war. First, "grievance"-based theories have argued that civil war is more likely to occur in nations characterized by high levels of poverty and state repression (e.g., Gurr
1970). Second, "greed"-based models focus on the presence of conditions that give
rebels an incentive and capacity to engage in organized armed violence, including the
presence of a large number of unemployed or underemployed young males (with low
opportunity costs for participation in armed conflict) and the presence of "lootable"
resources, such as illegal drugs or gemstones, that enable rebels to generate revenues
to sustain their operations (e.g., Collier and Hoeffler 2004). Third, others point to a
"weak state" syndrome that makes it possible for rebels to launch and sustain an insurgency (e.g., Fearon and Laitin 2003; chapter 4, this volume). Finally, an emerging
set of studies (e.g., Young 2013) point to state repression as the trigger that explains
both which nations in the risk set are likely to experience the onset of civil war and
when those conflicts are likely to erupt. Young argues in chapter 2 that we need to
move beyond greed versus grievance dichotomies for explaining civil war onset and
instead seek to understand the process by which insurgent groups emerge and make
decisions to challenge the central government.

While chapter 2 focuses on structural features of a state that might make it more susceptible to civil war, we know that not all civil wars are alike. One set of issues that is implicated in a large share of the conflicts that have erupted over the last half century is the presence of ethnic divisions within a nation-state. Among a large subset of civil wars, ethnic, religious, or other "identity" issues demarcate the divisions between rebels and government. Among those conflicts, a significant proportion involve rebel movements that seek not to seize political control over the existing state, but rather to secede from it and create a new nation-state out of some portion of the territory of the existing nation-state (i.e., secessionist movements). In chapter 3, Kathleen Gallagher Cunningham and Lee Seymour present an overview of theoretical arguments and empirical findings on how and why ethnic, religious, and other identity issues can increase the risk of civil war. This chapter also reviews the empirical findings on the causes and dynamics of identity-based civil wars. Are the causal dynamics of such conflicts different in significant ways from the causal dynamics of civil wars based on economic and other non-identity issues? What factors determine whether an identity-based rebellion will be secessionist or revolutionary in its goals?

While chapters 2 and 3 focus on motivations for civil war, the state itself, through its actions and its institutional capacity, is also implicated in civil war onset. Indeed, most contemporary theories of civil war onset point to "weak states" as being more susceptible to civil war (e.g., Fearon and Laitin 2003; Sobek 2010). One common theme in the civil war literature is that "weak states" are more susceptible to civil war, yet there is little consensus on what constitutes "state weakness" or which actions that weak states are inclined to take account for the greater risk of civil war among them. In chapter 4, Karl DeRouen and David Sobek identify the dimensions of state capacity (or incapacity) and the policies and practices of weak states that make nations more susceptible to civil war. Empirical studies of the weak state–civil war connection have employed a variety of measures of state capacity, such as gross domestic product (GDP) per capita, size of the army, or tax revenues. One dimension is the "domestic democratic peace" argument (Hegre et al. 2001): are democracies less susceptible to civil war than nondemocracies? Among nondemocracies, does the risk of civil war vary depending on whether the state is a military regime, a personalist dictatorship, or a one-party-dominant regime? A recent stream of works employs variants of Geddes's (1999a) nondemocratic regime type typology (e.g., personalist, military, one-party, monarchy) to model differences in the likelihood of civil war onset, duration, and outcomes across regime types (Fjelde 2010; Gurses and Mason 2010). Other studies focus on how variations in state capacity (the military, the bureaucracy, administrative and tax capacity, etc.) influence states' susceptibility to civil war (Hendrix 2010). DeRouen and Sobek analyze what the existing body of empirical findings on the weak state–civil war connection tell us about what we know and do not know about the role of the state in civil war onset and the attributes of state weakness that are associated with higher risks of civil war onset.

While civil wars are, by definition, armed conflict within a nation-state, the conflicts and their effects are rarely if ever confined within the boundaries of a single nation-state. In chapter 5, Erika Forsberg explores the international and transnational dimensions of civil war. When and under what conditions do civil wars diffuse across national boundaries? Does the occurrence of civil war in one country increase the risk of civil war in neighboring countries? Many rebel groups use cross-border safe havens as bases of operations. What conditions make this possible, and how does the existence of cross-border rebel operations affect the duration and outcome of a civil war? How does it affect the risk of civil war in the state where rebels maintain their safe havens? And does the presence of these safe havens increase the risk of interstate war between the civil war nation and its neighbors that harbor rebel base camps? Civil wars also generate refugee flows. How do refugee flows affect the risk of conflict within the host nation and between the host and source nation? Forsberg spells out these transnational dimensions of civil war in order to demonstrate their impact on the risk of conflict diffusion and on the duration and outcome of such conflicts. She argues that civil wars may cluster in space and time because conditions for civil wars are similar in neighboring countries, because conflicts spill over from one location to another, and because potential rebels may learn from the actions of neighboring states' rebel groups.

PART II: FACTORS THAT END CIVIL WARS AND PROMOTE PEACE

The second section of the book consists of a series of chapters on civil war outcomes. Once a civil war is underway, what accounts for whether it ends in a government victory, a rebel victory, a negotiated settlement, or some other outcome? We know that a large percentage of civil wars involve intervention by outside actors; they become internationalized. In chapter 6, Andrew Enterline and Christopher Linebarger analyze the impact of third-party intervention on the duration and outcome of civil wars. This chapter explores several factors that influence whether a conflict will end in a rebel victory, a government victory, or a negotiated settlement. One consistent finding across studies is that the outcome of a civil war is in part a function of its duration: the longer civil wars last, the less likely they are to end in military victory (Mason and Fett 1996; Mason, Weingarten, and Fett 1999). When governments defeat rebels, they usually do so early in the conflict, when they have a decided military advantage over a nascent rebel organization. Surprisingly, the evidence also indicates that rebel victories tend to occur early in conflicts. If neither side prevails early, then as the conflict endures, negotiated settlement becomes the most likely outcome of the civil war.

What, then, accounts for the duration of civil wars? A large proportion of the post–World War II civil wars have been "internationalized" in the sense that one or more nations intervened in the conflict on the side of the government or the rebels. One counterintuitive finding that emerged early in this stream of research is that third party interventions are associated with civil wars of longer duration (see Regan

1996, 2000; Balch-Lindsey and Enterline 2000). This is contrary to the expectation that intervention on the side of the government or the rebels would tip the balance on the battlefield so that the preferred side could achieve a decisive victory more quickly. That has not turned out to be the case. In exploring research on the impact of intervention on civil war duration and outcome, Enterline and Linebarger engage questions of (1) what forms third party intervention can take, (2) what factors make nation-states more or less likely to intervene in a given civil war, (3) when and why in the course of conflict other states are more or less likely to intervene, and (4) how international intervention affects the duration and outcome of such conflicts.

Since the end of the Cold War, more civil wars have ended by means of a negotiated settlement than by decisive military victory by either the rebels or the government. In chapter 7, Jacob Kathman and Megan Shannon explore research on the conditions and dynamics that make a negotiated settlement more likely. Theory has pointed to the emergence of a "hurting stalemate"—where neither side can defeat the other, but each side can prevent its rival from prevailing—as a condition that makes a conflict "ripe for resolution." However, even when both governments and rebels conclude that they would be better off with a peace agreement (compared to continuing to fight), they rarely can reach an agreement if left to their own devices because of credible commitment problems: both sides have incentives to cheat on an agreement, and they both know that they each have these same incentives. Therefore, they are unable to commit credibly to a peace agreement. Third party mediation has emerged as a critical conflict management device to resolve credible commitment problems and assist warring parties in negotiating a peace agreement. Kathman and Shannon explore what recent research has shown on such issues as (1) when is a conflict ripe for mediation, and (2) what characteristics of the mediator, the conflict, and the conflict participants are associated with success or failure of mediation efforts?

Once a civil war ends in a nation-state—whether in government victory, rebel victory, or negotiated settlement—that state has a high risk of relapsing into renewed war within a few years. That risk is especially high following wars that ended in negotiated settlements: one consistent finding across a number of studies is that, in general, negotiated settlements produce a less durable peace than decisive military victories (Licklider 1995a). However, Caroline Hartzell's work has shown that not all negotiated settlements are alike. With negotiated settlement having emerged as the modal outcome of civil wars since the end of the Cold War, it is important to examine how variations in the terms of a peace agreement affect the durability of the peace established by that agreement. Hartzell takes on this task in chapter 8. Early research pointed to a more stable peace following military victories; the peace established by negotiated settlements was alleged to be more likely to break down into renewed war than the peace established by a decisive victory that effectively destroyed one side's capacity to wage war. However, Hartzell's research has shown that, since the end of the Cold War, peace agreements have become more durable (see Hartzell and Hoddie 2003, 2007). Hartzell explains how the terms of the peace agreement—in particular, the presence or absence of multiple dimensions of power sharing spelled out in the agreement—contribute to the ability of the postwar regime to sustain the peace and avoid a relapse into renewed war. This research has identified military, political, economic, and territorial power sharing as the key elements of a peace agreement.

In civil wars that end with peace agreements, the risk of renewed war is high, especially in the immediate aftermath of the war. *Ceteris paribus*, the longer the peace endures, the less likely it is to fail. Therefore, the first task of postwar peacebuilding is simply sustaining the peace until the postwar political, social, and economic order can be consolidated. One thing we do know from numerous studies is that multinational peacekeeping operations substantially enhance the durability of the peace by (1) enforcing the terms of the agreement and (2) providing former protagonists on both sides with some assurance that their former enemies will not defect from the agreement and achieve through cheating the very military outcome they could not achieve on the battlefield. In chapter 9, Paul Diehl explains the theoretical arguments on how peacekeeping operations affect the durability of the post–civil war peace. Beyond the minimalist requirement of simply sustaining the peace after a civil war, postwar peacebuilding requires building the institutions of a viable postwar political regime, rehabilitating the economy, and encouraging the growth of civil society. Diehl spells out the special obstacles that post–civil war nations face with respect to installing effective institutions of governance and sustaining them over time.

We know that civil war is significantly more likely to occur in poor nation-states: low GDP per capita is one of the most robust predictors of which countries are at risk of experiencing civil war. This implies that stimulating economic growth is even more critical in post–civil war regimes if they are to avoid the conflict trap of a relapse into renewed civil war. Postwar regimes take power in poor nations that have been rendered even more impoverished by the destruction of years of armed conflict. The legacies of civil war are numerous and most of them are not favorable for sustaining the peace after civil war. In chapter 10, Clayton Thyne highlights what we know about those legacies of civil war and then identifies some policy levers that the international community can use to reduce the risk of renewed conflict through post-conflict reconstruction and rehabilitation of the economy and the society. Civil war kills people, destroys infrastructure, disrupts commerce, encourages capital flight (financial and industrial capital as well as human capital), and it does so in nations that, on average, had a deficit of those assets before the war began. It also contributes to the incidence and spread of disease because of a damaged health-care system (that was weak to begin with) that is often overwhelmed by injuries caused by war and the legacy of untreated diseases that results from the disruption and destruction of war (Ghobarah et al. 2003). Furthermore, civil war disrupts the education system, impeding the capacity of the nation to restore its already low stocks of human capital in the aftermath of war. What can be done to rebuild a postwar economy, and what are the impediments to postwar economic development that must be overcome? Thyne spells out the challenges of post–civil war economic and social development and what policies have succeeded (or failed) in producing sufficient economic growth to reduce the risk of a relapse into renewed armed conflict.

PART III: EMERGING TRENDS
IN CIVIL WAR RESEARCH

The third section of the book presents a set of chapters that deal with some new, important, and emerging topics in civil war research. The first of these new trends is the emergence of transitional justice mechanisms in the aftermath of civil war. Besides building the institutions of a viable postwar regime and rehabilitating the war-devastated economy, nation-states coming out of civil war are still marked by the social and psychological scars left by the violence of civil war. To paraphrase Roy Licklider (1995a), how can groups that have been killing each other with considerable enthusiasm and success for years now come live together in a single community? The fabric of social life is shredded by armed conflict. Transitional justice mechanisms, including both truth and reconciliation commissions (TRCs) and international criminal tribunals (ICTs), have evolved as instruments for reconciling former enemies, at least to the point that they can live together in peace with some hope for reviving a sense of shared community. In chapter 11, Jacqueline DeMeritt analyzes the current state of research on transitional justice processes in order to determine what we know about when and where TRCs and ICTs are employed and what determines how effective they are in bringing about some degree of post-conflict reconciliation. A variety of transitional justice institutions have evolved for the purpose of post-conflict reconciliation and justice. These include truth and reconciliation commissions (TRCs), international and national criminal tribunals, lustrations, and amnesties, all of which have emerged as mechanisms to bring about some sort of postwar reconciliation between former enemies. A growing body of research examines the effectiveness of different transitional justice institutions and processes for different transition justice goals (e.g., justice versus reconciliation). This chapter maps out this emerging stream of empirical research on how TRCs and postwar criminal tribunals contribute to a more durable peace following civil war.

Another emerging stream of research has brought to the forefront the question of what role women play in civil conflict, and how the status of women in a society affects the prospects for civil war occurrence and post–civil war peace (Hudson et al. 2012; Caprioli 2005; Melander 2005a). Traditionally, women have been viewed as passive victims of civil violence, as casualties caught in the crossfire of fighting between male combatants, and as victims of rape and other forms of sexual violence perpetrated by male combatants. Some research has explored women's participation in rebel movements, but these works tend to depict women as being confined to the roles of "keepers of the campfires," serving as cooks and nurses and in other support roles at best and as forced sex slaves at worst. Other works have examined the role of women as combatants in insurgent armies (Mason 1992). Recent works have gone beyond the anecdotal to explore more fundamental relationships between the status of women in a society—especially the presence or absence of patrimonial institutions, cultural norms, and practices—and a society's risk for civil war onset, as well as its capacity for sustaining the peace in the aftermath of civil war. These effects grow out of the more fundamental relationship between the status of women in society—including their access to education and jobs—and the nation's prospects for development along various dimensions. This developmental phenomenon was highlighted most recently in the World Bank's (2012) *World Development Report: Gender Equality and Development*. In chapter 12, Erik Melander maps out this emerging field of research on civil conflict. He analyzes how the status of women in a society affects (1) the nation's risk of civil war onset, (2) the likelihood of bringing civil conflicts to an earlier and less destructive end, and (3) a country's ability to sustain the peace in the aftermath of civil war and to build and sustain a viable democratic political system as well.

One cluster of civil war research that influenced Paul Collier's and Anke Hoeffler's "greed" hypothesis is the "resource curse" thesis: states that are endowed with rich stores of natural resources – especially oil, gemstones, and, in some cases, certain illegal drugs – are more likely to experience civil war, *ceteris paribus*. The resource curse has been implicated in civil war onset, duration, outcome, and post-conflict peace failure (Ross 2004a, 2004b). In chapter 13, Benjamin Smith examines these dimensions of the resource curse and assesses the often conflicting findings on whether certain types of resource endowments affect the risk of civil war as well as the duration and outcome of such conflicts. Rentier state theories support the notion that states that are dependent on oil exports are more susceptible to civil war onset than similar nations without major oil reserves. What are the causal dynamics that explain this relationship, and what is the empirical evidence on this relationship? Some have argued that "lootable" resources, such as gemstones and drugs, are associated with a greater risk of civil war; others contend that lootable resources may be more strongly related to the duration of civil war, as revenues from those resources can be used to sustain an armed rebellion. There has been less work on how the presence of lootable resources and other valued natural resources, such as oil, affects the outcome of civil wars, or the duration of the peace after civil war. Benjamin Smith sorts out some of these contending arguments.

Global concerns over climate change have fueled a new stream of research on the impact of climate change on the incidence and patterns of armed conflict in the world. In chapter 14, Cullen Hendrix, Halvard Buhaug, and Scott Gates review recent research on a variety of links in the causal chain between climate events and civil war. The premise of this research is the concern that climate change will lead to drought, floods, and other disruptive climate events, which will result in resource shortages. Water shortages and the loss of arable land will lead to increasing competition between communities and nations over those increasingly scarce resources. Climate and natural disaster events of this sort are also expected to produce famine and migration of populations away from drought- or flood-stricken regions, putting pressure on the resource base of the regions to which these populations migrate. The expectation is that these trends will contribute to increasing levels of violence, especially in nations that lack the economic wherewithal or the institutional capacity to mitigate the social and economic effects of climate events. Much of the violence may be local communal violence, as one community contests with a neighboring community over access to and control over increasingly scarce land, water, and food resources. This raises the question of whether otherwise sporadic local violence of this nature can coalesce into sustained organized armed rebellions, catalyzed by climatic events.

In the final chapter, David Cunningham, Kristian Gleditsch, and Idean Salehyan map out several important new trends in data collection that have emerged in recent years, each opening up new sets of research questions that can now be examined empirically. Among these are, first, the now fairly established and widely used dyadic datasets on civil wars. A second involves the coding of battles within civil wars. A third involves the coding of contentious events prior to, during, and after civil wars. A fourth area involves data collection on the characteristics of rebel groups. Extending existing country-year civil war datasets (such as COW and UCDP/PRIO's Armed Conflict Dataset) to the dyadic level emerged from the observation that a large proportion of civil wars involve more than one rebel group simultaneously sustaining an armed challenge to the same state (Cunningham, Gleditsch, and Salehyan 2009). UCDP/PRIO's dyadic datasets have enabled a number of studies on how the presence of multiple rebel groups affects the outcome and duration of civil wars as well as the duration of the peace after civil wars (Nilsson 2008b; Cunningham 2011). The dyadic analysis of civil war—using government-rebel dyad years rather than civil war years as the unit of analysis—has important implications for theories of the civil conflict process, for the empirical analysis of that process, and for the policy implications of empirical research on the civil conflict process. The ACLED dataset (Raleigh et al. 2010) and UCDP'S Georeferenced Event Data (Sundberg and Melander 2013) code the location, timing, duration, and destructiveness of battles within civil war spells. This represents an important addition to our tool set for studying how the shifting battlefield fortunes of governments and rebels during the course of a civil war can affect the duration, outcome, and destructiveness of civil wars. Up to now, most studies on duration and outcome employed covariates that were measured at the beginning of the conflict (or prior to it) and at the end of the conflict. History teaches us that the shifting tides of battle during a war can affect the duration and outcome in ways that preconditions would not enable us to predict. These battle datasets open the black box of civil war spells and allow us to examine the dynamics of conflict within the war itself. Projects such as the Social Conflict in Africa Database (SCAD) (Salehyan et al. 2012) use georeferenced data on social conflict events (e.g., protest, riots, communal violence) outside of civil war spells to map the spatial and temporal distribution of such events. Event data can be employed to develop more fine-grained models of how the dynamics of periods of contention outside of civil war spells can escalate to civil war or, alternatively, result in some other outcome.

With this overview of the organization of this volume, we now present the chapters. We are most grateful to the authors who devoted their time and energy to writing these chapters. Their dedication to the pedagogy and their knowledge of the subjects they address are reflected in the content of the chapters and their commitment to presenting this often complex material in a manner that is accessible to students and that stimulates their own thinking about what we do and don't know about civil wars. We hope the analyses presented and the unanswered questions revealed will motivate some of our readers to contribute to our work to expand our knowledge about the civil conflict process.

I

FACTORS THAT BRING ABOUT CIVIL WAR

1

Introduction—Patterns of Armed Conflict since 1945

Nils Petter Gleditsch, Erik Melander, and Henrik Urdal

In this chapter, we present data showing historical trends in armed conflict since 1945, focusing on the frequency, duration, severity, location, termination, and issues at stake in such wars. Since the end of World War II, civil war has been the most frequent form of armed conflict. Interstate wars were never very numerous at any one time in history, but many interstate wars involved many countries and resulted in a high number of fatalities. During the Cold War, there were up to fourteen on-going interstate conflicts at some point in a decade, whereas in the post–Cold War era, the number has been at most five in a decade. While interstate conflicts still on average claim more battle deaths than civil wars, we have to go back to the US-led invasion of Iraq in 2003 to find one with more than one thousand fatalities in a year and to the bloodiest year of the Vietnam War in 1972 to find one with more than two hundred thousand fatalities in a year. Civil wars now claim more lives overall than interstate war, and this has been true for every year since the mid-1970s. This is a dramatic shift in the global pattern of armed conflict. An even more significant shift is the clear but uneven decline in the lethality of war generally since the peak represented by World War II.

ARMED CONFLICT

In this chapter, we use the terminology of the Uppsala Conflict Data Program (UCDP) and refer to *armed conflict* as a contested incompatibility over government or territory where the use of armed force between two parties results in at least twenty-five battle-related deaths in a calendar year.[1] Of these two parties, at least one is the government of a state (Gleditsch et al. 2002: 618f). We shall refer to "war" as an armed conflict with more than one thousand battle-related deaths (military and civilian) in a given year. The dataset distinguishes between interstate armed conflict, intrastate armed conflict, and extra-systemic conflict (i.e., conflict between a state and a non-state group outside its own territory). Intrastate conflicts are subdivided into conflicts with and without intervention from other states. We return later to two other types of internal conflict that have occurred frequently during this period. We refer to intrastate armed conflicts as *civil conflicts*, or *civil wars* when they exceed the threshold of one thousand battle deaths.

HOW MANY?

Since the end of World War II and up until 2013, 567 conflict dyads have occurred in 259 conflicts in 159 countries (Pettersson and Wallensteen 2015). The number of conflict dyads exceeds the number of conflicts because many conflicts (interstate as well as intrastate) involve several parties on one side or both. For instance, in the territorial conflicts in Mindanao, the government of the Philippines is fighting three different insurgent groups. One conflict is with the Moro National Liberation Front (MNLF), a rebel group that has been fighting for territorial autonomy for the Bangsamoro ethnic population, concentrated in the islands of Mindanao, Sulu, Palawan, and Sabah. The Moro Islamic Liberation Front emerged from a faction of MNLF that opposed the peace agreement the MNLF signed with the government of the Philippines in 1976. The conflict with the Communist Party over government, however, is counted as a separate conflict with just one dyad. Figure 1.1 depicts the incidence (or occurrence) of armed conflicts (1946–2014). During this period, there have been four to five times as many civil conflicts as interstate ones and fifteen times as many conflict-years. While interstate wars have always been few in number, the incidence has declined even further in recent years. In nine of the years since the end of the Cold War (1989), no interstate conflicts were recorded, although an increasing number of civil conflicts have been internationalized—currently as much as one quarter of all armed conflicts. Extra-systemic conflict was more frequent than interstate conflict in the first thirty years after the end of World War II. These were primarily anticolonial conflicts. As the traditional colonial system was more or less wound up with the end of Portuguese colonial rule in the mid-1970s, this category is no longer used by the UCDP in coding new conflicts. The two last such conflict-years were Portugal versus Angola and Portugal versus Mozambique in 1974.

While interstate conflict has declined in frequency since World War II, the incidence of civil conflict increased markedly during the Cold War period, from less than ten ongoing conflicts in a given year in the first decade, to over forty in the final years of the Cold War. To some extent, this increase is due to the decolonization that gained speed after 1960. Internal conflicts in colonies would not have been recorded as state-based conflicts. After independence, they are counted as civil conflicts. Decolonization also involved arbitrary and sometimes disputed national

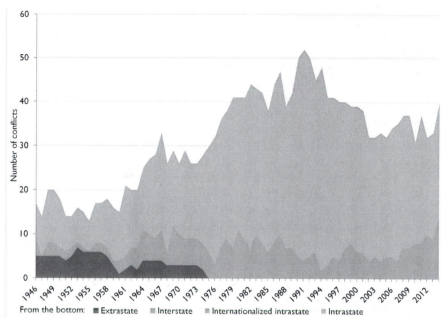

Figure 1.1. The Number of Ongoing Armed Conflicts by Type and Year, 1945–2014

Pettersson and Wallensteen (2015). The data are found at www.pcr.uu.se/research/ucdp/datasets/ucdp_prio_ armed_conflict_dataset.

Figure created by Ida Rudolfsen.

boundaries that easily developed into territorial conflicts. Many of the regimes in the new states were quite fragile and tempting targets for coups and other attempts to capture the government.[2] Decolonization also contributed to fragmentation of the state system—British India became two countries in 1947 (Burma had already been defined as a separate entity in 1937); a third was added with the independence of Bangladesh from Pakistan in 1971, the only successful secessionist conflict in the Cold War period. Worldwide, there were 74 independent countries in 1946 and 185 in 1991 (Gleditsch and Ward 1999). The probability that an independent country would experience civil war in a given year was 9 percent in 1960 and 18 percent in 1991. When taking into account the rising number of countries, we still see an increase in the risk of civil war for a given country during the Cold War period. But the figure is less dramatic than if we simply count the number of ongoing conflicts.

The end of the Cold War led to the breakup of Yugoslavia and the Soviet Union. Both of these involved violence, although not at a scale experienced in the collapse of Austria, Germany, Czarist Russia, and the Ottoman empires at the end of World War I. Most of the conflicts in the former federal states in the early 1990s ended relatively quickly. A number of Cold War–related conflicts in Africa and Central America also ended when the two superpowers lost interest in fighting by proxy.[3] Among these are the civil war in El Salvador, the Contra War in Nicaragua, and the Angolan civil war (although this conflict required multiple rounds of failed peace agreements before a lasting peace was established in 2002). Thus, around the turn of the millennium, the incidence of conflict had dropped by about 30 percent. Following the events of September 11, 2001, the decline halted and, in the period since then, the incidence of armed conflict has been relatively stable. Recent ups and downs are partly due to conflicts passing in and out of the "active" category when the number of battle deaths hovers around the lower threshold.

The total number of ongoing conflicts has remained at around thirty to thirty-five in the past decade, approximately the same level as in the mid-1970s. The probability that a given country would have a conflict on its territory declined in the first phase of the Cold War, increased during the heyday of decolonization and again quite recently, but declined markedly after the end of the Cold War, as shown by figure 1.2. The same statistic for war shows much less variation over time.

Somewhat paradoxically, the share of countries participating in armed conflict has increased in the past fifty years, as shown in figure 1.3. In other words, while a given country is less likely to have armed conflict on its territory, it is more likely to participate in armed conflict! The Nordic countries, for instance, have not experienced war on their own territory since World War II, but all of them have participated in

Figure 1.2. Share of Countries with Intrastate Armed Conflict on Their Territory, 1946–2014

Figure created by Ida Rudolfsen based on conflict locations reported by UCDP.

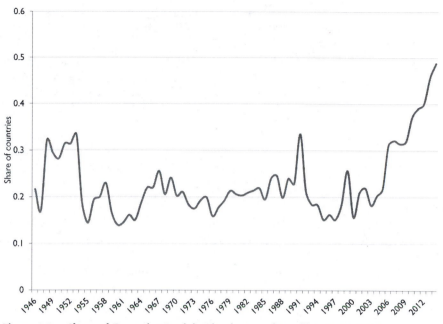

Figure 1.3.   **Share of Countries Participating in Armed Conflict, 1946–2014**
Figure created by Ida Rudolfsen on the basis of the UCDP/PRIO Armed Conflict Dataset. The number of independent countries from Gleditsch and Ward (1999).

armed conflict far from home several times after the end of the Cold War. A number of recent interstate and internationalized civil conflicts have been fought by large coalitions on one side. For instance, 28 countries fought against Iraq in the Gulf War of 1991, while the invasion of Afghanistan and the subsequent attempts at stabilizing and defending the new regime obtained the support of 29 countries. Although the United States only succeeded in enlisting two countries on its side (e.g., the coalition of the willing) when invading Iraq in 2003, no fewer than 36 countries eventually participated in the stabilization force. The first peak in figure 1.3 is due to a similar phenomenon—the large coalition fighting as a UN force in the Korean War. Of course, many countries participate in such coalitions mainly as acts of political solidarity; they make only very limited military contributions, and their governments tend to define it as peacekeeping or peacemaking rather than war.[4]

HOW LONG?

Almost every year, some new conflicts emerge while others end. Several new conflicts have ended very quickly. In 2013, for example, a new conflict broke out in Sabah in Malaysia in response to an old territorial claim by the Sultan of Sulu in the Philippines. After three weeks of fighting and seventy deaths, the conflict ended. Other conflicts are quite persistent. For instance, the conflict between Israel and the Palestinians goes back to the end of the 1940s, as does the territorial conflict in Kachin in Burma (Myanmar). Although ending such enduring intrastate rivalries has proved to be very difficult, the post–Cold War period has seen the end of major violence in some old conflicts such as those in the Basque region in Spain and in Northern Ireland, and there are hopes of a more peaceful future in Burma. The number of new conflicts in a given year is lower than during most of the Cold War era.[5]

HOW VIOLENT?

Armed conflicts vary enormously in their severity, measured by the number of battle-related deaths. The three bloodiest conflicts after World War II were the Vietnam War (2.1 million deaths), the Korean War (1.25 million), and the Chinese Civil War (1.2 million).[6] Yet to get a handle of the intensity, we must also consider how long conflicts endure. The Korean War and the Chinese Civil War lasted less than four years, so both exceeded the Vietnam War in annual battle deaths by a wide margin, even though they experienced fewer total battle-related deaths. At the other end of the scale, we find a number of conflicts that barely exceed the minimum threshold, such as the territorial conflict in India's Bodoland, which is recorded in the UCDP database with a "best estimate" (BE) of twenty-eight deaths in 2013. Thus, figures for the number of ongoing conflicts may present a somewhat misleading picture of the waxing and waning of war over time.

Figure 1.4 presents annual battle deaths over time for the period after World War II. The UCDP coding is a little more restrictive than that done at PRIO (Peace Research Institute Oslo); hence the UCDP curve is lower for the years that overlap. The trend over time is very similar for the two datasets. For 2014, the number of deaths is higher than at any previous time in the new millennium, but considerably lower than the peaks during the Cold War period.

Figure 1.4 makes a good case for the "waning of war" or "decline of violence," as forcefully argued in several recent books (Payne 2004; Goldstein 2011; Pinker 2011; see also Gleditsch et al. 2013).[7] Clearly, the aggregate figure for a given year is highly dependent on individual wars. The first peak is generated by the Chinese Civil War, immediately followed by the Korean War. The next peak is largely the Vietnam War. The third combines the Iran-Iraq interstate war plus the civil war in Afghanistan and the resistance to the intervention of the Soviet Union. The smaller peak in 1990–1991 is mainly due to Eritrea's fight for secession from the union with Ethiopia and the Gulf War between Iraq and the United States–led coalition, and the peak in 1999 stems from the interstate war between Eritrea and Ethiopia. The final peak, so far, chiefly results from the civil war in Syria. These peaks are progressively lower over time. The trend is clearly toward less bloody armed conflicts, but the decline is not linear, not even monotonic. The majority of battle deaths are located in a relatively small number of conflicts and countries.

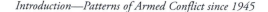

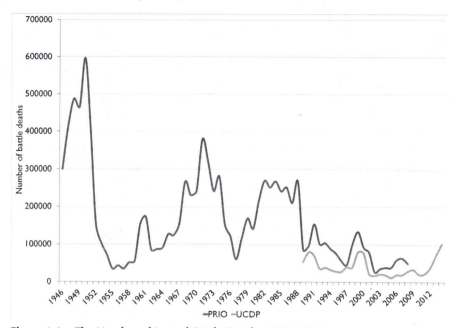

Figure 1.4.   The Number of Annual Battle Deaths, 1946–2014

Figure created by Ida Rudolfsen. The PRIO battle deaths data for 1946–2008 are found at www.prio.no/cscw/cross/battledeaths while the data from UCDP cover 1989–2014 and are found at www.ucdp.uu.se. Battle deaths data for 2014 for all conflicts are also found in Pettersson and Wallensteen (2015). All the numbers used here are best estimates (BE). The two sources also supply high and low estimates (HE, LE). Some PRIO figures lack a BE; we have used the average of the HE and the LE. BEs are not always available on an annual basis. The distribution of the total battle deaths over the years the war lasted is explained in Lacina (2006). While battle deaths have been declining, world population has increased almost threefold in the period since World War II. Had we used relative figures for the severity of conflict (i.e., measure the probability that a random person is killed in battle) the decline in the severity of war would have been even more pronounced. For graphs documenting this, see Pinker (2011: 301), Lacina, Gleditsch, and Russett (2006: 677), and figure 1.6.

A further argument for the waning of war is provided by a comparison of these figures with figures for the two world wars (Lacina, Gleditsch, and Russett 2006: 677, figure 1.2). Those two wars completely dwarf anything that has come later. Of course, the confrontation between the Soviet Union and the United States and its allies could have become a "third world war." Although the two opponents avoided direct military action, practiced considerable restraint, and left the fighting to smaller allies, the potential for a major confrontation was felt throughout the period. A direct nuclear confrontation between the two superpowers or between NATO and the Warsaw Pact would most probably have created a peak in the curve higher than those for the two world wars.

Some uncertainty surrounds all figures for battle deaths. How robust is the conclusion that battle deaths have declined during this period? The PRIO battle deaths data contain high estimates (HE) and low estimates (LE) in addition to the best estimates (BE) used in figure 1.4. If we plot the HEs and the LEs, they show the same jagged curve with declining peaks as we find for the BEs.[8] Using figures from the Correlates of War (COW) dataset, we also find a similar development over time.[9]

We obviously have more information on recent conflicts. In some of these, such as the 2003 invasion of Iraq and the ensuing civil conflict, there have been extensive efforts to measure conflict fatalities by surveys (Burnham et al. 2006; see also Spagat et al. 2009) as well as news reports. Many governments make persistent efforts to hide the extent of internal violence, but in the age of global news media, this is becoming increasingly difficult. If we had been able to obtain full information on the extent of internal violence in older conflicts, the waning-of-war argument would probably look even stronger.

The human cost of war extends beyond those killed in violent events, as major losses of life and negative health effects may stem from indirect and long-term consequences of armed conflict.[10] Cross-national studies have documented a considerable increase in overall mortality. For instance, Ghobarah, Huth, and Russett (2003) concluded that almost as many died from indirect causes attributable to civil war in the period 1991–1997 as those who died at gunpoint. Specifically, they found that some 8 million DALYs (disability-adjusted life years, with data from WHO) were lost in 1999 due to the overall long-term effects of the 1991–1997 civil wars, compared to some 8.4 million DALYs lost directly in international and civil wars globally in the same year. Other cross-national studies (Li and Wen 2005; Plümper and Neumayer 2006) also find considerable excess mortality both during and after conflict.

In order to assess the indirect effects of conflict in individual countries, one faces the challenge of establishing a reasonable counterfactual: What level of mortality would we have observed had it not been for the armed conflict? Such counterfactuals involve even greater uncertainties than estimates of battle-related deaths. Although it may be possible to come up with a plausible figure for war-related deaths for single conflicts, it seems unlikely that we will have reliable figures for global war deaths in the near future.

Civil wars also have clear detrimental effects on economic growth, the reduction of poverty, primary education, and access to drinkable water (Gates et al. 2012 and chapter 10 in this volume). In turn, these effects may also translate into increased long-term loss of human life.

Fazal (2014) claims that the reports of war's demise are exaggerated because there have been dramatic improvements in preventive care, in battlefield medicine, in evacuation time, and in protective equipment, all of which have reduced the proportion of battle casualties that become battle deaths. She has assembled data that show a reduction of killed-to-wounded ratios over time for a number of countries. These data are not directly comparable to standard battle-deaths data, since they relate only to combatants. Moreover, they include only interstate wars, and Fazal argues that collecting comparable data for civil wars is "virtually impossible." Moreover, the improvements of medical care in conflict zones may be influenced by the same humanitarian revolution that Pinker and others see as contributing to the decline of war. Fazal (2014: 116) concludes that her finding "tempers, but does not negate" the empirical claim of a decline of war.

WHERE?

Major parts of the world such as North America and most of Europe are now free of armed conflict. Figure 1.5 shows a map of conflict zones for the years 2006–2008. By *conflict zones*, we mean parts of a country that are directly affected by fighting. A similar map for countries involved in armed conflict or even for countries with armed conflict somewhere on their territory would portray armed conflict as much more extensive. For instance, Russia has a long-standing civil war in Chechnya, but the military action takes place only in a very small part of the country.

Broadly speaking, we can identify three clusters of conflict in the period after World War II. One extends through Central America and into South America. Most of these conflicts ended after the Cold War, and only the one in Colombia has persisted over a long period and was still active in 2014. A second cluster extends from the Middle East in a southeasterly direction all the way to the Philippines. In the 1990s this cluster extended all the way into former Yugoslavia on the Western side, and in the 1970s all the countries in Indochina were embroiled in wars of different kinds. Thus, this cluster is also now more limited geographically than it has been in the past. Finally, Africa has experienced a number of armed conflicts spread out over most of the continent. Of the fifty-four independent countries in the continent, forty-three have experienced civil armed conflict or interstate conflict after independence.[11] In the three years featured in this map, the African conflict cluster was concentrated in North and Central Africa, and this pattern largely persists today.

The geographical clustering of armed conflict is usually attributed to the similarity of neighboring countries in terms of conflict-inducing factors such as poverty and weak states. But there are also elements of contagion between conflicts generated, for instance, by refugees, rebel forces that seek sanctuaries across the border, or transnational ethnic ties (Buhaug and Gleditsch 2008).[12]

Europe was the main arena for war during the world wars, although Asia supplied a second important arena for war fighting in World War II. Following World War II, there have been major regional shifts in the incidence and severity of war (figure 1.6). Initially, the most serious armed confrontations occurred in East Asia; in fact, the three largest wars occurred there. The next peak was due to wars in West Asia (Afghanistan and Iran-Iraq). Currently, the largest wars are raging in the Middle East.

A regional breakdown does not reflect that many human losses are caused by countries from outside the region. In great-power interventions, fatalities among soldiers from outside powers are counted as casualties in the conflict area. However, the human losses suffered by the great powers are often small compared to losses among the local combatants. An arguably more significant factor in producing geographically skewed battle deaths is the fighting by proxy among the great powers. The enormous number of battle deaths in East Asia in the first three decades after World War II reflect this pattern (Tønnesson et al. 2013).

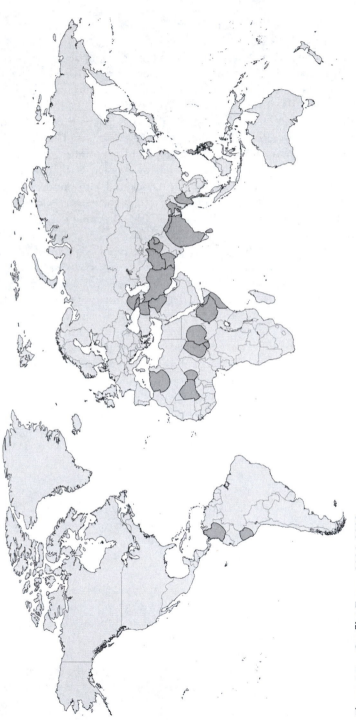

Figure 1.5. Conflict Zones, 2006–2008

Map created on the basis of data from Hallberg (2012). For updated information on what countries have civil conflict on their soil, see Pettersson and Wallensteen (2015) and earlier annual updates from UCDP.

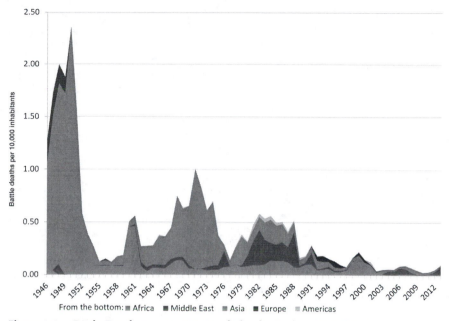

Figure 1.6.   Battle Deaths per 10,000 Population by Region, 1946–2014

Figure created by Ida Rudolfsen. PRIO battle deaths data to 2008, UCDP data for 2009–2014. The overall decline of violence is even more visible here than in figure 1.4, which shows absolute rather than relative figures.

Rather than comparing conventional geographical regions, Huntington (1996) proposed that the global pattern of conflict would increasingly be dominated by a "clash of civilizations," with a definition of civilization largely based on religion. Huntington was not alone in suggesting that conflicts between the Muslim world and the Christian West would be particularly serious. Although aspects of the conflicts after the end of the Cold War, notably in former Yugoslavia, ran along religious dividing lines, statistical studies have failed to find robust evidence of a greater incidence of conflict between than within civilizations (Russett, Oneal, and Cox 2000; Huntington 2000). However, Huntington (1996: 257f) had actually written that "Islam's borders are bloody and so are its innards." In fact, in 2012 there were only six intrastate conflicts reaching the level of war (one thousand battle deaths)—in Afghanistan, Pakistan, Sudan, Somalia, Syria, and Yemen. All of them occurred in countries with a majority of Muslims, and all of them involved Muslim insurgents (Rudolfsen and Gleditsch 2015). There is no evidence that there is a rise in conflicts in Muslim countries or involving Muslim insurgents. But the decline in other types of conflict means that the *share* of conflicts that involve Muslim insurgents or where a majority of the inhabitants are Muslims (or both) is increasing. Religion itself is not an issue in all these conflicts, though in some conflicts it clearly is. This point is also illustrated in figure 1.7. While the absolute number of wars with religious dimensions has been roughly level since the early 1980s, other wars have become so rare that religious war is now dominant.

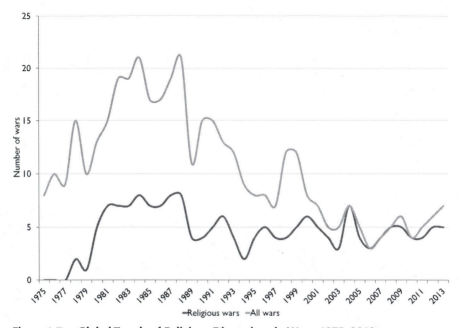

Figure 1.7.   Global Trends of Religious Dimensions in Wars, 1975–2013

Figure generated by Ida Rudolfsen on the basis of data in Svensson (2014b). Cf. also Svensson (2012). A war is considered to have a religious dimension if there was an explicit aspiration relating to religious issues (e.g., demands for Sharia law) at the onset of the conflict.

Finally, looking at figure 1.3 again, it is striking that conflicts tend to cluster around the Equator. Buhaug, Gleditsch, and Wischnath (2013) found that for countries that had not had any intrastate conflict since 1950, the distance from the capital to the Equator was on average 80 percent higher than for countries with at least one intrastate conflict. Nondemocratic regime types, weak states, low economic development, and Islam are also overrepresented in the low latitudes. The interactions between these factors and the role played by a tropical climate, if any, remain largely unexplored.

CONFLICTS BY ISSUE

There have been several calls for breaking down armed conflicts by issue (e.g., Diehl 1992), and the Issues Correlates of War (ICOW) project[13] maps territorial, river, maritime, and identity claims—but only for interstate conflict. A more limited typology is used by the UCDP, which distinguishes between conflicts over territory and over government. Conflicts over territory often involve secessionist movements, where an ethno-regional rebel movement seeks to create a new independent nation from a portion of an existing nation-state. The Eritrean rebellion in Ethiopia succeeded in gaining independence from Eritrea in 1993, following decades of armed conflict. The Biafra secessionist revolt in Nigeria from 1967 to 1970 failed to gain independence for the Igbo population that represents a majority of that region but a minority in the nation of Nigeria. Conflicts over the government include revolutionary civil conflicts in which the rebels seek to overthrow the incumbent regime and establish a new regime in a given nation. The Cuban revolution, the Sandinista revolution in Nicaragua, and the Khmer Rouge revolution in Cambodia are examples of rebel successes in conflicts over government. Figure 1.8 shows the trend in the two types of incompatibilities coded by UCDP. Whereas conflicts over government were relatively rare in the first decades after World War II, the number of governmental conflicts increased in the 1970s, and since then roughly half of all conflicts have been over territory and the other half over government.

The incompatibility distinction is key to a number of studies focusing on different explanations for conflict. Buhaug (2006) argued that the strength of the rebel group relative to the state would determine whether it was realistic to try to capture the state (conflict over government) or whether the rebels were more likely to aim for secession (conflict over territory). He also found that territorial and governmental conflicts are shaped by different causal mechanisms, with democratic countries experiencing territorial conflicts more frequently.

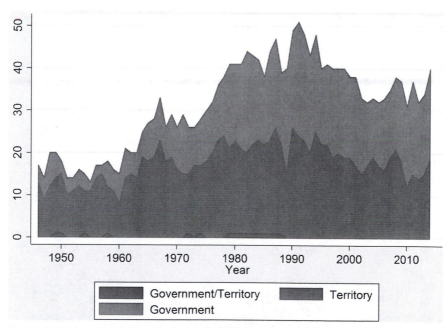

Figure 1.8. Armed Conflicts by Incompatibility, 1946–2014
Figure created by Erik Melander on the basis of the UCDP/PRIO Armed Conflict Dataset.

A majority of civil conflicts in the post–World War II period have been fought along ethnic lines. This is true for almost all conflicts over territory but even for almost half of the conflicts over government (Denny and Walter 2014). That does not, however, imply that ethnicity itself is the primary issue in civil wars. On the contrary, such conflicts appear to be driven by the same grievances that account for other conflicts as well (e.g., weak state, low income), but ethnicity provides a stable pattern of identification that facilitates the organization of an insurgency.[14]

HOW CONFLICTS END

For some countries, civil conflict has become a chronic condition. Approximately half of the nations that have experienced at least one onset of civil conflict later experienced a relapse into renewed conflict, even after several years of inactivity. Kreutz (2013) compares the number of civil conflict onsets with the number of civil conflict terminations over time. Figure 1.9 shows that, except for a few years, the rate of civil conflict onset was higher than the rate of termination throughout the Cold War, but the opposite has been true for the post–Cold War period with terminations outpacing onsets in all but a few years.

Figure 1.9.   Civil Conflict Onset and Terminations (Five-Year Averages), 1950–2014
Figure based on Kreutz (2013), updated to 2014 by Erik Melander using the UCDP/PRIO Armed Conflict Dataset.

A study of how civil conflicts ended in the period 1946–2005 (Kreutz 2010) found another striking difference between the Cold War period and the subsequent years. The percentage of civil conflicts ending with a peace agreement increased from 9 percent to 18 percent, whereas victories by either side decreased from 58 percent to 14 percent. Termination by cease-fire agreements also became much more frequent in the post–Cold War period.[15]

OTHER FORMS OF INTERNAL CONFLICT[16]

Two other forms of internal conflict are conceptually distinct, yet closely related to civil war. Conflicts between organized groups without the direct participation of the government are often called "intercommunal conflicts," or "non-state conflicts" in UCDP terminology. The UCDP codes three main types of non-state conflict: between rebel groups and other organized militias (e.g., the Free Syrian Army versus the Islamic State in Iraq and al-Sham/Syria); between supporters of different political parties (e.g., the Action Congress [ACN] versus the People's Democratic Party [PDP] in Nigeria); and between communal groups (e.g., between the Borana and the Turkana pastoralist peoples in Kenya). Such conflicts are currently as numerous as state-based conflicts, but on average less violent. They often come into being because the state is too weak to end them. If the state is strong enough to engage the warring parties, it exercises its power to quash the violence before it escalates. Alternatively, the state becomes the dominant actor on the other side and the conflict is classified as a civil conflict.

Second, many governments and organized non-state groups use violence against unorganized people. Such conflicts are not defined as civil conflicts, but rather as one-sided violence (see Eck and Hultman 2007 for UCDP data), or as genocide or politicide (Harff 2003) or an even broader category, democide (Rummel 1995, see also www.hawaii.edu/powerkills/). In the twentieth century, this form of conflict probably claimed more lives by a wide margin than all wars. Using Rummel's broad definition (which includes excess mortality in concentration camps and famines for which the government must be held responsible), democide claimed four to five times as many victims as war in the first three quarters of the twentieth century. The greatest catastrophe of its kind in the twentieth century, China's Great Leap Forward in 1958–1961—the policy of forced industrialization and collectivization of agriculture—is now estimated to have caused some 45 million deaths (Dikötter 2010), more than the total number of battle deaths in the twentieth century. Figure 1.10 shows the number of deaths combined for intrastate and non-state conflict as well as one-sided violence. In most years, victims in intrastate conflicts outnumber the two other forms of internal violence. The 1994 genocide in Rwanda represents a spike in casualties more than five times as high as any other year during the post–Cold War period.

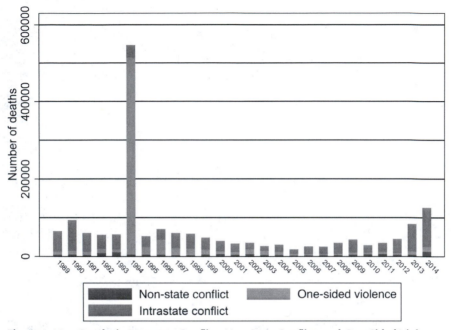

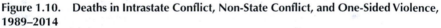

Figure 1.10.   Deaths in Intrastate Conflict, Non-State Conflict, and One-Sided Violence, 1989–2014
Figure created by Erik Melander on the basis of the UCDP data for the three categories of violence.

NEW WARS

According to a widespread claim, civilians suffer more from civil war and warlike situations today than in earlier times. The very nature of war has changed, according to several scholars. The most influential argument comes from Mary Kaldor (1999), who coined the term "New Wars." Kaldor identifies three particularly important historical developments: the increasing salience of identity in politics, the transformation of war economies, and the end of the bipolar world order of the Cold War. Wars based on identity politics are believed to be especially brutal toward members of the outgroup, transformed war economies means that armed groups increasingly come to depend on looting civilians, and the end of the rivalry between the superpowers removed their restraining influence over their allies. Critics have argued that the impact of these changes is misunderstood in the theorizing about the changing nature of civil war. For example, Kalyvas (2001: 116), in a review of ethnographical studies, finds that "both the perception that violence in old civil wars is limited, disciplined, or understandable and the view that violence in new civil wars is senseless, gratuitous, and uncontrolled fails to find support in the available evidence." The claim that civilian suffering has increased with the advent of the New Wars can be interpreted in two ways. Either other forms of organized mass violence taking place outside the context of traditionally defined state-based civil conflict have increased, or the severity of civilian victimization has increased in ongoing civil conflicts. Our data for other forms of organized violence in figure 1.10 suggest that the first possibility can be dismissed—there is no increasing trend since 1989 in non-state conflict or in one-sided violence. The genocide in Rwanda in 1994 stands out as an exceptionally destructive event in the post–Cold War period, but mass killings of civilians happened more frequently during the Cold War, according to data from the Political Instability Task Force (Center for Systemic Peace 2014).

In order to gauge the extent of civilian victimization in civil conflict, Melander, Öberg, and Hall (2009) analyzed the average levels of politicide/genocide and forced displacement in country-years with civil conflict. Taking into account other factors that might dampen the human impact of civil conflict, such as democracy and economic development, they found that to the extent there is any trend in the data, it is contrary to the New Wars thesis. In fact, the wars of the post–Cold War period are less atrocious on average. An update to 2014 shows a continued downward trend in the average magnitude of genocide during civil conflict (figure 1.11).[17] Greater civilian suffering could happen if civil conflicts cause other forms of violence to increase. While armed conflicts do seem to be associated with higher overall levels of homicide (Archer and Gartner 1984; Fox and Hoelscher 2012), it is not clear whether levels of homicide in conflict contexts have increased after the Cold War than in earlier periods. Cohen and Nordås (2014) find an increase in the use of sexual violence in

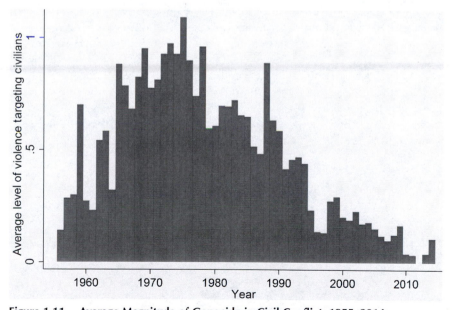

Figure 1.11.   Average Magnitude of Genocide in Civil Conflict, 1955–2014
Figure created by Erik Melander on the basis of UCDP/PRIO data for intrastate armed conflict and data on genocides from the Center for Systemic Peace (2015).

war from 1989 and up until around 2003, after which there has been a significant decrease. However, we do not have data for sexual violence predating the Cold War.

THE FUTURE OF CONFLICT

It is tempting to map the future of conflict by forecasting from current trends.[18] The decline in armed conflict after the end of the Cold War gave rise to widespread optimism about world peace built on democracy and the market economy. The events of September 11, 2001, and the drawn-out wars in Afghanistan and Iraq nullified much of this optimism. But such trend prolongation, whether optimistic or pessimistic, is a hazardous exercise. For one thing, as we have shown, the severity of armed conflict in a given year has traditionally been dependent on single conflicts. Had nuclear war between the two superpowers broken out during the Cold War, it would probably have given us a peak higher than World War II. If the current crisis between Russia and the West were to escalate, it could have a similar result, although most observers would rate this as much less likely than an escalation during the Cold War. The 1999 Kargil War, which barely made it over the one thousand battle deaths threshold, pitted two nuclear states, India and Pakistan, against each other. Had the conflict escalated to all-out war, the outcome would obviously have been much bloodier.

In order to make more realistic projections about the future, we need to look at reasonable prognoses for the main causal factors behind conflict. On the basis of our current knowledge about the main factors promoting conflict (such as Collier and Hoeffler 2004; Fearon and Laitin 2003; Hegre et al. 2001; Hegre and Sambanis 2006), Hegre et al. (2013) have worked out a forecasting model that projects a continued decline in the proportion of the world's countries that have intrastate armed conflict, from about 15 percent in 2009 to 7 percent in 2050. The substance of this forecasting model potentially spans the themes of all the other chapters of this book. As we gather more knowledge about the causes of civil war, we shall also be able to better assess its future.

2

Antecedents of Civil War Onset

Greed, Grievance, and State Repression

Joseph K. Young

When do civil wars begin? Some may point to John Brown's guerrilla strikes on Harper's Ferry, West Virginia, in 1859 as the precipitating event for the U.S. Civil War.[1] Brown, a radical abolitionist, along with over twenty other men, raided the town, took weapons from the local barracks, and seemed to demonstrate to the South that settlement of the slavery issue would require force (Howard 1978). Most historians date the beginning of the U.S. Civil War as the Battle of Fort Sumter in South Carolina, which raged from April 12 to April 14, 1861, two years after Harpers Ferry (Detzer 2001). Most courses on the U.S. Civil War, however, begin by discussing the constitutional issues of slavery, the Three-Fifths Compromise, then move to the Missouri Compromise, Bloody Kansas, and other events that were antecedents to formal declarations of war between the North and the South of the United States.[2] Which view of the beginning of the U.S. Civil War is the most accurate? On one hand, we might think about the onset of a new civil war. In this view, wars start like the beginning of the universe—with a big bang. Similar to religious and scientific arguments over this moment of creation, *big bang* civil war scholars argue that these conflicts just break out. The central debate is whether rebel opportunities to predate or challenge the state cause this outbreak or whether the intensity of group grievances is the proper tinder. On the other hand, *process*-oriented scholars suggest wars build up through a dynamic interaction of violence.

Let's consider a more contemporary example, the civil war in El Salvador that spanned from the 1970s to the early 1990s. Some scholars date the beginning of the war to a military coup that began in 1979 and ushered in a brutally repressive regime. Some accounts suggest the war began in 1980, sparked by events such as the murder of popular archbishop Monsignor Oscar Romero and other events orchestrated by an elite working in concert with the military (Stanley 1996). Later in the year, many rebel groups joined an alliance, the Farabundo Martí National Liberation Front (FMLN) to jointly challenge the regime and pursue civil war. Many of these groups, however, began their insurrection at least a decade prior, and some authors suggest the roots of the war were planted in a 1930s massacre by the government called *La Matanza* (Wood 2003). Again, in a *big bang* approach, we might search for a proximate event that led to conflict that exceeded a large number of deaths. If we consider the processes between the state and dissidents, our story will include events and interactions that preceded this catalyzing event.

The consequences of this implicit choice of studying a big bang or process influence how scholars conceptualize civil war, how they measure it, and how empirically civil war is modeled. In this chapter, I discuss the development of the quantitative civil war literature in the post–Cold War era. First, I discuss how civil war is defined and how different scholars measure this phenomenon. Second, I discuss some of the standard explanations for why civil war begins. Most of these explanations tend to follow a big bang approach that organizes a dichotomy between greedy rebels or aggrieved ones. The greed-versus-grievance arguments have been structured over a decade of civil war research. I argue for thinking about this more generally as an interaction between states and dissidents and integrating with process-oriented arguments built from the repression and dissent literature. Finally, based on a potential synthesis of standard approaches and a process approach, I discuss different future directions for the study of civil war, including how to integrate macro- and micro-level studies, how to best predict civil war, and how to think about strategic nonviolence as part of a larger repertoire of contention.

DEFINING CIVIL WAR

What is civil war? Useful definitions of critical concepts tell us what the phenomenon is and what it is not.[3] Standard definitions of civil war stress violence within a state, involving the national government and rebels, that produces deaths above a certain number. Focusing on the intrastate dimension helps distinguish civil war from the interstate variety. Specifying that the violence includes the national government *and* rebels helps to distinguish civil war from one-sided violence, such as politicide or genocide (Rummel 1995; chapter 1 this volume). Finally, using a death threshold distinguishes civil war from lower level conflict, such as terrorism.[4]

These differences among types of political violence may be more difficult to neatly discern as initially suggested. For example, war rarely is contained within a single country. Civil conflicts may bleed over into other states due to refugees fleeing the violence (Moore and Shellman 2007). Refugees may also be the cause of the civil conflict as they change local demographics, have ties to outside violent networks, and import ideas and materials for the production of violence (Salehyan and Gleditsch 2006). Additionally, these forms of political violence can occur at the same time. Terrorism, for example, often occurs in the context of civil war (Findley and Young 2012). Terror can be used to control populations (Kalyvas 2006) or spoil the peace (Kydd and Walter 2002) or as part of a larger strategy to force negotiations (Thomas 2014). Finally, an intrastate war may be interrupted by an external power or become *internationalized* (Themnér and Wallensteen 2014), such as in the current conflict in Syria. These issues make identifying a civil war separately from other forms of political violence complicated. In practice, however, scholars simplify the task by highlighting the reasons why civil war is distinct and uniquely destructive from other kinds of political violence.

MEASURING CIVIL WAR

So far, the discussion has focused on conceptually defining civil war and determining when a war begins. In the quantitative literature on civil wars, however, most scholars identify an operational definition of civil war, or a way to count what is and what is not civil war. The operational definition includes the relevant actors involved (e.g., government versus rebel group), the start date for the war, and a severity threshold that distinguishes civil wars from other forms of political violence (see, for example, Small and Singer 1982).

As Sambanis (2004) notes, in his work on defining and coding civil wars, a straightforward definition (e.g., war within a state, involving the state and rebels, that exceeds a battle-death threshold, such as one thousand deaths) leads to some inconsistencies and generates the need for ad hoc rules to deal with the complexity of defining the civil war concept. For example, how organized do the rebels need to be to be coded as a rebel group? If we use death thresholds to identify civil war, how do we deal with unreliable reporting? Since civil wars often proceed in fits and starts, how do we count the beginning of a new war as opposed to a continuation of an old war (Sambanis 2004: 816)?

Because of the complexity of creating an operational definition, several lists of civil wars are widely used in empirical research. Data projects by Fearon and Laitin (2003), the Correlates of War Project (Sarkees and Wayman 2010), and UCDP/PRIO have generated data on the onset of intrastate conflicts from 1816 to the present (Gleditsch et al. 2002). Regardless of how these projects produce different civil war lists (Hegre and Sambanis 2006), nearly all of the operational definitions of civil war include some death threshold or rules about counting a war within a particular range of battle deaths (Sambanis 2004). The UCDP data (Harbom and Wallensteen 2012) are unique in that they offer different thresholds for battle deaths to distinguish onsets of minor intrastate armed conflict (more than 25 battle deaths) from civil war (more than 1,000 battle deaths).[5] Sambanis (2004) suggests that coding a civil war by thinking about a more flexible interval of battle deaths might be a practical choice. More consistent with a process approach, we could consider an event as a civil war when aggregated deaths exceed a particular value (usually around 1,000 deaths) over the course of a conflict, but each year those casualties may vary and be less than 1,000.[6] This could also mitigate Sambanis's (2004) and others' concerns about unreliable reporting. Since we are not as concerned about being precise in the annual counts of battle deaths, we could minimize measurement error.

In deciding what is or is not a rebel group, we can again use some practical decision rules. Three considerations stand out: (1) rebel group goals, (2) difference from other actors (criminals), and (3) organizational structure. In terms of goals, rebel groups want to challenge the sovereignty of the state, or its monopoly over the use of legitimate violence (Tilly 1978). They may want to take over the state, transform it, or secede from it

(Gates 2002). In contrast to criminals, rebel groups have political motivations (Dugan and LaFree 2004). Finally, rebel groups have structure and are not a loose conglomerate of people (Weinstein 2006). Rebel groups create organized structures to organize group activities and leadership selection, with some groups even utilizing elections to select their leaders (e.g., groups in Ethiopia, India, and Somalia).

The final consideration is, how do we think about a civil war that proceeds in fits and starts? Classic coding provides an arbitrary time unit to separate new and old wars (see, for example, Collier and Hoeffler 2001). In a big bang approach, this choice may make sense. In short, conditions at one time led to an onset of war, time passed, and new conditions arose. In contrast, in a process approach, we would consider whether the underlying interactions between actors have changed. We consider whether the same actors were involved, and whether the incompatibility that began the first war was resolved prior to the onset of a new war.

Coding data and measuring concepts can influence the outcomes we develop. Since our empirical findings and policies are influenced by data, these data have to be as accurate as possible. Where these small changes in our data, due to rules like what counts as a rebel group or when a new civil war starts, influence *why* we think civil war began, we need to be open and clear and show these implications.[7]

Also implicit in this definitional approach is the belief that civil war begins once the right mix of ingredients is included. In short, civil war will break out when this mixture is right. Given this, an implicit assumption that needs to be explicit is to think about beginning a definition of civil war by acknowledging that it is a conflict caused by the interaction between states and dissidents.[8] In other words, there is a process of violence, action, and reactions by the state and dissidents that build to a civil war (Young 2008, 2013). This seems like a truism, but it has some critical, overlooked implications. If civil war is a *process* of violence, then defining it requires identifying the state and dissidents explicitly and acknowledging their contributions to the production of violence. Relatedly, if it is the interaction of these actors that gets a conflict above a certain death threshold, then we need to model dissent and repression and the consequences of this joint production of violence.[9]

EXPLAINING CIVIL WAR ONSET

The end of the Cold War brought a renewed interest to understanding the causes and consequences of civil wars.[10] As Fearon and Laitin (2003) showed, civil wars were not on the rise per se in terms of frequency, but they were far more deadly in the post–World War II world and more difficult to resolve than their interstate cousins (see also Walter 1997) and also tended to last far longer.[11] Early work on political violence suggested that grievances were the motivating factor for internal rebellion (Brinton 1938; Davies 1962; Gurr 1970). Whether these grievances were due to rising expectations and unfulfilled outcomes (Davies 1962) or relative deprivation (Gurr 1970), the root cause in revolutions lay in citizens' grievances, whether real or perceived. In this perspective, individual anger toward the government for unresolved religious, ethnic, or ideological reasons helps explain why individuals are moved to violence against the state. The state might be unable to satisfy these cleavages (Davies 1962), or coercion by the state helps create some of the grievances of the populace (Gurr 1988). Grievances are an intuitively plausible explanation for civil war as they are constantly expressed by the rebels and are often what media report as the underlying cause of the conflict. During the civil war in El Salvador, a rural participant suggested that people were moved to take part in mobilization against the state for religious reasons. They suggested that "[i]t was Biblical Study that made people conscious, a process that eventually took another form. By means of the Bible, it all began" (as quoted in Wood 2003: 89).

A standard critique of some grievance-based claims for civil war relates to difficulty in identifying subjective grievances (Walker and Pettigrew 1984) or the general ubiquitous nature of grievances across time and space (Muller and Weede 1994). For example, if groups have grievances over a long period of time, how can we explain why civil war breaks out in one year rather than another? Moreover, these approaches did not properly address how people banded together to collectively act on these grievances.[12] In many of the places of the world with the highest levels of economic inequality, such as Brazil, civil war is not common. Thus, even though citizens may have grievances toward the government, they do not always act upon those frustrations by forming or joining rebel groups.

Due, in part, to the inconsistency in empirical findings, grievance-based explanations fell out of favor in the post–Cold War literature.[13] Initially, there was an interest in *old* versus *new* wars. Kaldor (1999) suggested that *new* wars were based on identity rather than classic material concerns like territory and were excessively brutal, citing the Bosnian civil war as an example. These newer wars would be low intensity and both interstate and intrastate in scope. Kalyvas (2001), however, debunked this view as it pertained to civil wars, suggesting that it is difficult to ascertain a monocausal explanation of war, as individual motivations vary over even a single conflict and new *and* old civil wars are equally destructive and deadly. In the current civil war in Syria, for example, motivations for opposing the Assad regime could range from ideological to economic to religious to simple revenge for a disappeared or killed loved one.

In contrast, a new post–Cold War literature on civil war has tended to privilege structural explanations for civil war onset (Fearon and Laitin 2003, Collier and Hoeffler 2004).[14] In this work, opportunities for rebellion explain why we see civil war occur in some places but not others. For Collier and Hoeffler (2004), *greed* explains the onset of civil war. Greed can come in many forms, but it is prevalent where rebels have opportunities for predation and where opportunity costs of rebellion are low. In these structural situations where rebellion is low cost, we should expect the onset of civil war. In the first version, focusing on opportunities for predatory behavior, rebels can use natural resource endowments for financing attempts at becoming the sovereign or monopolizer of violence in a given territory (Grossman 1999). Natural resource endowments can take on several forms, including diamonds, oil, illicit drugs, or other so-called *lootable* resources (Ross 2006). While these arguments have suggested that many forms of primary commodities can be used to predate and finance rebellion, more nuanced claims suggest some resources are more easily lootable[15] or translated into rebel finance (Ross 2004a; Snyder and Bhavnani 2005).[16] Weinstein (2005, 2006) argues that how the rebels finance their conflict can influence not only who they recruit but also the groups' strategies for employing indiscriminate or targeted violence.

Beyond looting and natural resources, rebels' opportunity costs may influence the likelihood of civil war onset. Where the costs of rebelling are low relative to the opportunities for predation and eventual overtaking of the state, we might expect more civil war onsets (Collier and Hoeffler 2004). Conflicts in sub-Saharan Africa, such as in Liberia or Sierra Leone, seemed to be explained by this insight. These conflicts included a toxic mix of a weak state, opportunity to acquire natural resources to fuel violence, and lack of options for many citizens. While Collier and Hoeffler interpret poverty as the mechanism linking low income to civil conflict, this is not the only explanation (Sambanis 2004b). In short, and a point that will be developed later, the link between poverty could flow through the state, or weak states lead to civil conflict or to opportunity costs for rebels as Collier and Hoeffler (2004) suggest.

Collier and Hoeffler (2004) find that empirical proxies for greed, such as primary commodity exports, GDP per capita, and GDP growth, covary with the onset of civil war in their data. In their explanation and empirical model, they interpret this to mean that arguments about rebel opportunity costs are useful to explain onset of civil war. By contrast, they find less support for *grievances* or empirical proxies such as income inequality, ethnic fractionalization, or religious fractionalization that might explain variation in their civil war data. Importantly, this approach pointed scholars and policy makers toward focusing on a subset of at-risk, weak states as particularly prone to civil war.

Berdal (2005) and Ballentine and Sherman (2003) argued in favor of moving beyond the greed versus grievance story. Berdal (2005), in particular, suggested focusing on more local processes to understand individual conflict traps. By 2009, Collier and his colleagues made a similar set of arguments (Collier et al. 2009). Regardless, the greed story of rebellion had a large policy impact by permeating through the World Bank, leading to dozens of policy papers, a collection of case studies, and a legion of academic articles.[17]

Although they do not discuss greed and grievance, Fearon and Laitin (2003) offer a complementary approach, but suggest that state weakness explains the puzzle of civil war. Instead of linking rebel opportunity, via predation or poverty, to civil war onset, Fearon and Laitin suggest that states with *weak* counterinsurgent capabilities create opportunities for rebellion. These opportunities come in several forms, but factors that increase the probability that rebels can mount a credible offensive are the most important. Fearon and Laitin provide a comprehensive set of empirical evidence, including new data on coding civil war and detailed sensitivity analyses to make sure results are robust to alternative claims, such as grievances associated with religion or ethnicity.[18]

Similar data to Collier and Hoeffler's (2004) are used as empirical proxies of state capacity. Whereas Collier and Hoeffler find a strong link between measures of GDP and civil war and interpret this as support for the opportunity cost story, Fearon and Laitin find a similar empirical relationship and interpret low income per capita as the state's inability to effectively counter insurgencies (Sambanis 2004b). Fearon and Laitin find a robust relationship between GDP, mountainous terrain, and population and civil war onset and further see this as confirmation for their claims about weak state capacity increasing the risks for civil war. In sum, these important pieces suggest that opportunities for rebellion are the critical ingredient to explain the outbreak or big bang of civil war. They use different coding decisions and different data, but both studies find structural proxies of *opportunity* to be the most significant factors for understanding civil war onset.[19]

In an earlier article on interstate war, Starr (1978) suggested that *opportunity and willingness* were central ordering concepts in the study of war generally. In short, war should occur where there are opportunities for violence and willingness by each side for such acts. Fearon and Laitin (2003) and Collier and Hoeffler (2004) and subsequent research building on these pieces tend to focus on the opportunity side, albeit for different reasons. If opportunity and willingness help to explain actors' reasons for engaging in civil war, then this is analogous to greed and grievance, but the opportunity and willingness framework provides a more general way to think about conflict. Greed and grievance, then, are simply special cases of willingness and opportunity, respectively.

In many ways, Starr's work is similar to criminological studies that utilize so-called Routine Activities Theory (Osgood et al. 1996). In this framework, crime should occur when there is a motivated offender, a suitable target, and lack of a capable guardian. These three necessary conditions explain crime.[20] Both theories have been useful in outlining the total possibilities of explanations for violence at an individual or state level. Critiques of each approach have tended to suggest that they are true by definition, but cannot give more precise guidance about why some people will be violent or why some states are more prone to war than others (Henson et al. 2010). In the context of this post–Cold War quantitative civil war research, opportunities for civil conflict are privileged over willingness explanations. Assuming both portions of opportunity and willingness matter for civil war, willingness accounts are likely underrepresented.[21]

As with greed and opportunity, if we think of grievances as a special case of willingness to rebel, there are arguments beyond the simple grievance story. State repression is certainly an important source of grievance within any society. Lichbach (1987), among others, has examined whether state repression leads to mobilizing dissent or demobilizes it through deterrence. As Mason and Krane (1989) show, as the repression becomes more indiscriminate and the level of repression increases, the population moves away from supporting the state and is more likely to engage in civil conflict. The puzzle of why repression sometimes deters and at other times mobilizes may hinge on this issue of discrimination.

Bringing opportunity and willingness arguments together is a possible path forward. Certain configurations of different states and regime types likely breed more grievance than others (Hegre et al. 2001; Fjelde 2010; Gurses and Mason 2010). Hegre et al. (2001) argue that consolidated democracies that produce fewer grievances should be the least susceptible to civil war. Strong autocracies may produce willingness to rebel but offer little opportunity, lying in the middle of the regime spectrum where opportunities and willingness are both present and where civil war will occur.

Whether we adopt a greed/opportunity or grievance/willingness approach to explaining civil war, most research assumes civil war *breaks out* instead of building up through a process of interaction between states and dissidents. The quantitative tradition, in particular, models civil war empirically with a single equation that treats each additional variable as an extra covariate that can raise or lower the probability of a war breaking out in a given country-year.[22] Where this research has been most successful is in identifying a risk set of countries, generally with lootable resources, low GDP, or weak state institutions, and focusing scholarly and policy attention to these cases. This research can thus help explain *where* conflict is likely to erupt. The prevailing weakness, however, is that these models cannot tell us *when* conflict will occur. Using structural data, such as GDP or resource stocks, does not allow much variation in these cases over time. To understand the iterative processes that occur between the states and rebels and how these lead to more or less violent outcomes, we need data and models that bring time and interaction into the story.

Earlier work on repression and dissent tended to avoid discussions of civil war at all, instead focusing on how the two sides (states and dissidents) change their behavior conditional to the actions of each other (Lichbach 1987; Davenport 1995; Rasler 1996; Moore 1998, 2000). In this broad formulation, dissidents could rebel violently or nonviolently and states choose to repress or accommodate. Central questions relate to how these strategies or tactics interact, which strategies are more successful than others, and how to properly model this interaction. This research was inherently engaged in micro-level processes and data and was a precursor to the more recent disaggregating civil war movement in the mid-2000s (Cederman and Gleditsch 2009).

Work by Young (2013) and Lichbach et al. (2004) explicitly linked the repression and dissent literature with the newer work on civil war. Lichbach et al. (2004) criticized the literature generally, and Fearon and Laitin (2003) specifically, for not thinking about past conflict processes. Rather than assuming that past actions by the state and dissidents had no influence on an onset of civil war, Young (2008), used several modeling strategies[23] to explain first why states repress and why groups use dissent, and then how changes in repression and dissent lead to moving beyond a threshold we call civil war. Both Young (2013) and Lichbach et al. (2004) used measures of conflict between states and dissidents, or actual dynamic measures of interaction, rather than structural variables with little temporal variation. Young (2013) critiqued the dominant approach, building on claims by Ward et al. (2010) showing that typical civil war onset models were not good at predicting war. Most of the structural or opportunity models used data that varied across countries but not much over time. These models, in other words, could explain where civil war was likely but not predict *when* civil war was likely to occur. From a policy perspective, being able to incorporate temporal dynamics is an obvious reason for why models built on state-dissident interaction are inherently more useful than structural models.[24]

While Lichbach et al. (2004) used a conventional single-equation model to estimate the onset of civil war, Young (2013) suggested modeling the process in a two-stage procedure, which more accurately captured what first produced repression and dissent and then how repression and dissent escalated to civil war. Similarly to Shellman et al. (2013), Young (2013) did not completely reject the use of opportunity (e.g., structural or greed) measures, but argued for including measures of state and dissident choice to more accurately predict where civil war was likely to occur. With the inclusion of repression and dissent measures, Young's (2013) model provided better in-and-out of sample predictions of where and when civil war would occur. Importantly, like Mason and Krane (1989) and Rasler (1996), Young (2013) finds that repression is the key driver in the process of violence. In the first stage, where leaders are insecure or when they are likely to lose office, they are more likely to use repression. In the second stage, repression increases the likelihood of civil war dramatically. In 2011 in Syria, the president, Bashar al-Assad, felt insecure given the wave of activism spreading through the region. In response to some anti-regime graffiti, al-Assad jailed and tortured the youths held responsible. This repression sparked further mobilization against the regime. This dynamic process quickly developed into a bloody civil war still underway in 2015.

States, as Davenport (2007b) suggests, use a law of coercive responsiveness when challenged by dissidents, making repression a trigger for more conflict. After a more careful quasi-experimental design, opportunity explanations, which privilege GDP or population, still find support, but the overall effects are attenuated (Young 2008).

CONCLUSION

After tracing some of the progress of the quantitative study of civil war, this chapter showed two important developments. First, civil war studies can be enriched by incorporating the literature, modeling techniques, and insights of the repression and dissent literature. This literature's focus on process, interaction, and micro-level units of observation can be profitable when one is trying to model complex civil war violence. As violence by both sides can escalate conflicts, it helps to think about lower-level violence as an antecedent to civil war rather than civil war as something that just happens (e.g., a big bang). Second, thinking about a civil war does not have to be done using a dualist approach. Is it greed or grievance? Or opportunity and willingness? Or structure versus process? The best answer is probably all of the above. Rather than ignoring the insights of any of these literatures, a synthesis is the best approach. Macro-level studies can point us to cross-national differences and large structures that are more conducive to political violence. We can identify places with underlying greed/grievance motivations as risky. Coupled with escalatory behaviors by states and dissidents, we can establish a clearer picture of the pathways to civil war and the decisions made by actors that lead us in these directions. The future challenge is weighting the explanations based on context, timing, culture, and other micro-level factors.

While a disaggregation movement in civil war studies began in the mid-2000s, more recently there has been a micro-level turn. Lyall (2010), for example, collects data at precise spatial and temporal units of aggregation to investigate state-dissident interactions within a single country or a small set of countries.[25] This general approach favors studying civil war using a more process-oriented approach that incorporates repression and dissent. Cunningham et al. (chapter 15, this volume) discuss how micro-level data can account for the actors involved in conflict, where they choose to fight, and how they contest for power at the local level.

A challenge is, however, how do we scale these results up? A benefit of the quantitative studies in the early 2000s was their generalizability and the possibility that they represent big trends in post–World War II conflict. An obvious trade-off was the internal validity of the research as data were collected at higher levels of spatial and temporal aggregation. Micro-level studies tend to privilege the exact opposite. We can be more confident that *sweep* operations in Chechnya from 2000 to 2005 had a precise effect on violence in the region during this time period. We cannot be confident that this result can be applied to other kinds of counterinsurgency or applied to Afghanistan or Iraq or even to Chechnya from 1993 to 1999. We need studies that examine both micro- and macro-results, but macro-results work because lower barriers to entry have been more common.

Relatedly, there has been a recent turn toward studying strategic nonviolence. Chenoweth and Stephan (2011) and Stephan and Chenoweth (2008) along with work by Schock (2005) argue that strategic nonviolence is a more effective strategy when dissidents use it, as compared to violence, when challenging a state. Even when faced with a repressive state, possibly the critical driver of a civil war, the tactic of nonviolence can lead to strategic success. Since nonviolence attracts greater international support and sympathy as well as domestic involvement (Chenoweth and Stephan 2011), an increase in the use of this strategy could lead to larger reductions in civil war onsets while still allowing citizens to mobilize in the face of an unresponsive or repressive regime. In Tunisia, a pro-democracy, mainly nonviolent movement in 2011 brought down the regime. While the dictatorship in Tunisia did not repress its citizens as much as other states in the region, other nonviolent movements from South Africa (1983–1990) to the Philippines (1983–1986) brought down more repressive dictators without civil war (Schock 2005). This interest in nonviolence is inherently linked to a more process-oriented approach. If dissidents can choose these various tactics and be met by different responses, then the state, then only thinking about the big bang of civil war, will miss many of the antecedents and drivers of the conflict.

Finally, as the need for predictive models grows, incorporating dissident and state interactions along with structural models is likely the most comprehensive approach to explaining the onset of civil war. The quantitative civil war literature rightly pointed analysts, journalists, and observers to weak or poor states. Beyond this sorting mechanism, we still need to understand when these conflicts will develop to strengthen institutions and protect individuals. Early-warning models and prediction based on real-time data that deal with the interactions between the state and dissidents seemed highly unlikely a decade ago, but the reality is that this approach is both feasible and perhaps the best way to evaluate the factors that lead to civil war onset. For example, Jay Ulfelder, a political scientist and statistical modeler, developed an early-warning system paid for by the U.S. Holocaust Memorial Museum to provide policy makers with a predictive tool to head off these atrocities.[26] These data and models can help resolve academic debates and also improve the human condition. While debates over how we best think about and model the problem of civil war sometimes seem abstract, the consequences, unfortunately, for many people in affected areas are all too real.

3

Identity Issues and Civil War

Ethnic and Religious Divisions

Lee J. M. Seymour and Kathleen Gallagher Cunningham

Ethnic and religious identities are entangled in most civil wars. By some accounts, as many as 64 percent of civil wars have been fought along ethnic lines in recent decades (Denny and Walter 2014; Themner and Wallensteen 2012). As we write in late 2014, a bloody sectarian war in Syria fought mainly between Alawis and Sunnis has spilled over the borders into Iraq and threatens Lebanon's delicate sectarian politics. The explosive rise of the Islamic State in parts of Syria and Iraq demonstrates the potency of religious mobilization. Russia has annexed Crimea and intervened in Ukraine's civil war in defense of ethnic Russians. In South Sudan, feuding elites have mobilized tribal militias and disaffected army elements, with much fighting on the ground pitting rival Nuer and Dinka ethnic groups. These cases underscore the prevalence of ethnic and religious conflict, reinforce popular beliefs about the prevalence of identity conflict, and suggest the limits of ethnic and religious accommodation in many societies. Indeed, approximately 14 percent of the ethnic minorities in the world have been involved in significant violence against the state (Gurr 1996; Fearon 2008).

Yet most ethnic groups in most places live without experiencing large-scale, organized ethnic violence (Fearon and Laitin 1996). Indeed, much research suggests that the entanglement of ethnic and religious identity in political violence and civil war is highly complex. Even civil wars viewed as "ethnic" or "religious" in character are fought in ways that complicate popular understandings of the role being played by such identities (Kalyvas 2003). For instance, in the wars engulfing Syria and Iraq, notwithstanding the zeal of Sunni Salafists and Shi'a and Alawite radicals on either side, alliances between armed groups and the regional governments backing them appear largely opportunistic in nature. In eastern Ukraine, the roots of the current conflict between Ukrainians and Russians are arguably more economic than ethnic (Zhukov 2014). And in South Sudan, the logic of violence is essentially material rather than ethnic: "On the surface these appear to be ethnic conflicts, but that is a product of ethnic patronage that constitutes military units, not deep-rooted tribal animosities" (de Waal 2014: 362). Whereas most students would quickly point to ethnic identities as the main cause of civil war, the empirical findings are actually quite mixed.

Under what conditions are we likely to see violence organized around ethnic and religious cleavages, and what implications does this have for the dynamics of civil wars? We answer these questions by reviewing the voluminous literature on the identity dimensions of civil war.[1] We first define our terms, noting controversies over fundamental concepts such as ethnicity, identity, and nationalism. The second section then reviews what we think we know about the conditions under which identity matters for civil war, examining the role of identity in how wars begin, how they are fought, and how they end. We conclude by noting exciting directions for future research. While the findings are mixed and the mechanisms connecting identity to violence remain debated, the past three decades have seen considerable progress in our understanding of identity in civil wars.

ETHNIC AND RELIGIOUS IDENTITIES IN CIVIL WAR RESEARCH

The politics of identity came relatively late to the academic study of civil war. In 1970, for example, a decade after the turn to identity politics in the social sciences, Ted Gurr's path-breaking contribution *Why Men Rebel* made little direct reference to ethnic or religious identities. Literatures on political violence and social revolution, on one hand, and studies on ethnicity and nationalism, on the other hand, developed largely in parallel with each other. Only with Horowitz's (1985) *Ethnic Groups in Conflict* did the two large literatures come together. In the following two decades (1985–2005), the number of articles dealing with ethnicity and nationalism in political science roughly quadrupled (Cederman 2012). Civil war has been a major focus of this literature, alongside other violent episodes such as riots, terrorism, mass killing and genocide, and state violence and repression.

Several factors converged to drive this interest in the confluence of identity politics and civil war. These included the realization that violence is a key impediment to development, which raised the profile of identity politics in economics and political economy. Another reason for the focus on ethnic conflict was the marked decline in interstate war that saw a number of international relations specialists turn their attention to "internal" conflicts. Events themselves were a major driver, in particular the breakup of the Soviet and Yugoslav states in a burst of ethno-nationalism, with shocking violence in the interrelated separatist and irredentist wars in Yugoslavia. This coincided with emergence of a number of failed states racked by identity conflicts and incidents of ethnically motivated violence and mass killings, especially the 1994 Rwandan genocide.

Similarly, interest in religious identity, a relatively neglected area of study aside from the debate sparked by Huntington's *Clash of Civilizations* (1996),[2] surged after the terrorist attacks of September 11, 2001. The emergence and persistence of religiously inspired and organized insurgent groups in places such as Somalia, Kenya, Yemen, Nigeria, Chechnya, Syria, and Iraq has driven a renewed focus on religious identity. Despite echoes of a "clash of civilizations," these conflicts arguably have their roots in parochial tribal rivalries and historical relations between center and periphery, rather than transnational conflict between religiously organized civilizations. The murkiness and complexity of these conflicts underscores the need to shed light on the particular identities and grievances entangled in these wars.

Much research has focused on problems of defining and operationalizing key terms such as *identity*, *ethnicity* and *religion*. An identity is a social category denoting "some fundamental and consequential sameness" in which an individual is eligible to be a member (Brubaker and Cooper 2000). Hale (2004) conceives of identity as a kind of "social radar" that provides individuals with a point of reference, allowing them to situate themselves within a wider group and understand how their membership affects them in the social world, including relations with other groups.

Ethnic identity is correspondingly conceived as a subset of identities in which eligibility for membership is determined by attributes based on common descent (Horowitz 1985). A crucial property of these descent-based attributes is that they are both difficult to change in the short term and visible to other members of society (Chandra 2006). More specifically, "attributes associated with or believed to be associated with" ethnicity include

> those acquired genetically (e.g., skin color, gender, hair type, eye color, height, and physical features), through cultural and historical inheritance (e.g., name, language, place of birth, and origin of one's parents and ancestors), or in the course of one's lifetime as markers of such an inheritance (e.g., last name or tribal markings). Attributes "believed to be associated with descent" are attributes around which a credible myth of association with descent has been woven, whether or not such an association exists in fact. (Chandra 2006: 400)

Following Horowitz (1985: 46) and Rogowski (1985), we can distinguish the "strength of ethnic markers" as a function of how recognizable they are and how costly they are to change. This leads to two expectations: first, the stronger the ethnic markers that distinguish members of a group from its rival, the more easily members of one group can be singled out for discriminatory treatment by the members of the rival group; and second, the stronger those markers, the less likely is assimilation and the more likely conflict between the groups.

Religious identity is sometimes synonymous with ethnicity but, conceived in terms of the strength of ethnic markers, is generally harder to identify (or easier to conceal) and less costly to change. For some groups, religious and ethnic identities may be more or less the same, as with Armenians who are overwhelmingly Armenian Orthodox, or Ashkenazi Jews, whose ethnic identity is wrapped up in Judaism.

However, as Ashutosh Varshney notes, the distinction between ethnic and religious identity "becomes critical . . . when ethnicity and religion clash (East and West Pakistan before 1971, Kashmiri Hindus and Muslims, Irish Protestants and Catholics, black and white American Christians)" (Varshney 2009).

Thus, while religion is often an important feature of ethnicity, the two concepts are not synonymous. One way of thinking of religious identities as separate from national or ethnic identities is to emphasize the element of practices such as "sacrifice, prayer, meditation, pilgrimage, war, proselytization and charitable acts" (Toft 2011: 674). Religious identities are thus rooted in

> a system of practice and belief in the attainment of a beneficial personal or collective shift in existence (heaven, nirvana, paradise, salvation, ecstasy, transcendence, oneness, peace), by means of acting or not acting in specific ways which are constitutive of an established community practice, and for which empirical referents are either unnecessary or, indeed, anathema. (Toft 2011: 674)

Religion shares ethnicity's descent-based character insofar as one is often born into a religious identity, though the intensity of religious identities are potentially tied to the extent one ceases to practice and believe in a way that ethnicity is not. We understand what it might mean to be a lapsed Catholic who no longer attends church, or nonobservant Muslim who does not pray and enjoys the occasional whiskey, or an atheist Jew who eats bacon and shellfish. The same individuals can have tightly overlapping ethnic identities as, say, Poles, Somalis, or Jewish Americans, but ethnicity is not necessarily diminished by the same actions. Conversely, because ethnicity involves descent-based attributes, converting to Catholicism, Sunni Islam, or Judaism, does not necessarily make one ethnically Polish, Somali, or American Jewish.

These definitions are not without their critics. As an analytic category, identity is "riddled with ambiguity, riven with contradictory meanings, and encumbered by reifying connotations," so much so that some scholars propose dropping the term altogether (Brubaker and Cooper 2000: 34). Chandra has argued that many of the causal claims made for ethnicity in political science research concern properties that are not intrinsic to ethnic identity (2006). Such claims concern characteristics such as fixity, territorial concentration, dense social networks, cultural cohesiveness, or the emotional reactions that identities elicit, all of which vary across both ethnicities and other identity groups. Similarly, the relationship of clan, caste, tribal, sectarian, and linguistic identities to ethnicity, and of ethnicity to nationalism, remains contested (Calhoun 1993; Schatz 2013).

The ambiguity of identity complicates measurement and comparison, particularly in large-N datasets. Many arguments about ethnic identity stress the importance of diversity, with various measures aiming to capture *polarization* and *fractionalization* in a given population (Easterly and Levine 1997). Early measures of "ethno-linguistic fractionalization," or ELF, calculated a concentration index on the basis of Soviet ethnographic data collected in the 1960s and published in the *Atlas Narodov Mira* (1964).[3] A number of studies using ELF found that both very homogenous societies (with little to no diversity) and very diverse societies (where no single group can dominate the state easily) have a much lower risk of civil war. However, this measure has been much criticized as static and failing to account for the political salience of specific identities. Alternative measures emphasize different ways of calculating fractionalization or restricting which populations are included. For example, Fearon (2003) relies on linguistic difference to measure the overall diversity of a country. Posner (2004) offers an index of politically relevant ethnic groups (PREG) for forty-two countries in Africa. Montalvo and Reynal-Querol (2005) create an index of ethnic polarization that measures how far the distribution of groups is from a bipolar distribution, which captures the maximum degree of polarization.

While ELF and its successors all capture ethnic (and sometimes religious) diversity as a property of a country, another set of data projects centers on the ethnic or religious group as the central actor, rather than the state. Some of the earliest work to collect data about identity groups took place in the Minorities at Risk (MAR) project. While representing an important step in collecting data on groups at risk of rebellion, protest, or repression, the dataset effectively examined only a set of cases where identity already corresponded to mistreatment by the state, complicating testing against a wider set of ethnic groups not at risk. More recent data collection efforts, such as those behind the Ethnic Power Relations dataset, employ country expertise to capture the political relevance of different ethnic groups and patterns of horizontal inequality across them (Wimmer, Cederman, and Min 2009). This has also been paired with spatial modeling techniques to geographically reference identity groups. Thus, we now know much more about the geographic distribution of ethnic identity, even down to sub-ethnic segments defined by language and religion. This makes hypothesis testing possible on the basis of much more fine-grained data, enabling researchers to connect causal mechanisms to particular identity cleavages. Disaggregating among the elements of ethnic identity, for instance, one study finds that intrastate conflict is more likely within linguistic dyads than religious ones (Bormann, Cederman, and Vogt 2015).

Academic debates over how to define and measure these concepts have real-world relevance. One particular danger is that highly aggregated notions of identity shift from being categories of analysis employed by scholars to investigate social phenomena into categories of practice inherent in everyday social experience used by ordinary actors (Brubaker and Cooper 2000). By uncritically adopting certain identities as categories of analysis, scholars can reinforce and reproduce the efforts of political entrepreneurs who use ethnicity or religion as if they existed primordially and essentially, rather than as socially constructed categories—either as "invented traditions" (Hobsbawm and Ranger 1983) or "imagined communities" (Anderson 1991). For instance, in the Soviet Union, designation of certain ethnic groups as "nations" entitled to varying degrees of institutional status, a practice reflecting prevailing nationalist thinking, arguably contributed to the USSR's collapse through a series of national revolutions that led to still simmering civil wars (Bunce 1999; Beissinger 2002; Roeder 2007). Campbell (1998) argues that academic portrayals of ethnic violence in Bosnia during the bloody civil war of 1992–1995 played into the hands of ethno-nationalists who sought to portray the coexistence of multiple national groups on Bosnia's territory as unnatural and undesirable. Mahmood Mamdani (2010) makes a similar point about the way violence in Darfur was uncritically portrayed by the media and academics. Rather than viewing the war in Darfur as a messy insurgency involving communities with complex identities and histories, the violence was portrayed as a one-sided genocidal campaign pitting ethnic "Africans" versus "Arabs" in ways that sought to legitimate Western intervention (Seymour 2014). In sum, the act of designating certain ethnic or religious communities as groups and making claims about the consequences of groupness calls for careful attention, especially where violence is concerned (Brubaker 2004).

UNDER WHAT CONDITIONS AND HOW DOES IDENTITY MATTER IN CIVIL WARS?

Turning to explanations that situate identity in important civil war processes, we examine arguments examining ethnicity and religion in civil war onset, dynamics within wars, and their duration and termination. Taken together, this work makes a convincing case that identity is central to civil wars and political violence, but the causal connections are complex and often contingent.

Identity and the Causes of Civil Wars

Identity-based arguments have played an important role in explanations for how civil wars begin (see Young, chapter 2, this volume). Denny and Walter provide a useful summary of three key mechanisms linking ethnic identity to civil war: "Rebel movements are more likely to organize around ethnicity because ethnic groups are [1] more apt to be aggrieved, [2] better able to mobilize, and [3] more likely to face difficult bargaining challenges compared to other groups" (2014: 200). Following this insight, we focus on different theoretical propositions explaining how identity shapes patterns of grievance, mobilization, and bargaining behind the escalation to violent civil war.

For Horowitz (1985), ethnic conflict was rooted in the social psychology of group entitlements that evoked passions, anxieties, and apprehensions as rival groups contested their relative superiority within a state. "Ethnic conflict arises from the common evaluative significance accorded by the groups to acknowledged differences and then played out in public rituals of affirmation and contradiction" (1985: 227). Other authors make similar arguments linking ethnic grievances to contestation over the state or state-based discrimination (Gurr 1993; Gurr and Moore 1997). The social-psychological elements of Horowitz's arguments rest on a view of ethnicity rooted in kinship that, while fictive, is accepted by co-ethnics. This belief has particular relevance for how group members perceive threats. As Horowitz writes, "if group members are potential kinsmen, a threat to any member of the group may be seen in somewhat the same light as a threat to the family" (1985: 65). The conflation of ethnicity with kinship accounts for the increased probability and intensity of ethnic conflict in societies where political contestation becomes organized along ethnic lines.

Primordialist or essentialist arguments take this insight further, emphasizing the irrational psychological and emotional mechanisms behind the sense of kinship that pervades ethnically and religiously organized violence. As Connor argues, "people do not voluntarily die for things that are rational" (1994: 206). The symbols, poetry, songs, metaphors, and recurrent images behind ethnic appeals—"blood, family, brothers, sisters, mother, forefathers, ancestors, home"—tap into the sense of kinship that underlies ethnic and religious solidarities (Connor 1994; also Kaufman 2001). Structural changes can trigger emotional mechanisms of fear, hatred, and resentment that promote ethnic violence and conflict. Roger Petersen (2002) has taken this insight further in arguing that the same "ancient hatreds" many academics are quick to dismiss do in fact serve as "schema" that shape ethnic violence, with emotions catalyzing grievances and sustaining collective action (e.g., Petersen 2011; McDoom 2012; Pearlman 2013).

An important alternative to arguments based on seemingly innate identity emphasizes instrumentalization, particularly by entrepreneurial elites who exploit ethnicity's mobilizational advantages (Bates 1983). Against an essentialist view that identities endure and give rise to deep-seated grievances between groups competing for status, the instrumentalist argument portrays identity and the grievances to which it gives rise as malleable, or, at the extreme, even epiphenomenal. "Pure instrumentalists emphasize individual calculus in an identity marketplace in which ethnic entrepreneurs can create and sell new identity categories to willing buyers" (Sambanis and Shayo 2013: 299). The focus here shifts from the emotions and passions that ethno-nationalism and religion evoke to the strategic rationale behind promoting mobilization around particular identities according to self-interest. For example, V. P. Gagnon argues that "the violence in the former Yugoslavia was a strategic policy chosen by elites who were confronted with political pluralism and popular mobilization" (2006: 7). Valentino (2000) makes a comparable argument about the elite calculus behind mass killing, arguing that events like the 1994 Rwandan genocide reflect brutal strategies designed to counter threats to leaders' power and advance their interests. Another rationalist argument emphasizes that social mechanisms of sanctioning within groups promote cooperation and mobilization without elite manipulation. An experiment in a poor neighborhood in Kampala, Uganda, for instance, found that "co-ethnics play cooperative equilibria, whereas non-co-ethnics do not," and that "co-ethnics are more closely linked on social networks and thus plausibly better able to support cooperation through the threat of social sanction" (Habyarimana et al. 2007). Ethnicity is thus a potent cleavage around which to organize collective action because it is prone to manipulation from above and because ethnic homogeneity induces more cooperative behavior from below.

A different set of perspectives downplay the role of identity altogether. A number of scholars have emphasized the degree to which group mobilization and individual participation in violence can instead be linked to opportunity. While ethnicity gives would-be rebels a stronger base of support from which to recruit, a social base in a particular identity is insufficient without the opportunity to rebel afforded by financing or state weakness. Many ethnic (and some religious) groups tend to be geographically concentrated, making the physical act of mobilizing easier (Gates 2002; Toft 2003). Fearon and Laitin (2003) argue that state capacity is a key variable explaining rebellion. Insurgencies have the opportunity to mobilize in peripheral areas of weak state capacity with minimal police or military presence (see also Buhaug, Gates, and Lujala 2009). Others emphasize "greed" as a motive for rebellion (Collier and Hoeffler 2004), downplaying the role of grievances and emphasizing the gains to be had from lootable resources and diaspora funding that provide the key to financing wars (Le Billon 2001; Ross 2004a, 2004b). Mueller (2000) shows that even the disputes commonly considered "ethnic" (Yugoslavia and Rwanda) include high levels of apparently opportunistic participation in violence by antisocial elements of society. The role of opportunity factors, broadly construed, rather than identity factors, has been borne out in empirical work on civil war. "Cross national statistical studies find surprisingly few differences between the determinants of civil war onset in general, versus 'ethnic' civil wars in particular" (Fearon 2008, 857–58). However, a series of studies have presented counterevidence to this. For example, Hegre and Sambanis (2006) find that identity is associated with conflict at lower levels of armed conflict than are often used to test this empirically.

Another set of explanations for conflict outbreak and perseverance focus on the bargaining process from a rationalist perspective, observing the escalation to civil war as an outcome of a failure to achieve an *ex ante* settlement (Powell 2006; Walter 2002, 2009b). War, in this view, is "inefficient" in the sense that the costs incurred could be avoided through a negotiated compromise (Fearon 1995). Such arguments focus on the multiple ways states and ethnic groups are constrained in their ability to reach a negotiated agreement, which leads them into violent conflict. One insight is that a government has an incentive not to make concessions to one group if doing so exacerbates problems elsewhere by provoking similar demands by other groups (Toft 2003; Walter 2006). Cunningham and Weidmann (2010), for instance, show that local ethnic heterogeneity creates incentives for ethnic groups to oppose accommodation of others. In ethnically diverse localities dominated by one group, those excluded are more likely to resort to violence against a state that is constrained in its ability to mitigate their grievances. A related insight focuses on problems of "issue indivisibility" as ethnic groups construct claims to territory that make concessions difficult (Hassner 2003; Goddard 2006; Toft 2006). Ethnic identity and its associated political demands, unlike territory or income, tends to resist "splitting the difference" to reach a mutually acceptable bargain. Monica Toft (2006), for instance, shows how this worked to lead to war in Chechnya. The Russian government's fear of creating a precedent by bargaining over autonomy for Chechnya—not unfounded given the many other potential separatist groups on its territory—interacted with Chechens' refusal to concede on the issue of independence to collapse the bargaining space for a negotiated settlement that would have prevented war. Finally, credible commitment insights suggest that when engaged in a dispute with the state, the stability of group identity, paired with a history of grievance, can inhibit both states and ethnic rebels from making credible promises not to fight or abuse power again (Denny and Walter 2014).

Rather than thinking that explanations emphasizing grievance, opportunity, or bargaining failure are mutually exclusive, recent work tends to bridge these disparate explanations. Cederman, Wimmer, and Min (2010), for instance, put ethnic grievances alongside considerations of the military and economic feasibility of rebellion. Their account of the roots of ethnic grievance looks at differences in how states include or exclude ethnic groups from state power (see also Cederman, Gleditsch, and Buhaug 2013). Grievance is not immutably linked to ethnic or religious identity, but often develops and perseveres along those lines through political processes of exclusion and repression. The systematic marginalization of particular ethnic groups from the center of the state and the downgrading of ethnic groups removed from central power create conditions for violent mobilization when the group is relatively large. Sambanis and Shayo (2013) argue that while ethnic identities are socially constructed, historical and contemporary ethnic polarization is also an important part of the explanation for ethnic polarization and conflict driven by often small groups of radicals. Ellingsen (2000) examines heterogeneity in a number of ways, including the size of the largest group, the number of groups, and the size of the largest minority. While ethnic heterogeneity can promote conflict, she finds an even greater role played by political institutions and socioeconomic factors. These and other studies point toward integrated explanations and mark an important advance in our understanding of the role of identity factors in the causes of civil war.

Identity and Wartime Dynamics

Identity is an important factor in the risk of civil war onset that also shapes how wars are fought. Identities, in turn, are forged and transformed through wartime violence. Recent work has therefore sought to put wartime processes at the center of civil war research, much of which has traditionally focused on either how wars begin or how they end (e.g., Wood 2008). We briefly survey research highlighting a number of important processes linking identity to patterns of cohesion and fragmentation, civilian victimization and patterns of violence, recruitment and participation, and transnational processes. Together, this work tells us much about identity politics in wartime.

Early work applying the security dilemma to ethnic conflict noted how ethnic identity facilitated cohesion among co-ethnics and increased the probability of violent escalation. Ethnic and religious identities provide cohesive social bases for recruiting combatants and maintaining their allegiances (Gates 2002). Group cohesion, in turn, increases perceptions of vulnerability in neighboring ethnic groups. In an influential article, Barry Posen (1993) argued that the anarchy that followed the collapse of the Soviet Union and Yugoslavia resembled the security dilemma in international relations: preparations one ethnic group makes for its defense are perceived as threatening by others who fear these measures are offensive (particularly when there is a history of ethnic conflict), settlement patterns create incentives for ethnic cleansing, and windows of opportunity arise in the wake of state collapse. Chaim Kaufmann (1996) similarly argues that violence itself "hardens" ethnic identities in ways that promote ethnic cohesion, echoing a number of authors who provide explanations for the mechanics and effects of identity polarization (Kuran 1998; McDoom 2012).

Yet group cohesion may not always promote conflict. Fearon and Laitin (1996) suggest that in-group policing of deviant behavior within ethnic groups helps maintain cooperation across groups. Varshney (2001) shows that variation in social structure—whether dense civic networks are intercommunal rather than intracommunal—explains variation in the ability of Indian Hindu and Muslim communities to live together peacefully in some places but not others.

Kalyvas (2003, 2006) calls to question the centrality of "supralocal" identities in civil war, arguing that violence at the local level is often unrelated to overarching identity cleavages. "[W]e label political actors in ethnic civil wars as ethnic actors, the violence of ethnic wars as ethnic violence, and so on. Yet such characterization turns out to be trickier than anticipated, because civil wars usually entail a perplexing combination of identities and action" (Kalyvas 2003: 476). Drawing attention to endogenous processes of revenge and protection seeking, and the ways that local conflicts promote alliances with more powerful outside actors, Kalyvas notes that one finds fluid, fragmented alliances across identity cleavages rather than cohesive identity groups.

Other work demonstrates the weakness of ethnic identity in sustaining collective action. Even as ethnic and religious cleavages structure prominent incompatibilities at the macro level, there are important micro- and meso-level dynamics of contention and fragmentation within identity communities as rival organizations compete for representation, legitimacy and hegemony (Pearlman 2011; Lawrence 2013; Krause 2013). Cunningham (2014), for example, demonstrates that internal fragmentation in movements of self-determination is common. Bakke, Cunningham and Seymour (2012; also Bakke et al. 2012; Seymour et al. 2016) argue that fragmentation promotes violent conflict among co-ethnic factions and against co-ethnic civilian populations—think, for instance, of the fighting between Iraq's Kurds during the 1990s, or between Hamas and Fatah over the last decade. Staniland (2012, 2014) links societal structure to the organizational structure of rebels representing them, demonstrating that many armed groups are susceptible to state strategies to "flip" factions against their co-ethnics in counterinsurgency. In her study of alliance formation in Bosnia and Afghanistan, Christia (2012) demonstrates how the tenuous loyalty of fighters on the same "side" can be altered by wartime shifts in power.

The identity dimensions of violence against civilians have been an important line of investigation. Some research finds little connection between ethnicity and civilian victimization generally (Valentino, Huth and Balch-Lindsay 2004; Wood 2010), despite ample case studies suggesting the centrality of identity cleavages. Quantitative studies of conflict in ethnically fractionalized societies, for instance, find little evidence that ethnic polarization leads to more intense violence against civilians (Querido 2009). Others, however, drawing on disaggregated data, find some support for the notion that ethnic divisions promote more intense violence against civilians, whether through the interaction of macro-territorial motives that promote ethnic cleansing with micro-level polarization (Weidmann 2011), or through strategic incentives to target the civilian supporters of ethnic adversaries (Fjelde and Hultman 2014).

Civil war scholarship has been late to acknowledge the gendered dimensions of violence, especially sexual violence (see Melander, chapter 12, this volume). In examining the impact of civil wars on men and women, for instance, Plümper and Neumayer (2006) find that the adverse effects of conflict are notably higher for women than men in ethnic wars. Novel cross-national data on patterns of sexual violence reveal that ethnicity is the most common form of targeting choice, particularly for state militaries that commit most incidents of sexual violence (Cohen and Nordås 2014). Rape arguably follows from leaders' decisions to commit sexual violence against targeted ethnic groups, which can sometimes have a strategic dimension in identity wars (Wood 2006a). Far from being inevitable, however, wartime rape occurs when organizational norms and indiscipline allow combatants to do so, implying that it can also be stopped or limited (Wood 2009).

Another important line of research looks at how ethnic and religious identity shapes recruitment and participation patterns in civil war. Much of this work proceeds from the collective action problem facing rebels. Given the potentially high costs of participation in rebellion in pursuit of collective goods, we should see much free riding as rational individuals forgo the costs of participation (Moore 1995a; Lichbach 1995). From this perspective, the density of identity networks helps rebels solve the collective action problem through in-group policing and monitoring and sustains high-risk mobilization by rooting participation in quotidian social networks (Parkinson 2013). Groups with political agendas and social resources rooted in ethnic or religious identities are likely to behave differently. Jeremy Weinstein (2006) notes that groups with variable complements of resources will generate different types of rebellion, with economic endowments promoting opportunistic joiners, and social endowments such as ethnic and religious identities bolstering activist recruitment and participation. Yet there is nothing inevitable about ethnic conflict becoming "ethnic war," in which combatants recruit through ethnic networks, rather than irregular war, where violence is organized across ethnic lines (Kalyvas and Kocher 2007a). Many conflicts are marked by "ethnic defection" as co-ethnics are recruited by both insurgent and counterinsurgent armies and fight one another (Kalyvas 2008; Lyall 2010a; Staniland 2012; Seymour 2014b). This suggests a far more complex relationship between identity and participation in civil wars and violent acts taking place in the context of such wars.

Another important debate concerns how identity shapes the transnationalization and internationalization of civil war through mechanisms of diffusion (see Forsberg, chapter 5, this volume). Identity shapes how states and citizens react to both civil wars abroad and potentially rebellious minorities at home through several mechanisms. Domestic politics provides incentives to support ethnic kin entangled in foreign wars when their constituents share ethnicities with warring groups (Saideman 2002). Conversely, a state's external relations also influence how it treats unassimilated ethnic groups domestically (Jenne 2007). States are more likely to assimilate identity groups associated with their rivals, for instance, potentially triggering conflict (Mylonas 2012). Beyond states, recent research has looked at the identity politics behind non-state actors and civil war, whether refugee communities (Salehyan 2006, 2011), transboundary ethnic groups (Gleditsch 2007; Cederman et al. 2013; Forsberg 2008, 2014), or foreign fighters motivated to defend the transnational communities with which they identify (Hegghammer 2013; Malet 2013; Bakke 2014).

Identity and Ending Civil Wars

Scholars have also debated the role of identity on how to end civil wars, and related questions around civil war duration and recurrence. Insofar as ethnicity makes mobilization more likely and bargaining to resolve a dispute more difficult, factors associated with ethnicity are argued to increase war duration. Several studies have found this to be the case (Balch-Lindsay and Enterline 2000; de Rouen and Sobek 2004), with examples including multiple protracted civil wars in Myanmar, many dating back to independence in 1948. Montalvo and Reynal-Querol (2005) show a correlation between ethnic polarization and longer civil wars, for example. Others suggest that the relationship is nonlinear, that countries with a moderate degree of ethnic fractionalization have the longest wars because these are likely characterized by several distinct but large ethnic groups that can maintain cohesion vis-à-vis one another (Collier and Hoeffler 2004). Another set of studies sees important intervening variables between ethnicity and war duration. Cunningham et al. (2009) find that greater ethnic fractionalization is associated with shorter wars when we take into consideration a number of other characteristics of the rebel groups ignored in other studies. Another study suggests that institutions mediate the effects of ethnicity on civil war duration, as the politicization of identity backfires on governments unable to accept settlements to end protracted conflicts (Wucherpfennig et al. 2012).

Though religion has been studied less frequently in the quantitative literature, there are reasons to believe that religious conflicts are longer and harder to resolve because of the challenges posed by bargaining over sacred spaces or other seemingly indivisible issues. Ron Hassner argues that "conflicts over sacred space are a pervasive and global phenomenon" and that there are a variety of ways that they contribute to the outbreak and maintenance of conflict (2003: 4). Monica Toft (2003) furthers this logic, suggesting that nationalist homelands as well as religious belief can create indivisibility by changing the way people think about their own time-horizons and increase the value of seemingly insignificant territory (see also Goddard 2006).

The question of how to manage the challenges of ethnicity in the post-conflict phase has also generated robust debate. Arend Lijphart's (1977) work on power sharing offered an institutional response to bargaining and commitment challenges ethnic groups face by advocating a system in which each minority has a veto and a degree of political autonomy. The "consociational" model Liphart advocated, which emphasizes the cooperation of elites from different organized groups to promote stability and democracy while avoiding violence, has met with criticism (e.g., Roeder and Rothchild 2005; Horowitz 2014). Indeed, a vibrant debate has emerged over the prospects for different types of power sharing to end ongoing civil wars, prevent their recurrence, and forestall civil wars in countries susceptible to violence. Recent work has emphasized various types of institutional arrangement related to power sharing across ethnic and religious groups, such as territorial, political, and security sector power sharing, different electoral arrangements, or autonomy and federalism (e.g., Hartzell and Hoddie 2015; Cammet and Malesky 2012; Erk and Anderson 2013). Within this debate, scholars highlight concerns about the potential for institutional responses to identity conflict to exacerbate divisions, harden boundaries between groups, and ultimately limit the ability of individuals to exercise basic democratic principles in systems that reify ethnic or religious divisions (cf. Roeder and Rothchild 2005).

Donald Horowitz, in a bleak review of the challenges ethnic divisions pose to interethnic power sharing, argues that "many states that need conciliatory institutions will not get them; others will not keep them if majorities are able to break out of them; and still others will not change them when stalemate indicates that change is necessary" (2014: 18). Pessimism over the prospects for reconciling divided ethnonationalist and religious groups is mirrored in work on partition and secession as a solution to protracted violence. Some scholars advocate partition along ethnic lines as a last resort to identity conflicts, rooted in the insights of the security dilemma and primordialist views of identity. Partition, some argue, is the only way to separate warring groups into consolidated, defensible enclaves (e.g., Kaufmann 1996, 1998; Mearsheimer and Van Evera 1995). The theory has been criticized on empirical, pragmatic and ethical grounds (e.g., Sambanis and Schulhofer-Wohl 2009; Jenne 2012). Moving away from a primordialist reading of deeply rooted group hatreds driving conflict suggests different prescriptions. If, for instance, we believe in the malleability of intergroup cleavages and the ability to alter identities and their political salience, warring communities no longer have to be forcibly separated in the interests of peace. In sum, much of what we think about the conditions under which partition or power sharing are likely to succeed hinge on theoretical and empirical findings about the nature of identity itself.

CONCLUSION

While studies of identity divisions and civil war have made important strides in the past three decades, there is clearly much more work to be done. By way of conclusion, we chart several exciting avenues for future research, including interdisciplinarity; improved research designs, methods, and access to comparative data; unpacking identity politics; and theoretically integrated explanation.

First, while contemporary social science has been slow to study ethnicity and religion, identity is now a key conceptual category in political science, anthropology, economics, sociology, and history. There are promising avenues for connecting related research across these fields (Kanbur, Rajaram, and Varshney 2011). Recent studies demonstrate how political scientists can meaningfully engage questions of identity through theories and concepts from history (Mylonas 2012; Lawrence 2013), anthropology (Parkinson 2013; Autesserre 2014), sociology (Staniland 2014), economics (Bazzi and Blattman 2014), criminology (Skarbek 2014), and psychology (Pearlman 2013). Complementarities between fields, both theoretical and methodological, promise to advance our understanding of identity divisions. Political science, located between the deductive push of economics and the inductive focus of anthropology, and between society, markets, and the state, is well positioned to take advantage of insights from other disciplines.

Second, reflecting the influence of other fields, the study of identity and civil war has seen important advances in research design, methods, and data. Comparative case studies have become much richer, often informed by original data collection and mixed methods that build on extended fieldwork (e.g., Christia 2012; Driscoll 2012). The study of civil war has seen the increasing use of experiments, including field experiments, to improve the barriers to causal inference in violent, data-poor settings (Habyarimana, Humphreys, and Posner 2011; Fearon, Humphreys, and Weinstein 2009; Voors et al. 2009; Lyall, Blair, and Imai 2013; McCauley 2014). Large-N work has similarly improved with the refinement and disaggregation of data and better modeling techniques. Researchers can now look beyond aggregated country-level data into much more fine-grained phenomena, including ethnic power relations through the EPR-ETH dataset (Wimmer et al. 2009), geocoded civil wars data including ethnic settlement patterns through UCDP/PRIO GeoEPR, geocoded conflict events (UCDP Geo-referenced Events and ACLED), and even alternative strategies to war such as nonviolent campaigns for political change in NAVCO 2.0 (Chenoweth and Lewis 2013). An important next step is data collection at the organizational level below the level of "ethnic" and "religious" identity groups, with several projects already underway (Asal et al. 2008, D. Cunningham et al. 2013).

Third, while ethnicity has been the focus to date, the renewed prevalence of religious, linguistic, sectarian, tribal, clan, and kinship identities promises to be an exciting avenue of research. These identities, as much or more than ethnic ones, are at the center of protracted conflicts unfolding in Libya, Syria, Iraq, Afghanistan, and Somalia (Ahmed 2013). By only focusing on ethnic or religious cleavages, existing studies often ignore other important cleavages (Selway 2011). Whereas ethnic groups are hierarchically ordered, bounded units, other forms of social organization, such as tribal or clan identities, are relatively relational and situate shifting groups within more fluid social orders marked by the ability of conflict to scale up or down segmented lineages.

Finally, and in closing, after over three decades of research, the micro-foundations of identity-based conflict are still unclear (Blattman and Miguel 2010; Sambanis and Shayo 2013). Advances into our understanding of identification, identity mobilization, and processes of ethnification and increasing religiosity in conflict are likely to be made at the intersection of the theories surveyed above. Individuals are obviously self-interested, but at the same time also care about co-ethnics and co-religionists; instrumental rationality can be in tension with bounded and value rationality; identities change and identity repertoires shift, but slowly and within limits.

Scholars have spent decades exploring the role of identity in conflict and, while a great deal of progress has been made, this work has also generated new areas of inquiry. Though versions of the "ancient hatreds" thesis are still prevalent in public discourse and consciousness (including among our students), research has shown that the realities are far more complex. While there was little empirical support for the links between ethnicity and civil war in early cross-national studies, improved data and indicators are revealing the important role of ethnic and religious inequalities in sparking violence. In answering foundational questions—such as why people rebel, why ethno-nationalism is apparently so conducive to violence, or why ethnic and religious conflicts are so difficult to resolve—we now have a set of compelling answers, or at least an emerging consensus on the answers, driven by theoretical, empirical and methodological advances in the study of violence. A series of important new questions has also emerged along the way, particularly questions concerning the dynamics of conflict and violence, promising important insights in future research.

4

State Capacity, Regime Type, and Civil War

Karl DeRouen Jr. and David Sobek

The state plays an active role in whether civil war occurs. Skocpol (1979; see also Sobek 2010) concludes that when faced with a dissident challenge, the state can respond with repression or accommodation.[1] In this regard, states vary in terms of their ability to respond with military force or to seek accommodation. The state has various tools at its disposal when faced with armed domestic unrest, including broad decisions about whether to engage in accommodation (e.g., providing health service, sharing power with other groups) or coercion (e.g., repressing citizens with military force, denying groups the right to vote). The state's willingness to select these strategies depends on its strength, or what is often called state capacity. State capacity is a widely used term that is sometimes ambiguously defined. We adopt an intuitive definition (based on Arnold 1989 and used in DeRouen et al. 2010) as the state's ability to accomplish those goals it pursues, possibly in the face of resistance by actors within the state. Capacity is different from power in that in order to implement power, a state needs capacity. Put differently, capacity is a latent form of power.

Capacity is an important political concept in a number of ways; for instance state capacity is necessary for:

- *A large state army (coercive)*: A large government army has the capacity to maintain a monopoly of violence and to patrol all of the country's territory (Goodwin and Skocpol 1989; see also DeRouen and Goldfinch 2012).
- *Effective service delivery (accommodative)*: Improving service delivery is a key step in achieving the Millennium Development Goals (MDGs) (World Health Organization 2016; see also Goldfinch, DeRouen, and Pospieszna 2013). Service delivery in health, for example, includes MDGs of lowering child and maternal mortality in the developing world (World Health Organization 2008).

- *The implementation of peace agreements (accommodative)*: This is another common feature of civil wars in the developing world and typically rests with the state (DeRouen et al. 2010). A state lacking bureaucratic and security capacity will not readily be able to implement far-reaching peace agreements such as power sharing, constitutional reform, democratization, decentralization of authority, and others.
- *Public sector reform (accommodative)*: The neo-liberal good governance (GG) model of public sector reform relies upon the principle of state capacity. The GG agenda entails, for example, training public servants, control of corruption, maintaining and accounting for state assets, and tax revenue collection (Brinkerhoff 2005; Goldfinch, DeRouen and Pospieszna 2013). A state with low capacity along these dimensions could likely face challenges from armed insurgents.

Of course, the state is more than simply capacity in that the form of governance (e.g., democratic or autocratic) matters as well. In addition, the notion that the state is more than simply an arena in which actors compete is implicit in the contention that the form and degree of governance matter. The state is an actor (Skocpol, Evans, and Rueschemeyer 1985) that attempts to alter the outcomes of the political process in its favor.

This chapter takes a broad look at these concepts and the correlations that exist between state capacity, regime type, and civil war onset and outcomes. The chapter is organized as follows. First, we briefly discuss the concept of state capacity and identify the key empirical findings on the weak state–civil war connection. In addition to the role state capacity plays in civil war onset, we discuss the relevance of capacity to peace agreement implementation and civil war recurrence.

WEAK STATES AND CIVIL WAR[2]

This section reviews research on the weak state–civil war connection and identifies the dimensions of state capacity and what practices of weak states make nations more susceptible to civil war. We discuss the role of state capacity in both civil war onset and recurrence. From a broader theoretical perspective, this literature implies a role for the state that previous literature has left out. In particular, states have the ability to alter the risk of civil violence by their choices to coerce, accommodate, or do nothing.

Civil War Onset

Fearon and Laitin (2003) identify specific factors that can increase a state's vulnerability to insurgency. Rough terrain provides the insurgents an opportunity for cover to hide from the army. Fearon and Laitin contend that because rough terrain such as mountains or forests give the rebels a chance to regroup and offer protection, this factor increases the likelihood of civil war. Of course, rough terrain is largely outside the control of governments and as such, does not directly reflect the endogenous capacity of state institutions, but rough terrain can certainly degrade the ability of the state to act at a distance by increasing the cost and difficulty in travel.

A second factor that increases a state's vulnerability to insurgency is its power measured in terms of political and economic dimensions. Better equipped government armies can arguably prevent an insurgency from getting off the ground by utilizing coercion or repression early in the process. A country that is unstable politically also gives potential rebels the impression that an insurgency could succeed (see also DeRouen and Goldfinch 2012). The authors proxy economic power with GDP per capita. Fearon and Laitin (2003: 80) posit that GDP per capita has a negative effect on civil war onset because it captures the effectiveness of the state bureaucracy—including military, police, and administrative—and financial standing. Higher GDP per capita will also translate into better control of the state and a transportation network that effectively serves the entire nation. Unlike rough terrain, state power can be considered a better measure of state capacity as state actions can increase or decrease this value.

A third factor is the presence of a supportive rural base. If there is such a base that the rebels can exploit for food, shelter, and recruits, the insurgent army will be able to grow and prosper. The Cuban rebels used this feature to their advantage during their revolution. This indicator correlates with state capacity because a strong state will control peripheral populations, lest they fall under the influence of the rebels. In other words, high state capacity implies the state has administrative, political, and security control over all of its territory.

DeRouen and Sobek (2004) analyze the role state capacity plays in civil war outcomes. They hypothesize that high state capacity will undermine the probability of a rebel military victory. Their findings from multinomial logit models indicate that an effective bureaucracy staves off rebel victory, while as the size of the government army increases, the probability of the war continuing decreases and minimally increases the chances of a government victory. Democracy has no statistically significant effect on civil war outcomes. On the whole, state capacity does not have an overwhelmingly clear effect on civil war outcome beyond the finding that a state with an effective bureaucracy makes it harder for rebels to win militarily.

WHAT IS STATE CAPACITY?

While state capacity is to a certain extent an intuitive factor that can affect the onset and duration of civil conflicts, it can be difficult to operationalize. On one hand, measuring entails a critical assessment of relative strengths and weaknesses of alternative definitions of state capacity. Indicators such as income or infant mortality rate can be criticized on the grounds they do not directly reflect the state's ability to administer all of its territory, maintain a monopoly on the use of force, or deliver services. Below we describe some of the more recent empirical studies on the measurement of capacity measured at the state level.

MULTIDIMENSIONALITY AND THE ABILITY OF THE STATE TO EXTRACT

A number of studies have linked state capacity to civil war. Among the most prominent of these is Fearon and Laitin's (2003) work on the opportunity model (also known as the *insurgency model*) and civil war. The authors report that weak state capacity, measured as GDP per capita, plays a strong role in providing opportunity for rebellion. In other words, a weak state cannot prevent insurgencies from forming.[3]

But it is perhaps an oversimplification to measure state capacity with only one indicator. Hendrix (2010) uses fifteen measures to measure state capacity and argues these measures should not be considered in isolation as they cluster in distinct patterns. This is confirmed in a factor analysis. He demonstrates that state capacity is expressed in three dimensions: bureaucratic and administrative capacity, rentier-autocraticness, and neopatrimoniality. The bureaucratic and administrative dimension ranges from high-functioning democracies to bureaucratically weak autocracies. The second dimension is captured by a spectrum ranging from autocratic rentier states (states that receive a significant portion of their revenue from natural resources such as oil) that are successful in collecting revenue, to low-revenue and resource-poor states at the low end of the scale. The spectrum for the third dimension, neopatrimoniality, covers ground between states whose monarchs receive direct gain from natural resources (Hendrix lists Bahrain, Oman, and Kuwait as examples) with a low end on the spectrum that has no readily identifiable pattern (Hendrix 2010: 282). The author finds little evidence that size of government military is an important component of state capacity. Hendrix concludes state capacity should be treated as a multidimensional construct.

Ultimately, bureaucratic quality (see DeRouen and Sobek 2004) and total taxes as percentage of the state's gross domestic product (GDP) are suitable for empirical studies as they capture the three dimensions identified in the factor analysis (Hendrix 2010: 283). This indicates that state capacity may not be a single concept but a cluster of various dimensions, and the choice of measurement needs to be theory driven.

DeRouen and Goldfinch (2012) portray state capacity as the ability to conduct basic functions. Revenue extraction, for example, requires an effective bureaucracy to organize tax rolls, process tax payments, and punish those who do not pay their taxes. Those who pay taxes expect efficient service delivery from government. If the government does not extract revenue from the people and instead substitutes lucrative mineral lease payments, the social contract is undermined (e.g., Nigeria or Angola). Because leaders do not rely on taxes from the population, they are less accountable to the electorate.[4] Instead, corrupt leaders can share mineral wealth with a certain inner core of elites who, in return, help those leaders retain power. As a consequence, political leaders do not pursue legitimacy through the social contract, whereby they provide the general population with benefits in return for their political support.

To proxy revenue extraction DeRouen and Goldfinch (2012) use the variable "revenue excluding grants as percentage of GDP" to capture state capacity through revenue extraction. Specifically, the variable captures revenue extracted as "taxes, social contributions, fines, fees, rent and income from sales of property." This measure is taken from the United Nations (UNDATA, various years).

BUREAUCRACY AND GOVERNANCE MEASURES

Public goods provision is another indicator of capacity related to effective bureaucracy (DeRouen and Goldfinch 2012). These measures are proxied with state social spending. In particular, the authors use government spending on education as a percentage of GDP from the World Bank (various years) to proxy both social spending and public goods. The authors report that both (lagged) measures of state capacity enhance state stability.

In a related study of public sector performance, Goldfinch, DeRouen, and Pospieszna (2013: 55; see also Goldfinch and DeRouen 2014) derive a measure of the developing state's ability to implement public service sector reforms. One component of this index is state capacity operationalized using both income per capita and regulatory quality data. A second component is government effectiveness measured as the quality and competence of government bureaucracy. This variable is from the World Bank and is composed of perceptions of the civil and public services, the degree of its independence, and the ability of the government to formulate and implement policy (Kaufmann, Kraay, and Mastruzzi 2010) determined by expert assessment.

Clague et al. (1999) use contract-intensive money (CIM), a measure of the amount of currency in the form of contracts and promissory notes, to proxy state capacity. CIM captures "the enforceability of contracts and the security of property rights" (Fjelde and de Soysa 2009: 12; quoted from Clague et al. 1999). State capacity is required to perform these functions. Fjelde and de Soysa 2009) find CIM reduces the risk of civil war. They test two other measures of state capacity: relative political capacity (RPC) and government expenditures as a percentage of GDP. RPC proxies the state's ability to extract resources (in this case, taxes). Government expenditure is an indicator of the share of wealth in the hands of the state. The latter two measures are also associated with a lower risk of civil war. Taken together, each of these measures helps form a multifaceted understanding of state capacity and how it contributes to peace.

Fearon (2010) also points to the relevance of governance measures as predictors of civil war onset (see also Taydas and Peksen 2007). He discusses the connections between corruption, rule of law, political stability, regulatory quality, and civil war. In general, good scores on these governance indicators correlate with a reduced risk of civil war. He cautions that income typically correlates strongly with these measures. Further, endogeneity cannot be ruled out when using governance data (civil war may lead to an inference that governance is bad). Fearon does not state it explicitly, but we consider effective governance to be emblematic of state capacity.

Goodwin and Skocpol (1989) discuss the role of democracy, size of government army, and bureaucratic effectiveness in explaining revolutionary civil war. A democratic state would be expected to prevent a civil war from breaking out in the first place. Democratic regimes are expected to have fewer citizens willing to carry out acts of violence as they are designed to allow peaceful dispute resolution. A large army can better patrol the entire country and prevent potential rebels from taking advantage of safe havens. An effective bureaucracy is able to provide effective service delivery that meets the needs of the people. The presence of a strong bureaucracy means police, education, health care, and other service delivery capacity. These three indicators of capacity identified by Goodwin and Skocpol can also be applied to civil war outcome and duration as DeRouen and Sobek (2004) do in their study mentioned in the previous section. A bureaucracy is effective when there is an established process free of political pressure for recruiting and training bureaucrats. An effective bureaucracy also provides basic services.

Composite Index of National Capability (CINC) scores provide another means of measuring state capacity. These scores are based on the annual values for total population, urban population, iron and steel production, energy consumption, military personnel, and military expenditures (Singer, Bremer and Stuckey 1972). DeRouen et al. (2010) use these scores as a robustness measure in their exploration of civil war peace agreement implementation. CINC scores appear to be more consistent over time than does income.

No consideration of capacity would be complete without a consideration of natural resources. Thies (2010) posits that natural resource dependence, civil war onset, and state capacity should be modeled in a simultaneous system to avoid endogeneity. State capacity can be enhanced by natural resources, but an overreliance on natural resources rents can diminish capacity. A dependence upon natural resource rents increases the probability of civil war. Finally, state capacity can deter civil war but, when lacking, might increase the odds of civil war onset.

Thies (2010) measures capacity with three fiscal indicators (325–26): the amount of a society's resources consumed by government, a state's tax revenue as a percentage of GDP, and strength of the state relative to states with similar levels of resources and development. He reports that state capacity does not systematically lead to civil war, but if war breaks out, it will undermine future state capacity. Natural resources increase capacity, but do not increase the probability of civil war.

Thus, there are a number of ways to measure state capacity. In the end, researchers should choose a measure based on theory and not convenience. For example, studies of civil war victory might well use CINC data, while research on peacebuilding could rely, at least in part, upon level of democracy.

CIVIL WAR PEACE AGREEMENT IMPLEMENTATION

It has long been recognized that state capacity has implications for the type of peace agreement provisions that a state is able to implement (Peksen, Taydas, and Drury 2008). For starters, states must be able to fund the implementation process. As testament to this supposition, Hoddie and Hartzell (2003) find that higher levels of economic development are associated with greater probability of peace agreement implementation. For new states with very little state capacity, such as South Sudan, it is a Herculean task to undertake implementation. For other states, such as the United Kingdom after the Good Friday Peace Agreement, this task was a very reasonable expectation (see DeRouen et al. 2009). Low to medium state capacity was likely a determining factor in some failed agreements, such as the Tamanrasset Accord in Mali, the Comprehensive Ceasefire Agreement between the FNL and the government of Burundi, and various agreements in Somalia (DeRouen et al. 2009).

Peksen, Taydas, and Drury (2008) reported that states with high rates of taxation and redistribution (welfare) capabilities have lower probabilities of civil war onset. It is reasonable to expect that implementation of peace agreement provisions may vary across state capacity levels. Some states might appear to have the capacity to implement accords while others are so weak that mediators effectively become responsible for implementation (Peksen, Taydas, and Drury 2008: 14–16).

Taydas and Peksen (2007) similarly explored the impact of low state capacity on civil war onset. Their study employs "quality of government" as a proxy for state capacity. This measure is operationalized using data on corruption, rule of law, and contract enforcement. Like Peksen, Taydas, and Drury (2008) and Fearon and Laitin (2003), they also report that weak states are more prone to civil war. In addition, they find civil war recurrence after peace agreement is due to failure of agreement implementation.

DeRouen et al. (2010) continue this line of inquiry by exploring the specific role of state capacity on peace agreement implementation. They hypothesize that the state's ability to implement a peace agreement is a function of state capacity as this feature determines the functions the state is capable of carrying out. Therefore, peace agreements are less likely to be implemented in weak states because of a lack of capacity to implement the provisions of those agreements. It follows that since the state is called upon to implement structural agreement provisions, and post-conflict political institutions will have been decimated by the conflict, the state's ability to, for instance, hold new elections or adopt shared government may be severely compromised. In turn, unimplemented provisions may lead to a recurrence of war by impatient or skeptical rebels (Fearon 2004). Of course, this relationship could be influenced by the impact state capacity has on civil war onset and development as it is only the relatively weak states that have civil wars and are unable to have an outright victory. Even with that being said, the variation of state capacity seen between states attempting to implement peace accords impacts their likelihood of success.

Doyle and Sambanis (2000) build a three-pronged pyramid of civil war peace-building success in which one of the prongs is local capacity (the other two being international capacity and hostility level). They maintain that peacebuilding efforts are more likely to be successful when state capacity and international capacity are high and hostility levels are low. In this situation, the state has the resources to rebuild, administer, and carry out the implementation strategies. Rothchild (2002) also picks up on the relationship between capacity and agreement success. He argues that power-sharing agreements and provisions guaranteeing representation can shore up state capacity and in the long run even enhance it, so that implementation success is realized.

Thus, there is evidence in the literature that state capacity enhances the probability of successful implementation of postwar peace agreements—even in the absence of third party intervention. If state capacity is deficient, a third party may be needed to support implementation (see Arnault 2001; Walter 2002).

THE FORM OF GOVERNANCE VERSUS THE DEGREE

While measuring state capacity may be difficult, research seems to indicate that it does have an effect on the propensity for intrastate violence. States, however, can be defined by more than simply the degree of governance. In fact, it is the form of government that has generated one of the most significant bodies of literature in the study of interstate conflict (i.e., the democratic peace).[5] This naturally led researchers to wonder if regime type also influenced the risk of conflict at the domestic level (i.e., whether there is a democratic civil peace), and while parallels certainly exist, there is also a robust literature that has examined more than simply the role of democratic institutions.

WHY CIVIL WAR?

The form of governance does not act in a vacuum and can have multiple effects on behaviors, so perhaps the first question should be, how do civil wars develop, in general, and then we can address how regime type could affect that causal process. While there are various theories on the development of civil wars, they can be broadly categorized in terms of three main causes: civil wars occur due to a competition over resources, civil wars arise as a function of information asymmetries, or civil wars occur as a function of incomplete contracting.

Under the first argument, civil wars are simply competitions over some good, where the winning side is able to dictate the distribution of the good after the victory. For instance, using an explicit economic model, Garfinkel and Skaperdas (2007) see the winning side consuming the opponent's economic production. This model implies that factors increasing the probability of winning (Blattman and Miguel 2010: 10) or wealth (Grossman 1999; Dal Bó and Dal Bó 2004) affect the risk of conflict.

In addition, it means that a "civil war seems more likely when state wealth is easily appropriated or divorced from citizenry, as with some natural resource wealth and foreign aid flows" (Blattman and Miguel 2010: 10–11).

Of course, there are always resources under dispute, but there are not always conflicts, so wars might be driven by information asymmetries and incentives to misrepresent (Fearon 1995). In other words, these groups are making decisions without complete information as to the capability of their opponents. This lack of knowledge may lead the sides to overestimate their ability to win a conflict and thus engage in behavior that moves them into conflict even if neither actually wants a war. Governments or rebel groups might have incomplete information about their capabilities or resolve. These rationalist explanations for interstate war have also been applied to civil conflicts (Esteban and Ray 2001). In addition, this situation may be exacerbated domestically as the state may have significantly more information about capabilities than potential challengers (Dal Bó and Powell 2009). During times of economic troubles, the state may be seen as lowballing in their attempts to buy off opposition (Chassang and Padro i Miquel 2009).

The final broad explanation for civil conflict revolves around credible commitments. Leaders might be able to commit to a peace treaty today, but they could have incentives to renege on the agreement in the future, especially if the rebel group disarms. Commitment problems are particularly problematic for civil wars as the winner may take control of the state, leading to a significant shift in the future distribution of power, which exacerbates the ability to credibly commit to an agreement (Powell 2006). In fact, if a side can permanently eliminate its opponent, it can also gain a peace dividend (Garfinkel and Skaperdas 2000), which makes breaking a future commitment more likely (or perhaps a more attractive option). In addition, the ability to credibly commit may vary by regime type as authoritarian governments cannot ensure they will follow through with peace agreements as readily as democratic regimes (Acemoglu and Robinson 2006).

Conflicts can occur even if the two sides find a mutually acceptable agreement as they could see the deal as good but not trust the other side to uphold their commitment. This is not simply that they do not believe the opponent was not negotiating in good faith but that future circumstances might provide the incentive to renege. For instance, a rebel group may believe the government is providing a good deal, but what happens when the group disarms as part of the ending of the conflict? Do they believe the government will hold up its end when the rebels are in an inferior position? Thus, the ability of actors to credibly commit to upholding any deal increases the odds of a settlement and avoiding conflict.

WHY REGIME TYPE MATTERS

When researchers are looking for an effect of regime type on civil war onset, they are usually interested in whether democracies are more peaceful than nondemocracies.

While this is not always the case, it is a natural extension of the interstate democratic peace and has generated a significant amount of research. Why would democratic states be more peaceful? Perhaps the simplest explanation is simply the transference of the same causal mechanisms of the interstate democratic peace to the domestic realm, such as constraining institutions, improved information signaling, or norms of peaceful dispute resolution (Hegre 2014). But that does not exactly answer how those mechanisms operate domestically. If we assume that civil wars are a function of disputes over the distribution of goods, then democracies can be more peaceful if they have wealthier societies decreasing the incentive to challenge. In addition, wealthy democratic governments have more resources to buy off potential challengers and/or challengers have additional avenues to alter the *status quo* distribution of goods outside of armed challenges.

The link between democracy, wealth, and civil war is perhaps the most direct and hypothesized relationship. While Olson (1993) was not looking at civil conflict, he did make a strong claim that democracies would be more successful in providing growth and public goods, which would imply a lower risk of civil violence. Feng (1997) examined this possibility in the context of simultaneous regressions and found an indirect effect of democracy on growth that is mediated through the role that democracy has on the stability of regimes. In other words, "democracy provides a stable political environment which reduces unconstitutional government changes at the macro level; yet along with regime stability, democracy offers flexibility and the opportunity for substantial political change within the political system" (Feng 1997: 414).

While there appears to be a relatively consistent relationship between democracy, economic wealth, and domestic stability, the real debate revolves around the relative contributions of these three factors to peace. In other words, is the relationship between democracy and peace driven solely by the effect that democracy has on wealth, or do these factors have independent effects? Mousseau (2012) argues that it is capitalist development that drives these correlations and generates an unwarlike population, in the vein of Schumpeter (1955). Despite finding a strong role of capitalism and economic development, however, Mousseau (2012: 480) notes that regime type "still has a robust impact on conflict in ways that cannot be attributed to clientelist economy." This is in contrast to Fearon and Laitin (2003), who did not find a strong effect of democracy after controlling for wealth.

If we assume, however, that certain regime types are more likely to generate grievances, then it is not necessarily the case that there will be a linear relationship between regime type and the risk of civil violence. Hegre et al. (2001) argued that it is the institutional incoherence of anocracies that generates grievances leading to an increased risk of civil war. The problem is that anocracies are also regimes that have most likely experienced a regime change, which might have its own independent effect on the risk of civil war. Despite the potential confounding effect, Hegre et al. (2001) found an empirical relationship between anocracies and a higher risk of civil wars. In addition, states that have more recently experienced a regime change are also at increased risks for violence.

This nonlinear argument has theoretical roots in political opportunity structure theories (e.g., McAdams 1982; DeNardo 1985). In particular, Muller (1985) and Muller and Seligson (1987) argued that the ability to successfully organize under authoritarian regimes is low, making civil violence unlikely. In contrast, there are multiple avenues of contention in democracies, which makes the population less willing to engage in violent political action. As such, anocracies have the Goldilocks amount of grievances and potential for successful collective action.

Ginkel and Smith (1999) developed a game theoretic model that shows that rebellions under very repressive conditions are more likely to be successful, although that may or may not make them more likely to occur. In some ways, however, political violence may just be a function of more violent societies. Fox and Hoelscher (2012) note that it is the transitional regimes that are more likely to have social violence, indicating that both political and social violence may have similar underlying causal factors. This seems consistent with Lacina (2006) and Gleditsch, Hegre, and Strand (2009) who found that civil violence in democracies tended to be less violent.

Despite seemingly robust results that correlated anocracy with more civil conflict (e.g., Boswell and Dixon 1990; Muller and Weede 1990; Opp 1994; Fein 1995; Ellingsen and Gleditsch 1997; Sambanis 2001; Regan and Henderson 2002; Abouharb and Cingranelli 2007), questions remain. In particular, the results are only as good as the data they analyze. Scholars have noted that the Polity data used in these analyses might incorporate the presence of a civil war to code a state as anocratic. In other words, states that experience civil war are more likely to be coded as an anocracy, so researchers are really just finding a coding relationship as opposed to a causal relationship. Vreeland (2008: 419) empirically examined this possibility and found that "once the components defined with respect to political violence and civil war are removed from the index, the anocracy finding disappears." There does seem to be an inverted-U-shaped relationship in terms of political participation but a clear lack of relationship with other institutional measures.

Gleditsch and Ruggeri (2010) highlight another potential fault of the inverted-U-shaped relationship, and that is model misspecification. In particular, what often drive the civil violence are weak institutions, and this creates a political opportunity structure leading to more challenges. This does not mean there is no effect of regime type but that it is linear, meaning that democracies are more peaceful. When Gleditsch and Ruggeri (2010: 306) account for the coding decisions of Polity, "it seems reasonable to infer that there is a great deal more evidence of democracy having a negative effect on the risk of civil war."

One of the defining characteristics of the above literature is the focus on the first potential reason regime type may affect the risk of civil war. Democracy in these cases is generating wealth or minimizing the incentive to contest for resources through violence. It could also be the case that regime type can affect information asymmetries and the ability to provide credible commitments. While addressing the interaction of ethnic groups within a state, Fearon and Laitin (1996) show how in-group policing can keep peaceful interactions by addressing the lack of information and credible commitment problems.

Cunningham (2006) took this logic a step forward by noting that civil wars are not two-actor phenomena and may have multiple players who can veto outcomes. While this is not necessarily an analysis of civil war onset, Cunningham (2006) argued that the larger the number of veto players, the smaller the acceptable bargaining range and the more likely that information asymmetries are exacerbated. Ultimately this leads to longer civil wars, which he finds across a number of models and specifications. Given the role that veto players have on the duration of war, it may help explain why earlier studies found that regime type had no effect (Collier, Hoeffler and Soderbom 2004; Fearon 2004; and DeRouen and Sobek 2004).

A recurring theme in the early research on this topic is the focus on why democracies are different. This essentially treats authoritarian regimes as a single type. Geddes (1999a) splits from this by showing how incentive structures of military regimes differ from those of single party and personalistic regimes and how this relates to the stability or breakdown of these regimes. Fjelde (2010) builds on this insight to examine how authoritarian regimes may differ in their risk of civil war. In particular, single-party authoritarian regimes, such as China, should be the least likely to experience civil war. The single-party system offers the party an avenue to express preferences but, more importantly, it more easily allows for the co-option of potential threats (Fjelde and de Soysa 2009). The analyses confirm that while "coercion and co-optation, cannot be observed directly for these regime types, the empirical results support the proposed theoretical arguments" (Fjelde 2010: 215). On the other hand, personalist dictators (e.g., Saddam Hussein in Iraq) or military leaders (e.g., Pervez Musharraf in Pakistan) are more vulnerable to experiencing threats to their rule.

It seems clear that single-party regimes are unique among authoritarian governments. The findings of Fjelde (2010) nicely dovetail with Davenport (2007), who found single-party governments experience less repression by incorporating a larger portion of the population into the political process. Davenport (2007: 490) agrees with Geddes (1999b) that single party regimes are the least isolated politically and that "they do provide some venue within which discussion/aspirations/activism can take place—in a sense, it may be the only 'show in town' but at least there is a show." Ultimately this alternative method to express and address grievances decreases the amount of repression. Whether this decreased repression results in a lower risk of civil violence or whether these are both driven by the same underlying causal process is not clear, but it is clear that authoritarian regimes are not all the same in terms of how they deal with their domestic environment and how this affects the risk of civil war.

This also points to regime type as being a multifaceted concept and perhaps similar to state capacity in that it cannot be measured by a single variable. There may certainly be common threads between various types of regimes, but the idea that there is a single latent "regime type" concept is probably inaccurate, and it is much more likely the case that regimes differ across a number of separate dimensions.[6]

STATE CAPACITY, REGIME TYPE, AND CIVIL WAR: FUTURE DIRECTIONS

While there might not be a tremendous amount of agreement as to the precise role that state capacity and regime type play in civil conflict, there does seem to be more than enough evidence to strongly claim that there is a relationship. Of course, getting more specific, however, is where the difficulty lies. There is a correlation, but the exact form of that correlation and the causal process linking state capacity, regime type, and civil wars are not fully understood. The unresolved questions can be divided into three broad categories that dovetail into two new avenues of research.

QUESTION 1: ARE DOMESTIC INSTITUTIONS A PROXIMATE CAUSE?

Despite the numerous studies that find a correlation between either state capacity or regime type and civil conflict, it is not clear that the relationship is driven by the institutions or the effects that institutions have on more proximate causes. Perhaps the most common proximate cause in this vein is economic performance or wealth where either state capacity/stability/level of democracy increases the long-term performance of the economy, making wealthier and more peaceful domestic environments.

Mousseau (2012) is perhaps at the extreme of arguing for a minimal role of institutions, where it is their effect on capitalist development that is creating the peace. He still found an independent effect of regime type, but it is not a consistent finding. In Fearon and Laitin (2003), however, the effect of democracy was no longer statistically significant when controlling for the wealth of a state. In addition, it is not just that the level of democracy is correlated with wealth, but the strength of state institutions creates a positive environment for economic development (Lipset 1959).

In some ways, this debate is one of data in that there is a correlation between democracy, state capacity, and wealth, which makes it difficult, if not impossible, to empirically disentangle their independent effects. Ideally, the dataset would have wealthy and poor autocracies, wealthy and poor anocracies, and wealthy and poor democracies, but that is not the case. This essentially makes it impossible to definitively show an independent effect of each factor, but relatively easy to demonstrate that those factors as a group are significantly related to civil war onset. At least, that is the case as long as these factors are highly correlated.

QUESTION 2: DOES THE FORM OR DEGREE OF GOVERNANCE MATTER MOST?

There is more variation, however, between the form of governance and the degree of governance. In other words, there are high-capacity autocracies and democracies as well as low-capacity democracies and autocracies. Perhaps the only missing category would be high-capacity anocracies, but there is likely enough variation across regime types and state capacity to discern individual effects. In general, it appears that both have an independent effect on the odds of civil war, but there is certainly not a consensus as to what factor is most important.

Despite knowing the correlation between state capacity and civil war as well as the correlation between regime type and civil war, it remains unclear whether one is more important than the other. It could very well be the case that both are important causes of civil war, but there is also the potential that either state capacity or regime type drives the relationship. In other words, is the relationship between state capacity and civil war simply a reflection of the relationship of regime type and civil war? Further, understanding not just how these two factors affect the onset of civil war but also how they affect each other is important.

QUESTION 3: HOW DO WE CODE AND WHAT IS THE FUNCTIONAL FORM?

One of the recurring themes in the literature is either the difficulty in coding a concept or how the coding has affected the results. Obviously, problems with the data are problems for the empirical results, as even the best modeling cannot derive accurate results if the data are problematic. In some ways, it may be better to characterize the data issues as unresolved as opposed to problematic, but in either case they are critical to moving the research forward and accumulating knowledge.

In terms of state capacity, the larger issue is coding, and this is perhaps more related to the lack of conceptual clarity in early works that allowed for multiple ways to view the concept. At its heart, state capacity is not measurable as it is what a state could do, not what it has done; the realm of coded variables only includes those indicators that have some observable aspect. In other words, how would you know a state is high capacity unless it uses that capacity? Of course, you could assume that states and leaders have goals and that they would rarely have unused capacity, but that is an assumption.

Even if state capacity is an observable concept, what actions define it? This is where the literature focuses its discussion. In some ways, the economic measures are the most easily observable characteristics of state capacity but are clearly only part of the equation. Perhaps the key is not that there is a single best measure of state capacity, but there may be a single best measure of state capacity for a specific research question. This point is highlighted again in our concluding section.

The effect of regime type is a little different in that Polity is a commonly used and high quality measure for determining the form of governance. The problem is that the coding rules may have made it an inappropriate measure for determining the role of regime type in the civil war process as Vreeland (2008) and Gleditsch and Ruggeri (2010) aptly point out. Of course, this issue really only affects the finding on anocracies and the studies that looked at the democratic civil peace. Observed differences between autocratic regimes are mostly unaffected, but this still leaves open the question of whether there is something unique about anocracies.

FUTURE DIRECTION 1: DO CIVIL WARS AFFECT THE FORM AND DEGREE OF GOVERNANCE?

While scholars often view the intrastate and interstate causes of war as parallel developments, there is not always a strong connection. For instance, there is a robust literature that links the development of the state to interstate conflict. The basic idea is that wars force states to increase their extractive capacity, and if they are incapable, then they are removed from the system. There has not been a similar link made at the domestic level between civil wars and state development. Is this simply the result of inattention to this question or a more fundamental difference between domestic and interstate violence?

There are a couple of reasons why war domestically may not have the same state-building effect. First, these are conflicts that are based on a lack of trust/legitimacy in the domestic political institutions, where the losing side will remain within the confines of the territory as an implicit (if not explicit) challenge to the winner. This is not to say that interstate wars do not incorporate losing populations as territory conquest happens, but those are also seen as being more difficult to maintain. Second, civil wars may deplete domestic resources faster and more completely than interstate wars (on average), making it more difficult to consolidate any additional capacity gains. Regardless, it remains an interesting and open question as to the potential feedback from civil war to state capacity or regime type.

FUTURE DIRECTION 2: THE ROLE OF DOMESTIC INSTITUTIONS AT THE MICRO LEVEL

Civil wars do not occur simultaneously and evenly across a state. There are particular geographic distributions and patterns that researchers are now working to explicate. While institutional form may be constant across a state, it does not have to be, as federal systems allow for a degree of local autonomy. In addition, while there may be a single set of institutions for a state, that does not mean they are applied equally. State capacity could also vary, especially as one moves farther away from the seat of power(s).

What this ultimately means is that the surge in research on the micro-foundations of civil wars should also look at the micro-characteristics of the state. While the data resources on the micro-characteristics of states are not developed, there is little reason not to expect it to matter if one accepts the premise that the global characteristics of the state matter.

This also ties into a theme highlighted in the introduction. State capacity ultimately provides the state with options to coerce dissent or accommodate grievances, and more needs to be done to understand both when this happens and also how the state chooses between accommodation and coercion. While this could be broadly considered at the level of the state, it also makes sense that this decision is not universally applied across the state and that the decision to coerce or accommodate occurs at the micro level as well. Theoretical and empirical moves to the micro level will help civil war scholars understand more fully the relationships between state capacity, regime type, and political violence.

5

Transnational Dimensions of Civil Wars

Clustering, Contagion, and Connectedness

Erika Forsberg

In much of past research on civil war initiation, dynamics, and outcomes, the main focus has been to convey conflict as taking place within a single nation-state and involving two main adversaries pitted against each other: the ruling regime and a rebel group.[1] Picturing civil wars as domestic phenomena to some extent stems from the tradition of international relations to focus on borders as delimiting the political authority of states. This also explains why the most common unit of analysis for studying civil wars has been countries, where determinants of wars have been sought primarily in the institutional, socioeconomic, and demographic setup of those countries. When looking at cases and patterns of civil conflict across the globe, the reality is much more complex. Conflicts are geographically clustered, rebel groups move back and forth across porous borders, and cross-national networks of states and non-state actors are engaged in trading arms for natural resources. Thus, it is clear that the effects of civil war are felt far beyond the state in which the conflict is fought.

The notion that civil wars are not "internal" but display transnational dimensions has been increasingly acknowledged by recent scholarly accounts of civil war. Unless a conflict is very brief or located in an isolated place, the transnational dimensions are likely to be nontrivial (Fjelde 2012). Intrastate armed conflicts do not erupt and carry on in isolation within states, as the term *intrastate* would suggest. Quite the contrary, few if any civil wars are being fought without interference from actors, issues, and developments outside the country's border, and few if any conflicts fail to generate side effects outside the state where the war primarily takes place. The conflict in Syria exemplifies both. While the Free Syrian Army (FSA) was formed out of local militia groups and deserters from the military, it was clearly affected by the development in other parts of the Middle East, and, with time, jihadists from outside of Syria joined as well. In 2013, the Islamic State of Iraq and the Levant (ISIL) entered the Syrian civil war and included Sunni areas in Syria as part of their aim to establish an Islamic state. A year later, the group was renamed Islamic State (IS) and proclaimed a worldwide caliphate with religious authority over all Muslims worldwide. Syria's neighboring countries have also been active in providing arms and safe havens for rebel groups.

While one strand of scholarly work focuses on the cross-border (and beyond) effects of civil wars, another focuses on how external events and conditions shape the onset and dynamics of civil wars. Thus, a significant body of literature deals with the effects of civil war by focusing on refugee flows (Dowty and Loescher 1996; Lischer 2005; Loescher 1992; Salehyan and Gleditsch 2006), regional consequences for health (Davis, Iqbal, and Zorn 2003; Ghobarah, Huth, and Russett 2003) economic decline in the neighborhood (Murdoch and Sandler 2002, 2004), and contagion effects (Forsberg 2009; Lake and Rothchild 1998a). The second significant body of work instead focuses on the external events and conditions that make civil war in a country more likely or affect its durability or outcome. This includes focusing on political, economic, military, and other types of external support (Maoz and San-Akca 2012; Salehyan 2007, 2009; Salehyan, Gleditsch, and Cunningham 2011); how access to resources and trade networks in a region becomes a crucial driver of conflict and in the formation of war economies (Ballentine and Nitzschke 2005; Pugh and Cooper 2004); and how interstate relations affect the onset of civil war (Thyne 2006, 2009).

The present chapter categorizes the transnational dimensions into three clusters. First, the causes of civil conflict are *clustered*; second, an ongoing civil war spurs additional conflict in a proximate location due to *contagion*; and third, conflicts are *connected* within a region in terms of linkages between issues, actors, and motives. It should be noted that the three dimensions that help structure the present chapter are not fully mutually exclusive but may conceptually and empirically, to some extent, be difficult to discern from each other. The chapter then proceeds to discuss the implications of transnational dimensions for war-to-peace transitions and durable peace. Finally, the chapter concludes by discussing some of the remaining lacunae.

TRANSNATIONAL DIMENSION 1: CLUSTERING

Civil wars are clustered both in space and in time. The spatial clustering indicates that the likelihood of armed conflict in a country partly depends on the presence of armed conflicts in its neighborhood. These clustering patterns are found globally, regardless of which time period is examined. Moreover, it is not just a visual observation. Statistical research based on global data over time has found evidence for a so-called neighborhood effect of civil war (Buhaug and Gleditsch 2008; Gleditsch 2007; Hegre and Sambanis 2006; Sambanis 2001; Ward and Gleditsch 2002).[2] This suggests that a country is significantly more likely[3] to experience an eruption of internal conflict when one or more of its neighbors experiences civil conflicts. Thus, countries located in "bad neighborhoods," a term suggested by Michael E. Brown (1996), are increasingly likely to experience armed conflict themselves, compared to a country located in a region that is predominantly at peace. In fact, this finding has been shown to be one of the most robust predictors of civil war (Hegre and Sambanis 2006). Examples of such "bad neighborhoods" include West Africa in the 1990s and early 2000s, with civil wars raging in Liberia, Sierra Leone, Côte d'Ivoire, Guinea, and Guinea-Bissau, and Central America in the 1980s and early 1990s, with conflicts in El Salvador, Nicaragua, and Guatemala.

Some of the clustering may arise due to contagion effects, whereby conflict in one location brings about an increased risk of conflict elsewhere, as discussed in the next section. However, some of the clustering patterns are resulting from a corresponding spatial grouping of the factors that are related to conflict (Buhaug and Gleditsch 2008; Gleditsch 2002; Hegre et al. 2001; O'Loughlin et al. 1998; Ward 2005). What determinants of civil wars then are prone to clustering? Some of the factors that the scholarly community identifies as having a substantial impact on the risk of civil war tend to cluster geographically, just as civil conflicts do. For instance, countries geographically close to each other tend to have similar political systems and economic standards (Elkink 2011; Gleditsch 2002; Gleditsch and Ward 2000; O'Loughlin et al. 1998; Ward 2005). Democracies, anocracies, and autocracies, for example, often cluster together spatially (see chapter 4, this volume). In their test of spatial clustering of the determinants of civil war, Buhaug and Gleditsch's model includes political and economic measures (Buhaug and Gleditsch 2008). It is also possible that some more static conditions, such as some regions being rich in natural resources, may account for some of the clustering, as evidenced in West and Central Africa.

Observed geographical clustering (figure 5.1) of civil wars may hence be a consequence of a similar clustering of those factors that make conflict increasingly more likely. In such cases, the observed conflicts may in fact not be related to each other

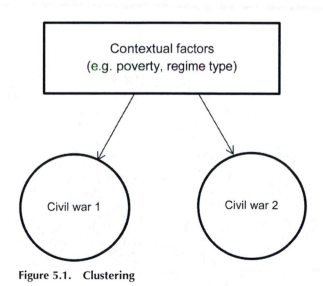

Figure 5.1.   Clustering

but generated by domestic processes. In other words, the clustering is not truly a "transnational dimension" of the civil wars in the sense that the conflicts are causally linked; rather, they are clustered because their determinants are. However, as mentioned previously, there is also evidence suggesting that some conflicts are in fact causally linked through contagion effects.[4] This process is outlined next.

TRANSNATIONAL DIMENSION 2: CONTAGION

The second transnational dimension discussed in this chapter involves the situation when civil war in one location renders civil war in a nearby location more likely. This process lacks conceptual consensus, and a plethora of terms is used including *contagion, diffusion, infection, bandwagoning, imitation, emulation,* and *horizontal escalation.* For simplicity, this chapter uses the term *contagion,* defined as a process whereby internal conflict in one location increases the probability of another internal conflict erupting in another location at a later point in time.[5] This is parallel to how diffusion is commonly defined in research on interstate war. For instance, Most and Starr (1990: 402) define "spatial diffusion" as a process in which "events of a given type in a given polity are conditioned by the occurrence of similar events in other polities at prior points in time." Figure 5.2 serves to illustrate contagion.

The fact that contagion is defined as a process and involves two units—one with conflict and one that is potentially affected (or infected) has led different studies to apply fundamentally different conceptualizations and empirical foci. I will return to some of the implications of these complexities later in this chapter. Below follows a review of existing explanations for contagion, categorized as tangible and intangible forms of contagion.

Tangible Forms of Contagion

Tangible forms of contagion relate to factors such as arms, refugees, and other factors linked to the spillover of conflict externalities across borders. Several mechanisms link these externalities to a heightened likelihood of civil war onset in neighboring states. First, both scholarly accounts and policy reports suggest that refugee

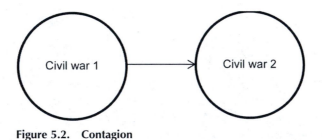

Figure 5.2.   Contagion

flows may contribute to the spread of civil conflict (Lischer 2005; Loescher 1992; Loescher and Monahan 1989; Salehyan and Gleditsch 2006; Stedman and Tanner 2003; Weiner 1992/1993, 1993; Whitaker 2003). Refugees from the Six Day War, for example, contributed to civil wars in Jordan and Lebanon. Several reasons are suggested, including that a large refugee flow may disrupt the demographic balance in the host state, exacerbate competition over scarce resources, or militarize people in refugee camps. These mechanisms are quite diverse. Since most previous empirical tests have relied on proxies and cross-national data, it has not been possible to distinguish the causal mechanisms from each other. Recent efforts to trace the ethnicity of refugees (Rüegger and Bohnet 2012) as well as the location of refugee camps (Bohnet, Cottier, and Hug 2013) are thus promising for disentangling what mechanisms are at work.

Second, when conflict is underway in one state, it often leads to an increased availability of arms. When border control is insufficient, these arms may be transferred to neighboring states where aggrieved groups may be willing to initiate violent conflict as soon as they have the ability to do so. The inflow of weapons at cheap rates may provide them with such capacity. Data scarcity has so far made it difficult to test this claim, but we see these dynamics in many cases. For example, after the fall of the Gaddafi regime of Libya in 2011, arms and fighters made their way to Mali and contributed to a rapid, and for many analysts rather unexpected, escalation of resentment felt among local Tuaregs against the Malian government (Allansson, Sollenberg, and Themnér 2013). This case also illustrates that while spillover of externalities primarily affect border areas, they sometimes travel farther.

Third, a civil war in one country affects the economy of the surrounding states. As noted by Murdoch and Sandler (2002, 2004), civil wars may lead to a reduction in trade and investment in proximate countries, in addition to the economic burden of hosting refugee flows. The economic costs of "collateral damage" are particularly likely with high-intensity civil wars and when the country shares a long border with countries with civil conflict. As lower income levels and low economic growth are among the most robust predictors of civil war (Hegre and Sambanis 2006), these externalities may indirectly heighten the probability of conflict in a civil war neighbor.

Fourth, characteristics of the border between the conflict country and a neighbor have been suggested to affect the likelihood of spillover. If two states share a mountainous border, it may make spillover less likely, since this would hamper the movement of arms and mercenaries from the conflict state to the neighboring state, for instance. It has also been suggested that spillover is more likely when two states share a long border. A long, shared border is more difficult to monitor; hence, it is associated with an increased likelihood that weapons and armed groups move from the conflict state to its neighbor. As an example, consider the Syrian civil war and the escalated violence in Iraq. With their shared border being little more than an imaginary line in the sand, spillover of combatants in both directions has been common. However, evidence that supports the proposition that long borders matter is lacking (Buhaug and Gleditsch 2008). Given that separatist conflicts typically are fought close to international borders, spillover effects may be more likely in such conflicts than in civil wars concerning the overthrow of the central government, as also demonstrated by Buhaug and Gleditsch (2008).

Intangible Forms of Contagion

Intangible contagion is the process whereby conflict in one country provides lessons, inspiration, and clues for actors in other countries. This can be in the form of strategic learning (for example, Bakke 2013; Elkins and Simmons 2005; Hill, Rothchild, and Cameron 1998) or because conflict in one location makes groups in other locations perceive an increased likelihood of success (for instance, Lake and Rothchild 1998b). Thus, conflict in one state may inspire one or more groups in another state to increase their own demands and decide to pursue demands using violent means (Byman and Pollack 2008). However, the effect is not clear-cut. While it is possible that conflict in one place may lead other actors to update their beliefs about the likelihood of success in such a way that conflict becomes more likely, it may also in some cases horrify rather than inspire. For instance, Buhaug and Gleditsch (2008) argue that more intense conflicts, in terms of fatalities, make contagion more likely. However, their analysis finds no support for this claim. One possible interpretation is that while high-intensity conflicts create more tangible spillover, they may also repel rather than inspire potential insurgents in other countries. This is parallel to the idea of war weariness in studies of interstate war (Levy and Morgan 1986; Richardson 1960).

Intangible forms of contagion may be conditioned by the characteristics of a civil war. As noted above, Buhaug and Gleditsch (2008) find that separatist conflicts are more likely to lead to contagion, compared to wars fought over government power. This may be due to more spillover effects, but also because such conflicts typically involve regional ethnic groups that have ties to kin across borders, who are more likely to act on demonstration effects. The importance of such transnational ethnic groups is noted by multiple researchers (for example, Ayres and Saideman 2000; Buhaug and Gleditsch 2008; Cederman, Girardin, and Gleditsch 2009; Forsberg 2008, 2013, 2014b; Gleditsch 2007; Saideman and Ayres 2000; Salehyan and Gleditsch 2006). In these studies, it is suggested, and generally supported empirically, that the involvement in conflict by a group in one country increases the likelihood of conflict erupting in a nearby country that shares the same group. One explanation for this finding is that such groups are more likely than other groups to be inspired to increase their own demands because the bonds and similar conditions shared with their kin involved in conflict are rendered salient (Forsberg 2014b). For instance, when the Kosovo Liberation Army (KLA) succeeded in gaining far-reaching autonomy for Albanians in Kosovo by using armed force, it appears to have inspired Albanian kin in Macedonia to launch their own struggle.

Last, it has been suggested that contagion is more likely when the rebel side is successful, supposedly due to stronger inspiration effects (Hill and Rothchild 1986; Hill, Rothchild, and Cameron 1998). Related to this, there is a widespread supposition that territorial concessions granted to separatist groups may spur other proximate ethnic groups to demand similar concessions. Within states, Walter (2003, 2006) has found evidence of such domino effects. However, until recently there has been scant investigation of the cross-border effects of granting territorial concessions. Using new data with global coverage, Forsberg (2013) finds no evidence of domino effects either across or within borders; territorial concessions granted to rebel groups do not appear to inspire other groups to rebel.

Susceptibility to Contagion

Regardless of the magnitude and severity of spillover, and regardless of the opportunities for strategic learning produced by a civil war, a country has to be conducive to conflict in order for a contagion process to transpire. As pointed out by Lake and Rothchild (1998b), conflict primarily spreads to those states that are already at risk of conflict and is, conversely, less likely to spread to countries with a low baseline probability of conflict in terms of domestic conditions. Arguments and findings in previous research point to a set of conditions that makes countries more or less likely to be "infected." First, proximity stands out as the primary medium in which contagion operates. Countries in the near proximity of a country involved in civil war are arguably more exposed both to spillover of externalities and to demonstration effects (Buhaug and Gleditsch 2008; Lake and Rothchild 1998b; Maves and Braithwaite 2013).[6]

Second, countries with higher levels of state capacity are suggested to be less susceptible to contagion, which is supported empirically (Braithwaite 2010b). With control of resource extraction and capacity to respond to instability, highly capable states have the tools to confine domestic unrest to legal action rather than rebellion. Also, such states are arguably better equipped to set up "firewalls" (Solingen 2012) through efficient border control and thus prevent some of the spillover of war externalities, such as the movement of arms and mercenaries across borders. Thus, states with high capacity (see chapter 4, this volume) have the ability to deter civil wars internally and decrease the chances of conflict spreading from neighboring countries.

Third, regime type may have an impact on a state's susceptibility to contagion. As suggested by Maves and Braithwaite (2013), among authoritarian states, those with elected legislatures are increasingly receptive to contagion since they may breed latent opposition groups. In addition to such institutional features, the ethnic composition of states may matter. Findings in Forsberg (2008) suggest that countries that are ethnically polarized, in the sense that there are a few roughly equally strong contenders, are more susceptible to contagion. Such societies supposedly form a delicate balance in which the input of a potentially inspirational conflict next door may create the momentum required for a group to challenge its own state with rebellion.

Contagion and Research Methodology

In studying contagion, researchers face a number of methodological challenges that prevent us from drawing strong conclusions about any of the findings just reviewed.[7] First, contagion is a process that, at least in a quantitative setting, is unobservable. What we do observe, and what we draw inference from, is a correlation in time and space whereby conflict in one location at t_1 is followed by conflict in a proximate location at t_2. Such strategy risks both over- and underestimating instances of contagion. The risk of overestimation stems from the fact that just because two conflicts erupted in sequence close to each other does not necessarily mean that they are linked, as determinants may be spatially clustered instead. The risk of underestimating cases of contagion comes from the fact that contagion may travel farther distances both in time (i.e., compared to any standard time lag) and in space (i.e., beyond the immediate neighborhood).

Second, contagion is complex to model empirically as it involves two units—one with conflict (a potential source or initial stimulus for contagion) and one that is potentially affected (a target of contagion). This has led researchers to apply different conceptualizations and empirical strategies when studying contagion. For instance, a question arises whether contagion should be studied with monadic or dyadic units of analysis. The most common approach in quantitative studies is to use the monadic country-year approach (Buhaug and Gleditsch 2008; Gleditsch 2007; Hegre and Sambanis 2006; Salehyan and Gleditsch 2006; Ward and Gleditsch 2002). In these studies, neighborhood conflict is either collapsed into a dichotomous variable (a spatial lag) or a summary measure of some kind (for example, a weighted index of conflict in the neighborhood). An alternative strategy is to use a dyadic setup, consisting of a state with conflict and one panel for each state considered at risk for contagion (Black 2012; Forsberg 2008, 2014b). As these two strategies follow different conceptualizations of conflict contagion, it is no surprise that they generate different findings (for a discussion, see Forsberg 2014a).[8] Since contagion is a process involving a chain of events and at least two units, there may not be one perfect modeling strategy. However, future work should strive to identify the unit of analysis that best captures contagion, while being cognizant of the inherent methodological challenges.

TRANSNATIONAL DIMENSION 3: CONNECTEDNESS

The third transnational dimension discussed in this chapter is termed *connectedness*. While *contagion* refers to a quite specific process involving a sequence of actions and a direction from one state to another, conflicts can also internationalize more broadly and involve a larger set of countries, issues, and actors. While potentially emanating from, or partly featuring, contagion or clustering processes, connections between different conflicts within a region can take on a broader transnational dimension. With time, actors from different conflicts may start to cooperate with each other, they may have similar goals or a common enemy, and they may share bonds through ethnic or ideological affiliation. It is also increasingly likely over time that there will be actors who see significant benefits from keeping the conflicts alive, such as mercenaries and traders involved in war economies.

In the extreme form, transborder connections between issues and actors within a region is referred to as a "regional conflict complex" (Wallensteen and Sollenberg 1998). In such cases, conflicts are mutually reinforcing to the extent that it may be infeasible to solve just one conflict without considering the regional aspects. While the concept of contagion implies a one-off event, or at least a directional process, interconnectedness between actors and issues can be much more long-standing and complex, as illustrated by figure 5.3.

To understand the transnational dimensions of civil war, and how wars may evolve into complex and enduring instability in a region, we thus need to address various cross-border linkages, including how factors such as transborder trade in arms and exploitation of resources play a role.

Connections between conflicts in a region influence both the incentives and capacity of a multitude of actors.[9] When conflicts are interlinked, it often means that conflict issues become more complex. In particular in regional conflict complexes, it will be difficult to separate different incompatibilities from each other and therefore difficult to solve any given conflict in isolation. Also, a larger set of actors is likely to have a stake in a given outcome, and as a consequence, there are more potential spoilers. With more reasons to choose to use violence, violence also becomes increasingly likely and more intense. When conflicts are interlinked, there is a large possibility that resources become more available—and more abundant. Easier access to resources then serves to strengthen warring parties' fighting capacity. Although difficult to resolve, regional conflict complexes are not completely intractable. Several of the regions that were categorized as conflict complexes not too long ago, such as Southeast Asia, southern Africa, and Central America, no longer exemplify regional conflict complexes.

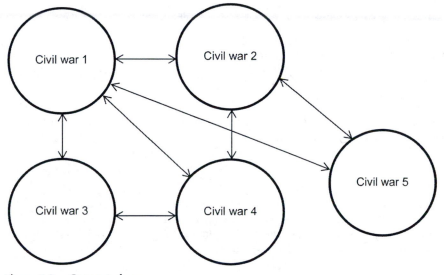

Figure 5.3.   Connectedness

Below follows a review of two important components of regional connections of civil wars: external support and war economies. These components often rely on preexisting networks based on ideological or ethnic affinity or stem from having a common adversary.

External Support and Proxy Warfare

Many conflicts experience some type of external involvement; in fact, according to the UCDP External Support Dataset, about 75 percent of all conflict dyads after 1975 have at some point received external support (Croicu et al. 2011; Högbladh, Pettersson, and Themnér 2011; Pettersson 2011). External support adds to the complexity of conflicts. Evidence suggests that insurgencies that receive outside support generally last longer (Balch-Lindsay and Enterline 2000; Hazen 2013), are more intensive in terms of combat fatalities (Lacina 2006), decrease the chance for a negotiated settlement (Cunningham 2006, 2010), and increase the likelihood of international disputes and conflicts (Gleditsch, Salehyan, and Schultz 2008). External support involves a diverse set of actors both on the supply and demand side: both rebel groups and regimes receive support and both state and non-state actors provide support, and the support varies in type and magnitude. For instance, states that are external to a civil war often seek influence by supporting one of the belligerents, either directly by participating with troops or indirectly by supplying arms, logistical assistance, or financial resources. Examples are abundant. Rebels from the Free Syrian Army seek shelter in neighboring Turkey, while the Kurdish Worker's Party fighting the government of Turkey relies on sanctuaries within Iraq. The Mozambican National Resistance (RENAMO) equipped and trained their fighters in neighboring South Africa during the civil war in Mozambique. Perhaps the most extreme form of cross-border military activity is military intervention by an outside power in an ongoing internal conflict. Examples include Vietnam's backing of the Kampuchean National United Front for National Salvation (KNUFNS) in Cambodia, and the intervention to support the Alliance of Democratic Forces for the Liberation of Congo-Zaire (AFDL) by Angola, Rwanda, and Uganda.

When a state provides support to a rebel group in another country, it is not always primarily driven by solidarity toward the rebel group, but often is meant to destabilize a rival regime (Byman 2005; Salehyan, Gleditsch, and Cunningham 2011). Such war by proxy is often bidirectional. For instance, the government of Uganda supported SPLA in Southern Sudan, while the government of Sudan supported the Uganda-based rebel group LRA. Uganda and Sudan also fought a similar undeclared war against each other in the DRC (Prunier 2004). In this way, two states can be engaged in an attempt to destabilize each other, eschewing the much more costly alternative of direct confrontation (Salehyan 2010). During the Cold War, the risk of nuclear war and mutual assured destruction prevented the United States and the Soviet Union from fighting each other directly; instead, they fought wars by proxy in, for example, Angola and Afghanistan. After the end of the Cold War, proxy wars have instead primarily involved states within the same regional security complex. Proxy wars are by definition a transnational dimension of contemporary warfare; moreover, they illustrate that the line between interstate and intrastate armed conflict is blurred (Gleditsch, Salehyan, and Schultz 2008b; Mumford 2013).

Apart from outside military support, ranging from sharing intelligence and allowing access to territory to overt military intervention, external support can also be financial. For instance, during much of the 1980s, South Africa provided extensive funding to the Angolan rebel group UNITA (UCDP). External economic support illustrates that the transnational dimension of external support may extend far beyond the immediate neighborhood of a civil war. Migrants living in far-off locations tend to transfer large amounts of resources to their kin. Evidence suggests that such support from diaspora and emigrant communities are crucial both for the initiation of rebellion (Collier and Hoeffler 2004; Miller and Ritter 2014) and for bolstering the fighting capacity of rebel groups engaged in conflict (Gunaratna 2003; Nitzschke and Studdard 2005).

As a final note, several propositions related to the causes and effects of external support have not been systematically tested due to data scarcity. For instance, several studies suggest that clandestine external support helps sustain and escalate conflict (Balch-Lindsay and Enterline 2000; Cunningham 2006, 2010). However, the fact that not all support is overt by definition makes it difficult to collect data with decent coverage.

Economic Linkages and War Economies

As mentioned above, many parties receive financial support during civil wars. However, the transnational economic factors of civil wars extend beyond issues of external support, especially in conflicts located in regions with lucrative resources. As argued by Ballentine and Sherman, economic dimensions of civil war may be those characterized with the largest degree of transnationalism: "Both the supply and demand sides of war-making have become internationalized as combatants have exploited the opportunities inherent in weakly regulated national and global marketplaces to trade lucrative natural resources for war materiel and financing" (Ballentine and Sherman 2003: 9).

When economic activity becomes militarized to a high extent and resources are mobilized to finance warring groups, war economies are formed (Ballentine and Sherman 2003; Berdal and Malone 2000; Pugh and Cooper 2004). In the type of war economies that often plague civil wars, predation, rent seeking, and illicit transfers of goods and services become prevalent. The consequences are often detrimental for state capacity, institutional growth, and economic prosperity. They also create blurred lines between political conflict and criminal activity. These war economies have a strong transnational character.

Many war economies center on illegal cross-border trade in natural resources, which may become a way of financing rebellions. When actors are involved in armed conflict, they are sometimes the target of international sanctions. To uphold fighting capacity, these actors may come to rely on regional trade networks as a way to escape formal sanctions. Not discounting that grievances and ideological conviction drive many conflicts, there are also many examples indicating that some actors are motivated by financial gain and profit from continued warfare. To provide some examples, alluvial diamonds were important in the conflicts in Sierra Leone, Liberia, and Angola; timber in Burma/Myanmar, the Philippines, and Cambodia; and drugs in the conflicts in Colombia and Afghanistan (Le Billon 2001).

A second important trade commodity in war economies is arms. More often than not, rebel groups fighting a civil war do so using weapons that originate outside their own state. Although most arms are manufactured legally in the industrialized world, once they make their way into conflict regions, they become an element of regional smuggling. Arms and natural resources are often part of the same trade network, whereby arms are procured in return for access to natural resources. For example, when Charles Taylor was ruling Liberia, he provided mercenaries, arms, and territorial bases for rebel groups operating in neighboring Sierra Leone. Doing so, he was motivated by an interest in gaining control of regional economic networks and diamond mines. In the end, this tactic led to the involvement of other states in West Africa, such as Guinea and Burkina Faso.

The illicit trade mentioned above—be it in arms, mercenaries, or resources such as drugs and diamonds—are often made available through various types of political and social networks, including ethnic ties. In addition, it should be noted that different types of links and networks often overlap. For instance, the establishment of illicit economic networks usually requires some preexisting network based on, for instance, political or ethnic affiliations. While political and social networks are based on affinity, the networks are often motivated by a shared animosity toward one or more other actors.

IMPLICATIONS FOR CIVIL WAR OUTCOMES

The fact that civil wars have external dimensions has a number of important implications for their duration and likelihood to transition from war to peace. It also entails that peace in one state may have effects that cross borders. The next sections explore some of the transnational dimensions that shape the prospects for a civil war to end and for peace to become durable.

External Dimensions That Obstruct Peace

The transnational dimensions of civil war have several implications that may make a war-to-peace transition less likely by involving more stakeholders, more resources to use for fighting (or fighting over), a wider set of issues, and the notion that peace in one place under certain conditions impacts other places negatively. The following section discusses these issues. First, when conflicts are connected across borders, there are more stakeholders. Particularly in regional-conflict complexes, there is a high risk that there are actors that benefit from continued warfare. This includes those involved in illicit trade and war economies, those who attempt to destabilize adversaries through proxy warfare, and mercenaries and private security firms. Many of these actors are not driven by grievances or ideological conviction. For them, peace could mean unemployment or the discontinuation of lucrative commerce. With more stakeholders involved, there is also increased uncertainty due to changing alliances. The war in the Democratic Republic of Congo/Zaire provides a vivid illustration. When the Mobutu-led Zairean government was challenged by the Kabila-led Alliance of Democratic Forces for the Liberation of Congo-Zaire (ADFL) in 1996, the rebel side was supported by Uganda, Rwanda, and Angola. After Kabila had toppled the regime and seized power, his former allies in Rwanda and Uganda soon shifted to support the emerging challenger Congolese Rally for Democracy (RCD), while the Kabila-led regime was instead supported by Zimbabwe, Angola, Namibia, and Chad. The internationalized civil war soon became known as "Africa's first world war" (UCDP). With a larger set of stakeholders, it will typically be more difficult to craft a settlement that all major parties conceive of as a better option than continued conflict. Hence, if a peace process is initiated, there are more internal and external spoilers (Stedman 1997).

Second, a common feature of highly internationalized conflicts is that more resources are available, and there may be more resources to fight for. When warring parties receive large amounts of economic and military support from external actors, they are likely more able and willing to continue fighting (Balch-Lindsay and Enterline 2000; Hazen 2013). With material inducement, warring parties may also consider a peace settlement as a less attractive alternative (Cunningham 2006, 2010). Thus, economic dimensions of war imply key challenges for peacemaking (Ballentine and Nitzschke 2005; Nitzschke and Studdard 2005).

Third, an increasing number of actors involved in conflict and more sustained cross-border linkages typically also bring a wider set of conflict issues and incompatibilities, for example related to refugee flows and repatriation. To exemplify, the armed conflicts in Southern Africa involved a set of deeply connected issues, such as the status of Namibia, the apartheid system, and South Africa's involvement in Angola and Mozambique (Wallensteen 2002). As a result, it proved difficult to settle just one conflict.

Fourth, peace processes that are successful in a national perspective may have negative consequences regionally. As with contagion of conflict, this process may manifest itself both as inspirational spillover and tangible material spillover. Peace has the potential of indirectly raising the probability of conflict elsewhere through demonstration effects (Kuran 1998; Lake and Rothchild 1998b). When a civil war ends by a negotiated settlement, rebel groups typically gain concessions. If such concessions are generous, they may inspire groups in neighboring countries to increase their own demands and challenge the ruling power, which may escalate to a violent outcome. Peace in one state may also cause tangible material spillover. This includes the transfer of weaponry and ex-combatants to new locations following a conflict resolution process, resulting from a failed disarmament, demobilization and reintegration (DDR) process. If weapons are not collected and ex-combatants are not provided with an alternative, former fighters may become mercenaries fighting wars in neighboring countries. If not fully integrated into post-conflict society, ex-combatants are easy targets for mobilization by other actors. By using existing networks and bonds of affinity, based on ethnicity or former military cooperation, armed groups in nearby countries can recruit demobilized combatants lacking economic opportunities in their home countries (Nilsson 2008a; Themnér 2011).

Aside from these comparative case studies, there are also studies that analyze the determinants of DDR success and failure using statistical analysis of micro-level data (see also chapter 11, this volume). Based on interviews and surveys in South Sudan, Phayal, Khadka, and Thyne (2015) find that ex-combatants are less aggrieved when offered job training and in the presence of the UN. In a survey of ex-combatants in Sierra Leone, Humphreys and Weinstein (2007) identify a range of factors associated with social, economic, and political reintegration. An avenue for future research could be to conduct a broader cross-case data collection regarding the success rate of DDR programs, which could help test the assertion that failed processes could lead to the movement of arms and ex-combatants to neighboring hot spots. Arms trade can also be a major problem that causes regional instability when conflict ends. When DDR programs fail, regional networks can take advantage of large quantities of arms becoming easily available to exploit. These arms can make their way into new areas, precipitating an eruption of new conflict somewhere else.

External Dimensions That Promote Peace

While cross-border linkages carry with them several complexities that work against a war-to-peace transition, there are also several external dimensions that could potentially promote peace.

First, the involvement of external actors through, for instance, third party mediation and peacekeeping missions have proven valuable to reach and sustain peace in many places. In the 216 peace agreements identified by the UCDP Peace Agreement Dataset in the 1975–2011 period, third parties were involved as mediators and/or signatories in more than 80 percent of the cases (Harbom, Högbladh, and Wallensteen 2006; Högbladh 2011). Also, third party mediation makes negotiated settlements more likely (Regan and Aydin 2006; see also chapter 7, this volume). Third party involvement from the outside not only helps reach and maintain peace but may also limit the risk of contagion effects to neighboring areas (Beardsley 2011; Kathman 2011, 2010).

Second, peace in one place, or a key event in one place, can bring with it a positive domino effect whereby additional conflicts are resolved. In other words, conflict resolution may have positive externalities: the settlement of one civil war may pave the way for settling other wars in the neighborhood. As noted by Wallensteen (2002), such peace spillover can transpire both as a consequence of settling the "hard case" (the most difficult conflict) first or by starting with the case most ripe for resolution. Evidence in favor of such "peace by piece" strategies has also been substantiated by Nilsson (2008b).

Third, a number of the regional obstacles identified above can also increase the prospects for peace if put in reverse. For instance, external support often prolongs and intensifies conflict by bolstering the parties' fighting capacity. Withdrawal of support may increase the prospects of the parties reaching a peaceful settlement, since lack of resources may push parties toward war weariness and a mutual hurting stalemate where a settlement becomes a more attractive option (Hazen 2013). As noted by Ballentine and Sherman (2003) such an effect was witnessed in Mozambique, El Salvador, and Nicaragua. Relatedly, regional trade networks increase the pool of resources available to warring actors and involve actors who profit from sustaining conflict. But a warring party that is reliant on a continuous flow of resources is also quite sensitive to disruptions (Hazen 2013). As a consequence, external efforts to obstruct illicit trade and monetary transfers may indirectly or directly work to promote peace (Hazen 2013). If warring parties rely on external parties to sustain their fighting capacity, then sanctions regimes and joint efforts to monitor illicit trade may, at least in theory, increase the likelihood of peace (Wallensteen 2011).

CONCLUSION

As evidenced by empirical patterns and systematic research, we can safely conclude that all civil wars have transnational dimensions, with variation found in magnitude and types. Several findings can be considered empirically robust. First, scholarly work points to the importance of war economies and crosscutting allegiances in sustaining conflicts. Second, there is strong support for a neighborhood effect of civil war, stemming from both clustering of civil war determinants and contagion effects. Third, external parties are important actors in both reaching negotiated settlements and in mitigating the regional effects of wars.

Yet many knowledge gaps remain, due to methodological challenges, data scarcity, and underdeveloped theories. Thus, future studies of the transnational dimensions should continue to strive for identifying the most appropriate unit of analysis and data sources to assess any given mechanisms. For many research questions, a mixed-method approach may be the most adequate strategy. If statistical analysis has established the strength and direction of a correlation, intense examination of strategically selected cases may provide additional insights into the causal process, especially when the temporal dimensions are not easily modeled over a large set of cases. This is often the case when a connection between two conflicts is established in the pre-war environment and, as a consequence, truncated in existing datasets of armed conflicts. Case study research may also serve to improve our understanding of the transnational dimensions of civil war by further studying puzzling variations and deviant cases. What has kept places like Malawi, Botswana, and Zambia from experiencing armed conflict when they, according to existing findings, should be high-risk cases? Zambia is located in a "bad neighborhood" with several civil war neighbors in the post–Cold War period (Angola, Democratic Republic of Congo, and Mozambique), has been exposed to spillover from these conflicts, and has itself meddled in conflicts by sending troops and other types of external support. In addition, Zambia has several domestic features that would make it likely to experience civil war, for example, ethnic competition and low GDP per capita. Yet, Zambia has not experienced civil war. Investigation of such deviant cases may uncover new and unspecified mechanisms (Gerring 2007).

II

FACTORS THAT END CIVIL WARS AND PROMOTE PEACE

6

Third Party Intervention and the Duration and Outcomes of Civil Wars

Christopher Linebarger and Andrew Enterline

For about a decade after the Cold War ended, civil wars ended at a faster rate than new wars began, resulting in a decline in the number of ongoing conflicts in the international system. This chapter will explore several factors that influence whether a conflict will end in rebel victory, a government victory, or a negotiated settlement. One consistent finding across studies is that the outcome of a civil war is, in part, a function of its duration: the longer civil wars last, the less likely they are to end in military victory. When governments defeat rebels, they usually do so early in the conflict, when they have a military advantage over a nascent rebel organization. The evidence also suggests that rebel victories tend to occur early in the conflict. If neither side prevails early, then after about five years, the most likely outcome is a negotiated settlement.

What, then, accounts for the duration of civil wars? One factor implicated in the duration—and, therefore, the outcome—of civil wars is that of third party intervention. A large proportion of post–World War II civil wars have been "internationalized" in the sense that one or more nations intervened on the government's or the rebel's side (see also chapter 5, this volume). The literature shows that these interventions are typically associated with civil wars of longer duration, contrary to the expectation that intervention might tip the balance on the battlefield.

This chapter focuses on the impact of third party interventions on the evolution and conclusion of civil wars. Specifically, the chapter identifies those factors that affect the duration and outcome of civil wars by engaging the following questions: (1) What are the forms of third party intervention? (2) What factors make nations more or less likely to intervene in a given civil war? (3) How does third party intervention affect the duration and outcome of such conflicts?

Several excellent reviews address questions pertaining to third party interventions into civil wars (e.g., Regan 2010; Shelton et al. 2013). Although we emulate these reviews by examining the literature on third party intervention, our primary goal is to suggest ways forward for future research, the task to which we devote the latter portion of the chapter. Moreover, we make note of the many conflicting findings uncovered by researchers. Although conflicting findings are partly the result of the varying definitions of civil war, intervention, and other data-related particularities, we argue that these disagreements offer a useful teaching tool. By identifying the way findings are affected by a researcher's theoretical focus and research design, the interested student is afforded an opportunity to reflect upon the social science craft.

THE DURATION AND OUTCOME OF CIVIL CONFLICTS

Civil conflicts are a particularly deadly and destructive form of conflict, with features that are noticeably different from their interstate counterparts. According to Brandt et al. (2008), there were more than four times as many civil wars as interstate wars in the world during the period 1946–1997. These conflicts, on average, last about four times as long as interstate wars, and the average duration of civil conflicts increased even as the number of new conflicts has declined since 1994 (Fearon and Laitin 2003). As a result, there was a steady accumulation of ongoing conflicts that did not diminish until several years after the end of the Cold War. After that point, the duration of civil conflicts actually fell, resulting in fewer ongoing wars overall.

These patterns are important, as the duration of civil conflicts is highly correlated with their overall destructiveness. Although civil conflict produces casualties at a lower rate than international conflict, their relatively longer duration results in a much higher cumulative death toll. Civil conflicts are also known for their unusually high stakes. The warring factions are locked together within the same borders and must coexist after the war concludes, and defeat often means elimination for rebel leadership and followers alike. As a result, protracted civil conflicts are extremely difficult to bring to an end (Brandt et al. 2008; DeRouen and Sobek 2004; Fearon 2004; Greig and Regan 2008; Licklider 1995a, 1995b; Mason and Fett 1996; Mason et al. 1999; Walter 1997, 2002; Zartman 1989).

There is a significant body of empirical research that explores the dynamics of civil war duration and outcome. This literature finds, among other things, that duration and outcome are functions of the strength or number of the various factions (Cunningham 2006, 2010; Cunningham et al. 2009; Mason and Fett 1996; Mason et al. 1999); the capacity of the state (DeRouen and Sobek 2004; Fearon 2004); or the strategy employed by the combatants (Arreguin-Toft 2001; Kalyvas 2006; Kalyvas and Kocher 2007b; Mack 1975; Mason and Krane 1989). The duration of civil conflicts is also directly implicated in their outcome, with Mason and Fett (1996) finding that the duration of a civil conflict is the single greatest predictor of whether a given war will end in a decisive victory or a negotiated settlement. Such logic leads Fearon (2004, 276) to conclude that "civil wars last a long time when neither side can disarm the other, causing a military stalemate. They are relatively quick when conditions favor a decisive victory."

Given these empirical regularities, it is no surprise that many social scientists and policy makers argue that it is imperative for third parties to intervene into civil wars in order to bring about as swift a conclusion as possible (Licklider 1995a, 1995b; Smith 1994). Yet there is serious disagreement in the extant scholarship on this point. For example, research finds that third party intervention can actually prolong civil wars (Balch-Lindsay and Enterline 2000; Cunningham 2006), and policy makers have expressed serious reservations about the efficaciousness of third party intervention. Luttwak (1999), for example, argues there is little that international parties can do to resolve a civil conflict, and that policy makers ought to "give war a chance." Only by allowing the grievances underlying a conflict to "burn out" on their own can a conflict ever be seriously resolved. To do otherwise risks freezing the conflict in place and delaying further hostilities for a later date.

That disagreement aside, civil conflict duration and outcomes are highly amenable to outside intervention (Brandt et al. 2008). One significant set of findings is that the apparent decline in civil wars after 1994 is a function of intervention by the international community, including the deployment of peacekeepers, negotiators, and mediators (Hegre 2004; Harbom et al. 2006). However, not all third party interveners act in order to resolve civil conflict. Some seek to deliberately prolong conflicts or alter the battlefield for their own purposes (Balch-Lindsay and Enterline 2000; Findley and Marineau n.d.; Gent 2008).

Third party interventions also vary widely in their forms and functions, ranging from the supplying of combat personnel and war material, to the direct use of military force by the third party (Regan 2010). This variation suggests that conflicts do not occur in isolation, waiting for outside powers to intervene but, rather, are deeply enmeshed in world politics. In the following four sections, we elaborate the ways in which international relations directly affect the duration and outcome of civil conflicts.

FORMS OF THIRD PARTY INTERVENTION

While it is possible to speak of purely "internal" conflicts, there is a long-standing recognition in the literature that the civil war process has a significant international component (Deutsch 1964; Modelski 1964; Rosenau 1964). Much of the contemporary research on civil war draws upon these foundational insights. A brief look at the early research on the subject is therefore necessary in order to provide context for contemporary advances.

Third party intervention encompasses an extremely broad class of behaviors, and it can be difficult to identify these behaviors because they are so easily conflated with policies that international actors undertake in order to influence the domestic politics of other states. However, as Rosenau (1968, 1969) discusses at some length, simple third party influence is a part of the ordinary course of international affairs. This distinction is crucial, as the earliest literature on third party intervention, according to Rosenau, fails to distinguish between military intervention and much larger classes of behavior, including propaganda (e.g., Fenwick 1941), diplomatic intervention (e.g., Wright 1939), and ideological persuasion (e.g., Morgenthau 1967). Although these latter phenomena might be seen as intervention, they are relatively more common than military force; moreover, they are well within established norms of international practice.

An overly vague definition of third party intervention also renders the topic nearly impossible to analyze. The topic therefore requires an operational definition that meets sharp criteria. Rosenau argues that such a definition must satisfy two general criteria. Intervention is: (1) convention breaking, meaning that it occurs outside the normal course of international politics; and (2) authority targeting, meaning that it is "directed at changing or preserving the structure of political authority in the targeted society" (Rosenau 1968: 167). By these criteria, the normal practices of international relations can be excluded (Regan 2000: 9). It should be noted, however, that these criteria are not necessarily concerned with civil wars, but with military interventions in general.

With respect to civil war, Regan (2000) offers a definition that satisfies Rosenau's criteria, namely, that third party intervention is the use of an actor's resources to affect the course of a civil conflict (Regan 2000: 9). These resources may be spent in a variety of ways that include, but are not limited to the following: (1) diplomatic methods, which can include mediation, arbitration, or the use of international forums (Regan 2000; Regan and Aydin 2006; Regan et al. 2009: 6–7); (2) economic intervention, including sanctions, inducements, and foreign aid (McNab and Mason 2007); (3) the deployment of peacekeepers (Fortna 2004); (4) covert or overt support for one of the warring factions in the form of funds, sanctuary, and weapons (Salehyan 2009; Salehyan et al. 2011); and, (5) direct military intervention (Balch-Lindsay and Enterline 2000; Balch-Lindsay et al. 2008; Mason and Fett 1996; Mason et al. 1999).

Diplomatic interventions, economic inducement, and the deployment of peacekeepers are covered elsewhere in this volume (see chapters 7, 8, and 9), and our focus in the remainder of this chapter is on external support and direct military intervention. This limit to the discussion is not unreasonable, as external support and military intervention are convention breaking and specifically designed to affect the balance of power on the battlefield. Such actions can also be extremely costly to the intervener. The decision-making processes underlying interventions therefore merit special attention.

WHAT FACTORS MAKE STATES MORE LIKELY TO INTERVENE?

Among the most important questions in the intervention literature are: Which third parties intervene? Where do third parties intervene? And why do third parties intervene? The conventional wisdom asserts that third parties intervene in order to engage in conflict resolution, thereby reducing the duration of civil war and increasing the odds of a negotiated settlement (Carment and Rowlands 1998; Krain 2005; Licklider 1995a, 1995b; Regan 2000). There is considerable debate on the plausibility of assuming the motives of third parties. Some scholars claim that third parties are rarely willing to pay the costs of intervention for purely humanitarian reasons (e.g., Morgenthau 1967), while others argue that third parties may intervene to pursue other, extra–civil war goals (e.g., Balch-Lindsay and Enterline 2000).

The management of civil conflicts gained considerable attention following the conclusion of the Cold War (e.g., Annan 1999; Deng 1995; Deng et al. 1996; Smith 1994; Stedman 1993; Wheeler 2000). The failure of the global community to prevent genocides in Rwanda and Bosnia generated a movement among policy makers commonly called the "Responsibility to Protect," or R2P, in which it is held as a duty of the international community to intervene in states that fail to prevent atrocity within their own borders. In a contrary assessment, Stedman (1993) argues that this post–Cold War tendency leads its advocates to engage in increasingly expansive and unrealistic interventions. Conversely, Finnemore (2004) tracked the evolving purpose of intervention, finding that assertions of universal human rights have become a common justification. However, the evidence seems to suggest that international interventions are remarkably successful in bringing about a negotiated settlement (Brandt et al. 2008; Mason et al. 1999).

Despite changing norms, empirical research shows that not all conflicts are likely to be targeted for intervention. Humanitarian interventions are conditioned by a selection effect. Specifically, the very process by which a civil conflict captures the attention of the global community, the requirements for achieving collective action among nations and obtaining consent from the UN Security Council, and then the assembling a peacekeeping force means that only the most difficult civil-conflict cases are the subjects of UN intervention (Gilligan and Stedman 2003). Thus, interveners and peacekeepers often become involved in the "hard cases" of civil wars that are most difficult to resolve.

Although it is clear that conflict management is an increasingly important motive, accumulating evidence shows that third parties are anything but selfless. Foremost among the ulterior motives of potential interveners is that of geopolitics, in which a civil conflict's regional environment motivates outside powers to action. The regional environment provides the necessary milieu for third party interaction with a civil conflict (Buhaug and Gleditsch 2008; Gleditsch 2007). Indeed, the earliest studies in this area suggest that the geographic proximity is one of the most influential factors in determining who intervenes and where (Pearson 1974).

Civil wars also generate considerable cross-national externalities within their regional environments by generating refugee flows, depressing regional economics, and destabilizing nearby states (Murdoch and Sandler 2004; Gleditsch 2007; Salehyan and Gleditsch 2006). Intergovernmental organizations may intervene in order to stabilize the conflict region (Beardsley 2011), and nearby states may become involved if their leaders believe that their own states are vulnerable to the spread, or contagion, of civil conflict (Kathman 2010, 2011). Third parties may also become involved in conflicts for purely material reasons, intervening in order to plunder resources or protect economic interests (Balch-Lindsay and Enterline 2000; Balch-Lindsay et al. 2008; Findley and Marineau n.d.; Koga 2011). The Congo Wars (1996–2003) remain the classic example of each of these phenomena. In those cases, a variety of states intervened in the civil war afflicting the Democratic Republic of Congo. Rwanda, for example, intervened in order to thwart Hutu raiders that had been expelled after that country's genocide, while Zimbabwe deployed military forces in order to extract a variety of precious stones and metals. Indeed, so many countries intervened in this "civil conflict" that, as noted in a previous chapter, it has often been called Africa's "first world war" (Stearns 2011).

Ethnicity also exerts a special kind of influence within the regional milieu, with cross-border communities and transnational diasporas providing a crucial link between interveners and their targets (Carment 1993; Carment and James 1996; Carment and Rowlands 1998; Davis and Moore 1997; Gleditsch 2007; Trumbore 2003). Which states are likely to intervene in favor of their co-ethnics is a source of considerable controversy. One piece of conventional wisdom holds that the norms of sovereignty within international society is a natural limit on intervention (e.g., Jackson and Rosberg 1982), while another is that states vulnerable to ethnic secession will be reluctant to intervene abroad in fear of encouraging their own aggrieved ethnicities to rebel (e.g., Herbst 1989; Touval 1972). Saideman (1997, 2001, 2002), by contrast, asserts that leaders of would-be interveners must pay attention to the preferences of the domestic constituencies that elevated them to power. Should these constituencies share an ethnic affinity with citizens of another state, rational and self-interested politicians may be forced to consider intervention into a conflict. Koga (2011) elaborates on the special role played by these kinds of domestic politics, finding that democratic states are especially likely to intervene in a civil war abroad if ethnic ties between the two are present.

Beyond the regional environment, world politics has a significant role to play. Research in this area is tentative, but a number of interesting conclusions have been reached. At this level of analysis, third parties are often less concerned with regional stability than with the possibility of undermining their interstate rivals (Akcinaroglu and Radziszewski 2005; Balch-Lindsay and Enterline 2000; Balch-Lindsay et al. 2008; Findley and Teo 2006). Moreover, the mere presence of a rivalry is enough to prolong a civil conflict because rebels expect the rival state to intervene on their behalf (Akcinaroglu and Radziszewski 2005). Examples from the Cold War are frequently invoked in this line of reasoning. In one classic case, American decision makers perceived the Soviet invasion of Afghanistan as a threat to U.S. interests in the Persian Gulf and therefore sought to aid rebels fighting in that conflict (Scott 1996: 42–43; Findley and Teo 2006).

The Cold War also highlights an interesting class of intervention, that of the "proxy war." Because intervention can be costly, and aiding a rival state's rebels constitutes a direct violation of sovereignty, many states wage war covertly or on the cheap, basically outsourcing their militaries. Research shows that rival states give sanctuary to one another's territories and supply rebel movements with men and materiel (Salehyan 2009; Salehyan et al. 2011). The supply of Angolan rebel groups like the MPLA and UNITA by the rival superpowers during the 1980s is an outstanding example—superpower proxy war was partly responsible for the multi-decade duration of that conflict. Salehyan et al. (2011) develop this logic within a principal-agent framework, arguing that foreign supply of patronage and the rebel demand for it are, in part, a function of rebel-group strength. The strongest rebel groups are unlikely to seek outside support, while foreign powers are unlikely to aid weak rebel groups. Similarly, rebel movements are more likely to receive support if they have an international audience or constituency, including ethnic and religious affinities (Jenne 2007; Saideman 1997, 2001, 2002; Trumbore 2003).

The Cold War is also interesting because of the way scholars model its effects in their statistical studies. Typically, the Cold War enters into a quantitative model as an atheoretical indicator variable marking the years 1946–1989. However, the Cold War was more than just a period of heightened tensions occurring in a particular time. Rather, it was a period in which policy makers observed the entire international system when considering the implications of their decisions. The United States' intervention in Vietnam (1964–1973), for example, was motivated by concerns over the security of regional states and over its reputation among American allies globally. Similarly, the Soviet Union intervened in Afghanistan (1979–1988) in order to uphold the so-called Brezhnev Doctrine that sought to maintain solidarity within the Soviet bloc. Finally, the United States decided against intervention during the Hungarian Revolt (1956) in order to avoid antagonizing the Soviets in a region they considered to be of vital interest. Interestingly, this latter case highlights a case of nonintervention, a phenomenon that has received little attention.

We therefore propose that military intervention and proxy war should be considered as components of a broad class of security-seeking behaviors engaged in by third parties in which third parties "observe" the entire international system when considering their actions. This kind of security-seeking decision making by policy makers may have diminished after the Cold War, yet we argue that political leaders still consider civil wars within global and regional systems. Research already shows that the Cold War directly affected the tactics by which civil wars are fought (Kalyvas and Balcells 2010), and Thyne (2009) shows that rebels and governments account for international relations when making decisions about the intrastate conflict environment. Thus, while it is widely accepted that third parties are strategic actors within the context of a conflict, their strategic interactions with the broader international environment is a neglected area of study.

WHEN AND WHY DO STATES INTERVENE OVER THE COURSE OF CONFLICT?

In this section, we address the question of the timing of third party intervention; that is to say, when and why do third party states intervene in conflict? The question of timing is naturally situated within the bargaining model of war (e.g., Fearon 1995;

Powell 2006; Reiter 2003; Walter 2009a). The bargaining model holds that conflicts are an information-revealing process in which the warring parties learn about one another's capability as combat ensues and then continually update their estimates of the utility for continuing the fight or seeking a negotiated settlement.

The bargaining model affords important insights for understanding the outcome and duration of civil wars. Given that capability and resolve are not normally known at the outset of conflict and because neither side is able to credibly commit to a peace agreement, war becomes the default solution (Walter 1997, 2002). War, then, is a bargaining failure, and if one side possesses an advantage in capability or resolve, then that side is likely to achieve victory quickly. However, because the state nearly always possesses an advantage, rebel victory is rare. When rebels actually succeed, they generally do so in the first few years of the conflict.

After about five years, the odds that either side will achieve victory in the civil war declines to nearly zero (Brandt et al. 2008; Mason and Fett 1996; Mason et al. 1999). Even after the odds of victory have fallen, however, protracted civil war may continue in a condition called a "mutually hurting stalemate" owing to the fact that neither side is able to credibly commit to peace (Zartman 1989). Third parties may provide the solution. International interveners are able to credibly commit to desegregating and demobilizing the warring factions, basically guaranteeing the peace (Carment and Rowlands 1998; Licklider 1995a, 1995b; Mason and Fett 1996; Regan 2000; Walter 1997, 2002).

The Rwandan Genocide of 1994 is one of the most notable examples of this logic. Walter (2002: 143–59), for example, shows how the failure of credible international commitments after a three-year civil war (1990–1993) contributed to the genocide. Under international supervision, the ethnic Tutsi rebels of the Rwandan Patriotic Front and the predominately Hutu government were actually willing to travel quite a distance down the road to peace, resulting in the signing of the 1993 Arusha Accords. Unfortunately, international commitment to these accords was revealed to be empty after United Nations peacekeepers were deliberately targeted. The UN's subsequent removal of the bulk of the force and overall refusal to reintroduce the peacekeepers exacerbated mutual security concerns among the Tutsi and Hutu communities, resulting in a resumption of hostilities and the initiation of genocide. In the aftermath of the killings, the Carnegie Commission for the Prevention of Deadly Conflict concluded that the reintroduction of even as few as five thousand peacekeepers could have prevented much of the violence (Walter 2002: 159). Although these arguments suggest great efficacy for humanitarian conflict management, they run directly counter to significant findings in the literature. Several scholars argue that third parties can intervene and lend their support to one side or the other in an attempt to alter the balance of power on the battlefield for their own interests (Balch-Lindsay and Enterline 2000; Balch-Lindsay et al. 2008). Some third party interveners are also more interested in looting resources or in undermining rival powers (Balch-Lindsay et al. 2008; Findley and Marineau n.d.; Ross 2004b). Thus, third party intervention can actually increase the duration of civil war for reasons of an entirely strategic nature unrelated to humanitarianism.

For these reasons, several studies have undertaken the crucial step of disaggregating interventions by type: government biased, rebel biased, and balanced (Balch-Lindsay and Enterline 2000; Balch-Lindsay et al. 2008; Collier et al. 2004; Mason and Fett 1996; Mason et al. 1999; Regan 2002; Regan and Aydin 2006). Balch-Lindsay and Enterline (2000) and Balch-Lindsay et al. (2008) find that interventions on behalf of the government decrease the time until negotiated settlement and increase the odds of such an outcome, but intervention on behalf of the rebels increases the odds of an opposition military victory. Balanced interventions in which third parties intervene on behalf of the government and rebels simultaneously, however, decrease the odds of negotiated settlement and lengthen the duration of hostilities.

These findings are not uncontested. Collier et al. (2004) show that rebel-biased interventions decrease the duration of civil wars, but interventions in favor of the government have no effect. Mason et al. (1999) find that third party intervention reduces the probability of settlement, regardless of its bias, although this effect attenuates with time—if a conflict becomes protracted, intervention and negotiated settlement become more likely. Finally, Regan (2002) and Regan and Aydin (2006) find that biased interventions have no effect.

Such a collection of contradictory findings poses an exceeding difficult puzzle for the literature. Gent (2008) argues these contradictions arise because the primary goal of an intervention is to affect the outcome of a civil war, not its duration. Because third parties are concerned mainly with outcome, they will intervene when military force will have the greatest marginal effect: "going in when it counts" to use Gent's turn of phrase. Because government forces are able to defeat weak rebels, government-biased intervention is unlikely to occur in such a case. Only when governments are on the verge of defeat by stronger rebels will government forces intervene. Conversely, weak rebels are unable to defeat the government even with military support; thus, third parties will intervene in favor of rebel forces only when they present a credible chance of victory over the government.

Regan (2010) further suggests that many of these contradictory findings are a result of the use of very different datasets, each with its own definition of civil war and intervention. It is further possible that interventions consisting in the actual deployment of military forces decrease the odds of a quick victory or negotiated settlement, but that less obtrusive interventions produce a more dramatic impact.

HOW DOES INTERNATIONAL INTERVENTION AFFECT THE DURATION AND OUTCOME OF CONFLICTS?

While the timing of intervention is subject to some debate, the mechanisms by which intervention affects duration and outcome are clearer. Scholarship in both the academic and policy arenas find that external patrons and military interventionists can dramatically assist rebel movements in their ability to challenge governments. Rebels are typically at a military disadvantage relative to the governments they seek the challenge, and so external support is one of the crucial determinants of rebel military success and decreased odds of government victory (Balch-Lindsay and Enterline 2000; Byman 2001; Connable and Libicki 2010; Mason et al. 1999; Record 2006, 2007; Salehyan 2007, 2009; Salehyan et al. 2011; Shelton et al. 2013). Only one study finds evidence that external support for rebellion decreases the odds of rebel military victory—Thyne (2009). Thyne argues that when particularly weak third parties support rebel movements, the odds of opposition success are greatly diminished.

Evidence in favor of government-biased interventions is less certain and conditional on highly nuanced factors. Sullivan and Karreth (n.d.) find that government-biased interventions are effective only when rebel capabilities match or exceed those of the state, and Lyall and Wilson (2009) find that government-biased intervention is counterproductive because it is perceived as illegitimate by the population, thereby increasing support for rebel movements within the conflict state.

Beyond biased intervention, outside actors can prolong civil wars and shape their outcome simply by being present (Mason and Fett 1996: 553). Indeed, the introduction of military forces by an outside power adds another actor whose consent is required in order for a negotiated settlement to occur (Cunningham 2006). This is especially problematic when intervening powers bring their own separate agendas to the negotiating table (Cunningham 2010).

Additional work examines the effect of intervention on war-fighting tactics and civilian victimization. Tactics are not directly the subject of this chapter, but the manner in which wars are fought is a product of international factors (e.g., Fearon 2004; Kalyvas and Balcells 2010), and, in turn, tactics directly impact civil war duration and outcome (e.g., Fearon and Laitin 2003; Enterline et al. 2013; Lyall 2010b; Lyall and Wilson III 2009; Paul et al. 2010; Sullivan 2007). Tactics may influence the duration and outcome of civil wars in two general ways: opposition use of insurgent tactics, and war-fighting methods that victimize civilians.

With respect to insurgency, nascent rebel organizations are frequently forced to hide from governmental forces (Arreguin-Toft 2001; Fearon and Laitin 2003; Lyall and Wilson III 2009). This tactic carries a political dimension, in that it seeks to prolong conflict beyond the patience of the incumbent authorities (Arreguin-Toft 2001; Mack 1975; Mason and Fett 1996; Record 2007). Many of the classic works on guerrilla strategy expound on the use of these tactics in such places as China, Vietnam, Cuba, and Algeria (e.g., Giap 1962; Guevara 1961; Mao 1961; Taber 1970).

Insurgent tactics frequently have an international origin. Fearon and Laitin (2003: 75) call them a "technology of military conflict" that may be passed around among rebel actors in the international system. Kalyvas and Balcells (2010) make a special point of this, noting that the Cold War was characterized by a transnational Marxist movement that was responsible for funneling thousands of insurgents into conflicts around the world. Modern civil conflicts find a counterpart in the transnational Islamist movement and the movement of foreign fighters around the globe (Hegghammer 2010, 2013).

The manner in which governments oppose insurgent tactics has a bearing on duration and outcome as well. Weak states afflicted with corruption, inept counter-insurgency practices, and authoritarian governments frequently lack the ability to even find insurgents and so react by "draining the sea"; that is to say, by disrupting the population that gives sanctuary to the rebels (Downes 2006, 2007; Mason and Krane 1989; Toft and Zhukov 2012; Valentino et al. 2004; Zhukov 2007). Rebels, too, often victimize civilians and prey upon the populations under their control (Hultman 2007; Kalyvas 2006; Wood 2010).

However, civilian victimization and harsh counterinsurgency carry significant risks because such tactics alienate the population and drive them into the arms of the opposing side (Kalyvas 2006; Kalyvas and Kocher 2007; Mason and Krane 1989; Zhukov 2007). More effective tactics try to recruit civilians through a "hearts and minds" style of war fighting (Enterline et al. 2013; Lyall 2010a). A shift to such a strategy was a notable feature of late-stage Vietnam, as well as Iraq after 2007.

Yet, if the use of harsh tactics by either side is so counterproductive, researchers must ask why combatants choose them in the first place. Recent work has thus opened up the "black box" of war and posited that as the various factions in a conflict gain or lose strength, they seek to impose costs on the other side or to extract resources from the population as capabilities decline (Hultman 2007; Kalyvas 2006; Wood 2010). Moreover, some warring factions in civil conflict come to rely on predation as a form of "taxation" that may be used to fund continued warfare. Wood et al. (2012) therefore conclude that because military intervention significantly adds to the strength of the supported faction, the side so supported will have less of a need to prey on civilians. However, the waging of proxy war below the threshold of direct military intervention also reduces the need for rebels to obtain the support of civilians in their area of control, but not to the point that they can function independently, thus encouraging predation of civilians by the rebels (Salehyan et al. 2014).

War-fighting tactics represent a rapidly growing area in the literature full of interesting puzzles and excellent research, but little work has actually connected them to civil war duration or outcomes. The work that does exist does not paint an optimistic picture for third party decision makers. Sullivan (2007) argues that the effect of military power and resolve on war outcomes varies, and that stronger states are likely to underestimate the costs of victory as the impact of resolve increases relative to war-fighting capacity. Thus, high-capacity democracies, which are so susceptible to public opinion, may be especially prone to defeat during insurgencies, although Lyall (2010b) contradicts this by finding no link between regime type and intervention outcome or duration. That said, one of the few studies on the long-term impact of third party counterinsurgent tactics on war outcomes finds that there is a "window of opportunity" for counterinsurgents to employ the hearts-and-minds strategy. The effectiveness of this strategy declines after about eight years (Enterline et al. 2013).

Because this area of research is relatively new, a number of interesting questions remain unresolved. For instance, in what ways does civilian victimization contribute to civil war duration? In what way does the defection of civilians from one side to the other affect war outcome? How does the prospect of international intervention affect the likelihood that a particular tactic will be adopted even before the intervention occurs? We return to these and other questions in the next section.

FUTURE RESEARCH

In this section, we identify unresolved puzzles in the literature and suggest directions for future research. These directions are (1) consideration of alternate units of analysis, (2) opening up the "black box" of third parties by examining the way in which domestic politics and institutions in third parties affect their decision making, and (3) a reintegration of research on intervention with the broader literature on world politics. We discuss each direction in turn.

Alternate Units of Analysis

One fact that stands out in the third party intervention literature is the presence of so many conflicting findings. Findley and Teo (2006) contend that this has occurred because much of the research has not actually studied third party intervention; rather, its focus is on those traits of civil wars that attract third party interveners. Indeed, the field has historically been *phenomenon-centric*, which is to say that the research has taken the civil war or the state in which the conflict occurs as its unit of analysis. However, such a focus causes the researcher to privilege a conflict's traits at the expense of "who intervenes, why, and on whose side" (Findley and Teo 2006: 828). Answering questions such as these requires an *actor-centric* approach in which the research examines the traits of actor, rather than the conflict.

Consistent with this insight is the recent rise of dyadic datasets that pair rebel actors with the governments with whom they are at war (see chapter 15). Among other things, these data have enabled a new stream of research to examine the effect of rebel military strength, command ability, territorial control, and transnational constituencies on conflict duration, peace processes, and the likelihood that external actors will provide arms and funding (Cunningham et al. 2009, 2013; Salehyan et al. 2011). A natural move for this literature is therefore to incorporate the involvement of third party militaries into the dyad, or to even move beyond the dyad into more complex units.

Another important data-related development is that of events-data, which catalog individual battles and atrocities within the conflict (see chapter 15). The emergence of such data allows researchers to explore the way in which intra-conflict events affect bargaining and, thus, the likelihood that third parties will intervene. Following from Gent (2008), it is known that third parties are more likely to intervene when they will have the greatest impact. Events on the battlefield should, therefore, provide this information to third parties, teaching them the utility of intervention and thereby affecting the timing of intervention.

There are several research questions that could take advantage of these new developments. For example, do battle outcomes affect the likelihood that third parties will intervene in civil war? Violence in places like Libya in 2011 and the Democratic Republic of Congo (DRC) in 1998 suggest that the answer to this question is yes. As battle events move toward strategic locations, such as capital cities, ethnic enclaves, or mineral and oil deposits, third parties may become more likely to interfere in order to protect their interests. In Libya, for example, the North Atlantic Treaty Organization (NATO) intervened as a result of rebel battle losses, while in the DRC, various governments intervened to support the government after it sustained losses at the hands of rebels.

Domestic Politics

The traits of warring factions and conflicts are a frequent object of study, but those of the third party state have received considerably less attention. Our second suggested area of focus is therefore the third party's decision calculus. Third party states must pay for the costs of intervention, including those paid in terms of casualties, monies, or the opportunity to carry out other international or domestic priorities. Indeed, the decision makers within these states, like all political actors (e.g., Bueno de Mesquita et al. 2003), must satisfy their domestic constituencies, and the costs attendant to intervention may make this impossible. The interventions of the United States in Vietnam and Iraq, or the Soviet Union in Afghanistan, were notable for the domestic dissatisfaction their costs incurred and subsequent ejection of political leaders from office. This link is well understood with respect to international conflict (e.g., Bueno de Mesquita and Siverson 1995), but civil war researchers have not focused much attention on the issue.

The domestic costs of intervention suggest a number of additional puzzles. Current literature examines the effect of war fighting on the public's willingness to absorb the costs, and the effect of war on democratic elections (Arena 2008; Sullivan 2008; Koch and Sullivan 2010). In the next wave of research, scholars should examine the way in which future-regarding leaders integrate the impact of public opinion into their initial intervention decisions. Third party decision makers are almost certainly aware of public opinion's effects on tenure. It therefore makes sense that they would consider it before even deciding whether or not to intervene. As with the effect of the Cold War on intervention, this insight on public opinion suggests that nonintervention is a significant problem that scholar must grapple with.

There are a large number of possible topics here, each of which examines the initial decision to intervene (or to abstain). For example, how and when do leader assessments of public opinion affect the scale of intervention? How do the outcomes of past interventions affect leader tenure in office? Relatedly, are all interventions the same, or does the level of commitment by the third party generate feedback into the domestic political system and, hence, affect the duration of the intervention and the outcome of the civil conflict? Moreover, does a costly military intervention render future leaders less likely to engage in them, effectively making them "learning" actors that take cues from events decades in the past? Initial research would suggest this to be the case (e.g., Pickering 2001).

There is also the issue of opportunity costs. Leaders come into office with a whole portfolio of international and domestic policy programs and preferences. Emphasizing one or the other reduces the time that can be spent on another, with increased military spending detracting from other domestic priorities. Lyndon Johnson learned that, much to his detriment, intervention in Vietnam crowded out funding for his Great Society programs and drained his political capital (Bernstein 1996). It is arguably the case that President George W. Bush's 2005 push for Social Security reform was similarly impacted by the war in Iraq.

This emphasis on domestic politics also suggests a need to "open the black box" of the third party state. To date, most of the quantitative literature treats the third party state as a unitary actor. Yet states are, in actuality, aggregations of multiple competing interests. Some important qualitative literature has examined this area. Scott (1996), for example, examines the effect of bureaucratic infighting on the development of the Reagan Doctrine of American intervention in Cold War–era conflicts. The final form of the doctrine was not simply a directive issued by Reagan and then seamlessly executed by the policy apparatus, but actually evolved out of the interaction of the president's ability to influence the bureaucracy, laws enacted by the Congress, and the preferences of various agencies. Although the peculiarities of the American political system are not generalizable across all potential interveners, their study does suggest that a leader's domestic prestige and a political system's institutional qualities affect the decision to intervene and, therefore, exert an influence on the duration and outcome of civil conflicts.

These puzzles therefore suggest that the duration and outcome of civil wars and the domestic policies of the would-be intervener are informed by multiple feedback loops. Because there are so many different possible causal chains in this area, researchers availing themselves of this dimension must give careful attention to causal mechanisms.

The World Politics of Intervention

In the last major area of research, we suggest increased attention to findings from other areas of international relations research and an effort to connect civil wars to insights in the broader world politics literature. In particular, we see a major division that separates existing work into two competing paradigms. The first such paradigm is that of realism, the traditional perspective among international relations scholars. Within this paradigm, scholars argue that concerns over security or power motivate third party intervention (Ayoob 1995; Buzan 1991; Heraclides 1990). Although realism contains several well-known flaws, particularly its inability to account for change and predict the future (e.g., Gaddis 1992), it is worth noting that some empirical researchers introduce realist expectations and variables into their statistical models (Regan 1998; Saideman 2001, 2002).

By contrast, modern research has given preference to a second paradigm—the bargaining model of war. In this model, conflicts and the actors within them are almost considered in isolation. Yet over forty years ago, Mitchell (1970) argued that there were four categories of factors generally responsible for influencing interventions: (1) the characteristics of the conflict state, (2) the characteristics of the intervener, (3) linkages between the target and intervener, and (4) the character of the international system.

The first three categories of factors are those preferenced by the bargaining model, with each responsible in some way for the duration and possible outcome of civil wars.

However, few present-day scholars give much attention to the fourth category—the international system—or to world politics more generally. To the extent that international factors enter into modern empirical work, it is through Mitchell's third category of factors—linkages between target and intervener—which includes ethnic affinities between the two, rivalry, or the regional political environment. To date, only a few scholars examine the way the system itself affects civil war duration and outcome. Fearon and Laitin (2003) and Hironaka (2005), for example, argue that decolonization produced a number of weak states that gave would-be rebels significant opportunities to mobilize and persist, resulting in an uptick in the number of civil war onsets and an increase in their duration during the Cold War. Kalyvas and Balcells (2010) go further, arguing that the tactics used by rebels for many decades was a product of the bipolar power struggle between the United States and the Soviet Union.

Given the interrelation between tactics, war duration, and outcome, it is a surprise that the international origins of these factors received so little attention in the research of the last twenty years. We therefore suggest a research agenda that integrates findings from a broad swath of the international relations subfield. Consider the following: At the end of World War II, much of the international system was organized around American hegemony and the community of powerful democratic nations. These states supported and, in some cases, installed authoritarian regimes around the world, a "firewall" against Soviet-supported states. That democratic states would engage in this behavior should not be surprising, as authoritarian states have less of a need to respond to large domestic constituencies and are more likely to deliver upon the preferences of their international patrons (Bueno de Mesquita and Downs 2006). In the case of the Cold War, the aims of such a foreign policy included the suppression of local communist movements and the containment of the Soviet Union (Westad 2005). Moreover, a view would later emerge among American policy makers that authoritarian regimes, however distasteful, were preferable to the totalitarian alternative, and also more likely to make the transition to democracy (e.g., Kirkpatrick 1982).

Decision makers thus choose to intervene, or not, based on their perception of the international system. The United States decided against intervention in 1956 Hungary, but in favor of such in 1960s Vietnam. Similarly, both the Americans and the Soviets intervened in the wars of southern Africa in the 1980s. In Hungary, deterrence played a role, with the United States unwilling to risk war with the Soviet Union. Vietnam, on the other hand, stood at risk of falling in the Soviet orbit, and American policy makers were determined to prevent that. Finally, in the case of Africa, policy makers in both superpowers were trying to outflank one another in order to aid or thwart revolution in South Africa. This highly strategic behavior occurred as a product of security seeking on the international level.

We do not argue that the bargaining model of war is somehow deficient; rather, its proponents have neglected to examine those international and strategic features that set the context of bargaining. As an example of this style of research, Daxecker (2011) argues that shocks to state capacity may prevent either the government or the state from credibly committing to peace. While these shocks may originate domestically, changes at the systemic level have their part to play as well, with global recession, defeat in war, or changes to the international balance of power complicating bargaining and, thus, contributing to civil war onset. Although this logic is primarily concerned with civil war onset, there is significant room for scholars to examine war duration and outcome as well.

Beyond these strategic factors, researchers should also consider the deeper historical contexts of the interventions in their datasets. For example, it is by this point well established that authoritarian regimes, lacking alternative policy tools for conflict resolution, are more likely to engage in the kind of repression that eventually aids recruitment into rebel organizations (Kalyvas and Kocher 2007; Mason and Krane 1989). From this perspective, then, civil war actually represents a kind of policy failure for the patrons of the repressive regimes. The revolutions and civil wars that overturned Soviet and American client states in Nicaragua, Iran, and Afghanistan in 1979 would seem to substantiate these points. Thus, intervention might be a reaction to this policy failure, with foreign patrons attempting to rectify the failure by supporting their preferred regime. Although this perspective is enmeshed in the logic of the Cold War, it is generalizable to all historical periods.

If, as we contend, many civil wars are international policy failures, then the way that empirical researchers treat civil conflicts should be reconceptualized. Rather than seeing these conflicts as the beginning of a process, they should instead be seen as one phase of continually evolving international relations. Systemic and dyadic relationships between and among states are established many decades before the onset of civil conflict, and these affect foreign aid flows, the repression that regimes engages in, and those states that interveners choose to target with military force. This "big picture" approach provides crucial context that is, at present, missing from the bargaining model.

To conclude, third party interventions are directly implicated in the way civil wars are fought. They affect the duration and the outcome of civil conflicts. The interest in intervention is long-standing, and modern empirical research has significantly expanded our understanding of the topic. Nevertheless, numerous puzzles remain, partly because researchers have, for reasons of both theory and data, focused almost entirely on the traits of the conflict or conflict-state. Although the literature risks becoming bogged down in conflicting findings and becoming stagnant, exciting new theoretical and data-driven developments should keep this from happening. Increasing precision in data and theory will allow researchers to provide key analyses to policy makers without becoming distracted by increasingly arcane details. In the present time, with policy debates raging over the Responsibility to Protect, the war in Iraq, and events in the Middle East, such research cannot be timelier.

7

Ripe for Resolution

Third Party Mediation and Negotiating Peace Agreements

Jacob D. Kathman and Megan Shannon

How does mediation influence belligerents in reaching a peace agreement to end civil wars? We often think of mediation as a process by which companies like Google and Microsoft seek an outside actor to help settle antitrust issues. Or we think of it as something Jimmy Carter uses to broker peace between the Israelis and the Egyptians. We less frequently think about how mediation affects negotiations and agreements between civil war combatants such as the Fuerzas Armadas Revolucionarias de Colombia (FARC) and the government of Colombia, or the Lord's Resistance Army (LRA) and the Ugandan government. This is surprising, given that civil wars are much more common than wars between countries and that mediation regularly occurs between civil war parties. Since the end of the Cold War, negotiated settlements have become the most frequent outcome of civil wars, and are often reached with the assistance of third party mediation. In fact, mediation as a conflict management tool has been used with increasing frequency in recent decades (DeRouen and Bercovitch 2012), and the scholarly literature on mediation in intrastate war has concurrently expanded (Svensson and Wallensteen 2014).

Mediation in civil wars is a very different process from mediation in interstate wars. First, it is much harder to get to mediation in civil wars than in interstate conflicts. Interstate rivals already have international recognition that is not necessarily compounded by the act of mediation. But governments facing civil insurgencies impart a level of legitimacy and possibly international recognition upon the rebels by agreeing to mediation. Governments will therefore avoid mediation so as not to hand the rebels a small victory. Second, civil wars have more acute commitment problems than interstate wars and tend to be more bloody, intractable, and seemingly difficult to settle with a peace agreement. Unlike interstate wars, reaching a peace agreement in civil conflicts necessitates disarming a combatant force. Yet the belligerents in civil war are reluctant to put down their weapons for fear of losing bargaining leverage and becoming vulnerable to annihilation by their rival. As a result, they are incentivized to continue fighting. Mediation therefore has less potential to produce peace agreements in civil wars than interstate wars, making it harder to compare across the two types of conflicts. For these reasons, mediation in civil wars should be studied as a distinct conflict resolution tool from mediation in interstate wars.

This chapter explores how often mediation occurs in civil wars, the types of mediation that are used, and the effectiveness of mediation in assisting the combatant parties in civil war to reach peace agreements. We assess what the literature has revealed about mediation processes, pointing to theoretical and empirical advances that indicate the conditions under which mediation appears to be more or less effective in bringing resolution to civil wars. We conclude by suggesting future research avenues that should prove productive to push the quantitative mediation literature forward and accumulate knowledge on mediation's effect on civil war processes.

WHAT IS MEDIATION?

While some disagreement exists on a specific definition of mediation, those who study it generally agree that it occurs when warring parties wish to try and resolve their differences, short of using violence. To help them reach a settlement, disputants seek the help of an outside actor who becomes the mediator (Bercovitch, Anagnoson, and Wille 1991: 8). The mediator brings the disputants together, facilitates talks, and makes suggestions toward a possible peace settlement. The mediator also generally refrains from aggression. Sometimes mediation is used in a procedural manner, to help the parties decide how they are going to manage a dispute. This may include, for example, the mediator setting the time or the agenda for talks. At other times, it is more substantive and addresses the substance of a dispute to help broker a settlement between the parties. An example is South African president Mbeki mediating an agreement in 2005 to give the Patriotic Movement of Ivory Coast rebel movement a role in the Ivory Coast government.

Mediation is more of a political than a legal process. While a third party helps disputants negotiate, disputants are not necessarily legally bound to reach a settlement or honor any agreement that they may eventually reach. This distinguishes mediation from more formal processes that incorporate law or legal processes, such as binding arbitration and adjudication (Gent and Shannon 2010). When the security environment within a country has degraded into civil war, the government has relatively little authority or ability to strong-arm opposition groups back to the negotiation table. Indeed, the fact that a rebel organization has confronted the government with organized violence is indicative of an extra-legal political process that operates outside of the state's formal institutional framework. Mediation in civil war is therefore a voluntary process on the part of the combatant factions, where the disputants decide if and when they want to peacefully settle grievances with the help of a third party. As such, the outside actor does not have the authority to impose a settlement between factions (Wall, Stark, and Standifer 2001: 375).

Mediation is a form of conflict resolution within a class of many types of third party conflict management efforts. These efforts vary in terms of the practices undertaken by the actors who use them, including the use of overt hostilities, the level of international coordination necessary for their execution, and the amount of cost borne by the third party. Scholars have analyzed such third party conflict management techniques as military intervention; economic sanctions; economic aid in the form of grants, loans, or other transfers; and peacekeeping efforts. These forms of conflict management are potential options available to third party states with interests in civil conflict processes and outcomes.

However, there are two characteristics of mediation worth noting that help to distinguish it from other forms of conflict management. First, the costs to the mediator for involvement in conflict differ in kind and size. Relative to military intervention, economic sanctions, aid, and peacekeeping activities, the material costs of mediation tend to be substantially lower. Mediation does not require the active use of the military or economic instruments common to other forms of third party involvement in order to engage the disputant factions in civil war. While the relative material costs may be low, the domestic- and international-audience costs associated with mediation may be substantial. This can be the case for both making the decision to engage in mediation and in the effectiveness of a mediation attempt. With regard to engaging in mediation, domestic audiences may motivate the mediation itself. For example, South Sudan mediated the conflict between the LRA and the government of Uganda because the LRA's repeated incursions threatened civil stability in South Sudan and complicated the conflict with the government of Sudan in Khartoum. Domestic and international audience costs are also important to mediation performance. Such costs include being caught providing incorrect or manipulated information, thus calling into question the mediator's credibility in the conflict resolution process and harming the mediator's international reputation for conflict management. The domestic-audience costs of mediation may also be considerable, particularly when mediation is perceived as failing in its objective to secure peace. Research has begun to tease out the contexts in which audience costs prove important to the choice to use mediation and its success in resolving conflict.[1] Still, the material costs of mediation are quite low with respect to the other alternatives mentioned.

A second distinguishing characteristic of mediation relative to other forms of third party involvement is that it has a sincere interest in conflict resolution. While research on third party economic and military intervention in civil war often starts with the claim that third parties generally seek an end to hostilities (Regan 2000), there is reason to believe that intervention actually worsens civil conflict (Regan 2002; Elbadawi and Sambanis 2000). An oft-mentioned example is the American intervention into the civil war in Afghanistan in the 1980s. The United States may have had an ulterior interest in imposing costs on the Soviet Union over a longer period of time. As National Security Advisor Zbigniew Brzezinski would later detail, the American strategy was to "make the Soviets bleed for as much and as long as is possible" (Brzezinski 1997). In fact, the finding that third party economic and military intervention tends to exacerbate civil wars has led to a series of subsequent studies that sought to unpack this seemingly counterintuitive finding.[2] Even if third parties generally do not intervene with sinister intentions to exacerbate a conflict, their involvement often worsens ongoing wars (Cunningham 2010).

By contrast, even when mediators are biased toward one conflict actor or in favor of a particular outcome, the mediator is generally understood to be seeking conflict resolution, since the perpetuation of hostilities is unlikely to benefit the mediator.[3] Thus, mediation is judged in its effectiveness in preventing or bringing an end to hostilities between the government and an insurgent organization. While this is often argued to be the motivation of other forms of third party involvement, like military intervention or economic sanctions, support for such suppositions is less well established.

In an attempt to determine the general effect of mediation as a tool of civil conflict management, scholars have recently constructed a number of rich datasets to identify instances of mediation in civil wars. These data projects code which actors mediate in civil conflict and how often they mediate and help to determine how successful mediation has been in civil war. The data they have gathered generally agree on the definition and identification of mediation efforts. However, the definition of civil conflict varies across datasets. Regan, Frank, and Aydin (2009) identify mediation in civil wars with a relatively high threshold of combat violence. These data use 200 battle deaths as its minimum level for which hostilities constitute civil war, indicating an end to war when six months have passed without reciprocated battlefield hostilities. Among the 153 civil conflicts identified from 1945 to 1999, there were 352 mediations among 438 diplomatic interventions.

DeRouen, Bercovitch, and Pospieszna (2011) create the Civil War Mediation (CWM) dataset to document mediation in a broader set of conflicts, as their definition of conflict includes a lower threshold for violence. The sample includes conflicts identified by the Conflict Termination Dataset (Kreutz 2010), which relies upon the Uppsala Conflict Data Program/Peace Research Institute, Oslo (UCDP/PRIO) Armed Conflict dataset. A conflict in these data is "a contested incompatibility that concerns government and/or territory where the use of armed force between two parties, of which at least one is the government of a state, and results in at least 25 battle-related deaths," (Gleditsch et al. 2002; Themner and Wallensteen 2014). Within the 319 conflicts in the sample, there occurred 460 mediation events, where a third party directly intervened and facilitated talks, either about the procedure for resolving the conflict or the actual disputed substance at the heart of the conflict (DeRouen, Bercovitch, and Pospieszna 2011).

Finally, the Managing Intrastate Low-Intensity Conflict (MILC) dataset, also using conflicts identified by the UCDP/PRIO Armed Conflict dataset, documents a wide range of preventive actions in civil wars from 1993 to 2004 (Melander, Möller, and Öberg 2009). The MILC dataset does not specifically refer to any actions as mediation, but it offers several categories of events that fall under a very broad definition of mediation, including good offices (359 incidents), direct talks (307 incidents), indirect talks (106 incidents), and fact finding (41 incidents), for a total of 813 third party efforts.

Mediators in civil wars can be individuals, nongovernmental organizations, countries, or international organizations. Research finds that, particularly in the post–Cold War era, the most frequent mediators are intergovernmental organizations (IGOs) such as the United Nations and the European Union (DeRouen, Bercovitch, and Pospieszna 2011; Grieg and Diehl 2012; Regan, Frank, and Aydin 2009). But state actors do not lag far behind IGOs in the frequency of mediation, with countries like the United States, United Kingdom, France, and Russia often serving as third party brokers (Grieg and Diehl 2012). The MILC data identify the United States as the most frequent mediator, with the UN the second most active. Private actors such as the Catholic Church are also called upon relatively frequently to facilitate talks (Regan, Frank, and Aydin 2009).

WHAT IS A PEACE AGREEMENT?

Now that a definition of mediation is established, allow us to discuss the occurrence of peace agreements in civil wars before turning to a discussion of if and how the two are linked. A peace agreement or settlement is a bargain that specifies who gets what and when they get it at the end of a civil war (Werner and Yuen 2005: 262). While this conceptual definition of peace agreement is somewhat easy to grasp, it is harder to identify, operationalize, and measure peace agreements. Doing so requires us to answer questions such as, what constitutes the end of a civil war? Does a civil war end when violence stops? Must combatants go further and sign a treaty or agreement or guarantee political or economic rights for particular groups? And if so, how long must an agreement last for it to be considered successful? One can imagine many ways to define and identify peace following civil wars, but perhaps the most utilized definition of peace agreement in the civil war literature comes from Walter's (1997) study of civil war settlements. She identifies peace agreements as capitulations or surrenders that keep opposition groups intact as a party to the peace process. The agreement must also end a civil war for at least five years (Walter 1997: 345). While a five-year threshold is admittedly arbitrary, it provides a systematic and concrete indicator by which we can explore the process of peace.

Peace agreements are difficult to reach in civil wars—more so than in wars between countries (Modelski 1964; Pillar 1983; Stedman 1996). Walter (1997) cites that between 1940 and 1990, only 20 percent of civil wars reached a peace agreement, compared to 55 percent of wars between countries. Kreutz (2010) similarly finds civil war peace agreements to be rare during the Cold War, occurring in only 8.4 percent of terminated conflicts between 1946 and 1990. Peace agreements have been brokered more frequently in civil wars after the Cold War comprising only 18.4 percent of 372 terminated episodes of conflict between 1991 and 2005.[4] However, when looking at wars as a whole, rather than just episodes, Harbom, Hogbladh, and Wallensteen (2008) find a higher percentage of peace agreements in civil conflicts than Kreutz, revealing that one-third of 231 civil conflicts ended in peace agreements. It seems that identifying how often peace agreements occur depends upon the time period for conflicts under study and the definition of conflict. Yet most studies agree that, compared to wars between countries, fewer civil wars end in negotiated peace settlements. As discussed in the following section, the unique bargaining structure within civil conflicts makes for long, violent wars with few peace agreements. Therefore, attempts to mediate and broker peace agreements must recognize and sufficiently address the unique bargaining obstacles in civil wars to be effective.

HOW MEDIATION ADDRESSES OBSTACLES TO CIVIL WAR RESOLUTION

What prevents civil war combatants from reaching peace agreements, and how can mediation help? In order to answer these questions, it is helpful to see civil war as a bargaining process, along the lines of the rationalist perspective (Wagner 2000). From the rationalist point of view, war is inefficient because it is costly relative to peaceful mechanisms of resolving disputes. The occurrence and perpetuation of war is puzzling because rational actors, which governments and rebel organizations are generally assumed to be, should prefer less costly and risky forms of dispute resolution. But because civil wars can and do occur, there must exist bargaining obstacles that prevent rational civil war combatants from reaching peace agreements. It is these bargaining obstacles that mediators seek to address in order to broker settlements.

The two categories of bargaining obstacles that have received the most attention in the civil war literature are information asymmetries and commitment problems (Fearon 1995).[5] For combatants to avoid conflict, they require information about one another that is difficult to acquire short of fighting. Such information includes knowledge of one another's strength, resolve, and potential negotiated agreements that each side would be willing to accept. Each actor's information is asymmetric: they know their own position, but lack similar knowledge of their opponent's preferences and capabilities. Acquiring this information is difficult, given the incentives of government and rebel forces to gain as much bargaining leverage as possible by misrepresenting their positions.

Fighting offers one means of revealing information. Once engaged in battle, combat events in civil war shed light on otherwise difficult-to-observe characteristics of combatant capabilities and resolve (Filson and Werner 2002; Ramsay 2008). The revelation of information through battlefield combat may explain the pattern in which costly civil wars arrive at negotiated conclusions more quickly than lower intensity conflicts (Balch-Lindsay and Enterline 2000; Brandt et al. 2008; Mason and Fett, 1996). Yet, given the asymmetric nature of civil conflict, "battlefield" hostilities may not fully reveal capabilities and resolve because insurgent organizations often seek to avoid overt combat in favor of hit-and-run attacks and guerrilla tactics. The government therefore attempts to root out insurgents, at least in the early stages of civil war, before insurgents gain strength and a greater foothold (Bapat 2005).

Fidel Castro's guerrilla insurgency in Cuba is one such example. Initially rather small in number, Castro's forces sought refuge in the mountainous and forested terrain distant from Havana, making it difficult for the Batista government to root out an otherwise weak rebel group. Castro's forces initially focused their energies on holding territory away from President Batista's centers of power. When fighting occurred, small skirmishes were common and were aimed at frustrating and confusing the government's forces over an extended period in an effort to slowly weaken the government's capability. It was only after years of guerrilla tactics that Castro's forces could then march on Havana. Among guerrilla conflicts more generally, such low-intensity and potentially infrequent combat engagements can make it difficult for belligerents to acquire necessary information quickly. Thus, civil wars can tend to be rather extended, making it difficult to arrive at an acceptable peace agreement relative to continued war.

Still, some civil wars endure for long periods even as battlefield interactions are frequent, pointing to causes of civil war beyond asymmetric information (Fearon 2004). Commitment problems also prevent negotiated resolutions, whereby an agreement that might be struck today could fail in the future if combatants' capabilities or resolve change, providing incentives for one side to renege on the agreement (Walter 1997, 2002; Cunningham 2006, 2011).[6] Unlike interstate wars, rebel and government factions cannot retreat behind internationally defined boundaries with the signing of a peace agreement. As Walter (2002) shows, this is particularly problematic for rebel organizations. For peace agreements to effectively end civil conflicts, rebels must put down their weapons and enter into the process of political reconciliation. But by virtue of doing this, the government and rebels essentially guarantee a destabilizing power shift in favor of the government side. When the rebels put down their arms, they sacrifice the ability to defend themselves. A window of opportunity opens for the government to subjugate the rebel forces and renege on the terms of a peace agreement. It is difficult for insurgents to commit to peace processes in the first place without credible guarantees of their future security (Walter 2002). As a result, civil wars often endure for extended periods of time and are difficult to settle with peace agreements.

Recognizing the importance of information asymmetries and commitment problems to civil war resolution, the mediation literature has sought to uncover means by which third parties might provide solutions to these issues. Because commitment problems are so prevalent and persistent in civil conflicts, mediation may be less effective as a singular intervention strategy than in tandem with stronger forms of intervention. Overcoming commitment problems requires strong third party enforcement of peace provisions and agreements. In interstate conflicts, such as the Yom Kippur War between Israel and Syria, a demilitarized zone can be established by an outside actor (e.g., the United Nations), which helps prevent the recurrence of fighting between forces in the area. When faced with persistent commitment problems, third parties may forgo the mediation strategy in favor of more coercive forms of intervention, to enforce and guarantee peace processes. For instance, Favretto (2009) argues that U.S. and European mediation efforts in the Balkan conflicts were unsuccessful at upholding cease-fires and peace agreements, so the United States turned to airstrikes. In an example of mediation working alongside more forceful diplomatic efforts, the United Nations combined mediation by the Secretary General with the deployment of a peacekeeping force in 2003 to help broker peace after Liberia's civil war. Scholars have sought to uncover the combinations of third party tactics in tandem with mediation that may provide leverage in getting combatants to agree to and abide by peace provisions. Such "mediation with muscle" helps the mediator overcome unwillingness from combatants to accept peace terms (Sisk 2009; Stedman 1996). As a result, one might expect powerful third parties to better mediate civil conflicts (Crocker 1992). Combined with the ability to enforce settlements, punish hostile behavior, and manipulate combatant incentives for continued conflict, mediation may be an important component of an overall intervention strategy for mitigating commitment problems faced by rebel and government forces.

Mediation as a solo tactic seems to have more potential in mitigating information asymmetries than commitment problems. Counter to conventional wisdom, a biased mediator may be more effective than a neutral one in producing peace agreements between civil war combatants. Biased mediators are those that want to see more benefits for one side to a conflict than another, and whose preferences are more aligned with a particular combatant. For example, the United States is a biased actor with preferences closer to Israel than to the Palestinians. A biased mediator may be more effective at getting its preferred side to back down, particularly if it has good information about the resolve of the opposing side (Kydd 2003). Biased mediators may also have greater leverage over their protégées and can therefore better convince one side to make concessions (Zartman 1995), which can be particularly valuable to civil war settlement. At the same time, biased mediators are also more likely to seek concessions for their preferred side (Svensson 2009), which has been shown to lead to richer peace settlements that have a greater potential for ending civil wars. In particular, mediation biased toward the government leads to more territorial power sharing and retributive justice, while mediation biased toward rebel opposition groups leads to more political power sharing and security guarantees (Svensson 2009).

IS MEDIATION EFFECTIVE IN
PRODUCING PEACE AGREEMENTS?

Practitioners, combatants, and civilians invariably have a stake in knowing how effective mediation is, but the success of mediation is difficult to determine. One reason is that the conflicts where mediation is used are not likely chosen at random. Instead, conflicts with mediation tend to be more intractable and less amenable to peace agreements. We therefore cannot easily compare mediated conflicts to those without mediation because conflicts where mediation is used already tend to be a more difficult set of conflicts to resolve. Evidence shows that, in fact, mediation is associated with shorter-lived settlements (Gartner and Bercovitch 2006) and is more likely in intense and longer conflicts (Greig and Regan 2008). Both findings are arguably due to the particularly thorny sample of conflicts in which mediation is used.

Even more so than interstate conflicts, mediation may be used in the most difficult civil wars because of the signal that accepting mediation sends. Governments resist mediation because it invites international recognition and legitimacy for rebel movements. It also sends the message that a government is not strong enough to control its territory (Clayton 2013; Greig and Regan 2008, Melin and Svensson 2009). Therefore, we should expect to see mediation in only the toughest cases, where the costs of ongoing conflict outweigh the domestic political costs of submitting to mediation. If that is the case, then any study that assesses the effectiveness of mediation must account for the sample selection processes behind the conflicts in which it is used.

Another complication with measuring the effectiveness of mediation is that it is frequently used in tandem with other mechanisms of conflict resolution. Conflict management is a process that often exhibits a range of resolution techniques, including bilateral negotiations, peacekeeping, arbitration, and military intervention (Diehl and Regan forthcoming). Mediation may precede or follow weaker diplomatic efforts or stronger intervention techniques. It may be used on multiple occasions and brokered by a variety of third parties.[7] Mediation is often not a singular or independent event, and it is therefore difficult to isolate the success of any given mediation effort.[8]

The success of mediation may depend on what it is being compared to. Melander, Moller, and Oberg (2009) find that among third party intervention tactics, some forms of mediation heighten conflict, while others dampen it. Specifically, UN mediation and mediation by neighbors are associated with increased escalation of war, while individual and NGO mediation seem to decrease war escalation. Svensson (2009) finds that, compared to unbiased mediation, biased mediation is more successful in producing peace agreements that are conducive to long-lasting peace. Böhmelt (2013) finds that, compared to initial attempts, later and cumulative mediation attempts are more effective.

Despite the research challenges noted above, scholars have measured success in a number of different ways and draw different conclusions about mediation's effectiveness. If full or partial settlements of civil conflict can be considered successful outcomes, then Regan et al.'s 2009 study concludes that mediation effectively ended 38 percent of conflicts in which it was used. Only 4 percent of attempts fail completely (Regan, Frank, and Aydin 2009). DeRouen, Bercovitch, and Pospieszna (2011), comparing among mediation attempts, estimate a slightly lower ratio of success, concluding that 15 percent of attempts result in a full peace settlement, while 18 percent result in a partial settlement. This however excludes the 13 percent of attempts that lead to process agreements, which may later lead to mediation success. About 24 percent of attempts were completely unsuccessful. It is difficult for mediation to succeed long-term in civil wars because civil wars are highly likely to restart following an initial cessation, even when the combatants agree to engage in negotiations. Only one-third of all such negotiations ended in an implemented peace agreement that resolved the conflict (Walter 2001). Yet given the devastating impacts of civil war on society (chapter 10, this volume), it is necessary for the international community to support mediation efforts, in hopes of ending the scourge of civil war.

FUTURE RESEARCH

While the literature on civil war mediation has expanded significantly, there are several ways in which future scholarship can move forward. In particular, as we and others have noted, research on civil war mediation would benefit from coding and analyzing data at finer levels of analysis by disaggregating information across actors and in time.

Many data projects have begun to disaggregate conflict phenomena both spatially and temporally beyond the state-year or dyad-year framework that has been the centerpiece of empirical studies of conflict processes. This has been especially necessary for data gathering projects focused on civil wars, as such conflicts are often complex. Countries may be embroiled in more than one conflict at a given time, fighting multiple rebel organizations within those conflicts. Also, rebel organizations may be wholly independent of one another or linked through security arrangements. Thus, the civil war literature has moved away from the country or the country-year as the unit of analysis and has begun to focus both theoretically and empirically on individual actors who constitute the conflict environment. Doing so allows researchers to conduct richer analyses of conflict and peace processes and offer new insights into civil war dynamics.

As an example of such progress, many advances have been made in data efforts linked to the Uppsala Conflict Data Program. In particular, data collection efforts have built greatly upon the UCDP/PRIO Armed Conflict Dataset (ACD) (Gleditsch et al. 2002). These data initially sought to provide information on conflict processes at a finer level than was previously available through other sources, such as the Correlates of War Intra-State War Data (Sarkees and Wayman 2010). Using a low threshold of only 25 annual battle deaths to categorize civil conflict, compared to the Correlates of War 1,000 combat casualties threshold, the UCDP/PRIO data program opened new opportunities for research at varying levels of conflict and war.

New data projects have begun collecting information on rebel groups and other non-state actors that were not previously available to researchers (see chapter 15, this volume). Linked to the UCDP/PRIO ACD, Harbom, Melander, and Wallensteen (2006) have identified each government-rebel dyad within civil conflicts. Cunningham, Gleditsch, and Salehyan (2009) have collected a wide variety of information on characteristics of each of these rebel groups, and Cunningham (2013) has disaggregated groups by their internal factions. These new data sources reveal a great deal of information about the actors engaged in civil conflict. Mediation studies could then analyze only combatant parties participating in mediation processes, rather than using a coarser state-centric conceptualization of negotiations.

Furthermore, the UCDP Geo-referenced Events Dataset (GED) (Melander and Sundberg 2013) disaggregates a variety of civil conflict phenomena to the events level. For instance, the GED provides event data on conflict violence in civil war, including monthly counts of battle-related deaths and civilian casualties. These data offer detailed information on the geographic location and timing of violence. Thus, not only have civil wars been delineated empirically by conflict actors, data collection efforts have disaggregated below yearly units of analysis.

Relying on such promising civil war data and armed with finer data on mediation processes,[9] scholars can pursue multiple interesting avenues of future research. First, evaluating mediation's effect at a finer temporal level among conflict actors would allow scholars to analyze different measures of mediation effectiveness. Much previous research assesses mediation effectiveness by relying on rather broadly defined indicators of success and failure: the cessation of conflict (Regan and Aydin 2006), signing of a peace accord (Savun 2008), or post-conflict transitions to democracy (Nathan 1999; chapter 9, this volume). These broadly measured outcomes are likely the product of the literature's reliance upon highly aggregated spatial-temporal research designs. Scholars should consider and pursue measures of mediation outcomes that are positive indicators of mediation success (Svensson 2009), even if the outcomes are not comprehensive peace agreements.[10]

This same issue of high-level aggregation has also been the standard empirical approach in related literatures, including research on sanctions, intervention, and peacekeeping. Yet progress has been made in disaggregating data to finer levels in these areas, and additional opportunities for exploiting such data are available. Take for example the peacekeeping literature. Data have historically relied upon simple dichotomous indicators of peacekeeping's presence or absence in a given conflict-year or post-conflict-year. New data collection efforts have revealed the size and type of personnel deployments to UN operations at the monthly level (Kathman 2013), events data on disputatious or cooperative behavior associated with missions (Ruggeri, Gizelis and Dorussen 2013), and the magnitude of efforts by states, regional organizations, and the UN in peacekeeping efforts that hold potential for use at sub-annual levels (Mullenbach 2013).

Evaluating mediation with similarly finely coded data would allow researchers to study micro-level conflict management processes. For instance, in evaluating mediation success, rather than relying on encompassing measures of success, scholars might well be interested in understanding whether mediation opens episodes of peace during which peace agreements become possible. Thus, we might think of mediation efforts as effective if they help create opportunities for such episodes of peace without which long-term peace would not be possible. As an example of similar research in a related field, Hultman, Kathman, and Shannon (2014) assess the effect of United Nations peacekeeping efforts in active civil conflicts. They find that as the UN deploys more troops to an ongoing civil war, battlefield violence declines. Moving from zero to 10,000 troops deployed, battlefield violence declines by approximately 70 percent. In their analysis of substantive effects, however, they point out that even with 10,000 troops deployed, on average the violence does not decline so low that conflict ceases completely. Indeed, using the UCDP standard of 25 battle deaths, civil conflict would still be coded as present. Thus, defining peacekeeping success simply as the full achievement of peace would ignore its relative effectiveness in ameliorating the hostilities and potentially opening a window of opportunity for the combatants to resolve their dispute in a less belligerent fashion.

More micro-level analyses of mediation effectiveness might be similarly revelatory, as even the opening of brief periods of peace may pay long-term dividends in seeking a sustainable end to conflict. Such analyses might also help to reveal the importance of mediation sequencing, in terms of the strategies used by mediators, the number and type of mediators, or the combined use of mediation as a tactic in tandem with other forms of third party involvement.[11]

Relatedly, more disaggregated analyses should improve our ability to deal empirically with the coordination problem in the study of mediation and help us infer which mediators lead the mediation efforts from multiple mediators in a given civil conflict. Assessing the timing of mediation by various actors with more finely disaggregated temporal units could shed light on the debate over the correlation between the number of mediators and the success of mediation (Beber 2010; Böhmelt 2012), including whether the number of mediators, mediation timing, or the tools used are more closely associated with the achievement of mediation objectives.

Finally, further disaggregated analyses would shed light on the choice of mediation and its effect in combination with or at the expense of other techniques of third party involvement. For instance, sub-annual temporal disaggregation may improve the ability of scholars to determine the more or less effective pairings of mediation with previous, concurrent, or subsequent military interventions, economic sanctions, or peacekeeping efforts. Observing the sequencing of these efforts at finer temporal levels is likely to be a productive enterprise in linking mediation to peace agreements as has been the recent experience of research in other literatures.

Ultimately, the literature would benefit from a greater amount and quality of research that can be conducted while exploiting more finely detailed data sources. This may have the benefit of expanding the common conceptions of mediation success and failure that pervade the literature. Additionally, the current literature tends to compare mediation only to other diplomatic tools of conflict resolution. Scholars should assess mediation against a broader range of tools of conflict intervention, including military intervention, aid, and economic sanctions. In doing so, scholars can offer richer suggestions regarding the most effective tools, sequences, actors, and combinations of peacemaking techniques.

8

Negotiated Peace

Power Sharing in Peace Agreements

Caroline A. Hartzell

Perhaps one of most contentious debates that has emerged regarding civil war focuses on what the "best" way is to end this type of conflict if a lasting peace is to be achieved. On one side of this debate can be found those who argue that the only way that long-term stability can be secured is for one of the parties to the conflict to score a decisive military victory. On the other side are those who claim that a negotiated agreement is not only a more humane way to end an intrastate conflict but also one that can, if designed properly, lead to a long-lasting peace. Both of these arguments are evaluated in this chapter. Although neither side has emerged as the clear-cut winner of this debate, the lion's share of the analysis in this chapter focuses on the negotiated settlement of civil wars. One reason for this is that during the past two and one-half decades, this has become the dominant means by which civil wars come to an end. The other reason, which is most likely related to the first, is that most of the data collection and research currently being done on civil war termination focus on negotiated agreements (see also chapter 7, this volume, for a discussion of mediation).

The content of this chapter is organized into four sections. In the first, I provide an overview of the debate regarding the relationship between settlement type and post-conflict stability as well as describing the pattern of civil war settlements in the post–World War II era. I then turn to negotiated settlements in the next section, focusing in particular on the role that power-sharing measures play in stabilizing the peace. I discuss emerging research on power sharing in the third section of the chapter and conclude with some thoughts regarding potential new research questions on power sharing and negotiated agreements in the final section of the chapter.

DEBATING THE "BEST" WAY TO END CIVIL WARS[1]

All civil wars end with a settlement of some type. These settlements, not all of which are necessarily recorded on paper, are bargains that "specify who gets what and when" at the end of a civil war (Werner and Yuen 2005, 262). In the absence of an outright victory by any of the parties to the conflict, adversaries can arrive at these bargains via negotiation. In the event that a group emerges as the victor in a civil war, it can dictate the terms of the settlement. In either case, the rationalist literature on war suggests that we should expect peace to last as long as the formerly warring groups remain committed to the bargain that they have struck (Fearon 1995, 1998; Reiter 2003). Adversaries should stick to their bargains, and the peace should prove stable, as long as the belligerents have similar expectations regarding the outcome of a future hypothetical civil war. If these expectations change, however, a settlement is not likely to stick, and war will become more likely (Wagner 1993; Werner 1999; Werner and Yuen 2005).

As this explanation for the recurrence of civil war makes clear, the challenge facing actors who want to foster a durable peace is "how best to reduce uncertainty and stabilize expectations among the parties to a settlement" (Hartzell 2009, 349). Two schools of thought exist regarding how these goals can best be accomplished. One, which until recently was the dominant view on this issue, contends that civil wars that end in a military victory will experience the most durable peace (Wagner 1993; Licklider 1995; Walter 1997; Luttwak 1999). According to this line of thinking, warring groups' expectations regarding any future deal that they may be able to obtain for themselves will be least likely to change in those cases in which the winning group or faction in a civil war demonstrates its supremacy. The victors of civil wars are posited to do this by destroying or dismantling the organizations of the adversaries they defeat, thus impeding the losers' ability to engage in future armed challenges. This is also thought to leave the losing parties with little doubt regarding the outcome of any potential future military encounters. Discouraged from thinking that they can gain a better deal for themselves by resorting to force of arms again, adversaries who have been militarily defeated are deemed to be more likely to stick to the bargain that ended the war. The civil war in Cuba (1958–1959) serves as a relevant example. Cuba has not seen a return to civil war in the years since Cuban president Fulgencio Batista was overthrown by forces led by Fidel Castro.[2]

Another school of thought, and one that has recently gained more traction, posits that it is possible for rivals to negotiate a war-ending settlement that stabilizes expectations and reduces uncertainty, thereby fostering a durable peace.[3] Scholars who advance this argument claim that it is the content of the bargain that is reached at the end of a civil war that exercises an impact on the potential for a long-lasting peace to take hold. This implies that we should be more concerned with the terms of settlements and the effects these have on warring actors' expectations for the future than on the outcome of a civil war (i.e., whether it ends in a military victory or a negotiated agreement). Although outcomes may affect the shape a bargain takes, other factors can as well. As a result, civil war settlements differ considerably in terms of questions regarding "who gets what and when."

What, according to the adherents of this second school of thought, are the characteristics of settlements negotiated by adversaries that can be expected to yield a durable peace? Scholars have hypothesized that settlements that distribute state power among adversaries, that make provisions for the groups' security, and that increase the costs of a return to armed conflict can help to give rival groups a stake in the peace and ensure that they remain committed to the bargain they have struck (Hartzell 1999; Hartzell and Hoddie 2007; Mattes and Savun 2009). It is important to note that at least some scholars working in this vein have observed that war-ending bargains with some of the features listed above are not unique to settlements that have been reached via negotiations; measures of this nature are characteristic of some settlements of civil wars that have ended in a military victory (Mukherjee 2006). While acknowledging this, other researchers have emphasized that the signaling or communication of a willingness to compromise that is involved in the process of negotiating a civil war settlement contributes to the durability of the peace and that such signaling is unlikely to take place when victors unilaterally construct the types of measures described above (Hartzell and Hoddie 2007).

How have these arguments fared in the face of empirical testing? For many years, efforts to test the proposition that some types of civil war settlements make for a more durable peace than others relied on the use of civil war outcomes as a proxy for the bargains reached at the war's end. Distinguishing between military victories and negotiated agreements, Licklider (1995a), in a pioneering study on civil war settlements, found that the latter means of ending a war was the one most likely to see parties return to armed conflict. Licklider attributed this result to the winning side's ability to vanquish the adversaries' fighting forces, a claim that is also affirmed in DeRouen and Bercovitch's (2008) work on the duration of peace following civil war. In contrast, Doyle and Sambanis (2006) find that negotiated agreements yield a durable peace, while military victories have no significant impact on postwar peace. Walter (2004) concludes that neither type of war outcome has a significant effect on peace duration. Fortna (2008a) finds that both military victories and negotiated settlements can produce a durable peace. Other researchers, arguing that the identity of the military victor has an impact on the stability of the peace, have distinguished between wars that end in a government victory, a victory by rebel forces, and a negotiated agreement. The results of these tests have proved mixed, providing support both for scholars who posit that rebel victories are more likely to produce a durable peace (Quinn, Mason, and Gurses 2007; Toft 2010; Mason et al. 2011) as well as for those who hypothesize that it is government victories that generate that outcome (Kreutz 2010).

What is one to make of these seemingly contradictory results? It should be noted that at least some of differences may stem from the fact that the studies in question draw on a variety of datasets, analyze different samples of intrastate conflicts, employ different model specifications, and make use of numerous methodologies. Having said that, the more important point that should be made is that none of the studies above really tests the argument advanced in the rationalist literature regarding the stability of war-ending bargains. Two observations undergird this claim. First, it is not clear that war outcomes are a reasonable proxy for settlement types. The means by which a civil war ends may shape the nature of the war-ending bargain, but it is not likely to be the only factor that does so. This implies that there may be real differences between war outcomes and war-ending bargains. For example, motivated by humanitarian concerns, the international community may exert pressure on warring parties to construct a settlement whose terms fail to match the adversaries' expectations of the outcome of the war (Werner and Yuen 2005). This appears to have occurred in Guatemala, where, although the Guatemalan National Revolutionary Unity (URNG) guerrillas essentially had been defeated militarily, the government of Guatemala was persuaded to agree to UN mediation of the conflict (Stanley and Holiday 2002). The outcome of this process was a peace agreement, signed in 1996, which preserved the organizational identity of the URNG.

Second, it is not clear whether the causal mechanisms associated with each of the types of civil war outcomes actually function as the rationalist literature claims they do. Scholars have assumed that military victories result in the destruction of the losing factions' organizational structures while negotiated agreements preserve them. However, none of the studies mentioned above have sought to test that proposition, thus making it difficult to conclude what effect the fate of factions has on the duration of the peace.[4] Nor do the studies cited above consider whether provisions for distributing power among adversaries, which are typically associated with negotiated agreements, were included as part of the bargain following a military victory. This means that even in those instances in which studies find an association between military victory, negotiated agreements, and the duration of the peace, we cannot be certain why the outcome has the effect that it does on the longevity of the peace. Civil war outcomes may have an impact on the peace, but it is not clear that we know exactly how and why that is the case.

Just how much does all of this matter? Arguably, determining what kind of civil war settlement can best help to sustain the peace, and how best it is arrived at, is a matter of more than just academic interest. Recent research indicates that negotiated ends to civil wars are a less costly means of terminating intrastate conflicts than waiting for one party to achieve a military victory. The death toll associated with conflicts that end in negotiated agreements is, on average, about half that of civil wars terminating in military victory. Additionally, in those instances in which a settlement breaks down and there is a return to the fighting, conflicts that recur following negotiated agreements prove much less deadly in nature than those that occur in the aftermath of military victory (Human Security Report 2012).

In light of this information regarding the relative costs associated with different means of terminating civil wars, there are obviously benefits associated with the fact that, for the last twenty-five years, negotiated agreements have become the modal way of ending an intrastate conflict. During the Cold War period, the majority of civil wars (69 percent) were concluded via military victory. The first post–Cold War decade saw a major shift in the way civil wars were ended, with 54 percent of the conflicts terminating via negotiated agreements and 23 percent ending in military victories.[5] Using different datasets, Mack (2008), Fortna (2009), and Toft (2010) identify the same trends in civil war termination for the Cold War and post–Cold War periods. The twenty-first century has seen the trend toward negotiated agreements become even more pronounced, with 75 percent of the civil wars ending between 2000 and 2007 seeing the warring parties negotiate an end to their respective conflicts (Hartzell 2012). One important factor that is believed to have helped to produce this trend is the increased deployment of international peacekeeping forces following the end of the Cold War (Fortna 2008a). Once the United States and the Soviet Union were no longer involved in sponsoring competing civil war forces and ceased impeding efforts by the United Nations and other actors to help end intrastate conflicts, civil war adversaries contemplating an end to a war became aware that there was a reasonably high likelihood that peacekeeping troops would be sent to their country if a settlement was reached. Reassured that peacekeeping troops would help to provide for their security, adversaries are thought to have become more willing to negotiate an end to civil wars in the years following the end of the Cold War.

Given the prevalence of civil war settlements arrived at via negotiations, it behooves us to learn more about the nature of these bargains. What do the terms of these settlements look like? How are the contents of these bargains thought to help keep the peace? What have tests of the impact that the contents of these settlements have on the duration of the peace found? It is to these questions that I now turn.

NEGOTIATED SETTLEMENTS AND POWER-SHARING INSTITUTIONS[6]

Questions regarding "who gets what and when?" lie at the heart of civil war settlements. In those instances in which armed opponents enter into negotiations in an effort to arrive at an answer to these questions, the outcome of that process, if successful, will be a bargain that specifies the institutions or rules of competition that are to govern them in the future. More specifically, the institutions at the heart of the settlement will be ones that determine the *distribution* of authority—through the sharing and the dividing of different elements of state power—among former rivals in the context of the postwar state. These power-sharing institutions, as they are commonly referred to, are a central component of civil war settlements. Characterized as "rules that, in addition to defining how decisions will be made by groups within the polity, allocate decision-making rights, including access to state resources, among collectivities competing for power" (Hartzell and Hoddie 2003: 320), power-sharing institutions are credited with being one of the key features of civil war settlements that, if designed correctly, can help to secure a durable peace.

There are three tasks power-sharing institutions perform that have been identified as contributing to the longevity of the peace. The first is to mitigate the security concerns of the warring parties. Accustomed to providing for their own security and those of their followers during the period in which a war has been ongoing, armed opponents worry about who will control the levers of state power once the war ends. Rivals who have been engaged in ongoing efforts to kill one another need some assurance that once they surrender their weapons, another party to the conflict will not seize the opportunity to threaten the group's continued existence. While peacekeeping forces can help to provide a sense of security during the process of disarmament and demobilization, civil war opponents know that peacekeeping forces are not a permanent feature of the post-conflict landscape and thus also seek to provide for their security through means such as integrating rebel troops into the state security forces. This was accomplished with great success in the Philippines, for example, where 5,750 Moro National Liberation Front combatants were integrated into the military following the 1996 peace agreement (Hall 2014). Adversaries also seek some guarantee that one group will not be able to use other forms of state power (e.g., control of the central government or access to state resources) to the detriment of its rivals. Power-sharing institutions can help to minimize these fears by distributing state power among the parties to the conflict. The fifty-fifty division of congressional seats between Colombia's Conservative and Liberal parties that was agreed to as part of the war-ending National Front Agreement in 1957, for example, served to reassure each group that the other would be unable to pass any policies inimical to its interests. Sudan's Comprehensive Peace Agreement also called for a similar division of power, although in that case, it focused on the revenues generated by oil, with 50 percent allocated to the government of Sudan and 50 percent to the Government of South Sudan (GoSS). In all of these instances, by constructing arrangements to share, divide, or otherwise balance different elements of state power among adversaries, groups sought to obtain a margin of security by making it extremely difficult for any one group to use the state's resources to increase its coercive capacity at the expense of the others.

Power-sharing institutions also help adversaries to signal their commitment to the peace. Negotiated civil war settlements are thought to suffer from a credible commitment problem that makes the bargains that they embody subject to potential failure. The potential for failure arises from the fact that, in order for a settlement to be considered credible, it must be in the interests of all of the parties that strike the bargain to abide by its terms (Fearon 1995). Doubts abound, however, about just how willing groups will be to stick to the bargain with the passage of time. Agreements by rival groups to share power can serve to signal a commitment on their part to build a lasting peace. What makes these actions credible signals of intentions are the costs associated with them. As Fearon (1997) observes, a commitment is only likely to be perceived as credible "when the act of sending it incurs or creates some cost that the sender would be disinclined to incur or create if he or she were in fact *not* willing to carry out" the obligation (69). Designing and implementing power-sharing institutions is not a cost-free process. Adversaries who agree to these measures must abandon their pursuit of monopoly control of the state. In addition, a group's leadership runs the risk of alienating supporters reluctant to share power with rivals who have only recently sought to kill them. The willingness of adversaries to endure these costs thus serves as a costly indicator of their commitment to a lasting peace.

Finally, power-sharing institutions also help to stabilize the peace by defining the means by which social conflict is to be managed in the postwar state. Constructing institutions that clarify how groups are expected to interact and compete with one another is particularly important in countries where previous conflict management institutions have come to be deemed illegitimate by some groups or may even have ceased to function. Power-sharing institutions provide a means for reconstructing domestic order following a civil war. Put another way, these institutions can serve as the basis for constructing the rule of law. If an enduring peace is to be secured, groups must have some means, other than relying on the use of force, for resolving their disagreements. By making the design of institutions a central part of the bargain that ends a civil war, adversaries lay the foundations necessary to build a lasting peace.

POWER-SHARING INSTITUTIONS: TYPES, TRENDS, AND A CAVEAT

There are four different types of power-sharing institutions that groups can design to help them accomplish the tasks outlined above. These institutions center on the dimensions of state power that civil war adversaries tend to be most concerned about with respect to the post-conflict environment. These four dimensions are those associated with the political, military, territorial, and economic bases of state strength. These components of state power prove a source of concern to groups because each could be used by one of the contending parties to add to its coercive capacity. The fact that these components of state power are fungible, meaning that control of them can shift among groups and thus affect power differentially, also makes them a source of concern to civil war adversaries. Motivated by these apprehensions, the architects of negotiated civil war settlements design institutions for sharing and dividing power across the following four dimensions of state power.

Political power-sharing institutions emphasize proportionality in the distribution of central state authority. Collectivities are guaranteed a degree of representation within governing institutions based on their group affiliation. The mechanisms that can be used to achieve this end are electoral proportional representation, administrative proportional representation, and proportional representation in the national government's executive branch. Electoral proportional representation lowers the minimum level of voter support that a candidate or party must achieve in order to gain political office, thus decreasing the intensity of political competition. Administrative proportional representation expands the opportunities for political participation by increasing groups' access to policy-making influence. Finally, proportional representation in the executive branch of the national government ensures groups a voice in the innermost circles of political power by appointing their members to ministerial, subministerial, and cabinet positions. An example of the latter may be found in Burundi, where Tutsis and Hutus agreed to share power at the political center by having the president assisted by two vice presidents, one from each ethnic group, as well as staffing the cabinet at a ratio of 60 percent Hutu to 40 percent Tutsi.

Military power-sharing institutions seek to distribute authority within the coercive apparatus of the state. The most straightforward means of sharing military power is integrating the antagonists' armed forces into a unified state security force. A proportional formula that reflects the relative size of the armed factions can be used to accomplish this or a strict balance in troop numbers can be established among the contending parties. The latter method was applied in Burundi where the state's security forces include equal numbers of Hutus and Tutsis. Alternately, military power can be distributed by appointing members of the subordinate group(s) to key leadership positions in the state's security forces. This occurred in the case of Nicaragua when President Violeta Barrios de Chamorro opted to retain Sandinista General Humberto Ortega as head of Nicaragua's armed forces in 1990. Last, in limited instances, striking a balance among the militaries of antagonists may involve allowing opposing sides to remain armed or to retain their own security forces.

Territorial power-sharing institutions seek to divide political influence among different levels of government by creating forms of decentralized government that are territorially based. Provisions for federalism or regional autonomy offer regionally concentrated groups a degree of power independent from the central government. In addition, regions within a federal system that are represented in the institutions of the federal government have the opportunity to monitor and check actions at the federal level that they fear may be inimical to their interests. An example of territorial power sharing as part of an effort to end civil war appears in Sudan's Addis Ababa Accords of 1972. The agreement provided southern Sudan with a degree of autonomy from the national government, and called for the establishment of an elected Southern Regional Assembly (Rothchild and Hartzell 1993).

Finally, it has been suggested that "[f]or minority groups, losing an election is a matter of not simply losing office, but of having no access to the resources of the state and thus losing the means for protecting the survival of the group" (Linder and Bächtiger 2005: 864).

Economic power-sharing institutions attempt to address exactly this type of concern regarding the question of access to and control of economic resources under the purview of the state. Designed to distribute wealth, income, or control of natural resources or production facilities on some group basis, economic power-sharing measures have been used in countries such as Sierra Leone and Indonesia. In the case of Sierra Leone's 1999 Lomé Peace Agreement, economic power sharing was apparent in the commitment to appoint rebel leader Foday Sankoh as chairman of the newly created Commission for the Management of Strategic Resources. This entity was to be responsible for overseeing the country's extensive gold and diamond resources (Melrose 2009: 136).

As part of a civil war settlement, adversaries can agree to construct institutions drawn from one or more of the four categories of power-sharing institutions identified above. Generally speaking, rival groups are likely to press for the creation of the type of power-sharing institutions that reflect the nature of their particular concerns. Those concerns are likely to emanate, in part, from their experiences before and during a civil war. If groups have experienced political marginalization or discrimination, they will be likely to seek access to political power. Groups that have experienced abuse at the hands of the state's security forces or fear threats to their existence by those forces will most likely be motivated to share military power. In some instances it may not make sense for groups to seek to design particular types of power-sharing institutions. Territorial power-sharing institutions, for example, are likely to hold little attraction for groups that lack a defined spatial distribution.

Table 8.1 shows the distribution of the power-sharing institutions agreed to as a part of civil war settlements—both negotiated and following military victories—for the period 1945–2006 (Hartzell and Hoddie 2015). Two interesting observations can be made based on the data reported in the table. First, the proportion of civil war settlements that include some form of power-sharing institution is much higher for wars that ended in the post–Cold War period than wars that ended between 1945 and 1989. This is not surprising, given two facts. One is the rising proportion of civil wars that ended via negotiated agreement during the post–Cold War period. The other is that nearly all civil wars ending in negotiated agreements call for at least one type of power-sharing institution, whereas very few wars ending in military victory call for even one such measure.

The second interesting observation has to do with the distribution in the types of power-sharing institutions agreed to as part of civil war settlements. As the far right column of table 8.1 indicates, political and military power-sharing institutions appear as part of civil war settlements far more often than do territorial and economic power-sharing institutions. While the relatively low number of territorial power-sharing institutions may reflect the fact that the geography of conflict does not lend itself to the use of this kind of measure in some cases, it is less clear why warring groups have made economic power-sharing institutions part of a settlement less often than they have political and military power-sharing institutions.

One potential explanation for the distribution of types of power-sharing institutions across civil war settlements is alluded to by studies that have distinguished among these institutions on the basis of the costliness of the concessions associated with each type of institution. Although these studies focus on the effects that the costs in question have on the duration of the peace rather than on the probability that certain types of institutions will be adopted, the arguments that they advance provide an interesting framework for thinking about the latter issue. Jarstad and Nilsson (2008), for example, posit that political power-sharing institutions are cheaper to implement than military and territorial power-sharing institutions. In their view, parties are less constrained by the former type of institution, and its implementation involves low material costs. DeRouen, Lea, and Wallensteen (2009), on the other hand, argue that governments find political power-sharing institutions more costly to adopt and implement than military and territorial power-sharing institutions.

This occurs, in part, because of the intangible costs associated with "legitimizing the rebels' struggle through political inclusion" (370). Although these two studies clearly do not agree on the relative costs associated with different types of power-sharing institutions, they do provide us with insight into one of the factors—the costs associated with adopting and implementing the institutions—that may have an effect on the frequency with which they appear in peace settlements.

Finally, a caveat regarding power-sharing institutions is in order. Although, as noted above, one of the means by which these types of institutions is hypothesized to help keep the peace is by providing a means for peacefully managing conflict, power-sharing institutions are not functionally equivalent to democracy (see also chapter 9, this volume). Power-sharing institutions do not require democracy in order to work. Government and rebel troops can be merged into a single army, for example, in the absence of democracy. And as in cases like Cambodia and Tajikistan, each of which saw its civil wars ended via a negotiated settlement that included power-sharing institutions, the use of power-sharing institutions does not guarantee that democracy will be established in the wake of civil war. In fact, several scholars have argued that power sharing is incompatible with democracy because it guarantees elites positions in government by virtue of a peace settlement rather than through the use of elections. Although recent empirical work suggests there may be reason to doubt this claim, it bears emphasizing that power sharing itself is not inherently democratic.

Table 8.1. Trends in the Use of Power Sharing in Civil War Termination, 1945–2006

Decade War Ended	Number of Civil Wars Ended in Decade	Number of Civil War Settlements Calling for Power Sharing	Distribution of Type of Power-Sharing Institutions[a]			
1945–1949	7	2 (28.5%)	political:	2	military:	0
			territorial:	1	economic:	1
1950s	11	2 (18%)	political:	2	military:	0
			territorial:	0	economic:	2
1960s	10	1 (10%)	political:	1	military:	0
			territorial:	0	economic:	0
1970s	21	8 (38%)	political:	7	military:	5
			territorial:	3	economic:	4
1980s	13	6 (46%)	political:	4	military:	4
			territorial:	3	economic:	2
1990s	46	34 (74%)	political:	26	military:	25
			territorial:	15	economic:	14
2000–2006	19	15 (79%)	political:	11	military:	13
			territorial:	7	economic:	6

Source: Hartzell and Hoddie (2015).
[a] The column labeled "Distribution of Type of Power-Sharing Institutions" sums the number of each type of power-sharing institution that appears in the settlements that call for power sharing in each decade.

POWER SHARING AND PEACE DURATION: THEORY

Although a growing number of scholars are in agreement regarding the broad outlines of power-sharing institutions sketched above as well as the potential such arrangements have to help stabilize the peace, important theoretical differences also exist in the research on power sharing. Most of these differences center on the causal mechanisms or the means by which scholars believe that power-sharing institutions help to produce a durable peace; others stem from disagreements regarding issues such as the intentions warring actors have in crafting these arrangements and questions regarding whose behavior it is that is influenced by the institutions. The following section is an overview of theoretical developments regarding the relationship between power-sharing institutions and the duration of the peace.

Initial works on power sharing emphasized the security-enhancing effects of these institutions. Invoking the concept of the security dilemmas, scholars noted that adversaries obliged to live within the borders of a country had real concerns about who would control the instruments of power in the post-conflict state. Addressing these concerns was important if there was to be a chance of ending a war via negotiation (Walter 1997). Furthermore, if the peace was to be stabilized, the means by which rivals' concerns were addressed should provide a basis for managing conflict in the postwar state (Hartzell 1999). Noting that civil war adversaries' concerns were often multifaceted—that is, rivals worried about control of more than one element of state power—early work on power sharing posited that it was more "institutionalized" civil war settlements, or those that called for an array of power-sharing institutions, that would be most likely to produce a durable peace (Hartzell and Hoddie 2003, 2007).

Other research soon emerged that elaborated on the theme of security as well as those of signaling and the credibility of commitments. Emphasizing the role that commitment problems play in civil war recurrence, Mattes and Savun (2009) hypothesized that power-sharing institutions serve as "fear-reducing provisions" that alleviate adversaries' concerns regarding opportunism by their opponents. Building on the idea that power-sharing institutions can serve as a signal of credible commitment by parties to a settlement, Jarstad and Nilsson (2008) advanced the argument that settlements that contain power-sharing institutions that are more costly and time-consuming to construct will be more durable. While Jarstad and Nilsson identify military and territorial forms of power sharing as the most costly and thus most effective power-sharing institutions, DeRouen, Lea, and Wallensteen (2009) conclude that settlements that contain military and territorial power-sharing provisions prove more durable because they are less costly to implement and therefore more likely actually to be put in place.

More recent work on civil war settlements has identified alternative causal mechanisms believed to account for the effect that power-sharing institutions have on settlement durability. Mason, Gurses, Brandt, and Quinn (2011) identify "multiple sovereignty" as a threat to the duration of the peace. A condition of multiple sovereignty exists when one or more organized armed challengers able to mobilize significant degrees of popular support remain in place following the end of a civil war. Power-sharing institutions help to buttress the peace, argue Mason et al., by dismantling or at least weakening multiple sovereignty.

Focusing on the size of the governing coalition, the group whose support a leader needs in order to claim political power over the rest of society, Joshi and Mason (2011) posit that larger governing coalitions are associated with a lower probability of peace failure. Because power-sharing institutions are inclusive in nature, settlements that call for such measures help to expand the size of the governing coalition. By including former enemies and newly mobilized groups within the postwar structures of power, power-sharing institutions help to minimize the likelihood that actors will destroy these structures by returning to war. This argument is one that appears in Binningsbø's (2011) work as well. This focus on the peace-enhancing characteristics of inclusion through power sharing, it should be noted, corresponds nicely with recent research that indicates that political and economic exclusion at the group level heightens the risk of ethnic civil war onset (Cederman, Gleditsch, and Buhaug 2013; see also chapter 3, this volume).

One of the most recent and more novel theories regarding the peace-augmenting effects of power-sharing institutions suggests that some of these measures contribute to the longevity of the peace through their effects on governance and public service delivery (Cammett and Malesky 2012). According to this line of thought, some forms of political power sharing undergird greater state capacity and facilitate the provision of public goods, thereby satisfying the welfare needs of a larger segment of the population. It is the higher quality of governance associated with some power-sharing institutions that helps to explain why civil wars are less likely to resume following settlements characterized by such measures.

The question of whether or not parties implement the terms of the peace settlements that they have agreed to is one of relevance to all of the theories enumerated above. While agreements to create power-sharing institutions carry costs for the parties involved and thus serve to signal the credibility of their commitment to the peace, full implementation of those agreements arguably carries higher costs and demonstrates an even more thoroughgoing commitment to abstain from returning to war (Hoddie and Hartzell 2003, Jarstad and Nilsson 2008, and Joshi and Mason 2011). Scholars have only recently directly tested this proposition. Employing a dataset that focuses on government-rebel dyads and the specific power-sharing measures to which they agree as part of a settlement, Ottmann and Vüllers find that while promises of military, economic, and territorial power sharing all reduce the risk of a return to war, when it comes to the implementation of power-sharing measures, only implemented promises of military power sharing extend the duration of the peace (2015). When power-sharing commitments and the subsequent implementation of those measures are looked at in conjunction, military, economic, and territorial power-sharing commitments all reduce the risk of conflict recurrence as does the implementation of political power sharing. Interestingly enough, the implementation of economic power-sharing measures is found to increase the risk of a return to civil war. This leads to the interesting conclusion on Ottmann and Vül-lers's part that "the promises of power-sharing and their subsequent implementation follow different bargaining logics" (2015: 346).

Finally, it should be noted that a number of scholars who have carried out research on power-sharing institutions have voiced doubts regarding the effects these arrange-ments have on the stability of the peace. Roeder and Rothchild (2005), for example, posit that power-sharing institutions generate incentives that encourage ethnic elites to escalate their claims for increased access to state resources. As a result, they ar-gue, power-sharing agreements may help end a war but only for the short term as renewed bargaining can be expected to lead to the reemergence of armed conflict. Other critics of power-sharing arrangements raise important questions regarding the beneficiaries of such measures. Tull and Mehler (2005) contend that the leaders of groups excluded from power-sharing arrangements might initiate further conflict in an effort to secure their own share of state power. Additionally, observes Mehler (2008), since it is by and large elites who profit from these arrangements, the masses are unlikely to demonstrate any real degree of commitment to the peace.

POWER SHARING AND PEACE DURATION: THE EMPIRICAL RECORD

Empirical tests of many of the hypotheses specified above have provided an expanding body of support for the proposition that power-sharing institutions can help to stabi-lize the peace following a civil war. Whereas initial tests of the influence power sharing has on the duration of the peace focused on the question of whether or not the fighting remained terminated for some period of time (e.g., for three years or five years follow-ing the end of the war), more sophisticated event-history models that consider the du-ration of a peace episode until (or if) a peace settlement fails have been used for the past several years.[7] These duration models have enabled scholars to observe that although settlements that include power-sharing measures have a higher likelihood of failing in the initial years following the end of a civil war, their stability-enhancing effects grow with the passage of time (Hartzell and Hoddie 2003; Joshi and Mason 2011).

Although empirical tests have helped to foster a growing consensus on the utility of power-sharing measures in helping to shore up the peace, important differences have also emerged from efforts to assess the effects of these measures. Most of the disparities that exist have to do with whether some forms of power sharing do a better job of help-ing to stabilize the peace than others. Some scholars find that military and territorial power sharing have a positive impact on peace duration, for example, while others find that political power sharing does this best, and yet others find that political power shar-ing has a negative (although not statistically significant) effect on settlement stability.[8]

Differences in the results of tests of the effects of power-sharing institutions are most likely the product of a variety of factors. These include the use of different da-tasets, with some scholars focusing only on conflicts that meet the Correlates of War threshold for civil wars and others employing more expansive datasets that employ the lower UCDP threshold of twenty-five conflict deaths. Another key difference among the empirical tests that have been conducted on power sharing is that many focus only on negotiated agreements of conflict, while more recently others have included wars that end in military victory by one side in their analysis as well. Finally, another important source of variation among studies that may account for some of the differences in empirical test results is that some scholars focus only on whether a settlement calls for the use of particular power-sharing institutions, while others code whether the power-sharing agreement was implemented.

EMERGING RESEARCH ON POWER SHARING AND CIVIL WAR SETTLEMENTS

The last few years have seen a broadening of the research being conducted on power sharing as part of peace settlements. Although new work regarding the impact that power-sharing institutions have on the duration of the peace continues to emerge, some scholars have begun to shift their attention to the effects that power sharing has on the quality of the peace that citizens experience in post-conflict states. Empirical work in this vein includes a study by Cammett and Malesky (2012) which finds that power sharing has a positive and significant effect on government spending on health, improved literacy rates, control of corruption, regulatory quality, and citizens' perceptions of government effectiveness in the post–civil war state. Tackling a long-running debate on the effects power-sharing institutions have on democracy, Hartzell and Hoddie (2015) find that states that adopt a range of these measures have a higher likelihood of establishing procedural democracy following the war's end. In the newest extension of this line of work, scholars have begun to examine the effects that power-sharing institutions have on human rights. Responding to concerns regarding the protections that power-sharing institutions sometimes provide to political elites with a history of human rights abuses, Hoddie (2014) finds no significant relationship between power-sharing settlements and violations of physical integrity rights in post-conflict states.

Many of the newest advances in the research on power sharing have been data driven. Seeking to understand what aspects of power sharing exercise influence on the duration and the quality of the peace, scholars have begun to employ more refined conceptions of power-sharing institutions. Rather than using political power sharing as an aggregated variable, for example, scholars have sought to determine what effects closed-list proportional electoral systems (Cammett and Malesky 2012) and executive-level coalitions (Martin 2013) have on the peace. Datasets that provide more fine-grained data on peace agreements offer researchers the potential more accurately to determine what aspects of power sharing—as well as other elements of peace agreements more generally—shape the duration and quality of the peace. Significant among these data collection efforts are the *UCDP Peace Agreement Dataset*

(Högbladh 2011), which contains information on the provisions of peace accords, and the Kroc Institute's *Peace Accords Matrix*, which provides details on fifty-one different topics that may fall within the scope of a peace agreement.

Advances in modeling in the last few years have also shaped the latest wave of research on peace settlements and power sharing. One of the problems to which the research on power sharing and its effects has been susceptible is that of endogeneity. In all likelihood, actors do not randomly adopt power-sharing institutions as part of settlements to end civil wars. It is possible, for example that civil war adversaries will prove most likely to agree to construct power-sharing institutions as a means of ending particularly difficult conflicts.[9] If this is the case and the peace is least likely to prove durable following these types of conflicts, then the failure to take this potential source of bias into account could lead researchers to miss the positive effect power-sharing institutions have on the duration of the peace. In order to deal with this issue, scholars have begun using two-stage approaches that include the use of an instrumental variable in the first or selection stage of the model. Using this approach, scholars have found that whereas single-stage models may find a negative association between power-sharing institutions and the duration of the peace, once reverse causality is accounted for, power-sharing institutions are found to have a positive and significant impact on the duration of the peace (Wucherpfennig 2011).

FUTURE RESEARCH ON POWER SHARING AND PEACE SETTLEMENTS

Power-sharing institutions have become an increasingly prominent aspect of civil war settlements. As such, it is important for the elites who agree to them, the actors and organizations that help to shape and implement them, and the citizens who live under them to learn more about their effects. Scholars can help with this task in a number of ways. I elaborate on some potential issues for further research in what follows.

Theory

Two principal themes seem likely to provide productive areas for future research. One of these involves the issue referenced at the beginning of this chapter—the terms of civil war settlements. Given that the dominant theories of war termination, including those regarding the role that power sharing plays in civil war settlements, are informed by bargaining models of war, scholars should strive more directly to test the propositions that stem from those models. Rather than assuming, for example, that conflicts that end in military victories see the organizational structures of all but one of the parties destroyed, empirical evidence regarding the fate of factions should be collected. Data of this nature could better help us to answer questions such as whether it is easier for parties to remobilize for armed conflict following negotiated settlements, as has long been claimed. Scholars should also strive to collect data regarding the terms of all kinds of settlements, not just those that end in negotiated agreements. In the absence of such data, we cannot, in Kreutz's words, determine "whether [or not] power sharing reduces the likelihood of [conflict] recurrence compared to all post-conflict situations" (2014: 357).

The second area that seems ripe for theoretical development is further exploration of the implications power-sharing institutions have for the peace. Thus far, scholars have been concerned with the pressing question of the effects that power sharing has on the duration of the peace. In light of growing evidence that there is a positive association between power sharing and the longevity of the peace, it seems worthwhile to turn to some of the follow-on effects these institutions might have. Given that power-sharing institutions have been described as providing a means for managing conflict in the wake of civil war, it seems reasonable to ask how such measures might shape other dimensions of relations among actors in the post-conflict state. If some power-sharing institutions provide groups with means of blocking the passage of laws that they perceive as negatively affecting their interests, for example, it would be of interest to explore whether this results in deadlocked and/or inefficient governments. Another topic of interest is the effect that power-sharing measures have on women's political participation, particularly since women are often excluded from participating in the peace processes where such institutions are designed. While a few incipient steps have been taken in this direction, there is a good deal of room for scholars to think about the ways in which institutions designed to end civil wars might shape the quality of the peace.

Data

A number of the criticisms that scholars have raised regarding power sharing concern their effects on non-elite actors. Power-sharing arrangements are designed and agreed to by elites who are generally the politico-military leaders of warring groups. The presumption that underlies the bargaining model of civil war is that these elites agree to these measures because they advance not only their interests but those of their followers as well. Scholars have increasingly raised questions regarding the validity of this assumption. The truth of the matter is that we have little way of knowing what effects power-sharing institutions have on the interests of different subsets of the population in post-conflict states. Do power-sharing institutions line the pockets of elite leaders at the expense of their followers, as some scholars have suggested (Devre 2011)? Although anecdotal evidence for countries like Lebanon and Nigeria suggests that this is the case, cross-national evidence in support of this claim is lacking. Do territorial autonomy arrangements improve the sense of security felt by individuals within the autonomous region or enhance their feelings of efficacy? Again, we currently lack the data to test such claims.

These observations suggest that data that could help us to assess the effects that power-sharing institutions have on politico-military elites, their followers, civil society, regionally based groups, and other sets of actors within post–civil war states would be extremely useful. Survey data seem to be a particularly fruitful way to get at important questions including the degree of knowledge that different groups have regarding the nature of power-sharing institutions, individuals' and groups' perceptions regarding the effects power-sharing measures have on their interests, and the manner in which all of this shapes their commitment to peace settlements.

Additional Topics

One of the topics that has been neglected in research on the role that power-sharing institutions play in peace settlements is the question of the factors that influence how parties come to agree to these terms. The bargaining literature generally has emphasized the role that combat or military means play in the bargaining process (Reiter 2003). Although combat may play an important role in structuring the terms of settlements in interstate wars, it is less clear that it plays as significant a role in intrastate conflicts, particularly in the post–Cold War period. One reason this is the case is that the often asymmetric, hit-and-run nature of civil wars makes for fewer clear signals where battlefield victories are concerned. Another important factor that bears consideration is the role of third party actors in shaping "the conditions under which . . . forms of conflict resolution are crafted" (Svensson 2014a: 370). Scholars should seek to determine whether mediators and other third party actors are pressing civil war adversaries to agree to power-sharing arrangements as a means of ending civil wars or whether those actors are arriving at such agreements organically. If such measures accord more with the interests of third parties than with the interests of the warring groups, the bargaining literature suggests that we should not expect such settlements to prove stable.

Researchers should also seek to develop a better understanding of the implementation of civil war settlements. We should seek to learn more about the conditions under which conflict parties are more likely to implement peace agreements as well as the factors that have an impact on how closely parties cleave to the letter of the agreement when implementing its provisions. While the cost associated with putting power-sharing institutions into place is likely to be one important determinant of implementation, other factors such as state capacity and the extent of external assistance and monitoring are sure to matter as well.

Finally, another subject worth exploring is the effect that components of civil war settlements other than power sharing have on the duration of the peace, both independently and in interaction with power-sharing institutions. Power-sharing institutions are not the only component of civil war peace settlements (and, in fact, may not figure at all in some settlements). Understanding how power-sharing measures interact with other terms of settlements such as transitional justice measures may be critical to understanding whether or not peace takes hold (see chapter 11, this volume). Power-sharing institutions are an important component of civil war settlements and as such deserve to be better understood. They are only one dimension of the terms of a settlement, though, and as such must also be put into perspective.

9

Breaking the Conflict Trap

The Impact of Peacekeeping on Violence and Democratization in the Post-Conflict Context

Paul F. Diehl

In the aftermath of civil wars, among the greatest challenges is to ensure that violence does not recur, undoing any agreement to end the conflict that might have been reached.[1] Yet we know that risk of return to warfare is quite high, with over 40 percent of states experiencing second (or more) civil wars (Quinn et al. 2007). One strategy for conflict mitigation in the short term is the deployment of peacekeeping forces to supervise the cease-fire and possibly to perform a series of other tasks, such as disarmament, conventionally referred to as *peacebuilding* missions. In the longer term, promoting democracy along the lines of Western liberalism is thought to create the conditions under which political violence is no longer an option with the rule of law and democratic processes channeling disagreements to peaceful means of conflict resolution.

Neither peacekeeping nor efforts at democratization is a panacea for the problems that plague post-conflict states. Yet under certain conditions, both can promote peace and stability. Nevertheless, to date, research on these strategies sometimes raises more questions than it resolves and contains a number of limitations that provides fruitful bases for future research.

This chapter reviews the state of knowledge in studies of peacekeeping,[2] specifically with respect to preventing violence renewal and democratization in post-conflict contexts. In terms of violence renewal, this chapter examines theoretical arguments on how peacekeeping operations affect the durability of the post–civil war peace, including the characteristics and missions of peacekeeping operations.[3] Beyond the minimalist requirement of simply sustaining the peace after a civil war, postwar peacebuilding requires building a viable political regime, among other tasks. Thus, this chapter explores the special obstacles that post–civil war nations face with respect to installing democratic institutions and sustaining them over time and the role that peacekeeping forces have in that process. Although preventing violence

139

and democratization are usually thought of as separate processes, they sometimes intersect in that peacekeepers can be assigned the role of election supervision, and peacebuilding operations might include assisting in the development of the rule of law. There is extensive research done on both peacekeeping and democratization separately, but there is less work on these phenomena in post-conflict periods, and there is reason to believe that this context poses some unique challenges to both; accordingly, this chapter discusses these as a prelude to a review of extant findings and the specification of agendas for future research.

PEACEKEEPING AND THE DURABILITY OF PEACE

In assessing the impact of peacekeeping in general, the predominant standard of success has been "peace duration," or the length of time following the deployment of peacekeepers to the next incidence of violence (see Diehl and Druckman 2010). In the context of civil wars, most research has focused on peacekeeping operations that occur in the aftermath of active fighting, whether following a peace agreement or not (see more below on cease-fires). Success is largely defined as the absence of a renewal of civil war.

The Post–Civil War Context for Peacekeeping

Many of the findings about the impact of peacekeeping mix different types of operations and different kinds of contexts, and thus it is difficult to discern the effectiveness of peacekeeping specifically in the aftermath of civil wars. Early studies of peacekeeping focused largely on interstate conflicts, primarily because that was the context in which operations were deployed until the late 1980s. Since then, more than 90 percent of peace operations have been deployed to conflicts with a significant, if not exclusive, internal conflict component; several operations in Haiti and the Congo, respectively, fit this profile.

Overall, peacekeeping has a mixed or "mediocre" (Bratt 1996) record of fulfilling its mandates, but this does not necessarily tell us about the context at hand, which mixes two elements that have been found to have opposite effects—civil war and post-conflict situations respectively.

Various case studies and other analyses suggest that peacekeeping encounters greater difficulties in monitoring cease-fires in civil wars than interstate conflicts (Diehl 1994; Wesley 1997). First, civil conflicts often involve more than two identifiable groups in conflict; by definition, an internationalized civil war involves more than two actors. In contrast, interstate disputes have been overwhelmingly dyadic, or fought between only two independent countries. As the number of actors in the dispute increases, so too does the likelihood that one or more of them will object to a cease-fire or settlement and the provisions for the deployment of the peace forces (Cunningham 2011); they may take military action against other actors or the peacekeeping soldiers. For example, U.S. and French peacekeepers came under fire from Lebanese factions during a 1980s deployment. Thus, there is more potential for "spoilers" in civil conflicts than interstate ones.

Beyond the difficulty of aggregating multiple preferences in support of a peace operation, the geographic requirements are different in a civil conflict from those in an interstate one. Civil instability may mean that several groups are operating in different parts of the country. This could lead to more violent incidents, as peacekeeping operations are typically small and unable to monitor large areas. Furthermore, unlike an identifiable international border or cease-fire line, such as the demilitarized zone in the Golan Heights between Israel and Syria, it may be impossible to demarcate a line or area separating the many sides in the conflict (e.g., Israeli settlers in the West Bank are interspersed with the Palestinian population). The cease-fire line between Ethiopia and Eritrea is much clearer than any separation between various groups in Sierra Leone. Being from the same state and often not wearing military uniforms (indeed, sometimes not being traditional military or paramilitary units at all), participants in a civil conflict are hard to identify, much less to separate when they occupy the same geographical space. Interstate disputants can more easily be identified and separated across internationally recognized borders or militarily defined cease-fire lines.

Civil conflict may be quite dangerous to peace forces, and the situation more difficult to control. James (1994: 17) notes that in civil conflict, "Arms are likely to be in the hands of groups who may be unskilled in their use, lack tight discipline, and probably engage in guerrilla tactics. Light arms are also likely to be kept in individual homes, and may be widely distributed." These conditions open the peacekeepers up to sniper fire and other problems, as well as making it virtually impossible to secure a given area fully.

Standard distinctions are made between wars in which ethnic fragmentation is involved and when it is not and, in a related fashion, between secessionist conflicts and those in which rebel groups seek to overthrow the government and seize control of the whole country. The evidence is mixed, however, on whether such distinctions affect peace operation success. Heldt (2001) notes that secessionist conflicts, such as during the Sudanese civil war, are no more difficult to handle than other civil conflicts. Fortna (2008a) suggests that ethnic conflicts are more prone to reignite, but her results are not statistically significant, and Heldt (2001) actually argues that ethnically divided societies are less war-prone following peacekeeping.

Peacekeeping in civil war contexts is problematic, but operations that occur in the post-conflict or fourth conflict phase (Diehl and Balas 2014) tend to be more successful than operations in earlier phases, including the third phase, when there is a cease-fire but no conflict resolution.[4] This is not necessarily attributable to any unique characteristics of peace operations in this phase. Rather, the post-conflict, agreement phase is one in which the conflicting parties (or a critical mass of them anyway) have agreed not only to stop fighting but also on how to resolve some of the differences that were the sources of violent conflict in the past. Peacekeeping plays a significant role in the implementation of such an agreement; for example, in the early 1990s, the United Nations Transitional Authority in Cambodia (UNTAC) successfully oversaw the repatriation of refugees and monitored democratic elections (over 90 percent of registered voters participated). Thus, the baseline probability of violence is lower in this phase, as opposed to cases in which fighting is ongoing or a cease-fire has occurred without any resolution of disagreements.

THEORETICAL EXPLANATIONS: WHY PEACEKEEPING WORKS

In general, scholars have long lamented the lack of peacekeeping-specific theory (e.g., Paris 2000); to the extent that theoretical formulations have been used to account for peacekeeping outcomes, they have been borrowed from other research milieus (Diehl 2014). Rather than coherent theory, peacekeeping studies have most often provided a series of variable-specific accounts for success and failure, with an emphasis on the latter more commonly than the former. Equally common have been attempts at providing ad hoc explanations *after* reporting empirical findings rather than starting with theoretically informed expectations that are subject to testing.

Generally, Fortna (2008a) offers what she describes as a "theory" to explain how peacekeeping works. In her conception, and reflective of past research on peacekeeping, the prevention of conflict renewal is achieved through a series of tasks that peacekeepers perform. By separating combatants at a physical distance, peacekeepers prevent the accidental engagement of opposing armies, thereby inhibiting small incidents that could escalate to renewed war; part of the success of peacekeepers in the Sinai can be attributed to separating Israeli and Egyptian forces. Peacekeepers also inhibit deliberate cheating on cease-fire agreements, as violations can be more easily detected. The physical separation of the protagonists provides early warning of any attack and thereby decreases the tactical advantages that stem from a surprise attack and increases the uncertainty of any side winning the next battle (Smith and Stam 2003). Renewed warfare in which the aggressor can be identified by the peacekeepers and in which peacekeepers are partly the target of that aggression is also likely to produce international condemnation. The costs in international reputation and possible sanctions, combined with the decreased likelihood of quick success, are designed to be sufficient to deter any attack (Fortna 2008a). Significantly, results from Mason et al. (2011) indicate that the conflict diminution effects are just as strong during the time that the peacekeepers are actually deployed as during the period *following* their withdrawal. This suggests that not only are the peacekeepers effective in directly deterring or preventing violence but that they also facilitate other processes that lay the groundwork for long-term peace.

With respect to post-conflict contexts, the purported success of peacekeeping has been explained through "credible commitment" theory, largely derived from the civil war literature (Walter 2002; see also Hartzell et al. 2001). The theoretical story flows from bargaining theory in that when parties to a conflict are ready for a settlement, they might need a third party to guarantee the implementation of that agreement, given that enemies do not trust each other and that there are incentives to undo the settlement in the future by one or both parties. Peacekeepers can play that role by performing or monitoring a series of tasks in the post-conflict context that disputants will not trust to one another; these include agreement provisions for demobilization, disarmament, and reintegration (DDR) and election supervision respectively. Peacekeeping personnel are usually regarded as impartial and therefore more likely to carry out these tasks in line with both the substance and spirit of the provisions crafted by the disputants, at least relative to the parties relying on each other. Thus, peacekeepers were trusted to monitor elections and the demobilization of troops in Namibia prior to its independence rather than relying on the outgoing South African administration.

Plans for peacekeeping are often part of a peace agreement as the parties would not accept the settlement without such a guarantee. That peacekeeping leads to better post-conflict outcomes is consistent with credible commitment theory. There are corollaries—foreign direct investment should increase with peacekeeping if the commitment is credible (Diehl 2014), but studies have not yet verified that effect. In addition, most peacekeeping operations after civil wars are relatively short, and it is not clear that long-term peace can be attributed to peacekeeping guarantees against reneging of the agreement.

EMPIRICAL EVIDENCE

Looking at the incidence of violent conflict's being renewed following a cessation of hostilities, there is clear evidence that peacekeeping works at least on the aggregate level. Depending on a variety of analyses and time periods, Fortna (2008a) notes that peace operations can reduce the renewal of civil warfare by 30 to 95 percent, a substantial effect. Because we know that peacekeepers are often sent to the most dangerous conflicts (Gilligan and Stedman 2003; Fortna 2004), she controls for the more difficult or severe conflicts into which peacekeepers are sent. Thus, comparisons of conflict outcomes between contexts with and without peace operations are not biased by the different initial conditions they face (see also Gilligan and Sergenti 2008 for an alternative approach). Doyle and Sambanis (2006) also confirm that putting UN peacekeepers in place after a civil war delays or prevents the renewal of violence. Similarly, Mason et al. (2011) report that the presence of peacekeepers reduces the likelihood of civil war renewal by over 70 percent (see also Quinn et al. 2007 for similar findings).[5]

Peacekeepers not only have a strong substantive effect on dissipating conflict renewal, they are also relatively important vis-à-vis other factors. Perhaps only a decisive victory by one side in a civil war has a stronger pacifying effect on future conflict. Notably, a series of other factors—for example ethnic and economic concerns—are likely to impact not only the dynamics of the original civil war, but also the prospects for its renewal.[6] Yet peacekeeping is one of the few factors that we can isolate as having an impact on civil war renewal and *not* on the original violence. There are a few studies that include a peacekeeping variable as a control or secondary concern in studies of power sharing and the durability of peace after a civil war; at least two of these studies (Jarstad 2009; Ottmann and Vüellers 2015) conclude that there is no effect or no value added from peacekeeping in the context of power-sharing peace agreements (more broadly, see chapter 8, this volume). It is not clear how this comports with the findings above or whether power-sharing cases are different than other post-conflict scenarios.

The above studies look at the aggregate effects of peacekeeping on conflict, focusing on whether a country as a whole experiences another civil war or not. Yet such analyses cannot precisely determine whether peacekeeping operations are *causally* related to the outbreak of war or violence. New civil wars might break out in substate geographic areas where no peacekeepers were deployed, but countries might remain stable in areas where such operations were ongoing (and vice versa); this could give a false sense of whether peacekeepers were effective. Accordingly, and consistent with a general trend in civil war studies, several works have sought to disaggregate civil conflict and peacekeeping deployment to pinpoint the locations of each and thereby better assess outcomes (see chapters 7 and 15, this volume). GIS and other geocoded data (e.g., ACLED) have allowed scholars to identify the specific areas where violence occurs. We also know that peacekeepers are never deployed in all parts of a country, given the relatively small size of most operations and often the large geographic areas to cover, such as the Congo. Indeed, there is some evidence that peacekeepers concentrate on areas where the government is involved in violent interactions, and they also cluster around transportation networks, densely populated areas, surface-based resources, and international borders (Townsen and Reeder 2014). Peacekeepers do go to substate areas with the greatest violence (Costalli 2014; Reeder et al. 2015), similar to the findings where the state was the unit of analysis.

When the spatial distribution of violence and peacekeepers are matched, it is less clear that peacekeeping really reduces conflict. Costalli (2014) reports that peacekeepers did *not* reduce subsequent violence in specific areas of deployment. Yet this study considers only Bosnia, a case classified as a failure and one that is an exemplar of the problems of peacekeeping in civil wars (Howard 2008). Beardsley (2011) examined the potential diffusion of conflict in the presence of peacekeeping operations and in their absence. In the absence of peacekeepers, there is substantial risk that the conflict will spread to a neighbouring rival state. Having peacekeepers in place significantly reduces that risk. For example, a UN operation in Macedonia is credited with preventing the spread of the Bosnian civil war to new areas.

A second way to disaggregate studies of peacekeeping is to consider more carefully the particular victims of civil conflict. Duration of peace measures focus on the achievement of certain thresholds of battle-related fatalities to signify the renewal of violence. Yet peacekeepers are increasingly charged with the protection of the civilian population. Thus, another standard for success is the ability of the operation to limit civilian casualties, which might (or might not) be correlated with the renewal of violence under other measures. Peacekeepers do not necessarily respond in terms of relocating to the risks associated with civilian casualties (Reeder et al., 2015), but there is clear evidence that when they are deployed, fewer civilian casualties result. Hultman et al. (2013) demonstrate that as the size of a peacekeeping force increases, it is better able to prevent civilian casualties.

Conventionally, studies compare situations with and without peacekeeping in order to analyse the efficacy of peace operations in preventing the renewal of civil war. This provides evidence on whether peacekeeping on average promotes peace, but it cannot help us understand variation *across* peace operations in their effectiveness, as there are numerous examples of failures even as the sum total produces a positive impact.

Fortna (2008a) is one of the few scholars to distinguish between different kinds of peace operations and how they impact peacekeeping effectiveness. First, she reports that both consent-based (in which combatants agree to the peacekeeping mission) and robust (involving greater military capacity and more permissive rules of engagement) forms of peacekeeping are effective in limiting future conflict, and neither type seems to have an advantage over the other in this respect. Fortna also breaks down consent-based operations in mission types: monitoring, traditional, enforcement, and multidimensional respectively. With the caveat that there are small numbers of cases in some categories, she concludes that the largest substantive impact comes from multidimensional missions (ones that carry out several tasks). Various European Union and UN missions in Kosovo collectively qualify as multidimensional; for example, the EU took over responsibility for reforming the criminal justice system there, including dealing with war crimes there.

Analysis of operational factors led Heldt (2001) to conclude in his systematic assessment of peace missions in civil wars that characteristics related to peacekeeping missions are insignificant, and most variation in the avoidance of war is accounted for by other factors related to the context of the conflict. Nevertheless, several recent works suggest that organizational elements are important, with the focus less on general differences across various international organizations and more on how the organizational culture and bureaucratic practices of the sponsoring agency (generally the UN) inhibits operational success. Such studies focus extensively on peacebuilding activities rather than traditional operational concerns of limiting armed conflict, and thus it is often difficult to disentangle these different goals and the causal factors affecting them.

Howard (2008) concentrates on organizational learning in the sponsoring organization as a partial cause of success and failure. Learning is determined, in part, by the effectiveness of the bureaucracy, emphasizing functions in the UN Secretariat rather than field actions taken by peacekeeping commanders, as was the case in early studies. Without this kind of learning, Howard (2008: 2) argues that "the operation is unable to implement its mandate or help to construct new domestic institutions that will solidify the peace." Such learning is considered to be a necessary condition for success, but she notes that the other elements—situational factors and cooperation from leading states—are also vital (see also Benner et al. 2011). Autesserre (2010) blames the dominant peacebuilding culture within the UN for failures to promote conflict resolution in Congolese society. Specifically, she criticizes the UN as having an incorrect, top-down view of conflict, with an emphasis on the superstructures of regional and global sources of tension. The result is that the needs of the local population are ignored, and rebuilding society after the conflict fails. A follow-up study (Autesserre 2014) reaches similar conclusions, noting that international aid workers (peacekeepers and beyond) are mismatched with the local needs and actors in terms of information gathering, expertise, and the dominant narratives employed. Such inconsistencies help account for problems encountered with peacekeeping in the Congo, Cyprus, Burundi, and elsewhere.

Beyond the contextual factors unique to civil wars discussed earlier, other factors have been associated with post-conflict success and failure. More severe wars (i.e., those with higher death tolls) and those that last longer also limit the prospects for lasting peace (Fortna 2008a). In each case, such conflicts heighten and harden feelings of enmity between the opposing sides. There is accordingly less inclination among the parties to grant concessions and reconcile with their enemies than if the conflicts are less serious. Furthermore, even leaders with such an inclination may be limited by public opinion and domestic political actors (e.g., military, political parties), who would find such actions unacceptable. Another contextual factor concerns the geographic configuration of the conflict and the accompanying peace operation deployment (Diehl 1994). Peace missions are most successful when deployed so as to detect cease-fire violations and monitor compliance with other mandates adequately; as noted above, this is problematic in civil war contexts such as in Liberia, where there were no clear cease-fire lines.

There is the broad generalization that the greater the number of different actors involved in a conflict, the more difficult it will be to achieve success (Diehl 1994; Doyle and Sambanis 2006). As the number of disputants increases, it becomes harder for any settlement or even a cease-fire agreement to be satisfactory to all parties (Cunningham 2011). Furthermore, there is increasing opportunity for any one party to undermine the operation, by refusing cooperation with state-building programs or, more seriously, by choosing to renew violence as a strategy to achieve goals. Thus, highly complex civil wars are the most difficult to resolve.

Most relevant are the actions of neighboring states (Pushkina 2006) or interested major powers (Bratt 1997). Third party states can influence the success of a peace operation in several ways (Urquhart 1983). Most obviously, they can directly intervene militarily in a conflict, causing a renewal of the fighting or jeopardizing the safety and mission of the operation. More subtly, they might supply arms and other assistance to one of the disputants (or to a sub-national actor) that serves to undermine the peace force's ability to limit violence, as was the case of Syrian and Iranian supply of arms to Hezbollah in southern Lebanon. Third parties might also bring diplomatic pressure to bear on one of the actors, such that the actor is more or less disposed to support the presence of the peace operation (Bratt 1997; Jett 2000; Diehl 1994). Third parties have the potential to play either a positive or a negative role in the performance of peace operations. Yet there are potentially more ways to complicate a peace operation than to assist it. Furthermore, a third party state that supports a peace operation likely stays out of the conflict, whereas, in opposition, it will tend to take a more active role.

LIMITATIONS AND FUTURE RESEARCH AGENDA

Behavioral or positivist research on peacekeeping is relatively young, dating only to the last two decades. Accordingly, the knowledge base is thin, and there are a number of limitations or problems associated with current studies, but these provide the basis for future research in this area. First, most of the studies confound simple cease-fires with situations in which the protagonists have signed an agreement resolving some or all of the disputed issues. Both contexts involve a halt to fighting, but the latter is likely to be less prone to resumption of hostilities than lulls in violence that are by definition designed to be temporary. In effect, the case selection confounds different phases of conflict.[7] The choice of mission type and the size of the force, and other factors associated with outcomes, are likely to be endogenous to the phase in which the operation is deployed. Distinguishing between these contexts in future research is essential to understanding the impact of peacekeepers, both empirically and theoretically.

Second, extant research relies too extensively on the "peace duration" conception of success; only a few studies have gone beyond this to consider protection of civilians, preventing the spread of violence, or the quality of postwar peace (see chapter 8, this volume). Looking at how long "peace" lasts seems to be more of a convenience of data availability and statistical technique (event history analysis) than necessarily driven by empirical or theoretical bases. There are multiple indicators of peacekeeping success available (Diehl and Druckman 2010), even if one concentrates on the single goal of preventing further violence (e.g., civilian casualties). In order to demonstrate the robustness of findings as well as uncover more nuanced effects of peacekeeping in the post-conflict context, scholarly research needs to look beyond peace duration as the dependent variable. Some other indicators that could be considered include whether the conflict simply moves to a new geographic area, whether weapon flows to disputants are reduced, and whether negotiations are begun and successful between the disputants.

Third, and related to the last point, if one does focus on peace duration, the threshold used for the renewal of violence—another civil war—is too high. Using the Correlates of War standard of one thousand or more deaths in a year to signify a civil war and coding renewal dichotomously (yes/no), studies miss lower-level and sporadic violence that might occur in the aftermath of a cease-fire. Nevertheless, setting the threshold too low (e.g., twenty-five or more fatalities as is common in many civil war studies) might imply that the peacekeeping force was a failure in instances in which it responded to the outbreak of violence and restored order quickly, thereby preventing escalation to full-scale war. Looking at interval levels of violence would allow the detection of such nuances as well as provide a better sense of *how* successful the peacekeeping operation was rather than merely whether it was successful vis-à-vis a high threshold event.

Fourth, post-conflict studies of peacekeeping largely ignore the other missions performed by operations that are often referred to as "peacebuilding"; these include election supervision, promoting the rule of law, and the like. This is not to say that research needs to examine the outcomes of every goal or mission of a peace opera- tion in a post-conflict context. Yet success (or failure) in those missions is likely to be intertwined with the ability of the operation to deter or prevent violence. There are causal concerns not only with how the outcomes of these tasks affect the renewal of conflict but also with whether the simultaneity or sequencing of missions and goals (see below) impact outcomes; these concerns have largely been unexplored, even as we know that peacekeeping operations in a post-conflict environment rarely are mandated to do only one thing.

Fifth, peacekeeping operations after civil wars do not represent the exclusive strat- egy of peacebuilding, nor are those soldiers the only actors performing peacebuild- ing duties. Generally, there are associated activities in economic development, civil society, and more, carried out by international organizations, NGOs, and foreign governments. These vary across post–civil war contexts and arguably might have a greater influence on the renewal of conflict than peace operations, especially if one adopts a long-term evaluation of conflict renewal. No large-N study has accounted for these activities and how they might interact with peace operations' ability to sus- tain cease-fires. This is a difficult challenge, but one that future research must tackle in order to draw the correct inferences about the impact of peacekeeping.

Finally, the standard peacekeeping study has considered only operations carried out by the United Nations, perhaps because data and information are more readily available for those operations as opposed to ones carried out by other agents. Never- theless, the UN now constitutes a minority of all peace operations (Diehl and Balas 2014), and increasingly operations are carried out by regional organizations, such as the European Union, alone and in conjunction with one another and the UN (Balas 2011). One should not automatically assume that non-UN actors intervene in the same conflicts or necessarily have the same record of success as the United Nations. Accordingly, future research might consider peace operations in general, rather than the more narrowly drawn set of UN operations.

PEACEBUILDING AND DEMOCRATIZATION

Following a civil war, the goals of the protagonists and the international community as a whole include more than preventing a renewal of violence. Creating or restoring democratic processes are often one of the goals. Indeed, the majority of post–civil war agreements contain provisions for elections (Jarstad 2009), and some 40 percent of more of civil wars end up producing democratic governments in their aftermath (Wantchekon 2004). Half of all democracies founded after 1945 were achieved in a postwar context, and a majority of these followed civil wars (Bermeo 2003).

Underlying the importance of democratization for breaking the conflict trap is the overarching democratic peace theory as applied to internal conflict. The general finding that democratic states do not fight each other has been extended to civil wars (Hegre et al. 2001; Gleditsch et al. 2009), with the rationale that democratic states are more responsive to citizen demands and have a series of institutional mechanisms (e.g., courts) to channel dissent and manage conflict. Thus, successful democratization could lessen the chances for civil war renewal in the longer term.

At the same time, the process of moving from nondemocracy to stable democracy has been subject to much academic debate, with some (Mansfield and Snyder 1995, 2005; Hegre et al. 2001) arguing that the risk of conflict is greatest in this transition phase (see also Cederman et al. 2010). Some controversy revolves around the timing of elections (see e.g., Brancati and Snyder 2012; Flores and Noorudin 2012) and how this has an effect on subsequent democratization and future conflict, elements that are intimately tied to one another. Democratization efforts cannot take place when violence re-erupts, and failed democratization tends to promote conflict.

The Post–Civil War Context for Democratization and Peacebuilding

Many studies make no distinction between post-conflict and other contexts for democratization (Bermeo 2003), even as they might include explanatory variables about the characteristics of the state involved (e.g., ethnic composition). Yet there are theoretical reasons to believe that post-conflict contexts pose special challenges to democratization not present in other scenarios.[8]

Hartzell and Hoddie (2015) note that civil wars can complicate or undermine a series of conditions that facilitate democratization. These include undermining modernization processes that are conducive to developing democracy. Economic costs of redevelopment (following especially destructive wars) might take away resources that would otherwise be used for institution building and provision of public goods that assist democracy efforts. Social capital might also be degraded because of the war. In addition, various actors might have a greater preference for order (Wantchekon 2004) than for rights and freedoms associated with democracy.

The post–civil war context also creates several insecurity and related commitment problems that are not present (or at least to the same degree) in other contexts. Leaders of different groups or factions, representing the concerns of their constituencies, will fear that rivals in power will use government institutions for repression or political advantage. For example, this was the situation in Rwanda (Samset 2011), when the victorious Tutsi rebels won the first election, and thousands of Hutus were killed thereafter, independent journalists were jailed, and some rival political parties were banned. This makes such leaders reluctant to cooperate in democratization efforts or play by the rules in a contested election. Because of the legacy of past violence, winners of the first election have incentives to use power to consolidate control over the state's apparatus, preventing the occurrence of a second election or ensuring its own victory in that election (Fearon, 2011). Losers, prospective and actual, recognize this and won't necessarily trust their enemies to continue with the democratization process.

Related to the commitment problem with respect to the renewal of violence, opposing sides will not trust each other to behave in such a way that free and fair elections will occur the first time or that the winning side will honor its commitment to democratic processes in the future. These are potential risks for any government transitioning to democracy, but the risks are acute when the most recent experience that groups had with one another was war.

The unique postwar context for democratization suggests that the democratization process might be less successful here than in other contexts and require special efforts to redress limitations. Nevertheless, from a causal standpoint, Fortna and Huang (2012) find that the same factors that influence democratization generally also apply to post-conflict contexts. This suggests that models might not need to be specific to that context, although this conclusion is dependent on specific empirical findings reported below, and these do not necessarily constitute a consensus.

THEORETICAL EXPECTATIONS: HOW DOES PEACEBUILDING HELP? (OR DOES IT?)

There are a myriad of factors that affect democratization and in multiple contexts, and this chapter will not review these. More specifically, the focus will be on how peacebuilding operations—essentially peacekeeping operations that can carry out and coordinate a series of other functions beyond conflict abatement—contribute to (or do not) the democratization process.

At the most basic level, the ability of an operation to prevent the renewal of violence contributes to democratization (Fortna 2008b), a process that requires stability and that cannot function in an environment of open warfare. Yet a peacekeeping operation is more likely to contribute to democratization when it is assigned a series of peacebuilding functions that complement efforts at democratization. One such mission is demobilization, disarmament, and reintegration (DDR). Peacekeepers supervise the turning in of weapons and demobilization of various armies and militias and, in some cases, the integration of those irregular forces into the national militaries as well. The African Union made this part of its mandate in sending a peace mission to Darfur, although its success in this task, and for the mission in general, is open to question. DDR makes the renewal of civil war less likely by limiting the ability of other forces to challenge the existing government (Wantchekon 2004; Brancati and Snyder 2011) or subvert democratic processes. Once again, peacekeepers provide a credible commitment in carrying out DDR supervision, actions that former enemies will not entrust to one another.

Most directly relevant to democratization is the role of peacekeepers in election supervision. Peacekeepers ensure that violence does not disrupt voter registration, campaigns, and voting in post-conflict elections; these tasks have been carried out by peacekeepers in Western Sahara, Nicaragua, Cambodia, and other locations. Working with international and national authorities, peacekeeping is designed to ensure that the elections are "free and fair." If successful, the election outcome is more likely to be accepted as legitimate by local groups and the international community, and such legitimacy is thought to decrease the chances that the losers would challenge the election with violence and outside parties would support such challenges.[9] Thus, peacekeepers provide a credible commitment to any agreement that democratic elections will be held (Brancati and Snyder 2011). Nevertheless, peacekeeping usually takes place only for the *first* election following a civil war, and thus does not and cannot address concerns of the losers with the post-election actions of the winner or the legitimacy of the *second* election; the latter is often a critical signpost for successful democratization in the long run.

Other peacebuilding missions might include facilitating the rule of law and promoting economic development; these are functions often carried out primarily by, or in conjunction with, other actors, including international agencies (e.g., World Bank) or nongovernmental organizations. Such peacebuilding helps create conditions more conducive to democracy efforts (e.g., economic development) or directly promotes components of democracy (e.g., creating a functioning judiciary system). This was the initial goal of peacekeeping efforts in East Timor, although a follow-up operation was needed there to deal with a renewal of violence. Finally, and related to the theoretical claims concerning credible commitment, peacekeepers can increase the flow of information between opposing sides and build the trust necessary for democratization to grow (Heldt 2011).

Much of the decidedly negative view of peacekeeping and democratization comes from critical theorists (e.g., Pugh 2004) who see peacekeeping as another form of imperialism and critique the fundamental assumption that Western liberalism and democracy should be encouraged by the international community in the aftermath of a civil war. Such studies generally lack a systematic empirical component. Perhaps the only exception is Marten's (2004) study of a handful of civil wars. She concludes that attempts to build democracy through the UN in these contexts is a "pipedream," although this might be read as an indictment of any attempts at democratization, whether through UN peace operations or otherwise.

The above explanations would seem to imply that peacebuilding has a uniformly positive or negative effect on democratization. Nevertheless, several scholars have identified what they term as "dilemmas" between peacekeeping and democratization such that they might work at cross purposes. Jarstad (2008) develops these in detail as a framework in which various authors examine individual cases (Jarstad and Sisk 2008). She describes peacebuilding and democratization as intersecting processes that have the potential to undermine one another. The *horizontal* dilemma refers to the degree to which all parties are included in a peace agreement and subsequent democratic efforts (as opposed to excluding certain elites or groups as has been the case in Somalia). Broad inclusion might be good for maintaining peace, but counter-productive for democratization. The *vertical* dilemma involves the trade-off between legitimacy and efficacy, again relating to issues of inclusion of the masses. Getting agreements to keep the peace might be elite driven, but ultimately democracy (and to some extent peace) depends on local factors and the cooperation of the mass public.

The third dilemma, labeled "systemic," deals with international versus local control of the peacebuilding processes. Peacekeeping involves external actors and resources, and these might be necessary to prevent the renewal of violence and carry out some of the tasks noted above. Yet democratization might depend on local ownership of activities. If the international community assumes too much responsibility for ac-tivities, then democratization and other efforts lack legitimacy from being imposed from outside (Autesserre 2010). There is also the concern that unless domestic actors take responsibility, democratization efforts will fail in the long run. Finally, *temporal* dilemmas suggest that short-term efforts might undermine long-term success. For example, efforts to keep the peace in the short term might involve substantial limits on democratic freedoms, such as public demonstrations. Initial efforts at democ-ratization might trigger violence and unravel the mechanisms for long-term peace.

The theoretical dilemmas of democracy and peacebuilding suggest a more ambiguous impact of peacekeeping on democratization. The value of promoting the stability necessary for democratization might be mitigated, canceled out, or overcome by the negative impact that peacebuilding has on democratization. The exact effects and their magnitude are largely empirical questions, and the results are reviewed in next section.

EMPIRICAL EVIDENCE

Does peacekeeping promote democratization? Authors in the Jarstad and Sisk (2008) collection find empirical support for the dilemmas noted above (see Sisk 2008 for an integrative summary), but it is not always clear whether these can be attributable to peacekeeping forces or other aspects (e.g., attempts to build civil society). Looking specifically at peacekeeping elements, empirical results present a mixed bag, although an emerging consensus suggests that peacekeeping has little effect on democratization.

Leaving aside some works that mix interstate and intrastate contexts (e.g., Picker-ing and Peceny 2006), early work found peacekeeping operations were positively associated with democracy formation. Most cited was the study by Doyle and Sam-banis (2006), which reports improvement in democracy scores two to five years after a civil war in the presence of a multidimensional peacekeeping force. Yet, as Fortna and Huang (2012) note, these and other studies of postwar democratization suffer from a number of methodological flaws. First, those works often compare pre- and postwar democracy levels but ignore that many of the changes in democracy levels occur *during* the war, thereby leading to misleading inferences about changes in democracy levels. Second, there might be differences in short- and long-term effects, the latter of which are not addressed in studies. Third, democracy scores based on Polity data include as components the presence or absence of political instability and violence (Vreeland 2008), thereby making claims partly tautological that limiting violence, for example from peacekeeping forces, promotes democracy.

A series of studies, some of which correct for the above concerns, have found that peacekeeping forces have no effect on democratization levels, suggesting that any positive effects from prompting stability are counteracted by negative impacts flowing from the dilemmas above. Directly addressing peacekeeping, Fortna (2008) concludes that even as peacekeeping forces are effective in preventing violence, they are not associated with higher democracy levels in the post-conflict context.[10] In a wide-ranging multivariate analysis, Fortna and Huang (2012) looked at peacekeeping along with a series of other factors thought to affect democratization (e.g., war outcome, oil) and also concluded that peacekeeping had no impact. Similarly, Gurses and Mason (2008) found that the presence of peacekeepers had no impact on democratization levels, even as they showed that strong institutions and other traditional correlates were important. Important exceptions are Heldt (2011) and Steinhart and Grimm (2015), who find support for the positive-effect position and for paying some attention to the mandates and capacities of the operations studied.[11]

The above studies look for direct effects of peacekeeping missions on democratization, comparing the presence or absence of forces with subsequent democracy levels. Yet peacekeeping operations might also have *indirect* effects on democratization, influencing other factors, which in turn are associated with democratization. Some factors identified in the literature are not or cannot be influenced by a post-conflict peacekeeping force, such as the outcome of the civil war or the ethnic composition of the state. Nevertheless, peacekeeping might be particularly influential in affecting the timing or sequencing of different peacebuilding tasks, and this in turn could affect post-conflict stability and the success of democratization.

Among the most controversial debates in scholarly studies of democratization is the timing of elections, specifically when they occur vis-à-vis the end of the civil war and other peacebuilding efforts such as promoting economic development. Jarstad (2008: 25) hails elections as "the crowning event" of peacebuilding, and international actors play a critical role in the peacebuilding strategy, including when certain tasks are performed. The preponderance of evidence suggests that holding elections "too early" is counterproductive in promoting democracy and indeed in preventing a renewal of violence (see, e.g., Brancati and Snyder 2012). Similarly, Paris (2004) reports that elections in advance of other peacebuilding missions undermine efforts at peace and other tasks. Brancati and Snyder (2011) contend that the UN and the international community have preferences for early elections to reassure the formerly warring parties; accordingly, the average time for the first election after a civil war has fallen to under three years. In addition, one might believe that the sponsoring agencies and troop suppliers of peace operations want early elections as it allows them to withdraw forces sooner in the post-conflict environment, rather than commit to long-term deployment. Thus, to the extent that early elections are undesirable, peace operations that encourage premature voting undermine democracy efforts in the long run. Early elections that are not accepted as free and fair might also have a negative feedback effect on the ability of the peace operation to preserve a cease-fire, as was the case following the 1992 elections in Angola.

LIMITATIONS AND FUTURE RESEARCH AGENDA

The empirical findings on the impact of peacekeeping on democratization are not encouraging, but they suffer from a number of limitations or deficiencies that need to be addressed before concluding that peacekeeping makes no difference. Regardless, it is likely that peacekeeping plays only a secondary role to a host of other factors that include the course of democracy in the post-conflict context.

First, it is not clear what a finding in existing studies that peacekeeping has no effect on democratization really means. It might indicate that there are no causal influences and peacekeeping is irrelevant. Within a given operation, it could also indicate that peacekeeping has some positive impacts that are canceled out in a symmetrical fashion by its negative influences. Null findings might also indicate that cross-sectionally, peacekeeping has positive effects in some cases and negative in others, with aggregate results masking these differences. There is also the possibility of a selection effect if peacekeeping guarantees, in peace agreements or election supervision, are only given to the most difficult cases, thus making it difficult to show democratization progress in comparison to other cases. Which, if any, of these possibilities holds empirically cannot be determined from extant studies, and this question deserves a place on a future research agenda.

Second, as with studies that focus on duration of peace, studies of peacekeeping and democracy often use only a dichotomous variable on whether peacekeeping forces were present or not. Yet some of the positive effects of peacekeeping theorized above are predicated on the performance of certain tasks, such as election supervision or DDR; it is not clear whether peacekeeping operations in many of these contexts were even mandated to perform such functions. Fortna (2008b), as well as Doyle and Sambanis (2006), look at different mission types, but even the classification "multidimensional" does not necessarily get at the specific and key functions that might be related to democratization. Heldt (2011) is perhaps the only study that considers whether democracy promotion was part of the peacekeeping mandate, and he indicates that 30 percent of positive effects from peacekeeping are the result of these democracy-support elements.

Third, even if one were to account for the particular missions performed, analyses must include some measure of success in order to tie the peacekeeping operation to successful democratization. The theoretical logics above presume such mission success for the democratizing effect to occur. It is not merely that the peacekeeping force was tasked with supervising an election or facilitating disarmament of militias; it must be that the force was able to achieve its goals. Thus, peacekeeping success with respect to one goal is a prerequisite for others, here democratization. Again, Fortna (2008a) is an exception to the standard study, but she only looks at whether the force was successful or not in limiting violence and not the other missions that might assist democratization. This is nonetheless critical, as a failure to keep the peace might scuttle any efforts at democratization and institution building. Therefore, future research must consider the success of other missions in assessing progress in democratization. An initial focus on DDR might be most desirable, given limited research on that mission and its apparent role as a prerequisite for achieving many other peace missions that follow it.

Fourth, temporal dynamics make it difficult to connect peacekeeping with democratization. Peacekeeping operations in post-conflict contexts are deployed for relatively short periods, with the average length of peacekeeping missions in civil wars being less than two and a half years (Wright and Greig 2012). In contrast, democratization tends to be a long-term process lasting decades before it becomes evident whether it has succeeded or not; even the time between the first and critical second elections is more than the conventional length of peacekeeping deployment. Thus, peacekeeping at best can affect some of the initial conditions that set a state on the path to democracy. Studies that report a positive effect on democratization do so only in a narrow time frame and do not assess the long-term impact (Heldt 2011). Yet even given lingering effects from those efforts, there are a multitude of other conditions and subsequent intervening variables that are more critical to successful democratization and, in any case, confound the peacekeeping-democratization connection. Understanding these other factors and the magnitude of their impact vis-à-vis peace operations is essential for assessing the latter, and therefore a worthy focus of future research.

Finally, and further complicating the making of causal inferences, peacebuilding after civil war involves multiple actors (IGOs, NGOs, other states) carrying out tasks independent of or in conjunction with peacekeepers. These do not always integrate well for common purposes and, accordingly, it is hard to parse out the effects of these efforts from those of peacekeeping, much less assess the interactive effects. Because the number of peacebuilding missions is relatively small, simply adding many control variables will not necessarily be an effective solution. In-depth case studies and ethnographic research (e.g., Autesserre 2014) might be the preferred research approach to disentangle these effects.

CONCLUSION

Breaking the conflict trap and therefore the renewal of civil war requires both short- and long-term strategies. This chapter assesses the state of knowledge with respect to the ability of peacekeeping operations to prevent the renewal of violence in the near term and then promote long-term peace by facilitating democratization.

We know considerably more about the short-term conflict abatement effects of peacekeeping. There, the consensus is that peacekeeping enhances stability in post-conflict environments by providing credible commitments to cease-fires and preventing accidental and deliberate engagement of forces through interposition. The literature on peacekeeping and democratization is less clear and less developed. Short-term orientations and the presence of many confounding factors make it problematic to establish whether peacekeeping really promotes democracy.

In conclusion, the reader should be reminded that peacebuilding operations in the twenty-first century do more than limit violence and promote democratization in post-conflict situations. As noted in passing above, they might also facilitate disarmament, deliver humanitarian assistance, and promote the rule of law among other missions. The success of these enterprises (see Diehl and Druckman 2010 for a discussion of different missions and indicators of success for each) might be as important as the two goals reviewed in this chapter.

In addition, whatever success peacekeepers have in helping countries recover from civil wars must be balanced against the harms that they cause. Peace operations also have a number of other outcomes, many of which are unintended and undesirable. Such unintended consequences come in a variety of forms. Some are gender based, as peacekeeping soldiers commit rapes against the local population, spread HIV/AIDS, and may perpetuate discriminatory hiring practices when employing the local population. For example, in 2007, UN peacekeepers (in the UNOCI mission in Côte d'Ivoire) were accused of rape and sexual abuse. Economic distortions include the creation of dual public-sector economies (that of the peacebuilding operation and that of the national government) and the undermining of local markets for services and products because of the displacement of the same by the peace operation. Political corruption, black market activity, and other effects are also possible; these might be committed by peacekeepers or facilitated by their presence, as was the case in Bosnia. These outcomes should not be ignored by either policy makers or scholars seeking to understand the impact of peace operations.

10

The Legacies of Civil War

Health, Education, and Economic Development

Clayton L. Thyne

The idea that war is harmful will attract few doubters. From the beginning of World War I to the end of the Cold War, an estimated 187 million people were killed or allowed to die due to human decisions (Hobsbawm 1994). Civil wars have been found to be particularly harmful, and this harm has perhaps increased over time as conventional wars have been replaced with new wars that are, in Mueller's (2003: 507) terms, "waged by packs—often remarkably small ones—of criminals, bandits and thugs." Indiscriminate use of force and violence against civilians are recurring themes in the current literature on civil wars (e.g., Eck and Hultman 2007; Stepanova 2009). Schools are destroyed, children attacked, rape is used as a fighting tactic, economies are left in tatters, and even professional soccer players from war-torn countries behave violently on the pitch (Collier et al. 2003; Miguel, Saiegh, and Satyanath 2011). With a mountain of evidence supporting this viewpoint, it is easy to take the harmful effects of civil war as a given and move on. To do so would be a mistake.

Understanding the harmful nature of civil wars is important for a variety of reasons. For one, intensive study of exactly how and what war harms puts policy makers in a better position in deciding where to invest scarce resources. A surprisingly meager investment of peacekeepers has been found to dramatically reduce violence against civilians during conflicts (Hultman, Kathman and Shannon 2013).[1] Similarly small investments in mental health and rebuilding schools are apt to support a country in the postwar period. Second, the effects of warfare are often not as obvious as one might suspect. Children exposed to warfare are surprisingly resilient, for example, and providing mental health support to parents has been found to have a trickle-down effect throughout the household (Rutter 1985). Likewise, pockets of enterprise can benefit economies even in the midst of civil conflicts, and refugees can serve as a boon to host economies (Alix-Garcia 2007; Whitaker 2002). Finally, understanding the harm caused by warfare puts both researchers and policy makers in a better position to prevent the recurrence of conflict. Dubbed the "conflict trap" by Paul Collier and his colleagues (2003), scholars increasingly understand that the factors causing wars to begin, such as weak economies and corrupt governance, often worsen during conflicts. Rates and sectors of decline differ, however. Understanding how war impacts a variety of factors, therefore, is an important step forward in moving conflict countries toward long-term peace.

Though kept separately to add coherence to the chapter, it will soon become clear that the factors discussed in this chapter—health, education, and economic development—are related to each other and in feedback loops with civil war. Education promotes individual and societal health, for example, and weaknesses in each of these factors can be both a cause and a consequence of civil wars. Covering the full scope of the endogenous relationship between these factors would be far too much for a single chapter. Thus, the primary focus of this chapter is on war as an independent variable, with less attention paid to the feedback mechanisms that may be at work. I begin by examining the influence of civil war on health, focusing on mortality, disabilities, and mental trauma. The chapter then moves to a discussion of education, parsing out where conflicts do the most harm and why. I end with a discussion of the impact of war on state economies and then discuss the path forward based on lessons learned.

CIVIL WAR AND HEALTH

Research on the effect of civil conflicts on health has burgeoned in recent years. Around a decade ago, Fearon and Laitin (2003) estimated the total deaths due to civil wars from 1945 to 1999 to be around 16 million. Since then, researchers have sought to uncover why and how these deaths come about, focusing on such things as deliberate targeting of civilians and less obvious mechanisms, like hunger and disease, by which people are killed during conflict. Researchers have also gained significant ground in looking beyond deaths to uncover the influence of civil conflicts on health more generally. Disabilities remain a key concern, and an expanding body of work focuses on how conflict influences mental health and sexual trauma. Little debate emerges from this body of literature. Civil wars are clearly harmful. The largest areas of innovation, as this chapter will seek to elucidate, come in uncovering the mechanisms behind the harm, figuring out where civil conflicts inflict the most damage, and attempting to provide useful policy recommendations. Figure 10.1 provides a summary of the areas of harm that will be covered, examples of evidence for each area, and a summary of the theoretical mechanisms used by past work to explain how and why civil wars produce these outcomes.

Estimates of deaths due to civil wars vary a fair amount. As noted above, the 16 million estimate provided by Fearon and Laitin (2003) has been cited dozens of times, and even shapes the title of Patrick Regan's (2009) analyses of how wars might

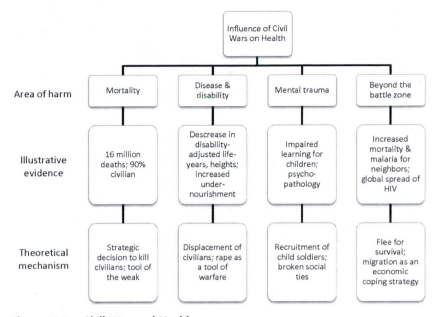

Figure 10.1. Civil Wars and Health

be brought to an end—his effort to understand how to prevent 16 million from becoming "Sixteen Million One." An effort to present more recent and robust battle death estimates is led by scholars at the Uppsala Conflict Data Program (UCDP).[2] Covering 1989 to 2013, the most recent presentation of these data shows that deaths due to civil conflicts have *not* coincided with the decline in civil conflicts since the early 1990s. Instead, deaths are sporadic, and recent trends show an increase mainly due to the increased intensity of fighting in Central and South Asia (mainly Afghanistan, Pakistan, and Sri Lanka). Though down from two earlier peaks (1991 and 1999, due to conflicts in the Horn of Africa), there is little doubt that death due to civil conflicts remains a blight on many states (Themnér and Wallensteen 2014; Guha-Sapir and Van Panhuis 2002; Hoeffler and Reynal-Querol 2003).

Understanding that a single death due to civil war is one too many, scholars have sought to uncover why civil wars are exceedingly bloody. Understanding why millions die in interstate wars is simple in comparison. When two or more well-trained and well-equipped militaries face off on the battlefield, deaths are likely. However, deaths of this type account for a surprisingly small portion of deaths due to warfare. According to Holsti (1992), only around one-third of the 22 million casualties due to warfare between 1945 and 1989 were due to combat between organized armies of states. The remaining two-thirds were due to less conventional civil wars. And among the 14 million or so deaths due to civil wars during this time period, an astounding 90 percent were civilians (Cairns 1997).

Recognizing that the sheer numbers of civilian deaths are too large to cast aside as a mere by-product of conflict, recent work has gained significant ground in explaining both why civil wars are so bloody and why civilians are so commonly the victims of the bloodshed. Leading theories focus on the power dynamics that emerge between competing intrastate actors to explain the intentional use of violence against civilians in civil wars (e.g., Hultman 2007; Kalyvas 2006; Wood 2010). From this viewpoint, violence against civilians is employed because it produces positive returns, altering the conflict landscape in favor of the belligerents who attack civilians. Several mechanisms explain how these positive returns come about, and recent work helps explain why we might see violence against civilians be either collective or targeted.

Regarding collective violence, a central argument contends that success in conflict is largely determined by combatants' control of territory. Violence is used to intimidate the population, helping to deter civilian defection and secure the civilian support that is necessary to control territory (Kalyvas 1999, 2006; Kalyvas and Kocher 2007b). Though coerced, the resulting support allows those who perpetrate the violence to obtain information about their adversary, fill their ranks with new recruits, and acquire food, shelter, and arms (Wood 2010; Wood, Kathman, and Gent 2012). For example, FRELIMO (Mozambique Liberation Front) shelled villages to show that the Portuguese colonizers could not protect the civilians. Rather than resist FRELIMO and risk death, the shelling led to both recruits and indirect collaboration from civilians (Henriksen 1983). Targeting civilians also makes it increasingly difficult for opponents to operate in contested areas, which may coerce opponents into concessions (Azam and Hoeffler 2002; Valentino, Huth, and Balch-Lindsay 2004; Balcells 2011; Vinci 2005). Though one might suspect that such tactics come solely from rebel organizations that lack the capabilities to control territory using more conventional approaches, this is not the case. Like rebels, governments use collective targeting of civilians to clear territory and "drain the sea" of support around insurgents (Valentino, Huth and Balch-Lindsay 2004; Kalyvas and Kocher 2007; Lichbach 1995). And while sustained levels of collective violence may produce a backlash in the long run (Mason and Krane 1989; Kalyvas 2006; Kalyvas and Kocher 2007), the short-term benefits of such violence often outweigh the uncertain long-term consequences (Arendt 1970).

Moving beyond the need to control territory that is common to all belligerents, we see a growing consensus among scholars who focus on the balance of capabilities to explain widespread, indiscriminate violence. This work is closely tied to more general efforts to explain how the balance of capabilities influences the type of warfare that belligerents choose (Buhaug 2006; Balcells 2010; Kalyvas 2005; Lockyer 2010). The main idea is that weaker parties are apt to choose strategies like guerrilla warfare and terrorism and then move toward more conventional approaches as they strengthen (Byman 2008; Butler and Gates 2009). In a similar vein, weak actors are apt to kill civilians indiscriminately. Kalyvas (2006) links this to information. Though selectively targeting individuals or groups may be the preferred approach, weak actors lacking the information and capabilities for selective targeting are more likely to choose indiscriminate violence. Work from Hultman (2007) largely supports this viewpoint, finding that civilians are increasingly attacked after forces suffer battlefield losses. In contrast, such violence is unnecessary following battlefield gains because victories elicit popular support as civilians update their beliefs and seek to join the winning side to assure that they have a part in the benefits that an eventual outcome may produce (Gates 2002; Lichbach 1995; Wood 2003). The most recent work in this area brings in international actors, finding that civilian victimization increases as one's opponent receives external support (Wood, Kathman, and Gent 2012).

DISEASE AND DISABILITIES

Deaths remain the focal point among civil war scholars, but what about the survivors? Several bodies of work move beyond deaths to understand the broader consequences of war on health. Formative work in this vein focuses on "disability-adjusted life expectancy" (DALEs) and "disability-adjusted life years" (DALYs). Compiled by the World Health Organization (WHO), these measures capture both years of life lost due to disease and injury and years of healthy life lost due to long-term disability. An early World Health Organization (2000) report estimated that wars in 1999 alone accounted for 8.44 million DALYs lost. Ghobarah, Huth and Russett (2003) extend this work both theoretically and empirically. Arguing that civil wars hurt health due to changes in living conditions that make staying healthy more difficult (termed "technical regress") and reducing the pool of government resources that can be spent on public health, these authors find strong evidence that wars harm health in the immediate term. Importantly, they also demonstrate the long-term effects of war on health. On top of the 8.44 million DALYs lost due to direct warfare in 1999, they estimate that another 8.01 million were lost in 1999 due to the lingering effects of civil wars from 1991 to 1997.

More recent attempts to further uncover both the short-term and long-term consequences of civil conflicts on health have moved the literature a step further. Iqbal's (2010) study is impressive in this regard. In studying the health consequences of interstate and civil conflicts, Iqbal situates the discussion within the "human security" agenda. Different from more common theoretical approaches that focus on the consequences of warfare for states or leaders, the human security agenda recognizes that "it is the security of populations . . . that makes the world more secure" (5). Moving beyond deaths and disabilities, therefore, Iqbal shows that wars are harmful for a variety of indicators that directly capture the effects on the general population, including fertility rates, infant mortality, life expectancy, immunizations, diversion of funds from health to the military, and refugee flows. Coupled with earlier studies, the message from this work is clear: civil wars are harmful both in the immediate term, and their effects on health linger far into the future.

More fine-grained analyses often focus on specific cases to understand the harmful effects of warfare. Using child height as a useful proxy for the health impacts of civil

wars, a variety of studies have shown that exposure to civil war has a significant negative effect. For example, Bundervoet et al. (2009) find that while all child heights in
Burundi were significantly lower than those for similarly aged children in the United
States, children with direct exposure to conflict were significantly shorter than nonaf-
fected children. Studies showing similar effects come from places like Zimbabwe (Alderman, Hoddinot, and Kinsey 2006), Rwanda (Akresh, Verwimp, and Bundervoet
2011), and Iraq (Guerrero-Serdán 2009). The mechanism behind these deleterious
health effects is largely undernourishment due to the displacement of individuals. A
2009 UNICEF report claims that two-thirds of the undernourished under five years
of age—a full 98.5 million children—live in conflict-affected countries.

Another mechanism that has been analyzed is rape, which has greatly contributed
to the spread of HIV and other diseases, particularly in Africa (Carballo and Solby
2001; Cohen and Nordås 2014). In places like Rwanda, rape was used as a weapon
of war, resulting in an increase of HIV prevalence rates from around 3 to 11 percent
(DelaCruz 2007). In other instances, girls exchange sex for security, forging relationship with officers in what has been termed "survival sex" (Schoepf 2002; Zack-
Williams 1999). Thus, while studies on the impact of civil wars have often focused
on the abduction of boys to be used as child soldiers, more recent work has shown
that girls are also used as soldiers and have the added burden of sexual exploitation
and forced marriage (Geneva Declaration 2008; WCRWC 2006).

Taken together, work on the nonlethal impacts of civil war on health paints a dire
picture. While battlefield deaths are clearly common, an emerging consensus demonstrates that hunger and disease are likely more lethal than munitions (Ghobarah,
Huth and Russett 2003; Guha-Sapir 2005). Child deaths due to hunger and diseases
accounted for almost half of the 5.4 million deaths from fighting in the Democratic
Republic of Congo from 1998 to 2007 (Coghlan et al. 2008), for example, and diar-
rhea was the biggest killer in Darfur from 2004 to 2007 (Degomme and Guha-Sapir
2010; Depoortere et al. 2004). Though deaths directly tied to warfare should continue to be an important area of study, we must clearly think beyond the battlefield
to understand the true health impacts of civil wars.

MENTAL HEALTH

One final area that has received increasing attention in the literature is the psychological harm caused by civil wars. Much of this work focuses on children—both
those who fought and those who suffered away from the battlefield. Regarding the
former, a commonly cited figure claims that anywhere from 200,000 to 300,000
children are being used by both governments and rebels in ongoing armed conflicts
(Human Rights Watch 2007). Noncombatant children include around 20 million
homeless and another 1 million separated from their parents (Betancourt and Khan
2008). Though nascent, researchers have gained significant ground in understanding
how either direct combat or exposure to warfare influences mental health.

Work coming from both psychology and sociology has long understood that social ties like being in "connected" neighborhoods or schools and belonging to youth groups are integral to positive mental health outcomes (Kliewer et al. 1998; Kliewer et al. 2001; Hirschi 1969). The importance of these attachments is even more profound when children attempt to cope in difficult circumstances (Rutter 1985; Werner 1989). Landmark studies from scholars like Freud and Burlingham (1943) and Henshaw and Howarth (1941) found that exposure to caring adults was integral to children being able to cope with their exposure to warfare in World War II.

More recent studies focused directly on civil wars yield similar conclusions both in terms of the harmful negative effects of conflicts and the mechanisms by which children learn to cope with warfare. Studies have shown that war-related traumatic events contribute to both short-term health distress and longer-term psychopathology in both children and adolescents (Lustig et al. 2004; Barenbaum et al. 2004; Betancourt and Williams 2008; Sany 2010). These effects are astounding when we consider the sheer number of children affected by warfare. Recent studies have shown that 39 percent of Iraqi refugee children in Jordan had lost someone close to them, and 43 percent had directly witnessed violence (Clements 2007). Evidence elsewhere demonstrates how these experiences influence a variety of outcomes, such as impaired learning and poor achievement in Afghanistan, Bosnia and Herzegovina, Gaza, and Sierra Leone (Betancourt et al. 2008; Elbert et al. 2009; Tamashiro 2010).

HEALTH BEYOND THE BATTLE ZONE

Though most studies focus on the health of individuals either directly in war-torn states or the health of those who have fled, a growing body of work analyzes the health impact on people who have no direct ties to civil conflicts. Most of this work focuses on how the spread of refugees can have deleterious consequences for host states (Siverson and Starr 1991; Gleditsch 2007). Migration of individuals away from conflict areas is usually forced, as individuals flee their homes to survive. Migration can also be thought of as an economic coping strategy (Lindley 2007; Czaika and Kis-Katos 2009). Either way, we have sufficient evidence to suggest that migrants bring diseases with them when they spread to new areas. A study from Baez (2011) in Tanzania, for example, found that the civil war in Rwanda negatively affected adult height and child mortality and spread infectious diseases. This case coincides with Montalvo and Reynal-Querol's (2007) broader study, which shows an increase in malaria rates for countries that host refugees. And while neighbors bear the brunt of the negative health affects due to migration, at least some evidence suggests that civil wars can have a global effect on health. For example, Smallman-Raynor and Cliff (1991) trace the global HIV epidemic to the Ugandan civil war in 1979, where rape and refugee flows contributed to the spread of HIV throughout the world.

CIVIL WAR AND EDUCATION

Civil wars can devastate a state's education system. Both the reasons why this happens and the long-term consequences largely mimic those from the discussion of health. Education systems are harmed as the by-product of warfare at times, and are deliberately targeted at others. The effects are often immediate and long lasting, contributing to health declines and slower economic growth. In this section, I review the consequences of civil wars on education and seek to shed light on the causal processes behind the destruction. To help guide the discussion, the primary areas to be covered in this section—areas of harm, evidence, and theoretical mechanisms—are presented in figure 10.2.

The Nature of the Problem

Like health, civil wars are destructive at many levels. The destruction of the educational infrastructure has led schools to be closed in a variety of locations (Abdi 1998). For example, begun in 1983, the Sudanese civil war devastated the education infrastructure of Sudan, particularly in the south (CIA 2005). Among the few schools that remained open, class sizes averaged ninety-four students per teacher, and few buildings had qualified teachers or necessary materials like desks or textbooks (Shalita 1994; Brander 1996). Lai and Thyne's (2007) cross-national study of the impact of civil war on education from 1980 to 1997 shows that countries at war experience an average enrollment decline anywhere from 1.6 to 3.2 percent.

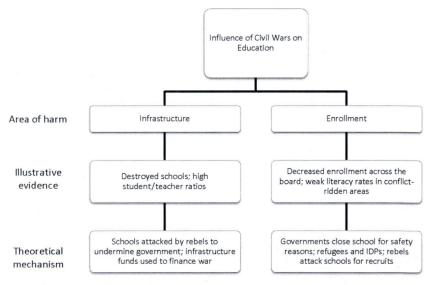

Figure 10.2.   Civil Wars and Education

Research focusing on individual countries yields similar conclusions, including work from Rwanda (Akresh and de Walque 2008), Cambodia (De Walque 2004), Tajikistan (Shemyanika 2011), Guatemala (Chamarbagwala and Morán 2011), and Côte d'Ivoire (Dabalen and Paul 2012). A recent report by UNESCO (2011) on the state of global education provides useful detail. Examining thirty-five states that experienced conflict from 1999 to 2008, they find that 42 percent (28 million) of the world's out-of-school, primary-age children come from conflict states. Gross enrollment ratios for secondary schools likewise lag nonconflict areas by 30 percent (48 percent versus 67 percent). Unsurprisingly, literacy rates, perhaps the most useful tool for examining basic educational attainment across states, sit at a meager 79 percent for the youth and 69 percent for adults in conflict-ridden areas.

MECHANISMS BEHIND THE HARM

Civil wars destroy many types of physical capital, including roads, bridges, and livestock, and other productive assets (Bruck 2001; Bundervoet and Verwimp 2005; Shemyakina 2011). They also damage human capital, resulting in deaths, disabilities, and mental trauma. Schools are no different in this regard. Research has revealed two main mechanisms to explain why civil wars have such disastrous consequences for schools.

First, schools make ripe targets for belligerents. Diverse places like Mozambique, Sudan, Angola, Guatemala, Colombia, Afghanistan, and the Philippines have seen rebels attack schools to undermine the government (Pedersen 2002). This has led state leaders to close schools in the interest of safety. Schools have been closed for months at a time due to the long-running Israeli-Palestinian conflict (Greenberg 1994), for instance, and Sengupta (2003) claims that the closure of schools has made the innocence of youth the biggest victims of the civil war in the Congo. Beyond undermining the government, both governments and rebels have found schools to be useful sources for the forced recruitment of child soldiers (O'Malley 2010). During the Sudanese civil war, for example, it was not uncommon for the military to raid schools to acquire troops (Amnesty International 2000). The long-term devastation as a result of targeting schools is revealed quite well in Liberia. During fourteen years of warfare, 80 percent of the state's 2,400 schools were put out of operation. Around 800,000 children were driven from schools during this period, explaining the meager 28 percent literacy rate seen in the country afterward (Dukuly 2004).

The second way in which civil wars can harm schools is less direct, but equally harmful. As discussed in the next section, civil wars are devastating for a state's economy. The drop in revenue provides a smaller budgetary piece of the pie to be allocated toward education. Compounding the decline in revenue is the shift in government expenditures toward the military in times of conflict. Sen (1990) indicates that poor states, where we see the bulk of civil conflicts, are often unable to meet the basic needs of their citizens due to high military spending and foreign debt. This problem is amplified by civil conflict, as states push even more of their declining revenues to the war effort. The government in Sudan increased military expenditures from around 10 to 20 percent during their most recent civil war (Mohammed 1999), for example. This is consistent with Collier and his colleagues' more systematic study (2003), which reports a nearly twofold increase in military expenditures (2.8 to 5 percent of GDP) during periods of warfare. Though Lai and Thyne (2007) do not find evidence of a direct shift from education to military expenditures, they do find an average decrease in educational expenditures of between 3.1 to 3.6 percent due to civil wars.

Taken together, the evidence clearly indicates that civil wars are harmful for education, whether the path is direct targeting or indirect budgetary problems. Education is strongly linked to the other two processes focused upon in this chapter. Schools can mitigate the mental trauma inflicted by warfare, restore predictability, and provide social support to children (Elbedour et al. 1993; Aguilar and Retamal 1998). Education is also directly linked to individual and state economic health. Psacharopoulos and Patrinos (2004) find that an additional year of education adds around 10 percent to one's pay in a low-income country. A plethora of work reveals a similarly strong connection between education and economic growth (e.g., Sianesi and Van Reenen 2003). Thus, understanding how civil wars influence education helps reveal important mechanisms at work when we discuss other consequences of conflict. I now turn to a specific focus on how civil wars influence economic growth.

CIVIL WAR AND ECONOMIC GROWTH

The link between civil conflict and economic growth is perhaps not as obvious as one might suspect. The conventional wisdom is that civil conflicts disrupt economies for a variety of reasons, ranging from destruction of human capital, physical capital, and the diversion of money from economically beneficial activities like infrastructure development to less beneficial activities like weapons procurement and production. Contrasting viewpoints point to two main areas. First, conflict may spur economic development if investments to fight the conflict result in positive externalities for the economy. Second, while the correlation between civil wars and economic growth may be negative, some scholars question whether we can clearly differentiate between cases where conflict is hurting an economy and cases where poor economies promote conflict. Empirical analyses derived from both case studies and cross-national work reveal some ambiguities. However, the overwhelming evidence indicates that civil wars cause economies to weaken. Beyond reviewing the evidence and providing support for this contention, this section attempts to clearly define the causal mechanisms by which civil wars degrade economic growth, which should put policy makers in a better position to understand what factors can best be addressed in order to put a postwar country on the firmest footing possible to improve the state's economic environment.

Understanding the Debate

Scholars are not in complete agreement on how war influences a state's economy, particularly when we consider both interstate and intrastate conflicts. Occasionally referred to as the "war renewal" school, some scholars suggest that war may produce beneficial effects for the economy by improving efficiency, reducing the power of special interests, spurring technological innovation, and advancing human capital (Olson 1982; Organski and Kugler 1980; Chan 1987; Diehl and Goertz 1985; Russett 1970; Benoit 1973, 1978). This work points to places like post–World War II Europe to explain that wars can help develop strong institutions, which promote economic growth in the long run (Tilly 1975; Blattman and Miguel 2010). Wider, cross-national studies have revealed similar outcomes (Stewart 1991; Yildirim, Sezgin, and Ocal 2005). It is important to note, though, that most studies that reveal a positive influence of war on a state's economy focus on interstate conflicts. However, some debate remains when focusing on civil wars. During the latter stages of the Salvadoran civil war (1979–1992), for instance, Stanley (1996: 237) explains that remittances from Salvadorans abroad had become the "life blood of the economy." Likewise, Sri Lanka averaged a 5 percent annual growth rate during its thirty-year civil war, though evidence of the harmful economic effects of civil war in places like Afghanistan, Burundi, and Somalia fall in line with more conventional wisdom (Snodgrass 2004; Wijeweera and Webb 2009; Ganegodage and Rambaldi 2011).

The bulk of theories and evidence point to an overall harmful effect of warfare in general and civil wars specifically. Coined the "war ruin" school, scholars have provided a plethora of mechanisms to explain why civil wars harm economic growth. The empirical work supporting this viewpoint is vast. Cross-national studies reveal a strong, negative impact of civil wars on both short-run and long-term economic growth (Chen, Loayza, and Reynal-Querol 2008; Murdoch and Sandler 2002; Kang and Meernik 2005; Collier 1999; Gyimah-Brempong and Corley 2005; Flores and Nooruddin 2009; Garriga and Phillips 2014). In two studies focused specifically on the influence of civil wars on economic growth, Collier (2007) and Hoeffler and Reynal-Querol (2003) estimate that civil war reduces average yearly economic growth by about 2.3 percent. Studies of individual cases reveal similar trends, though variations are quite wide compared to these average effects. For example, Stewart and Humphreys (1997) compare nine countries at war to average growth rates for states in the same region not at war. Their estimates indicate that war costs ranged from a high of 113.4 percent of GDP for Nicaragua to a much lower 7.8 percent in Somalia.

Taken together, we see both theories and evidence to support both the "war renewal" and the "war ruin" points of view when we consider all types of conflict. The overwhelming consensus for studies focused on civil wars, however, reveals that internal conflicts are harmful for economies both in the short and long term. In the next section, I probe the causal mechanisms that drive poor economic performance for states at war. As with the two earlier sections, figure 10.3 provides a road map of how civil wars influence economic growth.

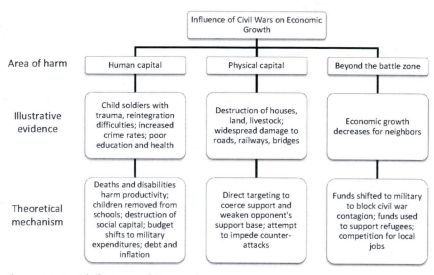

Figure 10.3.   Civil Wars and Economies

Human and Physical Capital

One way that we can better understand the harmful effects of civil wars on economic growth is by focusing on the types of damage that conflicts produce. A useful way to differentiate between types of damage is to focus on human capital (human characteristics like knowledge, skills, and health) and physical capital (factors of production like machinery, buildings, and roads), both of which contribute to economic growth. Though scholars recognize the endogeneity between these concepts, such that physical capital should have a positive effect on human capita, and vice versa (Caballe and Santos 1993; Graca, Saqib, and Philippopoulos 1995), differentiating between the two remains a well-used tool to understand the harmful effects of warfare because the type of capital destroyed influences the rate of recovery (Barro and Sala-i-Martin 2004).

The toll that civil war takes on physical capital is vast, as fighting and looting damage houses, land, livestock, and other productive assets (Bruck 2001; Bundervoet and Verwimp 2005; Shemyakina 2011). Individual production is decreased due to these damages because they remove the means by which individuals can earn a living, making it difficult to recover in post-conflict settings (Justino and Verwimp 2006; Verpoorten 2009). Far from doomed, research shows that some private enterprises can benefit from warfare, and pockets of resilience emerge in all conflict settings (McDougal 2008). Producers of staple goods, for example, can benefit from market shocks if their physical capital goes undamaged. However, the net effect of losses in physical capital is almost always negative because most individuals are consumers, and transaction costs increase when infrastructure like roads and train lines is destroyed.

Scholars have increasingly turned to human capital to understand the harshest effects of civil wars. While destruction of physical capital harms economic growth, rebounding from such destruction is relatively swift because replacements can be imported, buildings and roads can be rebuilt, and physical capital is often quite weak in conflict states before the war began (Miguel and Roland 2011; Cerra and Saxena 2008; Collier and Duponchel 2013). Thus, scholars increasingly claim that human capital losses reveal the harshest long-term economic impacts of civil war (Barro and Sala-i-Martin 2004; Bellows and Miguel 2006).

Three main pathways help explain how destruction in human capital contributes to slow or negative economic growth. The first is directly related to the earlier discussions on health and education. Deaths, disabilities, and psychological trauma due to warfare reduce or remove individuals' abilities to contribute to household income, which can push vulnerable households below the critical threshold of survivability (Beegle 2005; Bruck and Schindler 2007). When households suffer deaths or injuries due to conflict, they often choose to replace otherwise productive adults with child workers to compensate for lost income (Dasgupta 1993; Duryea, Lam, and Levinson 2007). Though this may help household survival in the short term, the impact of lost schooling on the economy is to deplete the future generation's stock of human capital (Akresh and de Walque 2008; Swee 2009; Merrouche 2006; Rodriguez and Sanchez 2009; Case and Paxson 2006; Maccini and Young 2009; Psacharopoulos and Patrinos 2004). Both forced and voluntary recruitment of child soldiers likewise hurts the capacity of the youth to accumulate skills and education, trapping them in long-term, low-productive activities (Blattman and Annan 2010).

A second mechanism by which civil wars hurt economies is by destroying social capital, which refers to societal norms and structures that yield trust, cooperation, and strong governance (Fukuyama 2001; Poder 2011; Kitissou and Yoon 2014; Putnam 1993). Social capital reduces transaction costs from asymmetric information, increasing cooperation in ways that allow for efficient functioning of modern economies (Algan and Cahuc 2010; Knack and Keefer 1997). As explained by Fukuyama (2001), social capital cannot be easily created or rebuilt because it derives from factors outside the government's control, such as religion, tradition, and shared experiences. Low social capital has been linked to the onset of economic and social failures, including civil war, and further destruction of social capital during conflict is apt to make postwar economic growth all the more difficult (Robinson and Schmid 1994). Recounting his childhood experience during the 1990s civil war in Sierra Leone, for example, Ishmael Beah's (2007) bestseller, *A Long Way Gone: Memoirs of a Boy Soldier*, vividly captures the destruction of social capital in his home country. Renowned for its brutality, the leading RUF (Revolutionary United Front) rebel group employed child soldiers extensively. As Beah and other children fled the conflict, they found no assistance because people had learned to fear even young children as potential killers. As he explains, "Everyone stopped feeling for anyone at all." Thus, even basic social norms like protecting children can quickly unravel during civil conflicts.

A final way in which civil wars damage human capital is the result of how states allocate funds when responding to threats. Early work often claimed that military strength was a modernizing force that promoted economic growth by maintaining stability for effective policy implementation and by controlling actors who would otherwise be slow to change (Halpern 1963; Levy 1966). More recent work, often referred to as the "guns for butter" theory, claims that money allocated to the military takes away resources from social programs (Adeola 1996). Empirical analyses largely support the latter viewpoint, as numerous studies have shown the deleterious effect of military spending on social programs that are needed for economic growth (Russett 1969; Dixon and Moon 1986; Huang and Mintz 1990; Looney 1990; Apostolakis 1992; Collier et al. 2003; Galvin 2003). Beyond crowding out investment in social programs, military spending harms economic development by increasing inflation as money is printed to pay for the war effort (Deger 1986), increasing external debt as states seek to cover war costs (Smyth and Narayan 2009), and diverting labor from more productive sectors (Deger 1985). These processes are likely in any state, but they are compounded by warfare as governments face revenue declines due to lost foreign direct investment, reduced tourism, and capital flight (Phillips 2014).

Though some debate remains, the bulk of theoretical arguments and empirical evidence indicates that civil wars damage state economies, and scholars have gained significant ground in clarifying the mechanisms by which civil wars harm economic growth. One final area deserving of consideration is the influence that civil wars have on neighboring and global economies.

Economies beyond the Conflict Zone

The bulk of the literature linking civil wars to economic growth rightly focuses on the states that experience the conflict, as these actors are likely to face the largest challenges in postwar recovery. As discussed in Erika Forsberg's earlier chapter (chapter 5, this volume), however, a newer and growing body of literature looks beyond the warring states' borders, seeking to understand how civil wars influence neighbors and other actors in the region. Scholars like Murdoch and Sandler (2002, 2004), for example, have shown that having a neighbor involved in a civil war reduces economic growth. Two main mechanisms, both of which are linked to literature on the contagion effects of civil wars, shed light on this process (Collier et al. 2003; Gleditsch 2002).

First, having a neighbor at war may threaten a government because conflicts often provide cheap arms and cross-border sanctuaries to potential rebels within their own country, decreasing the opportunity costs of challenging the government. Neighboring conflicts might also produce an emulation effect as citizens see people rebelling due to conditions that they also face, particularly if ethnic similarities span the border (Kuran 1998; Lake and Rothchild 1998b; Halperin 1998). The likely response by governments in these situations is to move resources to the military to deter rebellion, which (as discussed above) is likely to harm economic growth.

Second, refugees fleeing a neighboring conflict are likely to harm the host state's economy due to uncompensated public expenditures related to the care of the refugee population (World Bank 2011). Likewise, economies can be harmed as refugees challenge neighbors for jobs (Lischer 2003) and pressure host governments to get involved in the conflict (Salehyan 2009; Salehyan and Gleditsch 2006). The influence of refugees on a host country's economy is not altogether bleak, however, and a strong body of evidence points toward several positive economic benefits. Farmers in Tanzania benefited greatly from the increased demand for agricultural goods due to the influx of refugees from Rwanda, for example (Alix-Garcia 2007; Whitaker 2002). A recent study on the refugee camp in Daadab, Kenya, likewise revealed several positive impacts of refugees on the host country's economy, including increased trading opportunities and lower food prices (Nordic Agency for Development and Ecology 2010). Other studies point to a variety of positive impacts for host countries, including the entry of well-educated refugees to staff host country hospitals and universities (Crisp et al. 2009) and economic growth spurred by remittances sent to refugees (Jacobsen 2002; Horst and Van Hear 2002). Though it would be a stretch to say that the economic benefits to countries that host refugees outweigh the costs, there is certainly evidence to suggest that civil wars create trade-offs when it comes to the movement of people.

THE PATH FORWARD

The overall notion that civil war is harmful to health, the economy, and education likely surprises no one. As this chapter has addressed, however, the consequences of civil wars often range beyond the obvious. We have seen instances where civil wars have helped specific sectors of economies, for example, and have uncovered commonly overlooked consequences like mental health, school enrollments, and social capital. In this final section, I conclude by focusing on two paths forward. First, I discuss a few areas of research that have sought to uncover mechanisms by which policy makers can ease the deleterious consequences of civil conflict. Second, I highlight areas that are particularly fruitful for further research.

Avenues for Policy

As with the flow of the chapter, I begin with health. Delineating the specific ways in which these wars harm health—whether it is by intentional targeting of civilians, undernourishment and rape, refugee flows, or some other process—is useful because it provides avenues for further study and influences policy decisions about where to invest. Death and warfare go hand in hand, and civil wars are particularly harmful due to the high rate in which noncombatants are targeted. One study that seeks to develop specific recommendations for how to limit these deaths comes from Hultman, Kathman, and Shannon (2013). These scholars seek to explain how UN interventions in civil conflicts influence the targeting of civilians. Using unique, monthly level data on the type and magnitude of UN interventions and the number of civilians killed from 1991 to 2008, these authors find that robust UN peacekeeping missions—those that employ military and police forces—dramatically reduce the number of civilians targeted with violence. Their results are robust and astonishing. For example, placing a small UN police force of 200 personnel reduces expected civilian deaths from around 100 to only 14, and a force of 500 police brings the estimates to near zero. Given that the UN often gets involved in the most difficult conflict cases (Gilligan and Stedman 2003), the promising conclusion from this line of work is that UN interventions save lives.

Regarding mental health, a plethora of work has linked social support to helping individuals overcome the consequences of their war experience. Three sources of social support have been outlined to be particularly important: instrumental support (assistance with carrying out necessary tasks), informational support (information and guidance to carry out day-to-day activities successfully), and emotional support (caring and comfort provided by others) (Sherbourne and Stewart 1991). Work focusing on various providers of social support indicates that family members, peers, and the larger community are integral to postwar psychological health. Betancourt (2005), for example, found that war-affected Chechen adolescents internalized emotions less and had fewer behavioral problems when their connectedness to these groups increased. Similar findings come from postwar studies in Colombia (Kliewer et al. 2001), Palestine (Barber 2001) and Kuwait (Llabre and Hadi 1997).

Two particularly promising findings focused on children point to avenues for policy intervention. First, caregivers can play a role in providing a "protective shield" during hardship, even if the children have lost their parents (Dybdahl 2001; Miller 1996). Second, supporting the mental health of parents, particularly mothers, has been shown to have positive effects for children (Locke et al. 1996; Dybdahl 2001). This work is important because it shows that interventions can help war-exposed individuals deal with mental trauma even if they are cut off from their immediate sources of support—their families. Likewise, supporting adults as they deal with mental trauma can have a trickle-down effect to children, magnifying such an investment. Given that most war-torn states have little access to health care of any type, even a meager attempt to deal with mental trauma is likely to have a significant impact on improving lives.

Improving a state's education system offers many promising avenues for postwar investment. Evidence indicates that the harm done by civil wars lies both in underinvestment, as resources are devoted to the war effort, and in destruction of both physical and human capital necessary for a well-functioning system of education (Lai and Thyne 2007). Thus, reallocation of funds back toward education following a conflict should be a priority. Investing in the physical educational infrastructure is likely to produce positive gains not only to education, but in economic growth as a whole.

A second main point of emphasis for improving education is devising a way to train those who have already lost years of schooling by either fighting or fleeing the conflict. A recent UNESCO (2011) report claims that 69 percent of primary school–age refugees in UNHCR (United Nations High Commissioner for Refugees) camps were attending school in 2008. Though this number is respectable under the circumstances, wide variation exists from one site to another, education rarely extends beyond the secondary level, and raw statistics hide high student-to-teacher ratios and weak infrastructure. Thus, improving access to and the quality of education remains a key avenue for further investment. Recent work focusing on demobilization, disarmament, and reintegration (DDR) sheds some light on one promising avenue for further investment in education. Phayal, Khadka and, Thyne (2015) and Humphreys and Weinstein (2007) find that those who were educated either prior or during wars face difficulties with postwar reintegration. However, even meager training opportunities during the DDR process are apt to ease the reintegration process considerably.

Moving to economic growth, at first blush, we see reason for optimism. Scholars have found that countries coming out of civil wars experience higher growth rates than the global average. However, while places like Algeria and Peru saw strong postwar recovery, economic growth following wars in Burundi and Nicaragua has been far weaker (Hoeffler et al. 2011). A recent study by Hoeffler (2012) helps shed light on why we see these disparate outcomes. In reviewing previous work and providing original analyses, she explains that foreign aid following conflicts is supportive of economic growth. However, she finds that just under half of all foreign aid is allocated to fragile states, which includes postwar states that are unable to provide basic security and economic opportunities to their citizens (Chauvet et al. 2011). Thus, postwar economic recovery could be enhanced by both increasing the volume of aid directed toward postwar states and by reallocating aid to states that are most in need of recovery.

Understanding that giving postwar states more money is perhaps unrealistic or even unhelpful if it falls into the wrong hands, scholars have gone a step further to better understand where investments should be made to spur postwar economic growth. Collier (2009) explains that the best strategy includes low taxation, increased aid, increased oversight of public spending, and low inflation. More specifically, Collier calls for a focus on employing youth with major investments in infrastructural projects. Given that postwar states often lack the capacity to efficiently allocate funds to projects like these, he also calls for a partnership between local governments, nongovernmental organizations (NGOs), and private firms to deal with public administration and spending decisions. Though we lack strong evidence indicating whether such policies would be effective, we do have evidence that postwar states, when left on their own, are largely ineffective at spurring economic growth (Kimenyi and Ajakaiye 2012; Gauthier and Wane 2007). Thus, more active support, both in terms of aid and allocation and administration of funds, is apt to support economic growth.

AREAS FOR FUTURE RESEARCH

This chapter has revealed a plethora of information about what we know regarding the harmful effects of civil wars on health, education, and economic development. Though impressive, this review has also begun to highlight places where we are in need of further discovery. The purpose of this final section is to add some clarity to these needs. I will begin with the link between academia and policy and then move toward more explicit directions for future research.

Two decades ago, Will Moore (1995b: 130) urged the following: "Given the consequences [civil] conflicts produce, it is incumbent on social scientists to provide a better understanding of these conflicts so that we may put policy makers in a better position to minimize them and, thereby, improve the human condition." In the two decades since Moore articulated this goal, scholars have gained significant ground in producing research that reveals specific and attainable ways to reduce civil violence and to ameliorate the consequences of conflicts that arise. And as articulated in the first chapter of this book, we have seen an appreciable decline in the level and frequency of civil violence as a result. However, we can point to two main areas where scholars could do more to inform policy makers.

First, though we have evidence of what is harmed by civil conflicts and what can be fixed in order to avoid the recurrence of violence, we know little about the actors that do the best job in solving postwar problems. The UN seems to be quite effective in establishing postwar peace, but we know little about which actors are best at dealing with mental trauma, rebuilding schools, or administering a postwar state's finances. As discussed above, Collier (2009) provides advice on an array of ways that actors can better deal with postwar situations, focusing largely on the economy, but we have little evidence on whether these ideas might actually work. Likewise, we have little idea whether some policies might work in one situation but not the next. The termination of secessionist conflicts, for example, may require different policies from those needed in fights over control of the state (Lasley and Thyne 2015). Likewise, postwar democracies may have different needs from postwar authoritarian regimes. Thus, a larger focus on both the actors involved in postwar recovery and the diversity of civil war types and outcomes is warranted.

Second, implications from research should continually be tempered by the fact that policy makers are under severe resource constraints in terms of human capacity and finances. Quadrupling aid to postwar countries may improve the situation, for example, but the likelihood of this happening is poor at best (Hoeffler 2012). Thus, researchers should improve their focus on where policy makers can get their biggest "bang for the buck." Some problems may sort themselves out on their own. We may see private investment increase with no policy intervention as corporations see profit in the postwar climate, for example. Likewise, rebuilding infrastructure may harness multiple goals simultaneously by spurring economic growth and providing employment. Other issues, such as dealing with mental trauma and recovering lost education for child soldiers, likely demand more long-term investments. Thus, though researchers have defined the problems with civil wars quite well, we have done far less to provide specific solutions to the problems and have done even less to inform policy makers about what solutions should take priority over others.

Beyond providing a more useful set of policy recommendations, researchers would do well to focus on three main areas for future development. First, the way in which we design studies could be improved by considering the counterfactual situations. That is, given that states experiencing civil wars likely had poor health, education, and economies to begin with, how can we be sure that the supposed harmful effects of civil conflicts would not have been bad in the absence of conflict? Multiple regression estimations can do a fair job in estimating the independent effects of variables like civil war, though trends like matching methods that we see in other areas of literature and have seen in some earlier areas of civil war work (Stewart and Humphreys 1997) would likely be worthwhile.[3]

Second, researchers could push further in understanding when and where we might see disparate civil war consequences. We have seen pockets of economic development within civil wars, for example, but we know little about where these pockets might be expected to develop elsewhere, or how they may be harnessed for more widespread growth. We also know little about what might condition the influence that civil wars have on health, education, and economic growth. Do we see the harshest effects when the government is authoritarian, for example, or when the civil war is of a particular type or involves multiple rebel groups? Moving beyond civil war as a simple dummy variable will improve our understanding of these questions.

Finally, research would be advanced by speaking across disciplinary boundaries. The work reviewed earlier on mental health rarely considers economic or political factors, for example, drawing primarily on psychological and sociological studies. The link between economists and political scientists is stronger, though many economic studies continue to ignore important political variations, just as politics-focused studies continue to ignore economic intricacies. Work on education from both political and economic camps uses only the most basic measures of educational infrastructure and competency, ignoring the vast body of comparative education work that taps into the quality of education. If we are to improve our understanding of the consequences of civil conflicts and, in Moore's words, "improve the human condition," then scholars must continually push beyond their comfort zones, be realistic about constraints for postwar development, and continue to strive to ask difficult research questions that have clear and attainable policy implications.

III

EMERGING TRENDS IN CIVIL WAR RESEARCH

11

Transitional Justice

Prospects for Postwar Peace and Human Rights

Jacqueline H. R. DeMeritt

In early 2011, Egyptians inspired by the Tunisian revolution launched a wave of popular protests. President Mubarak's National Democratic Party and his military responded with violence, culminating in the February 2 attacks on demonstrators in Tahrir Square. Allegations of torture, killings, and sexual assaults surfaced, and on February 11, Mubarak stepped down. Power was transferred to Egypt's Supreme Council of Armed Forces, which suspended the constitution and dissolved parliament. They vowed to transfer power to an elected civilian government, and Mohamed Morsi of the Muslim Brotherhood became Egypt's first democratically elected president in June of 2012. Yet discontent increased and ultimately, millions took to the streets and called for Morsi to relinquish power. Egypt's army intervened and took the reins of power in July 2013. Once again, the military suspended the constitution. Police backed by armored vehicles and bulldozers violently dispersed groups of Morsi's supporters; hundreds were killed.

Political upheaval, civil war, and human rights are inextricably linked. State-perpetrated abuse of fundamental human rights leads to popular dissent, mobilizing the opposition and risking escalation to war (e.g., Gurr 1970; Lichbach 1995; Tilly 1978; Young 2012 and this volume). Abuse is more widespread and severe during war than at other times, as states employ repression to defeat their opposition (e.g., Hibbs 1973; Kalyvas 2000; Mason and Krane 1989; Poe and Tate 1994). And genocide, often considered the most heinous form of abuse, occurs almost exclusively in the context of civil and interstate war (e.g., Harff 2003; Krain 1997; Licklider 1995a; Valentino 2005).[1]

When international war ends, opponents return to their own distinct territories. But when civil war ends, the people remain together in the same country. To paraphrase Licklider (1993: 4), how do groups of people who have been killing one another with considerable enthusiasm and success come together in a single community? How can you coexist with the people who imprisoned, disappeared, tortured, or killed your parents, your children, your friends or lovers? How can Egyptians who lived through the recent uprising stabilize their world and move forward together?

Transitional justice (TJ) is the implementation of measures designed to redress legacies of mass human rights abuses during periods of radical political change, including democratization and civil war (Teitel 2000). As the International Center for Transitional Justice (ictj.org) notes, "it seeks recognition for the victims and to promote possibilities for peace, reconciliation, and democracy." In Egypt, the Ministry for Transitional Justice and National Reconciliation was created in June 2014; it will consider the variety of institutions and processes that have evolved in pursuit of these goals, including (for example) criminal prosecutions, truth commissions, lustrations, and amnesties.[2]

The *prima facie* argument for transitional justice is clear. Advocates argue that holding individuals accountable for their abhorrent treatment of others satisfies fundamental principles of fairness. It pressures governments to adhere to publicly known and widely accepted standards of conduct and represents a break with a past in which the government failed to abide by those standards. And it offers victims a sense of justice, which promotes healing and reconciliation while dampening the desire for retribution. In short, transitional justice helps metamorphosing states establish a foundation for a peace (e.g., Akhavan 2001; Goldstone 1996; Malamud-Goti 1990; Méndez 1997).

Others have been less optimistic. Skeptics argue that dredging up the recent past will undermine efforts to move on, sharpening societal divisions in ways that exacerbate or renew conflict, weaken fledging democratic institutions, and generally "cause more harm than the original crime it purports to address" (Goldsmith and Krasner 2003: 51; see also Grono and O'Brien 2008; Huntington 1991; O'Donnell and Schmitter 1986; Vinjamuri and Snyder 2004; Zalaquett 1992).

Recently, the use of transitional justice in the aftermath of atrocities has become increasingly accepted and increasingly common. Until 2002, for example, the international community had to establish ad hoc tribunals like the International Criminal Tribunal for the Former Yugoslavia (ICTY) and the International Criminal Tribunal for Rwanda (ICTR) in order to criminally prosecute perpetrators of egregious human rights abuse. Since 2002, that role has been transferred to the permanent International Criminal Court. More generally, there has been a "rapid and dramatic shift in the legitimacy of the norms of individual criminal accountability for human rights violations and an increase in actions (such as trials) on behalf of those norms" (Sikkink and Kim 2013: 170). In the context of civil war, TJ in one form or another is now a part of most postwar peace processes, and trials and truth commissions in particular have emerged as "staple[s] of post-conflict peacebuilding efforts" (Brahm 2007: 16; Bates et al. 2007; Thoms, Ron, and Paris 2010). Scholars have called this the *justice cascade* (e.g., Lutz and Sikkink 2001; Savelsberg 2010; Sikkink 2011; Sikkink and Kim 2013), and it has spawned a new wave of social scientific research on the origins, spread, and effectiveness of transitional justice.

As other chapters in this volume make clear, the post–civil war period is not characterized by a durable peace, stability, or prosperity. In chapter 9, for example, Diehl notes that current civil war begets future civil war in over 40 percent of states. Thyne describes in chapter 10 how health, education, and the economy suffer. These deleterious effects may be mitigated through negotiated settlements, the deployment of peacekeeping missions, policy interventions, and the promotion of democracy (see chapters 8–10, this volume). But none of these strategies is a panacea for the common afflictions of post-conflict states. Can transitional justice ameliorate these problems?

This chapter maps out the emerging stream of systematic empirical research on how transitional justice affects the prospects for postwar peace, focusing particularly on its effects on recurrent conflict and government respect for human rights.[3] After introducing the most common mechanisms of transitional justice, I summarize the universe of existing empirical results in the political science literature linking TJ to two state-level outcomes: civil war and postwar human rights. Despite a growing number of systematic studies, this literature is still in its very early stages, and our cumulative understanding of the effects of transitional justice in the context of civil war is limited. I argue that this limitation follows from a lack of rigorous causal theory, which produces ungrounded differences in scope conditions and the operationalization of key concepts across existing studies. These differences prevent the literature as a whole from making compelling correlational or causal claims. I identify new goals that I believe transitional justice scholars should pursue, discuss several new datasets that are well equipped to help in that pursuit, and raise a series of as-yet unasked questions about transitional justice, civil war, and human rights.

TJ INSTITUTIONS AND PROCESSES

Transitional justice mechanisms include criminal prosecutions, truth commissions, reparations, memory projects, lustrations, amnesties, purges, and exiles. *Criminal prosecutions*, including trials and tribunals, are retributive mechanisms aimed at holding perpetrators accountable and punishing them for abuse (Elster 2004). Many prosecutions, such as those in Peru, Venezuela, and Egypt, occur within the society where the crimes occurred. When societies emerging from transition lack the capacity or political will to prosecute perpetrators domestically, justice may be pursued through hybrid courts that include international and domestic actors and draw upon international standards and practices; this was the case in Sierra Leone, Kosovo, Bosnia, Timor-Leste, and Cambodia. Finally, prosecution may occur in a purely international context, through ad hoc tribunals like the ICTY and ICTR, or through the International Criminal Court. Regardless of the context in which it occurs, advocates believe that establishing criminal responsibility offers victims a sense of justice, deters future abusers, and strengthens the rule of law (e.g., Akhavan 2001; Kritz 1996; Minow 1998; Stromseth 2003). Alternatively, one might argue that the pursuit of justice through prosecution undermines the goal of reconciliation.

Other TJ mechanisms are nonretributive, designed to offer reparation or compensation to victims (Gloppen 2005). *Truth commissions*, like the South African Truth and Reconciliation Commission and the Chilean Comisión Nacional de Verdad y Reconciliación, are temporary, nonjudicial bodies that are officially sanctioned, authorized, or empowered by the state to investigate a pattern of abuses over a period of time (Hayner 2001: 14). They create historical records of human rights abuse that help victims find closure by learning more about the events they suffered, making it difficult to deny or rewrite history, and signaling an official commitment to prevent recurrent atrocities (Brahm 2007; Goldstone 1996). *Reparations* may be material, such as financial payments and social services like education or health care. They may also be symbolic, such as public acknowledgment or apology. In East Timor, for example, perpetrators made amends by rebuilding homes that had been destroyed or providing a set number of hours of community service (Magarrell 2007). *Memory projects*—like the monuments, annual prayer ceremony, and mass grave in northern Uganda—create records and preserve memories of people or events (Shaw et al. 2010). Proponents believe that these nonretributive measures pave the way for reconciliation by helping victims acknowledge and recover from the physical, psychological, and social damage caused by past brutality (e.g., Aukerman 2002; Borer 2006; Drumbl 2007; Long and Brecke 2003). Alternatively, one might argue that these measures sacrifice people's desire for justice in the hopes of achieving reconciliation.

A third set of TJ mechanisms has both retributive and nonretributive elements. *Lustration* identifies politicians who collaborated with past abusive regimes and either limits their access from public office or disqualifies them from holding office entirely. This helps to ensure that the new government will neither appear nor behave like the old regime, and signals a new chapter in state history (Cohen 1995; David 2011; Kaminski and Nalepa 2006; Nalepa 2010). *Amnesties* are granted by passing retroactive laws "to eliminate any record of crimes occurring by barring criminal prosecutions and/or civil suits. In extinguishing liability for a crime, amnesty assumes that a crime has been committed" (Mallinder 2009: 2–3). They are typically granted in exchange for truth, and mark a turning point between the conflict-ridden climate of the past and a new, more peaceable social climate (Cobban 2007: 199; see also Huyse 1995; Kritz 1995). Finally, *purges* remove perpetrators from public office, while *exiles* remove them from the state. Like lustrations, these mechanisms impose tangible punishment for abuse while also providing a psychological break with the past (Arthur 2009; Elster 2004; Teitel 2000, 2003).

These TJ institutions and processes are not mutually exclusive, and multiple mechanisms are often used in a single case. In the aftermath of its 1994 genocide, for example, Rwanda adopted mechanisms including domestic criminal prosecution (the Gacaca courts), international criminal prosecution (the International Criminal Tribunal for Rwanda), and a truth commission (the National Unity and Reconciliation Commission).[4] More generally, almost two-thirds of transitional countries that established truth commissions between 1979 and 2004 also held trials, and many of these had amnesties as well (Sikkink and Walling 2007: 430).

EMPIRICAL EVIDENCE OF TJ'S EFFECTS

So how do the various TJ mechanisms described above affect civil war and postwar human rights? I explore this question in this section by reviewing empirical work on the topic.

Effects of Individual Mechanisms

Between 1991 and 2001, as Yugoslavia dissolved, a series of separate but related military conflicts occurred within its boundaries.[5] In April 1992, the Yugoslav republic of Bosnia-Herzegovina declared its independence and the Bosnian War began. Bosnian Serb forces, backed by the Serb-dominated Yugoslav army, set out to "cleanse" their territory of Bosnian Muslims (known as Bosniaks) and Bosnian Croats (Croatian civilians). By 1995, around one hundred thousand people were dead. Eighty percent of the victims were Bosniak (Malcolm 1996).

The most famous and deadly event was the July 1995 massacre at Srebrenica, a Bosniak-dominated town under the watch of UN peacekeepers. Serb general Ratko Mladić and his forces entered the town and murdered roughly seven thousand men and boys; it was the single largest massacre in Europe since World War II. Many of those who survived the initial massacre were sent to concentration or detention camps where they were beaten, tortured, and executed en masse. Srebrenica women were often taken to rape camps, there to be raped and tortured until they became pregnant (Honig 1996).

The International Criminal Tribunal for the former Yugoslavia was established in 1993 to prosecute war crimes committed during each of the Yugoslav Wars, including the events at Srebrenica and other instances of ethnic cleansing that occurred in Bosnia-Herzegovina. Ratko Mladić was arrested on May 26, 2011, and was charged with two counts of genocide, five counts of crimes against humanity, and four counts of violations of the laws or customs of war. His trial began in May 2012, and judgment is expected in November 2017.[6] More generally, the ICTY's prosecutions have "dramatically changed the civil landscape and permitted the ascendancy of more moderate political forces backing multiethnic co-existence and nonviolent democratic process" (Akhavan 2001: 9). In Bosnia-Herzegovina and throughout the former Yugoslavia, the ICTY seems to have played an appreciable role in preventing a relapse to civil war and limiting postwar human rights abuse.

This case narrative suggests that retributive TJ improved the prospects for postwar peace and human rights in the former Yugoslavia. Is this result generalizable? The earliest empirical research of TJ's effects on postwar peace looked at the impacts of retributive mechanisms (i.e., criminal prosecutions) like the ICTY. With respect to recurrent civil war, anecdotal evidence suggests that criminal prosecutions reduce the risk of recurrent conflict (Akhavan 2001), while several systematic studies find that prosecutions have no discernable effect on recurrent conflict (Meernik 2005; Sikkink and Walling 2007; Lie, Binningsbø, and Gates 2007; Meernik, Nichols, and King

2010; Sikkink 2011). In a more nuanced analysis, Loyle and Appel (2014) find that trials selectively and solely targeting the opposition do not affect the risk of relapse to civil war, while comprehensive trials targeting both governments and rebels do reduce the risk of recurrence.

Research into criminal prosecutions' effects on postwar human rights produces two contrasting findings. Several studies (Sikkink and Walling 2007; Kim and Sikkink 2010, 2013; Sikkink 2011; Sikkink and Kim 2013) find that prosecutions improve state respect for human rights,[7] while another study (Meernik, Nichols, and King 2010) finds that prosecutions have no effect on state respect for human rights.

With respect to nonretributive mechanisms, scholars have focused specifically on truth commissions. Some analyses (Long and Brecke 2003; Snyder and Vinjamuri 2003/2004; Lie, Binningsbø, and Gates 2007; Loyle and Appel 2014) suggest that such commissions reduce the risk of recurrent civil war. Wiebelhaus-Brahm (2010) examines truth commissions' effect on state respect for human rights; his multimethod approach produces two very different results, suggesting first that truth commissions improve respect for human rights, and then that these commissions actually worsen respect for human rights. Last, Lie, Binningsbø, and Gates (2007) examine the effects of reparations on recurrent civil war. They find that reparations have no effect on recurrence in all states taken together, or in authoritarian regimes considered alone. However, reparations do reduce the risk of civil war relapse in democracies.

Finally, with respect to mechanisms with both retributive and nonretributive elements, four studies examine the effects of amnesties on the risk of recurrent civil war. Both Loyle and Appel (2014) and Snyder and Vinjamuri (2003/2004) find that amnesties reduce the risk of civil war recurrence. The two remaining studies find that amnesty's impact depends on political institutions (i.e., regime type): Lie, Binningsbø, and Gates (2007) find that amnesties have no effect on recurrence in all states taken together, or in authoritarian regimes on their own. In democracies, amnesties appear to increase the risk of relapse to civil war. Melander (2013) finds that amnesty provisions in peace agreements reduce the risk of civil war recurrence, but only in authoritarian regimes; in democracies or regimes in flux, his results show no significant effect of amnesties on a return to civil war.

Beyond amnesties, Lie, Binningsbø, and Gates (2007) find that the effect of exiles depends on regime type, such that they reduce the risk of recurrent civil war in democracies but have no significant effect in other regimes. And purges, in their results, have no effect on recurrent civil war regardless of the type of regime in which they occur. Last, Loyle and Appel (2014) find that reparations are associated with a reduced risk of recurrence.

EFFECTS OF MULTIPLE MECHANISMS

The findings described above examine the effects of one transitional justice mechanism in isolation, or consider them as independent influences in multivariate analyses.

Yet as mentioned above, multiple mechanisms are often used in a single case. When considered as an additive index (so that the presence of one more TJ mechanism increases the amount of TJ by a value of one), the use of additional mechanisms has no significant impact on the recurrence of civil wars (Lie, Binningsbø, and Gates 2007).

When considered as available "packages" of TJ, however, anecdotal evidence suggests that different combinations of mechanisms may reduce the risk of civil war relapse. Consider, for example, East Timor. Following the 1974 Portuguese revolution, Portugal abandoned its colony on Timor; in 1975, civil war broke out between East Timorese political parties. Indonesia invaded shortly thereafter, fearing a communist state in the region. The Indonesian occupation lasted for twenty-four years, and was marked by violence and brutality. East Timorese civilians suffered displacement, sexual violence, and torture. Approximately 18,600 civilians were killed, and another 84,200 died from hunger and illness (Burgess 2004).

In 1999, the UN organized a referendum on autonomy of East Timor. In the months leading up to the vote, paramilitary groups attacked independence activists and warned of a "bloodbath" in the event of a vote for independence (Nevins 2005: 91). When 78.5 percent of East Timorese voted for independence, Indonesian security forces and their militia began attacking civilians and setting fires around the capital city, Dili. Ultimately, more than 1,400 lives were lost (Nevins 2005).

In the wake of the Indonesian occupation and post-referendum violence, three separate TJ institutions were established. In 1999 the UN set up the Serious Crimes Investigations and Prosecutions Process to investigate serious crimes committed during the conflict and indicted nearly four hundred subjects. In 2002, the independent Commission for Reception, Truth, and Reconciliation (CAVR) was established to "inquire into human rights violations committed on all sides, between April 1974 and October 1999, and facilitate community reconciliation with justice for those who committed less serious offenses."[8] In 2005, Indonesia and East Timor established the bilateral Commission for Truth and Friendship (CTF). Perhaps as a result of these efforts at transitional justice, East Timor has seen neither recurrent civil war nor exceptionally high levels of repression since the 1999 referendum.

Trials and truth commissions also reduced the risk of recurrence in the former Yugoslavia (except Macedonia) and Peru. Formal amnesties combined with truth commissions reduced the likelihood of civil war renewal in El Salvador and South Africa; and the combination of de facto amnesty and a truth commission reduced the risk of relapse in Guatemala (Snyder and Vinjamuri 2003/2004).

The effects of multiple mechanisms on state respect for human rights are cohesive and suggest that different combinations of mechanisms lead to less human rights abuse then we might otherwise expect. Snyder and Vinjamuri (2003/2004) suggest that the TJ packages that reduced the risk of recurrent civil war also contributed to improved human rights practices in those same states. Sikkink and Walling (2007) show that the combination of trials and truth commissions improves human rights performance more than trials alone. Olsen, Payne, and Reiter (2010b, 2010c) find that trials and amnesties, as well as trials, amnesties, and truth commissions, generate improvements in state respect for human rights. In short, transitional justice mechanisms may be more effective in reducing conflict and human rights abuses in the long term when multiple TJ approaches are adopted in the post-conflict environment.

SYNTHESIS AND LIMITATIONS

The empirical study of transitional justice's impacts on postwar peace and human rights has made great strides in the past decade. Perhaps the most notable development has been a move away from the earlier tendency to concentrate only on cases that have experienced TJ (Thoms et al. 2010: 346). Certainly this literature has followed a pattern common to many areas of conflict studies, starting with historiographic description and debate that relied on anecdotal evidence and suffered from sample selection bias, and then growing more sophisticated in both case selection criteria and methods of analysis. Of the sixteen empirical tests discussed above, only two focus solely on cases where transitional justice was used; the other fourteen examine both positive and negative cases. With respect to methodology, only one of the studies relies exclusively on anecdotal evidence. Four others use correlational statistics, eight make use of multivariate analysis, and the remaining three employ some combination of these methods.

Overall, most studies find that TJ has either desirable or negligible effects, and evidence of strong negative impacts is relatively rare. This conclusion is tenuous, however, largely because extant work has privileged ad hoc hypotheses over causal logic. Scholars have tended to ask whether transitional justice strengthens postwar peace and human rights rather than focusing on how and why these improvements occur. When scholars have developed causal logic that points the way to new research questions and empirical expectations, others in the community have failed to engage. This failure has also led to major differences in scope conditions and in the operationalization of key concepts across empirical efforts. Consequently, the literature has been unable to achieve the kind of cumulative knowledge that allows social scientists to make compelling causal—or even correlational—claims.

CAUSAL THEORY?

A rigorous theory should explain known empirical patterns, rendering facts informative by specifying logical linkages among the terms in our hypotheses. It should also point the way forward, guiding the search toward new questions and new empirical regularities. Consider, for example, this simple stylized story. Assume that state leaders are driven to maintain power and a monopoly on the forces of coercion within their borders. When faced with domestic challenges, such leaders are likely to respond with human rights abuses. Repression, after all, is a highly effective and relatively inexpensive way to quell dissent, dissuade future opposition to the regime, and consolidate power and control.

If all this is true, then one way for transitional justice to reduce repression is to deter leaders from abusing their citizens by threatening their grasp on power. Retributive TJ is capable of imposing such a threat, while wholly nonretributive TJ is not. Thus, we might expect that criminal prosecutions would reduce postwar human rights abuse, while truth commissions would not. This explains findings in Lie, Binningsbø, and Gates (2007), Sikkink and Walling (2007), Kim and Sikkink (2010, 2013), Sikkink (2011), and Sikkink and Kim (2013). Because the causal pressure here is the *threat* of retributive TJ, we should expect these mechanisms to reduce human rights abuse when and where they are applied *and* anywhere else they raise leaders' expectations of punishment for abuse. Thus retributive TJ may have deterrent effects for the postwar leadership, or in states that share borders or other linkages with the state where TJ is used. And, in fact, Sikkink and Kim (2013) find just such a neighborhood effect.

This causal logic also implies that leaders are most vulnerable when their transgressions are readily identified as well as punished. Thus, human rights abuse should be deterred more in the context of both truth commissions *and* trials than in the presence of trials alone. Empirical results from Snyder and Vinjamuri (2003/2004), Sikkink and Walling (2007), Olsen, Payne, and Reiter (2010b, 2010c) support these expectations.

This brief exercise demonstrates the power of careful theorizing. While the empirical studies of TJ's effects on human rights do not advance a causal logic, two studies focused on civil war recurrence do invest in theory.[9] For Melander (2013), the research question is whether amnesty provisions in peace agreements reduce the likelihood of civil war recurrence. His theoretical argument begins with the claim that amnesties are only effective (i.e., capable of increasing societal peace and reducing the risk of conflict recurrence) when they are credible and enforceable. In democratic states and regimes in flux, leadership changes are likely, and the political future is uncertain. Authoritarian regimes, in contrast, are both less changeable and more certain. Because authoritarian regimes are more credible, then, amnesties in these states are more likely to be enforced and less likely to be undermined. Thus, amnesties should reduce the risk of conflict recurrence, but only when political institutions are authoritarian.

Empirical results support Melander's expectations. Perhaps more importantly, his theoretical framework points the way to new and promising research questions and empirical expectations. Do political institutions condition the effectiveness of other forms of transitional justice? Truth commissions, for example, depend on individual victims to identify perpetrators; if victims are unwilling to come forward, then crimes cannot be acknowledged and truth cannot be told. Might victims be unwilling to name names in the shadow of uncertainty cast by regularized leadership change? If so, then truth commissions in democracies seem less likely to reduce political violence than comparable commissions in an autocratic context. Lustrations ban collaborators with abusive regimes from participation in the new government. Might they be poorly equipped to prevent a return to civil war or widespread abuse when the new government is likely to be replaced in a relatively short time, through regularly scheduled elections or another institutionalized political process?

For Loyle and Appel (2014), the research question is whether post-conflict justice (i.e., transitional justice occurring in the aftermath of civil war) reduces the risk of recurrent civil war. Building on the civil conflict literature cited throughout this volume, they argue that recurrence depends on how easily conflict entrepreneurs can mobilize former rebels and their supporters against the government. Mobilization is easier when potential opponents feel aggrieved against the government, so one way to avoid recurrence is to address and lessen those grievances. Post-conflict justice is well equipped to mitigate grievances that result from a previous conflict; it also signals the post-conflict government's continued commitment to addressing future grievances as they arise. Thus, post-conflict justice attenuates conflict entrepreneurs' ability to mobilize would-be opponents by addressing and alleviating their motivations to rebel.

Empirical results support the insight that TJ reduces the likelihood of civil war relapse only when it helps alleviate grievances. Loyle and Appel's theoretical framework suggests some new and promising research questions and empirical expectations. Might nonretributive TJ mechanisms increasingly reduce the likelihood of civil war recurrence as they are increasingly able to address lingering or new grievances at civil war's end? If so, then truth commissions with broad investigatory powers may reduce political violence more than comparable commissions that are limited in the issues they can engage. Reparations can be either material or symbolic; is one form more powerful for reducing grievances than the other? Given a limited pool of resources, might reparations spread more thinly but extended to more potential opponents more effectively reduce political violence than larger reparations packages offered to fewer potential opponents?

Theoretical logic can also be found in research that does not contain systematic empirical tests. Hayner (2010: 182) suggests that truth commissions aim to prevent further violence and rights abuse "by breaking the cycle of revenge and hatred between former enemies, somehow encouraging reconciliation between opposing groups who may feel they have much to hate or fear in the other, or a history to avenge." These attempts are embedded in truth commission reports and include recommended prosecutions, reparations, lustrations, apologies, and political and institutional reforms. Their success has varied widely but systematically, based on several factors. Does the truth commission have the power to make binding recommendations? If so, does it have direct powers of enforcement to ensure that those recommendations are implemented? Success also varies, Hayner argues, with the specificity of the recommendations and the international community's willingness to push national authorities toward implementation. The United Nations, for example, led a strong push for implementation in El Salvador, but was "considerably less assertive" in its stance toward implementation in Sierra Leone (Hayner 2010: 194). Thus Hayner lays out a clear causal pathway for TJ influence and provides some observable indicators likely to covary with success. Yet this process, and the hypotheses it implies, has not yet been engaged by the empirical literature.

Rather than engage these new questions and expectations, or develop new causal arguments, most extant work has used empirical analysis to test ad hoc hypotheses—expectations based on hunches rather than carefully derived from a logical framework (Zinnes 1976). As a result, it is difficult to know how to interpret puzzling empirical results. Scholars have relied on post hoc explanations, which do little to further our cumulative understanding of how, why, or under which conditions TJ improves the prospects for postwar peace.

SCOPE CONDITIONS AND OPERATIONAL CHOICES?

The lack of careful and rigorous theorizing has also led to problematic differences in scope conditions and operationalization of key concepts across existing research efforts. A theory's scope is "a set of conditions such that, if the conditions are satisfied, the theory will not be found false" (Walker and Cohen 1985: 291; see also Freese 1980; George and Bennett 2004; Toulmin 1957). It is, in other words, a domain of applicability or a context within which a given hypothesis is expected to hold. A central goal of the empirical transitional justice literature has been to construct general theories of TJ's effects. Thus, hypotheses take the general form "the presence of transitional justice mechanisms decreases the likelihood of civil war (or increases human rights performance)." Nonetheless, nearly every study reviewed above imposes systematic and consequential restrictions on the sample subjected to empirical testing. Of the eighteen tests discussed in this chapter, two are case specific. Three include only states undergoing democratic transition in Latin America, and five include only democratic transitions without regional limitation. Six include only countries emerging from civil war, one includes only post–civil war democracies, and one imposes no scope restrictions whatsoever. Because results within one context cannot be assumed to generalize outside that context, and in the absence of theoretical justification for limited scope, the literature's ability to make broad claims about the effects of transitional justice is limited.

Accumulation of knowledge has been limited, too, as a result of differences in operationalization. With respect to independent variables, different scholars have operationalized transitional justice differently. Most tests are designed to assess the effects of a specific TJ mechanism, and authors are careful to limit their conclusions appropriately. The problem arises within these subsets, when one concept is operationalized in multiple ways *but conclusions about that concept's (in)effectiveness are largely unqualified*. With respect to criminal prosecutions, for example, some studies (e.g., Kim and Sikkink 2010) allow trials to affect their outcomes of interest only in years in which a trial was ongoing (country prosecution years). Others (Meernik et al. 2010) allow domestic prosecutions to have an effect beginning in the year the first trial began and continuing for the five-year period after the trial's end, allowing international tribunals to have an effect beginning in the year of establishment and continuing throughout their temporal domain.

Regarding truth commissions, one study (Long and Brecke 2003) investigates the impacts of reconciliation events including but not limited to truth commissions, while another (Wiebelhaus-Brahm 2010) examines the presence/absence of a truth commission as well as its issuance of a final report. And in the case of studies investigating multiple TJ institutions and processes, those mechanisms are sometimes considered independent influences (e.g., Snyder and Vinjamuri 2003/2004), and at other times they are treated additively (e.g., Sikkink and Walling 2007). These studies also measure specific mechanisms differently. Sikkink and Walling (2007), for example, measure the presence or absence of trials at any part of the prosecution process, while Olsen, Payne, and Reiter (2010b, 2010c) account only for trials that ended in verdicts.

Measurement choices also commonly differ across studies purporting to engage the same dependent variable. Most studies of TJ's effects on wars leverage data from the PRIO/Uppsala Armed Conflict Database (e.g., Kim and Sikkink 2010, 2013; Lie et al. 2007; Meernik et al. 2010), but one relies instead on a thirty-two-death threshold (Long and Brecke 2003). Differences also exist within the subset of studies using the PRIO/Uppsala data: some (e.g., Sikkink and Walling 2007; Sikkink 2011) combine civil and interstate wars into a single outcome of interest, while others (Lie et al. 2007; Meernik et al. 2010) focus only on civil war. And while all studies of TJ's effects on human rights use the Political Terror Scale (PTS), the Cingranelli-Richards Physical Integrity Index (CIRI), or both, there are differences in how those data are employed: some (e.g., Olsen et al. 2013b, 2013c; Wiebelhaus-Brahm 2010) use the levels of the relevant measure(s), while others (e.g., Meernik et al. 2010; Sikkink and Walling 2007) use binary indicators of positive change.[10]

Operational differences, then, are quite common in both independent and dependent variables. More importantly, these differences appear to be random rather than driven by different—and explicit—theoretical concepts. Scholars tend not to place their own measurement choices in the context of the broader literature or consider how different decisions may lead to different conclusions without casting doubt on earlier work. Without this type of cross-study engagement, and careful grounding in conceptual definitions, empirical results cannot come together to advance our collective knowledge of postwar transitional justice.

PATHS FORWARD

In this penultimate section, I suggest two ways that the limitations noted above might be addressed, I describe two new TJ data collection efforts and suggest some profitable future data collection possibilities, and I raise some as-yet unasked questions about how TJ relates to postwar peace and human rights.

NEW GOALS

To some extent, scholars have already begun to engage scope conditions as described above. Meernik et al., for example, consider the potential effects of domestic trials independent of international tribunals, and vice versa. Wiebelhaus-Brahm investigates whether truth commissions have differential impacts when they do or do not publicly issue a final report. Long and Brecke find that reconciliation events produce a lasting peace only when they involve public truth telling and the redefinition of perpetrators' identities and social roles. Snyder and Vinjamuri find that TJ success depends on weak spoilers, a strong judiciary, and well-established democratic institutions. And Lie et al. find that TJ has effects in post-conflict democracies that are not clear across all post-conflict states. The trouble stems not from a lack of attention, but from a lack of systematic and rigorous causal logic. An abundance of post hoc theorizing and the failure to make scope conditions explicit are symptomatic of this problem.

Cumulation in social science can (perhaps should) begin with precise theorizing, which leads naturally to the thoughtful identification of suitable samples and operationalization of key concepts both within and across individual efforts. One goal of future research should be the careful development of causal arguments, particularly with regard to context. As noted earlier, researchers should ask not only *whether* transitional justice strengthens postwar peace and human rights, but also *how* and *why* these improvements occur. They should be mindful of circumstances in which their arguments may not apply, including limitations with respect to transition type, regime type, geography, time, and other characteristics. And they should test their theories aptly, measuring concepts and defining samples in ways that reflect theoretical expectations.

Currently, scholars impose scope conditions and operationalize concepts implicitly. A second goal of future research, related to and following naturally from the first, should be to state theoretically grounded assumptions and choices explicitly. The more transparent a research effort is, the more directly it can be engaged by future efforts and the more easily we can pursue a collective understanding of postwar TJ. A discussion of the generalizability of results would be another welcome addition to any (or every) new empirical contribution.

NEW DATA

The push for cumulation can also be pursued through data. Heretofore, most TJ researchers have coded their own data.[11] This isolation inevitably leads to a diverse set of coding rules. As more scholars test theoretical expectations using data born of a single set of coding rules, the reliability of the literature's results—taken as a set—can only grow. The recent introduction of two publicly available data collection efforts should make this goal increasingly easy to achieve.[12]

First, the Justice Data Project is meant for scholars wishing to test hypotheses about transitional justice in both the wartime and postwar environments (Binningsbø, Loyle, Elster, and Gates 2012a, 2012b). The project includes two distinct datasets: the Post-Conflict Justice (PCJ) dataset contains information on TJ in the aftermath of all internal, internationalized internal, and extra-systemic armed conflicts identified by the PRIO/Uppsala Armed Conflict Dataset between 1946 and

2006, and version 1 is available in its entirety; these are the data used by Loyle and Appel (2014) as discussed above. The During-Conflict Justice (DCJ) dataset expands the PCJ scope of inquiry to include TJ processes implemented while conflict is still ongoing. DCJ data collection is complete, and the data are being finalized for public release. Both datasets contain detailed information on TJ processes including criminal prosecutions, truth commissions, reparations, amnesties, purges, and exiles.

Second, the Transitional Justice Research Collaborative allows scholars to test hypotheses about transitional justice during regime shifts toward democracy (Payne and Sikkink 2014), including democratization on the heels of civil war. The data include information on TJ in the context of 109 democratic transitions in 86 countries around the world between 1970 and 2012. Detailed information on criminal prosecutions, truth commissions, and amnesties is currently available, and data collection on four additional mechanisms—civil trials, vetting and lustration, reparations, and customary forms of justice—is underway.

These new datasets will enable scholars to test many hypotheses derived from systematic causal theories about TJ's impacts on postwar peace. As our theories grow more nuanced and sophisticated, though, they may produce expectations that cannot be engaged with data focused on the configuration and operation of TJ institutions themselves. Many of the causal mechanisms proposed throughout this chapter, for example, emphasize individual-level factors including norms, beliefs, opinions, and preferences. Testing the observable implications of these mechanisms, and discriminating between them, will require more fine-grained micro-level data. Interviews with survivors and victims' relatives, human rights advocates, and scholars may provide such data, as might interviews with officials from governments and TJ institutions themselves (e.g., Brounéus 2008; Hayner 2001, 2010; Nalepa 2010). Surveys, and perhaps survey experiments, may also prove valuable in the collection of micro-level data (e.g., Brounéus 2010; Gibson 2004a, 2004b; Nalepa 2010). While undoubtedly time- and resource-intensive, such efforts will further advance our understanding of transitional justice, including its ability to limit recurrent civil war and human rights abuse.

NEW DIRECTIONS

In addition to reconciling existing issues within the postwar TJ literature, these new datasets—both those being collected and those as yet undeveloped—will facilitate the asking and answering of new research questions. Many such questions are suggested by the ad hoc hypotheses and post hoc explanations that typify the state of the literature.

Long and Brecke, for example, find that where reconciliation events led to a lasting peace, the events involved a protracted process of public truth telling, the redefinition of the identities and social roles of perpetrators, and "partial justice short of revenge." They infer that "reconciliation events are often, but not uniformly, correlated with restoration of civil . . . order" (Long and Brecke 2003: 13). Their conclusion taps into the causal process suggested by Hayner (2001, 2010), suggesting that transitional justice may work indirectly. In particular, it may work by changing societal norms and individual-level beliefs and preferences in ways that make political violence less likely.

The current literature tends to focus on efforts initiated by the state in which atrocities occurred, or those initiated by the international community. Yet unofficial or bottom-up institutions and processes also exist, both in cases where state actors have shown little interest in pursuing justice and alongside these top-down TJ mechanisms. These endeavors are often truth-telling initiatives and may be initiated by local communities or civil society organizations (Bickford 2007). Examples include Brazil's *Nunca Mais*, Zimbabwe's *Breaking the Silence*, and Northern Ireland's *Ardoyne Commemoration Project*. If TJ works by influencing norms and preferences at the individual level, then these unofficial mechanisms may also be equipped to enact desirable change. Is the establishment of these unofficial mechanisms a developing trend in transitional justice or a small set of isolated cases? Where, when, and under what conditions are they established? What effects—if any—do unofficial TJ efforts have on postwar peace, human rights performance, or other outcomes of interest to the TJ community? Do these effects differ from those resulting from official mechanisms and, if so, why? What is the relationship between these efforts and those initiated at the state level? These are interesting but as-yet unasked questions, and their answers seem likely to inform both scholars and policy makers focused on transitional justice.

If TJ works through changing norms and preferences, should studies of transitional justice and human rights look beyond abuses perpetrated by the state? Other actors also abuse human rights; in the context of civil war, insurgents are especially likely to engage in civilian victimization (e.g., Kalyvas 2006; Eck and Hultman 2007; Wood 2010). Does transitional justice implemented during ongoing conflict reduce human rights abuse by non-state actors? When implemented after war's end, does it prevent rebel groups that oppose the state and engage in atrocities from regrouping or rearming in ways that lead to recurrent war? Broadening the scholarly focus beyond state-perpetrated abuse, and focusing also on non-state actors, may reveal new opportunities for transitional justice to beget positive change.

Next, in a conclusion they term the justice balance, Olsen, Payne, and Reiter submit that both trials and amnesties are essential to advancing human rights because "trials provide accountability and amnesties provide stability" (Olsen et al. 2010c: 980). Results also imply that truth commissions serve a positive role, but only when combined with trials and amnesties. This, again, is in line with Hayner; it echoes her claim that truth commissions are most effective when they lead to the implementation of additional TJ mechanisms, and from there produce political and institutional reforms.

If TJ leads to political and institutional reforms, it seems likely to affect other war-related outcomes, including many that are particularly relevant for those interested in the relationship between transitional justice and civil war. Can transitional justice initiated during civil war reform institutions in ways that affect the severity of that war? Can such reforms affect the length of time that passes before the war ends, or influence whether that end comes via military victory or negotiated settlement? When implemented in the post-conflict environment, does transitional justice affect peace duration directly? Or might reforms affect the underlying mechanisms (greed and grievance, for example, or ethnic fractionalization) that lead to outbreak and relapse? Does TJ reduce violence, regardless of when it is implemented, by changing the decision calculus of state and rebel leaders (i.e., principals)? Might it also deter individuals on the ground (i.e., agents) from taking actions that prolong or renew conflict? Focusing on conflict-related effects of TJ other than its direct impact on recurrence, and particularly on effects resulting from political and institutional reforms, seems one promising avenue for future research in this area.

Note, too, that not all TJ mechanisms actually produce the kinds of reforms that seem likely to encourage postwar peace. Yet to a large extent, current work relies on binary indicators of the presence or absence of a given TJ mechanism. Those exceptions that exist tend to be additive indices of the number of institutions or processes operating in a given observation. In chapter 8 of this volume, Hartzell suggests that not all peace agreements are alike in determining the durability of peace. Similarly, transitional justice may matter not merely because it exists, but also because of how it is implemented (Wiebelhaus-Brahm 2010). Hayner suggests that specificity and international support affect TJ's impacts. The transparency or perceived legitimacy and fairness of these institutions may also matter, as might any number of other measures of TJ quality. A small number of studies now underway move beyond a binary conceptualization of transitional justice (Loyle and Appel 2014; Miller 2014; Nichols 2014), and there remains much more to explore.

Finally, Snyder and Vinjamuri (2003/2004) conclude that TJ works only under specific conditions: trials contribute to ending human rights abuse only when peace spoilers are weak and the domestic justice infrastructure is already well established, and truth commissions have negligible or harmful impacts unless employed in countries where democratic institutions are already fairly well established. In addition, truth commissions often provide political cover for amnesties; whether formal or de facto, amnesties with effective political backing and institutions capable of enforcement can help pave the way for peace. These suggestions are in line with Melander's (2013) general claim that the effectiveness of transitional justice depends on the context in which it occurs, including the nature of political institutions.

Might context also condition the effectiveness of transitional justice for other outcomes, including some that affect the prospects for postwar peace? Extant research on TJ's impact on human rights is focused exclusively on state-perpetrated violations of physical integrity rights, but group rights—and particularly women's rights—may also be affected in desirable ways. There is strong evidence of the link between gender equality and various facets of civil war. As women increasingly participate in society, economics, and politics, the likelihood of involvement in civil war declines (Caprioli 2005; Melander 2005a). When paired with peacekeeping operations, female participation in post–civil war society reduces the likelihood of renewed conflict within five years (Gizelis 2009). Female participation also reduces the risk of relapse to civil war (DeMeritt, Nichols, and Kelly 2014). Gender equality is linked to lower levels of the physical integrity abuse that so often precedes and occurs in the context of civil war (Melander 2005b). Given this set of results, does transitional justice affect women's rights in ways that reduce the likelihood of civil war occurrence or recurrence? If so, is this a general effect or is it specific to certain TJ institutions or processes? Is it specific to TJ implemented under certain scope conditions? Clarifying the effects of transitional justice on civil war and human rights may mean pushing this line of inquiry past its current focus on physical integrity abuse.

CONCLUSION

Transitional justice has become increasingly common, and scholars have increasingly turned their attention to its outcomes and consequences. In line with this volume's theme, I have generally focused on the state-level effects of transitional justice in the context of civil war. Simply put, and despite great strides forward in recent years, the state of our collective knowledge remains relatively weak. Few studies find that TJ has negative effects on civil war or postwar human rights, but evidence on whether its overall impact is desirable or negligible is mixed.

I argue that moving the empirical TJ literature toward consensus will require more careful attention to causal forces, which will also enable explicit decisions and statements about scope conditions and how we operationalize key concepts. The pursuit of consensus is important and worthwhile, as scholarly insights have the potential to affect developing policy standards and practices. Current discussions of transitional justice are largely faith based rather than fact based (Thoms et al. 2010); moving toward the latter will enable scholars to make recommendations and offer advice to those who design and implement TJ but will be difficult in the absence of cohesive and coherent evidence.

As is true of any young literature, the empirical study of transitional justice is rich with untapped potential. In addition to the need for the reconciliation of existing evidence, there is a wealth of unasked questions about the various effects of transitional justice. Some of these questions are already being engaged, but opportunities abound for new studies, and new scholars, with an interest in the relationships among transitional justice, human rights, and civil war.

12

Gender and Civil Wars

Erik Melander

The strongest pattern in civil war is probably its gendered nature, meaning that men and women tend to assume different roles in civil war and that differences in the status of men and women in a society correlate strongly with aspects of civil war such as onset and recurrence. The gendered nature of civil war can be found on different levels of analysis. To give some examples, which will be discussed in more detail later in the chapter: on the individual level, the overwhelming majority of civil war combatants are men (Henshaw 2013, 2015; Thomas and Bond 2015); on the sub-national level, organizations engaged in contentious politics are less likely to use violence if they espouse a gender-inclusive ideology; on the country level, the countries with the smallest difference in the status of men and women are the least likely to experience civil war. Several studies show that the gendered nature pertains to the origins, dynamics, and resolution of civil wars. It follows that explaining this pattern should shed light on strong causal forces at work.

However, unless plausible theoretical arguments are given for why and how gender matters, any empirical associations are likely to be dismissed as spurious, random flukes, or flawed findings. For this reason this chapter will open with a presentation of the main theoretical arguments that have been offered for why gender matters for civil war. After the theory has been introduced, key empirical results concerning the gendered nature of civil war are presented. The section after that deals with alternative explanations implying that the gendered nature of civil war is spurious. Most research on civil war does not even consider gender as an alternative explanation or include measures related to gender as control variables. Implicitly, then, most civil war scholars dismiss the relevance of gender without engaging with the research. For the field to advance in this regard, a debate is needed in which the arguments related to gender are explicitly pitted against the alternative explanations, taking into account empirical patterns. The penultimate section of this chapter is intended as a beginning of such a debate, in which alternative explanations are discussed. The chapter ends with avenues for future research.

THEORY

The World Health Organization defines *gender* as referring to "the socially constructed roles, behaviors, activities, and attributes that a given society considers appropriate for men and women," whereas *sex* refers to "the biological and physiological characteristics that define men and women" (World Health Organization). This is useful, although the distinction between what is biological and physiological on one hand and socially constructed on the other is not always clear-cut. So why would gender equality be related to civil peace? The theoretical arguments can be divided into two categories. The essentialist argument holds that gender equality is related to civil peace because women are more peaceful than men, and when women are empowered in more equal societies, the more pacific women will influence political outcomes in a more peaceful direction. It is assumed that peacefulness is inherent in the essential nature of women. The constructivist argument, in contrast, explains the association between gender equality and peace by pointing to the intolerant and warlike norms that are strong among both men and women in gender-unequal societies. These norms are assumed to be socially constructed. Figure 12.1 is a scheme of the arguments.

At the top of the figure, there are headings indicating whether the explanatory factors in the boxes below are considered to be ultimate causes or proximate causes. Prominent work on the relationship between gender equality and peace draws on

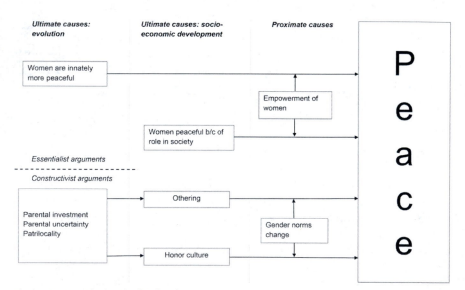

Figure 12.1.   Theoretical Scheme

evolutionary biology and psychology, arguing that the ultimate causes of human behavior are to be found in natural selection (e.g., Hudson et al. 2009). Whereas humans cannot control how we have been shaped by evolution, it is possible to consciously try to influence how much power is held by women. We can also question or promote different norms that prescribe appropriate behavior. The empowerment of women and normative changes are more proximate causes in the arguments linking gender equality and peace. It is not necessary to go back so deeply in the causal chain as to invoke evolution in order to provide more ultimate causes for why gender matters for peace (Goldstein 2001, chapter 3). As will be discussed below, deep patterns having to do with gender can be explained with reference to socioeconomic developments instead. In this connection, it should be noted that neither evolution nor socioeconomics imply deterministic relationships as far as gender is concerned. Rather, we find tendencies involving complex interactions and great variation among individuals.

ESSENTIALIST ARGUMENTS

The essentialist argument is built on an assumption that women are innately more peaceful than men, either because of upbringing and position in society, or because of biological difference. It is further argued that when women are empowered, this female peacefulness will impact on societal outcomes so that more civil peace results. In contrast, the constructivist argument assumes that socially constructed ideas about gender roles influence how conflict is dealt with, and as gender roles are redefined in the direction of increased equality between men and women, norms about conflict change as a result. In particular, as gendered norms about dominance and honor change, peace benefits. The essentialist and constructivist arguments are not mutually contradictory on logical grounds, and each may thus have some explanatory power (Tickner 1992, 1997; Caprioli 2000, 2005; Goldstein 2001; Melander 2005a).

In the essentialist argument, empowerment of peaceful women is hence the more proximate cause linking gender equality and more peaceful outcomes. Numerous studies show that women tend to have more peaceful attitudes than men (Frankovic 1982; Smith 1984; de Boer 1985; Shapiro and Mahajan 1986; Fite, Genest, and Wilcox 1990; McGlen and Sarkees 1993; Togeby 1994) and that women play crisis games and behave in simulated negotiations in a less confrontational style than men (e.g., McDermott et al. 2007). Thus, there seems to be some support for the notion that women in general are more peaceful. A complication is that there are also studies that show that the gender gap in warlike attitudes goes away when attitudes to gender equality are taken into account: both men and women who are more favorable to gender equality tend to hold more peaceful attitudes (Cook and Wilcox 1991; Tessler and Warriner 1997; Tessler et al. 1999; Brooks and Valentino 2011). This suggests that the gender gap is not about inherently peaceful women but about ideas about gender among both sexes. The essentialist explanation has also been questioned on the grounds that it would seem unrealistic that the peaceful women should be able to substantially impact outcomes, given how male dominated the sphere of war and peace is (e.g., Bjarnegård and Melander 2013).

CONSTRUCTIVIST ARGUMENTS

In the constructivist argument, normative change among both men and women, and perhaps in particular among men, is the more proximate cause of peace. This argument is about how socially constructed gender roles, which may also in part be shaped by evolutionary forces, have consequences for tolerance and attitudes to violence. Two mechanisms through which gender roles influence war and peace can be identified: othering and honor culture.

Psychological studies show that almost from infancy, individuals notice three basic differences in people: age, gender, and race. Furthermore, the first adults that children observe regularly interacting are their parents. The way men and women relate to each other therefore becomes the fundamental template for differentiating between groups of people, and to the extent that the father dominates and controls the mother, this model teaches the child that domination by one group over another is appropriate and normal. Much psychological research also shows that children who grow up in violent homes have a greater tendency to become violent themselves. In harshly patriarchal societies, the lives of women and girls are clearly less valued than the lives of men and boys, and it is argued that this kind of othering facilitates the dehumanizing of others, which is almost a precondition for war and genocide. On the other hand, Hudson and den Boer hold that "the first 'other' is always women, and if one can make peace with the first other without resorting to coercion, one will have a template in place to know how to do so with other 'others'" (2012: 317). That is to say, when patriarchal dominance by men over women is reduced, the type of othering that breeds intolerance and violence is weakened, and more companionate marriages instead serve as templates for respectful and equal interaction with others (Hudson et al. 2009; Hudson and den Boer 2012; Hudson et al. 2012)

Honor culture refers to a system in which individuals are assigned status and right to precedence based on how well one lives up to a code of honor that entails deterring or redressing affronts with violence for men, and chastity and family fidelity for women. Traditional ideals of manhood prescribe, at least to some extent, that men have a superior position relative to women and that men must be warlike and dominant. Real men are supposed to be tough, brave, resistant to pain, and able to steel themselves against the potentially weakening influences of soft emotions. For men, violence or the threat of violence is an appropriate response to affronts, and men who back down lose honor and status. Moreover, the male privileges vis-à-vis women are linked to their role as warriors or potential warriors, and these privileges tend to be seen as natural. A man of honor is also expected to act as the head of the family and to guard over the chastity of female family members. Women tend to espouse and perpetuate this understanding of what manhood means. This honor culture, although present to some degree in all societies, is changeable. Furthermore, individuals, both men and women, differ with regard to how much they accept traditional honor culture or, rather, adopt more modern and less warlike and oppressive ideals. Hence, this argument implies that individuals who embrace a more traditional honor culture should hold more warlike attitudes as well as attitudes that men should be privileged vis-à-vis women, both in society and in the home. Also, societies with stronger honor culture should as a consequence be more violent and warlike (Tickner 1992, 2001; Enloe 1993; Gibson 1994; Nisbett and Cohen 1996; Gill 1997; Goldstein 2001; Pin-Fat and Stern 2004).

SOCIOECONOMIC FACTORS

As figure 12.1 illustrates, both the essentialist and the constructivist arguments are compatible with and draw on more ultimate causes for why women supposedly are more peaceful than men and why gendered othering and honor culture exist, respectively. These ultimate causes can be found in socioeconomic developments and in evolutionary psychology. The socioeconomic explanations do not depend on the evolutionary arguments, but they are generally compatible. That is to say, there are socioeconomic explanations for why women would be more peaceful than men, and for why gendered othering and honor cultures exist. Likewise, there are evolutionary explanations for why women would be more peaceful than men, and for why gendered othering and honor cultures develop.

A socioeconomic argument for why women would be at the same time more peaceful than men, and subordinated to men, can be made as follows. Because women have less power and privilege than men, wars and other forms of organized violence tend to be decided upon by men and benefit men primarily. Women can therefore become a peaceful influence if empowered. Because of gender roles, women are furthermore trained to deal with conflict in a less confrontational way than men. Proponents of this line of reasoning do not claim that these differences between men and women are deterministic, but instead talk about more or less pronounced tendencies. The socioeconomic reasons for why women are subordinated to men, and for traditional gender roles, relate to social consequences of the different reproductive roles of men and women. Where fertility rates and infant mortality are high, life spans are short, and where there are few safe alternatives to breastfeeding infants, women tend to spend a large part of their adult lives either pregnant or breastfeeding infants. This has been the pattern up until relatively recently, and it is still the case in the poorest societies. Men have been much freer in this regard, and hence able to accrue advantages in the public sphere, including consolidating a hegemonic ideology legitimizing male superiority. Having many (surviving) children used to be a means for the family patriarch to leverage power and secure his old age. Although these patterns are pervasive, they also change: when life spans increase, infant mortality rates go down, and wealth becomes delinked from the number of children, lower fertility rates leave room for women to be more than mothers at the same time as the role of the male patriarch becomes less functional and dominant (MacInnes 1998). This line of reasoning invoking socioeconomic developments to explain why societies with less oppression of women are more peaceful does not require any assumption about women being inherently more peaceful than men in terms of biologically inherited predispositions. The most common perspective is that these differences, instead, are socially constructed and can develop relatively fast when constraints and opportunities change (Hudson and den Boer 2012).

Also, the evolutionary argument for why gender equality is related to civil peace eschews determinism and instead refers to tendencies and changing patterns. Evolutionary biology and psychology take note of the many patterns that recur in some recognizable form in almost all known human cultures, such as the gendered nature of war, invoking natural selection to explain why these patterns can be found to some extent almost everywhere. Yet evolutionary forces only predispose males and females to particular behaviors under certain conditions. Humans of both sexes are prone to both aggression and cooperation, both cruelty and altruism, and so on, depending on the circumstances. Evolutionary-derived predispositions are shaped by culture, in which changes occur much faster than in evolution. Despite the existence of human universals, and striking patterns regarding masculine ideals, male privileges, and so on, culture can be seen as more important for understanding human behavior today, even in an evolutionary perspective.

The evolutionary argument revolves around the different reproductive roles of males and females. Because of pregnancy and breastfeeding, females inevitably have a higher initial investment in producing offspring than men. A basic evolutionary principle is that the sex with higher parental investment becomes a limiting resource, and the other sex therefore competes more intensively for reproductive access. Furthermore, a consequence of internal female fertilization is, in the words of Lord Kilbrandon, that "maternity is a matter of fact, paternity one of mere inference" (cited in Potts and Hayden 2008: 58). It follows that sexual jealousy has been selected for more strongly among men than among women. Higher female parental investment and paternity uncertainty result in sexual conflict. Intense male competition for reproductive partners and male control over female sexuality are accordingly evolutionary-favored adaptations that can be found in most known cultures. The great majority of traditional cultures are patrilocal, meaning that after marriage, the wife moves to her husband's household. As a consequence, women tend to be at a disadvantage relative to their husband in terms of availability of kin, whereas the men are more closely related. These conditions are conducive to male-male alliances that cooperate in controlling women and warring against outgroup male coalitions. Whereas a male-dominant hierarchy structure dampens male-male competition within the group, competition for status has nevertheless been particularly important for reproductive success for males. For these reasons, evolution has selected for a predisposition among men to strive to be (or be perceived to be) fierce, so as to deter affronts and gain status and be controlling in relation to women, loyal to male kin (or perceived kin), and ruthless toward outgroup male competitors. Hence, it is possible to provide evolutionary arguments for why a culture of honor develops, in which men must prove their manhood by acting tough and warlike.

To summarize, socioeconomic developments and evolutionary forces provide explanations for why gender should be related to patterns of war and peace. Three more precise arguments were identified, which are compatible with both types of explanations. First, women may be more peaceful on average than men. Second, when, in patriarchal societies, men in the family dominate women, this oppressive othering serves as a template for how other "others," such as political opponents and ethnic and religious minorities, are treated. Third, honor culture trains men that violence is the appropriate way of dealing with affronts and proving one's manhood. The proximate causes condition these three mechanisms. Empowerment of women enables the more peaceful women to impact outcomes in a more peaceful direction. Changing norms regarding gendered othering and honor culture influence both men and women, and perhaps in particular men, to be less warlike in their attitudes and behaviors.

EMPIRICAL RESULTS AT THE INDIVIDUAL LEVEL OF ANALYSIS

Civil war is a subcategory of the broader phenomenon of war, which also encompasses interstate wars. War in general is extremely gendered with regard to the identity of participants. Most strikingly, Goldstein assesses that less than 1 percent of all warriors throughout history have been women (2001: 10). There are reasons to believe that the rate of female participation is higher in civil war than in interstate war, but as will be discussed below, the empirical evidence shows that the actual fighting in civil wars is overwhelmingly done by males. At the same time, many women have participated in different capacities, including in combat roles, in numerous civil wars, and this female civil war participation has often been downplayed and overlooked. Both of the patterns, that most warriors are men and that female participation in fighting has been overlooked, are telling and speak to the peculiar gendered nature of civil war and the study of civil war.

The skewed distribution of male and female civil war combatants can hardly be explained by innate qualities of the biological sexes that would make men suitable for the warrior role and women unsuitable. There is an abundance of evidence that women can be extremely capable fighters, and if those individuals who are the most suitable filled the ranks of civil war fighters, the distribution between men and women would be much closer to fifty-fifty. Clearly something else is going on in addition to innate differences between the sexes in terms of warrior qualities (Goldstein 2001).

A handful of studies use statistical methods of inference to test for generalizable explanations for why some individuals take up arms in situations of civil conflict or genocide, while most people do not. It is perhaps unsurprising but nevertheless striking that the male sex turns out to be an extremely strong predictor of participation in civil conflict violence. Yet gender is typically treated merely as a necessary control variable, and no explanations are offered or tested for why men are so much more prone to civil-conflict violence than women (e.g., Verwimp 2005; Humphrey and Weinstein 2008; McDoom 2013). The strongly gendered nature of the use of violence in civil conflict is seemingly taken as a given and in need of no explanation. But if the male sex is the strongest individual-level predictor of use of violence in civil conflict, this cries out for an explanation.

Henshaw (2013, 2015) has carried out the most ambitious study of the extent to which men and women, respectively, participate in civil conflict. She maps female participation in a random sample of seventy-two rebel groups active between 1990 and 2008. In more than two-thirds of the rebel groups, the active combatants (i.e., those participating in direct armed attacks) are exclusively male. In groups with female direct participation in fighting, male active combatants outnumber the women. The male numerical dominance is less pronounced, but still strong, when female insurgents who fulfill other roles than direct participation in armed attacks are taken into account. It is reported that if taking into account females participating in all capacities, several exceptional rebel movements may have somewhere between almost one-third to almost one-half female participation (e.g., the Tamil Tigers of Sri Lanka, the Communist Party of Nepal, Farabundo Martí National Liberation Front of El Salvador, and the Revolutionary Armed Forces of Colombia). The data collected by Henshaw thus show a very strong male overrepresentation in participation in rebel groups, which is particularly pronounced for active participation in combat and leadership roles (see also Thomas and Bond 2015). Thus, participation remains extremely gendered in contemporary civil conflict.

At the same time, the decision of many women to take up arms or join an armed group needs to be explained and cannot be assumed away as a matter of their merely following males. In an early study of women's agency in civil war fighting, Mason (1992) argues that women joined the leftist guerrillas of El Salvador and Nicaragua for the same basic reasons as the male guerrillas, namely, economic hardships and regime repression. Mason stresses that many of these women were mobilized independently of their spouses and did not simply follow them to the hills. Henshaw (2013) points out that her data show that female participation in rebel groups is "much greater than what is recognized by current scholarship" (8), and she identifies and addresses an important and overlooked variation in need of explanation, that some rebel groups attract large numbers of female participants while other groups attract none or very few. Her study presents several findings on what differentiates rebel groups with female participation from other rebel groups. For example, rebel groups with a leftist, redistributive ideology along Marxist or socialist lines are more likely to have female participants. She also situates her study in a discussion of scholarly work suggesting that female combatants may be undercounted because they are pressured to deny their participation, and that female combatant participation is minimized both in the social context in which it occurred as well as in research (Sharlach 1999; Enloe 2000; Sjoberg and Gentry 2007; MacKenzie 2009, 2012; McEvoy 2009).

Indeed, it seems that both among people embroiled in war or preparing for war and among many students of war, there is an unstated assumption that fighting is a male thing and that this is the natural order and the way it should be. Clearly this has more to do with imagined differences in warrior qualities and beliefs about proper gender roles than any actual differences between men and women with regard to the capacity to become a warrior. The extent to which war fighting is unreflectively treated as a male sphere shows the strength of warrior masculinity, that is, the notion that war, preparation for war, and warlike behavior is what being a real man is perceived to be about, and also what distinguishes real men from the contrast category of submissive and nursing women. Indeed, recognizing the capacity of women to fight, and the actual track record of women fighters, threatens to undo the ultimate test of manhood, which is also the way men are goaded into becoming warriors: real men prove their worth and gain precedence by acting warlike and tough so that the weak women are protected (which often entails control by the men). This concern is reflected in this quote by a U.S. Marine Corps general on the effect of female participation in combat: "War is man's work. . . . It would be an enormous psychological distraction for the male who wants to think that he's fighting for that woman somewhere behind, not up there in the same fox hole with him. It tramples the male ego. When you get right down to it, you've got to protect the manliness of war" (cited in Enloe 1993: 153–54).

Naturally, the gendered nature of civil war is reflected also in patterns of victimization. This is yet another issue on which we do not have complete data, but from different fragments of information, several distinct patterns emerge. When data disaggregated by gender are available, men turn out to be the overwhelming majority of those killed and injured by direct violence (Obermayer et al. 2008). For example, 99 percent of the combatants killed in the war in Bosnia-Herzegovina in 1992–1995 were male, as were 78 percent of the civilians killed (Zviwezchowski and Tabeau 2010). The wound database of the International Red Cross covers all patients admitted to Red Cross hospitals in a number of conflicts from several continents. Out of 18,877 individuals wounded by bullets, fragmentation munitions, or mines, men aged 16–49 constituted 74 percent (Coupland and Samnegaard 1999). Given that most of the actual fighting in civil wars is done by males, it is to be expected that most of the combatant victims are male as well. But as the numbers above illustrate, men seem to suffer more from direct violence also among noncombatants. Conflict-related sexual violence is an exception and a form of direct violence in which women are the majority of the victims. The problem with lack of reliable data is even more pronounced when sexual violence is concerned because of the stigma and shame often experienced by victims. This stigma and shame may be stronger for male victims and hence underreporting may be even greater for men than for women (Solangon and Patel 2012). A few studies investigate the extent to which both men and women were victims of sexual violence in armed conflict. For example, survey results representative of the Liberian adult population in 2008 show that 9.2 percent of the noncombatant women and 7.4 percent of the noncombatant males had experienced sexual violence. Among combatants, the rates were much higher: 42.3 percent of the combatant women and 32.6 percent of the men (Johnson et al. 2008). In a survey representative of the adult population in territories of the eastern Democratic Republic of Congo, 18 percent of the women reported having been raped compared to 4 percent of the men (Johnson et al. 2010). In recent years, several important studies have been published on conflict-related sexual violence (e.g., Cohen 2013a, 2013b; Cohen, Green, and Wood 2013; Cohen and Nordås 2014; Wood 2006a, 2006b, 2009).

Several studies deal with indirect suffering from civil war. Ghobarah et al. estimate that at least as many people die during the first postwar years as during the years of fighting because of lingering consequences, many of which seem to be gendered (2003). In this vein, Urdal and Che find that maternal mortality rates are elevated in conflict countries (2013). Plümper and Neumayer (2006) conclude that indirect negative consequences of civil war affect women more than men. However, Iqbal (2010) finds that whereas there is a negative effect of war on male life expectancy, no negative effect can be found on female life expectancy of war. Men and women are forced to become refugees to roughly the same extent. UNHCR reports that "over the past 10 years the total number of male refugees has consistently been slightly higher than the total number of female refugees." (UNHCR: 51)

While most combatants are male, it is at the same time true that most men never mobilize for war and instead remain civilians (cf. Kidron and Smith 1991: 33). For example, the male population of Afghanistan aged 15 to 54 is almost 8.4 million. A recent estimate puts the number of Taliban insurgents at over 60,000 (Dawi 2014), whereas the forces on the government side numbered just over 360,000. These numbers suggest that not much more than 5 percent of the Afghan males of military age can be active combatants in that ongoing civil war. Carpenter discusses how and why it has become common to essentialize the civilian/combatant distinction, so that men are associated with combatants and women and children with civilians, despite the fact that most men never mobilize for war while some women do. When studying civil war, we must be able to see both the gendered nature of war and avoid oversimplifying proxies such as equating "women and children" with civilians. Civilian adult men, child soldiers, and women combatants are all made invisible with this trope (2005).

EMPIRICAL RESULTS AT THE
SUB-NATIONAL UNITS OF ANALYSIS

Asal et al. seek to explain why some organizations engaged in contentious politics chose violent tactics, nonviolent tactics, or a mix of both, specifically investigating the effect of an organization's ideology relating to gender. In a sample of 104 ethno-political organizations in the Middle East, they find that organizations with a gender-inclusive ideology are much more likely to engage in protest and less likely to use a violent or mixed strategy compared to other groups. With regard to theory, the authors state that "Much of the feminist literature . . . suggests that gender-inclusive ideologies should make organizations more peaceful" and that "theorists argue that the choice of violence is related to patriarchal attitudes, while the choice of non-violent resistance is explicitly connected to a feminist perspective" (308). It is not clearly stated, however, what the theoretical explanation is for why gender-inclusive ideology is associated with nonviolent tactics, and why and how patriarchal attitudes lead to violence. One has to go to the cited works to find out what causal mechanisms the authors found plausible and relied on to formulate their hypothesis. The authors' selection of cited works gives the impression that they agree with the analysis that patriarchy leads to violence through othering and its concomitant fostering of violent domination. There is no indication that the authors believe that participation by inherently peaceful women in itself influences organizations to be less violent. Instead they emphasize that "there is a world of difference between a movement that includes women, while still advocating policies that may prove damaging to women's interests in the long run, and one that actively advocates for their inclusion" (308). It seems clear that the authors rely on a constructivist view on gender and peace rather than the essentialist perspective, but this kind of work probably needs to spell out the theoretical argument more fully in order to seem convincing to readers who are not familiar with gender theory.

EMPIRICAL RESULTS AT THE COUNTRY LEVEL OF ANALYSIS

Before research on the causes of civil war began to use statistical methods to test for associations derived from gender theory about a decade ago, a number of cross-cultural studies drawing on anthropological research examined whether pre-industrial societies with more inequality between men and women were more warlike. The distinction between civil war and interstate war does not apply directly to pre-state societies, but in this context, it is nevertheless relevant to note that a review of the cross-cultural anthropology studies concludes that "overall, women's low status correlates somewhat with frequent warfare" (Goldstein 2001: 397). The idea guiding the study of gender and civil war onset is similarly that countries with a lower status for women should be more prone to civil war. A challenge for these studies is in coming up with measures of the relative status of women that are available for most or all countries of the world and for long periods of time, since onset of civil war is quite rare and statistical tests aiming to parse out the effects of different but correlated explanatory factors require many observations and a good deal of variation in the dependent variable. This has necessitated the use of rough proxy measures, and most studies use several alternative measures for gender equality to compensate for the potential weaknesses of the individual measures.

In her pioneering study, Caprioli (2005) uses two different proxies for gender equality, namely, fertility rate and female labor-force participation. The dependent variable is the incidence of intrastate armed conflict, and her models take into account prior conflict and the length of any preceding peace spell, among several other control variables. Higher fertility rates and lower female labor-force participation significantly predict intrastate armed conflict.

In line with her previous work on gender and interstate conflict (2000), and building on a large, cited feminist literature, Caprioli discusses two main theoretical arguments for why gender equality matters for civil conflict. She argues that gender inequality amounts to cultural violence and norms that legitimize violence, and that militarization of masculinity feeds into a gendered nationalism that helps mobilize people to fight other groups. Clearly Caprioli draws primarily on a constructivist perspective.

Melander (2005a) tests for the effect of three independent variables: (1) an indicator of whether the highest leader of a state is a woman; (2) the percentage of women in parliament; (3) the female-to-male higher education attainment ratio. The dependent variable is an ordinal measure taking the values of no intrastate armed conflict, minor intrastate armed conflict, and full-scale civil war, and the models include a lagged dependent variable (as well as numerous controls) so that what is explained is change in the level of intrastate armed conflict. Melander finds no effect of the female leadership indicator but strong pacifying effects of the other two measures of gender equality. Melander also tests for interaction between democracy and female parliamentary representation and finds that the pacifying effect of gender equality in parliament is greatest in democracies.

The theoretical framework draws on the distinction in Caprioli (2000) and the feminist literature cited above in identifying ways in which gender equality may influence civil conflict, namely, empowerment of more peaceful women (the essentialist argument), othering, and militarized masculinity (the constructivist argument). That female leadership has no effect, also when parsing out the potential effect of female leaders who came to power for dynastic reasons, could be interpreted as suggesting that the constructivist argument fares better than the essentialist argument, although the number of observations in which the highest leader of a state was a woman is low. The study concludes that although the effect of gender equality is evident, the results do not provide grounds for concluding whether the essentialist or the constructivist argument has more explanatory power.

Gleditsch et al. (2011) find that an index representing the degree to which women's equal political, social, and economic rights are respected in a country is significantly associated with a lower risk of civil war onset. The authors also examine the effect of polygyny, since a previous study claimed to have found a strong relationship between polygyny and civil war (Kanazawa 2009). Gleditsch et al. conclude that their results are difficult to reconcile with a claim about "civil war emanating from reproductive frustration in polygynous groups," and instead emphasize how socially constructed gender roles legitimizing violence provide a more plausible explanation.

DeMeritt et al. (2014) investigate whether the peace following terminated civil wars is more likely to hold when female participation is higher in different spheres of society. They find that two measures of gender equality are associated with a reduced risk of civil war relapse, namely, the female-to-male literacy rate and female parliamentary representation. Contrary to the some of the other results presented here, they find that female labor force participation predicts an increased risk of relapse. Like most works reviewed above, DeMeritt et al. invoke both the essentialist argument and the constructivist arguments to motivate their hypotheses.

Gizelis (2009) studies the prospects for peacebuilding success using a dependent variable that reflects avoiding conflict relapse as well as meeting democratic standards in societies emerging from civil conflict. She finds that there is a statistically significant interaction between the female-to-male life expectancy ratio and United Nations peacebuilding operations, so that UN peacekeeping is much more likely to succeed in societies in which the status of women is higher before the onset of the civil war. In line with previous research, Gizelis refers to both the essentialist argument and the constructivist argument. She adds that gender equality entails higher social capital in that the traditional exclusion of competent individuals who are women is diminished, and that peacekeeping forces thereby gain more effective local partners. Interestingly, Gizelis notes that her argument does not require that equal societies be more peaceful, and she stresses that "higher social capital and domestic capacity could also make countries or communities more able to organize collective violence" (509). This suggests that in line with a constructivist perspective, the effect of female participation is not hardwired but depends on the context.

ALTERNATIVE EXPLANATIONS

In 2004, Paul Collier and Anke Hoeffler published their famous article "Greed and Grievance in Civil War." They contrasted two arguments explaining civil war: rebellions are caused by atypical opportunities for building a rebel organization or by atypically severe grievances. Using proxy measures that they admit are open to different interpretations, the authors conclude that "the grievances that motivate rebels may be substantially disconnected from the large social concerns of inequality, political rights, and ethnic or religious identity" (2004: 589). This study generated enormous interest and has been cited more than four thousand times. The following year, Mary Caprioli published the first quantitative study on the relationship between gender equality and civil peace. Using two proxy measures for gender equality, she concluded that "states characterized by gender inequality are more likely to experience intrastate conflict" (2005: 161). She also noted that "the insignificance of average GDP per capita growth rate suggests that poverty or growth rates whether negative or positive are not in themselves a predictor of internal violent conflict without gendered structural violence supporting norms of violence" (174). Except for those studies aiming to test hypotheses derived from feminist theory, only a handful of studies on civil conflict and related phenomena have cited these findings. As a rule, mainstream research on civil war does not consider gender equality as an alternative explanation and does not include measures of gender equality as control variables. The study of civil war would benefit from a debate and accumulation of studies on which explanatory factors that may conceivably cancel out the findings on the effects of gender equality. This section briefly discusses a few alternative explanations.

It could be that the association found between gender equality and peace is spurious in that both phenomena may be driven by some larger normative change entailing that violence and domination in general is viewed as less acceptable. It should be acknowledged that in any observational study, the possibility always exists that some third factor would explain away the findings if taken into account. But a general objection of such a sweeping and unspecified character carries little weight unless that potential third factor supposedly driving a general normative change devaluing violence can be specified theoretically, operationalized, and then shown empirically to make the relationship between gender equality and peace go away. A second problem with this objection (that there might be a larger normative change that the studies on gender do not capture) is that it comes close to being circular: violence in general becomes less common because violence in general becomes less popular. In contrast, the arguments tested in the reviewed studies imply an empirical association between two quite different phenomena: gender equality and peace. Hence, the gender argument is far from circular or tautological.

A related possible objection is that measures of gender equality actually tap into economic development in general, and that the tests pick up a causal relationship between development and peace, rather than between gender equality and peace. However, the reviewed studies each control for one or several standard measures of development, and the variables reflecting gender equality are statistically significant, whereas the measures of development often are not. The onus is therefore on the skeptics to present the correct, and theoretically justified, measure of development and to demonstrate that the relationship between gender equality and peace no longer exists when a superior measure of development is used.

At the same time, and as previously noted, it seems highly likely that various aspects of development, such as changes in means of production and technological innovations, are important drivers of gender equality. This means that development causes gender equality, which in turn causes peace. Gender equality would then be the mechanism through which development impacts peace. This is an interesting possibility, but the reviewed results also show that the pacifying effect of gender equality cannot be reduced solely to development having an indirect effect through gender equality since the measures of gender equality remain significant when controlling for measures of development. Instead, in several of the studies, development in general seems to have no direct effect on peace when gender equality is taken into account. A vague speculation that the relationship between gender equality and peace would be entirely driven by development in some form can of course be correct nevertheless, but it lacks empirical support so far. That is to say, no large study has been published that demonstrates that gender equality can be crowded out as a significant predictor of civil peace by development indicators. At the very least, and given the record of published studies, it seems reasonable that gender equality would have a pacifying effect, given equal levels of economic development. For example, contraceptive pills may become available at a low cost as a consequence of economic development, but men may refuse women the freedom to use them. Such differences in the treatment of women, given equal levels of economic development, should, according to the theoretical arguments dealt with in this chapter, be related to peace, and if this is so, gender equality and economic development would be complementary and partially overlapping drivers of peace.

Whereas development in the study of civil war typically is conceived of as a societal-level variable, alternative explanations operate also on the individual level. In particular, honor ideology may correlate with conservatism and social dominance orientation (SDO), and either of these two variables may explain both the variation in honor ideology as well as proneness to violence, so that any association on the individual level between honor ideology and violence would be spurious. Scruton defines conservatism as "the political outlook which springs from a desire to conserve existing things, held to be either good in themselves, or better than the likely alternatives, or at least safe, familiar, and the objects of trust and affection" (90). Individual-level measures of conservatism (other than those that simply rely on self-identification) are based on the notion that conservatism consists of resistance to change and endorsement of inequality (Wilson and Sibley 2013). Given these views of conservatism, it is hard to see the logic that would predispose conservatives to take up arms in civil conflicts more often than other people. Sometimes militaristic views are considered to indicate conservatism, or to be part of the definition of conservatism, but in this context, that only muddies the water: including the endorsement of violence in the definition or measurement of conservatism brings dependent and independent variables closer to each other by definition or measurement, and gives no explanatory leverage. What is more, conservatism is mute with the regard to the gendered pattern of war. If conservatism were the main cause of violent participation in civil conflict, then we would expect to see almost as many female and male combatants (since women are only a little less conservative than men). The fact that warriors traditionally have been men does not help the conservatism explanation but only begs the question of why this tradition has evolved in the first place, which again cannot be explained by invoking conservatism. Granted, individuals who are more conservative tend to be less favorably disposed to equal rights for women, but again conservatism is no explanation for why power, war, and political violence are coded masculine.

The same argumentation can be used to counter the possibility that SDO provides a better explanation for the pattern of gender equality correlating with civil peace. SDO is an individual-difference variable that captures "a general attitudinal orientation toward intergroup relations, reflecting whether one generally prefers such

relations to be equal, versus hierarchical, that is ordered along a superior-inferior dimension" (Pratto et al. 1994: 742). Social dominance theory provides an explanation
for why a lot of people would like to discriminate against and dominate other groups
but does not explain the gendered nature of war and political violence. There is a
weak, or at best moderately strong correlation, between sex and SDO, meaning that
men tend to have higher SDO than women, but this moderate difference can hardly
explain the overwhelming male dominance in war and violence in general. Also,
SDO provides no explanation for the human universal that men dominate women,
and not the other way around. Hence, invoking SDO cannot negate the need for
theory that explicitly deals with the gendered nature of war and power.

It seems reasonable to expect that individuals who espouse honor culture and
othering tend to be high on SDO, and conservatives more often than not, because
of the overlapping element of endorsing inequality. But there is no theoretical logic
that would entail that conservatism or SDO explains individual-level participation in
civil conflict better than honor ideology and othering, nor can conservatism or SDO
explain the gendered nature of war and violence. The exact interrelationship between
honor ideology, conservatism, and SDO is an important area for future research.

The preceding pages exemplify how one may begin to contrast and evaluate different competing (or complementary) explanations for the empirical regularities that
have been found concerning gender and civil war. It seems certain that more engagement of this type with the arguments and empirics will be useful even if agreement
or consensus on the relationship between gender and civil war should remain elusive.

AVENUES FOR FUTURE RESEARCH

A key challenge in the research on gender and civil war is in developing tests that are
closer to the operation of the theorized causal mechanisms. This entails making the
theoretical arguments more precise as well. Exactly how do empowered women effect
change in processes of conflict formation, mobilization, escalation, de-escalation,
resolution, and prevention? How, more precisely, does gendered othering result in
more civil conflict, and how does reduced othering translate into civil peace? What
is the exact relationship between honor cultures and civil conflict at the level of the
society or culture, and how does individual adherence to honor culture result in
civil-conflict participation? Future research should try to establish whether the causal
mechanisms indeed are at work as the more coarse tests carried out so far imply.
When developing new tests, researchers should aim to be able to distinguish between
the impact of empowered peaceful women, othering and honor culture, and the new
arguments that will be developed.

Much leverage on the gendered nature of civil war can probably be gained by conducting more research seeking to explain relevant variation in individual-level dependent variables such as participation in civil conflict or peacemaking. Such research
is in many ways more demanding and sensitive than the kind of studies reviewed

in this chapter, but such a development would be in line with the current boom in micro-level studies on issues of peace and conflict. For example, unpublished research suggests that adherence to honor culture is an individual-difference variable that can be measured in surveys, and that predicts the use of violence in contentious politics. Bjarnegård et al. (2014) carried out a survey in Thailand in 2012 of both a nationally representative sample and a special sample of hardcore political activists. The authors show that self-reported political violence (bringing a weapon to a political protest, using a weapon, or causing material damage) is significantly and strongly predicted by the interaction of an index measuring patriarchal values (male privilege and dominance in society as well as in the family, extending to control over female sexuality) and a question measuring the ideal of male toughness (a man shouldn't show emotions and weakness). This result holds also in the nationally representative sample when the sampled activists are removed. This is potentially an important step forward in that previous research on the role of gender attitudes has identified effects on other attitudes (e.g., militarism) or behavior outside the realm of participation in political violence (e.g., street crime, sexual violence in peacetime).

A methodologically more ingenious example, but in the context of interstate conflict, is an unpublished study by Dafoe and Caughey (2012). Previous research has identified the American South as a case of honor culture. The authors treat the haphazard variation in the cultural backgrounds of U.S. presidents as a natural experiment and analyze the effect of a southern background on U.S. behavior in international militarized disputes. Using matching and taking into account other characteristics, they find that disputes under southern presidents are approximately twice as likely to involve U.S. uses of force. This study shows that the effects of honor culture on military conflict can be studied at the level of the highest decision maker of a state.

Another important area for future research is endogeneity and reverse causality. It is conceivable that gender inequality, and in particular the militarized masculinity of honor cultures, is the consequence of experiencing war and turmoil and the concomitant need to foster warriors. One way in which studies could be designed to get at this problem on the individual level of analysis is suggested by a study of determinants of value change among Swedish soldiers deployed to Afghanistan (Sundberg 2016). The author surveys the same soldiers before and after deployment, and also exploits the largely haphazard variation in combat exposure during deployment, to investigate how the experience of war influences personal values. The results show that although combat exposure increases the probability of value change, the overall conclusion is that values tend to remain stable. This study does not investigate gender values or honor culture, but the unusual research design and the result that personal values tend to be resilient are relevant.

A general challenge for the research on gender and civil war is how to deal with the gendered nature of civil war without blinding oneself to relevant variation and falling prey to oversimplifications. For example, the pattern that active combatants in all war, including civil war, tend overwhelmingly to be male has, on the one hand, been ignored or taken for granted. This means that the many women who have participated as active combatants are overlooked or defined away as uninteresting in research. In practice, female combatants have, as mentioned above, been actively pressured to deny their experience and discriminated against in post-conflict situations. This has of course been very detrimental to advancing our deeper understanding of war, and not the least to the women affected. In practical work, it is essential to see the needs and capabilities of individuals regardless of sex. The agency of women in various capacities in civil war is clearly underresearched. At the same time, the strongly gendered nature of civil war seems to hold also with a more nuanced and less stereotypical view of female agency. Hence, a full understanding of the phenomenon of civil war requires explanations that can account for the gendered nature of civil war. Theories are needed that are nuanced enough to deal with this kind of complexity.

13

Exploring the Resource–Civil War Nexus

Benjamin Smith

Since Paul Collier and Anke Hoeffler (1998) suggested nearly twenty years ago that economic incentives were a major determinant of civil wars, the exploration of possible links between natural resources and conflict has grown dramatically. Given the prevalence of intrastate violent conflicts in the post–Cold War world, interest in this possible relationship has grown all the more, leading to major investments in research by the World Bank and other international organizations. As it has grown, however, scholars have collectively accumulated a mass of conclusions that sometimes contradict one another. This lack of consensus makes it difficult to extract solid implications, with a majority of researchers finding a positive link between resources and conflict, but a sizable minority either finding no relationship or a negative (conflict-reducing) role.[1] The growing divergence of conclusions warrants some stocktaking, for two reasons. First, the question of whether or not there exists a "resource curse" is a major one in the social sciences, and its scope extends well beyond the study of civil war to tracing the determinants of long-term economic development, the prospects for democracy, and broader political stability. Second, this is a widely important substantive question in international politics. Just within one "resource," in the global oil sector, there are at least fifty states that can be classified as major oil producers (Ross 2012: 20–21). One-quarter of the world's independent states falling into the "resource-rich" category, based on just one nonrenewable resource, merits close attention by both scholars and policy makers for analytic and prescriptive reasons.

This chapter outlines the state of current research on the resources–civil war linkage. I would note up front that it is an intentionally nontechnical review of the research. There are a number of excellent but more technical complements to this chapter, among them Ross (2014), Koubi et al. (2014), and Humphreys (2005). Also, I focus primarily, although not exclusively, on fuel resources—in particular oil and natural gas (hereafter simply "oil"). I do so because oil is the most important nonrenewable commodity resource in the world, accounting for the vast majority of commodity trade globally.[2]

The chapter proceeds as follows. First, I outline the origins of the hypothesis that oil would increase the likelihood of violent intrastate conflict. Second, I explore the various linking mechanisms that have been theorized to tie oil wealth to conflict. Third, I discuss briefly how scholars typically *measure* oil wealth and conflict—after all, a hypothesis cannot be tested until we find a way to measure the concepts in it. Fourth, I summarize the current debate over whether national- or sub-national–level research is the more appropriate level of focus, highlighting where results differ as a function of this decision. Finally, I suggest some of the more promising avenues for future research, noting in particular the valuable new contributions stemming from locational data on oil fields. To summarize my conclusions briefly, the jury is still out on whether resources are a direct determinant of violent civil conflict or whether they are a result of weak state institutions along *with* such conflict. As a result, the weak-states variant of the resources and conflict thesis is less compelling than the possibility that aspects of resource wealth—in particular its location in regions populated by excluded or dominated minorities—might conditionally shape the likelihood of violent conflicts erupting.

ORIGINS OF THE THESIS THAT OIL BREEDS CONFLICT

The end of the Cold War brought, among other things, a fairly large number of civil wars into sharp focus for both the international and scholarly communities. Conflicts that had often been folded into manifestations of superpower rivalry, or whose ideological meta-narratives (Kalyvas 2001) had been only lightly questioned, lost that cover with the collapse of the Soviet Union. At the same time, a number of new conflicts within the former Soviet Union and outside of it broke out in the first half of the last decade of the twentieth century. These conflicts took place historically outside the Cold War, pulling back a convention to ascribe loose left-right division to violent internal conflicts and demanding a new set of explanations. A number of the conflicts—in Angola, Algeria, and the Republic of Congo among others—resonated with the apparent lessons of Iran's 1979 revolution and Nigeria's Biafra war to generate a sense that resource-rich countries might be more prone to civil war outbreak than others. This was particularly true in sub-Saharan Africa, where a full third of the civil wars of the 1990s took place (Ross 2004; 47).

At the same time, countries that were both resource rich and either politically unstable, autocratic, or economically stagnant continued to proliferate. Civil wars in Algeria, Liberia, Sierra Leone, and Angola, to take just a handful, were tied to those countries' ample diamond and oil wealth. Authoritarianism and oil were tied together, too, in an important article by Ross (2001). Economic variants of the resource curse accompanied these political ones. The economic resource curse was centrally about "Dutch Disease," a dynamic in which a booming resource sector (e.g., the discovery of North Sea oil resources in the Netherlands) inflates a country's currency value, pricing its agricultural and manufacturing sectors out of global competitiveness and later undermining growth and diversification (Sachs and Warner 2001; Frankel 2010). Nigeria's trajectory from strong agricultural producer to heavy agricultural importer between independence and 1990 illustrates this: as the country's oil sector grew, it drew investment away from agriculture so completely that Nigeria must import the majority of its produce.

Another major economic strand of the resource curse is persistently lower economic performance over time. Ross (2012) explains that on average, oil producing countries should have grown substantially faster than their oil-poor counterparts but instead barely broke even with them: it was as if the hundreds of billions of dollars in oil revenues accomplished nothing. As we shall see, slow growth and failed development are then centrally implicated in conflict outbreak. In short, the economics of the resource curse—stagnating non-resource sectors and slow growth—highlighted the material factors that could lower the perceived opportunity costs to rebelling.

Paul Collier and Anke Hoeffler (1998) inaugurated the political-economy approach to civil war studies with a path-breaking effort to tease out a possible link between resources and conflict and catalyzed a new greed-based approach to studying civil war onset: "War occurs if the incentive for rebellion is sufficiently large relative to the costs" (563). Pairing a utility model of rebellion with data capturing primary exports as a share of GDP, they found that resource wealth both increased the risk of civil wars and prolonged those that did break out. The logics were twofold for both center-seeking and secession wars. First, the possibility of capturing a state bringing in such immense revenue with virtually no social cost (as with taxation) was a strong incentive for leaders to organize, and for followers to join, rebellions. Second, the prospect of taking a resource-rich region to independence promised future benefits far outweighing the costs of a secessionist rebellion. The authors uncovered a positive correlation between primary commodity dependence and the onset of major intrastate conflict. This original finding underlays much of the subsequent research on civil war causes.

Some aspects of this starting point are worth noting. First, Collier and Hoeffler conceptualized all primary commodities through the same lens: oil, palm oil, coffee, gold, and diamonds would be considered functionally the same, and presumed to have the same effect on the calculus of would-be rebels. As scholars pushed this research program forward, it became clear that this was a problematic assumption. Second, no apparent realization that commodity export dependence can be endogenous to political strife is evident. We have come to realize that countries undergoing civil war or a number of other forms of internal strife tend to see both foreign and domestic investment shrink as a function of shortened time horizons and uncertain stability and to see economic activity in general contract. This dynamic shrinks the size of the non–commodity sectors of the economy, thereby reducing the size of the overall GDP and boosting the size of the commodity revenue to GDP ratio. Third,

Collier and Hoeffler found a non-linear (inverse U-curved) relationship between resource wealth and conflict, with the effect initially increasing to a threshold and then providing a stabilizing effect. This nonlinear relationship harbored implications for future conditional analyses. Finally, the actual exploration of possible causal links between resources and conflict is thin, and the theoretical framework for the original paper is entirely formal with no direct empirical inquiry as to causation. As a result, it left open questions of the causal chains that might be shown to tie resource wealth to the onset and duration of civil wars. The next section turns to this last issue: the exploration in subsequent research of causal links.

THEORIZING THE MECHANISMS AND MOTIVES

Despite the somewhat coarse nature with which the greed-grievance dichotomy was originally spelled out (see chapter 2, this volume), the theorized mechanisms linking resource wealth to civil conflict track fairly well along a grievance-greed continuum. It is important to keep in mind that the "greed" end of it has come to suggest a broader set of economic reasons than simply economic gain—ranging from greed to basic needs provision or subsistence—but as outlined below, this range captures the set of mechanisms adequately. On the grievance end, we see two main lines of argument. The first is one related to the initial development of the rentier state theory (Mahdavy 1970; Beblawi and Luciani 1987; Delacroix 1980). This theory held that oil contributed directly to weak-state capacity by obviating the need to build an effective extractive apparatus for collecting revenue. It was deeply influenced by European-derived theories of state formation that centered on the need to raise revenues to support standing professional armies during the formative centuries of nation-state building in Western Europe. The rentier state thesis of conflict is basically this: oil leads to weak state formation or to state decay. The concomitant lack of ability to collect revenues effectively leads to broader state decay, eroding public goods provision capabilities. This in turn generates the kinds of grievances that can lower the cost-to-benefit ratio of rebelling.

The weak-state argument has been used in numerous ways, both to link resources and conflict and as a stand-alone hypothesis. Fearon and Laitin (2003) use income per capita as a proxy for state strength and find, unsurprisingly, that it reduces the risk of civil war. They do not explore whether resource wealth has an independent effect on state strength as an intervening variable. What they do instead is to theorize that weak states are incapable of policing their territory—the classic Weberian state imperative—and thus are likely to fail at suppressing insurgents. Macartan Humphreys (2005) also theorizes this way, and finds that although oil appears to weaken state capacity, its main conflict-inducing effect is not through that mechanism. It is important to note that Humphreys does not model civil war onset with a state capacity indicator; I discuss this more below. Cullen Hendrix directly explores the state capacity thesis, employing factor analysis to explore fruitful strategies for making the broad concept operationally manageable (2010). Thies (2010) and Mitchell and Thies (2012) find, respectively that civil war weakens state capacity and that resource dependence is endogenous to ongoing conflict. Both of these cast doubt on the independent role of state capacity in fomenting conflict and on the indirect effect of resources influencing conflict by eroding state capacity. For the most part, the rentier-state variant of the grievance mechanism is thought to shape the risk of center-seeking wars breaking out, both by weakening the state's capacity to provide public goods and by reducing its ability to maintain social order or to quell rebellions.

The second broad strand of grievances has to do with inequitable distribution of the goods that resource revenues can provide. Particularly in states geographically divided along ethnic lines, weak states are predisposed to favor some regions and groups over others (Wimmer 2012). Ethnic favoritism makes this starker, raising the likelihood of the emergence of a sense of relative deprivation by have-not groups. Recent research at the sub-national level has engaged this dynamic with promising new data and detail, and as I discuss below, has helped to put empirical richness into this particular strand of the grievance thesis while providing more nuanced understanding of the interplay between the economic incentives in natural resources and the grievances that state management of them can catalyze.

The broad set of economic incentives for both rebel leaders and for potential followers—what has come to be simply called the "greed thesis"—was nicely spelled out in two edited volumes on the topic (Berdal and Malone 2000; Collier and Sambanis 2005). The contributors to the Berdal and Malone book mostly devoted themselves to fleshing out both macro- and micro-variants of economic explanations, often going beyond the original hypotheses laid out by Collier and Hoeffler. This first set of chapters established a number of durable war economy equilibria—situations likely to arise in civil war settings that powerful actors might find profitable to sustain. A second set of chapters proposed international remedies for this growing set of wartime economic incentives.

Ross (2004) explored causal mechanisms inductively with a sample of thirteen civil wars from the thirty-six that took place during the 1990s. On one hand, it is worth noting that the other twenty-three civil wars appeared to have had little to do with resources. On the other hand, Ross finds in the resource-linked civil wars evidence for a causal onset effect in just two, with no evidence to bolster the looting mechanism and little to support a grievance hypothesis. In assessing duration, however, Ross finds some strong support for the looting hypothesis: in ten of thirteen of the conflicts, looting appeared to have kept them in motion. This is fully in line with the first set of chapters in Berdal and Malone, which developed a number of rich accounts of wartime economic orders that go well beyond a simple "looting" model and explored a wide range of ways that actors might profit from the continuation of conflict. Ross's additional insight is that, while rebel actors may not originally be motivated by prospects for material gain, their understandings and preferences can shift during the conflict itself, so that what may not have been a powerful motive at the outset can become one later.

In addition, Ross found evidence of two previously understudied mechanisms: foreign intervention and what he termed "booty futures." In the latter, rebels bargain with the future value of extraction rights on territory they hope to conquer (58).[3] Perhaps most importantly, in assessing the effect of resources on conflict, Ross finds multiple causes at work in the resource curse: no single mechanism appears in more than nine of thirteen cases, suggesting multiple pathways. He concludes that "this multiplicity of causal linkages . . . may help account for the analytical muddle, and contradictory findings, of earlier studies" (2004b: 62)

The contributors assembled by Collier and Sambanis (2005) explored fifteen different civil war case studies to assess the utility of Collier's and Hoeffler's greed and grievance mechanisms in explaining the outbreak and unfolding of each case. The general conclusion emerging from this collection of cases was essentially that motives tend to be more complex than a single "greed" or "grievance" lens can capture. Indeed, as the editors note, "case studies offer a more textured and nuanced view of civil war and show that the distinction between 'greed' and 'grievance' in the CH model should be abandoned for a more complex model that considers greed and grievance as inextricably fused motives for civil war" (2).

Edward Aspinall's analysis (2007a, 2007b) of the evolution of Acehnese identity and incorporation of the region's oil and gas reserves into that narrative illustrates nicely how resource wealth can be woven into aspects of both economic motives for gain and of anti-state grievance. In this case, he argues, the Free Aceh Movement (GAM, for *Gerakan Aceh Merdeka*) built a narrative of economic deprivation of Aceh's rightful gains from its oil. This became a powerful part of a broader identity frame of resistance to the Indonesian government, particularly for urban and more educated Acehnese. Moreover, Aspinall is careful to distinguish the role that the resource narrative played among different strata of Acehnese society. Less well-educated and rural Acehnese GAM recruits and supporters were much less influenced by it, largely joining instead for reasons related to direct experience of state violence and family lineage in past rebellions. This qualified role of Aceh's resource wealth in the broader narrative is an important corrective to macro-accurate but micro-inaccurate accounts such as that provided by Kell (1995). What I mean by this is that scholars who proceed in this vein sometimes neglect to explore the salience of resources and their monopolization by central governments as a reason for participating in rebellion. Aspinall, by contrast, does exactly this, asking a wide array of former GAM supporters and fighters about the role of resources and finds that a small, mostly urban and highly educated subset were convinced by the resource narrative. I return to this theme in the conclusion.

Among other things, the insights afforded by Aspinall's extensive ethnographic research in Aceh provide a research design link to a prominent research program in civil war studies that focused on why ordinary people are willing to incur extreme risk to themselves and their families to participate in a rebellion. Drawing such links can facilitate broader inquiry that normalizes resource-related rebellions in a fuller set of civil conflicts. To take one non-resource-related example, Elizabeth Wood's

(2003) work on the civil war in El Salvador exemplifies this ecumenical approach to theorizing and explaining participation as a dual function of both material and nonmaterial considerations. Since resource issues are of course a powerful additional layer on what are already complex motivating factors in the choice to join a rebel group, our limited vistas of what this kind of micro-qualitative research can uncover should prompt more inquiry along the same lines.

An additional methodological cautionary note from the Collier-Sambanis case study war project is the danger of spurious correlation. As Sambanis puts it, in a number of important cases "the narratives in this volume show that those natural resources were neither a motive for the war nor a means to sustain rebellion" (309). In others, as in the Democratic Republic of the Congo, it was not resource wealth per se but its concentration in the country's east, where ethnically dominant regional groups threatened secession, and the resource-poor but nationally dominant west felt there was no alternative but to exercise substantial state repression. This conditional relationship between ethnicity, inclusion/exclusion, and resources turns up again in Ross's chapter in the volume on Aceh, as well as in more recent econometric work discussed below.

CAPTURING THE CONCEPT OF "RESOURCE WEALTH": MEASUREMENT ISSUES AND LEVELS OF ANALYSIS

Scholars who explore the onset of civil wars quantitatively face several measurement choices. The initial generation focused exclusively at the national level, drawing on publicly available indicators. The first widely used continuous measure of natural resource wealth, drawing on the Sachs and Warner (1995) and Collier and Hoeffler (1998) precedents, was to take commodity export revenues as a share of GDP. This measure captured the relative economic dependence of a country—thus of both its government and of its populace—on the resource sector. Capturing the concept this way became the standard not just for civil war studies but also for work on the effect of oil on regime type and durability (Ross 2001; Smith 2004, 2007; Morrison 2009).

Measuring it this way, however, created problems of endogeneity. Poorer countries—less industrialized, more dependent on agriculture, and with a smaller non-oil economy—looked more *resource dependent* even if they were not necessarily more oil *abundant* due to their baseline GDP being smaller overall. Another problem with this measure was that by focusing only on revenues derived from the export of oil, it biased the indicator against economically diverse countries that consumed most of what they produced. The United States, for example, has been one of the world's largest oil producers in volume for the last four decades, but as the world's largest economy, it consumes nearly all of its produced oil. In the last two decades a number of increasingly well-governed and economically diversified countries—Brazil is one notable example—have tapped massive new oil and gas reserves and expanded their economies so far beyond just commodities that their resource-revenues-to-GDP ratios would look relatively small. In short, while earlier indicators provided a useful way to think about resource dependence, they are less useful for measuring abundance.

A bevy of studies not specifically focused on resource wealth as the explanatory variable of choice have employed different dummy variables to capture one aspect or another of the concept—among them OPEC membership, oil exports of more than 50 percent of total exports, oil exports of more than 25 percent of GDP, and a host of others. These were more problematic by far than the oil-export-revenues-to-GDP measure. Today, for example, OPEC countries make up only a quarter or so of the major oil producers in the world. Moreover, we have no good analytical reason to believe that arbitrary threshold points such as 25 or 50 percent demarcate a point at which oil suddenly begins to have political importance. Finally, coding country years as "1" if oil exports comprised more than half of total exports told us nothing about the importance of exports in a country's economy. A large, prosperous country with a sizeable domestic consumer market would have a smaller export-to-GDP ratio than a smaller, equally prosperous country (such as Norway), but this figure would not tell us as much as we would want to know to think about the empirical importance of oil wealth.

Subsequently, scholars (Humphreys 2005; Ross 2012) constructed a new measure, based on fuel income per capita. This indicator, not dependent on a GDP denominator for its magnitude, solved the problem of being endogenous to a country's level of development and provided a consistent, easy-to-measure standard. It also captures the conceptual half of resource wealth that we think of as abundance—the total amount of wealth per person that accrues to a nation's economy from the production and sale, abroad or at home, of natural resources. It does not tell us (Smith 2014) how relatively important the fuel income per person is in differing contexts, however, and this point raises the issue of thinking about two kinds of oil wealth: dependence and abundance. Ratio measures with GDP in the denominator capture the former, oil income per capita the latter.

A number of recent studies (Basedau and Lay 2009; Lederman and Maloney 2007; Dunning 2008a) have found both oil abundance and dependence to be statistically significant and substantively important for predicting civil war onset, although sometimes in the opposite direction. Given the analytical differences between the two dimensions of resource wealth, and their contradictory effects, best practices at least in preliminary empirical analysis, would suggest employing a measure for each.

A third set of studies attempts to move beyond income from oil and gas to reserves and in some cases to pursue an instrumental-variables approach.[4] Cotet and Tsui (2013) use data on oil discoveries, the value of oil reserves, and on natural disasters in producing countries. Their goal in developing and employing alternate measures to fuel income is to sidestep the endogeneity problems inherent in production value-based measures. Here, in contrast to the "resource curse" thesis, they find no relationship between oil and conflict, after controlling for country fixed effects.[5] They do find that oil-rich countries spend more on defense, which may provide an explanation for the lack of an effect, but in essence their conclusion is that omitted variables specific to countries matter much more than the fact of national-level oil wealth.

Brunnschweiler and Bulte (2009) similarly attempt to attenuate the risk of endogeneity by using per capita reserves and production figures as proxies for resource abundance. Their conclusions are further still from the conventional wisdom: resource abundance is strongly associated with less risk of conflict onset, and resource dependence is not only not a cause of conflict but appears to be a systematic effect of it. In other words, as discussed above, the effect that conflict has on non-resource economic productivity is strongly negative and enough to depress overall GDP in that reducing the size of the denominator produces the statistical appearance of "resource wealth." As mentioned above, Mitchell and Thies (2012) find similar endogeneity to exist between conflict and resource production.

LEVELS OF ANALYSIS

For much of the two decades during which serious comparative work was ongoing in this research program, it was focused at the national level, as discussed above with regard to measurement. The question in cross-country research effectively asked whether countries rich in natural resources were more likely to suffer conflict than their resource-poor counterparts. Indeed, the strongest book-length case for the resource curse (Ross 2012) is subtitled "Petroleum Wealth and the Development of *Nations*" [my italics]. There are multiple reasons for this. First, both development economics and the political science subfields of comparative and international politics were for a very long time all focused squarely on national states as the units of analysis. Most of the outcomes of interest for scholars across these disciplines therefore manifested at that level, and with the study of civil wars and of the effect of resources on their onset, it was a natural extension to continue the nation focus. Second, it was equally the case that until relatively recently, we lacked data at the sub-national level for enough states to conduct representative comparative research. The Correlates of War Project, and then the Armed Conflict Data project,[6] both originally measured conflict only at the national level, as did the Polity and Freedom House regime datasets, World Bank, International Monetary Fund, and Penn World Tables data projects, meaning that not only our dependent variables (wars) but our independent and control variables, too, were captured at the national level. Finally, nearly all of the original body of theory we have to guide us in exploring the politics of resource wealth points directly to national states as the main locus of causality.

Rentier states, national-level corruption, ethnic favoritism, and similar theoretical frameworks all rely on the presumption that states are the main targets in town, both for scholarly inquiry and for the potential rebels seeking either to capture the center or to exit from it. Is this a problem? To the extent that national-level data cloud potential sub-national dynamics in the resource-conflict relationship, yes. To the extent that national-level data are arguably plagued by causal identification problems that could be addressed with more fine-grained data, again, yes. These two arguments are at the center of critiques of past research (see Ross 2014 and Koubi et al. 2014 for summaries). Two trends in conflict-research data may offer partial solutions to these problems. First, research on variation across space during civil wars (for example Straus 2006; Kalyvas 2006; Balcells 2010) helped to focus the attention of scholars on why some parts of countries during civil war were so much more violent than others. In each of these cases—Rwanda, Greece, Spain—the civil wars under discussion have not been argued to have been shaped by resource wealth. Rather, each of these conflicts turns out to have evinced important variation across even very small national territories, opening a new line of inquiry. And, the increasing turn to sub-national exploration of patterns of violence during civil wars has in turn helped to reshape the contours of research specifically focused on the resource link. It has in part been motivated by scholars convinced that the national-level confusion of findings is a function of sub-national variation.

One of the strongest new lines of inquiry to have emerged in the broader civil wars research program in the last five to ten years has been the proliferation of sub-national analyses versus national-level ones (see chapter 15, this volume). Considering the growing improvement of data quality at the sub-national level, and the volume of non-resource-focused research on violence during civil wars (for example Balcells 2010; Kalyvas 2006) this is a welcome direction for research. In particular, sub-national research promises to help develop answers to two sets of questions. First, do ethnic minorities or sub-national regions launch violent challenges to governments more often when the resource reserves are located within their regions? Second, do we see sub-national variation within national settings that might help to explain the inconsistency of country-level research?

In addition to these problems is the reality that all of the above-mentioned measurement strategies focus only at the national level. If the effects of resource wealth on conflict accrue *only* there, this could be a reasonable strategy. At this point, however, many recent studies have shown systematic sub-national and micro-level dynamics at work, pointing strongly to the need for careful analysis below the level of national states. These dynamics take two broad forms: rebel recruitment through lootable resources (individual level), and regional inequities and resource location (group/regional level). I address these in order below.

REBEL RECRUITMENT AND LOOTABLE RESOURCES

Any rebellion must recruit and retain fighters to be viable. A central question related to resources and recruitment is lootability—put simply, the ease with which rebel organizations can seize and allocate the resources themselves. Weinstein (2007) points to coca cultivation in Colombia as one source of easily looted wealth. Secondary (the so-called blood) diamonds are another—because they require no logistically expansive mining, rebels who hold the territory in which they are located can make use of them. More recently, our awareness that ISIS has developed an expansive smuggling network for selling Syrian oil from territory it controls (through Turkey), along with

Mexican cartel looting of oil in the northern parts of the country, suggest that we should devote further inquiry to the issue. This prospect could, like the primary versus secondary diamond bifurcation, create two tracks of argument about oil reserves and micro-level conflict dynamics.

At the level of rebel organizations, scholars have theorized that resource allocations shape both rebel groups themselves and the kinds of recruits who are attracted to the movement. Weinstein (2007) illustrates how groups with greater resource endowments tend to more effectively attract opportunistic recruits and to become more loot-driven themselves. Buhaug et al. (2009) find that rebel movements originating in mineral-rich regions can sustain much more durable violent conflicts with the governments they challenge. Gates (2002: 115) models a dynamic in which "loot-seeking groups generally possess more resources than other types of rebel groups." While this latter logic leans toward the circular, it fits into a broader line of inquiry seeking to uncover the extent to which rebel leaders benefit from having access to resources they can offer to potential recruits.

REGIONAL INEQUITIES IN RESOURCES

Since many countries at risk for civil war are also deeply divided along regional, ethnic, or religious lines, the prospect for resources affecting those cleavages has also produced a growing research program. One line of argument suggests simply that rebels—ethnic or otherwise—located in resource-rich regions are more likely to rebel, and more likely to succeed when they do. Related to this, the development of the Minorities at Risk[7] and then the Ethnic Power Relations projects enabled the analysis of ethnically charged conflicts at the group level. This made it possible to analyze center-seeking civil wars distinct from separatist ones, and also to explore the role that political exclusion plays in group mobilization against the state. These trends helped to push research forward by encouraging scholars to ask whether resource location, too, might be a promising direction, in essence allowing us to explore not whether a country was resource-rich, but where resources are produced across its territory. Hunziker and Cederman (2012) for example, find a strong difference in the conflict proclivities of ethnic minority regions based on (a) whether or not they enjoy meaningful access to political authority and (b) whether or not their regions are home to resource reserves. Sorens (2011) finds that while the presence of mineral riches in an ethnic minority region discourages center-seeking conflicts, it enhances the risk of separatist ones by providing a base for thinking about post-independence economic sustainability. This is in line with Ross's (2003) analysis of the independence narrative of the Free Aceh Movement in Indonesia, whose leaders looked to nearby Brunei as a model of oil-funded small-country success. Oyefusi (2008) similarly finds a strong positive relationship between the size of the oil sector in Nigerian communities and the willingness of individuals to participate in rebellions.

It is reasonable to ask simply whether the large number of different measures used to capture the concept of "resource wealth" might be driving increasingly divergent results. The answer to that question is of course impossible to know unless we could convince all of these scholars to use the same indicators. But there are some important implications of the measure debate for future research. The first is that, while more challenging, national-level analysis based on cross-country data is not by any means a dead end. Instead, we find scholars working diligently to craft measures that deal with endogeneity problems, constructing research designs that account for the uncertain but inevitably missing variables in explaining the onset of civil conflict, and in general taking careful steps to improve the quality of data and the reliability of results. It is worth noting that the current uncertainty in cross-country research is by no means unique in political science and political economy research. One could say the same about the development-democracy nexus, and as a result, I would caution against arguing for a shift away from national-level research simply because causal identification is challenging. Rather, as those who argue for a resource curse and those who argue against it continue to accumulate findings, it would be well worth trying to bridge the disparity of conclusions with explicit efforts to isolate a smaller number of measures of resource wealth. This if nothing else would allow for genuine knowledge accumulation around a consistent set of indicators and would make it possible to focus on the other differences of specification, design, and analysis. Another strategy, one I detail more in the conclusion, is to pair cross-country aggregate data analysis with structured qualitative comparisons arguably better suited to teasing not just causality but the mechanisms underpinning them. Despite the clear accomplishments of the World Bank case study war project (Collier and Sambanis 2005), we have seen too little of this multi-method research.

None of this is to say that cross-country research, either econometric or small-N comparative historical, is dead or on the way out. Because resource revenues are overwhelmingly owned by national states,[8] and because states are the most frequent arbiters of who gets exploration and production contracts as well as the last line of responsibility, national governments will continue to play a central practical role in determining the future of the politics of resource wealth. Accordingly, problems with national-level data such as endogeneity or the likelihood of disparateness stemming from sub-national variation, are ones that we ought to tackle to improve, not ones we ought to use to justify ending, cross-country research. This is simply to say that we need to address squarely the data and theoretical problems that have challenged cross-national research in the past.

A very promising avenue of research, as I suggested with reference to cross-country studies, is the exploration of conditional relationships between sub-national resource wealth and conflict. For example, rather than simply asking whether oil-rich regions rebel more, Hunziker and Cederman (2012) ask whether oil-rich regions that have been excluded from political power are more likely rebel than oil-rich regions that are included. Similarly, Østby, Nordås, and Rød (2009) find that the presence of oil fields in ethnic regions only makes those regions more likely to rebel when they are relatively economically deprived compared to the national average. The slow but steady erosion of monotonic findings at the country level suggests strongly that as more scholars pursue research below the national level, more important conditional relationships are likely to emerge. Moreover, in the same way that conditional institutional quality-resource linkages led to "institutions, not resources" conclusions (see for example Brunnschweiler 2008; Menaldo 2014), and as we develop better ways of capturing sub-national political dynamics, we may well discover that they are similar to country-level ones. In short, while at this time scholars are finding strong sub-national relationships between resources and conflict, ten to fifteen years ago exactly the same thing would have been true about country-level relationships, and the important point is that we are early in our empirical understanding of the sub-national dynamics.

LOOKING FORWARD

As the volume and quality of research on the relationship between resources and conflict has expanded, so too has the discord in conclusions. While acknowledging that there are multiple views on why this is the case, my sense is that it is normal in social science. "Civil wars" are big events and conceptually complicated ones. Measuring civil war itself is a debated topic, and the standard threshold of 1,000 battlefield deaths raises questions about why 999 would be substantively different from 1,001. Notwithstanding that, there are a number of areas in which it seems most fruitful to encourage future research to push forward. In this concluding section, I outline five main priorities of focus: the direction of causality in the institutions-resources nexus, endogeneity concerns, measurement choice, levels of analysis, and the promise of multi-method research. Two—the question of whether resource wealth is a product of, or a cause of, weak institutions and the issue of multi-method inquiry—could be called meta-theoretical and research design–level issues, respectively. The other three are essentially concept and measure questions.

One conceptual area that stands out—both in terms of links to broader questions in comparative politics and political economy—as needing closer consideration is the relationship between resource wealth and state capacity (or institutional quality). Although Humphreys (2005) concluded that the weak-states mechanism was more consistent with the empirics than others linking resources to conflict, it was inferred rather than directly explored. And, subsequent research has increasingly suggested three things. First, resource wealth does not appear to have any direct weakening effect on state capacity or on the quality of institutions. Ross (2012) in fact finds a small but significant strengthening effect of oil wealth on institutional quality, and Smith (2012) finds the same in a sample of Southeast Asian countries. In short, the net effect of resources often seems to enhance, not undercut, government performance.

Second, several recent studies have concluded that it is institutional quality that determines resource "wealth" rather than the other way around, via two processes.

Brunnschweiler and Bulte (2009) found that countries with weaker institutions tend not to adopt economic policies that encourage diverse growth and development. As a result, the resource sector's share of the total GDP increases, effectively making "resource wealth" endogenous to prior institutions. In line with this, Menaldo (2014) demonstrates that rulers in countries with weak institutions tend to turn to resource-sector development to compensate for their inability to accomplish broader development. Hence, there are really two mechanisms at work, both of which plausibly boost the size of the resource sector. Moreover, the established effects of conflict in increasing a country's resource dependence, plus the frequency of repeated conflicts in war-prone countries, suggest a further endogeneity effect. In a research program in which it is very often taken as a given that resources are granted a priori by nature—and by definition exogenous to the political and social worlds due to their natural occurrence—this new insight is among the most important in moving forward. If this is the case, the scholarly community ought to cease advising policy makers on how to combat the resource curse and instead focus on improving the quality of institutions and battling corruption.

Third, the exploration for and discovery of resource reserves is highly endogenous to politics and governance. Collier (2010) notes that in the developed world, we estimate that 80 percent of actual reserves have already been discovered, with just 20 percent remaining. He notes further that the estimates are reversed for much of the developing world. The reason? Oil exploration firms facing limited asset mobility, once "sunk," have been much more hesitant to commit to investing in unstable, poorly governed states than in stable, well-governed ones. The extent to which known reserves are thus a function of, rather than a cause of, state capacity provides yet a third compelling reason to think of resource wealth itself as an outcome to be explored, and as potentially a sub-outcome of state weakness alongside conflict. Thinking of it this way then would make the conflict-resources link seem less surprising. If it is the case that governments in command of weak states both tend to over-rely on resource sectors and fail in promoting economic diversification *and* to suffer more internal conflicts than others, scholars would do well to start conceptualizing resource dependence as a potential warning sign rather than strictly an independent variable.

Another line of promising future inquiry has to do with data. As data quality continues to increase at multiple levels, two major areas of potential scholarly gains appear most fruitful. One is the prospect of synthesizing national and sub-national research. Recognizing that this scope of inquiry is most likely to be book length, or at least on the longer end of what journals in political science are generally willing to accept, it is the case that a growing consensus that if there is a relationship between resources and the likelihood (or duration) of violent conflict, it is a conditional or nonlinear one. This consensus appears to be emergent at both levels, and while I am sensitive to critiques of national-level data analysis for the reasons of difficulty in causal identification and in sorting out endogenous relationships, the substantive importance of continuing to explore dynamics at this level is simply too great to lose.

However, to the extent that analysis of empirics at both levels is feasible—and I do not mean simply two levels of statistical data but a wider array of potential multi-method design options—we stand a much better change of nailing down robust conclusions (see for example Balcells and Justino 2014).

Another issue in need of attention as civil war scholars move forward on the resource angle is some consistency in measurement choice. There are three main clusters of indicators commonly employed as measures of resource wealth: resource abundance (resource income per capita, most commonly), resource dependence (resource income as a share of some measure of average income per capita), and a variety of efforts to instrument for resource wealth (known reserves, giant oil fields, proven reserves, etc.). Yet I catalogued more than one dozen separate measures including dummy variables for either OPEC membership or various thresholds of dependence (Smith 2014). Since it is the case in a number of recent studies that indicators capturing abundance and dependence either have opposite effects or varying ones, and since this broad concept of resource wealth has a number of dimensions, it makes sense that scholars ought to explore resource-conflict linkages using an array of measures. Given the wide availability and consistency of fuel income per capita, this indicator would seem the best for capturing abundance. I have argued elsewhere for employing rent leverage as the best measure of dependence. And while efforts to find instruments for oil wealth continue to be endogenous in some way to politics, non-income-based measures ought to continue to play a role. As a result, best practices would argue for multiple measures, with one from each of the above-mentioned three categories.

A final avenue for future research at the micro level has to do with the dovetailing looting mechanisms in a host of case-driven studies. As conflict dynamics change, so too might the balance of grievance-to-greed motives, affecting individuals over time but also the kind of individuals who join into conflicts at specific points in their duration. Aspinall's in-depth analysis of joining dynamics during the Aceh conflict in Indonesia illustrates this point well. In the late 1990s and early 2000s, there took place a change in the central motives of joiners. Immediately after the fall of the Suharto regime in Jakarta, the Free Aceh Movement (*Gerakan Aceh Merdeka*, or GAM) found itself with greatly expanded freedom to mobilize. As a result, in addition to political activists, GAM's ranks swelled with low-level criminals, for whom the payoffs of taking part at that moment far outweighed the costs. Beginning in 2001, however, with the declaration of a military emergency in the province, state coercion increased dramatically. The years following this change subsequently saw the defection from GAM of many if not most of the wave of opportunistic joiners.

Micro-focused research is most likely to continue to illuminate such dynamics as these. There has been relatively less ethnographic research on the resource-conflict link to compare to work such as that of Elizabeth Wood (2003), which holds much promise for sorting out just which motives appear most salient for individuals in deciding whether to participate in rebellions. And while we have seen valuable insights emerge from survey research (Humphreys and Weinstein 2008; Barron, Humphreys,

Paler, and Weinstein 2009), it is also likely that these more formalized, less ethnographically embedded research strategies may miss many of the honest and rich responses that more in-depth research might provide. This would argue for equal emphasis on the micro-qualitative side of civil war research. In short, a clearer focus on supporting the collection of quality ethnographic as well as quantitative data on the micro-dynamics of how resources shape conflict proneness could take us far in understanding the tough decisions that individuals make about whether or not to participate in rebellions.

14

Environment and Conflict

Cullen Hendrix, Scott Gates, and Halvard Buhaug

How do environmental conditions and resource scarcity affect civil war? Between July 2011 and August 2012, a severe drought and resultant famine killed as many as 260,000 people—half of whom were under the age of six—in Djibouti, Ethiopia, Somalia, and northern Kenya.[1] The drought marked the first time since the 1980s that famine had been declared in the Horn of Africa. Though the famines were as different as they were alike—the epicenters (southern Somalia in the 2010s, Ethiopia in the 1980s) were different, the rapidity of international response varied—they had one important commonality: both occurred against a backdrop of civil war. In the 1980s, the Ethiopian government faced armed challenges from a variety of peripheral ethnic groups seeking independence, most importantly the Eritrean Liberation Front and the Oromo Liberation Front. In the 2010s, Somalia's battle against al-Shabaab rebels drew in African Union–sponsored forces from Burundi, Kenya, and Uganda, resulting in retaliatory terror attacks against those countries' civilian populations.

The notion that scarcity fuels conflict by amplifying societal grievances and sparking distributional conflicts over scarce natural resources (food, water, arable land) was central to popular reporting on both conflicts. Indeed, these conflicts have taken place in locations marked by high levels of chronic food insecurity and environmental degradation, suggesting a causal relationship between scarcity and civil strife. However, a closer look at conflict dynamics in Somalia reveals a more complex relationship between scarcity and violence. The drought and resultant scarcity may have actually weakened al-Shabaab. Drought forced farmers and herders to flee the rural areas that are considered al-Shabaab strongholds, undercutting the economic base of the movement and making it harder to sustain its forces (Roble 2011). Moreover, al-Shabaab's blockage of food aid angered tribal groups in areas it controls and its resource constraints contributed to its unexpected withdrawal from Mogadishu in August 2011 and Kismayo in 2012. In short, the prolonged drought and famine in the region may have made it more difficult for al-Shabaab to sustain rebellion. This case highlights the complex and potentially countervailing effects environmental conditions and resource scarcity may have on civil war.

The chapter reviews the state of knowledge linking environmental conditions and resource scarcity to civil war. It begins with a review of the origins of environmental security thinking before briefly outlining the first wave of empirical research, featuring resource scarcity as the main mechanism through which environmental factors lead to armed civil conflict (see also chapter 13, this volume). It then presents the second wave of research, featuring the direct and indirect effects of weather-related variables such as change in rainfall and temperature on armed conflict. This is followed by a discussion of the reverse causal relationship—how armed conflict affects the environment. Given the failure of extant research to find conclusive evidence of a single, direct, and general relationship between the environment and conflict, it then presents a set of critical challenges and opportunities for future research with respect to quantitative research design and the theoretical/empirical identification of more nuanced, context-specific causal mechanisms. It concludes with a discussion of paths forward for future research.

ENVIRONMENT AND CONFLICT: A BRIEF INTELLECTUAL HISTORY

Attempts to link environmental conditions to conflict go back at least as far as the eighteenth century, to the writings of Montesquieu (1748) and Malthus (1798). Montesquieu contended that climatic conditions, in particular temperature, determined the nature of individual behavior. Those living in cooler northern climates, while brave and vigorous, were less suspicious of others and less desirous of revenge. Inhabitants of warmer climates, though predisposed toward idling, had strong passions that led to more violent and criminal behavior. So began a long tradition of environmental determinism in Western thought, even if recent research tends to support the notion that anomalously high temperatures can lead to more aggressive, violent behavior at the interpersonal level (Jacob et al. 2007; Larrick et al. 2011). Whether this relationship holds for civil conflict, however, is more contested (see the section on climate change and conflict).

Malthus was perhaps the first to directly link environmental resource constraints—in particular, food—with human conflict. He noted that while human populations grow at an exponential rate (i.e., in percentage terms, with a compounding effect over time), the food supply, at least in early Industrial Revolution England, appeared to increase only linearly, as more land was brought under cultivation. The implication of this insight was straightforward: the human population would outpace its food supply, resulting in competition for ever-diminishing shares of the pie. Human populations would be kept "equal to the means of subsistence" by a mixture of disease, starvation, and violent death.

Though Malthus did not explicitly link food shortages with political violence, the term "Malthusian" has come to describe those who argue that human conflict will occur when a population's resource needs surpass the carrying capacity of their environment, sparking distributive conflicts. In more modern times, this logic has been expanded to include not just basic necessities—food and water—but any competition over natural resources that are rivalrous in their consumption and are either nonrenewable (coal, oil) or exhaustible due to overexploitation (farmland, rivers). Malthus appears to have been wrong on both counts. Human population growth is not exponential, but rather logistic, and the food supply has increased faster than population since the 1800s. However, such findings have not materially diminished the intuitive appeal of his logic.

Modern scholarly interest in environmental conflict has three main historical antecedents: (1) the centrality of territorial conquest to both Nazi and Imperial Japanese ideologies; (2) the rise of U.S. and European environmental movements in the late 1960s; and (3) several high profile conflicts of the 1980s and 1990s, particularly those of Ethiopia and Rwanda. Following World War II, many observers linked Germany's and Japan's territorial ambitions to their pre-war population problems and the need to expand territorially in order to reduce demographic pressure. In Germany, the notion of *Lebensraum* ("living space," and the need for the German people to expand territorially to accommodate their numbers) was a key component of Nazi thought and served as a justification for Germany's territorial expansion into the Sudetenland, annexation of Austria, and ultimate invasions of Poland and the Soviet Union. Similarly, Japan's annexation of Manchuria was understood in part as the result of Japan's high population density and need to expand its agricultural base.

Second, environmental issues in general rose to prominence as a result of environmental movements in Western democracies. The 1960s and early 1970s saw the publication of influential commentaries on rapid population growth and declining natural resource stocks: *The Population Bomb* (Ehrlich 1968) and *The Limits to Growth* (Meadows et al. 1972). Even Russell (1964) theorized that one of the most plausible causes of thermonuclear war would be overpopulation leading to starvation, impoverishment, and competition for depopulated arable land. Finally, several African conflicts of the 1980s and 1990s seemed to provide ample support for Malthus's hypothesis. Images of famine-stricken Ethiopian children—dual victims of hunger and the country's brutal civil war—catalyzed global action in the 1980s and seemed to underscore a causal link between acute food scarcity and conflict, even if this dominant narrative had the causal logic reversed (see "Conflict Effects on the Environment" section of this chapter). This notion was reinforced by the Rwandan civil war and genocide, which occurred in Africa's most densely populated rural society (Uvin 1996, Esty et al. 1998).

The resulting generation of scholarship on environmental effects on civil conflict developed much more nuanced, contextual models. Demographic pressures and resource constraints (specifically, declining stocks of renewable resources) still played a primary role in affecting outcomes, but it focused more on inequality of access to resources and the role of mediating variables. Homer-Dixon (1991, 1994, 1999) and Kahl (1998, 2006) moved beyond simple neo-Malthusian propositions to highlight specific causal pathways—migration and economic contraction—linking environmental scarcity to conflict. Both authors emphasized the role of state capacity as a factor that might condition the effects of environmental stress: in Homer-Dixon's work, state capacity was weakened by migration and economic contraction, resulting in decreased capacity to deter violent challenges and, therefore, an increased likelihood of ethnic conflicts, coups d'état, and "deprivation conflicts": civil strife and insurgency.

Kahl's analysis highlighted two more important factors: ethnic cleavages ("group-ness") and institutional inclusivity—whether there were significant constraints on the executive and whether there were divisions within ruling elites—in determining whether "demographic-environmental stress (DES)" would result in civil strife. Where ethnic cleavages were not highly salient, environmental stress did not manifest in intergroup conflict; where institutions were inclusive, alternative, nonviolent mechanisms existed for resolving environmental conflicts. His work highlighted the role of the state as well, but introduced the concept of "state exploitation": environmental conflict that resulted from the state sponsoring the migration of favored groups into lands inhabited by marginalized or excluded peripheral ethnic groups. These so-termed "sons of the soil" conflicts, though discussed in the 1970s (Weiner 1978), would eventually become a substantial focus of the literature in the 2000s (Fearon 2004; Hegre 2004; Fearon and Laitin 2011).

Derived from qualitative case studies, these models were highly nuanced and contextual. However, this was not universally perceived as a virtue. Gleditsch (1998) criticized this literature for developing such large and complex models that they were essentially untestable and for selecting on the dependent variable: by focusing on cases where environmental stress appeared to lead to conflict, the studies neglected the prospect that similar environmental conditions might also be associated with peace, rendering their causal import unknowable. Owing partly to poor time-series data on environmental factors and obvious methodological challenges related to reverse causality, the neo-Malthusian thesis has been subject to less systematic scientific scrutiny than one might think, considering the widespread support for the notion of scarcity-driven social tensions among dominant policy and NGO actors.

EMPIRICAL FINDINGS

First Wave: Resource Scarcity and Conflict

In the late 1990s, the first comparative large-N studies of the environment-conflict nexus emerged with the near simultaneous publication of the State Failure Task Force's (now Political Instability Task Force) second report (Esty et al. 1998) and Hauge and Ellingsen's (1998) statistical analysis of civil war occurrence. The two studies reported somewhat different findings; the latter was more supportive of a robust correlation between resources and civil wars, although it concluded that economic and political factors are more decisive in predicting conflict. A later study that sought to reconcile the confusing differences in findings among these early investigations found little support for the scarcity thesis, but pointed to a number of problems with sample coverage and data quality, including mostly static measures of environmental conditions such as deforestation and soil degradation (Theisen 2008).

More recent assessments of environmental change and civil conflict have resulted in mixed findings. For example, de Soysa (2002) found that abundance of nonrenewable resources increases civil war risks, presumably by providing a contestable resource base over which to fight (the "honeypot" hypothesis), whereas scarcity of renewables has little effect (see chapter 13, this volume); Raleigh and Urdal (2007) showed that local conflict risk is associated with high population density but not with resource scarcity per se. The study by Gizelis and Wooden (2010) is more supportive of the general scarcity narrative as it reports evidence of a direct link between water scarcity and conflict as well as an indirect association, conditioned by political institutions. Alternately, Koubi et al. (2014) find that resource abundance, rather than scarcity, is associated with armed conflict, providing some support for de Soysa's "honeypot" hypothesis.

Second Wave: Climate Variability and Conflict

Much of the early statistical research on the scarcity thesis suffered from poor data, usually limited to snapshot observations of highly volatile environmental phenomena such as de- and reforestation, desertification, soil depletion, and freshwater availability. Increasing availability of digitalized remote sensing data[2] over the past decade has ensured significant progress in the field in this regard, although it also has resulted in an analytical shift of focus toward meteorological patterns and climatic changes, rather than studying environmental degradation and renewable resource scarcity more generally.

A pioneering study spearheading the second wave of quantitative environment-conflict research reported a significant relationship between decreased rainfall and increased civil war risk in Sub-Saharan Africa, operating through its effect on economic growth (Miguel et al. 2004). However, rainfall was introduced by the authors as a suitable exogenous instrument for economic growth rather than as a variable for environmental conditions. Boosted by the UN Intergovernmental Panel on Climate Change (IPCC) Fourth Assessment report (2007) and the contemporaneous Nobel Peace Prize award to the IPCC and former U.S. vice president Al Gore, research on climate and conflict quickly gained prominence and media attention. Around the same time, the first journal special issue on climate change and conflict was published in *Political Geography* (Nordås and Gleditsch 2007). A contribution to that issue by Hendrix and Glaser (2007) expanded Miguel et al.'s work by showing that both long-term and short-term shifts in precipitation patterns affect conflict risk, although their simulation of implications of alternative future climate change scenarios returned few significant results.

More recent investigations of the rainfall-conflict link have provided mixed support (e.g., Jensen and Gleditsch 2009; Ciccone 2011; Koubi et al. 2012), and a follow-up study by the original authors of Miguel et al. found that temperature matters much more for civil war risk than variations in rainfall levels (Burke et al. 2009). The unequivocal conclusions of that study, alongside the gloomy quantitative projections about implications of future global warming for African peace and security, stirred a vocal debate that has continued to until this day (see, e.g., Buhaug 2010, 2014; Cane et al. 2014; Hsiang and Meng 2014; O'Loughlin et al. 2014a, 2014b; Raleigh et al. 2014).

In 2012, the second major compilation of climate-conflict research was published as a special issue of the *Journal of Peace Research* (Gleditsch 2012). Overall, the contributions provided mixed and inconclusive evidence for a systematic climate effect. For example, Hendrix and Salehyan (2012) and Raleigh and Kniveton (2012) found that both positive and negative deviations from normal rainfall increase conflict risk (although the exact shape of the relationship differs between different conflict types). In other words, countries can face increased risk for civil wars in the face of too little or too much rainfall.

Among studies focusing squarely on local communal violence, Meier et al. (2007) reported a weak and insignificant effect of rainfall on conflict in East Africa. Their conclusion that cattle raiding occurs more frequently during times of ample vegetation density also contradicts the traditional scarcity narrative, hinting at predation and looting behavior being shaped more by environmental and military-tactical opportunities than classical grievances. Benjaminsen et al.'s (2012) study of land-use disputes in Mali concluded that climate variability at best has a trivial effect, whereas Theisen (2012) found that below-average rainfall is associated with a reduction in conflict events across Kenya (see also Witsenburg and Adano 2009). Other studies have contributed to the confusion by reporting that negative deviations from normal rainfall either increase conflict risk (Fjelde and von Uexkull 2012), have little effect (O'Loughlin et al. 2012), or are associated with a lowered incidence of conflict (Detges 2014; Salehyan and Hendrix 2014). The origin of such discrepancies in findings may be traced to differences in conflict data, level of aggregation, sample coverage, and model specification.

The most up-to-date research, epitomized by a third special issue on climate change and conflict (Salehyan 2014), has done little to rectify the confusing and contradictory empirical results of climate impacts on violent conflict. Some have concluded that the contradictory results are driven primarily by modeling choices: some studies exclude control variables that might plausibly be affected by climatic factors—like a drought exerting a drag on economic growth, which might also affect conflict onset—and thus produce biased coefficient estimates, and instead use time and country fixed effects and panel-specific or region-specific time trends to identify the impact of climatic fluctuations on conflict (Burke et al. 2009; Hsiang et al. 2013). Others (Buhaug 2010; O'Loughlin, Linke, and Witmer 2014b; Theisen et al. 2011/2012) argue that control variables are necessary to place the relative causal weight of climatic factors in context, to facilitate modeling interactive and conditional relationships, and to address the confounding effects of factors (such as economic development) that may also trend over time. At least one recent study attempts to reconcile findings across these different model specifications, finding a positive relationship between rainfall abundance and conflict (Salehyan and Hendrix 2014).

There is somewhat more empirical support for a link between anomalous weather and low-intensity communal conflict (e.g., von Uexkull 2014) than between climate variability and civil conflict (e.g., Buhaug et al. 2014), although any manifestation of a causal climate effect is likely to depend on contextual conditions and the vulnerability of the local population that hitherto has not been properly modeled and understood (see Busby et al. 2014; Ide et al. 2014). We return to the significance of indirect mechanisms and context below. Tellingly of the state of the art, recent reviews of the literature almost uniformly conclude that there is a lack of convergence on the climate-conflict relationship (Adger et al. 2014; Bernauer et al. 2012; Buhaug et al. 2014; Klomp and Bulte 2013; Meierding 2013; Salehyan 2014; for a dissenting voice, see Hsiang et al. 2013).

Indirect Effects and Mediated Effects

Save for some work linking environmental conditions to conflict via either economic growth (Miguel et al. 2004) or food prices and agricultural productivity (Smith 2014; Wischnath and Buhaug 2014), discussions of indirect causation largely have been absent from analyses of environmental impacts on conflict. To the extent that the conflict literature has addressed environmental variables, these variables are typically included on the right-hand side of the equation along with other economic, political, and geographic factors, such as economic development, the strength and coherence of political institutions, and primary commodity dependence. Setting aside the various problems of endogeneity that arise from the interplay of political institutions, patterns of economic development, and resource dependence, part of the effect of environmental factors on conflict may flow through these indirect channels. That is, environmental factors may help explain why some countries are wealthier (poorer) and have stronger (weaker) institutions, and are more (less) commodity-dependent and thus are less (more) conflict prone.

Environmental factors play a large indirect role in political and economic development. Olsson and Hibbs (2004) use prehistorical data on initial biological endowments at the time of the transition to agriculture to estimate present-day levels of wealth, finding that areas with appropriate endowments of domesticable plant and animal life are indeed wealthier than those with less accommodating biological endowments, even in the presence of controls for institutional quality. Acemoglu, Johnson, and Robinson (2001) and Rodrik, Subramanian, and Trebbi (2004) find that environmental conditions have a strong indirect effect on economic growth by influencing the quality of political and legal institutions.

These arguments hinge on the effects of disease environments on settler mortality rates and on the types of political and legal institutions that developed. Where environmental conditions approximated those in continental Europe, colonizers were more likely to establish large European-descended populations and European-like political and legal institutions, with protections on private property and checks and balances against government expropriation. Where environmental conditions did not sustain large settler populations due to high disease burdens and mortality rates, more extractive, bureaucratically weak institutions were put in place. In general, these insights have not been widely incorporated by the scholarly community studying environmental impacts on conflict, but they suggest that many factors related to the onset of civil war (e.g., political institutions, economic growth) may be related to environmental conditions in a country's historical development.

There is also evidence that environmental impacts on conflict are more likely to emerge in particular political, socio-demographic, and economic contexts. While linkages at the global scale are contested, more consistent evidence for environmental influences on conflict has emerged at the regional scale in Africa and Asia, two regions characterized by low state capacity and weak legal institutions, comparatively exclusionary patterns of rule, and high levels of ethnic polarization (Meier, Bond, and Bond 2007; Hendrix and Glaser 2007; Eck 2014; Salehyan and Hendrix 2014). While Salehyan and Hendrix (2014) find a positive relationship between precipitation anomalies and various conflict indicators in a global sample, these correlations are both statistically and substantively much stronger when the sample is stratified according to economic development (below 50th percentile), agriculture as a percent of GDP (above 50th percentile), and region, with both Africa and Asia showing stronger correlations. These findings suggest that one way to break any link between environmental conditions and conflict outcomes is for societies to develop economically to the point where economic conditions are not so tightly coupled with environmental conditions.

CONFLICT EFFECTS ON THE ENVIRONMENT

While the causal relationship of environmental conditions on conflict is contested, evidence for the reverse relationship—that conflict has negative consequences for the environment—is much less controversial. Conventional interstate warfare often created "warzone refugia," or zones where human activity was curtailed due to fighting, where ecosystems could flourish. Examples include the rebound in North Atlantic fish populations as a result of fishing pressure curtailed by submarine warfare and the protected ecosystem that flourishes in the Korean demilitarized zone (Martin and Szuter 1999; Jennings, Kaiser, and Reynolds 2001). Modern civil conflicts, however, have more uniformly negative effects on wildlife and wildlife habitats (Dudley et al. 2002), with particularly devastating effects for large mammals that require large habitats or are a source of food during crises.

Conflict adversely affects environmental conditions through four primary mechanisms: (1) population displacement and unsustainable coping strategies, (2) counterinsurgency strategy, (3) "crowding out" effects and shortened time horizons, and (4) the emergence of destructive wartime political economies. Via these mechanisms, conflict can create further resource competition, contributing to a cycle of violence (UNEP 2009).

Violence and the fear of future violence create incentives to migrate in search of safety, both across borders and within affected countries (Collier et al. 2003; Moore and Shellman 2004, 2007). The choice to leave is often an arduous one: Staying and risking harm must be balanced against flight to safety, which entails the loss of property, livelihood, and community. This is especially impoverishing for rural populations whose main store of wealth is often livestock. For example, 80 percent of Mozambique's cattle stocks were liquidated during the peak years of combat between the FRELIMO government and RENAMO rebels (Collier et al. 2003).

Refugees often wind up inhabiting marginal lands with few economic prospects, making them dependent on humanitarian assistance and unsustainable foraging strategies for food, shelter, and energy (Jacobsen 1997; Gleditsch and Salehyan 2006). For example, refugees of the Rwandan civil war in the Democratic Republic of Congo deforested roughly 3,800 hectares (38 km²) within three weeks of their arrival in and around Goma (Biswas and Tortajada-Quiroz 1996). These unsustainable foraging strategies extend to combatants as well: armed groups in the eastern Congo were implicated in the slaughter of gorillas, a highly endangered species, for meat (Draulans and Van Krunkelsven 2002). In general, these foraging practices harm ecosystems and the wildlife they support.

In an analysis using matching techniques, Monte Carlo simulations and other statistical techniques of how armed civil conflict affects the Millennium Development Goals, Gates et al. (2012) find that armed conflict was significantly associated with degradation of potable water, which in turn is associated with increased infant and child mortality rates. Especially in unplanned camps, poor sanitation and human waste treatment can foul local water supplies, further exacerbating problems of access to drinking water (Connolly et al. 2004). Over the longer term, political instability inhibits the ability of the state to engage in disease eradication programs and extend public health systems into rural areas. Countries where conflict has been prevalent in the post–World War II era have performed much worse in eradicating malaria than countries where political stability has prevailed (Hendrix and Gleditsch 2012).

Environmental destruction and degradation can also be part of deliberate counterinsurgency operations. Insurgent forces are almost always outnumbered and outgunned by the state forces against which they rebel. As such, they tend to rely on guerrilla tactics that make use of cover provided by forests, tall grasslands, and marshes, as well as local communities (Mao 1961; Guevara 1968). Frustrated by these tactics, governments often respond with a strategy of "draining the sea": denying the insurgents operating space by inflicting hardships on the local population and removing the cover from which they launch attacks (Valentio, Huth, and Balch-Lindsay 2004; Downes 2007). In some instances, this means targeting the food supply through crop burning, salting of fields, and cutting off access to markets (Hendrix and Brinkman 2013). In conflicts ranging from the Second Boer War (1899–1902) to the Ethiopian-Eritrean civil war (1964–1991), food denial has been a central component of many counterinsurgency campaigns.

In others, it means denying insurgents cover by destroying the forests they use for concealment. Strategic deforestation was pursued famously by the United Kingdom during the Malay Emergency (1948–1960) and the United States during the Vietnam War under the auspices of Operation Ranch Hand (1962–1971). In both instances, counterinsurgency operations involved aerial spraying of herbicides and pesticides to deprive the insurgents of food (targeting rice paddies) as well as cover and supply lines (forests). Variants of this strategy, however, have been used for centuries: Russian forces cut down forests to deny Chechen rebels sanctuary during the Caucasian War (1817–1864), and Julius Caesar's legions were known to cut down adjacent forests in order to prevent hit-and-run attacks while on campaign in Gaul (Archer et al. 2002; Caesar 1907).

Civil conflicts can contribute to increased environmental degradation by "crowding out" other forms of economic activity and making populations more reliant on natural resource extraction as a means of survival. Many types of economic activity that make intense use of movable assets (light manufacturing, services) also take flight from conflict zones, leaving those activities that make use of fixed assets—like many natural resources—as the default sector (Boix 2008).

Because civil conflict often entails a breakdown in state authority structures, property rights become insecure, encouraging actors to harvest natural resources at unsustainable rates for fear they will not have access to those resources in the future and therefore not benefit from current conservation efforts. A 2003 post-conflict environmental assessment in Afghanistan found that half the country's natural pistachio woodlands had been cut down in order to sell the wood or hoard it for fuel due to fears that the communities would lose access to these woodlands in the future (UNEP 2003). While this relationship holds for many primary commodities and foraged goods, exploitation of diamonds, oil, and fisheries appears to decline during conflict (Hendrix and Glaser 2011; Mitchell and Thies 2012). However, it is likely that these declines are in part due to the breakdown of property rights and evasion of taxation through sale on black markets.

Whereas the previous mechanism regards the coping strategies of conflict-affected populations, the final mechanism regards opportunistic behavior by conflict actors. The same breakdown in state authority provides insurgents, local warlords, and often members of the military with opportunities to enrich themselves through the illegal harvesting of natural resources, including mineral resources (diamonds, gold, tin, tungsten, tantalum, etc.), forest resources ("conflict timber," generally exotic hardwoods), and wildlife (illegal poaching, either for bush meat or for international markets for exotic animal products, e.g., rhino horn and elephant tusks) (Bannon and Collier 2003). This mechanism has received the most international attention due to its reliance on international markets and trade and the role Western consumers have played in first creating and later attempting to deny export markets for these goods, sometimes with negative consequences for legal mining operations in conflict-affected countries (Haufler 2009; Autesserre 2012). Other work has highlighted the effectiveness of transboundary management of gorilla populations, including anti-poaching activities, in the Virunga Massif, one of the most conflict-affected regions in central Africa (Martin et al. 2011).

REMAINING CHALLENGES AND RESEARCH PRIORITIES

Methodological Challenges: Data Quality and Appropriate Research Design

One of the critical problems in the examination of the causal relationship between the environment and civil conflict has been the lack of distinction between different forms of conflict.[3] The UCDP[4] dataset differentiates the various forms of civil conflict in terms of political incompatibility, severity, and the actors involved. For any type of armed conflict to be considered to be active, at least one of the parties of the primary dyad (pair of actors) comprising the conflict must incur twenty-five battle casualties in a calendar year. Armed civil conflict involves the state and at least one non-state actor. Non-state conflict involves two non-state actors. One-sided violence involves the state or a non-state actor that kills at least twenty-five unorganized civilians in a year. Given the distinct nature of these three forms of conflict, to presume that environmental factors would affect all forms of conflict through the same causal pathways is untenable.

The quantitative analysis of the effect of environmental factors on civil conflict must address a number of problems relating to the characteristics of cross-national, cross-temporal intrastate conflict data (or conflict panel data). The fundamental advantage of studying civil conflict through the use of conflict panel data is that the cross-sectional characteristics allow for greater flexibility in modeling differences across countries. Single-country cross-temporal cross-sectional studies (where the units of analysis are sub-national entities, such as administrative regions, grid cells, or distinct population groups) offer opportunities to better understand micro-motives underlying the relationship between the environment and armed conflict. Conflict data are based on the concept that armed civil conflict is an event. Such analyses, therefore, constitute some form of event analysis, regarding armed conflict onset. Conflict data tend to suffer from three fundamental problems: non-independence, endogeneity, and omitted variable bias (including unmeasured heterogeneity bias). Different statistical techniques are better at dealing with each of these problems than others. The following paragraphs elaborate on these challenges.

Conflict data tend to be characterized by complex dependence structures. As noted above, a country's conflict history significantly affects the risk of civil conflict. Obviously civil conflicts are temporally dependent. They also may be spatially dependent, though this finding is less clear from the literature. Any statistical analysis of civil conflict must account for this lack of independence across cases. Fortunately, a variety of statistical techniques have been designed to address the problems of spatial and temporal dependence. The lack of independence of events is particularly problematic for the analysis of environment on conflict. For example, a society's previous experiences with environmental shocks will affect future shocks.

A related limitation is the almost exclusive focus on the environment as a possible driver of conflict outbreak or of specific conflict events. Extant research offers little insight on how environmental conditions and changes affect the dynamics of conflict, such as escalation, duration, and diffusion of hostilities, as well as the prospect for successful and lasting conflict resolution. Even though resource scarcities may be weakly related to civil conflict risk in general, this cannot be taken as evidence that renewable resources are always unrelated to conflict. For example, some see the durable drought and resultant agricultural decline in Syria in the years preceding the civil war as a contributing cause to the initial antigovernment protests in 2011 (Kelley et al. 2015), although existing political and socioeconomic stressors, influx of arms and know-how from proximate war zones, and the wave of ideological awakening that swept across the Middle East and North Africa certainly laid the ground for the hostilities.

Endogeneity, or the potential that the outcome (conflict) is actually the cause of the purported cause (environmental scarcity/degradation) is another problem. Most econometric studies of civil war have examined the onset of armed conflict. They have not, however, accounted for the endogenized effect of civil war on other variables. Countries racked by years of war will tend to be characterized by a lack of economic development. Similarly, democratic institutions are often weakened by civil conflict. This weakening in turn is often associated with political change and instability. The relationship between environment and armed conflict is wrought with endogeneity. If environmental factors alter the probability of conflict onset, the conflict itself is likely to alter the environment. Indeed, the average conflict probably has a much larger negative impact on local environmental conditions than the other way around. Analyzing the effect from degradation to conflict without accounting for the reverse relationship thus will produce biased estimates.

One way to address problems of endogeneity is to design an experiment to assess causality. A classic experimental design would involve subjecting two similar areas to two conditions: a treatment (e.g., climate change) and a control (e.g., no climate change). For civil war research, such an experiment would be infeasible, unadvisable, and unethical. Rather than employing a classical experimental design, the use of an instrumental variable (IV) allows us to perform a kind of post hoc quasi-experiment. The trick is to find an IV that is uncorrelated with the error term (thus meaning it is uncorrelated with the dependent variable) while correlated with the explanatory variable. The instrument predicts the treatment (the explanatory variable in question—in our case an environmental indicator) but does not affect the outcome (the onset of armed conflict) other than through the treatment. The IV estimate thus provides an estimate of the average treatment effect for those whose behavior is affected in the manner predicted.

As mentioned above, an early application of an IV approach to the study of civil war onset was Miguel et al. (2004), who asked: Do economic conditions affect civil conflict? The endogeneity problem is that civil war is bad for an economy. The dependent variable (Y) is the presence of an UCDP armed civil conflict in a country year. The explanatory variable (X) measuring the economy is per capita income growth. The posited relationship is X causes Y, but we have good evidence that Y affects X. To address the endogeneity problem, the authors employ an instrumental variable, change in annual rainfall, which is correlated with X, but not with Y. Note the relationship—change in rainfall was not associated with armed conflict onset.

(We discuss this below.) The problem with instrumental variables is that identifying an IV is more art than science. Finding an IV that is correlated with X and not with Y is often extremely difficult; in particular, rainfall may affect conflict patterns through mechanisms other than economic growth (Dunning 2008b). The more one knows about the factors that affect X, the more likely a good IV can be found, but it often requires some creativity and thinking outside the box.

Omitted variable bias is an even stickier problem for the quantitative analysis of the effect of environmental factors on civil conflict onset. A posited theoretical relationship typically does not specify all the variables that should be held constant when estimating the relationship. As our understanding of civil war, and more particularly of the relationship between environment and armed conflict, is underdeveloped, omitted variable bias will often be present. An omitted variable (e.g., colonial legacy) that is correlated with both the explanatory (e.g., resource dependence) and outcome variable (e.g., political instability) will lead to a biased estimation of the causal relationship under investigation.

The art of research design is to combine theory, data, and statistical analysis to produce credible causal inference. Good designs address the problems of non-independence, endogeneity, and omitted variable bias. A theoretical focus on mechanisms and causal processes is essential to the development of a good design.

Theoretical Challenges: Identifying Causal Mechanisms and Context

Armed conflicts originate, persist, and terminate with human decisions. To have armed conflict, people must make the decision to take up arms and engage in violence. The manner in which violence is engaged, and who it is that engages, will shape the nature of the conflict. It also determines whether and how environmental factors affect the onset of armed conflict. Civil conflict varies in form according to the nature of combat, the actors involved, severity, duration, location, capability ratios, and goals of actors.

Location and nature of combat are closely linked, serving to define the form of armed conflict fought. One form of communal violence (classified as non-state actor conflict by UCDP) typically involves violent cattle-rustling taking place in rural settings. Another form of communal violence occurs in urban settings, pitting one group against another—often manifest in ethnic clashes, but it could pit the general public in rioting against shopkeepers. The settings vary, pitting two non-state actors against one another, and the resulting violence also tends to be similar in that such events tend to be limited to sporadic violence often far below the twenty-five-battle-death threshold. But here's the rub—the mechanisms that causally link environmental factors to armed conflict differ completely. In the rural setting, contestation over property plays a central role, either in the form of land or cattle (especially for pastoral people). In an urban setting, economic shocks, such as rising food prices—which may or may not be related to environmental conditions—mediated by government policies are more important for triggering violence (Smith 2014).

The manner in which environmental factors may exacerbate contestation over property is varied. Such conflicts often tend to fall along the lines of social cleavages, particularly in terms of ethnic (religious, racial, linguistic) polarization. Such cleavages serve to unite one group against another through identity. Migration induced by environmental factors is one way that could possibly spark a fight over property, particularly if one ethnic group moves into the territory dominated by another group. Among pastoral peoples, the movement of a group and their cattle into another group's traditional grazing grounds, farms, or waterholes might lead to contested property rights, wherein the cattle, the water, and the land are all forms of property. For example, migratory Fulani herders have been expelled periodically from Ghana to Nigeria following clashes with local farmers.

State strength or at least degree of legal authority, especially with regard to enforcing property rights, is another factor that may affect the chances of violent conflict over property rights. Weak states are thereby presumed to be less able to mitigate conflict induced by environmental shocks. Enforcement of property rights alone, however, is insufficient. Biased property rights, whereby one ethnic group is favored at the expense of another, are likely to increase the chances of armed conflict, since the disadvantaged group has little legal recourse to solve the contestation over property (Butler and Gates 2012). Such bias in property rights protection is likely to be reflected in patterns of social, political, and economic exclusion manifest in horizontal inequality (Murshed and Gates 2003; Østby 2008; Cederman, Gleditsch, and Buhaug 2013). The discriminatory treatment of the Maasai, a pastoralist people in Tanzania, serves as an example. "Villagization" policies and reforms in property rights have fostered an anti-pastoral environment in Tanzania. Livestock are confined to "pastoral villages," but these villages lack adequate pastures and water supplies. Competition over these resources (water and pastureland) often leads to violence. In order to understand such farmer-herder conflict, one also must take political factors into account, such as policies related to land tenure, livestock confinement, and villagization (Benjaminsen et al 2009).

As for the logic of cattle raiding, fat healthy cattle should be more desirable than those starving or diseased; hence we should expect, all things being equal, that resource abundance leads to more cattle rustling. Plenty of rainfall (without extensive flooding) will result in good grazing and healthy fat cattle. But if resource allocations are highly asymmetric, a poorly endowed group would be expected to engage in raids and the richer group to retaliate. In this regard, arguments of resource plenty and scarcity are insufficient. Relative allocation of resources between groups is critical to understanding how environment is causally linked to armed civil conflict.

In an urban environment (or at least in environments of dense population), the mechanisms by which environmental factors would affect armed civil conflict tend to be economic in nature, whereby the general public or a group reacts to an economic shock and riots. Economic growth (or growth shocks), food price shocks, and food shortages (in the extreme leading to famine) are often posited to be the critical links of causality. Whether these shocks are transitory or permanent could be important.

On occasion, these events can escalate. Riots can continue for days. More and more people may join the protest, culminating in mass movements. The riots spread. The government's response in turn plays a big role in shaping the escalatory process and the death toll. These escalation dynamics serve to sustain violence affecting duration and severity. In Syria, the al-Assad regime refused to grant significant concessions to the protesters, and the uprising of 2011 quickly turned into a bloody war, in contrast to the relatively swift "Jasmine Revolution" in Tunisia only weeks earlier.

While a riot or a violent dispute over property may occur more or less spontaneously, sustained violence requires organization and leadership. Recruitment and mobilization play a central role. The composition of the population in terms of ethnic or regional identity and polarization will affect the degree to which a group can mobilize support. The more people become involved, the more likely the state will become involved if it is not already part of the conflict from the beginning. In this way, non-state conflicts can evolve into armed civil conflict involving the state and non-state actors. In rural settings, the conflict may develop into an insurgency. In an urban setting a riot may become a revolution. Environmental factors spark violence through an intervening mechanism (such as a food price shock or a dispute over property). The initial violence may be localized and involve few or no casualties, but if the conflict escalates it is likely to be more severe.

Escalatory dynamics allow for non-state actor conflict to escalate to civil conflict when the state becomes involved as a belligerent. One-sided conflict as it relates to environmental factors is not so clearly related. Brutal authoritarian governments such as that of North Korea and the Derg in Ethiopia have used famine as a political tool of oppression. But this is a case of political opportunism, rather than a case of famine causing one-sided conflict. We will therefore not consider one-sided violence in this chapter.

The theoretical focus on the causal link between environment and armed conflict has shifted from a general consideration of resource scarcity (or plenty) to specific aspects of weather that relate to climate change, such as rainfall and temperature deviations. Rainfall (whether too much, resulting in flooding, or too little, which leads to drought) fits nicely in the framework of resource scarcity and plenty, exclusion and privilege. High temperatures do not fit so nicely. Of course, sustained high temperatures will be associated with inadequate water for plants or animals or humans, which highlights scarcity. But high temperatures are often seen to be associated with violent behavior in general, taking on an individual psychological dimension. If high temperatures occur in association with a highly polarized environment pitting one group against another, violence may be triggered and escalate.

More and more research has begun to link the environment/climate variables to conflict via identified and explicitly tested intermediate effects, such as agro-economic shocks, migration, the role of the state in enforcing property rights, and degree of ethnic polarization (e.g., Koubi et al. 2012; Wischnath and Buhaug 2014). The use of rainfall deviation as an instrument for economic shocks serves to model the role of economic shocks as an intervening variable between environment and armed conflict and to account for the endogenous relationship between conflict and economic growth. We need to explore more fully how environmental factors interact with other forces that increase the risks for civil wars.

CONCLUSION

Despite an intellectual history that dates back at least three centuries, the links between environmental conditions, resource scarcity, and civil war have yet to be fully disentangled. Nevertheless, the last twenty years have seen significant progress in understanding how environmental conditions affect conflict, both directly and through their effects on the developmental trajectories of states against which rebellion occurs. Moreover, the recognition that conflict itself exerts significant environmental tolls constitutes an important series of findings that make conflict an environmental—not just humanitarian, political, or economic—issue.

This chapter reviews the now considerable literature on environmental conditions and conflict, concluding that no single, universal relationship between environmental scarcity and conflict exists, but rather that relationships are largely scale dependent and contingent on other social, political, and demographic factors. However, it finds more uniformly negative effects of conflict on environmental conditions. Finally, while this literature has expanded rapidly in the past decade, especially following the 2007 Nobel Peace Prize awarded to the IPCC for its work on climate change, it is still in its relative infancy. The chapter concludes with challenges and opportunities for future research with respect to research design and the theoretical/empirical identification of more nuanced, context-specific causal mechanisms.

To many, the idea that human interactions—in particular, peace and conflict—could be shaped by their environment will be a source of consternation. The idea that humans are not masters of their environment, but rather products of it, goes against the concepts of human agency and choice, which are ingrained in both our philosophical and normative notions of what makes us human in the first place. Whatever the ultimate resolution of scholarly debates discussed herein, this chapter does not treat environmental conditions as determinative of human behavior, but rather as embedding human interactions within a system of incentives and constraints. This perspective is consistent with the generally accepted notion that institutions, by establishing incentive structures and norms of interaction, affect human interactions. Given the magnitude of environmental shifts that have attended industrialization, globalization, and climate change, a better understanding of the ways environmental conditions shape peace and conflict is crucial.

15

Trends in Civil War Data

Geography, Organizations, and Events

David E. Cunningham, Kristian Skrede Gleditsch, and Idean Salehyan

Why are some countries trapped in cycles of civil conflict while others are relatively peaceful? Why do some dissident groups use nonviolent strategies while others resort to arms? When do combatants in a civil war choose to negotiate and come to a settlement rather than continue to fight? Such questions are at the heart of contemporary civil war research, and scholars have advanced several theories of conflict onset, duration, and resolution, among other topics. While theories of conflict can often be abstract, they usually suggest empirical implications that can be tested against observable data. Ultimately, a theory is primarily helpful insofar as it helps us resolve puzzles. The best test of this is normally whether the theory makes predictions about behavior in the real world and whether these predictions are consistent with the best available evidence. This evidence can be qualitative or quantitative; it can be based on surveys and interviews or archival research; or it can be taken from current news sources. The task of the researcher is to identify what types of evidence are needed to corroborate or falsify a hypothesis and subject one's theories to empirical scrutiny.

In this chapter, we focus specifically on large-scale, quantitative data on civil war that compares across countries as well as historical periods. While much can be learned by examining a single case, conflict scholars are usually concerned about general trends or seek to develop theories that are more general in nature. Empirical studies of civil conflict and political violence have progressed at a rapid pace over the last several years. These developments have been driven in part by the many exciting new data sources that have become available. The Correlates of War (COW) project[1] is a long-standing research project commonly used in studies of international as well as civil conflict. Drawing on various earlier data collection efforts, including most notably Richardson's data (1960) on wars from 1815 to 1945, the COW Project provided the first comprehensive dataset on civil wars from 1816, defined as domestic conflicts requiring at least one thousand battle-related deaths (Small and

Singer 1982; Sarkees and Wayman 2010). Later, the Uppsala Conflict Data Project and Peace Research Institute Oslo introduced the Armed Conflict Dataset (ACD) with a lower battle-deaths threshold of twenty-five in a calendar year, although this dataset remains limited to the post–World War II era (Gleditsch et al. 2002). The Cross-Polity Time-Series Data project by Banks (1971) provided counts of different types of conflictual events, including riots and demonstrations, based on newspaper reports. For those interested in ethnic protests and rebellions, the Minorities at Risk Project (Gurr 2000)[2] provides useful information on the use of political violence by ethno-national groups around the world. Each of these resources has its strengths and weaknesses and continues to be used by the scholarly community, attesting to the staying power of such comprehensive data projects.

Until recently, quantitative studies on civil war largely used binary indicators of the presence/absence of a civil war in a particular country during a given year (e.g., Collier and Hoeffler 1998; Fearon and Laitin 2003). However, scholars have increasingly come to recognize the limitations of using the country/year as the unit of analysis and a simple dichotomy of war and peace (or, more appropriately, absence of war). Conceptually, civil conflict is not a binary "state of affairs" but reflects a number of social, geographic, and organizational dynamics that early quantitative studies of war did not take into account. Looking at countries as a whole, for example, masks considerable variation across geographic space where fighting occurs. For example, civil conflicts in the Caucasus region of Russia have been relatively confined within a small geographic area that differed significantly from the rest of the country, while country-level data would simply code the entire state of Russia as being "at war." Covariates of civil conflict, such as mountainous terrain, oil dependence, ethnic fractionalization, gross domestic product, and so on, for a country as large and complex as Russia, could hardly capture the local-level context of the Chechen conflict. And while the country may be too encompassing as a unit in some cases, in other contexts the state may be too limiting as a conceptual unit. The wars in the Great Lakes region of Africa, for example, have witnessed rebel groups that were not constrained by borders, but that exhibited strong transnational linkages across the Democratic Republic of Congo, Rwanda, Burundi, and Uganda.

Scholars have also paid greater attention to dynamic processes and conflict escalation/de-escalation at different temporal intervals. Some civil wars last only a few weeks or months; the Libyan conflict in 2011 lasted from February to October, for example. Moreover, there is often a series of conflictual events—protests, riots, small-scale armed attacks—that precipitate an outbreak of full-scale armed violence. The Syrian crisis, for instance, began with a series of protests across the country, but quickly escalated to bloodshed as militant groups began to target the state and government sympathizers. These escalatory dynamics from low-level unrest to war belies a simple dichotomous accounting of the presence or absence of conflict. Binary indicators of war cannot account for variation in conflict intensity, as measured by the number of deaths or the frequency of armed attacks within a given year. Across civil conflicts around the world, some are clearly more intense and cause many more deaths and displacements than others. Even within a single conflict, there are often periods of intense fighting and other periods of relative calm.

Finally, country-level indicators could not account for the particular actors who fight and contest power in civil wars. In this regard, studies of civil war stand in stark contrast to studies of international conflict. In looking at international war, scholars have a relatively well-defined set of recognized states. This enables researchers to look at dyadic interactions and relative capabilities across countries. Findings in the international conflict literature demonstrate that pairs of democratic states are less likely to fight one another (Oneal and Russett 1999), that the *relative* military capabilities between states are important for the risk of war (Bremer 1992), and that *dyadic* commercial ties incline states toward peace (Gartzke 2007). Each of these findings implies comparisons and interactions between state actors. In the civil war literature, researchers cannot adequately evaluate theories of rebel-government interactions through analyses employing crude country/year data and a dichotomous war/peace dependent variable. Scholarship was therefore largely focused on structural covariates of conflict, such as oil dependence or per capita Gross Domestic Product, and variables that measured features of the state, such as the level of democracy. This approach was far removed from the theoretical arguments that motivated empirical analysis in the first place such as the opportunity costs of rebels (Collier and Hoeffler 2004) or the role of state capacity in fighting insurgents (Fearon and Laitin 2003). In assessing key questions such as the duration of conflict, war outcomes, third party interventions, and so on, ignoring factors such as rebel strength, organizational structure, and funding sources omits several important features of the war and ignores variation across rebel movements.

Earlier generations of data collection on civil war were quite impressive and continue to be used by researchers. Yet with the advent of the Internet, online archives, social media, and near real-time reporting on conflict, current generations of researchers have far more access to information than ever before. This has enabled the rapid accumulation of new data on conflict events, locations, and actors. We now have much more fine-grained data on conflict and multiple data structures and units of analysis to choose from. There has been a move toward temporal and geographic disaggregation of data (i.e., looking at shorter time intervals and smaller geographic units): using organizations as the unit of analysis, collecting information on particular events such as battles and protests, as well as using new technologies such as web-scraping and natural language processing to automate data generation. In this chapter, we examine several new data sources on conflict and point to promising areas for future refinement and data collection. To be sure, new data are being collected even as we write. Therefore, one critical challenge for the future will be to enable scholars to quickly and reliably sort through this glut of information and to ensure that data projects are mutually reinforcing rather than redundant or incompatible.

In this chapter, we assess three main areas into which conflict data have expanded over the last several years. First, we look at a growing trend toward collecting fine-grained, geographically disaggregated data on civil conflict. These data have enabled analyses at the sub-national level and are now a mainstay of conflict research. Second, we discuss data collected on rebel organizations. These data have enabled new research agendas on the organizational characteristics of militant groups and dyadic analyses of rebel-government interactions. Third, we examine new trends in event data, which seek to provide precise information on particular conflict interactions between dissidents and the state. Such data enable researchers to address temporal sequencing and conflict escalation and to examine particular actions taken by protagonists in conflict. The overarching theme, then, is the disaggregation of civil war into more nuanced temporal, geographic, and organizational units instead of a simple war/peace distinction. In a final section, because new data projects are currently or soon to be underway, we discuss a series of best practices for the collection of data. We emphasize how the research community must seek to be as transparent as possible and, when applicable, provide data in such a format as to be compatible with other projects. Users of conflict data in turn must pay close attention to the documentation and try to ensure that the data they consider reflect as best as possible their concept of interests.

NEW DATA ON GEOGRAPHIC FEATURES OF CONFLICT

As noted earlier, previous generations of conflict data often used the entire country as the unit of analysis. However, conflict also has a geographic component, with conflictual events taking place within specific locations. There is a long-standing interest in the impact of geographical features of conflict, especially in international relations. An early example includes Richardson's (1960) pioneering work on borders and conflict, which pointed to the role of territory as a potential motivation for conflict between countries and for opportunities for violent clashes. Drawing in part on Lanchester's (1956) work examining the relative power of antagonists in conflict, Boulding (1965) examined the relationship between distance and opportunities for conflict. He highlighted the role of the "loss of strength gradient," where the ability of an actor to project force declines with geographical distance. Standard models of dyadic conflict opportunities typically include a number of geographical measures such as contiguity and distance between states to consider motivation and opportunities for conflict (see, e.g., Bremer 1992; Oneal and Russet 1999). Finally, many studies have looked at the potential for spread of conflict between countries (e.g., Gleditsch 2002; Siverson and Starr 1991).

Despite this interest in geography in international relations, civil conflict data lacked a clear geographic representation, typically just including the country as a whole where conflict occurs. The lack of geographical referents entails a number of problems for evaluating arguments about conflict. In the case of interstate war, there is an essential difference in the specific locations where a conflict is fought between two actors. For example, although the United States may have claimed to feel threatened by Iraq prior to the 2003 invasion, we clearly had an asymmetric situation, where the United States was able to invade the territory of Iraq, while Iraq lacked the ability to threaten the United States at home. In civil war, it is also often the case that actors have differential ability to take the conflict to the enemy. It is rare that conflict engulfs an entire country, and normally civil wars take place in confined areas, often in the periphery. For example, the civil wars in India have taken place mainly in Kashmir and the northeast. If we believe that civil wars are driven by local factors, it would be misleading to look at the country as a whole, and not consider possible differences between active conflict areas and the rest of the country, such as the presence of ethnic groups that perceive themselves to be marginalized.

More recently, there have many efforts to develop new and more comprehensive data representing the geographical features of conflict. In the case of civil wars, Buhaug and Gates (2002) developed a new dataset that identified the midpoint and geographic extent of all the conflict zones in the PRIO/Uppsala Armed Conflict dataset. These data allowed them to calculate new measures of the distance between conflict zones and capitals as well as their relationship to borders. In brief, they find that civil war conflict zones tend to be located far away from capitals (where the government presumably has the best ability to project force) and were more likely to abut international borders, suggesting that transnational features shape the risk of civil wars (Salehyan 2009). Finally, Buhaug and Gates (2002) also find that civil wars far away from the capital tend to be more persistent.

The original data developed by Buhaug and Gates were relatively crude, and simply assumed a constant radius beyond the midpoint. The core data were subsequently refined to form a spatial polygon, using a GIS data format, clipped to national boundaries and with a more refined coding of the actual location of conflict. The most recent version of these data is discussed by Hallberg (2012) and Buhaug et al. (2011) and identify the specific location of the initial conflict onset and the subsequent reach of the conflict. For example, for India there are ten distinct conflicts over the period 1989–2008, taking place in different and non-overlapping areas of the country, such as Nagaland in the northeast and Kashmir in the northwest. Spatial data with explicit geographical representation tend to be more complex than traditional data, which can be represented in relatively simple tables. We refer to Gleditsch and Weidmann (2012) for more details on how such data are collected and organized and on the added complexity in analyses.

A different approach to geographic disaggregation uses specific events or battle locations, represented as points on a map, rather than polygons depicting the conflict zone. One of the earliest efforts, which looks at both events and locations, the Armed Conflict Location and Event Data project (see Raleigh et al. 2010), identifies individual events within civil war such as battles and the taking of strategic territory and their specific location. These data have been used to examine issues such as the relationship between population distributions and conflict (Raleigh and Hegre 2009) or the relationship between poverty and conflict events (Hegre et al. 2009). Other event data projects have similarly started including geographic coordinates, often relying on automated computing techniques to locate a geographical location for events (but see Hammond and Weidmann 2014 for a discussion of some of the shortcomings).

The new emphasis on geocoded events has also led to a new approach to coding conflict at the Uppsala Conflict Data Program, which launched the Geocoded Event Data (GED) project (Sundberg and Melander 2013), covering both civil wars as well as non-state or intercommunal conflict. The available data currently cover Africa from1989 to 2010, although there are efforts underway to expand the coverage. The GED have proposed a new approach to identifying conflict zones, based on the explicit location of individual battle events and the drawing of conflict polygons around the extent of fighting. This avoids some of the potential problems in the Buhaug and Gates (2002) approach, where the entire area within the circular space does not necessarily see battle events. Beardsley, Gleditsch, and Lo (2015) use the GED polygons to study the geographic extent of conflict, and how they are affected by the characteristics of rebel groups. They show that groups with a clearly define core territory are more likely to fight in a well-defined consistent theater, while groups without strong ethnic ties and lacking sufficient military strength to compete with government forces in conventional warfare are more likely to roam or fight over a wider area. Beardsley and Gleditsch (2015) use these data and provide evidence suggesting that more robust peacekeeping with larger troop numbers help contain conflicts.

Although much of the development of spatial conflict data has focused on civil war, there have also been similar developments for other types of conflict data. In the case of interstate wars, Braithwaite (2010a) developed a new dataset called MIDLOC, identifying the geographical location of interstate disputes. These data have been used to revisit research on borders of conflict, which had typically been carried out the country level and without distinguishing location (Brochman et al. 2012); the data have also been used to look at the relationship between climate and interstate conflict (Gartzke n.d.). There have also been many analyses looking at the location of terrorist attacks, using the geographic coordinates in the Global Terrorism Database (Findley and Young 2012). The new interest in the geography of conflict has also benefited from a new wave of development of related spatial data, including new data on the geography of states and changing borders (Weidmann et al. 2010); the settlement areas of ethnic groups (Wucherpfenning et al. 2011); and survey data with spatial locations, and satellite data as well as approaches to develop spatially varying measures of wealth and population distributions (Nordhaus and Chen 2009). Geographically disaggregated data has also led to new interest in the appropriate units of analysis to evaluate specific propositions and to some researchers using disaggregated grid cell analysis to reflect geographically disaggregated characteristics (Buhaug and Rød 2006; Tollefsen et al. 2012).

One challenge with geographically disaggregated data is that there are few standard approaches for analyzing smaller units than nation-states. Determining the "appropriate" basis for disaggregation is ultimately a theoretical question and involves many practical challenges in combining and integrating data collected at different geographical scales. There have been promising efforts to integrate standard formats for geographic data that reduce some of the practical challenges for researchers and may be helpful for many purposes. The PRIO-GRID data structure uses a standardized spatial grid, with cells that are 0.5 by 0.5 degrees in area, that contain information on conflict locations, socioeconomic data, and climatic variables, among others (Tollefsen et al. 2012). The GROWup platform, hosted at the Swiss Federal Institute of Technology, is intended to facilitate geographic analyses of conflict and allows researchers to visualize and integrate data on ethnic settlement patterns, administrative units, population, wealth, conflict, and other variables in a user-friendly manner.[3]

Yet, the choice of geographic unit—whether country, administrative division, grid cell, and so on—is not a trivial one. The well-known Modifiable Areal Unit Problem (MAUP) occurs when analyzing data at different geographic scales yields different results (Rød and Buhaug 2006). This is similar to the problems that may arise for the temporal resolution, where aggregation to longer intervals may change results (Shellman 2008). Typically, researchers do not have good theoretical priors about the appropriate geographic size of the unit of analysis. For example, grid cells can be defined at any potential resolution—50 by 50km, 100 by 100km, 250 by 250km, and so on. Administrative units can be defined at the provincial, district, or municipal level. Without theoretical guidance about which unit to choose, research projects can potentially become incommensurable with one another, and results at one geographical scale may not hold at a different scale. Ideally, researchers should test their hypotheses at a variety of scales to ensure robustness.

NEW DATA ON ORGANIZATIONAL CHARACTERISTICS OF REBEL GROUPS

Civil wars occur because opposition groups choose to use violence in disputes.[4] Conflicts continue because these organizations choose to keep fighting, and they terminate when all but one actor either cannot fight or actors agree on settlement terms. Understanding the onset, duration, and termination of conflicts, then, requires understanding why these actors make the choices they do, and empirical analysis of these conflict dynamics requires information on how characteristics of the actors involved influence their behavior.

Despite the clear importance of organizations to the dynamics of conflict, until recently, quantitative studies of civil war tended to focus solely on the characteristics of states. Prominent studies of civil war onset, such as Fearon and Laitin (2003) and Collier and Hoeffler (2004) did not include any information about dissidents in their analyses. Likewise, early studies of the duration and outcome of conflict, such as Mason and Fett (1996), Collier, Hoeffler, and Söderbom (2004), and Fearon (2004) only included information, about the country or the government in analyses, on why some conflicts last longer than others. This country-level approach stood in sharp contrast to the dyadic approach common in studies of interstate war and was likely the result of a lack of data. Early civil war datasets, such as Correlates of War data, Fearon and Laitin's (2003) data, and Doyle and Sambanis's (2000) dataset, included no information on the actors involved, not even a list of rebel groups participating in conflict.

Over the last decade, the amount of data available on characteristics of states and rebel groups has expanded greatly, and many scholars have taken advantage of these data to examine how the characteristics of actors influence conflict dynamics. The most comprehensive and systematic data on rebel groups comes from the Uppsala Armed Conflict Dataset, which identifies all rebel groups participating in internal armed conflicts.[5] The UCDP Dyadic Dataset (Harbom, Melander, and Wallensteen 2008 and Themner and Wallensteen 2014) splits all of the ACD conflicts into state-rebel dyads, allowing researchers to examine relationships between the state and the opposition over time.

The Non-State Actor (NSA) data (Cunningham et al. 2009, 2013) provide a variety of additional information on each of these rebel groups, expanding the ACD. These indicators include the strength of each group (relative to the government); the ability of the group to fight, mobilize support, and procure arms (again relative to the government); the command structure of the group; and indicators of whether the group controls territory and if so, where. Additionally, a series of variables in the NSA data provide information about the transnational dimensions of state-rebel group dyads, including whether either side receives support from an external state (and, if so, what type), indicators of transnational constituency for groups, the use of external rebel bases, and other factors.

The NSA data have been used in a variety of statistical studies to analyze how characteristics of groups influence the duration and outcome of conflict (Cunningham et al 2009). Salehyan et al. (2014) examine how rebel group characteristics and the regime type of external supporters influence rebel decisions to attack civilians. Additionally, other scholars have incorporated further information into these data. For example, Stanton (2013), Fortna (2015), and Polo and Gleditsch (n.d.) collect information on the use of terrorism by rebel groups in civil war and analyze how group characteristics affect whether or not they target civilians. Wucherpfennig et al. (2012) link the ethnic groups in the Ethnic Power Relations (EPR) project, which details the political status of ethnic groups around the world, to rebel groups in the ACD. This allows for analyses of how the characteristics of ethnic groups influence the behavior of rebels, indicating, for example, that larger excluded ethnic groups are more likely to experience civil war, while large included groups are not, and that excluded ethnic groups tend to be involved in longer civil wars (Cederman, Gleditsch, and Buhaug 2013, Wucherpfennig et al. 2012). Thomas (2014) identifies the demands that rebel groups make and examines how these demands influence the way governments respond to them. Ongoing data projects analyze how characteristics of the leaders of rebel groups, such as whether they are "responsible" for starting the war (Prorok n.d.) or how they come into office, influence the duration and termination of conflict (Cunningham and Sawyer n.d.).

The proliferation of data on rebel groups has allowed for much more direct testing of theoretical arguments about the behavior of states and rebel groups in civil war. These studies have significantly advanced our understanding of what shapes the duration and outcome of civil war, as well as of the behavior of warring parties, such as civilian targeting and participation in negotiations. The shift to dyadic analyses of civil war has primarily involved analyses of the dynamics of ongoing civil wars. Studies of civil war onset, by contrast, still rarely take into account the characteristics of potential rebel groups as determinants of whether or not civil wars occur. Identifying a sample of dissident organizations with the potential to turn to violence is more challenging than identifying the rebel groups involved in ongoing conflicts.

Despite these challenges, several data projects do provide information on a variety of non-state actors that are not directly involved in violence. K. Cunningham (2013, 2014) has identified over 1,200 organizations representing 147 self-determination movements active from 1960 to 2005. She examines how the number of organizations representing each group affects civil war between states and self-determination groups. This step opens up the study of violent or nonviolent strategies by opposition groups as an important area of inquiry (Chenoweth and Stepan 2008).

Indeed, one promising development in the study of civil unrest is the turn toward combining studies of protest movements and violent dissent. The MAROB project (Wilkenfeld et al. 2012) identifies information on ethno-political organizations in the Middle East and post-Soviet states. These data have been used to examine how characteristics of organizations influence whether or not they use violence. K. Cunningham et al. (2012) examine how organizational competition affects whether organizations decide to abandon nonviolent tactics and take up arms.

The growth in data on rebel groups and other non-state dissident actors has led to significant empirical progress and is a thriving area of research. However, limitations remain. In particular, two problems stand out. First, the use of this ever-increasing amount of data is limited due to difficulties with merging different datasets with one another. While scholars of interstate war can use commonly agreed upon state names and identification codes to combine information across datasets, data on non-state actors often are based on different datasets, use different names, and identify groups or collective actors in different ways (Asal et al. 2015). The various projects that are based on the UCDP Dyadic Dataset address this problem because they collect information on a common set of actors. However, for many other datasets listing different actors, combining information is problematic.

Second, while there has been growth in the availability of data on organizations in countries and periods without active civil war, these data are still limited to specific regions (such as the Middle East) or specific types of actors (ethno-political groups or self-determination movements). The studies using these data are informative, but their generalizability may be limited by their specific scope. Systematic data on dissident organizations with the potential to violently rebel would increase scholars' ability to examine the determinants of the onset of civil war. However, this requires systematic theorizing about which groups to include and what types of information should be collected.

NEW DIRECTIONS IN EVENT DATA

The final area of data expansion and disaggregation is on the temporal level. Instead of looking at the entire calendar year, event data allow researchers to look at particular actions in a conflict at a daily level. Armies and rebel groups attack each other (or possibly civilians), and these actions can have significant influence on war outcomes, conflict management, and post-conflict politics. Historically, cross-national analyses of civil war have largely ignored dynamics within conflicts. Some scholars have focused on specific features within conflicts, including how territorial control (Kalyvas 2006), electoral competition (Balcells 2010), or international conflict (Davis and Moore 1997) affects levels of violence or the relationship between repression and dissent (Moore 1998, Dugan and Chenoweth 2012). These events studies, however, have generally focused on a single or a small number of countries. The above studies, for example, focus on Greece, Spain, Zaire, Peru and Sri Lanka, and Israel.

In recent years, several new datasets have emerged, providing information on conflict events across a range of disputes, allowing for cross-national analyses using events data. The UCDP Geo-referenced Event Dataset discussed previously identifies instances of violence involving organizations that resulted in at least one fatality (Sundberg and Melander 2013). These events include violent events occurring within state-rebel group interactions, events that take place as part of conflict between non-state actors, and instances of violence against civilians. Because the UCDP project uses a threshold of twenty-five deaths in a calendar year to identify conflicts, only those violent events that take place as part of a dispute reaching that threshold are included in the GED, and any violence outside these is not included.[6] In addition, the UCDP-GED data are currently limited to Africa for the period 1989–2010.

Another large dataset providing cross-national data on conflict events is the Armed Conflict Location Event Dataset (Raleigh et al. 2010). Unlike the UCDP-GED, ACLED provides information about political violence events without regard to whether they take place within a full-scale insurgency or civil war. Additionally, ACLED includes both violent and nonviolent events. Thus, there is a wider range of events available in the ACLED data than in the UCDP-GED. However, some have argued that the UCDP-GED has more precise definitional requirements for which events are included in its dataset, and thus its data are potentially more comparable across countries.[7]

ACLED and the UCDP-GED are the most comprehensive events datasets focused specifically on civil conflict. Other data have been developed to capture different forms of conflict. Terrorism is particularly well covered, with several datasets seeking to provide comprehensive data on the occurrence of domestic and transnational terrorism. The Global Terrorism Database (GTD) is perhaps the most comprehensive, with data on terrorist events from 1970 to 2013.[8] While many of the terrorist attacks in the GTD occur in the context of civil war, the data also identify smaller scale, sporadic uses of terrorism. Other events datasets seek to cover a broader range of events. The Social Conflict in Africa Database (SCAD) (Salehyan et al. 2012): for example, identifies events related to protests, riots, strikes, intercommunal conflict, violence against civilians by the government, and others.[9] SCAD also contains information on actors and targets of conflict events, the number of participants, the number of deaths, the use of repression, and the issue-area of the event. These data are also fully geocoded, allowing for spatial analyses of civil unrest.

The increasing availability of events data has allowed scholars to more directly examine the determinants of violence both within and outside of civil conflicts. Hultman, Kathman, and Shannon (2013) aggregate the events in the UCDP-GED to code monthly counts of the number or civilians killed by governments and rebel groups in civil conflicts, and then examine how the composition of peacekeepers influences this. They find that civilian killings decline when there are more peacekeepers in a country. This analysis revisits the question of whether "peacekeeping works" (Fortna 2008) by looking at its effect on prolonging cease-fires and also demonstrates that peacekeeping can reduce civilian victimization.

Events data also provide opportunities for researchers to analyze different forms of violence in conjunction with one another. Findley and Young (2012), for example, examine the overlap between terrorist attacks and civil war, and find that about 56 percent of all terrorist attacks take place within geographical areas with ongoing civil war. An increasing number of researchers seek to use information from different event and nonevent datasets, but the ability to do so is limited by the difficulty with attribution and re-aggregation. While it is possible to link events to specific countries, it is more difficult to link events to the specific actors responsible for them. Ascertaining responsibility is often contested as actors either claim responsibility for attacks they did not commit or deny involvement in other attacks. Nonetheless, an important step for future research would be to better integrate organizational data with event data.

One promising direction in the collection of event data is the use of fully automated or computer-assisted techniques to extract information from news sources (Bond et al. 1997; King and Lowe 2003; D'Orazio et al. 2014). With the plethora of information readily available through online sources and archives, it is practically impossible for human researchers to easily sort through massive amounts of text on conflict events. Use of technology, including web-scraping, document classification, and natural language processing has certainly come a long way and can be used to aid human researchers in their efforts, or replace human coding altogether.[10] Such methods have the prime advantage of being able to code millions of data points relatively quickly. However, for certain more complex tasks—for example, arbitrating between conflicting accounts of the number of fatalities or event attribution to the correct group—the currently available software is limited in its ability to interpret events.

BEST PRACTICES IN DATA COLLECTION

Undoubtedly, there are exciting new data projects currently being developed or in the early planning stages. The availability of information about conflict events, especially through online sources, has been a tremendous asset to conflict researchers. Researchers are making use of news archives, social media, pictures and video, and crowd sourcing technologies to develop ever more sophisticated data. Several older data projects were not archived or documented very well, making it difficult for others to validate the final product or understand what the coding and assigned values are based on. For current and future data projects, we urge researchers to collect data in such a way that others can, as closely as possible, replicate and verify the data-generation process. In addition, as data are meant to be integrated with other data, we call on scholars to present data in a format that is compatible with existing resources. In this section, we discuss a series of best practices in the collection of data, in the hope that these will be useful to those contemplating creating data (Salehyan 2014).

First, researchers should be transparent and systematic about the sources they consulted for each data point. Others should be able to consult the same sources and come to the same conclusions about a conflict event, rebel organization, or other attribute of the war. Often, sources contain conflicting information, particularly about sensitive subjects such as sexual violence or mass killings. Therefore, researchers should be as clear as possible as to how final coding decisions were made and how discrepancies in source material are dealt with.

Second, scholars should be aware of reporting bias in their sources. One type of bias involves nonreporting on a point of interest. Are conflict events more likely to be reported in certain areas of the country (e.g., urban centers) than in peripheral rural areas? Do journalists, nongovernmental agencies, and other reporting sources lack access to certain information, such as the internal politics of rebel organizations? Are certain types of events more likely to be reported on than others? For example, the media tend to report on violent events more than peaceful action. Such reporting bias may require additional effort to find information about certain features of the conflict. Some have suggested potential remedies for the problem, such as including covariates of detection or estimating the rate at which data are missing for specific observations (Hug 2003; Li 2005; Drakos and Gofas 2006; Hendrix and Salehyan 2015). Another type of bias pertains to the information that is presented in a report. Activist groups may have an incentive to inflate the number of people they brought out to the streets, government sources may wish to cast blame on rebels for atrocities, and journalists may not be entirely neutral when covering events. Comparing the information across sources and being transparent about which sources are used, which are discarded, and the degree of certainty is essential to arbitrate between potentially biased accounts (see Davenport and Ball 2002; Poe et al. 2002).

Third, researchers should have clear coding rules and ensure the reliability of numeric values. The "real world" is complex and each conflict undoubtedly has unique characteristics. The task of collecting data requires that trained researchers sort through this complexity and provide relatively simple, quantitative representations of the facts of a particular case. Clear coding rules must be developed and presented along with the data such that others can assess how judgments are made. Scholars should also report inter-coder reliability statistics—or the rate of agreement across coders—along with their data, especially for values that are potentially ambiguous. Difficult cases, or those that do not quite fit the strictures of a coding rule, should be noted and documented along with the researcher's justification for why a decision was made.

Finally, researchers should share their data on easily accessible platforms and ensure that their data are compatible with other resources. Too often, data are stored on personal websites, which require others to be familiar with that person's work in order to find and access the data. Free resources such as the Dataverse Network project[11] allow researchers to post their work along with metadata, allowing others to easily search and find the data they need. In addition, as data are typically meant to be joined with other information (e.g., conflict data is often combined with data on political institutions) the use of common handles and identifiers can greatly assist with data integration.

CONCLUSION

Research on civil war has seen many exciting developments over recent years, driven in part by new data development. Data are useful to theoretical progress insofar as they help us evaluate implications of our theories and new theoretical understandings of civil war processes. Current research in civil war discusses the role of factors such as resource dependence, external intervention, the organizational structure of rebel groups, and ethnic inequality in driving civil war onset, duration, and resolution. Our understanding of conflict is surely driven by advances in theory, but a striking feature of recent research on civil conflict is the close interaction and synergies between theory and data development. Data development projects are driven by theoretical developments, which clarify what sort of information would be required to evaluate specific propositions and highlight limitations with current resources. However, data sources often turn out to be useful for many purposes other than their original motivation, and often lead to a reevaluation or refinement of theoretical perspectives. Based on the high level of activity in conflict data development, we expect this cumulative trend in progressive research to continue.

There is a clear need for continued progress in data collection—in particular, in identifying factors that lead to the outbreak of violence. The growth in data on the timing and location of specific acts of violence and the organizations participating in violence allow for examining the dynamics of ongoing conflicts. However, there is still a significant gap in our understanding of why violent civil conflict begins in some places at some times and not in others. Much of this gap is driven by lack of data. Identifying a set of potential civil conflicts, some of which do and others of which do not, become civil wars is difficult, but without this comparison set it is difficult to address important questions such as whether and how specific actions increase or decrease the likelihood of escalation to violence. Going forward, we would gain a greater understanding of the determinants of civil war by having better data on both violent and nonviolent organizations, as well as on the timing and location of nonviolent acts of dissent than could occur in the lead-up to civil conflict. Our understanding of civil conflict would be improved with more comprehensive data that examines conflictual interactions outside of the context of violence.

Notes

CHAPTER 1: INTRODUCTION—PATTERNS OF ARMED CONFLICT SINCE 1945

1. Chapter 15 discusses the UCDP and other databases of importance to the study of civil war. See also chapter 2 on what civil war is, and particularly on when and how civil war begins. For a broader discussion on the collection of conflict data, see the special section of the *Journal of Peace Research*, "Best Practices in the Collection of Conflict Data," issue 52(1), January 2015, including a discussion of how "unclear cases" are dealt with by UCDP (Kreutz 2015).

2. Chapter 4 deals with weak state capacity as a risk factor for civil war onset. It is often argued that in poor countries with high incomes from natural resource extraction, the temptation to try to take over the state by force becomes greater. On the resource curse and civil war, see chapter 13.

3. Proxy warfare is discussed in chapter 5 of this volume.

4. Third party military intervention in civil war is dealt with in chapter 6.

5. Most analyses of the causes of armed conflict (e.g., Hegre and Sambanis 2006) use the *onset* of new conflicts as the dependent variable. In order to gauge the amount of conflict, as we do here, the *incidence* of conflict is the better measure. For a study showing the varying impact of democracy on the onset, incidence, and duration of civil war, as well as its severity, see Gleditsch, Hegre, and Strand (2009).

6. Lacina and Gleditsch (2005: 154). The Chinese Civil War 1946–1949 was a direct continuation of armed conflict that began before World War II.

7. For a challenge to this interpretation and a response, see Gohdes and Price (2013) and Lacina and Gleditsch (2013).

8. See figure A.1 in the online appendix to this chapter, available at https://rowman.com/ISBN/9781442242258.

9. See figure A.2 in the online appendix.

10. Recently, conflict-related sexual violence has received a great deal of attention. Chapter 12 on gender and civil war reviews some of the relevant findings.

11. Or after World War II, in the rare cases where independence occurred first.

12. See chapter 5 for more on the transnational dimensions of civil war.

13. www.icow.org.

14. The role of ethnic and religious divisions in civil war is treated in chapter 3.

15. The factors that determine how a civil war ends are discussed in chapter 6. Chapter 7 deals with third party mediation to end civil wars and chapter 8 discusses how power sharing influences whether peace takes hold or not. Chapter 9 presents research on the role of peace-keeping and democratization in preventing the recurrence of civil wars, whereas chapter 10 focuses specifically on transitional justice and its effect on the aftermath of civil war.

16. We do not consider interpersonal violence. Roughly nine times as many people die from homicide worldwide than from civil war (Hoeffler and Fearon, 2014).

17. An update to 2008 also shows that there is no upward trend in forced displacement. Cf. figure A.6 in the online appendix.

18. A common concern is that global warming and other environmental problems will be a more prominent cause of civil war in the future; see chapter 14.

CHAPTER 2: ANTECEDENTS OF CIVIL WAR ONSET: GREED, GRIEVANCE, AND STATE REPRESSION

1. Some would argue that this, in fact, was the second U.S. civil war, counting the revolution in 1776 as the first civil war.

2. See David Blight's course at Yale as an exemplar of a course that explains the antecedents, conduct, and aftermath of the U.S. Civil War: http://oyc.yale.edu/history/hist-119.

3. See Goertz (2006) for a complete discussion on how to develop and use concepts for social science and with specific applications to the study of war.

4. See Hoffman (2013) for an extensive discussion on defining terrorism, and Young and Findley (2011) for how defining terrorism can influence inferences. See Fein (1990) for a complete discussion on defining genocide.

5. Codebook accessed on September 19, 2014: http://www.pcr.uu.se/digitalAssets/124/1 24922_1onset2012pdf.pdf

6. In practice, this is most similar to how Fearon and Laitin (2003) code civil wars. It does require, however, some retrospective decisions. In short, it may be difficult to determine when we are in a civil war as opposed to coding this ten years later.

7. Sometimes quantitative researchers change these coding decisions and then re-analyze the data. This is often called a "robustness check" or a "sensitivity analysis."

8. Regardless of intensity, this assumes that violent conflict between two non-state actors is *not* civil war. Studies on topics such as ethnic riots focus on intrastate conflict that does not necessarily include the state (see Varshney 2003).

9. See Young (2013) for an extended discussion of related points and for a formal derivation of this definition.

10. Classic studies of internal conflict, such as Gurr (1970), either looked at a range of types of political violence or focused more on revolution (e.g., Skocpol 1979).

11. Fearon (2004) shows this empirically and offers a model to explain why.

12. See Lichbach (1995) for potential solutions to getting people to act together for rebellion. See Gates (2002) for a formal theory on the micro-foundations of rebellion.

13. More recently, horizontal inequalities or inequalities between culturally defined groups, have been a popular explanation for how grievance relates to conflict. See, for example, Cederman et al. (2013).

14. While these two papers are far from the only work in this tradition, each established a following in the literature, and each structures the debate even today (Collier and Hoeffler 2004 has 4,580 Google Scholar citations and Fearon and Laitin 2003 has 4,234). DeRouen and Sobek in chapter 4 offer more detailed explanations for how one important structure, the state and its capacity, relates to civil war.

15. For example, diamonds found in a stream are more easily taken by rebels than diamonds that have to be extracted from a mine. Additionally, oil fields are more easily pillaged than offshore oil rigs that require boats to reach them.

16. Smith in chapter 13 offers a comprehensive discussion of the natural resource–civil war nexus.

17. See, for example, Collier (2003), Collier and Sambanis (2005), De Soysa (2002) and Regan and Norton (2005).

18. See Gallagher and Seymour's discussion in chapter 3 of how ethnicity and religion can influence civil war processes.

19. I do not have the space nor is this the place to offer a complete critique of their empirical approaches. However, both studies tend to examine correlations between weak proxies of concepts with their coded onset of civil war variables. Using quasi-experimental methods, such as propensity score matching, to better identify causal effects suggests that many of the key results are overestimated (Young 2008).

20. In international relations, because of anarchy, there is a general lack of a capable guardian.

21. It is difficult to account for precise proportions of how each matter. The more general point is that neither is trivial.

22. There are obviously many other ways to model civil war. More recently, a micro turn in the study of civil war has led to more precision in modeling and data collection. See Cederman and Gleditsch (2009) and Cunningham et al. (2009) as examples.

23. To do so requires multistage models that first predict an outcome like repression and then how factors that lead to repression indirectly lead then to civil war.

24. See Thyne (2006) for a related discussion. See Mack (2002) for a discussion about how current quantitative civil war literature could better communicate results to the policy world.

25. Schrodt and Gerner (1994) pioneered this approach in conflict studies decades ago, but the more mainstream adoption just recently began.

26. See the Mass Atrocities Early Warning Project as an example: https://cpgearlywarning.wordpress.com/.

CHAPTER 3: IDENTITY ISSUES AND CIVIL WAR: ETHNIC AND RELIGIOUS DIVISIONS

1. Notably, we focus throughout on the study of civil war in political science. We therefore set aside the relationship between identity and interstate conflict, as well as growing literatures on civil war in economics and anthropology (e.g., Blattman and Miguel 2010; Kanbur, Rajaram, and Varshney 2011).

2. In brief, Huntington hypothesized that future conflicts would be primarily cultural, with the fault lines drawn between civilizations defined in cultural and religious terms.

3. This is essentially an index that measures the chance that two randomly selected people drawn from a country will belong to different ethno-linguistic groups.

CHAPTER 4: STATE CAPACITY, REGIME TYPE, AND CIVIL WAR

1. We appreciate the comments and suggestions of David Mason, Sara Mitchell, Erik Melander, Lars-Erik Cederman, Samantha Lange, and participants at the Shambaugh Conference, September 2014, University of Iowa.

2. Portions of this section draw from work by DeRouen et al. (2009).

3. Young (chapter 2 of this volume) also notes GDP per capita has been used to measure state capacity and rebel greed arguments. In the case of greed, a low GDP per capita reflects low opportunity costs for rebellion.

4. The resource curse or rentier literature identifies a general connection between the production of oil and diminished provision of social services.

5. The democratic peace is a broad set of theories and empirical findings that show why no fully democratic states have fought interstate wars against other democracies (Russett and Oneal 2001).

6. Regimes can be categorized along many aspects. Some groups focus on the institutions of the state, such as voting laws and/or how power is separated. Others focus on the rights regimes provide regardless of the institutions, such as political, civil, economic, and/or women's rights. There is no generally accepted best measure, but scholars use the measure that can best test their hypothesis.

CHAPTER 5: TRANSNATIONAL DIMENSIONS OF CIVIL WARS: CLUSTERING, CONTAGION, AND CONNECTEDNESS

1. A number of people have contributed to the present book chapter, including the book editors, T. David Mason and Sara Mitchell, and the participants of the book workshop, in particular Clayton Thyne and Christopher Linebarger; my colleagues Mats Hammarström, Magnus Öberg, Hanne Fjelde, Marga Sollenberg, and Niklas Karlén; and Tanja Börzel, Etel Solingen, Aida Hozic, Detlef Jahn, Thomas Risse, and Arthur Stein.

2. See also Gleditsch, Melander, and Urdal in this volume (2016).

3. Gleditsch (2007) estimates that for a country with conflict present in a neighboring country, the probability of civil war onset increases by almost two-thirds, when the country profile in other respects has an average estimated risk of onset.

4. For many phenomena it is difficult to distinguish between diffusion and spatial clustering. Ross and Homer provide an illustrative example of this problem, typically termed *Galton's problem* (Galton 1889). Conditions relating to weather, such as average temperatures and precipitation, are clustered geographically just like the technologies for farming usually are. However, the fact that farmers adopt similar technologies may not necessarily stem from

them mimicking each other (contagion) but may simply be the result of the farmers being exposed to the same conditions favoring a specific technique. Thus, if two conflicts correlate in space and time, one may incorrectly conclude that one conflict led to another through contagion, when in fact both conflicts arose from the same set of determinants that were clustered, such as poverty. With the contribution by Buhaug and Gleditsch (2008), there seems to be evidence of both processes in place. Thus, spatial clustering of relevant country characteristics like poverty and regime type generates a neighborhood effect of conflict, but even when removing the impact of these determinants some clustering remains, lending support for contagion effects.

5. This definition is in line with the commonly used definition of diffusion as an event or transition in one place affecting the likelihood of a similar event or transition happening at another place at a later point in time (Elkins and Simmons 2005; Strang 1991).

6. However, it should be noted that spatial proximity has typically not been treated as an important determinant of contagion, but as a selection criterion used to identify high-risk cases of contagion. This hampers our ability to draw inference about its relative importance.

7. These problems are discussed in more detail in Forsberg (2014a)

8. The dyadic approach allows for testing explanations for contagion that vary across pairs of states. For instance, it has been suggested that refugees fleeing from a conflict to a neighboring country may cause conflict contagion. With the dyadic setup, it is possible to examine the number of refugees fleeing from the conflict country to an at-risk country, to examine whether at-risk countries are at greater risk of contagion if hosting many refugees compared to an at-risk country not receiving any (or fewer) refugees. With the monadic country-year design, all refugees hosted by a given state are aggregated, with no reference to their origin.

9. For an excellent review of how the reasons, resources, and resolve of actors (i.e., the Triple-R typology suggested by Ohlson [2008]) relate to transnational linkages of conflicts, see Fjelde (2012).

CHAPTER 7: RIPE FOR RESOLUTION: THIRD PARTY MEDIATION AND NEGOTIATING PEACE AGREEMENTS

1. See for example Beardsley (2010) and Crescenzi et al. (2011).

2. See for example Balch-Lindsay, Enterline, and Joyce (2008), Cunningham (2010), Thyne (2006), and chapter 6 in this volume.

3. The caveat to this is that biased or strategic mediators may have interests over outcomes such that potential resolutions to conflict may be dismissed when they fall outside the mediator's own set of acceptable outcomes. In this way, continued conflict may be the consequence of mediator interests over outcomes. Yet, in the discussion above, we only mean to suggest that the literature generally assesses the effectiveness of mediation in achieving resolution to conflict as the central goal of mediation efforts, even when mediator bias for certain outcomes or actors is present. This is not necessarily the case for all forms of third party involvement in civil conflicts.

4. Kreutz's finding of the rarity of peace agreements may be attributed to how he defines conflict. His data take conflicts and split them into episodes, making the chance than any one episode ends in an agreement less likely.

5. Fearon (1995) also addresses issue indivisibilities as a bargaining obstacle that leads to war. Indivisible issues may include ethnicity, religion, and culture, such as Israeli and Palestinian claims to sacred sites in Jerusalem. However, in the broader rationalist literature, and in the study of civil war, support is limited for the role of issue indivisibilities in explaining war processes. See Fearon and Laitin (2000) for a convincing perspective that seemingly indivisible issues in civil conflict can be constructed and manipulated. Some also argue that issue indivisibilities are not a separate bargaining obstacle, but are a special type of commitment problem (Powell 2006). Because information asymmetries and commitment problems have garnered substantially more attention in the study of conflict and civil war, we focus on those bargaining problems here.

6. Commitment problems also persist in interstate wars (Powell 1999, 2006, 2012).

7. Greig and Diehl (2012), in a study of interstate and civil mediation, estimate that one-third of all mediation attempts are carried out by repeat mediators.

8. Diehl and Regan, in the introduction to a special forthcoming issue of *Conflict Management and Peace Science*, discuss options for accounting for interdependence between mediation attempts. The special issue challenges the assumption of independence of mediation attempts within conflicts, across conflicts, and with regard to other events that occur over the course of a conflict.

9. For example, see the Managing Intrastate Low-Intensity Conflict dataset (Melander, Möller, and Öberg 2009), which offers events data on civil conflict management efforts that include mediation attempts, albeit for a limited time frame. Additionally, DeRouen, Bercovitch, and Pospieszna's (2011) Civil War Mediation dataset offers start and end dates, when available, of mediation in civil war by conflict episode, thus allowing for further temporal disaggregation to match related datasets.

10. Also, disaggregation may offer means by which contradictory empirical findings in the literature can be resolved. High levels of aggregation may combine otherwise nuanced information into overly coarse categorizations. Sensitivity analyses with disaggregated data would be one positive way of checking the robustness of previously reported results. Given the sensitivity of some results in the civil war literature more generally (Hegre and Sambanis 2006), further tests of past empirical analyses are welcome.

11. See, for example, Heldt (2009).

CHAPTER 8: NEGOTIATED PEACE: POWER SHARING IN PEACE AGREEMENTS

1. This section of the paper draws on Hartzell (2009, 2012).

2. Counterrevolutionary forces, trained and funded by the U.S. Central Intelligence Agency, sought to overthrow the Castro regime via the Bay of Pigs invasion in 1961 but were handily defeated by the Cuban Revolutionary Armed Forces.

3. It should be emphasized that those who adopt this line of thinking claim that, if properly constructed, negotiated agreements can be used to stabilize the peace, not that they are the only means of doing so.

4. Hartzell (2009) tests this proposition for all civil wars ending between 1945 and 2006 and finds that slightly more than 40 percent of the conflicts that ended in a military victory saw more than one faction preserve its organization identity.

5. The other 23 percent of the settlements ended in negotiated truces. Identification of trends based on author's data.

6. This section of the paper draws on Hartzell and Hoddie (2015).

7. Event history models take into account the fact that datasets are "right censored," meaning that an event such as a settlement failure may not have occurred by the last period of time covered by the dataset.

8. Jarstad and Nilsson (2008) find that military and territorial power sharing have a positive impact on peace duration. Mattes and Savun (2009) conclude that political power sharing best extends the duration of the peace while DeRouen, Lea, and Wallensteen (2009) find that political power sharing has a negative but statistically insignificant impact on the stability of the peace.

9. Agreements to share power may resemble mediation in this respect. Mediation also has been found to take place in the most difficult cases in which disputants cannot agree bilaterally to settle their differences (Gartner and Bercovitch 2006). See chapter 7, this volume.

CHAPTER 9: BREAKING THE CONFLICT TRAP: THE IMPACT OF PEACEKEEPING ON VIOLENCE AND DEMOCRATIZATION IN THE POST-CONFLICT CONTEXT

1. An earlier version was presented at the workshop "What Do We Know about Civil Wars?" at the University of Iowa, September 26–27, 2014. The author would like to thank Jacob Kathman, Patrick Regan, Sara Mitchell, David Mason, and other workshop participants for their comments and suggestions. In addition, gratitude is expressed to Caroline Hartzell, and Jose Cheibub for their advice, and to Jason Renn and David Bowden for their editing and revision suggestions.

2. The conventional term "peacekeeping" and the broader term "peace operation" are used interchangeably here. These terms refer to the range of conflict management operations in which third parties deploy a small number of lightly armed soldiers to supervise cease-fires, monitor elections, and perform other duties in support of efforts to prevent the renewal of war and facilitate long-term peace and stability; an example is the United Nations Peacekeeping Force in Cyprus (UNFICYP), in place since 1964. For a discussion of different terms and meanings, including peacebuilding, see Diehl and Balas (2014).

3. This chapter largely covers the literature in the behavioral or positivist research tradition, namely those traditions driven by a theoretical orientation to explain causal relationships and ones in which those theoretical arguments are tested by reference to historical cases, often in a large-N and statistically dependent research design.

4. Conflict phases from the vantage point of peacekeeping can be broken into first (pre-violence), second (active violence), third (cease-fire, pre-resolution), and fourth (post-conflict, agreement) phases (Diehl and Balas 2014).

5. Yet this depends on the winner of the war, with no peacekeeping effect when the government is the victor.

6. See Gartner and Melin (2009) for a good review of such factors as well as some discussion about assessing durability of conflict management outcomes.

7. Studies tend to confound the third and fourth phases, in that violence has halted, but there is a major difference concerning whether an agreement between disputants has been reached or not.

8. Democratization is unlikely *during* an active civil war when parties are focused on attaining military victory on the battlefield, rather than through political institutions. Indeed, aspects of democracy might be diminished during this time as personal liberties are violated and executive powers are enhanced. Thus, democratization efforts occur *after* the conclusion of civil wars.

9. This presumes, however, that election monitoring is able to detect fraud and manipulation. Daxecker (2012) reports a higher risk of violence when results are manipulated and international observers are present.

10. There are some differences in mean democracy levels (at 1, 2, and 5 years after the war) for conditions of no peacekeeping, consent-based peacekeeping, and enforcement-based peacekeeping. Yet, most of these are not statistically significant or inconsistently so. In any case, these disappear when peacekeeping is part of a multivariate analysis.

11. There are some drawbacks, however, in focusing too much on formal mandates. The mandates given for operations, especially those directed by large-membership international organizations, are the products of political deliberation and compromise, and the result is that they are frequently vague. For example, the UN Security Force (UNSF) in West Guinea was charged with maintaining law and order, but how this was to be achieved was not specified.

CHAPTER 10: THE LEGACIES OF CIVIL WAR: HEALTH, EDUCATION, AND ECONOMIC DEVELOPMENT

1. See chapter 9 (this volume) for a more thorough discussion of the influence of peacekeepers on civilian deaths and conflict more generally.

2. See chapter 1 (this volume) for a more thorough discussion of deaths and civil conflict.

3. Matching is a statistical technique that attempts to approximate true experiments in studies where the treatment is not randomly assigned. Attempting to capture how a civil war influences a state's economy is difficult, for example, because we cannot (and would not want to) randomly assign civil wars to states to see how the conflicts influence treated cases versus nontreated (i.e., control) cases. With matching, researchers attempt to match treated units (those that experienced civil war) with similar nontreated units (states at peace) based on similar observable characteristics (e.g., similar levels of wealth, democracy, ethnic heterogeneity), leaving the treatment (civil conflict) as the primary factor that can account for variations in the dependent variable (e.g., economic growth or decline).

CHAPTER 11: TRANSNATIONAL JUSTICE: PROSPECTS FOR POSTWAR PEACE AND HUMAN RIGHTS

1. Genocide is the extermination or attempted extermination of a people because of their indelible group membership (race, ethnicity, religion, or language).

2. I define these terms in greater detail later in this chapter.

3. Other empirical work falls outside the scope of this chapter, but may be of interest to this volume's audience. First, scholars have investigated the conditions under which states pursue transitional justice, both in general and with respect to specific mechanisms or packages (see, for example, Dancy et al. 2010; Dancy and Poe 2006; Elster 1998; Kim 2012; Mallinder 2008, 2009; Nalepa 2010; Olsen, Payne and Reiter 2010a; Powers and Proctor 2015; Roper and Barria 2009; Skaar 1999). Second, studies have probed impacts of transitional justice not covered here,

including democratization, the rule of law, and reconciliation (e.g., Call 2007; de Brito et al. 2001; Gibson 2004b, 2006; Goldstone 1995; Kenney and Spears 2005; Stromseth et al. 2006).

4. The Gacaca courts also have nonretributive objectives, including the reconstruction of what happened during the genocide and the reconciliation of all Rwandans (Daly 2002).

5. In addition to the Bosnian War discussed here, conflicts occurred in Slovenia, Croatia, Kosovo, the Preševo Valley, and the Republic of Macedonia.

6. For updates and the full criminal proceedings of the ICTY, visit www.icty.org.

7. Here, *human rights* refers to physical integrity rights including freedom from extrajudicial killing, torture, imprisonment for political views, and disappearances (e.g., Cingranelli and Richards 2010; Poe and Tate 1994; Wood and Gibney 2010).

8. For the full text of the CAVR mandate, see http://www.cavr-timorleste.org.

9. Another example of rigorous theory and research design is Nalepa (2010), whose focus is on the strategic conditions that make TJ implementation both possible and desirable. In particular, she engages decisions (not) to lustrate in Eastern Europe.

10. PTS ranges from 1 to 5 with higher values capturing increasing government violations of physical integrity rights including extrajudicial killing, torture, disappearances, and political imprisonment. CIRI ranges from 0 to 8 with higher values capturing increasing government respect for the same set of physical integrity rights. For more on PTS, see Wood and Gibney (2010) or www.politicalterrorscale.org. For more on CIRI, see Cingranelli and Richards (2010) or www.humanrightsdata.com.

11. Meernik et al. (2010) is an exception, as these authors leveraged Kim and Sikkink's prosecutions data rather than coding the same concept on their own.

12. This is not an exhaustive list; mechanism-specific datasets are also newly and publicly available. Perhaps most notably, Mallinder's Amnesty Law Database (http://incore.incore.ulst .ac.uk/Amnesty/) contains information on over 520 amnesty laws in 138 countries since the end of World War II and Powers and Proctor's (2015) data records which countries awarded and paid out reparations in each year from 1969 to 2006.

CHAPTER 13: EXPLORING THE RESOURCE–CIVIL WAR NEXUS

1. Full disclosure: this author generally comes down in the conflict-reducing camp.

2. In this broader research program, scholars also address the conflict implications of extractive sectors such as minerals, diamonds, and timber. More expansively, we see exploration of still more commodities: water, agricultural production, fisheries, etc.

3. For example, in advance of the American-British invasion of Iraq in 2003, Iraqi Kurds began making public statements indicating that they would view partnerships with American and British oil companies favorably in a post-Saddam Iraqi political economy.

4. When scholars suspect that explanatory (causal) variables are correlated with a model's statistical error term, they sometimes employ an instrumental variables (IV) approach, which is simply indicators related to the explanatory variables but not to the error term. In political economy research, many factors such as resource wealth are prone to this problem, hence the increasing commonness of IV analysis.

5. Fixed effects analyses are common in political economy research when scholars suspect that the units of analysis—especially countries—may have time-invariant traits not accounted for in the set of variables included but that might be causally important. Concretely, a scholar asks, "are there things about Nigeria (or any other country) that could influence the dependent

variable but that we haven't identified or measured?" Fixed effects models account for these potential omitted variables.

6. Archived at http://www.correlatesofwar.org/ and http://www.pcr.uu.se/research/ucdp/datasets/, respectively.

7. Including the Minorities at Risk data project here is not intended to minimize the selection bias problems that have been pointed out with it—i.e., sampling only groups that are discriminated against. Rather, I mention it here to note the real benefit for scholars of having access to publicly available group year level data.

8. This is the case everywhere in the world other than in the United States.

CHAPTER 14: ENVIRONMENT AND CONFLICT

1. Associated Press, "Somalia: Famine Toll in 2011 Was Larger than Previously Reported," *New York Times* April 29, 2013.

2. Remote sensing data are normally acquired from satellite images and adapted to a common data framework (e.g., grid cells or countries) for use in statistical analysis. Examples of such data used in conflict studies include climatological indices, land use and forest cover, and night light emission data.

3. Given that this book is about civil war, we have deliberately not considered interstate conflict.

4. UCDP is the most commonly used dataset for the analysis of armed civil conflict. For a more detailed description of UCDP datasets, see Gleditsch et al. (2002) and Themnér and Wallensteen (2014), or http://www.pcr.uu.se/research/ucdp/definitions.

CHAPTER 15: TRENDS IN CIVIL WAR DATA: GEOGRAPHY, ORGANIZATIONS, AND EVENTS

1. Data available at: www.correlatesofwar.org. Access date: November 18, 2014.

2. Data available at: http://www.cidcm.umd.edu/mar/. Access date: September 22, 2014.

3. See http://growup.ethz.ch/ for more details. Access date: September 22, 2014.

4. Civil wars require that both states and non-state actors use organized violence. States can also use violence outside of formal civil war, for example when using repression against unorganized civilians or actors that do not use violence.

5. For a rebel group to be listed in the ACD, it has to be engaged in dyadic violent conflict with the state, resulting in at least twenty-five battle-related deaths in a calendar year.

6. The latest version of the data recently released includes events taking place in "inactive years" involving organizations that were involved in dyadic conflicts leading to twenty-five deaths in other years.

7. For a comparison of UCDP-GED and ACLED, see Eck (2012).

8. See Enders, Sandler, and Gaibulloev (2011) for a discussion of GTD and other terrorism databases.

9. See Schrodt (2012) for a survey of various events datasets.

10. See the Computational Event Data System website for applications and software: http://eventdata.parusanalytics.com/index.html. Access date: September 22, 2014.

11. Available at: http://thedata.org/. Access date: November 18, 2014.

References

Abdi, Ali A. 1998. "Education in Somalia: History, Destruction, and Calls for Reconstruction." *Comparative Education* 34(3):327–40.

Abouharb, M. Rodwan, and David Cingranelli. 2007. *Human Rights and Structural Adjustment.* Cambridge: Cambridge University Press.

Acemoglu, Daron, Simon Johnson, and James A. Robinson. 2001. "The Colonial Origins of Comparative Development: An Empirical Investigation." *American Economic Review* 91(5):1369–401.

Acemoglu, Daron, and James A. Robinson. 2006. *Economic Origins of Dictatorship and Democracy.* New York: Cambridge University Press.

Adeola, Francis. 1996. "Military Expenditures, Health, and Education: Bedfellows or Antagonists in Third World Development?" *Armed Forces & Society* 22(3):441–55.

Adger W. Neil, et al. 2014. "Human Security." In *Climate Change 2014: Impacts, Adaptation, and Vulnerability. Part A: Global and Sectoral Aspects. Contribution of Working Group II to the Fifth Assessment Report of the Intergovernmental Panel on Climate Change,* edited by Christopher B. Field, Vicente R. Barros, David Jon Kokken, Katharine J. Mach, and Michael D. Mastrandrea, 755–91. Cambridge, UK: Cambridge University Press.

Aguilar, Pilar, and Gonzalo Retamal. 1998. "Rapid Educational Response in Complex Emergencies: A Discussion Document." Geneva, Switzerland: International Bureau of Education.

Ahmed, Akbar S. 2013. *The Thistle and the Drone: How America's War on Terror Became a Global War on Tribal Islam.* Washington, DC: Brookings Institution Press.

Akcinaroglu, Seden, and Elizabeth Radziszewski. 2005. "Expectations, Rivalries, and Civil War Duration." *International Interactions* 31(4):349–74.

Akhavan, Payam. 2001. "Beyond Impunity: Can International Criminal Justice Prevent Future Atrocities?" *American Journal of International Law* 95(1):7–31.

Akresh, Richard, and Damien de Walque. 2008. "Armed Conflict and Schooling: Evidence from the 1994 Rwandan Genocide." IZA Discussion Papers 3516, Institute for the Study of Labor (IZA), HiCN Working Paper no. 47.

Akresh, Richard, Philip Verwimp, and Tom Bundervoet. 2011. "Civil War, Crop Failure, and Child Stunting in Rwanda." *Economic Development and Cultural Change* 59(4):777–810.

Alderman, Harold, John Hoddinott, and Bill Kinsey. 2006. "Long Term Consequences of Early Childhood Malnutrition." *Oxford Economic Papers* 58(3):450–74.

Algan, Yann, and Pierre Cahuc. 2010. "Inherited Trust and Growth." *The American Economic Review* 100(5):2060–92.

Alix-Garcia, Jennifer. 2007. *The Effects of Refugee Inflows on Host Country Populations: Evidence from Tanzania.* University of Montana. http://ssrn.com/abstract=836147.

Allansson, Marie, Margareta Sollenberg, and Lotta Themnér. 2013. "Armed Conflict in the Wake of the Arab Spring." In *SIPRI Yearbook 2013: Armaments, Disarmament and International Security,* edited by SIPRI. Oxford: Oxford University Press.

Amnesty International. 2000. *Annual Report.* http://web.amnesty.org/report2000/.

Anderson, Benedict. 1991. *Imagined Communities: Reflections on the Origin and Spread of Nationalism.* London: Verso Books.

Annan, Kofi. 1999. "Two Concepts of Sovereignty." *The Economist.* September 18.

Apostolakis, Bobby E. 1992. "Warfare-Welfare Expenditure Substitutions in Latin America, 1963–1987." *Journal of Peace Research* 29(1):85–98.

Archer, Christon I., John R. Ferris, Holger H. Herwig, and Timothy H. E. Travers. 2002. *World History of Warfare.* Lincoln, NE: University of Nebraska Press.

Archer, Dane, and Rosemary Gartner. 1984. *Violence and Crime in Cross-National Perspective.* New Haven, CT: Yale University Press.

Arena, Philip. 2008. "Success Breeds Success? War Outcomes, Domestic Opposition, and Elections." *Conflict Management and Peace Science* 25(2):136–51.

Arendt, Hannah. 1970. *On Violence.* New York: Harcourt, Brace & World.

Arreguin-Toft, Ivan. 2001. "How the Weak Win Wars: A Theory of Asymmetric Conflict." *International Security* 26(1):93–128.

Arthur, Paige. 2009. "How 'Transitions' Reshaped Human Rights: A Conceptual History of Transitional Justice." *Human Rights Quarterly* 31(2):321–67.

Asal, Victor, Ken Cousins, and Kristian Skrede Gleditsch. 2015. "Making Ends Meet: Combining Organizational Data in Contentious Politics." *Journal of Peace Research,* 52(1):134–138.

Asal, Victor, Richard Legault, Ora Szekely, and Jonathan Wilkenfeld. 2013. "Gender Ideologies and Forms of Contentious Mobilization in the Middle East." *Journal of Peace Research* 50(3):305–18.

Asal, Victor, Amy Pate, and Jonathan Wilkenfeld. 2008. "Minorities at Risk Organizational Behavior Data and Codebook Version 9/2008." http://www.cidcm.umd.edu/mar/data.asp.

Aspinall, Edward. 2007a. *Islam and Nation.* Stanford: Stanford University Press.

Aspinall, Edward. 2007b. "The Construction of Grievance: Natural Resources and Identity in a Separatist Conflict." *Journal of Conflict Resolution* 51(6):950–72.

Aukerman, Miriam J. 2002. "Extraordinary Evil, Ordinary Crime: a Framework for Understanding Transitional Justice." *Harvard Human Rights Journal* 15:39.

Autesserre, Séverine. 2010. *The Trouble with the Congo: Local Violence and the Failure of International Peacebuilding.* Cambridge: Cambridge University Press.

Autesserre, Séverine. 2012. "Dangerous Tales: Dominant Narratives on the Congo and Their Unintended Consequences." *African Affairs* 111(443):202–22.

Autesserre, Séverine. 2014. *Peaceland: Conflict Resolution and the Everyday Politics of International Intervention.* Cambridge: Cambridge University Press.

Ayoob, Mohammed. 1995. *The Third World Security Predicament: State Making, Regional Conflict, and the International System.* Boulder, CO: Lynne Rienner Publishers.

Ayres, R. William, and Stephen Saideman. 2000. "Is Separatism as Contagious as the Common Cold or as Cancer? Testing International and Domestic Explanations." *Nationalism and Ethnic Politics* 6(3):91–113.

Azam, Jean-Paul, and Anke Hoeffler. 2002. "Violence against Civilians in Civil Wars: Looting or Terror?" *Journal of Peace Research* 39(4):461–85.

Baez, Javier E. 2011. "Civil Wars beyond Their Borders: The Human Capital and Health Consequences of Hosting Refugees." *Journal of Development Economics* 96(2):391–408.

Bakke, Kristin M. 2013. "Copying and Learning from Outsiders? Assessing Diffusion from Transnational Insurgents in the Chechen Wars." In *Transnational Dynamics of Civil War*, edited by Jeffrey T. Checkel. Cambridge: Cambridge University Press.

Bakke, Kristin M. 2014. "Help Wanted? The Mixed Record of Foreign Fighters in Domestic Insurgencies." *International Security* 38(4):150–87.

Bakke, Kristin M., Kathleen G. Cunningham, and Lee J. M. Seymour. 2012. "A Plague of Initials: Fragmentation, Cohesion, and Infighting in Civil Wars." *Perspectives on Politics* 10(2):265–83.

Balas, Alexandru. 2011. "It Takes Two (or More) to Keep the Peace: Multiple Simultaneous Peace Operations." *Journal of International Peacekeeping* 15:384–421.

Balcells, Laia. 2010. "Rivalry and Revenge Violence against Civilians in Conventional Civil Wars." *International Studies Quarterly* 54(2):291–313.

Balcells, Laia. 2011. "Continuation of Politics by Two Means: Direct and Indirect Violence in Civil War." *Journal of Conflict Resolution* 55(3):397–422.

Balcells, Laia, and Patricia Justino. 2014. "Bridging Micro and Macro Approaches on Civil Wars and Political Violence: Issues, Challenges and the Way Forward." *Journal of Peace Research* 58(8):1–17.

Balch-Lindsay, Dylan, and Andrew J. Enterline. 2000. "Killing Time: The World Politics of Civil War Duration, 1820–1992." *International Studies Quarterly* 44(4):615–42.

Balch-Lindsay, Dylan, Andrew J. Enterline, and Kyle Joyce. 2008. "Third-Party Intervention and the Civil War Process." *Journal of Peace Research* 45(3):345–63.

Ballentine, Karen, and Heiko Nitzschke. 2005. "The Political Economy of Civil War and Conflict Transformation." Berghof Research Center for Constructive Conflict Management.

Ballentine, Karen, and Jake Sherman, eds. 2003. *The Political Economy of Armed Conflict: Beyond Greed and Grievance.* Boulder, CO: Lynne Rienner Publishers.

Banks, Arthur S. 1971. *Cross-Polity Time-Series Data.* Cambridge, MA: MIT Press.

Bannon, Ian, and Paul Collier, eds. 2003. *Natural Resources and Violent Conflict: Options and Actions.* Oxford, UK: Oxford University Press.

Bapat, Navin. 2005. "Insurgency and the Opening of the Peace Process." *Journal of Peace Research* 42(6):699–717.

Barber, Brian K. 2001. "Political Violence, Social Integration, and Youth Functioning: Palestinian Youth from the Intifada." *Journal of Community Psychology* 29(3):259–80.

Barenbaum, J. Joshua, Vladislav Ruchkin, and Mary Schwab-Stone. 2004. "The Psychosocial Aspects of Children Exposed to War: Practice and Policy Initiatives." *Journal of Child Psychology and Psychiatry* 45(1):41–62.

Baron de Montesquieu, Charles de Secondat. 1748. *The Spirit of the Laws.*

Barro, Robert J., and Xavier Sala-i-Martin. 2004. *Economic Growth.* MIT Press, Second Edition.

Barron, Patrick, Macartan Humphreys, Laura Paler, and Jeremy Weinstein. 2009. "Community Based Reintegration in Aceh." *Indonesian Social Development Papers* 12.

Basedau, Matthias, and Jann Lay. 2009. "Resource Curse or Rentier Peace? The Ambiguous Effects of Oil Wealth and Oil Dependence on Violent Conflict." *Journal of Peace Research* 46(6):757–76.

Bates, Robert. 1983. *Essays on the Political Economy of Rural Africa*. Cambridge: Cambridge University Press, 1983.

Bates, Robert, Fen Osler Hampson, Margaret Levi, and Mark Howard Ross. 2007. "Consolidating Peace and Mitigating Conflict in the Aftermath of Violence." Washington, DC: APSA Task Force on Political Violence and Terrorism.

Bazzi, Samuel, and Christopher Blattman. 2014. "Economic Shocks and Conflict: Evidence from Commodity Prices." *American Economic Journal: Macroeconomics* 6:1–38.

Beah, Ishmael. 2007. *A Long Way Gone: Memoirs of a Boy Soldier*. New York: Farrar, Straus and Giroux.

Beardsley, Kyle. 2010. "Pain, Pressure and Political Cover: Explaining Mediation Incidence." *Journal of Peace Research* 47(4):395–406.

Beardsley, Kyle. 2011. "Peacekeeping and the Contagion of Armed Conflict." *The Journal of Politics* 73(4):1051–64.

Beardsley, Kyle, and Kristian Skrede Gleditsch. 2015. "Peacekeeping as Conflict Containment." *International Studies Review* 17(1):67–89.

Beardsley, Kyle, Kristian Skrede Gleditsch, and Nigel Lo. 2015. "Roving Bandits? The Geographical Evolution of African Armed Conflicts." *International Studies Quarterly*, 59(3): 503–516.

Beber, Bernd. 2010. "The (Non-)efficacy of Multi-Party Mediation in Wars Since 1990." Unpublished manuscript, New York University, https://files.nyu.edu/bb89/public/files/ Beber_MultipartyMediation.pdf.

Beblawi, Hazem, and Giacomo Luciani, eds. 1987. *The Rentier State*. New York: Croom Helm.

Beegle, Kathleen. 2005. "Labor Effects of Adult Mortality in Tanzanian Households." *Economic Development and Cultural Change* 53(3):655–83.

Beissinger, Mark R. 2002. *Nationalist Mobilization and the Collapse of the Soviet State*. Cambridge: Cambridge University Press.

Bellows, John, and Edward Miguel. 2009. "War and Local Collective Action in Sierra Leone." *Journal of Public Economics* 93(11–12):1144–57.

Benjaminsen, Tor A., Koffi Alinon, Halvard Buhaug, Jill Tove Buseth. 2012. "Does Climate Change Drive Land-Use Conflicts in the Saleh?" *Journal of Peace Research* 49(1):97–111.

Benjaminsen, Tor A., Faustin P. Maganga, and Jumanne Moshi Abdallah. 2009. "The Kilosa Killings: Political Ecology of a Farmer-Herder Conflict in Tanzania." *Development and Change* 40(3):423–45.

Benner, Thorsten, Stephan Mergenthaler, and Philipp Rotmann. 2011. *The New World of UN Peace Operations: Learning to Build Peace*. Oxford: Oxford University Press.

Benoit, Émile. 1973. *Defense and Economic Growth in Developing Countries*. Lexington, MA: Lexington Books.

Benoit, Émile. 1978. "Growth and Defense in Developing Countries." *Economic Development and Cultural Change* 26(2):271–80.

Bercovitch, Jacob, J. Theodore Anagnoson, and Donnette L. Wille. 1991. "Some Conceptual Issues and Empirical Trends in the Study of Successful Mediation in International Relations." *Journal of Peace Research* 28(1):7–17.

Berdal, Mats. 2005. "Beyond Greed and Grievance-and Not Too Soon . . ." *Review of International Studies* 31(4):687–98.

Berdal, Mats R., and David Malone. 2000. *Greed & Grievance: Economic Agendas in Civil Wars*. Boulder, CO: Lynne Rienner.

Bermeo, Nancy. 2003. "What the Democratization Literature Says—Or Doesn't Say—About Postwar Democratization." *Global Governance* 9:159–77.

Bernauer Thomas, Tobias Böhmelt, and Vally Koubi. 2012. "Environmental Changes and Violent Conflict." *Environmental Research Letters* 7:1–8.

Bernstein, Irving. 1996. *Guns or Butter: The Presidency of Lyndon Johnson*. New York: Oxford University Press.

Betancourt, Theresa. 2005. "Stressors, Supports and the Social Ecology of Displacement: Psychosocial Dimensions of an Emergency Education Program for Chechen Adolescents Displaced in Ingushetia, Russia." *Culture, Medicine & Psychiatry* 29(3):309–40.

Betancourt, Theresa S., and Kashif T. Khan. 2008. "The Mental Health of Children Affected by Armed Conflict: Protective Processes and Pathways to Resilience." *International Review of Psychiatry* 20(3):317–28.

Betancourt, Theresa S., Stephanie Simmons, Ivelina Borisova, Stephanie E. Brewer, Uzo Iweala, and Marie de la Soudière. 2008. "High Hopes, Grim Realities: Reintegration and the Education of Former Child Soldiers in Sierra Leone." *Comparative Education Review* 52(4):565–87.

Betancourt, Theresa S., and Timothy Williams. 2008. "Building an Evidence Base on Mental Health Interventions for Children Affected by Armed Conflict." *International Journal of Mental Health, Psychosocial Work and Counseling in Areas of Armed Conflict* 6(1):39–56.

Bickford, Louis. 2007. "Unofficial Truth Projects." *Human Rights Quarterly* 29(4):994–1035.

Binningsbø, Helga Malmin. 2011. *A Piece of the Pie: Power Sharing and Postconflict Peace.* PhD thesis, Department of Sociology and Political Science, Norwegian University of Science and Technology.

Binningsbø, Helga Malmin, Cyanne E. Loyle, Jon Elster, and Scott Gates. 2012a. "Justice Data," available online at http://www.justice-data.com.

Binningsbø, Helga Malmin, Cyanne E. Loyle, Jon Elster, and Scott Gates. 2012b. "Armed Conflict and Post-Conflict Justice, 1946–2006: A Dataset." *Journal of Peace Research* 49(5):731–40.

Biswas, Asit K., and H. Cecilia Tortajada-Quiroz. 1996. "Environmental Impacts of the Rwandan Refugees on Zaire." *Ambio* 25(6):403–8.

Bjarnegard, Elin, Karen Brouneus, and Erik Melander. 2014. "Patterns of Peace in Thailand: Exploring the Relationship between Attitudes to Gender Equality and Violent Behavior." Paper presented at the annual meeting of the American Political Science Association.

Bjarnegård, Elin, and Erik Melander. 2013. "Revisiting Representation: Communism, Women in Politics, and the Decline of Armed Conflict in East Asia." *International Interactions* 39(4):558–74.

Black, Nathan. 2012. *The Spread of Violent Civil Conflict: Rare, State-Driven, and Preventable.* Department of Political Science: Massachusetts Institute of Technology.

Blattman, Christopher, and Jeannie Annan. 2010. "The Consequence of Child Soldiering." *The Review of Economics and Statistics* 92(4):882–98.

Blattman, Christopher, and Edward Miguel. 2010. "Civil War." *Journal of Economic Literature* 48(1):3–57.

Böhmelt, Tobias. 2012. "Why Many Cooks if They Can Spoil the Broth? The Determinants of Multiparty Mediation." *Journal of Peace Research* 49(5):701–15.

Böhmelt, Tobias. 2013. "Failing to Succeed? The Cumulative Impact of International Mediation Revisited." *Conflict Management and Peace Science* 30(3):199–219.

Bohnet, Heidrun, Fabien Cottier, and Simon Hug. 2013. "Conflict-Induced IDPs and the Spread of Conflict." Paper prepared for presentation at the European Political Science Association (EPSA) in Barcelona, June 20–22, 2013.

Boix, Carles. 2008. "Economic Roots of Civil Wars and Revolutions in the Contemporary World." *World Politics* 60(3):390–437.

Bond, Douglas, J. Curt Jenkins, Charles L. Taylor, and Kurt Schock. 1997. "Mapping Mass Political Conflict and Civil Society: Issues and Prospects for the Automated Development of Event Data." *Journal of Conflict Resolution* 41(4):553–79.

Borer, Tristan Anne, ed. 2006. *Telling the Truth: Truth Telling and Peace Building in Post-Conflict Societies.* Notre Dame, IN: University of Notre Dame Press.

Bormann, Niels-Christian, Lars-Erik Cederman, and Manuel Vogt. 2015. "Language, Religion and Ethnic Civil War." *Journal of Conflict Resolution.*

Boswell, Terry, and William J. Dixon. 1990. "Dependency and Rebellion." *American Sociological Review* 55:540–59.

Boulding, Kenneth E. 1963. *Conflict and Defense: A General Theory.* New York: Harper and Row.

Brahm, Eric. 2007. "Uncovering the Truth: Examining Truth Commission Success and Impact." *International Studies Perspectives* 8(1):16–35.

Braithwaite, Alex. 2010a. "Midloc: Introducing the Militarized Interstate Dispute." *Journal of Peace Research* 47(1):91–98.

Braithwaite, Alex. 2010b. "Resisting Infection: How State Capacity Conditions Conflict Contagion." *Journal of Peace Research* 47(3):311–19.

Brancati, Dawn, and Jack L. Snyder. 2011. "Rushing to the Polls: The Causes of Premature Postconflict Elections." *Journal of Conflict Resolution* 55:469–92.

Brancati, Dawn, and Jack L. Snyder. 2012. "Time to Kill: The Impact of Election Timing on Postconflict Stability." *Journal of Conflict Resolution* 57:822–53.

Brander, Bruce. 1996. "Sudan's Civil War: Silent Cries to a Deaf World." http://www.worldvision.org.

Brandt, Patrick T., T. David Mason, Mehmet Gurses, Nicolai Petrovsky, and Dagmar Radin. 2008. "When and How the Fighting Stops: Explaining the Duration and Outcome of Civil Wars." *Defence and Peace Economics* 19(6):415–34.

Bratt, Duane. 1996. "Assessing the Success of UN Peacekeeping Operations." *International Peacekeeping* 3:64–81.

Bratt, Duane. 1997. "Explaining Peacekeeping Performance: The UN in Internal Conflicts." *International Peacekeeping* 4:45–70.

Bremer, Stuart A. 1992. "Dangerous Dyads: Conditions Affecting the Likelihood of Interstate War, 1816–1965." *Journal of Conflict Resolution* 36(2):309–41.

Brinkerhoff, Derick. 2005. "Rebuilding Governance in Failed States and Post-Conflict Societies: Core Concepts and Cross-Cutting Themes." *Public Administration and Development* 25:3–14.

Brinton, Crane. 1938. *Anatomy of a Revolution.* New York: Vintage Press.

Brochmann, Marit, Jan Ketil Rød, and Nils Petter Gleditsch. 2012. "International Borders and Conflict Revisited." *Conflict Management and Peace Science* 29(2):170–94.

Brooks, Deborah Jordan, and Benjamin A Valentino. 2011. "A War of One's Own: Understanding the Gender Gap in Support for War." *Public Opinion Quarterly* 75(2):270–86.

Brounéus, Karen. 2008. "Truth-Telling as Talking Cure? Insecurity and Retraumatization in the Rwandan Gacaca Courts." *Security Dialogue* 39(1):55–76.

Brounéus, Karen. 2010. "The Trauma of Truth Telling: Effects of Witnessing in the Rwanda Gacaca Courts on Psychological Health." *Journal of Conflict Resolution* 54(3):408–37.

Brown, Michael E. 1996. "The Causes and Regional Dimensions of Internal Conflict." In *The International Dimensions of Internal Conflict*, edited by Michael E. Brown. Cambridge, MA: MIT Press.

Brubaker, Rogers. 2004. *Ethnicity without Groups*. Cambridge, MA: Harvard University Press.

Brubaker, Rogers, and Frederik Cooper. 2000. "Beyond 'Identity.'" *Theory and Society* 29(1): 1–47.

Brubaker, Rogers, and David D. Laitin. 1998. "Ethnic and Nationalist Violence." *Annual Review of Sociology,* 423–52.

Brück, Tilman. 2001. "Mozambique: The Economic Effects of the War." In *War and Underdevelopment*, Vol. 2, edited by Francis Stewart and Valpy Fitzgerald, 56–88. Oxford: Oxford University Press.

Brück, Tilman, and Kati Schindler. 2007. "The Impact of Conflict: A Conceptual Framework with Reference to Widow and Refugee Households." Paper presented at the second annual workshop of the Household in Conflict Network, Antwerp, January 19–20.

Brunnschweiler, Christa. 2008. "Cursing the Blessings? Natural Resource Abundance, Institutions, and Economic Growth." *World Development* 36(3):399–419.

Brunnschweiler, Christa N., and Erwin H. Bulte. 2009. "Natural Resources and Violent Conflict: Resource Abundance, Dependence and the Onset of Civil Wars." *Oxford Economic Papers* 61(4):651–74.

Brzezinski, Zbigniew. 1997. "Interview with Zbigniew Brzezinski." Interviewed at George Washington University, Washington, DC. *National Security Archive,* June 13, 1997. http://www.gwu.edu/~nsarchiv/coldwar/interviews/episode-17/brzezinski1.html.

Bueno de Mesquita, Bruce, and George W. Downs. 2006. "Intervention and Democracy." *International Organization* 60(3):627–49.

Bueno de Mesquita, Bruce, and Randolph M. Siverson. 1995. "War and the Survival of Political Leaders: A Comparative Study of Regime Types and Political Accountability." *American Political Science Review* 89(4):841–55.

Bueno de Mesquita, Bruce, Alistair Smith, Randolph M. Siverson, and James D. Morrow. 2003. *The Logic of Political Survival*. Cambridge, MA: MIT Press.

Buhaug, Halvard. 2006. "Relative Capability and Rebel Objective in Civil War." *Journal of Peace Research* 43(6):691–708.

Buhaug, Halvard. 2010. "Climate Not to Blame for African Civil Wars." *Proceedings of the National Academy of Sciences* 107(38):16477–82.

Buhaug, Halvard. 2014. "Concealing Agreements over Climate-Conflict Results." *Proceedings of the National Academy of Sciences of the United States of America* 111(6):E636.

Buhaug, Halvard, and Scott Gates. 2002. "The Geography of Civil War." *Journal of Peace Research* 39(4):417–33.

Buhaug, Halvard, Scott Gates, and Paivi Lujala. 2009. "Geography, Rebel Capability and the Duration of Civil Conflict." *Journal of Conflict Resolution* 53(4):544–69.

Buhaug, Halvard, and Kristian Skrede Gleditsch. 2008. "Contagion or Confusion? Why Conflicts Cluster in Space." *International Studies Quarterly* 52(2):215–33.

Buhaug, Halvard, Kristian Skrede Gleditsch, Helge Holtermann, Gudrun Østby, and Andreas Forø Tollefsen. 2011. "It's the Local Economy, Stupid! Geographic Wealth Dispersion and Conflict Outbreak Location." *Journal of Conflict Resolution* 55(5):814–84.

Buhaug, Halvard, and Jan Ketil Rød. 2006. "Local Determinants of African Civil Wars, 1970–2001." *Political Geography* 25(3):315–35.

Buhaug, Halvard, Jonas Nordkvelle, Thomas Bernauer, Tobias Böhmelt, Michael Brzoska, Joshua W. Busby, Antonio Ciccone, Hanne Fjelde, Erik Gartzke, Nils Petter Gleditsch, Jack A. Goldstone, Håvard Hegre, Helge Holtermann, Vally Koubi, Jasmin S. A. Link, P. Michael Link, Päivi Lujala, John O'Loughlin, Clionadh Raleigh, Jürgen Scheffran, Janpeter Schilling, Todd G. Smith, Ole Magnus Theisen, Richard S. J. Tol, Henrik Urdal, and Nina von Uexkull. 2014. "One Effect to Rule Them All? A Comment on Climate and Conflict." *Climatic Change* 127(3–4):391–97.

Buhaug, Halvard, Gerdis Wischnath, and Nils Petter Gleditsch. 2013. "War(m) Zones: Climate, Geography, and Civil Conflict." Paper presented to the 54th Annual Convention of the International Studies Association, San Francisco, CA, April 3–6.

Bunce, Valerie. 1999. *Subversive Institutions: The Design and the Destruction of Socialism and the State*. Cambridge: Cambridge University Press.

Bundervoet, Tom, and Philip Verwimp. 2005. "Civil War and Economic Sanctions: An Analysis of Anthropometric Outcomes in Burundi." HiCN Working Paper no. 11, Households in Conflict Network.

Bundervoet, Tom, Philip Verwimp, and Richard Akresh. 2009. "Health and Civil War in Rural Burundi." *Journal of Human Resources* 44(2):536–63.

Burgess, Patrick. 2004. "Justice and Reconciliation in East Timor: The Relationship Between the Commission for Reception, Truth and Reconciliation and the Courts." In *Truth Commissions and Courts*, edited by William Schabas and Shane Darcy. New York: Springer.

Burke, Marshall B., Edward Miguel, Shanker Satyanath, John A. Dykema, and David. B. Lobell. 2009. "Warming Increases the Risk of Civil War in Africa." *Proceedings of the National Academy of Sciences* 106(49):20670–74.

Burnham, Gilbert, Riyadh Lafta, Shannon Doocy, and Les Roberts. 2006. "Mortality after the 2003 Invasion of Iraq: A Cross-Sectional Cluster Sample Survey." *Lancet* 368(9545):1421–28.

Busby, Joshua W., Todd G. Smith, and Nisha Krishnan. 2014. "Climate Security Vulnerability in Africa Mapping 3.0." *Political Geography* 43:51–67.

Butler, Christopher, and Scott Gates. 2009. "Asymmetry, Parity, and (Civil) War: Can International Relations Theories Help Us Understand Civil War?" *International Interactions* 35(3):330–40.

Butler, Christopher K., and Scott Gates. 2012. "African Range Wars: Climate, Conflict, and Property Rights." *Journal of Peace Research* 49(1):23–34.

Buzan, Barry. 1991. *People, States & Fear: An Agenda for International Security Studies in the Post–Cold War Era*. Colchester: ECPR Press.

Byman, Daniel. 2001. *Trends in Outside Support for Insurgent Movements*. Santa Monica: Rand Corporation.

Byman, Daniel. 2005. *Deadly Connections: States that Sponsor Terrorism*. Cambridge: Cambridge University Press.

Byman, Daniel. 2008. "Understanding Proto-insurgencies." *Strategic Studies* 31(2):165–200.

Byman, Daniel L., and Kenneth M. Pollack. 2008. *Things Fall Apart: Containing the Spillover from an Iraqi Civil War*. Washington, DC: Brookings Institution Press.

Caballe, Jordi, and Manuel S. Santos. 1993. "On Endogenous Growth with Physical and Human Capital." *Journal of Political Economy* 101(6):1042–67.

Caesar, Julius. 1907. *Caesar's Gallic War*. Glenview, IL: Scott Foresman.

Cairns, Edmund. 1997. *A Safer Future: Reducing the Human Cost of War*. Oxford: Oxfam Publications.

Calhoun, Craig. 1993. "Nationalism and Ethnicity." *Annual Review of Sociology* 19:211–39.

Call, Charles T., ed. 2007. *Constructing Justice and Security after War*. Washington, DC: United States Institute of Peace Press.

Cammett, Melani, and Edmund Malesky. 2012. "Power Sharing in Postconflict Societies: Implications for Peace and Governance." *Journal of Conflict Resolution* 56(6):982–1016.

Campbell, David. 1998. *National Deconstruction: Violence, Identity, and Justice in Bosnia*. Minneapolis: University of Minnesota Press.

Cane, Mark A., Edward Miguel, Marshall Burke, Solomon M. Hsiang, David B. Lobell, Kyle C. Meng, and Shanker Satyanath. 2014. "Temperature and Violence." *Nature Climate Change* 4:234–35.

Caprioli, Mary. 2000. "Gendered Conflict." *Journal of Peace Research* 37(1):51–68.

Caprioli, Mary. 2005. "Primed for Violence: The Role of Gender Inequality in Predicting Internal Conflict." *International Studies Quarterly* 49(2):161–78.

Carballo, Manuel, and Steve Solby. 2001. "HIV/Aids, Conflict and Reconstruction in Sub Saharan Africa." Paper presented at the conference for Preventing and Coping with HIV/Aids in Post-Conflict Societies: Gender Based Lessons From Sub Saharan Africa. Durban, March 26–28.

Carment, David. 1993. "The International Dimensions of Ethnic Conflict: Concepts, Indicators, and Theory." *Journal of Peace Research* 30(2):137–50.

Carment, David, and Patrick James. 1996. "Two-Level Games and Third-Party Intervention: Evidence from Ethnic Conflict in the Balkans and South Asia." *Canadian Journal of Political Science* 29(3):521–54.

Carment, David, and Dane Rowlands. 1998. "Three's Company: Evaluating Third-Party Intervention in Intrastate Conflict." *Journal of Conflict Resolution* 42(5):572–99.

Carpenter, Charli R. 2005. "Women, Children and Other Vulnerable Groups: Gender, Strategic Frames and the Protection of Civilians as a Transnational Issue." *International Studies Quarterly* 49(2):295–334.

Case, Anne, and Christina Paxson. 2006. "Stature and Status: Height, Ability, and Labor Market Outcomes." *Journal of Political Economy* 116(3):499–532.

Cederman, Lars-Erik. 2012. "Nationalism and Ethnicity in International Relations." In *Handbook of International Relations*. Second edition, edited by Walter Carlsnaes, Thomas Risse, and Beth A. Simmons. Los Angeles: Sage.

Cederman, Lars-Erik, Luc Girardin, and Kristian S. Gleditsch. 2009. "Ethnonationalist Triads: Assessing the Influence of Kin Groups on Civil Wars." *World Politics* 61(3):403–37.

Cederman, Lars-Erik, and Kristian Skrede Gleditsch. 2009. "Introduction to Special Issue on 'Disaggregating Civil War.'" *Journal of Conflict Resolution* 53(4):487–95.

Cederman, Lars-Erik, Kristian Skrede Gleditsch, and Halvard Buhaug. 2013. *Inequality, Grievances, and Civil War*. New York: Cambridge University Press.

Cederman, Lars-Erik, Kristian S. Gleditsch, Idean Salehyan, and Julian Wucherpfennig. 2013. "Transborder Ethnic Kin and Civil War." *International Organization* 67(2):389–410.

Cederman, Lars-Erik, Simon Hug, and Lutz F. Krebs. 2010. "Democratization and Civil War: Empirical Evidence." *Journal of Peace Research* 47:377–94.

Cederman, Lars-Erik, Andreas Wimmer, and Brian Min. 2010. "Why Do Ethnic Groups Rebel? New Data and Analysis." *World Politics* 62(1):87–119.

Center for Systemic Peace. 2015. *Political Instability Task Force (PITF), State Failure Problem Set, 1955–2013,* www.systemicpeace.org/inscrdata.html.

Central Intelligence Agency (CIA). 2005. "Sudan." https://www.cia.gov/cia/publications/factbook/geos/su.html.

Cerra, Valerie, and Sweta C. Saxena. 2008. "Growth Dynamics: The Myth of Economic Recovery." *American Economic Review* 98(1):439–57.

Chamarbagwala, Rubiana, and Hilcías E. Morán. 2011. "The Human Capital Consequences of Civil War: Evidence from Guatemala." *Journal of Development Economics* 94(1):41–61.

Chan, Steve. 1987. "Growth with Equity: A Test of Olson's Theory for the Asian Pacific Rim Countries." *Journal of Peace Research* 24(2):135–49.

Chandra, Kachan. 2006. "What Is Ethnic Identity and Does It Matter?" *Annual Review of Political Science* 9:397–424.

Chassang, Sylvain, and Gerard Padro i Miquel. 2009. "Economic Shocks and Civil War," *Quarterly Journal of Political Science* 4:211–28.

Chauvet, Lisa, Paul Collier, and Anke Hoeffler. 2011. "The Cost of State Failure and the Limits to Sovereignty." In *Fragile States: Causes, Costs, and Responses,* edited by Wim A. Naudé, Amelia U. Santos-Paulino, and Mark McGillivray, 91–110. Oxford: Oxford University Press.

Chen, Siyan, Norman V. Loayza, and Marta Reynal-Querol. 2008. "The Aftermath of Civil War." *The World Bank Economic Review* 22(1):63–85.

Chenoweth, Erika, and Maria J. Stephan. 2008. "Why Civil Resistance Works: The Strategic Logic of Nonviolent Conflict." *International Security* 33(1):7–44.

Chenoweth, Erica, and Maria J. Stephan. 2011. *Why Civil Resistance Works: The Strategic Logic of Nonviolent Conflict.* New York: Columbia University Press.

Christia, Fotini. 2012. *Alliance Formation in Civil Wars.* Cambridge: Cambridge University Press.

Ciccone, Antonio. 2011. "Economic Shocks and Civil Conflict: A Comment." *American Economic Journal: Applied Economics* 3(4):215–27.

Cingranelli, David L., and Thomas E. Pasquarello. 1985. "Human Rights Practices and the Distribution of US Foreign Aid to Latin American Countries." *American Journal of Political Science* 29:539–63.

Cingranelli, David L., and David L. Richards. 2010. "The Cingranelli and Richards (CIRI) Human Rights Data Project." *Human Rights Quarterly* 32(2):401–24.

Clague, Cristopher, Philip Keefer, Stephen Knack, and Mancur Olson. 1999. "Contract-Intensive Money: Contract Enforcement, Property Rights, and Economic Performance." *Journal of Economic Growth* 4:185–211.

Clayton, Govinda. 2013. "Relative Rebel Strength and the Onset and Outcome of Civil War Mediation." *Journal of Peace Research* 50(5):609–22.

Clements, Ashley J. 2007. "Trapped! The Disappearing Hopes of Iraqi Refugee Children." Geneva, Switzerland: World Vision.

Cobban, Helena. 2007. *Amnesty after Atrocity? Healing Nations after Genocide and War Crimes.* Boulder, CO: Paradigm Publishers.

Coghlan, Benjamin, Pascal Ngoy, Flavien Mulumba, Colleen Hardy, Valerie N. Bemo, Tony Stewart, Jennifer Lewis, and Richard Brennan. 2008. "Mortality in the Democratic Republic of Congo: An Ongoing Crisis." New York: International Rescue Committee.

Cohen, Dara Kay. 2013a. "Female Combatants and the Perpetration of Violence: Wartime Rape in the Sierra Leone Civil War." *World Politics* 65(03):383–415.

Cohen, Dara Kay. 2013b. "Explaining Rape During Civil War: Cross-National Evidence (1980–2009)." *American Political Science Review* 107(03): 461–77.

Cohen, Dara Kay, Amelia Hoover Green, and Elisabeth Jean Wood. 2013. "Wartime Sexual Violence." United States Institute of Peace. Washington, DC: United States Institute of Peace. Copy at http://www.is.gd/LJg3tr.

Cohen, Dara Kay, and Ragnhild Nordås. 2014. "Sexual Violence in Armed Conflict: Introducing the SVAC Dataset, 1989–2009." *Journal of Peace Research* 51(3):418–28.

Cohen, Stanley. 1995. "State Crimes of Previous Regimes: Knowledge, Accountability, and the Policing of the Past." *Law and Social Inquiry* 20(1):7–50.

Collier, Paul, 1999. "On the Economic Consequences of Civil War." *Oxford Economic Papers* 51(1):168–83.

Collier, Paul. 2007. "Economic Causes of Civil Conflict and their Implications for Policy." In *Leasing the Dogs of War: Conflict Management in a Divided World*, edited by Chester A. Crocker, Fen Osler Hampson, and Pamela All, 197–218. Washington, DC: United States Institute of Peace Press.

Collier, Paul. 2009. "Post-Conflict Recovery: How Should Strategies be Distinctive?" *Journal of African Economies* 18:99–131.

Collier, Paul. 2010. *The Plundered Planet*. Oxford: Oxford University Press.

Collier, Paul, and Marguerite Duponchel. 2013. "The Economic Legacy of Civil War: Firm-Level Evidence from Sierra Leone." *Journal of Conflict Resolution* 57(1):65–88.

Collier, Paul, V. L. Elliott, Håvard Hegre, Anke Hoeffler, Marta Reynal-Querol, and Nicholas Sambanis. 2003. *Breaking the Conflict Trap: Civil War and Development Policy*. Oxford,: Oxford University Press.

Collier, Paul, and Anke Hoeffler. 1998. "On Economic Causes of Civil War." *Oxford Economic Papers* 50(4):563–73.

Collier, Paul, and Anke Hoeffler. 2004. "Greed and Grievance in Civil War." *Oxford Economic Papers* 56(4):563–95.

Collier, Paul, Anke Hoeffler, and Dominic Rohner. 2009. "Beyond Greed and Grievance: Feasibility and Civil War." *Oxford Economic Papers* 61(1):1–27.

Collier, Paul, Anke Hoeffler, and Månd Söderbom. 2004. "On the Duration of Civil War." *Journal of Peace Research* 41(3):253–73.

Collier, Paul, and Nicholas Sambanis, eds. 2005. *Understanding Civil War: Africa*. Vol. 1. World Bank Publications.

Connable, Benjamin, and Martin C. Libicki. 2010. *How Insurgencies End*. Santa Monica: Rand Corporation.

Connolly, Máire A., Michelle Gayer, Michael J. Ryan, Peter Salama, Paul Spiegel, and David L. Heymann. 2004. "Communicable Diseases in Complex Emergencies: Impact and Challenges." *The Lancet* 364(9449):1974–83.

Connor, Walker. 1994. *Ethnonationalism*. Princeton: Princeton University Press.

Cook, Elizabeth Adell, and Clyde Wilcox. 1991. "Feminism and the Gender Gap—A Second Look." *The Journal of Politics* 53(04):1111–22.

Costalli, Stefano. 2014. "Does Peacekeeping Work? A Disaggregated Analysis of Deployment and Violence Reduction in the Bosnian War." *British Journal of Political Science* 44: 357–80.

Cotet, Anca M., and Kevin K. Tsui. 2013. "Oil and Conflict: What Does the Cross Country Evidence Really Show?" *American Economic Journal: Macroeconomics*, 5(1):49–80.

Coupland, Robin M., and Hans O. Samnegaard. 1999. "Effect of Type and Transfer of Conventional Weapons on Civilian Injuries: Retrospective Analysis of Prospective Data from Red Cross Hospitals." *BMJ* 319(7207):410–12.

Crescenzi, Mark J. C., Kelly M. Kadera, Sara McLaughlin Mitchell, and Clayton L. Thyne. 2011. "A Supply Side Theory of Mediation." *International Studies Quarterly* 55(4):1069–94.

Crisp, Jeff, Jane Janz, Jose Riera, and Shahira Samy. 2009. *Surviving in the City, A Review of UNHCR's Operation for Iraqi Refugees in Urban Areas of Jordan, Lebanon and Syria.* United Nations High Commissioner for Refugees, Switzerland.

Crocker, Chester A. 1992. "Conflict Resolution in the Third World: The Role of Superpowers." In *Resolving Third World Conflict: Challenges for a New Era,* edited by Sheryl J. Brown and Kimber M Schraub, 193–210. Washington, DC: United States Institute of Peace Press.

Croicu, Mihai, Stina Högbladh, Thérèse Pettersson, and Lotta Themnér. 2011. *UCDP External Support Project—Disaggregated/Supporter Dataset Codebook,* Version 1.0-2011. Uppsala: Department of Peace and Conflict Research.

Cunningham, David E. 2006. "Veto Players and Civil War Duration." *American Journal of Political Science* 50(4):875–92.

Cunningham, David E. 2010. "Blocking Resolution: How External States Can Prolong Civil Wars." *Journal of Peace Research* 47(2):115–27.

Cunningham, David E. 2011. *Barriers to Peace in Civil War.* Cambridge: Cambridge University Press.

Cunningham, David E., Kristian Skrede Gleditsch, and Idean Salehyan. 2009. "It Takes Two: A Dyadic Analysis of Civil War Duration and Outcome." *Journal of Conflict Resolution* 53(4):570–97.

Cunningham, David E., Kristian Skrede Gleditsch, and Idean Salehyan. 2013. "Non-state Actors in Civil Wars: A New Dataset." *Conflict Management and Peace Science* 30(5):516–31

Cunningham, Kathleen G. 2013. "Actor Fragmentation and Civil War Bargaining: How Internal Divisions Generate Civil Conflict." *American Journal of Political Science* 57(3):659–72.

Cunningham, Kathleen G. 2014. *Inside the Politics of Self-Determination.* Oxford: Oxford University Press.

Cunningham, Kathleen G., Kristin M. Bakke, and Lee J. Seymour. 2012. "Shirts Today, Skins Tomorrow: Dual Contests and the Effects of Fragmentation in Self-Determination Disputes." *Journal of Conflict Resolution* 56(1):67–93.

Cunningham K. G., Marianne Dahl, Anne Fruge and Kenneth Mattis. 2013. "Strategies of Dissent: Organizational Behavior in Self-Determination Disputes." Working paper.

Cunningham, Kathleen G., and Katherine Sawyer. N.d. "Rebel Leader Selection, Legitimacy, and Civil War Termination." Manuscript, University of Maryland.

Cunningham, Kathleen G., and Nils B. Weidmann. 2010. "Shared Space: Ethnic Groups, State Accommodation, and Localized Conflict." *International Studies Quarterly* 54(4):1035–54.

Czaika, Mathias, and Krisztina Kis-Katos. 2009. "Civil Conflict and Displacement: Village-Level Determinants of Forced Migration in Aceh." *Journal of Peace Research* 46(3):399–418.

Dabalen, Andrew L., and Saumik Paul. 2012. "Estimating the Causal Effects of War on Education in Cote D'Ivoire." *Households in Conflict Network.* HiCN Working Paper no. 120.

Dafoe, Allan, and Devin Caughey. 2012. "Honor and War: Southern US Presidents and the Effects of Concern for Reputation." Paper presented at the annual meeting of the International Studies Association.

Dal Bó, Ernesto, and Pedro Dal Bó. 2004. "Workers, Warriors, and Criminals: Social Conflict in General Equilibrium." Working paper, 1–33.

Dal Bó, Ernesto, and Robert Powell. 2009. "A Model of Spoils Politics." *American Journal of Political Science* 53:207–22.

Daly, Erin. 2002. "Between Punitive and Reconstructive Justice: The Gacaca Courts in Rwanda." *New York University Journal of International Law and Politics* 34:355–96.

Dancy, Geoff, Hunjoon Kim, and Eric Wiebelhaus-Brahm. 2010. "The Turn to Truth: Trends in Truth Commission Experimentation." *Journal of Human Rights* 9(1):45–64.

Dancy, Geoff, and Steven C. Poe. 2006. "What Comes before Truth? The Political Determinants of Truth Commission Onset." Paper presented at the Annual International Studies Association conference.

Dasgupta, Partha. 1993. *An Inquiry into Well-Being and Destitution.* Oxford: Clarendon Press.

Davenport, Christian. 1995. "Multi-Dimensional Threat Perception and State Repression: An Inquiry into Why States Apply Negative Sanctions." *American Journal of Political Science* 39(3):683–713.

Davenport, Christian. 2007a. "State Repression and the Tyrannical Peace." *Journal of Peace Research* 44:485–504.

Davenport, Christian. 2007b. "State Repression and Political Order." *Annual Review of Political Science* 10:1–23.

Davenport, Christian, and Patrick P. Ball. 2002. "Views to a Kill: Exploring the Implications in Source Selection in the Case of Guatemalan State Terror, 1977–1995." *Journal of Conflict Resolution* 46(3):427–50.

David, Roman. 2011. *Lustration and Transitional Justice: Personnel Systems in the Czech Republic, Hungary, and Poland.* Philadelphia: University of Pennsylvania Press.

Davies, James C. 1962. "Toward a Theory of Revolution." *American Sociological Review* 27(1):5–19.

Davis, David R., Zaryab Iqbal, and Christopher Zorn. 2003. "Conflict and Public Health: Modeling Spatial Effects." Presented at the "Geography, Conflict and Cooperation" workshop of the Joint Sessions of Workshops, European Consortium for Political Research. March 28–April 2. Edinburgh, Scotland.

Davis, David R., and Will H. Moore. 1997. "Ethnicity Matters: Transnational Ethnic Alliances and Foreign Policy Behavior." *International Studies Quarterly* 41(1):171–84.

Dawi, Akmal. 2014. "Despite Massive Taliban Death Toll No Drop in Insurgency." Voice of America, March. http://www.voanews.com/content/despite–massive–taliban–death–toll–no–drop–in–insurgency/1866009.html.

Daxecker, Ursula E. 2011. "Shocks, Commitment, and the Risk of Civil War." *International Interactions* 37(1):29–54.

Daxecker, Ursula. 2012. "The Costs of Exposing Cheating: International Election Monitoring, Fraud, and Post-Election Violence in Africa." *Journal of Peace Research* 49:503–16.

de Boer, Connie. 1985. "The Polls: The European Peace Movement and Deployment of Nuclear Missiles." *Public Opinion Quarterly* 49(1):119–32.

de Brito, Alexandra Barahona, Carmen González-Enríquez, and Paloma Aguilar, eds. 2001. *The Politics of Memory: Transitional Justice in Democratizing Societies.* New York: Oxford University Press.

Deger, Saadet. 1985. "Human Resources, Government Education Expenditure and the Military Burden in Less Developed Countries." *Journal of Developing Areas* 20(1):37–48.

Deger, Saadet. 1986. "Economic Development and Defense Expenditure." *Economic Development and Cultural Change* 35(1):179–96.

Degomme, Oliver, and Debarati Guha-Sapir. 2010. "Patterns of Mortality Rates in Darfur Conflict." *The Lancet* 375(9711):294–300.

Delacroix, Jacques. 1980. "The Distributive State in the World System." *Studies In Comparative International Development* 15(3):3–21.

Delacruz, Juan. 2007. "A Brief Contribution to the Debate Over the Impact of HIV/AIDS on Economic Growth." MPRA Paper 10841, University Library of Munich, Germany.

DeMeritt, Jacqueline H. R., Angela D. Nichols, and Eliza G. Kelly. 2014. "Female Participation and Civil War Relapse." *Civil Wars* 16(3):346–68.

DeNardo, James. 1985. *Power in Numbers.* Princeton: Princeton University Press.

Deng, Francis M. 1995. "Frontiers of Sovereignty: A Framework of Protection, Assistance, and Development for the Internally Displaced." *Leiden Journal of International Law* 8(2):249–86.

Deng, Francis M., Sadikiel Kimaro, Terrence Lyons, Donald Rothchild, and I. William Zartman. 1996. *Sovereignty as Responsibility: Conflict Management in Africa.* Washington, DC: Brookings Institution Press.

Denny, Elaine K., and Barbara F. Walter. 2014. "Ethnicity and Civil War." *Journal of Peace Research* 51(2):199–212.

Depoortere, Evelyn, Francesco Checchi, France Broillet, Sibylle Gerstl, Andrea Minetti, Olivia Gayraud, Virginie Briet, Jennifer Pahl, Isabelle Defourny, Mercedes Tatay, and Vincent Brown. 2004. "Violence and Mortality in West Darfur, Sudan (2003–04): Epidemiological Evidence from Four Surveys." *The Lancet* 364(9442):1315–20.

DeRouen, Karl Jr., and Jacob Bercovitch. 2008. "Enduring Internal Rivalries: A New Framework for the Study of Civil War." *Journal of Peace Research* 45(1):43–62.

DeRouen, Karl, and Jacob Bercovitch. 2012. "Trends in Civil War Mediation" in *Peace and Conflict 2012*, edited by Joseph J. Hewitt, Jonathan Wilkenfeld, and Ted Robert Gurr. Boulder, CO: Paradigm Press, 59–70.

DeRouen, Karl, Jacob Bercovitch, and Paulina Pospieszna. 2011. "Introducing the Civil Wars Mediation (CWM) Dataset." *Journal of Peace Research* 48(5):663–72.

DeRouen, Karl, Mark Ferguson, Jenna Lea, Ashley Streat-Bartlett, Young Park, and Sam Norton. 2010. "Civil War Peace Agreement Implementation and State Capacity." *Journal of Peace Research* 47:333–46.

DeRouen, Karl, and Shaun Goldfinch. 2012. "What Makes a State Stable and Peaceful? Good Governance, Legitimacy and Legal-Rationality Matter Even More for Low-Income Countries." *Civil Wars* 14:499–520.

DeRouen, Karl Jr., Jenna Lea, and Peter Wallensteen. 2009. "The Duration of Civil War Peace Agreements." *Conflict Management and Peace Science* 26(4):367–87.

DeRouen, Karl, and David Sobek. 2004. "The Dynamics of Civil War Duration and Outcome." *Journal of Peace Research* 41:303–20.

De Soysa, Indra. 2002. "Paradise Is a Bazaar? Greed, Creed, and Governance in Civil War, 1989–99." *Journal of Peace Research* 39(4):395–416.

Detges, Adrien. 2014. "Close-up on Renewable Resources and Armed Conflict: The Spatial Logic of Pastoralist Violence in Nothern Kenya." *Political Geography* 42(1):57–65.

Detzer, David. 2001. *Allegiance: Fort Sumter, Charleston, and the Beginning of the Civil War.* New York: Harcourt.

Deutsch, Karl. 1964. "External Involvement in Internal War." In *Internal War*, edited by Harry Eckstein, 100–10. New York: The Free Press.

Devre, Gülsen. 2011. "State Corruption in Post-War Lebanon: The Relation Between Post-War Inclusive Institutions and State Corruption." *Bilge Strateji* 3, 5:221–43. Accessed at http://www.academia.edu/2606743/state_corruption_in_post-war_lebanon_the_rela tion_between_post-war_inclusive_institutions_and_state_corruption.

de Waal, Alex. 2014. "When Kleptocracy Becomes Insolvent: Brute Causes of the Civil War in South Sudan." *African Affairs* 113(452):347–69.

de Walque, Damien. 2004. "The Long-Term Legacy of the Khmer Rouge Period in Cambodia." Policy Research Working Paper Series 3446, The World Bank.

Diehl, Paul F. 1994. *International Peacekeeping,* Revised edition. Baltimore: Johns Hopkins University Press.

Diehl, Paul F. 2014. "Behavioural Studies of Peacekeeping Outcomes." *International Peacekeeping* 21:484–91.

Diehl, Paul F., and Alexandru Balas. 2014. *Peace Operations,* 2nd ed. Cambridge: Polity Press.

Diehl, Paul F., and Daniel Druckman. 2010. *Evaluating Peace Operations.* Boulder, CO: Lynne Rienner.

Diehl, Paul, and Gary Goertz. 1985. "Trends in Military Allocations Since 1816: What Goes Up Does Not Always Come Down." *Armed Forces and Society* 12(1):134–44.

Diehl, Paul F., and Patrick Regan. 2015. "The Interdependence of Conflict Management Attempts." *Conflict Management and Peace Science* 32(1):99–107.

Dikötter, Frank. 2010. *Mao's Great Famine. The History of China's Most Devastating Catastrophe, 1958–62.* London: Bloomsbury.

Dixon, William, and Bruce Moon. 1986. "The Military Burden and Basic Human Needs." *Journal of Conflict Resolution* 30(4):660–84.

D'Orazio, Vito, Steven T. Landis, Glenn Palmer, and Philip Schrodt. 2014. "Separating the Wheat from the Chaff: Applications of Automated Document Classifications Using Support Vector Machines." *Political Analysis* 22(2):224–42.

Downes, Alexander B. 2006. "Desperate Times, Desperate Measures: The Causes of Civilian Victimization in War." *International Security* 30(4):152–95.

Downes, Alexander B. 2007. "Draining the Sea by Filling the Graves: Investigating the Effectiveness of Indiscriminate Violence as a Counterinsurgency Strategy." *Civil Wars* 9(4):420–44.

Dowty, Alan, and Gil Loescher. 1996. "Refugee Flows as Grounds for International Action." *International Security* 21(1):43–71.

Doyle, Michael W., and Nicholas Sambanis. 2000. "International Peacebuilding: A Theoretical and Quantitative Analysis." *American Political Science Review* 94(4):779–801.

Doyle, Michael W., and Nicholas Sambanis. 2006. *Making War and Building Peace: United Nations Peace Operations.* Princeton: Princeton University Press.

Drakos, Konstaninos, and Andreas Gofas. 2006. "The Devil You Know but Are Afraid to Face: Underreporting Bias and Its Distorting Effects on the Study of Terrorism." *Journal of Conflict Resolution* 50(5):714–35.

Draulans, Dirk, and Ellen Van Krunkelsven. 2002. "The Impact of War on Forest Areas in the Democratic Republic of Congo." *Oryx* 36(1):35–40.

Driscoll, Jesse. 2012. "Commitment Problems or Bidding Wars? Rebel Fragmentation as Peace Building." *Journal of Conflict Resolution* 56(1):118–49.

Drumbl, Mark A. 2007. *Atrocity, Punishment, and International Law.* Cambridge: Cambridge University Press.

Dudley, Joseph P., Joshua R. Ginsberg, Andrew J. Plumptre, John A. Hart, and Liliana C. Campos. 2002. "Effects of War and Civil Strife on Wildlife and Wildlife Habitats." *Conservation Biology* 16(2):319–29.

Dugan, Laura. 2004. "How Does Studying Terrorism Compare to Studying Crime?" *Sociology of Crime Law and Deviance* 5:53–74.

Dugan, Laura, and Erika Chenoweth. 2012. "Moving beyond Deterrence: The Effectiveness of Raising the Expected Utility of Abstaining from Terrorism in Israel." *American Sociological Review* 77(4):597–624.

Dukuly, Abdullah. 2004. "Education-Liberia: Civil War Leaves School System in Tatters." *Inter Press Service*, June 16.

Dunning, Thad. 2008a. *Crude Democracy*. New York: Cambridge University Press.

Dunning, Thad. 2008b. "Model Specification in Instrumental-Variables Regression." *Political Analysis* 16(3):290–302.

Duryea, Suzanne, David Lam, and Deborah Levinson. 2007. "Effects of Economic Shocks on Children's Employment and Schooling in Brazil." *Journal of Development Economics* 84:118–214.

Dybdahl, Ragnhild. 2001. "Children and Mothers in War: An Outcome Study of a Psychosocial Intervention Program." *Child Development* 72(4):1214–30.

Easterly, William, and Ross Levine. 1997. "Africa's Growth Tragedy: Policies and Ethnic Divisions." *The Quarterly Journal of Economics*: 1203–50.

Eck, Kristine. 2012. "In Data We Trust? A Comparison of UCDP GED and ACLED Conflict Events Datasets." *Cooperation and Conflict* 47(1):124–41.

Eck, Kristine. 2014. "The Law of the Land: Communal Conflict and Legal Authority." *Journal of Peace Research* 51(4):441–54.

Eck, Kristine, and Lisa Hultman. 2007. "One-Sided Violence against Civilians in War: Insights from New Fatality Data." *Journal of Peace Research* 44(2):233–46.

Ehrlich, Paul R. 1968. *The Population Bomb*. New York: Sierra Club/Ballantine Books.

Elbadawi, Ibrahim, and Nicholas Sambanis. 2000. "External Interventions and the Duration of Civil Wars." World Bank Policy Research Working Paper no. 2433, Washington, DC.

Elbedour, Salman, Robert ten Bensel, and David T. Bastien. 1993. "Ecological Integrated Model of Children of War: Individual and Social Psychology." *Child Abuse & Neglect* 17:805–19.

Elbert, Thomas, Maggie Schauer, Elisabeth Schauer, Bianca Huschka, Michael Hirth, and Frank Neuner. 2009. "Trauma-Related Impairment in Children: A Survey in Sri Lankan Provinces Affected By Armed Conflict." *Child Abuse & Neglect* 33(4):238–46.

Elkink, Johan A. 2011. "The International Diffusion of Democracy." *Comparative Political Studies* 44(12):1651–74.

Elkins, Zachary, and Beth Simmons. 2005. "On Waves, Clusters, and Diffusion: A Conceptual Framework." *The Annals of the American Academy of Political and Social Science* 598(1):33–51.

Ellingsen, Tanja. 2000. "Colorful Community or Ethnic Witches' Brew? Multiethnicity and Domestic Conflict During and After the Cold War." *Journal of Conflict Resolution* 44(2):228–49.

Ellingsen, Tanja, and Nils P. Gleditsch. 1997. "Democracy and Armed Conflict in the Third World." In *Causes of Conflict in Third World Countries,* edited by Ketil Volden et al., 69–81. Oslo: North-South Coalition and International Peace Research Institute.

Elster, Jon. 1998. "Coming to Terms with the Past: A Framework for the Study of Justice in the Transition to Democracy." *European Journal of Sociology* 39(1):7–48.

Elster, Jon. 2004. *Closing the Books: Transitional Justice in Historical Perspective*. New York; Cambridge: Cambridge University Press.

Enders, Walter, Todd Sandler, and Khusrav Gaibulloev. 2011. "Domestic versus Transnational Terrorism: Data, Decomposition, and Dynamics." *Journal of Peace Research* 48:319–37.

Enloe, Cynthia H. 1983. *Does Khaki Become You? The Militarisation of Women's Lives*. Boston: South End Press.

Enloe, Cynthia H. 1993. *The Morning After: Sexual Politics at the End of the Cold War*. Berkeley: University of California Press.

Enloe, Cynthia H. 2000. *Maneuvers: The International Politics of Militarizing Women's Lives*. Berkeley: University of California Press.

Enterline, Andrew J., Emily Stull, and Joseph Magagnoli. 2013. "Reversal of Fortune? Strategy Change and Counterinsurgency Success by Foreign Powers in the Twentieth Century." *International Studies Perspectives* 14(2):176–98.

Erk, Jan, and Lawrence M. Anderson, eds. 2013. *Paradox of Federalism: Does Self-Rule Accommodate or Exacerbate Ethnic Divisions?* London: Routledge.

Esteban, Joan, and Debraj Ray. 2001. "Social Decision Rules are Not Immune to Conflict." *Economics of Governance* 2:59–67.

Esty, Daniel C., Jack A. Goldstone, Ted Robert Gurr, Barbara Harff, Marc Levy, Geoffrey D. Dabelko, Pamela T. Surko, and Alan N. Unger. 1998. *State Failure Task Force: Phase II Findings*. McLean, VA: Science Applications International, for State Failure Task Force.

Favretto, Katja. 2009. "Should Peacemakers Take Sides? Major Power Mediation, Coercion, and Bias." *American Political Science Review* 103(2):248–63.

Fazal, Tanisha M. 2014. "Dead Wrong: Battle Deaths, Military Medicine, and Exaggerated Reports of War's Demise." *International Security* 39(1):95–125.

Fearon, James D. 1995. "Rationalist Explanations for War." *International Organizations* 49:379–414.

Fearon, James D. 1997. "Signaling Foreign Policy Interests: Tying Hands versus Sinking Costs." *Journal of Conflict Resolution* 41(1):68–90.

Fearon, James D. 1998. "Commitment Problems and the Spread of Ethnic Conflict." In *The International Spread of Ethnic Conflict*, edited by David A. Lake and Donald Rothchild. Princeton: Princeton University Press.

Fearon, James D. 2003. "Ethnic and Cultural Diversity by Country." *Journal of Economic Growth* 8(2):195–222.

Fearon, James D. 2004. "Why Do Some Civil Wars Last so Much Longer than Others?" *Journal of Peace Research* 41(3):275–301.

Fearon, James D. 2008. "Ethnic Mobilization and Ethnic Violence." In *The Oxford Handbook of Political Economy*, edited by Barry R. Weingast and Donald A. Wittman. Oxford Handbooks Online.

Fearon, James. 2010. "Do Governance Indicators Predict Anything? The Case of 'Fragile States' and Civil War," unpublished manuscript, Stanford University. Available at http://www.operationspaix.net/DATA/DOCUMENT/6663~v~Do_Governance_Indicators_Predict_Anything__The_Case_of.pdf.

Fearon, James D. 2011. "Self-Enforcing Democracy." *The Quarterly Journal of Economics* 126:1661–708.

Fearon, James D., Macartan Humphreys and Jeremy M. Weinstein. 2009. "Can Development Aid Contribute to Social Cohesion after Civil War? Evidence from a Field Experiment in Post-Conflict Liberia." *American Economic Review: Papers and Proceedings* 99:287–91.

Fearon, James D., and David D. Laitin. 1996. "Explaining Interethnic Cooperation." *American Political Science Review* 90:715–35.

Fearon, James D., and David D. Laitin. 2000. "Violence and the Social Construction of Ethnic Identity." *International Organization* 54(4):845–77.

Fearon, James D., and David D. Laitin. 2003. "Ethnicity, Insurgency, and Civil War." *American Political Science Review* 97(1):75–90.

Fearon, James D., and David D. Laitin. 2011. "Sons of the Soil, Migrants, and Civil War." *World Development* 39(2):199–211.

Fein, Helen. 1990. *Genocide: A Sociological Perspective*. Newbury, CA: Sage.

Fein, Helen. 1995. "Murder in the Middle: Life-Integrity Violations and Democracy in the World, 1987." *Human Rights Quarterly* 17:170–91.

Feng, Yi. 1997. "Democracy, Political Stability, and Economic Growth." *British Journal of Political Science* 27:391–418.

Fenwick, Charles G. 1941. "Intervention by Way of Propaganda." *American Journal of International Law* 35:626–31.

Filson, Darren, and Suzanne Werner. 2002. "A Bargaining Model of War and Peace: Anticipating the Onset, Duration, and Outcome of War." *American Journal of Political Science* 46(4):819–37.

Findley, Michael G., and Josiah F. Marineau. 2015. "Lootable Resources and Third-Party Intervention into Civil Wars." *Conflict Management and Peace Science* 32(5):465–486.

Findley, Michael G., and Tze Kwang Teo. 2006. "Rethinking Third-Party Interventions into Civil Wars: An Actor-Centric Approach." *Journal of Politics* 68(4):828–37.

Findley, Michael G., and Joseph K. Young. 2012. "Terrorism and Civil War: A Spatial and Temporal Approach to a Conceptual Problem." *Perspectives on Politics* 10(2):285–305.

Finnemore, Martha. 2004. *The Purpose of Intervention: Changing Beliefs about the Use of Force*. Ithaca, NY: Cornell University Press.

Fite, David, Marc Genest, and Clyde Wilcox. 1990. "Gender Differences in Foreign Policy Attitudes: A Longitudinal Analysis." *American Politics Research* 18(4):492–513.

Fjelde, Hanne. 2010. "Generals, Dictators, and Kings: Authoritarian Regimes and Civil Conflict, 1973–2004." *Conflict Management and Peace Science* 27(3):195–218.

Fjelde, Hanne. 2012. "Transnational Dimensions of African Civil Wars and the Triple-R Framework." In *From Intra-State War to Durable Peace: Conflict and Its Resolution in Africa after the Cold War*, edited by Thomas Ohlson, 59–78. Dordrecht: Republic of Letters.

Fjelde, Hanne, and Indra de Soysa. 2009. "Coercion, Co-optation, or Cooperation?" *Conflict Management and Peace Science* 26:5–25.

Fjelde, Hanne, and Lisa Hultman. 2014. "Weakening the Enemy: A Disaggregated Study of Violence against Civilians in Africa." *Journal of Conflict Resolution* 58:1230–57.

Fjelde, Hanne, and Nina von Uexkul. 2012. "Climate Triggers: Rainfall Anomalies, Vulnerability, and Communal Conflict in Sub-Saharan Africa." *Political Geography* 31:444–53.

Flores, Thomas Edward, and Irfan Nooruddin. 2009. "Democracy under the Gun: Understanding Postconflict Economic Recovery." *Journal of Conflict Resolution* 53(1):3–29.

Flores, Thomas Edward, and Irfan Nooruddin. 2012. "The Effect of Elections on Postconflict Peace and Reconstruction." *The Journal of Politics* 74:558–70.

Forsberg, Erika. 2008. "Polarization and Ethnic Conflict in a Widened Strategic Setting." *Journal of Peace Research* 45(2):283–300.

Forsberg, Erika. 2009. "Neighbors at Risk: A Quantitative Study of Civil War Contagion." PhD Dissertation: Department of Peace and Conflict Research, Uppsala University.

Forsberg, Erika. 2013. "Do Ethnic Dominoes Fall? Evaluating Domino Effects of Granting Territorial Concessions to Separatist Groups." *International Studies Quarterly* 57(2):329–40.

Forsberg, Erika. 2014a. "Diffusion in the Study of Civil Wars: A Cautionary Tale." *International Studies Review* 16(2):188–98.

Forsberg, Erika. 2014b. "Transnational Transmitters: Ethnic Kinship Ties and Conflict Contagion 1946–2009." *International Interactions* 40(2):143–65.

Fortna, Virginia Page. 2004. "Does Peacekeeping Keep Peace? International Intervention and the Duration of Peace after Civil War." *International Studies Quarterly* 48:269–92.

Fortna, Virginia Page. 2008a. *Does Peacekeeping Work? Shaping Belligerents' Choices after Civil War.* Princeton: Princeton University Press.

Fortna, Virginia Page. 2008b. "Peacekeeping and Democratization." In *From War to Democracy: Dilemmas of Peacebuilding*, edited by Anna K. Jarstad and Timothy D. Sisk, 39–79. Cambridge: Cambridge University Press.

Fortna, Virginia Page. 2009. "Where Have All the Victories Gone? Peacekeeping and War Outcomes." Working paper, Columbia University, available at http://www.columbia/edu/~vpf4/victories%20Sept%202009.pdf.

Fortna, Virginia Page. 2015. "Do Terrorists Win? The Use of Terrorism and Civil War Outcomes 1989–2009." *International Organization* 69(3):519–56.

Fortna, Virginia Page, and Lisa Morjé Howard. 2008. "Pitfalls and Prospects in the Peacekeeping Literature." *Annual Review of Political Science* 11:283–301.

Fortna, Virginia Page, and Reyko Huang. 2012. "Democratization after Civil War: A Brush-Clearing Exercise." *International Studies Quarterly* 56:801–08.

Fox, Sean, and Kristian Hoelscher. 2012. "Political Order, Development, and Social Violence." *Journal of Peace Research* 49:431–44.

Frankel, Jeffrey. 2010. "The Natural Resource Curse: A Survey." National Bureau of Economic Research Working Paper 15836.

Frankovic, Kathleen A. 1982. "Sex and Politics—New Alignments, Old Issues." *PS: Political Science & Politics* 15(03):439–48.

Freese, Lee. 1980. "The Problem of Cumulative Knowledge." In *Theoretical Methods in Sociology: Seven Essays*, edited by Lee Freese. Pittsburgh: University of Pittsburgh Press.

Freud, Anna, and Dorothy T. Burlingham. 1943. *War and Children.* Ann Arbor, MI: University of Michigan Press.

Fukuyama, Francis. 2001. "Social Capital, Civil Society and Development." *Third World Quarterly* 22(1):7–20.

Gaddis, John Lewis. 1992. "International Relations Theory and the End of the Cold War." *International Security* 17:5–58.

Gagnon, V. P. 2006. *The Myth of Ethnic War: Serbia and Croatia in the 1990s.* Ithaca, NY: Cornell University Press.

Galton, Francis. 1889. "Comment on E.B. Tylor 'On a Method of Investigating the Development of Institutions: Applied to Laws of Marriage and Descent.'" *Journal of the Royal Anthropological Institute* 18:268–69.

Galvin, Hannah. 2003. "The Impact of Defence Spending on the Economic Growth of Developing Countries: A Cross-Section Study." *Defence and Peace Economics* 14(1):51–9.

Ganegodage, K. Renuka, and Alicia. N. Rambaldi. 2011. "The Impact of Education Investment on Sri Lankan Economic Growth." *Economics of Education Review* 30(6):1491–502.

Garfinkel, Michelle R., and Stergios Skaperdas. 2000. "Conflict without Misperceptions or Incomplete Information: How the Future Matters." *Journal of Conflict Resolution* 44:793–807.

Garfinkel, Michelle R., and Stergios Skaperdas. 2007. "Economics of Conflict: An Overview." In *Handbook of Defense Economics, Volume 2, Defense in a Globalized World*, edited by Todd Sandler et al., 649–709. Amsterdam and Oxford: Elsevir, North-Holland.

Garriga, Anna C., and Brian J. Phillips. 2014. "Foreign Aid as a Signal to Investors: Predicting FDI in Post-Conflict Countries." *Journal of Conflict Resolution* 58(2):280–306.

Gartner, Scott Sigmund, and Jacob Bercovitch. 2006. "Overcoming Obstacles to Peace: The Contribution of Mediation to Short-Lived Conflict Settlements." *International Studies Quarterly* 50:819–40.

Gartner, Scott Sigmund, and Molly M. Melin. 2009. "Assessing Outcomes: Conflict Management and the Durability of Peace." In *Sage Handbook on Conflict Resolution*, edited by Jacob Bercovitch, Victor Kremenyuk, and I. William Zartman, 564–79. Thousand Oaks, CA: Sage.

Gartzke, Erik. N.d. "Blame It on the Weather: Seasonality in Interstate Conflict." Typescript, University of California, San Diego.

Gartzke, Erik. 2007. "The Capitalist Peace." *American Journal of Political Science* 51(1):166–91.

Gates, Scott. 2002. "Recruitment and Allegiance The Microfoundations of Rebellion." *Journal of Conflict Resolution* 46(1):111–30.

Gates, Scott, Håvard Hegre, Håvard Mokleiv Nygård, Håvard Strand. 2012. "Development Consequences of Armed Conflict." *World Development* 40(9):1713–22.

Gauthier, Bernard, and Waly Wane. 2007. "Leakage of Public Resources in the Health Sector: An Empirical Investigation of Chad." Policy Research Working Paper WPS 4351. Washington, DC: The World Bank.

Geddes, Barbara. 1999a. "What Do We Know about Democratization after Twenty Years?" *Annual Review of Political Science* 2:115–44.

Geddes, Barbara. 1999b. "Authoritarian Breakdown: Empirical Test of a Game Theoretic Model." Los Angeles, CA: University of California at Los Angeles.

Geneva Declaration. 2008. "Global Burden of Armed Violence." Geneva, Switzerland, Geneva Declaration on Armed Violence and Development, Geneva Declaration Secretariat.

Gent, Stephen E. 2008. "Going in When It Counts: Military Intervention and the Outcome of Civil Conflicts." *International Studies Quarterly* 52(4):713–35.

Gent, Stephen E., and Megan Shannon. 2010. "The Effectiveness of Arbitration and Adjudication: Getting Into a Bind." *Journal of Politics* 72(2):366–80.

George, Alexander L., and Andrew Bennett. 2004. *Case Studies and Theory Development in the Social Sciences*. Cambridge, MA: MIT Press.

Gerring, John. 2007. *Case Study Research: Principles and Practices*. New York: Cambridge University Press.

Ghobarah, Hazem Adam, Paul Huth, and Bruce Russett. 2003. "Civil Wars Kill and Maim People—Long After the Shooting Stops." *American Political Science Review* 97(2):189–202.

Giap, Vo Nguyen. 1962. *People's War, People's Army*. Washington, DC: Department of Defense.

Gibson, James L. 2004a. "Overcoming Apartheid: Can Truth Reconcile a Divided Nation?" *Politikon* 31(2):129–55.

Gibson, James L. 2004b. "Does Truth Lead to Reconciliation? Testing the Causal Assumptions of the South African Truth and Reconciliation Process." *American Journal of Political Science* 48(2):201–17.

Gibson, James L. 2006. "The Contributions of Truth to Reconciliation Lessons From South Africa." *Journal of Conflict Resolution* 50(3):409–32.

Gibson, James William. 1994. *Warrior Dreams: Violence and Manhood in Post-Vietnam America.* New York: Hill and Wang.

Gill, Lesley. 1997. "Creating Citizens, Making Men: The Military and Masculinity in Bolivia." *Cultural Anthropology* 12(4):527–50.

Gilligan, Michael, and Ernest Sergenti. 2008. "Do UN Interventions Cause Peace? Using Matching to Improve Causal Inference." *Quarterly Journal of Political Science* 3:89–122.

Gilligan, Michael, and Stephen J. Stedman. 2003. "Where Do the Peacekeepers Go?" *International Studies Review* 5(4):37–52.

Ginkel, John, and Alastair Smith. 1999. "So You Say You Want a Revolution: A Game Theoretic Explanation of Revolution in Repressive Regimes." *Journal of Conflict Resolution* 43:291–316.

Gizelis, Theodora-Ismene, 2009. "Gender Empowerment and United Nations Peacebuilding." *Journal of Peace Research* 46(4):505–23.

Gizelis, Theodora-Ismene, and Amanda E. Wooden. 2010. "Water Resources, Institutions, and Intrastate Conflict." *Political Geography* 29(8):444–53.

Gleditsch, Kristian Skrede. 2002. *All International Politics Is Local: The Diffusion of Conflict, Integration, and Democratization.* Ann Arbor, MI: University of Michigan Press.

Gleditsch, Kristian Skrede. 2007. "Transnational Dimensions of Civil War." *Journal of Peace Research* 44(3):293–309.

Gleditsch, Kristian Skrede, and Andrea Ruggeri. 2010. "Political Opportunity Structures, Democracy, and Civil War." *Journal of Peace Research* 47:299–310.

Gleditsch, Kristian Skrede, and Idean Salehyan. 2006. "Refugees and the International Spread of Civil War." *International Organization* 60(2):335–66.

Gleditsch, Kristian Skrede, Idean Salehyan, and Kenneth Schultz. 2008a. "Fighting at Home, Fighting Abroad: How Civil Wars Lead to International Disputes." *Journal of Conflict Resolution* 52(4):479–506.

Gleditsch, Kristian Skrede, and Michael D. Ward, MD 1999. "Interstate System Membership: A Revised List of Independent States Since 1816." *International Interactions* 25(4):393–413.

Gleditsch, Kristian Skrede, and Michael D. Ward. 2000. "War and Peace in Space and Time: The Role of Democratization." *International Studies Quarterly* 44:1–29.

Gleditsch, Kristian Skrede, Julian Wucherpfennig, Simon Hug, and Karina Garnes Reigstad. 2011. "Polygyny or Misogyny? Reexamining the 'First Law of Intergroup Conflict.'" *The Journal of Politics* 73(01):265–70.

Gleditsch, Kristian Skrede, and Nils B. Weidmann. 2012. "Richardson in the Information Age: GIS and Spatial Data in International Studies." *Annual Review of Political Science* 15:461–81.

Gleditsch, Nils Petter. 1998. "Armed Conflict and the Environment: A Critique of the Literature." *Journal of Peace Research* 35(3):381–400.

Gleditsch, Nils Petter. 2012. "Whither or Weather? Climate Change and Conflict." *Journal of Peace Research* 49(1):3–9.

Gleditsch, Nils Petter, Håvard Hegre, and Håvard Strand. 2009. "Democracy and Civil War." In *Handbook of War Studies III*, edited by Manus Midlarsky, 155–92. Ann Arbor, MI: University of Michigan Press.

Gleditsch, Nils Petter, Steven Pinker, Bradley A. Thayer, Jack S. Levy, and William R. Thompson. 2013. "The Forum: The Decline of War." *International Studies Review* 15(3):396–419.

Gleditsch, Nils Petter, Peter Wallensteen, Mikael Eriksson, Margareta Sollenberg, and Håvard Strand. 2002. "Armed Conflict 1946–2001: A New Dataset." *Journal of Peace Research* 39(5):615–37.

Gloppen, Siri. 2005. "Roads to Reconciliation: A Conceptual Framework." In *Roads to Reconciliation*, edited by Elin Skar, Siri Gloppen, and Astrid Suhrke. Lanham, MD: Lexington Books.

Goddard, Stacie E. 2006. "Uncommon Ground: Indivisible Territory and the Politics of Legitimacy." *International Organization* 60(1):35–68.

Goertz, Gary. 2006. *Social Science Concepts: A User's Guide*. Princeton: Princeton University Press.

Gohdes, Anita, and Megan Price. 2013. "First Things First: Assessing Data Quality before Model Quality." *Journal of Conflict Resolution* 57(6):1090–108.

Goldfinch, Shaun, and Karl DeRouen. 2014. "In It for the Long Haul? Lessons from Post-Conflict Statebuilding, Peacebuilding and Good Governance in Timor-Leste." *Public Administration and Development* 36:96–108.

Goldfinch, Shaun, Karl DeRouen and Paulina Pospieszna. 2013. "Flying Blind: Evidence for Public Sector Reform in Low Income Countries, Good Governance Agendas, Good Governance Implementation, and Development Outcomes as Measured by Changes in Millennium Development Goals." *Public Administration and Development* 33:50–61.

Goldsmith, Jack, and Stephen D. Krasner. 2003. "The Limits of Idealism," *Daedalus* (2003):47–63.

Goldstein, Joshua. 1992. "A Conflict-Cooperation Scale for WEIS International Events Data." *Journal of Conflict Resolution* 36:369–85.

Goldstein, Joshua S. 2001. *War and Gender: How Gender Shapes the War System and Vice Versa*. Cambridge: Cambridge University Press.

Goldstein, Joshua S. 2011. *Winning the War on War: The Decline of Armed Conflict Worldwide*. New York: Dutton.

Goldstone, Jack A., Robert H. Bates, David L. Epstein, Ted R. Gurr, Michael Lustik, Monty G. Marshall, Jay Ulfelder and Mark Woodward. 2010. "A Global Model for Forecasting Political Instability." *American Journal of Political Science* 54:190–208.

Goldstone, Richard J. 1995. "Exposing Human Rights Abuses—A Help or Hindrance to Reconciliation?" *Hastings Constitutional Law Quarterly* 22:607–21.

Goldstone, Richard J. 1996. "Justice as a Tool for Peacemaking: Truth Commissions and International Criminal Tribunals." *New York University Journal of International Law and Politics* 28(3):485–503.

Goodwin, Jeff, and Theda Skocpol. 1989. "Explaining Revolutions in the Contemporary World." *Politics and Society* 17:489–509.

Gourevitch, P. A. 1979. "The Reemergence of 'Peripheral Nationalisms': Some Comparative Speculations on the Spatial Distribution of Political Leadership and Economic Growth." *Comparative Studies in Society and History* 21(03):303–22.

Graca, Job, Jafarey Saqib, and Apostolis Philippopoulos. 1995. "Interaction of Human and Physical Capital in a Model of Endogenous Growth." *Economics of Planning* 28:93–118.

Greenberg, Joel, 1994. "Building Peace in Palestinian Schools." *New York Times*, January 9.

Greig, J. Michael, and Paul F. Diehl. 2012. *International Mediation*. Malden, MA: Polity Press.

Greig, J. Michael, and Patrick M. Regan. 2008. "When Do They Say Yes? An Analysis of the Willingness to Offer and Accept Mediation in Civil Wars." *International Studies Quarterly* 52(4):759–81.

Grono, Nick, and Adam O'Brien. 2008. "Justice in Conflict? The ICC and Peace Processes." In *Courting Conflict? Justice, Peace and the ICC in Africa*, edited by Nicholas Waddell and Phil Clark. London: Royal African Society.

Grossman, Herschel I. 1999. "Kleptocracy and Revolutions." *Oxford Economic Papers* 51(2):267–83.

Guerrero-Serdan, Gabriela. 2009. "The Effects of the War in Iraq on Nutrition and Health: An Analysis Using Anthropometric Outcomes of Children." World Bank Report.

Guevara, Ernesto. 1961. *Che Guevara on Guerrilla Warfare*. New York: Praeger.

Guevara, Ernesto. 1968. *Guerrilla Warfare*. New York: Monthly Review Press.

Guha-Sapir, Debbie. 2005. "Viewpoint: Counting Darfur's Dead Isn't Easy." London, Reuters.

Guha-Sapir, Debbie, and Willem Van Panhuis. 2002. *Mortality Risks in Recent Civil Conflicts: A Comparative Analysis*. Brussels: Centre for Research on the Epidemiology of Disasters.

Gunaratna, Rohan. 2003. "Sri Lanka: Feeding the Tamil Tigers." In *The Political Economy of Armed Conflict: Beyond Greed and Grievance*, edited by Karen Ballentine and Jake Sherman. Boulder, London: Lynne Rienner.

Gurr, Ted Robert. 1970. *Why Men Rebel*. Boulder, CO: Paradigm Publishers.

Gurr, Ted R. 1993. *Minorities at Risk: A Global View of Ethnopolitical Conflicts*. Washington, DC: US Institute of Peace Press.

Gurr, Ted R. 1996. *Minorities at Risk III Dataset: User's Manual*. CIDCM, University of Maryland. http://www. cidcm.umd.edu/inscr/mar/home.htm.

Gurr, Ted R., ed. 2000. *Peoples versus States: Minorities at Risk in the New Century*. Washington, DC: United States Institute of Peace Press.

Gurr, Ted R., and Will H. Moore. 1997. "Ethnopolitical Rebellion: A Cross-Sectional Analysis of the 1980s with Risk Assessments for the 1990s." *American Journal of Political Science* 41(4):1079–103.

Gurses, Mehmet, and T. David Mason. 2008. "Democracy Out of Anarchy: The Prospects for Post-Civil-War Democracy." *Social Science Quarterly* 89:315–36.

Gurses, Mehmet, and T. David Mason. 2010. "Weak States, Regime Types, and Civil War." *Civil Wars* 12(1–2):140–55.

Gyimah-Brempong, Kwabena, and Marva E. Corley. 2005. "Civil Wars and Economic Growth in Sub-Saharan Africa." *Journal of African Economies* 14(2):270–311.

Habyarimana, James, Macartan Humphreys, Daniel Posner, and Jeremy M. Weinstein. 2007. "Why Does Ethnic Diversity Undermine Public Goods Provision?" *American Political Science Review* 101(4):709–25.

Habyarimana, James, Macartan Humphreys, Daniel N. Posner, and Jeremy M. Weinstein. 2009. *Coethnicity: Diversity and the Dilemmas of Collective Action*. New York: Russell Sage Foundation.

Hale, H. E. 2004. "Explaining Ethnicity." *Comparative Political Studies* 37(4):458–85.

Hall, Rosalie Arcala. 2014. "From Rebels to Soldiers: An Analysis of the Philippine Policy of Integrating Former Moro National Liberation Front Combatants into the Armed Forces." In *New Armies from Old: Merging Competing Military Forces after Civil Wars*, edited by Roy Licklider. Washington, DC: Georgetown University Press.

Hallberg, Johan Dittrich. 2012. "PRIO Conflict Sites 1989–2008: A Geo-Referenced Dataset on Armed Conflict." *Conflict Management and Peace Science* 29(2):219–32.

Halperin, Sandra. 1998. "The Spread of Ethnic Conflict in Europe: Some Comparative–Historical Reflections." In *The International Spread of Ethnic Conflict*, edited by David A. Lake and Donald Rothchild, 151–84. Princeton: Princeton University Press.

Halpern, Manfred, 1963. *The Politics of Social Change in the Middle East and North Africa.* Princeton: Princeton University Press.

Hammond, Jesse, and Nils B. Weidmann. 2014. "Using Machine-Coded Event Data for the Micro-Level Study of Political Violence." *Research & Politics* 1(2):1–8.

Harbom, Lotta, Stina Högbladh, and Peter Wallensteen. 2006. "Armed Conflict and Peace Agreements." *Journal of Peace Research* 43(5):617–31.

Harbom, Lotta, Erik Melander, and Peter Wallensteen. 2008. "Dyadic Dimensions of Armed Conflict, 1946–2007." *Journal of Peace Research* 45(5):697–710.

Harbom, Lotta, and Peter Wallensteen. 2012. "Armed Conflict, 1989–2011." *Journal of Peace Research* 49(4):565–75.

Harff, Barbara. 2003. "No Lessons Learned from the Holocaust? Assessing Risks of Genocide and Political Mass Murder since 1955." *American Political Science Review* 97(1):57–73.

Hartzell, Caroline A. 1999. "Explaining the Stability of Negotiated Settlements to Intrastate Wars." *Journal of Conflict Resolution* 43(3):3–22.

Hartzell, Caroline A. 2009. "Settling Civil Wars: Armed Opponents' Fates and the Duration of the Peace." *Conflict Management and Peace Science* 26(4):347–65.

Hartzell, Caroline A. 2012. "Transitions from War to Peace." In *Elgar Handbook of Civil War and Fragile States,* edited by Graham K. Brown and Arnim Langer. Cheltenham, UK: Edward Elgar.

Hartzell, Caroline A., and Matthew Hoddie. 2003. "Institutionalizing Peace: Power Sharing and Post–Civil War Conflict Management." *American Journal of Political Science* 47(2):318–32.

Hartzell, Caroline A., and Matthew Hoddie. 2007. *Crafting Peace: Power-Sharing Institutions and the Negotiated Settlement of Civil Wars.* University Park, PA: Pennsylvania State University Press.

Hartzell, Caroline, and Matthew Hoddie. 2015. "The Art of the Possible: Power Sharing and Post–Civil War Democracy." *World Politics* 67(01):37–71.

Hartzell, Caroline, Matthew Hoddie, and Donald Rothchild. 2001. "Stabilizing the Peace after Civil War: An Investigation of Some Key Variables." *International Organization* 55:183–208.

Hassner, Ron E. 2003. "'To Halve and To Hold': Conflicts over Sacred Space and the Problem of Indivisibility." *Security Studies* 12(4):1–33.

Haufler, Virginia. 2009. "The Kimberley Process Certification Scheme: An Innovation in Governance and Conflict Prevention." *Journal of Business Ethics* 89 (4):409–16.

Hauge, Wenche, and Tanja Ellingsen. 1998. "Beyond Environmental Scarcity: Causal Pathways to Conflict." *Journal of Peace Research* 35(3):299–317.

Hayner, Priscilla B. 2001. *Unspeakable Truths: Facing the Challenge of Truth Commissions.* New York: Routledge.

Hayner, Priscilla B. 2010. *Unspeakable Truths: Facing the Challenge of Truth Commissions,* Second edition. New York: Routledge.

Hazen, Jennifer M. 2013. *What Rebels Want: Resources and Supply Networks in Wartime.* Ithaca, NY: Cornell University Press.

Hegghammer, Thomas. 2010. "The Rise of Muslim Foreign Fighters: Islam and the Globalization of Jihad." *International Security* 35(3):53–94.

Hegghammer, Thomas. 2013. "Should I Stay or Should I Go? Explaining Variation in Western Jihadists' Choice between Domestic and Foreign Fighting." *American Political Science Review* 107(1):1–15.

Hegre, Håvard. 2004. "The Duration and Termination of Civil War." *Journal of Peace Research* 41(3):243–52.

Hegre, Håvard. 2014. "Democracy and Armed Conflict." *Journal of Peace Research* 51:159–72.

Hegre, Håvard, Tanja Ellingsen, Scott Gates, and Nils Petter Gleditsch. 2001. "Toward a Democratic Civil Peace? Democracy, Political Change, and Civil War, 1816–1992." *American Political Science Review* 95(1):33–48.

Hegre, Håvard, Joakim Karlsen, Håvard Nygård, Håvard Strand, and Henrik Urdal. 2013. "Predicting Armed Conflict, 2011–2050." *International Studies Quarterly* 57(2):250–70.

Hegre, Håvard, Gudrun Østby, and Clionadh Raleigh. 2009. "Poverty and Civil War Events: A Disaggregated Study of Liberia." *Journal of Conflict Resolution* 53(4):598–623.

Hegre, Håvard, and Nicholas Sambanis. 2006. "Sensitivity Analysis of Empirical Results on Civil War Onset." *Journal of Conflict Resolution* 50(4):508–35.

Heldt, Birger. 2001. "Conditions for Successful Intrastate Peacekeeping Missions." Paper presented at Euroconference, San Feliu de Guixols, Spain, October 6–11.

Heldt, Birger. 2005. "Can Peacekeeping Operations Promote Democracy?" *International Studies Review* 7:304–07.

Heldt, Birger. 2009. "Sequencing of Peacemaking in Emerging Intrastate Conflicts." In *War and Peace in Transition*, edited by Karin Aggestam and Annika Bjorkdahl. Lund, Sweden: Nordic Academic.

Heldt, Birger. 2011. "Peacekeeping and Transitions to Democracy." In *Building Peace, Creating Conflict? Conflictual Dimensions of Local and International Peacebuilding*, edited by Hanne Fjelde and Kristine Höglund. Lund, Sweden: Nordic Academic Press.

Hendrix, Cullen. 2010. "Measuring State Capacity: Theoretical and Empirical Implications for the Study of Civil Conflict." *Journal of Peace Research* 47:273–85.

Hendrix, Cullen S., and Henk-Jan Brinkman. 2013. "Food Insecurity and Conflict Dynamics: Causal Linkages and Complex Feedbacks." *Stability: International Journal of Security and Development* 2(2):Art-26.

Hendrix, Cullen S., and Sarah M. Glaser. 2007. "Trends and Triggers: Climate, Climate Change, and Civil Conflict in Sub-Saharan Africa." *Political Geography* 26(6):695–715.

Hendrix, Cullen S., and Sarah M. Glaser. 2011. "Civil Conflict and World Fisheries, 1952–2004." *Journal of Peace Research* 48(4):481–95.

Hendrix, Cullen S., and Kristian Skrede Gleditsch. 2012. "Civil War: Is It All about Disease and Xenophobia? A Comment on Letendre, Fincher & Thornhill." *Biological Reviews* 87(1):163–67.

Hendrix, Cullen S., and Idean Salehyan. 2012. "Climate Change, Rainfall, and Social Conflict in Africa." *Journal of Peace Research* 49(1):35–50.

Hendrix, Cullen, and Idean Salehyan. 2015. "No News Is Good News? Mark and Recapture for Event Data When Reporting Probabilities Are Less than One." *International Interactions* 41(2):392–406.

Henriksen, Thomas. 1983. *Revolution and Counterrevolution: Mozambique's War of Independence, 1964–1974*. Westport, CT: Greenwood.

Henshaw, Alexis Leanna. 2013. "Why Women Rebel: Understanding Female Participation in Intrastate Conflict." Dissertation. University of Arizona.

Henshaw, Alexis Leanna. 2015. "Where Women Rebel." *International Feminist Journal of Politics* 14 (20150522): 1–22.

Henshaw Edna M., and H. E. Howarth. 1941. "Observed Effects of Wartime Condition of Children." *Mental Health* 2:93–101.

Henson, Billy, Pamela Wilcox, Bradford W. Reyns, and Francis T. Cullen. 2010. "Gender, Adolescent Lifestyles, and Violent Victimization: Implications for Routine Activity Theory." *Victims and Offenders* 5(4):303–28.

Heraclides, Alexis. 1990. "Secessionist Minorities and External Involvement." *International Organization* 44(3):341–78.

Herbst, Jeffrey. 1989. "The Creation and Maintenance of National Boundaries in Africa." *International Organization* 43(4):673–92.

Hibbs, Douglas A. 1973. *Mass Political Violence: A Cross-National Causal Analysis* (Vol. 253). New York: Wiley.

Hibbs, Douglas A. Jr., and Ola Olsson. 2004. "Geography, Biogeography, and Why Some Countries Are Rich and Others Are Poor." *Proceedings of the National Academy of Sciences* 101(10):3715–20.

Hill, Stuart, and Donald Rothchild. 1986. "The Contagion of Political Conflict in Africa and the World." *Journal of Conflict Resolution* 30(4):716–35.

Hill, Stuart, Donald Rothchild, and Colin Cameron. 1998. "Tactical Information and the Diffusion of Peaceful Protests." In *The International Spread of Ethnic Conflict: Fear, Diffusion, and Escalation*, edited by David A. Lake and Donald Rothchild. Princeton: Princeton University Press.

Hironaka, Ann. 2005. *Neverending Wars: The International Community, Weak States, and the Perpetuation of Civil War*. Cambridge, MA: Harvard University Press.

Hirschi, Travis. 1969. *Causes of Delinquency*. Berkeley, CA: University of California Press.

Hobsbawm, Eric, J. 1994. *The Age of Extremes: A History of the World, 1914–1991*. London: Michael Joseph.

Hobsbawm, Eric, and Terence Ranger, eds. 1983. *The Invention of Tradition*. Cambridge: Cambridge University Press.

Hoddie, Matthew. 2014. "Power Sharing and Physical Integrity Rights in Post–Civil War States." Unpublished manuscript, Towson University.

Hoddie, Matthew, and Caroline Hartzell. 2003. "Civil War Settlements and the Implementation of Military Power-Sharing Arrangements." *Journal of Peace Research* 40(3):303–20.

Hoeffler, Anke. 2012. "Growth, Aid and Policies in Countries Recovering from War." OECD Development Co-Operation Working Papers, WP 1/2012.

Hoeffler, Anke, and James D. Fearon. 2014. *Benefits and Costs of the Conflict and Violence Targets for the Post-2015 Development Agenda*. Post-2015 Consensus. Copenhagen: Copenhagen Consensus Center, www.copenhagenconsensus.com/sites/default/files/conflict_assessment_–hoeffler_and_fearon_0.pdf.

Hoeffler, Anke, Syeda S. Ijaz, and Sarah von Billerbeck. 2011. "Post-Conflict Recovery and Peace Building." Background Paper for the *World Development Report 2011*.

Hoeffler, Anke, and Marta Reynal-Querol. 2003. "Measuring the Costs of Conflict." Working paper, Centre for the Study of African Economie.

Hoffman, Bruce. 2013. *Inside Terrorism*. New York: Columbia University Press.

Högbladh, Stina. 2012. "Peace Agreements 1975–2011—Updating the UCDP Peace Agreement Dataset." In *States in Armed Conflict 2011*, edited by Thérése Pettersson and Lotta Themnér. Uppsala University: Department of Peace and Conflict Research Report 99.

Högbladh, Stina, Thérése Pettersson, and Lotta Themnér. 2011. "External Support in Armed Conflict 1975–2009: Presenting New Data." Unpublished manuscript presented at the International Studies Association Convention in Montreal, 2011.

Holsti, Kalevi. 1992. "International Theory and War in the Third World." In *The Insecurity Dilemma: National Security of Third World States*, edited by Brian Job, 37–62. Boulder, CO: Lynne Rienner.

Homer-Dixon, Thomas F. 1991. "On the Threshold: Environmental Changes as Cause of Acute Conflict." *International Security* 16(2):76–116.

Homer-Dixon, Thomas F. 1994. "Environmental Scarcities and Violent Conflict: Evidence from Cases." *International Security* 19(1):5–40.

Homer-Dixon, Thomas F. 1999. *Environment, Scarcity, and Violence*. Princeton: Princeton University Press.

Honig, Jan Willem. 1996. *Srebrenica: Record of a War Crime*. New York: Penguin Books.

Hooper, Charlotte. 2001. *Manly States: Masculinities, International Relations, and Gender Politics*. New York: Columbia University Press.

Horowitz, Donald L. 1985. *Ethnic Groups in Conflict*. Los Angeles: University of California Press.

Horowitz, Donald L. 2014. "Ethnic Power Sharing: Three Big Problems." *Journal of Democracy* 25(2):5–20.

Horst, Cindy, and Nicholas Van Hear. 2002. "Counting the Cost: Refugee, Remittances and the War on Terrorism." *Forced Migration Review*, No. 14. University of Oxford.

Howard, Lise Morjé. 2008. *UN Peacekeeping in Civil Wars*. Cambridge: Cambridge University Press.

Howard, Victor B. 1978. "John Brown's Raid at Harpers Ferry and the Sectional Crisis in North Carolina." *The North Carolina Historical Review*: 396–420.

Hsiang, Solomon M., Marshall Burke, Edward Miguel. 2013. "Quantifying the Influence of Climate on Human Conflict." *Science* 341(6151).

Hsiang, Solomon M., and Kyle C. Meng. 2014. "Reconciling Disagreement Over Climate-Conflict Results in Africa." *Proceedings of the National Academy of Sciences* 111(6):2100–2103.

Huang, Chi, and Alex Mintz, 1990. "Ridge Regression Analysis of the Defense-Growth Tradeoff in the United States." *Defense Economics* 2(1):29–37.

Hudson, Valerie, Bonnie Ballif-Spanvill, Mary Capriolo, and Chad Emmett. 2012. *Sex and World Peace*. New York: Columbia University Press.

Hudson, Valerie M, Mary Caprioli, Bonnie Ballif-Spanvill, Rose McDermott, and Chad F. Emmett. 2009. "The Heart of the Matter: The Security of Women and the Security of States." *International Security* 33(3):7–45.

Hudson, Valerie M., and Andrea M. den Boer. 2012. "A Feminist Evolutionary Analysis of the Relationship between Violence against and Inequitable Treatment of Women, and Conflict within and between Human Collectives, Including Nation-States." In *The Oxford Handbook of Evolutionary Perspectives on Violence, Homicide, and War*, edited by Tood K. Shackelford and Viviana A. Weekes-Schackelford, 301–23. Oxford: Oxford University Press.

Hug, Simon. 2003. "Selection Bias in Comparative Research: The Case of Incomplete Datasets." *Political Analysis* 11(3):255–74.

Hultman, Lisa. 2007. "Battle Losses and Rebel Violence: Raising the Cost of Fighting." *Terrorism and Political Violence* 19(2):205–22.

Hultman, Lisa, Jacob Kathman, and Megan Shannon. 2013. "United Nations Peacekeeping and Civilian Protection in Civil War." *American Journal of Political Science* 57(4):875–91.

Hultman, Lisa, Jacob D. Kathman, and Megan Shannon. 2014. "Beyond Keeping Peace: United Nations Effectiveness in the Midst of Fighting." *American Political Science Review* 108(4):737–753.

Human Rights Watch. 2007. "Child Soldiers." http://www.hrw.org/.

Human Security Report. 2012. *Sexual Violence, Education, and War: Beyond the Mainstream Narrative.* Simon Fraser University, Burnaby, BC: Human Security Report Project.

Humphreys, Macartan. 2005. "Natural Resources, Conflict, and Conflict Resolution." *Journal of Conflict Resolution* 49(4):508–37.

Humphreys, Macartan, and Jeremy M. Weinstein. 2007. "Demobilization and Reintegration." *Journal of Conflict Resolution* 51(4):531–67.

Humphreys, Macartan, and Jeremy Weinstein. 2008. "Who Fights? The Determinants of Participation in Civil War." *American Journal of Political Science* 52(2):436–55.

Huntington, Samuel P. 1991. *The Third Wave: Democratization in the Late Twentieth Century.* Norman, OK: University of Oklahoma Press.

Huntington, Samuel P. 1996. *The Clash of Civilizations and the Remaking of World Order.* New York: Simon & Schuster.

Huntington, Samuel P. 2000. "Try Again: A Reply to Russett, Oneal & Cox." *Journal of Peace Research* 37(5):609–10 .

Hunziker, Phillippe, and Lars-Erik Cederman. 2012. "No Extraction without Representation." Presented at the 2012 annual meeting of the American Political Science Association, New Orleans, LA.

Huyse, Luc. 1995. "Justice after Transition: On the Choices Successor Elites Make in Dealing with the Past," *Law & Social Inquiry* 20(1):51–78.

Ide, Tobias, Janpeter Schilling, Jasmin S. A. Link, Jürgen Scheffran, and Grace Ngaruiya. 2014. "On Exposure, Vulnerability and Violence: Spatial Distribution of Risk Factors for Climate Change and Violent Conflict across Kenya and Uganda." *Political Geography* 43:68–81.

Iqbal, Zaryab. 2010. *War and the Health of Nations.* Stanford, CA: Stanford University Press.

Jackson, Robert H., and Carl G. Rosberg. 1982. "Why Africa's Weak States Persist: The Empirical and the Judicial in Statehood." *World Politics* 35(1):1–24.

Jacob, Brian, Lars Lefgren, and Enrico Moretti. 2007. "The Dynamics of Criminal Behavior: Evidence from Weather Shocks." *Journal of Human Resources* 42(3):489–527.

Jacobsen, Karen. 1997. "Refugees' Environmental Impact: The Effects of Patterns of Settlement." *Journal of Refugee Studies* 10(1):19–36.

Jacobsen, Karen. 2002. *Livelihoods in Conflict: the Pursuit of Livelihoods by Refugees and the Impact on the Human Security of Host Communities.* Expert Working Paper, Prepared for the Center for Development Research Study: Migration-Development, Evidence and Policy Options. Feinstein International Famine Center, Tufts University.

James, Alan. 1994. "Internal Peacekeeping." In *Peacekeeping and the Challenge of Civil Conflict Resolution*, edited by David Charters, 44–58. New Brunswick: Centre for Conflict Studies, University of New Brunswick.

Jarstad, Anna K. 2008. "Dilemmas of War-to-Democracy Transitions: Theories and Concepts." In *From War to Democracy: Dilemmas of Peacebuilding*, edited by Anna K. Jarstad and Timothy D. Sisk, 17–36. Cambridge: Cambridge University Press.

Jarstad, Anna K. 2009. "The Prevalence of Power Sharing: Exploring the Patterns of Post-Election Peace." *African Spectrum* 46:41–62.

Jarstad, Anna K., and Desirée Nilsson. 2008. "From Words to Deeds: The Implementation of Power-Sharing Pacts in Peace Accords." *Conflict Management and Peace Science* 25(3):206–23.

Jarstad, Anna K., and Timothy D. Sisk, eds. 2008. *From War to Democracy: Dilemmas of Peacebuilding.* Cambridge: Cambridge University Press.

Jenne, Erin K. 2007. *Ethnic Bargaining: The Paradox of Minority Empowerment*. Ithaca, NY: Cornell University Press.

Jenne, Erin K. 2012. "When Will We Part with Partition Theory?" *Ethnopolitics*: 1–13.

Jennings, Simon, Michel J. Kaiser, and John D. Reynolds. 2001. *Marine Fisheries Ecology*. Oxford: Blackwell Science.

Jensen, Peter Sandholt, and Kristian Skrede Gleditsch. 2009. "Rain, Growth, and Civil War: The Importance of Location." *Defense and Peace Economics* 20(5):359–72.

Jett, Dennis C. 2000. *Why Peacekeeping Fails*. New York: St. Martin's Press.

Johnson, C. 2008. "Partitioning to Peace: Sovereignty, Demography and Ethnic Civil Wars." *International Security* 32(4):140–70.

Johnson, Kirsten, Jana Asher, Stephanie Rosborough, Amisha Raja, Rajesh Panjabi, Charles Beadling, and Lynn Lawry. 2008. "Association of Combatant Status and Sexual Violence with Health and Mental Health Outcomes in Postconflict Liberia." *JAMA* 300(6):676–90.

Johnson, Kirsten, Jennifer Scott, Bigy Rughita, Michael Kisielewski, Jana Asher, Ricardo Ong, and Lynn Lawry. 2010. "Association of Sexual Violence and Human Rights Violations with Physical and Mental Health in Territories of the Eastern Democratic Republic of the Congo." *JAMA* 304(5):553–62.

Joshi, Madhav, and T. David Mason. 2011. "Civil War Settlements, Size of Governing Coalition, and Durability of Peace in Post–Civil War States." *International Interactions* (37)4:388–413.

Justino, Patricia, and Philip Verwimp. 2006. "Poverty Dynamics, Conflict and Convergence in Rwanda." Working Paper no. 16, Households in Conflict Network. www.hicn.org.

Kahl, Colin H. 1998. "Population Growth, Environmental Degradation, and State-Sponsored Violence: The Case of Kenya, 1991–1993." *International Security* 23(2):80–119.

Kahl, Colin H. 2006. *States, Scarcity, and Civil Strife in the Developing World*. Princeton: Princeton University Press.

Kaldor, Mary. 1999. *New and Old Wars: Organized Violence in a Global Era*. Stanford, CA: Stanford University Press.

Kalyvas, Stathis. 1999. "Wanton and Senseless? The Logic of Massacres in Algeria." *Rationality and Society* 11(3):243–85.

Kalyvas, Stathis N. 2001. "'New' and 'Old' Civil Wars: A Valid Distinction?" *World Politics* 54(1):99–118.

Kalyvas, Stathis. 2005. "Warfare in Civil Wars." In *Rethinking the Nature of War*, edited by Isabelle Duyvesteyn and Jan Angstrom, 88–108. London: Frank Cass.

Kalyvas, Stathis N. 2006. *The Logic of Violence in Civil War*. Cambridge: Cambridge University Press.

Kalyvas, Stathis N. 2008. "Ethnic Defection in Civil War." *Comparative Political Studies* 41(8):1043–68.

Kalyvas, Stathis N., and Laia Balcells. 2010. "International System and Technologies of Rebellion: How the End of the Cold War Shaped Internal Conflict." *American Political Science Review* 104(3):415–29.

Kalyvas, Stathis N., and Matthew A. Kocher. 2007a. "Ethnic Cleavages and Irregular War: Iraq and Vietnam." *Politics and Society* 35(2):183–223.

Kalyvas, Stathis, and Matthew Kocher. 2007b. "How 'Free' is Free Riding in Civil Wars? Violence, Insurgency, and the Collective Action Problem." *World Politics* 59(2):177–216.

Kaminski, Marek M., and Monika Nalepa. 2006. "Judging Transitional Justice: A New Criterion for Evaluating Truth Revelation Procedures." *Journal of Conflict Resolution* 50(3):283–408.

Kanazawa, Satoshi. 2009. "Evolutionary Psychological Foundations of Civil War." *Journal of Politics* 71:25–34.

Kanbur, Ravi, Prem Kumar Rajaram, and Ashutosh Varshney. 2011. "Ethnic Diversity and Ethnic Strife: An Interdisciplinary Perspective." *World Development* 39(2):147–58.

Kang, Seonjou, and James Meernik. 2005. "Civil War Destruction and the Prospects for Economic Growth." *Journal of Politics* 67(1):88–109.

Kathman, Jacob D. 2010. "Civil War Contagion and Neighboring Interventions." *International Studies Quarterly* 54(4):989–1012.

Kathman, Jacob D. 2011. "Civil War Diffusion and Regional Motivations for Intervention." *Journal of Conflict Resolution* 55(6):847–76.

Kathman, Jacob D. 2013. "United Nations Peacekeeping Personnel Commitments, 1990–2011." *Conflict Management and Peace Science* 30(5):532–49.

Kaufmann, Chaim. 1996. "Possible and Impossible Solutions to Ethnic Civil Wars." *International Security* 20(4):136–75.

Kaufmann, Chaim. 1998. "When All Else Fails: Ethnic Population Transfers and Partitions in the Twentieth Century." *International Security* 23:20–56.

Kaufmann, Daniel, Aart Kraay, and Massimo Mastruzzi. 2010. "The Worldwide Governance Indicators: Methodology and Analytical Issues," *World Bank, Draft Research Policy Working Paper*. Available at http://info.worldbank.org/governance/wgi/pdf/WGI.pdf.

Kaufman, Stuart J. *Modern Hatreds: The Symbolic Politics of Ethnic War*. Ithaca, NY: Cornell University Press, 2001.

Kell, Timothy. 1995. *The Roots of the Acehnese Rebellion, 1989–1992*. Cornell Modern Indonesia Project Publication No. 74.

Kelley, Colin P., Shahrzad Mohtadi, Mark A. Cane, Richard Seager, and Yochanan Kushnir. 2015. "Climate Change in the Fertile Crescent and Implications of the Recent Syrian Drought." *Proceedings of the National Academy of Sciences* 112(11):3241–46.

Kelly, John D. 2010. "Seeing Red: Mao Fetishism, Pax Americana, and the Moral Economy of War." In *Anthropology and Global Counterinsurgency*, edited by John D. Kelly et al., 77. Chicago: University of Chicago Press.

Kenney, Charles D., and Dean E. Spears. 2005. "Truth and Consequences: Do Truth Commissions Promote Democratization?" Annual Meeting of the American Political Science Association, Washington DC.

Kidron, Michael, and Dan Smith. 1991. *The New State of War and Peace: An International Atlas: A Full Color Survey of Arsenals, Armies and Alliances Throughout the World*. New York: Simon & Schuster.

Kim, Hun Joon. 2012. "Structural Determinants of Human Rights Prosecutions after Democratic Transition." *Journal of Peace Research* 49(2):305–20.

Kim, Hun Joon, and Kathryn Sikkink. 2010. "Explaining the Deterrence Effect of Human Rights Prosecutions for Transitional Countries." *International Studies Quarterly* 54:939–63.

Kim, Hun Joon, and Kathryn Sikkink. 2013. "How Do Human Rights Prosecutions Improve Human Rights after Transition?" *Interdisciplinary Journal of Human Rights Law* 7.

Kimenyi, Mwangi S., and Olu Ajakaiye. 2012. *Institutions and Service Delivery in Africa*. African Economic Research Consortium and the World Bank.

King, Gary, and Will Lowe. 2003. "An Automated Information Extraction Tool for International Conflict Data with Performance as Good as Human Coders: A Rare Events Evaluation Design." *International Organization* 57(3):617–42.

Kirkpatrick, Jeane J. 1982. *Dictatorships and Double Standards: Rationalism and Reason in Politics.* New York: Simon & Schuster.

Kitissou, Kpoti, and Bong Joon Yoon. 2014. "Africa and Social Capital: From Human Trade to Civil War." *The Journal of Pan African Studies* 6(8):146–69.

Kliewer, Wendy, Stephen J. Lepore, Deborah Oskin, and Patricia D. Johnson. 1998. "The Role of Social and Cognitive Processes in Children's Adjustment to Community Violence." *Journal of Consulting and Clinical Psychology* 66:199–209.

Kliewer, Wendy, Lenn Murrelle, Roberto Mejia, Yolanda Torres, and Adrian Angold. 2001. "Exposure to Violence against a Family Member and Internalizing Symptoms in Colombian Adolescents." *Journal of Consulting and Clinical Psychology* 69(6):971–82.

Klomp, Jeroen, and Erwin Bulte. 2013. "Climate Change, Weather Shocks, and Violent Conflict: A Critical Look at the Evidence." *Agricultural Economics* 44:63–78.

Knack, Stephen, and Philip Keefer. 1997. "Does Social Capital Have an Economic Payoff? A Cross-Country Investigation." *The Quarterly Journal of Economics* 112(4):1251–88.

Koch, Michael T., and Patricia L. Sullivan. 2010. "Should I Stay or Should I Go Now? Partisanship, Approval, and the Duration of Major Power Democratic Military Interventions." *The Journal of Politics* 72(03):616–29.

Koga, Jun. 2011. "Where Do Third Parties Intervene? Third Parties' Domestic Institutions and Military Interventions in Civil Conflicts." *International Studies Quarterly* 55(4):1143–66.

Koubi, Vally, Thomas Bernauer, Anna Kalbhenn, and Gabriele Spilker. 2012. "Climate Variability, Economic Growth, and Civil Conflict." *Journal of Peace Research* 49 (1): 113–27.

Koubi, Vally, Gabriele Spilker, Tobias Böhmelt, and Thomas Bernauer. 2014. "Do Natural Resources Matter for Interstate and Intrastate Armed Conflict?" *Journal of Peace Research* 51(2):227–43.

Krain, Matthew. 1997. "State-Sponsored Mass Murder: The Onset and Severity of Genocides and Politicides." *Journal of Conflict Resolution* 41(3):331–60.

Krain, Matthew. 2005. "International Intervention and the Severity of Genocides and Politicides." *International Studies Quarterly* 49(3):363–88.

Krause, Peter. 2013. "The Structure of Success: How the Internal Distribution of Power Drives Armed Group Behavior and National Movement Effectiveness." *International Security* 38(3):72–116.

Kreutz, Joakim. 2010. "How and When Armed Conflicts End: Introducing the UCDP Conflict Termination Dataset." *Journal of Peace Research* 47(2):243–50.

Kreutz, Joakim. 2013. "A Model of Peace?" Paper prepared for the Workshop on the Depth of the East Asian Peace, Uppsala, Sweden, June 6–8.

Kreutz, Joakim. 2014. "How Civil Wars End (and Recur)." In *Routledge Handbook of Civil Wars,* edited by Edward Newman and Karl DeRouen Jr. London: Routledge.

Kreutz, Joakim. 2015. "The War That Wasn't There: Managing Unclear Cases in Conflict Data." *Journal of Peace Research* 52(1):120–24.

Kritz, Neil J., ed. 1995. *Transitional Justice: How Emerging Democracies Reckon with Former Regimes.* Vol. 2. Washington, DC: US Institute of Peace Press.

Kritz, Neil J. 1996. "Coming to Terms with Atrocities: A Review of Accountability Mechanisms for Mass Violations of Human Rights." *Law and Contemporary Problems* 59(4):127–52.

Kuran, Timor. 1998. "Ethnic Dissimilation and Its International Diffusion." In *The International Spread of Ethnic Conflict: Fear, Diffusion, and Escalation,* edited by David A. Lake and Donald Rothchild, 35–60. Princeton: Princeton University Press.

Kuran, Timur. 1998. "Ethnic Norms and Their Transformation Through Reputational Cascades." *The Journal of Legal Studies* 27(S2):623–59.

Kydd, Andrew. 2003. "Which Side Are You on? Bias, Credibility, and Mediation." *American Journal of Political Science* 47(4):597–611.

Kydd, Andrew. 2005. *Trust and Mistrust in International Relations.* Princeton: Princeton University Press.

Kydd, Andrew, and Barbara F. Walter. 2002. "Sabotaging the Peace: The Politics of Extremist Violence." *International Organization* 56(2):263–96.

Lacina, Bethany. 2006. "Explaining the Severity of Civil Wars." *Journal of Conflict Resolution* 50(2):276–89.

Lacina, Bethany, and Nils Petter Gleditsch. 2005. "Monitoring Trends in Global Combat: A New Dataset of Battle Deaths." *European Journal of Population* 21(2–3):145–66.

Lacina, Bethany Ann, and Nils Petter Gleditsch. 2013. "The Waning of War is Real: A Reply to Gohdes and Price." *Journal of Conflict Resolution* 57(6):1109–27.

Lacina, Bethany Ann, Nils Petter Gleditsch, and Bruce Russett. 2006. "The Declining Risk of Death in Battle." *International Studies Quarterly* 50(3):673–80.

Lacina, Bethany, with Gabriel Uriarte. 2009. *The PRIO Battle Deaths Dataset, 1946– 2008, Version 3.0. Documentation of Coding Decisions for Use with Uppsala/PRIO Armed Conflict Dataset, 1946–2008, Version 4.0,* www.prio.org/Global/upload/CSCW/Data/PRIObd3.0_documentation.pdf.

LaFree, Gary, and Laura Dugan. 2004. "How Does Studying Terrorism Compare to Studying Crime." In *Terrorism and Counter-Terrorism,* edited by Mathieu Deflem. Bingley, UK: Emerald Group Publishing Limited.

Lai, Brian. 2003. "Examining the Goals of US Foreign Assistance in the Post–Cold War Period, 1991–96." *Journal of Peace Research* 40(1):103–28.

Lai, Brian, and Clayton L. Thyne. 2007. "The Effect of Civil War On Education, 1980–97." *Journal of Peace Research* 44(3):277–92.

Lake, David A., and Donald Rothchild. 1998a. *The International Spread of Ethnic Conflict: Fear, Diffusion, and Escalation.* Princeton: Princeton University Press.

Lake, David A., and Donald Rothchild. 1998b. "Spreading Fear: The Genesis of Transnational Ethnic Conflict." In *The International Spread of Ethnic Conflict: Fear, Diffusion, and Escalation,* edited by David A. Lake and Donald Rothchild. Princeton: Princeton University Press.

Lanchester, Frederick. W. 1956. "Mathematics in Warfare." In *The World of Mathematics.* Vol. 4, edited by James R. Newman, 2138–57. New York: Simon & Schuster.

Larrick, Richard P., Thomas A. Timmerman, Andrew M. Carton, and Jason Abrevaya. 2011. "Temper, Temperature, and Temptation: Heat-Related Retaliation in Baseball. *Psychological Science* 22(4):423–28.

Lasley, Trace, and Clayton L. Thyne. 2015. "Secession, Legitimacy and the Use of Child Soldiers." *Conflict Management and Peace Science* 32 (3):289–308.

Lawrence, Adria. 2013. *Imperial Rule and the Politics of Nationalism: Anti-colonial Protest in the French Empire.* Cambridge: Cambridge University Press.

Le Billon, Philippe. 2001. "The Political Ecology of War: Natural Resources and Armed Conflicts." *Political Geography* 20(5):561–84.

Lederman, Daniel, and William F. Maloney, eds. 2007. *Natural Resources: Neither Curse Nor Destiny.* Washington, DC: Stanford University Press and World Bank.

Levy, Jack S., and T. Clifton Morgan. 1986. "The War-Weariness Hypothesis: An Empirical Test." *American Journal of Political Science* 30(1):26–49.

Levy, Marion, 1966. *Modernization and the Structure of Societies*. Princeton: Princeton University Press.

Li, Quan. 2005. "Does Democracy Promote or Reduce Transnational Terrorist Incidents?" *Journal of Conflict Resolution* 49(2):278–97.

Li, Quan, and Ming Wen. 2005. "The Immediate and Lingering Effects of Armed Conflict on Adult Mortality: A Time-Series Cross-National Analysis." *Journal of Peace Research* 42(4):471–92.

Lichbach, Mark Irving. 1987. "Deterrence or Escalation? The Puzzle of Aggregate Studies of Repression and Dissent." *Journal of Conflict Resolution* 31(2):266–97.

Lichbach, Mark I. 1995. *The Rebel's Dilemma*. Ann Arbor, MI: University of Michigan Press.

Lichbach, Mark Irving, Christian Davenport, and Dave Armstrong. 2004. "Contingency, Inherency, and the Onset of Civil War." Unpublished manuscript, University of Maryland.

Licklider, Roy. 1993. "How Civil Wars End: Questions and Methods." In *Stopping the Killing: How Civil Wars End,* edited by Roy Licklider, 3–19. New York and London: New York University Press.

Licklider, Roy. 1995a. "The Consequences of Negotiated Settlements in Civil Wars, 1945–1993." *American Political Science Review* 89(3):681–90.

Licklider, Roy. 1995b. *Stopping the Killing: How Civil Wars End*. New York: New York University Press.

Luttwak, Edward N. 1999. "Give War a Chance." *Foreign Affairs* 78(4):36–44.

Lie, Tove Grete, Helga Malmin Binningsbø, and Scott Gates. 2007. "Post-Conflict Justice and Sustainable Peace." World Bank Policy Research Working Paper 4191.

Lijphart, Arend. 1977. *Democracy in Plural Societies: A Comparative Exploration*. Yale University Press.

Linder, Wolf, and André Bächtiger. 2005. "What Drives Democratization in Asia and Africa?" *European Journal of Political Research* 44(6):861–80.

Lindley, Anna. 2007. "Remittances in Fragile Settings: A Somali Case Study," HiCN Working Paper no. 27, Households in Conflict Network. www.hicn.org.

Lipset, Seymour. 1959. "Some Social Requisites of Democracy: Economic Development and Political Legitimacy." *American Political Science Review* 53(1):69–105.

Lischer, Sarah K. 2003. "Collateral Damage: Humanitarian Assistance as a Cause of Conflict." *International Security* 28(1):79–109.

Lischer, Sarah Kenyon. 2005. *Dangerous Sanctuaries: Refugee Camps, Civil War, and the Dilemmas of Humanitarian Aid*. Ithaca, NY, and London: Cornell University Press.

Llabre, Maria, and Foaziah A. Hadi. 1997. "Social Support and Psychological Distress in Kuwaiti Boys and Girls Exposed to the Gulf Crisis." *Journal of Clinical Child Psychology* 26(3):247–55.

Locke, Catherine J., Karen Southwick, Laura A. McCloskey, and Maria E. Fernandez-Esquer. 1996. "The Psychological and Medical Sequelae of War in Central American Refugee Mothers and Children." *Archives of Pediatric Adolescent Medicine* 150:822–28.

Lockyer, Adam. 2010. "The Dynamics of Warfare in Civil War." *Civil Wars* 12(1):91–116.

Loescher, Gil. 1992. "Refugee Movements and International Security." Adelphi Papers, 268, London: IISS.

Loescher, Gil, and Laila Monahan. 1989. *Refugees and International Relations*. Oxford and New York: Oxford University Press.

Long, William J., and Peter Brecke. 2003. *War and Reconciliation: Reason and Emotions in Conflict Resolution*. Cambridge, MA: MIT Press.

Looney, Robert E. 1990. "Militarization, Military Regimes, and the General Quality of Life in the Third World." *Armed Forces and Society* 17(1):127–39.

Loyle, Cyanne E., and Benjamin J. Appel. 2014. "Conflict Recurrence and Post-Conflict Justice: Addressing Motivations for Sustainable Peace." Working paper.

Lustig, Stuart L., Maryam Kia-Keating, Wanda G. Knight, Paul Geltman, Heidi Ellis, and J. David Kinzie. 2004. "Review of Child and Adolescent Refugee Mental Health." *Journal of the American Academy of Child and Adolescent Psychiatry* 43(1):24–36.

Luttwak, Edward N. 1999. "Give War a Chance." *Foreign Affairs* 78(4):36–44.

Lutz, Ellen, and Kathryn Sikkink. 2001. "The Justice Cascade: The Evolution and Impact of Foreign Human Rights Trials in Latin America." *Chicago Journal of International Law* 2:1–33.

Lyall, Jason. 2010a. "Are Coethnics more Effective Counterinsurgents? Evidence from the Second Chechen War." *American Political Science Review* 104(01):1–20.

Lyall, Jason. 2010b. "Do Democracies Make Inferior Counterinsurgents? Reassessing Democracy's Impact on War Outcomes and Duration." *International Organization* 64(1):167–92.

Lyall, Jason, and Isaiah Wilson III. 2009. "Rage against the Machines: Explaining Outcomes in Counterinsurgency Wars." *International Organization* 63(1):67–106.

Lyall, Jason, Graeme Blair, and Kosuke Imai. 2013. "Explaining Support for Combatants During Wartime: A Survey Experiment in Afghanistan." *American Political Science Review* 107(4):679–705.

Maccini, Sharon, and Dean Young. 2009. "Under the Weather: Health, Schooling, and Economic Consequences of Early-Life Rainfall." *American Economic Review* 99(3):1006–26.

MacInnes, John. 1998. "Capitalist Development: Creator of Masculinity and Destroyer of Patriarchy?" Men and Masculinities and Gender Relations in Development Conference Seminar, Bradford, UK.

Mack, Andrew. 1975. "Why Big Nations Lose Small Wars: The Politics of Asymmetric Conflict." *World Politics* 27(02):175–200.

Mack, Andrew. 2002. "Civil War: Academic Research and the Policy Community." *Journal of Peace Research* 39:315–525.

Mack, Andrew. 2008. "Human Security Brief 2007." Simon Fraser University, Vancouver, available at http://www.humansecuritybrief.info/HSR_Brief_2007.pdf.

MacKenzie, Megan. 2009. "Securitization and Desecuritization: Female Soldiers and the Reconstruction of Women in Post-Conflict Sierra Leone." *Security Studies* 18(2):241–61.

MacKenzie, Megan H. 2012. *Female Soldiers in Sierra Leone: Sex, Security, and Post-Conflict Development*. NYU Press.

Magarrell, Lisa. 2007. *Reparations in Theory and Practice*. New York: Reparative Justice Series, International Center for Transitional Justice.

Mahdavy, Hossein. 1970. "The Patterns and Problems of Economic Development in Rentier States: The Case of Iran." In *Studies in Economic History of the Middle East*, edited by M. A. Cook, 428–67. London: Oxford University Press.

Malamud-Goti, Jaime. 1990. "Transitional Governments in the Breach: Why Punish State Criminals?" *Human Rights Quarterly* 12(1):1–16.

Malcolm, Noel. 1996. *Bosnia: A Short History*. New York: New York University Press.

Malet, David. 2013. *Foreign Fighters: Transnational Identity in Civil Conflicts*. Oxford: Oxford University Press.

Mallinder, Louise. 2008. *Amnesty, Human Rights and Political Transitions: Bridging the Peace and Justice Divide*. Oxford and Portland, OR: Hart Publishing.

Mallinder, Louise. 2009. *Exploring the Practice of States in Introducing Amnesties.* Berlin: Springer.

Mamdani, Mohammed. 2010. *Saviors and Survivors: Darfur, Politics, and the War on Terror.* New York: Random House.

Mansfield, Edward D., and Jack Snyder. 1995. "Democratization and the Dangers of War." *International Security* 20:5–38.

Mansfield, Edward D., and Jack Snyder. 2005. *Electing to Fight: Why Emerging Democracies Go to War.* Cambridge: MIT Press.

Mao, Zedong. 1961. *On Guerrilla Warfare.* Champaign, IL: University of Illinois Press.

Maoz, Zeev, and Belgin San-Akca. 2012. "Rivalry and State Support of Non-State Armed Groups (NAGs), 1946–20011." *International Studies Quarterly* 56(4):720–34.

Marten, Kimberly Zisk. 2004. *Enforcing the Peace: Learning from the Imperial Past.* New York: Columbia University Press.

Martin, Adrian, Eugene Rutagarama, Ana Cascão, Maryke Gray, and Vasudha Chhotray. 2011. "Understanding the Co-existence of Conflict and Cooperation: Transboundary Ecosystem Management in the Virunga Massif." *Journal of Peace Research* 48(5):621–35.

Martin, Paul S., and Christine R. Szuter. 1999. "War Zones and Game Sinks in Lewis and Clark's West." *Conservation Biology* 13(1):36–45.

Martin, Philip. 2013. "Coming Together: Power-Sharing and the Durability of Negotiated Peace Settlements." *Civil Wars* 15(3):332–58.

Mason, T. David. 1992. "Women's Participation in Central American Revolutions: A Theoretical Perspective." *Comparative Political Studies* 25(1):63–89.

Mason, T. David. 2004. *Caught in the Crossfire: Revolution, Repression, and the Rational Peasant.* Boulder, CO: Rowman & Littlefield.

Mason, T. David, and Patrick J. Fett. 1996. "How Civil Wars End: A Rational Choice Approach." *Journal of Conflict Resolution* 40(4):546–68.

Mason, T. David, Mehmet Gurses, Patrick T. Brandt, and Jason Michael Quinn. 2011. "When Civil Wars Recur: Conditions for Durable Peace after Civil Wars." *International Studies Perspectives* 12:171–89.

Mason, T. David, and Dale Krane. 1989. "The Political Economy of Death Squads." *International Studies Quarterly* 33(2):175–98.

Mason, T. David Jr., Joseph P. Weingarten, and Patrick J. Fett. 1999. "Win, Lose, or Draw: Predicting the Outcome of Civil Wars." *Political Research Quarterly* 52(2):239–68.

Mattes, Michaela, and Burcu Savun. 2009. "Fostering Peace after Civil War: Commitment Problems and Agreement Design." *International Studies Quarterly* 53(3):737–59.

Maves, Jessica, and Alex Braithwaite. 2013. "Autocratic Institutions and Civil Conflict Contagion." *The Journal of Politics* 75(2):478–90.

McAdam, Doug. 1982. *Political Process and the Development of Black Insurgency.* Chicago: University of Chicago Press.

McCauley, John F. 2014. "The Political Mobilization of Ethnic and Religious Identities in Africa." *American Political Science Review* 108(04):801–16.

McCormick, James M., and Neil Mitchell. 1988. "Is US Aid Really Linked to Human Rights in Latin America?" *American Journal of Political Science*: 231–39.

McDermott, Rose, Dominic Johnson, Jonathan Cowden, and Stephen Rosen. 2007. "Testosterone and Aggression in a Simulated Crisis Game." *The Annals of the American Academy of Political and Social Science* 614(1):15–33.

McDoom, Omar Shahabudin. 2012. "The Psychology of Threat in Intergroup Conflict: Emotions, Rationality, and Opportunity in the Rwandan Genocide." *International Security* 37(2):119–55.

McDoom, Omar Shahabudin. 2013. "Who Killed in Rwanda's Genocide? Micro-Space, Social Influence and Individual Participation in Intergroup Violence." *Journal of Peace Research* 50(4):453–67.

McDougal, Topher L. 2008. "Mars the Redeemer: What Do Civil Wars and State-Led Industrialization Have in Common?" Unpublished manuscript, MIT. Paper presented at the WIDER/HiCN Conference on Entrepreneurship and Conflict.

McEvoy, Sandra. 2009. "Loyalist Women Paramilitaries in Northern Ireland: Beginning a Feminist Conversation about Conflict Resolution." *Security Studies* 18(2):262–86.

McGlen, Nancy E., and Meredith Reid Sarkees. 1993. *Women in Foreign Policy: The Insiders.* New York: Routledge.

McNab, Robert M., and Edward Mason. 2007. "Reconstruction, the Long Tail and Decentralisation: An Application to Iraq and Afghanistan." *Small Wars & Insurgencies* 18(3):363–79.

Meadows, Donella H., Dennis L. Meadows, Jørgen Randers, and William W. Behrens III. 1972. *The Limits to Growth.* New York: Universe Books.

Mearsheimer, John, and Steven Van Evera. 1995. "When Peace Means War: The Partition That Dare Not Speak Its Name," *The New Republic* 18:16–21.

Meernik, James D. 2005. "Justice and Peace? How the International Criminal Tribunal Affects Societal Peace in Bosnia." *Journal of Peace Research* 42(3):271–89.

Meernik, James, Eric L. Krueger, and Steven C. Poe. 1998. "Testing Models of US Foreign Policy: Foreign Aid during and after the Cold War." *Journal of Politics* 60(1):63–85.

Meernik, James D., Angela Nichols, and Kimi L. King. 2010. "The Impact of International Tribunals and Domestic Trials on Peace and Human Rights after Civil War." *International Studies Persepctives* 11:309–34.

Mehler, Andreas. 2008. "Not Always in the People's Interest: Power-Sharing Arrangements in African Peace Agreements." GIGA Working Paper, no. 83, Hamburg: GIGA. http://www .giga-hamburg.de/en/system/files/publications/wp83_mehler.pdf.

Meier, Patrick, Doug Bond, and Joe Bond. 2007. "Environmental Influences on Pastoral Conflict in the Horn of Africa." *Political Geography* 26(6):716–35.

Meierding, Emily. 2013. "Climate Change and Conflict: Avoiding Small Talk about the Weather." *International Studies Review* 15: 185–203.

Melander, Erik. 2005a. "Gender Equality and Intrastate Armed Conflict." *International Studies Quarterly* 49(4):695–714.

Melander, Erik. 2005b. "Political Gender Equality and State Human Rights Abuse." *Journal of Peace Research* 42(2):149–66.

Melander, Erik. 2013. "Does Amnesty Benefit Peace? The Role of Amnesties in Ending Civil Wars." Working paper.

Melander, Erik, Frida Möller, and Magnus Öberg. 2009. "Managing Intrastate Low–Intensity Armed Conflict 1993–2004: A New Dataset." *International Interactions* 35(1):58–85.

Melander, Erik, Magnus Öberg, and Jonathan Hall. 2009. "Are 'New Wars' More Atrocious? Battle Severity, Civilians Killed and Forced Migration before and after the End of the Cold War." *European Journal of International Relations* 15(3):505–36.

Melander, Erik, and Ralph Sundberg. 2013. "Introducing the UCDP Georeferenced Event Dataset." *Journal of Peace Research* 50(4):523–32.

Melin, Molly M., and Isak Svensson. 2009 "Incentives for Talking: Accepting Mediation in International and Civil Wars." *International Interactions* 35(3):249–71.

Melrose, Joseph H. Jr. "The Sierra Leone Peace Process." In *Human Rights and Conflict Resolution in Context: Colombia, Sierra Leone, and Northern Ireland,* edited by Eileen F. Babbitt and Ellen L. Lutz. Syracuse, NY: Syracuse University Press.

Menaldo, Victor. 2014. "From Institutions Curse to Resource Blessing." Manuscript, University of Washington.

Méndez, Juan E. 1997. "In Defense of Transitional Justice." in *Transitional Justice and the Rule of Law in New Democracies*, ed. A. James McAdams. Notre Dame, IN: University of Notre Dame Press.

Merrouche, Ouarda. 2006. "The Human Capital Cost of Landmine Contamination in Cambodia," HiCN Working Paper no. 25, Households in Conflict Network.

Miguel, Edward, and Gérard Roland. 2011. "The Long Term Impact of Bombing Vietnam." Mimeo Berkeley University.

Miguel, Edward, Sebastián M. Saiegh, and Shanker Satyanath. 2011. "Civil War Exposure and Violence." *Economics and Politics* 23(1):59–73.

Miguel, Edward, Shanker Satyanath, and Ernest Sergenti. 2004. "Economic Shocks and Civil Conflict: an Instrumental Variables Approach." *Journal of Political Economy* 112(4):725–53.

Miller, Gina Lei, and Emily Hencken Ritter. 2014. "Emigrants and the Onset of Civil War." *Journal of Peace Research* 51(1):51–64.

Miller, Jennifer L. 2014. "Justice in Action: The Institutional Design and Implementation of Transitional Justice." Unpublished doctoral dissertation, University of Arizona.

Miller, Kenneth E. 1996. "The Effects of State Terrorism and Exile on Indigenous Guatemalan Refugee Children: A Mental Health Assessment and an Analysis of Children's Narratives." *Child Development* 67:89–106.

Minorities at Risk Project. 2009. "Minorities at Risk Dataset." College Park: Center for International Development and Conflict Management. http://www.cidcm.umd.edu/mar/.

Minow, Martha. 1998. *Between Vengeance and Forgiveness: Facing History after Genocide and Mass Violence.* Boston, MA: Beacon Press.

Mitchell, Christopher R. 1970. "Civil Strife and the Involvement of External Parties." *International Studies Quarterly* 14:166–94.

Mitchell, Sara McLaughlin, and Cameron Thies. 2012. "Resource Curse in Reverse: How Civil Wars Influence Natural Resource Production." *International Interactions* 38(2):218–42.

Modelski, George. 1964. "International Settlement of Internal War." In *International Aspects of Civil Strife,* edited by James Rosenau. Princeton: Princeton University Press.

Mohammed, Nadir, 1999. "Civil Wars and Military Expenditures: A Note." Paper Presented At the World Bank's Development Economic Research Group (DECRG) Launch Conference On "Civil Conflict, Crime and Violence," World Bank, Washington, DC, 22–23 February. http://www.worldbank.org/research/conflict/papers/civil.pdf.

Montalvo, Jose G., and Martha Reynal-Querol. 2005. "Ethnic Polarization, Potential Conflict, and Civil Wars." *American Economic Review* 95(3):796–816.

Montalvo, J. Garcia, and Marta Reynal-Querol. 2007. "Fighting against Malaria: Prevent Wars While Waiting for the 'Miraculous' Vaccine." *The Review of Economics and Statistics* 89(1):165–77.

Moore, Will H. 1995a. "Rational Rebels: Overcoming the Free-Rider Problem." *Political Research Quarterly* 48(2):417–54.

Moore, Will H. 1995b. "Action-Reaction or Rational Expectations? Reciprocity and the Domestic-International Conflict Nexus During the 'Rhodesia Problem.'" *Journal of Conflict Resolution* 39(1):129–67.

Moore, Will H. 1998. "Repression and Dissent: Substitution, Context, and Timing." *American Journal of Political Science* 42(3):851–73.

Moore, Will H. 2000. "The Repression of Dissent: A Substitution Model of Government Coercion." *Journal of Conflict Resolution* 44(1):107–27.

Moore, Will H., and David R. Davis. 1998. "Ties that Bind? Domestic and International Conflict Behavior in Zaire." *Comparative Political Studies* 31(1):45–71.

Moore, Will H., and Stephen M. Shellman. 2004. "Fear of Persecution and Forced Migration, 1952–1995." *Journal of Conflict Resolution* 48(5):723–45.

Moore, Will H., and Stephen M. Shellman. 2007. "Whither Will They Go? A Global Study of Refugees' Destinations, 1965–1995." *International Studies Quarterly* 51(4):811–34.

Morgenthau, Hans J. 1967. "To Intervene or Not to Intervene." *Foreign Affairs* 45(3):425–36.

Murdoch, James C. and Todd Sandler. 2004. "Civil Wars and Economic Growth: Spatial Dispersion." *American Journal of Political Science* 48(1):138–51.

Morrison, Kevin. 2009. "Oil, Nontax Revenue, and Regime Stability." *International Organization* 63:107–38.

Most, Benjamin A., and Harvey Starr. 1990. "Theoretical and Logical Issues in the Study of International Diffusion." *Journal of Theoretical Politics* 2(4):391–412.

Mousseau, Michael. 2012. "Capitalist Development and Civil War." *International Studies Quarterly* 56: 470–83.

Mueller, John. 2000. "The Banality of 'Ethnic War.'" *International Security* 25(1):42–70.

Mueller, John. 2003. "Policing the Remnants of War." *Journal of Peace Research* 40(5):507–18.

Mukherjee, Bumba. 2006. "Why Political Power-Sharing Agreements Lead to Enduring Peaceful Resolution of Some Civil Wars, but Not Others?" *International Studies Quarterly* 50(2):479–504.

Mullenbach, Mark J. 2005. "Deciding to Keep Peace: An Analysis of International Influences on the Establishment of Third-Party Peacekeeping Missions." *International Studies Quarterly* 49:529–56.

Mullenbach, Mark J. 2013. "Third-Party Peacekeeping in Intrastate Disputes, 1946–2012: A New Dataset." *Midsouth Political Science Review* 14(1):103–33.

Muller, Edward N. 1985. "Income Inequality, Regime Repressiveness, and Political Violence." *American Sociological Review* 50:47–61.

Muller, Edward N., and Mitchell A. Seligson. 1987. "Inequality and Insurgency." *American Political Science Review* 81:425–52.

Muller, Edward N., and Erich Weede. 1990. "Cross-National Variations in Political Violence: A Rational Action Approach." *Journal of Conflict Resolution* 34:624–51.

Muller, Edward N., and Erich Weede. 1994. "Theories of Rebellion Relative Deprivation and Power Contention." *Rationality and Society* 6(1):40–57.

Mumford, Andrew. 2013. "Proxy Warfare and the Future of Conflict." *The RUSI Journal* 158(2):40–46.

Murdoch, James C., and Todd Sandler. 2002. "Economic Growth, Civil Wars, and Spatial Spillovers." *Journal of Conflict Resolution* 46(1):91–110.

Murdoch, James C., and Todd Sandler. 2004. "Civil Wars and Economic Growth: Spatial Dispersion." *American Journal of Political Science* 48(1):138–51.

Murshed, S. Mansoob, and Scott Gates. 2005. "Spatial-Horizontal Inequality and the Maoist Insurgency in Nepal." *Review of Development Economics* 9(1):121–34.

Mylonas, Harris. 2012. *The Politics of Nation-Building: Making Co-Nationals, Refugees, and Minorities.* New York: Cambridge University Press.

Nalepa, Monika. 2010. *Skeletons in the Closet: Transitional Justice in Post-Communist Europe.* Cambridge: Cambridge University Press.

Nathan, Laurie. 1999. "When Push Comes to Shove: The Failure of International Mediation in African Civil Wars." *Track Two* 8(2):1–23.

Nevins, Joseph. 2005. *A Not-So-Distant Horror: Mass Violence in East Timor.* Ithaca, NY: Cornell University Press.

Nichols, Angela D. 2014. "Understanding the Limitations of Truth Commission Impact." Unpublished doctoral dissertation, University of North Texas.

Nilsson, Anders. 2008a. *Dangerous Liaisons: Why Ex-Combatants Return to Violence, Cases from the Republic of Congo and Sierra Leone.* Uppsala: Department of Peace and Conflict Research, Uppsala University.

Nilsson, Desirée. 2008b. "Partial Peace: Rebel Groups Inside and Outside of Civil War Settlements." *Journal of Peace Research* 45(4):479–95.

Nisbett, Richard E., and Dov Cohen. 1996. *Culture of Honor: The Psychology of Violence in the South.* New York: Westview Press.

Nitzschke, Heiko, and Kaysie Studdard. 2005. "The Legacies of War Economies: Challenges and Options for Peacemaking and Peacebuilding." *International Peacekeeping* 12(2):222–39.

Nordås, Ragnhild, and Nils Petter Gleditsch. 2007. "Climate Change and Conflict." *Political Geography* 26(6):627–38.

Nordhaus, William D., and Xi Chen. 2009. "Geography: Graphics and Economics." *The B.E. Journal of Economic Analysis & Policy* 9(2):1–12.

Nordic Agency for Development and Ecology (NORDECO). 2010. "Impacts of Dadaab Refugee Camps on Host Communities." Draft Study Report.

Obermeyer, Ziad, Christopher J. L. Murray, and Emmanuela Gakidou. 2008. "Fifty Years of Violent War Deaths from Vietnam to Bosnia: Analysis of Data from the World Health Survey Programme." *British Medical Journal* 336(7659):1482A–86.

O'Donnell, Guillermo, and Phillipe C. Schmitter. 1986. *Transitions from Authoritarian Rule: Tentative Conclusions about Uncertain Democracies.* Baltimore, MD: Johns Hopkins University Press.

Ohlson, Thomas. 2008. "Understanding Causes of War and Peace." *European Journal of International Relations* 14(1):133–60.

O'Loughlin, John, Andrew M. Linke, Frank D. W. Witmer. 2014a. "Effects of Temperature and Precipitation Variability on the Risk of Violence in Sub-Saharan Africa, 1980–2012." *Proceedings of the National Academy of Sciences* 111(47):16712–17.

O'Loughlin, John, Andrew M. Linke, and Frank D. W. Witmer. 2014b. "Modeling and Data Choices Sway Conclusions About Climate-Conflict Links." *Proceedings of the National Academy of Sciences* 111(6):2054–55.

O'Loughlin, John, Michael D. Ward, Corey L. Lofdahl, Jordin S. Cohen, David S. Brown, David Reilly, Kristian Skrede Gleditsch, and Michael Shin. 1998. "The Diffusion of Democracy, 1945–1994." *Annals of the Association of American Geographers* 88(4):545–74.

Olsen, Tricia D., Leigh A. Payne, and Andrew G. Reiter. 2010a. "Transitional Justice in the World, 1970–2007: Insights from a New Dataset." *Journal of Peace Research* 47:803.

Olsen, Tricia D., Leigh A. Payne, and Andrew G. Reiter. 2010b. *Transitional Justice in Balance: Comparing Processes, Weighing Efficacy.* Washington, DC: United States Institute of Peace Press.

Olsen, Tricia D., Leigh A. Payne, and Andrew G. Reiter. 2010c. "The Justice Balance: When Transitional Justice Improves Human Rights and Democracy." *Human Rights Quarterly* 32(4):980–1007.

Olson, Mancur. 1982. *The Rise and Decline of Nations.* New Haven: Yale University Press.

Olson, Mancur. 1993. "Dictatorship, Democracy, and Development." *American Political Science Review* 87:567–76.

O'Malley, Brendan. 2010. "Education under Attack 2010." Paris, UNESCO.

Oneal, John R., and Bruce M. Russett. 1999. "The Kantian Peace: The Pacific Benefits of Democracy, Interdependence, and International Organizations, 1885–1992." *World Politics* 52(1):1–37.

Opp, Karl-Dieter. 1994. "Repression and Revolutionary Action." *Rationality and Society* 6:101–38.

Organski, A. F. K., and Jacek Kugler. 1980. *The War Ledger*. Chicago: Chicago University Press.

Osgood, D. Wayne, Janet K. Wilson, Patrick M. O'Malley, Jerald G. Bachman, and Lloyd D. Johnston. 1996. "Routine Activities and Individual Deviant Behavior." *American Sociological Review*: 61 (4):635–55.

Østby, Gudrun. 2008. "Polarization, Horizontal Inequalities and Violent Civil Conflict." *Journal of Peace Research* 45(2):143–62.

Østby, Gudrun, Ragnhild Nordås, and Jan Ketil Rød. 2009. "Regional Inequalities and Civil Conflict in Sub-Saharan Africa." *International Studies Quarterly* 53(2):301–24.

Ottmann, Martin, and Johannes Vüellers. 2015. "The Power-Sharing Event Dataset(PSED):A New Dataset on the Promises and Practices of Power-Sharing in Post-Conflict Countries." *Conflict Management and Peace Science* 32(3):327–50.

Oyefusi, Aderoju. 2008. "Oil and the Probability of Rebel Participation Among Youths in the Niger Delta of Nigeria." *Journal of Peace Research* 45(4):539–55.

Paris, Roland. 2000. "Broadening the Study of Peace Operations." *International Studies Review* 2:27–44.

Paris, Roland. 2004. *At War's End: Building Peace after Civil Conflict*. Cambridge: Cambridge University Press.

Parkinson, Sarah E. 2013. "Organizing Rebellion: Rethinking High-Risk Mobilization and Social Networks in War." *American Political Science Review* 107(3):418–32.

Paul, Christopher, Colin P. Clarke, and Beth Grill. 2010. *Victory Has a Thousand Fathers: Sources of Success in Counterinsurgency*. Santa Monica: Rand Corporation.

Payne, James L. 2004. *A History of Force: Exploring the Worldwide Movement against Habits of Coercion, Bloodshed, and Mayhem*. Sandpoint, ID: Lytton.

Payne, Leigh A., and Kathryn Sikkink. 2014. "Transitional Justice Research Collaborative." Available online at http://www.transitionaljusticedata.com.

Pearlman, Wendy. 2011. *Violence, Nonviolence, and the Palestinian National Movement*. Cambridge: Cambridge University Press.

Pearlman, Wendy. 2013. "Emotions and the Microfoundations of the Arab Uprisings." *Perspectives on Politics* 11(2):387–409.

Pearson, Frederic S. 1974. "Geographic Proximity and Foreign Military Intervention." *Journal of Conflict Resolution* 18(3):432–60.

Pedersen, Duncan. 2002. "Political Violence, Ethnic Conflict, and Contemporary Wars: Broad Implications for Health and Social Well-Being," *Social Science and Medicine* 55(2):175–90.

Peksen, Dursun, Zeynep Taydas, and A. Cooper Drury. 2008. "Taxation, State Building, Welfare Policy and Civil Wars," paper presented at the Annual Convention of the International Studies Association, San Francisco, CA.

Petersen, Roger D. 2002. *Understanding Ethnic Violence: Fear, Hatred, and Resentment in Twentieth-Century Eastern Europe*. Cambridge: Cambridge University Press.

Petersen, Roger D. 2011. *Western Intervention in the Balkans: The Strategic Use of Emotion in Conflict*. Cambridge: Cambridge University Press.

Pettersson, Therése. 2011. "Pillars of Strength: External Support to Warring Parties." In *States in Armed Conflict 2010*, edited by Therése Pettersson and Lotta Themnér. Uppsala: Department of Peace and Conflict Research, Uppsala University.

Pettersson, Therése, and Lotta Themnér, eds. 2012. *States in Armed Conflict 2011*. Research Report 99. Uppsala: Department of Peace and Conflict Research, Uppsala University.

Pettersson, Therése, and Peter Wallensteen. 2015. "Armed Conflicts, 1946–2014." *Journal of Peace Research* 52(4):536–50.

Phayal, Anup, Prabin Khadka, and Clayton L. Thyne. 2015. "What Makes an Ex-Combatant Happy? A Micro Analysis of Disarmament, Demobilization and Reintegration in South Sudan." *International Studies Quarterly*, 59:654-668.

Phillips, Brian J. 2014. "Civil War, Spillover and Neighbors' Military Spending." *Conflict Management and Peace Science* 32(4):425–42.

Pickering, Jeffrey. 2001. "The Conflict-Prone and the Confict-Weary: War Outcomes and Types of Military Intervention, 1946–1996." *Journal of Political and Military Sociology* 29(2):221–39.

Pickering, Jeffrey, and Mark Peceny. 2006. "Forging Democracy at Gunpoint." *International Studies Quarterly* 50:539–60.

Pillar, Paul. 1983. *Negotiating Peace: War Termination as a Bargaining Process*. Princeton: Princeton University Press.

Pin-Fat, Véronique, and Maria Stern. 2005. "The Scripting of Private Jessica Lynch: Bio-politics, Gender, and the 'Feminization'? of the US Military." *Alternatives: Global, Local, Political* 30(1):25–53.

Pinker, Steven. 2011. *The Better Angels of Our Nature: The Decline of Violence in History and Its Causes*. New York: Penguin.

Plümper, Thomas, and Eric Neumayer. 2006. "The Unequal Burden of War: The Effect of Armed Conflict on the Gender Gap in Life Expectancy." *International Organization* 60(3):723–54.

Poder, Thomas G. 2011. "What Is Really Social Capital? A Critical Review." *The American Sociologist* 42(4):341–67.

Poe, Stephen, Sabine Carey, and Tania Vazquez. 2001. "How Are These Pictures Different? A Quantitative Comparison of US State Department and Amnesty International Human Rights Reports, 1976–1995." *Human Rights Quarterly* 23(3):650–77.

Poe, Steven C., and C. Neal Tate. 1994. "Repression of Human Rights to Personal Integrity in the 1980s: A Global Analysis." *American Political Science Review* 88(4):853–72.

Pollan, Michael. 2006. *The Omnivore's Dilemma: A Natural History of Four Meals*. New York: Penguin.

Posen, Barry R. 1993. "The Security Dilemma and Ethnic Conflict." *Survival* 35:27–47.

Posner, Daniel N. 2004. "Measuring Ethnic Fractionalization in Africa." *American Journal of Political Science* 48(4):849–63.

Potts, Malcolm, and Thomas Hayden. 2008. *Sex and War: How Biology Explains Warfare and Terrorism and Offers a Path to a Safer World*. Dallas: BenBella Books.

Pouligny, Beatrice. 2006. *Peace Operations Seen from Below: UN Missions and Local People*. London: C. Hurst and Co.

Powell, Robert. 1999. *In the Shadow of Power: States and Strategies in International Politics*. Princeton: Princeton University Press.

Powell, Robert. 2006. "War as a Commitment Problem." *International Organizations* 60:169–203.

Powell, Robert. 2012. "Persistent Fighting and Shifting Power." *American Journal of Political Science* 56(3):620–37.

Powers, Kathy L., and Kim Proctor. 2015. "Victim's Justice in the Aftermath of Political Violence: Why Do Countries Award Reparations?" forthcoming in *Foreign Policy Analysis*.

Pratto, Felicia, Jim Sidanius, Lisa M Stallworth, and Bertram F Malle. 1994. "Social Dominance Orientation: A Personality Variable Predicting Social and Political Attitudes." *Journal of Personality and Social Psychology* 67(4):741.

Prorok, Alyssa. N.d. "Leader Incentives and the Termination of Civil War." Manuscript, University of Iowa.

Prunier, Gérard. 2004. "Rebel Movements and Proxy Warfare: Uganda, Sudan and the Congo (1986–99)." *African Affairs* 103(412):359–83.

Psacharopoulos, George, and Harry A. Patrinos. 2004. "Returns to Investment in Education: A Further Update." *Education Economics* 12(2):111–34.

Pugh, Michael. 2004. "Peacekeeping and Critical Theory." *International Peacekeeping* 11:39–58.

Pugh, Michael, and Neil Cooper. 2004. *War Economies in a Regional Context*. Boulder, CO: Lynne Rienner.

Pushkina, Darya. 2006. "A Recipe for Success? Ingredients of a Successful Peacekeeping Mission." *International Peacekeeping* 13:133–49.

Putnam, Robert D. 1993. *Making Democracy Work: Civic Traditions in Modern Italy*. Princeton: Princeton University Press.

Querido, Chyanda M. 2009. "State-Sponsored Mass Killing in African Wars—Greed or Grievance?" *International Advances in Economic Research* 15:351–61.

Quinn, J. Michael, T. David Mason, and Mehmet Gurses. 2007. "Sustaining the Peace: Determinants of Civil War Recurrence." *International Interactions* 33:167–93.

Raleigh, Clionadh, and Håvard Hegre. 2009. "Population, Size, and Civil War: A Geographically Disaggregated Analysis." *Political Geography* 28(4):224–38.

Raleigh, Clionadh, and Dominic Kniveton. 2012. "Come Rain or Shine: An Analysis of Conflict and Climate Variability in East Africa." *Journal of Peace Research* 49(1):51–64.

Raleigh, Clionadh, Andrew Linke, Håvard Hegre, and Joakim Karlsen. 2010. "Introducing ACLED: An Armed Conflict Location and Event Dataset." *Journal of Peace Research* 47(5):651–60.

Raleigh, Clionadh, Andrew Linke, and John O'Loughlin. 2014. "Extreme Temperatures and Violence." *Nature Climate Change* 4(2):76–77.

Raleigh, Clionadh, and Henrik Urdal. 2007. "Climate Change, Environmental Degradation and Armed Conflict." *Political Geography* 26(6):674–94.

Ramsay, Kristopher. 2008. "Settling It on the Field: Battlefield Events and War Termination." *Journal of Conflict Resolution* 52(6):850–79.

Rasler, Karen. 1996. "Concessions, Repression, and Political Protest in the Iranian Revolution." *American Sociological Review*: 132–52.

Record, Jeffrey. 2006. "External Assistance: Enabler of Insurgent Success." *Parameters* 36(3):36.

Record, Jeffrey. 2007. *Beating Goliath: Why Insurgencies Win*. Washington, DC: Potomac Books.

Reeder, Bryce W., Ashly Adam Townsen, and Matthew Powers. 2015. "Hot Spot Peacekeeping." *International Studies Review* 17(1):46–66.

Regan, Patrick M. 1996, "Conditions of Successful Third-party Intervention in Intrastate Conflicts." *Journal of Conflict Resolution* 40(2): 336–59.

Regan, Patrick M. 1998. "Choosing to Intervene: Outside Interventions in Internal Conflicts." *Journal of Politics* 60(3):754–79.

Regan, Patrick M. 2000. *Civil Wars and Foreign Powers: Outside Intervention in Intrastate Conflict*. Ann Arbor, MI: University of Michigan Press.

Regan, Patrick M. 2002. "Third Party Interventions and the Duration of Intrastate Conflict." *Journal of Conflict Resolution* 46(1):55–73.

Regan, Patrick M. 2009. *Sixteen Million One: Understanding Civil War*. Boulder, CO: Paradigm Publishers.

Regan, Patrick M. 2010. "Interventions into Civil Wars: A Retrospective Survey with Prospective Ideas." *Civil Wars* 12(4):456–76.

Regan, Patrick M., and Aysegul Aydin. 2006. "Diplomacy and Other Forms of Intervention in Civil Wars." *Journal of Conflict Resolution* 50(5):736–56.

Regan, Patrick M., Richard W. Frank, and Aysegul Aydin. 2009. "Diplomatic Interventions and Civil War: A New Dataset." *Journal of Peace Research* 46(1):135–46.

Regan, Patrick M., and Errol A. Henderson. 2002. "Democracy, Threats and Political Repression in Developing Countries: Are Democracies Internally Less Violent?" *Third World Quarterly* 23:119–36.

Regan, Patrick M., and Daniel Norton. 2005. "Greed, Grievance, and Mobilization in Civil Wars." *Journal of Conflict Resolution* 49(3):319–36.

Reiter, Dan. 2003. "Exploring the Bargaining Model of War." *Perspectives on Politics* 1(1):27–43.

Richardson, Lewis Fry. 1960. *Arms and Insecurity: A Mathematical Study of the Causes and Origins of War*. Pittsburgh: Boxwood Press.

Robison, Lindon J., and A. Allan Schmid. 1994. "Can Agriculture Prosper without Increase Social Capital?" *Choices* 9(4):29–31.

Roble, Muhaydin Ahmed. 2011. "Somalia's Famine Contributes to Popular Revolt against al-Shabaab Militants." *Terrorism Monitor* 9(32):3–5.

Rodriguez, Catherine, and Fabio Sánchez. 2009. "Armed Conflict Exposure, Human Capital Investments and Child Labour: Evidence from Colombia." HiCN Working Paper no. 68, Households in Conflict Network. www.hicn.org.

Rodrik, Dani, Arvind Subramanian, and Francesco Trebbi. 2004. "Institutions Rule: The Primacy of Institutions over Geography and Integration in Economic Development." *Journal of Economic Growth* 9(2):131–65.

Roeder, Philip G. 2007. *Where Nation-States Come From: Institutional Change in the Age of Nationalism*. Princeton: Princeton University Press.

Roeder, Philip G., and Donald S. Rothchild. 2005. *Sustainable Peace: Power and Democracy after Civil Wars*. Ithaca, NY: Cornell University Press.

Rogowski, Ronald. 1974. *Rational Legitimacy: A Theory of Political Support*. Princeton: Princeton University Press.

Roper, Steven D., and Lilian A. Barria. 2009. "Why Do States Commission the Truth? Political Considerations in the Establishment of African Truth and Reconciliation Commissions." *Human Rights Review* 10(3):373–91.

Rosenau, James N. 1964. "Internal War as an International Event." In *International Aspects of Civil Strife*, edited by James N. Rosenau, 14–44. Princeton: Princeton University Press.

Rosenau, James N. 1968. "The Concept of Intervention." *Journal of International Affairs* 22(2):165–76.

Rosenau, James N. 1969. "Intervention as a Scientific Concept." *Journal of Conflict Resolution* 13(2):149–71.

Ross, Michael L. 2001. "Does Oil Hinder Democracy?" *World Politics* 53(3):325–61.

Ross, Michael L. 2003. "Resources and Rebellion in Aceh, Indonesia." Unpublished manuscript, University of California, Los Angeles.

Ross, Michael L. 2004a. "What Do We Know about Natural Resources and Civil War?" *Journal of Peace Research* 41(3):337–56.

Ross, Michael L. 2004b. "How Do Natural Resources Influence Civil War? Evidence from Thirteen Cases." *International Organization* 58(1):35–67.

Ross, Michael L. 2006. "A Closer Look at Oil, Diamonds, and Civil War." *Annual Review Political Science* 9:265–300.

Ross, Michael L. 2012. *The Oil Curse.* Princeton: Princeton University Press.

Ross, Michael L. 2014. "What Have We Learned about The Resource Curse?" Manuscript, UCLA.

Rothchild, Donald. 2002. "Settlement Terms and Post-Agreement Stability." In *Ending Civil Wars: The Implementation of Peace Agreements*, edited by Stephen John Stedman, Donald Rothchild, and Elizabeth Cousens. Boulder, CO: Lynne Rienner.

Rothchild, Donald, and Caroline Hartzell. 1993. "The Peace Process in Sudan, 1971–1972." In *Stopping the Killing: How Civil Wars End*, edited by Roy Licklider. New York: New York University Press.

Rothchild, Donald, and Philip G. Roeder. 2005. "Dilemmas of State-Building in Divided Societies." In *Sustainable Peace: Power and Democracy after Civil Wars*, edited by Philip Roeder and Donald Rothchild. Ithaca, NY, and London: Cornell University Press.

Rudolfsen, Ida, and Nils Petter Gleditsch. 2015. "Are Muslim Countries More Warprone?" *Policy Brief.* Oslo: PRIO, www.prio.org/Publications/Publication/?x=8645.

Rüegger, Seraina, and Heidrun Bohnet. 2012. "No Undifferentiated Mass: Introducing a Quantitative Data Set on the Ethnic Composition of Refugee Movements." Paper prepared for presentation at ENCoRe Meeting in Oslo, September 21–22.

Ruggeri, Andrea, Theodora-Ismene Gizelis, and Han Dorussen. 2013. "Managing Mistrust: An Analysis of Cooperation with UN Peacekeeping in Africa." *Journal of Conflict Resolution* 57(3):387–409.

Rummel, Rudolph J. 1995. "Democracy, Power, Genocide, and Mass Murder." *Journal of Conflict Resolution* 39(1):3–26.

Russell, Earl Bertrand, and Arthur William. 1964. "Population Pressure and War." In *The Population Crisis and the Use of World Resources: World Academy of Art and Science Volume II*, edited by Stuart Mudd, 1–5. The Hague: Springer.

Russett, Bruce M. 1969. "Who Pays for Defense?" *American Political Science Review* 63(2):412–26.

Russett, Bruce M. 1970. *What Price Vigilance?* New Haven, CT: Yale University Press.

Russett, Bruce M. and John R. Oneal. *Triangulating Peace: Democracy, Interdependence, and International Organizations.* New York: Norton.

Russett, Bruce M., John R. Oneal, and Michaeline Cox. 2000. "Clash of Civilizations, or Realism and Liberalism Déja Vu? Some Evidence." *Journal of Peace Research* 37(5):583–608.

Rutter, Michael. 1985. "Resilience in the Face of Adversity: Protective Factors and Resistance to Psychiatric Disorder." *British Journal of Psychiatry* 147:598–611.

Sachs, Jeffrey, and Andrew Warner. 2001. "The Curse of Natural Resources," *European Economic Review* 45(4–6):827–38.

Saideman, Stephen M. 1997. "Explaining the International Relations of Secessionist Conflicts: Vulnerability versus Ethnic Ties." *International Organization* 51(4):721–53.

Saideman, Stephen. 2001. *The Ties That Divide: Ethnic Politics, Foreign Policy and International Conflict.* New York: Colombia University Press.

Saideman, Stephen M. 2002. "Discrimination in International Relations: Analyzing External Support for Ethnic Groups." *Journal of Peace Research* 39(1):27–50.

Saideman, Stephen M., and R. William Ayres. 2000. "Determining the Causes of Irredentism: Logit Analyses of Minorities at Risk Data from the 1980s and 1990s." *Journal of Politics* 62(4):1126–44.

Salehyan, Idean. 2007. "Transnational Rebels: Neighboring States as Sanctuary for Rebel Groups." *World Politics* 59(2):217–42.

Salehyan, Idean. 2009. *Rebels Without Borders: Transnational Insurgencies and World Politics.* Ithaca, NY: Cornell University Press.

Salehyan, Idean. 2010. "The Delegation of War to Rebel Organizations." *Journal of Conflict Resolution* 54(3):493–515.

Salehyan, Idean. 2014. "Climate Change and Conflict: Making Sense of Disparate Findings." *Political Geography* 43:1–5.

Salehyan, Idean. 2015. "Best Practices in the Collection of Conflict Data." *Journal of Peace Research* 52(1):105–9.

Salehyan, Idean, and Kristian Skrede Gleditsch. 2006. "Refugees and the Spread of Civil War." *International Organization* 60(2):335–66.

Salehyan, Idean, Kristian Skrede Gleditsch, and David E. Cunningham. 2011. "Explaining External Support for Insurgent Groups." *International Organization* 65(4):709–44.

Salehyan, Idean, and Cullen S. Hendrix. 2014. "Climate Shocks and Political Violence." *Global Environmental Change* 28:239–50.

Salehyan, Idean, Cullen S. Hendrix, Jesse Hamner, Christina Case, Christopher Linebarger, Emily Stull, and Jennifer Williams. 2012. "Social Conflict in Africa: A New Database." *International Interactions* 38(4):503–11.

Salehyan, Idean, Dean Siroky, and Reed Wood. 2014. "External Rebel Sponsorship and Civilian Abuse: A Principal-Agent Analysis of Wartime Atrocities." *International Organization* 68(3):633–61.

Sambanis, Nicholas. 2001. "Do Ethnic and Nonethnic Civil Wars Have the Same Causes? A Theoretical and Empirical Inquiry (Part 1)." *Journal of Conflict Resolution* 45(3):259–82.

Sambanis, Nicholas. 2004a. "What Is Civil War? Conceptual and Empirical Complexities of an Operational Definition." *Journal of Conflict Resolution* 48(6):814–58.

Sambanis, Nicholas. 2004b. "Using Case Studies to Expand Economic Models of Civil War." *Perspectives on Politics* 2(02):259–79.

Sambanis, Nicholas and Jonah Schulhofer-Wohl. 2009. "What's in a Line? Is Partition a Solution to Civil War?" *International Security* 34:82–118.

Sambanis, Nicholas, and Moses Shayo. 2013. "Social Identification and Ethnic Conflict." *American Political Science Review* 107(2):294–325.

Samset, Ingrid. 2011. "Building a Repressive Peace: The Case of Post-Genocide Rwanda." *Journal of Intervention and Statebuilding* 5:265–83.

Sany, J., 2010. "Education and Conflict in Cote d'Ivoire." USIP Special Report. United States Institute of Peace. http://www.usip.org/files/resources/sr235sany_final_lowres–1.pdf.

Sarkees, Meredith Reid, and Frank Whelon Wayman. 2010. *Resort to War: A Data Guide to Interstate, Extra-state, Intra-state, and Non-state Wars, 1816–2007.* Washington, DC: CQ Press.

Savelsberg, Joachim. 2010. *Crime and Human Rights: Criminology of Genocide and Atrocities.* London: Sage.

Savun, Burcu. 2008. "Information, Bias, and Mediation Success." *International Studies Quarterly* 52(1):25–47.

Schatz, Edward. 2013. *Modern Clan Politics: The Power of "Blood" in Kazakhstan and Beyond.* Seattle: University of Washington Press.

Schock, Kurt. 2005. *Unarmed Insurrections: People Power Movements in Nondemocracies.* Minneapolis: University of Minnesota Press.

Schoepf, Brooke G. 2002. "'Mobutu's Disease': A Social History of AIDS in Kinshasa." *Review of African Political Economy* 29(93–94):561–73.

Schrodt, Phillip A. 2012. "Precedents, Progress, and Prospects in Political Event Data." *International Interactions* 38(4):546–69.

Schrodt, Philip A., and Deborah J. Gerner. 1994. "Validity Assessment of a Machine-Coded Event Data Set for the Middle East, 1982–92." *American Journal of Political Science* 38(3): 825–54.

Schumpeter, Joseph. 1955. *Imperialism; Social Classes: Two Essays.* Translated by Heinz Norden. New York: Meridian Books.

Scott, James M. 1996. *Deciding to Intervene: The Reagan Doctrine and American Foreign Policy.* Durham, NC: Duke University Press.

Scruton, Roger. 1983. *A Dictionary of Political Thought.* London: Pan Books.

Selway, Joel S. 2011. "Cross-Cuttingness, Cleavage Structures and Civil War Onset." *British Journal of Political Science* 41(1):111–38.

Sen, Somnath. 1990. "Debt, Financial Flows and International Security." In *SIPRI Yearbook, World Armament and Disarmament,* 203–17. New York: Oxford University Press.

Sengupta, Somini, 2003. "Innocence of Youth as Victim of Congo War." *New York Times,* June 23.

Seymour, Lee J. M. 2014a. "Let's Bullshit! Arguing, Bargaining and Dissembling over Darfur." *European Journal of International Relations* 20(3):571–95.

Seymour, Lee J. M. 2014b. "Why Factions Switch Sides in Civil Wars: Rivalry, Patronage and Realignment in Sudan." *International Security* 39(2):92–131.

Seymour, Lee J. M., Kristin M. Bakke, and Kathleen G. Cunningham. 2016. "E Pluribus Unum, Ex Uno Plures: Competition, Violence, and Fragmentation in Ethnopolitical Movements." *Journal of Peace Research* 53(1):3–18.

Shalita, Nicholas. 1994. "The Sudan Conflict (1983–)." In *The True Cost of Conflict,* edited by Michael Cranna, 135–54. London: Earthscan.

Shapiro, Robert Y., and Harpreet Mahajan. 1986. "Gender Differences in Policy Preferences: A Summary of Trends from the 1960s to the 1980s." *Public Opinion Quarterly* 50(1):42–61.

Sharlach, Lisa. 1999. "Gender and Genocide in Rwanda: Women as Agents and Objects of Genocide." *Journal of Genocide Research* 1(3):387–99.

Shaw, Rosalind, Lars Waldorf, and Pierre Hazan, eds. 2010. *Localizing Transitional Justice: Interventions and Priorities after Mass Violence.* Stanford: Stanford University Press.

Shellman, Stephen M. 2004. "Time Series Intervals and Statistical Inference: The Effects of Temporal Aggregation on Event Data Analysis." *Political Analysis* 12(1):97–104.

Shellman, Stephen M. 2006. "Process Matters: Conflict and Cooperation in Sequential Government-Dissident Interactions." *Security Studies* 15(4):563–99.

Shellman, Stephen M., Brian P. Levey, and Joseph K. Young. 2013. "Shifting Sands Explaining and Predicting Phase Shifts by Dissident Organizations." *Journal of Peace Research* 50(3):319–36.

Shelton, Allison M., Szymon M. Stojek, and Patricia L. Sullivan. 2013. "What Do We Know about Civil War Outcomes?" *International Studies Review* 15(4):515–38.

Shemyakina, Olga. 2011. "The Effect of Armed Conflict on Accumulation of Schooling: Results from Tajikistan." *Journal of Development Economics* 95(2):186–200.

Sherbourne, Cathy D., and Anita L. Stewart. 1991. "The MOS Social Support Survey." *Social Science and Medicine* 32(6):705–14.

Sianesi, Barbara, and John Van Reenen. 2003. "The Returns to Education: Macroeconomics." *Journal of Economic Surveys* 17(2):157–200.

Sibley, Chris G, Andrew Robertson, and Marc S. Wilson. 2006. "Social Dominance Orientation and Right-Wing Authoritarianism: Additive and Interactive Effects." *Political Psychology* 27(5):755–68.

Sikkink, Kathryn. 2011. *The Justice Cascade: How Human Rights Prosecutions Are Changing World Politics*. New York: W.W. Norton & Company.

Sikkink, Kathryn, and Hun Joon Kim. 2013. "The Justice Cascade: The Origins and Effectiveness of Prosecutions of Human Rights Violations." *Annual Review of Law and Sociology* 9:269–85.

Sikkink, Kathryn, and Carrie Booth Walling. 2007. "The Impact of Human Rights Trials in Latin America." *Journal of Peace Research* 44:427.

Singer, J. David, Stuart Bremer, and John Stuckey. 1972. "Capability Distribution, Uncertainty, and Major Power War, 1820–1965." In *Peace, War, and Numbers*, edited by Bruce M. Russett. Beverly Hills: Sage.

Sisk, Timothy D. 2008. "Peacebuilding as Democratization: Findings and Recommendations." In *From War to Democracy: Dilemmas of Peacebuilding*, edited by Anna K. Jarstad and Timothy D. Sisk, 239–59. Cambridge: Cambridge University Press.

Sisk, Timothy D. 2009. *International Mediation in Civil Wars: Bargaining with Bullets*. London: Routledge.

Siverson, Randolph M., and Harvey Starr. 1991. *The Diffusion of War: A Study in Opportunity and Willingness*. Ann Arbor, MI: University of Michigan Press.

Sjoberg, Laura, and Caron E Gentry. 2007. *Mothers, Monsters, Whores: Women's Violence in Global Politics*. London and New York: Zed Books.

Skaar, Elin. 1999. "Truth Commissions, Trials—or Nothing? Policy Options in Democratic Transitions." *Third World Quarterly* 20(6):1109–28.

Skarbek, David. 2014. *The Social Order of the Underworld: How Prison Gangs Govern the American Penal System*. Oxford: Oxford University Press.

Skocpol, Theda. 1979. *States and Social Revolutions: A Comparative Analysis of France, Russia and China*. Cambridge: Cambridge University Press.

Skocpol, Theda, Peter B. Evans, and Dietrich Rueschemeyer, eds. 1985. *Bringing the State Back In*. New York and Cambridge: Cambridge University Press.

Small, Melvin, and J. David Singer. 1982. *Resort to Arms: International and Civil War, 1816–1980*. Beverly Hills, CA: Sage.

Smallman-Raynor, Matthew R., and Andrew D. Cliff. 1991. "Civil War and the Spread of AIDS in Central Africa." *Epidemiology and Infection* 107(1):69–80.

Smith, Alastair, and Allan Stam. 2003. "Mediation and Peacekeeping in a Random Walk Model of Civil and Interstate War." *International Studies Review* 5:115–35.

Smith, Benjamin. 2004. "Oil Wealth and Regime Survival in the Developing World, 1960–1999." *American Journal of Political Science* 48(2):232–46.

Smith, Benjamin. 2007. *Hard Times in the Lands of Plenty: Oil Politics in Iran and Indonesia.* Ithaca, NY: Cornell University Press.

Smith, Benjamin. 2012. "Oil Wealth and Political Power in Southeast Asia." In Robert E. Looney, ed. *Handbook of Oil Politics.* New York: Routledge.

Smith, Benjamin. 2015. "Resource Wealth as Rent Leverage: Rethinking the Oil-Stability Nexus." *Conflict Management and Peace Science* forthcoming.

Smith, Todd G. 2014. "Feeding Unrest: Disentangling the Causal Relationship between Food Price Shocks and Sociopolitical Conflict in Urban Africa." *Journal of Peace Research* 51(6):679–95.

Smith, Tony. 1994. "In Defense of Intervention." *Foreign Affairs* 73(6): 34–46.

Smyth, Russell, and Paresh K. Narayan. 2009. "A Panel Data Analysis of the Military Expenditure-External Debt Nexus: Evidence from Six Middle Eastern Countries." *Journal of Peace Research* 46(2):235–50.

Snodgrass, Donald R. 2004. "When States Fail: Causes and Consequences." In *Restoring Economic Functioning in Failed State*, edited by Robert I. Rotberg, 256–68. Princeton: Princeton University Press.

Snyder, Jack, and Leslie Vinjamuri. 2003/2004. "Trials and Errors: Principles and Pragmatism in Strategies of International Justice." *International Security* 28(3):5–44.

Snyder, Richard, and Ravi Bhavnani. 2005. "Diamonds, Blood, and Taxes: A Revenue-Centered Framework for Explaining Political Order." *Journal of Conflict Resolution* 49(4):563–97.

Sobek, David. 2010. "Masters of Their Domains: The Role of State Capacity in Civil Wars." *Journal of Peace Research* 47:267–71.

Solangon, Sarah, and Preeti Patel. 2012. "Sexual Violence against Men in Countries Affected by Armed Conflict." *Conflict, Security & Development* 12(4):417–42.

Solingen, Etel. 2012. "Of Dominoes and Firewalls: The Domestic, Regional, and Global Politics of International Diffusion." *International Studies Quarterly* 56(4):631–44.

Sorens, Jason. 2011. "Mineral Production, Territory, and Ethnic Rebellion: The Role of Rebel Constituencies." *Journal of Peace Research* 48(5):571–85.

Spagat, Michael, Andrew Mack, Tara Cooper, and Joakim Kreutz. 2009. "Estimating War Deaths: An Arena of Contestation." *Journal of Conflict Resolution* 53(6):934–50.

Staniland, Paul. 2012. "Between a Rock and a Hard Place: Insurgent Fratricide, Ethnic Defection, and the Rise of Pro-State Paramilitaries." *Journal of Conflict Resolution* 56(1):16–40.

Staniland, Paul. 2014. *Networks of Rebellion: Explaining Insurgent Cohesion and Collapse.* Ithaca, NY: Cornell University Press.

Stanley, William. 1996. *The Protection Racket State: Elite Politics, Military Extortion, and Civil War in El Salvador.* Philadelphia: Temple University Press.

Stanley, William, and David Holiday. 2002. "Broad Participation, Diffuse Responsibility: Peace Implementation in Guatemala." In *Ending Civil Wars: The Implementation of Peace Agreements*, edited by Stephen John Stedman, Donald Rothchild, and Elizabeth M. Cousens. Boulder, CO: Lynne Rienner.

Stanton, Jessica A. 2013. "Terrorism in the Context of Civil War." *Journal of Politics* 75(4):1009–22.

Starr, Harvey. 1978. "'Opportunity' and 'Willingness': Empirical and Theoretical Research in International Relations." *International Interactions* 4:363–87.

Stearns, Jason. 2011. *Dancing in the Glory of Monsters: The Collapse of the Congo and the Great War of Africa.* New York: Public Affairs.

Stedman, Stephen John. 1993. "The New Interventionists." *Foreign Affairs* 72(1):1–16.

Stedman, Stephen J. 1996. "Negotiation and Mediation in Internal Conflict." In *The International Dimension of Internal Conflict*, edited by Michael Edward Brown, 341–76. Cambridge, MA: MIT Press.

Stedman, Stephen J. 1997. "Spoiler Problems in Peace Processes." *International Security* 22(2):5–53.

Stedman, Stephen J., and Fred Tanner. 2003. *Refugee Manipulation: War, Politics, and the Abuse of Human Suffering*. Washington, DC: Brookings Institution Press.

Steinert, Janina Isabel, and Sonja Grimm. 2015. "Too Good to Be True? United Nations Peacebuilding and the Democratization of War-torn States." *Conflict Management and Peace Science* 32:513–35.

Stepanova, Ekaterina. 2009. "Trends in Armed Conflicts: One-Sided Violence against Civilians." In *SIPRI Yearbook 2009: Armaments, Disarmament and International Security*, 39–68. New York: Oxford University Press.

Stephan, Maria J., and Erica Chenoweth. 2008. "Why Civil Resistance Works: The Strategic Logic of Nonviolent Conflict." *International Security* 33(1):7–44.

Stewart, Douglas B. 1991. "Economic Growth and the Defense Burden in Africa and Latin America: Simulations from A Dynamic Model." *Economic Development and Cultural Change* 40(1):189–207.

Stewart, Frances, and Frank Humphreys. 1997. "Civil Conflict in Developing Countries over the Last Quarter of a Century: An Empirical Overview of Economic and Social Consequences." *Oxford Development Studies* 25(1):11–41.

Strang, David. 1991. "Global Patterns of Decolonization, 1500–1987." *International Studies Quarterly* 35(4):429–54.

Straus, Scott. 2006. *The Order of Genocide: Race, Power and War in Rwanda*. Ithaca, NY: Cornell University Press.

Stromseth, Jane E. 2003. "Introduction: Goals and Challenges in the Pursuit of Accountability." In *Accountability for Atrocities: National and International Responses*, edited by Jane E. Stromseth. Ardsley, NY: Transnational Publishers.

Stromseth, Jane E., David Wippman, and Rosa Brooks. 2006. *Can Might Make Rights? Building the Rule of Law After Military Interventions*. New York: Cambridge University Press.

Sullivan, Patricia L. 2007. "War Aims and War Outcomes: Why Powerful States Lose Limited Wars." *Journal of Conflict Resolution* 51(3):496–524.

Sullivan, Patricia L. 2008. "Sustaining the Fight: A Cross-Sectional Time-Series Analysis of Public Support for Ongoing Military Interventions." *Conflict Management and Peace Science* 25(2):112–35.

Sullivan, Patricia L., and Johannes Karreth. Forthcoming "The Conditional Impact of Military Intervention on Internal Armed Conflict Outcomes." *Conflict Management and Peace Science*.

Sundberg, Ralph. 2016. "Value Stability and Change in an ISAF Contingent." *Journal of Personality* 84(1):91–101.

Sundberg, Ralph, and Erik Melander. 2013. "Introducing the UCDP Georeferenced Event Dataset." *Journal of Peace Research* 50(4):523–32.

Svensson, Isak. 2007. "Fighting with Faith Religion and Conflict Resolution in Civil Wars." *Journal of Conflict Resolution* 51(6):930–49.

Svensson, Isak. 2009. "Who Brings Which Peace? Biased versus Neutral Mediation and Institutional Peace Arrangements in Civil Wars." *Journal of Conflict Resolution* 53(3):446–69.

Svensson, Isak. 2012. *Ending Holy Wars: Religion and Conflict Resolution in Civil Wars*. Brisbane: University of Queensland Press.

Svensson, Isak. 2014a. "Conflict Resolution in Civil Wars." In *Routledge Handbook of Civil Wars,* edited by Edward Newman and Karl DeRouen Jr. London: Routledge.

Svensson, Isak. 2014b. "The Missing Jihad: The East Asian Peace and the Global Patterns of Religious Conflict." Paper presented to the 4th Annual Conference of the East Asian Peace Program, Beijing, October 30–November 1.

Swee, Eikl L. 2009. "On War and Schooling Attainment: The Case of Bosnia and Herzegovina." HiCN Working Paper no. 57, Households in Conflict Network. www.hicn.org.

Taber, Robert. 1970. *The War of the Flea: A Study of Guerrilla Warfare Theory and Practice.* London: Paladin.

Tamashiro, Tami. 2010. "Impact of Conflict on Children's Health and Disability." Background paper for EFA Global Monitoring Report 2011.

Taydas, Zeynep, and Dursun Peksen. 2007. "State Capacity, Quality of Governance and Civil War Onset," paper presented at the 48th Annual Convention of the International Studies Association, Chicago, IL.

Teitel, Ruti G. 2000. *Transitional Justice.* Oxford: Oxford University Press.

Teitel, Ruti G. 2003. "Transitional Justice Genealogy." *Harvard Human Rights Journal* 16:69.

Tessler, Mark, Jodi Nachtwey, and Audra Grant. 1999. "Further Tests of the Women and Peace Hypothesis: Evidence from Cross-National Survey Research in the Middle East." *International Studies Quarterly* 43(3):519–31.

Tessler, Mark, and Ina Warriner. 1997. "Gender, Feminism, and Attitudes toward International Conflict: Exploring Relationships with Survey Data from the Middle East." *World Politics* 49(02):250–81.

Theisen, Ole Magnus. 2008. "Blood and Soil? Resource Scarcity and Internal Armed Conflict Revisited." *Journal of Peace Research* 45(6):801–18.

Theisen, Ole Magnus, Helge Holtermann, and Halvard Buhaug. 2011/2012. "Climate Wars? Assessing the Claim that Drought Breeds Conflict." *International Security* 36(3):79–106.

Themnér, Anders. 2011. *Violence in Post-Conflict Societies: Remarginalization, Remobilizers and Relationships*: New York: Routledge.

Themnér, Lotta, and Peter Wallensteen. 2012. "Armed Conflicts, 1946–2011." *Journal of Peace Research* 49(4):565–75.

Themnér, Lotta, and Peter Wallensteen. 2014. "Armed Conflicts, 1946–2013." *Journal of Peace Research* 51(4):541–54.

Thies, Cameron. 2010. "Of Rulers, Rebels, and Revenue: State Capacity, Civil War Onset, and Primary Commodities." *Journal of Peace Research* 47(3):321–32.

Thomas, Jakana. 2014. "Rewarding Bad Behavior: How Governments Respond to Terrorism in Civil War." *American Journal of Political Science* 58(4):804–18.

Thomas, Jakana L, and Kanisha D. Bond. 2015. "Women's Participation in Violent Political Organizations." *American Political Science Review* 109(03):488–506.

Thoms, Oskar N. T., James Ron, and Roland Paris. 2010. "State-Level Effects of Transitional Justice: What Do We Know?" *International Journal of Transitional Justice* 4:329–54.

Thyne, Clayton L. 2006. "Cheap Signals with Costly Consequences: The Effect of Interstate Relations on Civil War." *Journal of Conflict Resolution* 50(6):937–61.

Thyne, Clayton L. 2009. *How International Relations Affect Civil Conflict: Cheap Signals, Costly Consequences* Lexington, MA: Lexington Books.

Tickner, J. Ann. 1992. *Gender in International Relations: Feminist Perspectives on Achieving Global Security.* New York: Columbia University Press.

Tickner, J. Ann. 2001. *Gendering World Politics: Issues and Approaches in the Post-Cold War Era.* New York: Columbia University Press.

Tilly, Charles. 1975. "Reflections on the History of European State-Making." In *The Formation of National States in Western Europe,* edited by Charles Tilly, 3–83. Princeton: Princeton University Press.

Tilly, Charles. 1978. *From Mobilization to Revolution.* New York: McGraw-Hill.

Toft, Monica D. 2003. *The Geography of Ethnic Violence: Identity, Interests, and the Indivisibility of Territory.* Princeton: Princeton University Press.

Toft, Monica Duffy. 2010. *Securing the Peace: The Durable Settlement of Civil Wars.* Princeton: Princeton University Press.

Toft, Monica D. 2011. "Religion in International Relations." In *Handbook of International Relations,* Second Edition, edited by Walter Carlsnaes, Thomas Risse, and Beth A. Simmons. Thousand Oaks, CA: Sage.

Toft, Monica Duffy, and Yuri M. Zhukov. 2012. "Denial and Punishment in the North Caucasus Evaluating the Effectiveness of Coercive Counter-Insurgency." *Journal of Peace Research* 49(6):785–800.

Tollefsen, Andreas F., Håvard Strand, and Halvard Buhaug. 2012. "PRIO–GRID: A Unified Spatial Data Structure." *Journal of Peace Research* 49(2):363–74.

Tønnesson, Stein, Erik Melander, Elin Bjarnegård, Isak Svensson, and Susanne Schaftenaar. 2013. "The Fragile Peace in East and South East Asia." In *SIPRI Yearbook 2013,* 28–42. Oxford: Oxford: Oxford University Press.

Toulmin, Stephen. 1957. *The Philosophy of Science (Volume 14).* Genesis Publishing Pvt. Ltd.

Touval, Saadia. 1972. *The Boundary Politics of Independent Africa.* Cambridge, MA: Harvard University Press.

Townsen, Ashly Adam, and Bryce W. Reeder. 2014. "Where Do Peacekeepers Go When They Go? Explaining the Spatial Heterogeneity of Peacekeeping Deployments." *Journal of International Peacekeeping* 18:69–91.

Trumbore, Peter F. 2003. "Victims or Aggressors? Ethno-Political Rebellion and Use of Force in Militarized Interstate Disputes." *International Studies Quarterly* 47(2):183–201.

Tull, Denis M., and Andreas Mehler. 2005. "The Hidden Cost of Power-Sharing: Reproducing Insurgent Violence in Africa." *African Affairs* 104(416):375–98.

UCDP. *UCDP Conflict Encyclopedia*: Uppsala Conflict Data Program, Uppsala University. Available at http://www.ucdp.uu.se/database. (Accessed September 9, 2013).

UN Environmental Programme (UNEP). 2003. *Afghanistan Post-Conflict Environmental Assessment.* Geneva, Switzerland: UNEP.

UN Environmental Programme (UNEP). 2009. *From Conflict to Peacebuilding: The Role of Natural Resources and the Environment.* Nairobi, Kenya: UNEP.

UNESCO. 2011. "The Hidden Crisis: Armed Conflict and Education." *EFA Global Monitoring Report.*

UNHCR. 2013. *UNHCR Statistical Yearbook 2012.* December. http://www.unhcr.org/52a7213b9.html.

UNICEF. 2009. "Machel Study 10-Year Strategic Review: Children and Conflict in a Changing World." New York, UNICEF/office of the Special Representative of the Secretary-General for Children and Armed Conflict.

Urdal, Henrik, and Chi Primus Che. 2013. "War and Gender Inequalities in Health: The Impact of Armed Conflict on Fertility and Maternal Mortality." *International Interactions* 39(4):489–510.

Urquhart, Brian. 1983. "Peacekeeping: A View from the Operational Center." In *Peacekeeping: Appraisals and Proposals,* edited by Henry Wiseman, 161–74. New York: Pergamon.

Uvin, Peter. 1996. "Tragedy in Rwanda: The Political Ecology of Conflict." *Environment: Science and Policy for Sustainable Development* 38(3):7–29.

Valentino, Benjamin. 2000. "Final Solutions: The Causes of Mass Killing and Genocide." *Security Studies* 9(3):1–59.

Valentino, Benjamin A. 2005. *Final Solutions: Mass Killing and Genocide in the 20th Century.* Ithaca, NY: Cornell University Press.

Valentino, Benjamin, Paul Huth, and Dylan Balch-Lindsay. 2004. "'Draining the Sea': Mass Killing and Guerrilla Warfare." *International Organization* 58(2):375–407.

Varshney, Ashutosh. 2001. "Ethnic Conflict and Civil Society." *World Politics* 53(3):362–98.

Varshney, Ashutosh. 2003. *Ethnic Conflict and Civic Life: Hindus and Muslims in India.* New Haven, CT: Yale University Press.

Varshney, Ashutosh. 2009. "Ethnicity and Ethnic Conflict." In *Oxford Handbook of Comparative Politics*, edited by Carles Boix and Susan C. Stokes. Oxford: Oxford University Press.

Verpoorten, Marijke. 2009. "Household Coping in War and Peacetime: Cattle Sales in Rwanda, 1991–2001." *Journal of Development Economics* 88:67–86.

Verwimp, Philip. 2005. "An Economic Profile of Peasant Perpetrators of Genocide: Micro-Level Evidence from Rwanda." *Journal of Development Economics* 77(2): 297–323.

Vinci, Anthony. 2005. "The Strategic Use of Fear by the Lord's Resistance Army." *Small Wars and Insurgencies* 16(3):360–81.

Vinjamuri, Leslie, and Jack Snyder. 2004. "Advocacy and Scholarship in the Study of International War Crimes Tribunals and Transitional Justice." *Annual Review of Political Science* 7:345–62.

von Uexkull, Nina. 2014. "Sustained Drought, Vulnerability and Civil Conflict in Sub-Saharan Africa." *Political Geography* 43(1):16–26.

Voors, Maarten J., Eleonora E. M. Nillesen, Philip Verwimp, Erwin H. Bulte, Robert Lensink, and Daan P. Van Soest. 2012. "Violent Conflict and Behavior: A Field Experiment in Burundi." *American Economic Review* 102(2):941–64.

Vreeland, James R. 2008. "The Effect of Political Regime on Civil War: Unpacking Anocracy." *Journal of Conflict Resolution* 52:401–25.

Wagner, Robert Harrison. 1993. "The Causes of Peace." In *Stopping the Killing: How Civil Wars End*, edited by Roy Licklider. New York: New York University Press.

Wagner, Robert Harrison. 2000. "Bargaining and War." *American Journal of Political Science* 44(3):469–84.

Walker, Henry A., and Bernard P. Cohen. 1985. "Scope Statements: Imperatives for Evaluating Theory." *American Sociological Review* 50(3):288–301.

Walker, Iain, and Thomas F. Pettigrew. 1984. "Relative Deprivation Theory: An Overview and Conceptual Critique." *British Journal of Social Psychology* 23(4):301–10.

Wall, James A., John B. Stark, and Rhetta L. Standifer. 2001. "Mediation: A Current Review and Theory Development." *Journal of Conflict Resolution* 45(3):370–91.

Wallensteen, Peter. 2002. *Understanding Conflict Resolution: War, Peace and the Global System.* London: Sage.

Wallensteen, Peter. 2011. *Peace Research: Theory and Practice.* London and New York: Routledge.

Wallensteen, Peter, and Margareta Sollenberg. 1998. "Armed Conflict and Regional Conflict Complexes, 1989–97." *Journal of Peace Research* 35(5):621–64.

Wallensteen, Peter, and Isak Svensson. 2014. "Talking Peace: International Mediation in Armed Conflicts." *Journal of Peace Research* 51(2):315–327.

Walter, Barbara F. 1997. "The Critical Barrier to Civil War Settlement." *International Organization* 51(3):335–64.

Walter, Barbara F. 2002. *Committing to Peace: The Successful Settlement of Civil Wars.* Princeton: Princeton University Press.

Walter, Barbara F. 2003. "Explaining the Intractability of Territorial Conflict." *International Studies Review* 5(4):137–53.

Walter, Barbara F. 2004. "Does Conflict Beget Conflict? Explaining Recurring Civil War." *Journal of Peace Research* 41(3):371–88.

Walter, Barbara F. 2006. "Information, Uncertainty, and the Decision to Secede." *International Organization* 60(1):105–35.

Walter, Barbara F. 2009a. "Bargaining Failures and Civil War." *Annual Review of Political Science* 12:243–61.

Walter, Barbara F. 2009b. *Reputation and Civil War: Why Separatist Conflicts Are So Violent.* Cambridge: Cambridge University Press.

Wantchekon, Leonard. 2004. "The Paradox of Democracy: A Theoretical Investigation." *American Political Science Review* 98:17–33.

Ward, Geoffrey C. and Ken Burns. 2007. *The War: An Intimate History, 1941–1945,* 52. New York: Knopf.

Ward, Michael D. 2005. *What Are the Neighbors Doing?* Unpublished manuscript, University of Washington.

Ward, Michael D., and Kristian Skrede Gleditsch. 2002. "Location, Location, Location: An MCMC Approach to Modeling the Spatial Context of War and Peace." *Political Analysis* 10(3):244–60.

Ward, Michael D., Brian D. Greenhill, and Kristin M. Bakke. 2010. "The Perils of Policy by P-Value: Predicting Civil Conflicts." *Journal of Peace Research* 47(4):363–75.

WCRWC. 2006. "Beyond Firewood: Fuel Alternatives and Protection Strategies for Displaced Women and Girls." Women's Commission for Refugee Women and Children, New York

Weidmann, Nils B. 2011. "Violence 'From Above' or 'From Below'? The Role of Ethnicity in Bosnia's Civil War." *The Journal of Politics* 73(4):1178–90.

Weidmann, Nils B., Doreen Kuse, and Kristian Skrede Gleditsch. 2010. "The Geography of the International System: The Cshapes Dataset." *International Interactions* 36(1):86–106.

Weiner, Myron. 1978. *Sons of the Soil: Migration and Ethnic Conflict in India.* Princeton: Princeton University Press.

Weiner, Myron. 1992/1993. "Security, Stability, and International Migration." *International Security* 17(3):91–126.

Weiner, Myron. 1993. *International Migration and Security.* Boulder, San Francisco, and Oxford: Westview Press.

Weinstein, Jeremy M. 2005. "Resources and the Information Problem in Rebel Recruitment." *Journal of Conflict Resolution* 49(4):598–624.

Weinstein, Jeremy M. 2006. *Inside Rebellion: The Politics of Insurgent Violence.* Cambridge: Cambridge University Press.

Weinstein, Joshua I. 2009. "The Market in Plato's *Republic.*" *Classical Philology* 104: 440.

Werner, Emmy E. 1989. "High-Risk Children in Young Adulthood: A Longitudinal Study from Birth to 32 Years." *American Journal of Orthopsychiatry* 59(1):72–81.

Werner, Suzanne. 1999. "The Precarious Nature of Peace: Resolving the Issues, Enforcing the Settlement, and Renegotiating the Terms." *American Journal of Political Science* 43(3):912–34.

Werner, Suzanne, and Amy Yuen. 2005. "Making and Keeping Peace." *International Organization* 59(2):261–92.

Wesley, Michael. 1997. *Casualties of the New World Order: The Causes of Failure of UN Missions to Civil Wars*. New York: St. Martin's Press.

Westad, Odd Arne. 2005. *The Global Cold War: Third World Interventions and the Making of Our Times*. Cambridge: Cambridge University Press.

Wheeler, Nicholas J. 2000. *Saving Strangers: Humanitarian Intervention in International Society*. Oxford: Oxford University Press.

Whitaker, Beth Elise. 2002. "Refugees in Western Tanzania: The Distribution of Burdens and Benefits among Local Hosts." *Journal of Refugee Studies* 15(4):339–58.

Whitaker, Beth Elise. 2003. "Refugees and the Spread of Conflict: Contrasting Cases in Central Africa." *Journal of Asian and African Studies* 38(2–3):211–31.

Wiebelhaus-Brahm, Eric. 2010. *Truth Commissions and Transitional Societies: The Impact on Human Rights and Democracy*. London and New York: Routledge.

Wijeweera, Albert, and Matthew J. Webb. 2009. "Military Spending and Economic Growth in Sri Lanka: A Time Series Analysis." *Defence and Peace Economics* 20(6):499–508.

Wilkenfeld, Jonathan, Victor Asal, and Amy Pate. 2008. "Minorities at Risk Organizational Behavior (MAROB) Middle East, 1980–2004." http://hdl.handle.net/1902.1/15973 UNF:5:qvN7+gsRsnFRvZpkEupM1A== Center for International Development and Conflict Management(CIDCM): University of Maryland, Department of Government and Politics [Distributor] V1 [Version].

Wimmer, Andreas. 2002. *Nationalist Exclusion and Ethnic Conflict: Shadows of Modernity*. Cambridge: Cambridge University Press.

Wimmer, Andreas. 2012. *Waves of War: Nationalism, State-Formation and Ethnic Exclusion in the Modern World*. New York: Cambridge University Press.

Wimmer, Andreas, Lars-Erik Cederman, and Brian Min. 2009. "Ethnic Politics and Armed Conflict. A Configurational Analysis of a New Global Dataset." *American Sociological Review* 74(2):316–37.

Wischnath, Gerdis, and Halvard Buhaug. 2014. "Rice or Riots: On Food Production and Conflict Severity across India." *Political Geography* 43(1):6–15.

Witsenburg, Karen M., and Wario R. Adano. 2009. "Of Rain and Raids: Violent Livestock Raiding in Northern Kenya." *Civil Wars* 11(4):514–38.

Wood, Elisabeth Jean. 2003. *Insurgent Collective Action and Civil War in El Salvador*. Cambridge: Cambridge University Press.

Wood, Elisabeth J. 2006a. "Variation in Sexual Violence During War." *Politics and Society* 34(3):307–42.

Wood, Elisabeth J. 2006b. "Sexual Violence during the War: Towards an Understanding of Variation." *Gender, War, and Militarism: Feminist Perspectives* no.124–38.

Wood, Elisabeth J. 2008. "The Social Processes of Civil War: The Wartime Transformation of Social Networks." *Annual Review of Political Science* 11:539–61.

Wood, Elisabeth J. 2009. "Armed Groups and Sexual Violence: When Is Wartime Rape Rare?" *Politics and Society* 37(1):131–61.

Wood, Reed M. 2010. "Rebel Capability and Strategic Violence against Civilians." *Journal of Peace Research* 47(5):601–14.

Wood, Reed M., and Mark Gibney. 2010. "The Political Terror Scale (PTS): A Re–introduction and a Comparison to CIRI." *Human Rights Quarterly* 32(2):367–400.

Wood, Reed M., Jacob D. Kathman, and Stephen E. Gent. 2012. "Armed Intervention and Civilian Victimization in Intrastate Conflicts." *Journal of Peace Research* 49(5):647–60.

World Bank. 2011. "The Impacts of Refugees on Neighboring Countries: A Development Challenge." *World Development Report: Background Note.*

World Bank. 2012. *World Development Report: Gender Equality and Development.* Washington, DC: World Bank.

World Health Organization. 2016. "Millenium Development Goals (MDGs)." Available at http://www.who.int/topics/millennium_development_goals/en/ (2016).

Wright, Quincy. 1939. "The Munich Settlement and International Law." *American Journal of International Law* 33:12–32.

Wright, Thorin M., and J. Michael Greig. 2012. "Staying the Course: Assessing the Durability of Peacekeeping Operations." *Conflict Management and Peace Science* 29:127–47.

Wucherpfenning, Julian. 2011. "Fighting for Change: Onset, Duration, and Recurrence of Ethnic Conflict." Doctoral dissertation thesis, ETH Zurich.

Wucherpfennig, Julian, Nils B. Weidmann, Luc Girardin, Lars-Erik Cederman, and Andreas Wimmer. 2011. "Politically Relevant Ethnic Groups across Space and Time: Introducing the Geo-EPR Dataset." *Conflict Management and Peace Science* 28(5):423–37.

Wucherpfennig, Julian, Nils W. Metternich, Lars-Erik Cederman, and Kristian Skrede Gleditsch. 2012. "Ethnicity, the State, and the Duration of Civil War." *World Politics* 64(1):79–115.

Yildirim, Julide, Selami Sezgin, and Nadir Ocal. 2005. "Military Expenditure and Economic Growth in Middle Eastern Countries: A Dynamic Panel Data Analysis." *Defence and Peace Economics* 16(4):283–95.

Young, Joseph K. 2008. "Repression, Dissent and the Onset of Civil War: Understanding the Interaction of States and Dissidents in the Production of Violent Conflict." PhD dissertation, Florida State University.

Young, Joseph K. 2013. "Repression, Dissent, and the Onset of Civil War." *Political Research Quarterly* 66(3):516–32.

Young, Joseph K., and Michael G. Findley. 2011. "Promise and Pitfalls of Terrorism Research." *International Studies Review* 13(3):411–31.

Zack-Williams, Afred B. 1999. "Sierra Leone: The Political Economy of Civil War, 1991–98." *Third World Quarterly* 20(1):143–62.

Zalaquett, Jose. 1992. "Balancing Ethical Imperatives and Political Constraints: The Dilemma of New Democracies Confronting Past Human Rights Violations." *Hastings Law Journal* 43:6–16.

Zartman, William. 1989. *Ripe for Resolution: Conflict and Intervention in Africa.* New York: Oxford University Press.

Zartman, I. William. 1995. *Elusive Peace: Negotiating an End to Civil Wars.* Washington, DC: Brookings Institution.

Zhukov, Yuri M. 2007. "Examining the Authoritarian Model of Counter-Insurgency: The Soviet Campaign against the Ukrainian Insurgent Army." *Small Wars & Insurgencies* 18(3):439–66.

Zhukov, Yuri M. 2014. "Rust Belt Rising: The Economics behind Eastern Ukraine's Upheaval." *Foreign Affairs.*

Zinnes, Dina A. 1976. *Contemporary Research in International Relations: A Perspective and a Critical Appraisal.* New York: Free Press.

Index

abuse, 129, 156, 179, 181–82, 187, 193, 195

accommodation, 43, 50, 59, 74

ACD (Armed Conflict Dataset), 118, 248, 254, 270

Aceh, 220–21, 229

Acemoglu, Daron, 67, 237

ad hoc tribunals, 180–81

adversaries, 53, 75, 84, 87, 122–28, 131, 160

Afghanistan, 19–20, 23, 25, 32, 42, 52, 56, 84, 86, 98–99, 105, 108, 111, 159, 163, 165, 167, 206, 213, 240

Africa, 1, 5, 17, 23, 47, 77, 83, 86–87, 98, 107, 159, 162, 231, 233, 238, 248, 252, 256

African Union, 150, 231

aggregation, 41, 106, 119, 236, 253, 266; temporal, 42, 317

aggression, 110, 142, 202

agreements, 3, 8–9, 65–67, 71, 109–10, 113, 115, 128, 131–32, 137, 139, 141–43, 147, 151–52, 167, 212, 259, 265, 267; power-sharing, 66, 133–34; provisions, 65, 143

agriculture, 29, 217, 221, 233, 237–38

aid, 99, 107, 111, 120, 156, 173, 257; foreign, 96, 173

Akhavan, Payam, 180–81, 183

Akresh, Richard, 162, 165, 169

Algeria, 102, 173, 216

Alix-Garcia, Jennifer, 157, 171

alliances, 33, 43, 52, 84, 87, 202

amnesties, 10, 180–82, 184–85, 187, 192–94

ancient hatreds, 49, 57

Angola, 16, 18, 62, 84–87, 90, 98, 154, 165, 216

anocracies, 68–69, 71–73, 77

antecedents, 4-5. 33, 41–42, 233, 262

arbitration, 96, 110, 117, 226, 257

armed conflict, ix, 1, 4–6, 9–10, 15–16, 18–20, 22–23, 26–27, 31–32, 35, 50, 75–76, 85, 87, 89–90, 112, 123, 133, 135, 205, 208, 232, 235, 239, 241–46, 261; attacks, 204, 248; ongoing, 17, 162; patterns of, 1, 5, 11, 15, 17, 19, 21, 23, 25, 27, 29, 31, 261

Armed Conflict Data. See ACD

armies, 6, 10, 53, 59–61, 64, 130, 142, 150, 159, 218

arms, 75–76, 78–79, 81, 83–84, 86, 88, 103–4, 115, 122, 141, 146, 160, 170, 203–4, 211, 242–43, 247, 254–55

Arreguin-Toft, Ivan, 94, 102

Asal, Victor, 56, 206, 255

Asia, 1, 5, 23, 238
atrocities, 42, 97, 104, 180, 182, 193, 258
attacks, 142, 179, 257; hit-and-run, 114,
    240; terrorist, 45, 231, 252, 256–57
Autesserre, Severine, 56, 146, 152, 155, 240
authority, 60, 76, 96, 110, 125, 128; legal,
    244, 286; political, 75, 96, 225
autocracies, 60, 62, 71–72, 77, 216
autonomy, 16, 50, 55, 73, 80, 128, 185
Aydin, Aysegul, 88, 96, 101, 112–13, 117,
    119

Bakke, Kristin, 52, 54, 80
Balas, Alexandru, 141, 148, 267
Balcells, Laia, 99, 102, 107, 160, 224, 229,
    256
Balch-Lindsay, Dylan, 8, 53–54, 84–85, 87,
    95–98, 100–102, 114, 160, 239, 265
Ballentine, Karen, 38, 76, 85, 87, 89
Bangladesh, 3, 17
bargaining, 48, 50–51, 54–55, 70, 104,
    108, 113, 122-27, 133, 137, 143;
    failures, 51, 100; leverage, 109, 114;
    model of war, 99–100, 106–8, 135–36;
    obstacles, 114, 266; process, 50, 114,
    137
Bates, Robert, 49, 180
battle deaths, 15–16, 18, 20–23, 25, 29, 32,
    35, 112, 118, 120
battlefield, 8–9, 22, 93, 95–96, 100,
    104, 114–15, 137, 159, 161–62, 268;
    hostilities, 112, 114
battle-related deaths, 15, 20, 22, 112, 119,
    247, 270
battles, 12, 21, 33, 104, 114, 142, 249, 251
Beardsley, Kyle, 88, 97, 144, 252, 265
beliefs, 36, 46, 48, 80, 161, 192, 205
belligerents, 84, 109, 115, 122, 160, 165,
    245
Bercovitch, Jacob, 109–10, 112–13, 116–
    17, 123, 266–67
Biafra, 3, 27
bias, 101, 135, 186, 241, 243-44, 258
Binningsbø, Helga, 132, 183–85, 187, 191
Bjarnegård, Elin, 200, 213
Blattman, Christopher, 56–57, 66–67, 167,
    169, 263

Böhmelt, Tobias, 117, 120
Bond, Doug, 82, 238, 257
borders, 23, 43, 75, 78–81, 86–87, 94, 97,
    131, 170, 186–87, 239, 248, 250–52;
    international, 80, 144, 251
Bosnia-Herzegovina, 48, 52, 97, 144, 156,
    163, 181, 183, 205
Bosnian War, 37, 144, 183, 269
Braithwaite, Alex, 81, 252
Brancati, Dawn, 149–51, 153
Brandt, Patrick, 94–95, 97, 100, 114, 131
Brazil, 37, 193, 221
Brecke, Peter, 182, 184, 189–93
Bremer, Stuart, 64, 249–50
Bueno de Mesquita, Bruce, 105, 107
Buhaug, Halvard, 11, 23, 26–27, 50–51,
    76–77, 79–82, 97, 132, 160, 225, 231–
    32, 234, 236–38, 240, 242, 244–46,
    251–54, 265
Bulte, Erwin, 223, 228, 237
Bundervoet, Tom, 162, 165, 168
bureaucracy, 6, 61–64, 106, 145
Burma, 17, 20, 86
Burundi, 65, 128, 146, 162, 167, 173, 231,
    248

Cambodia, 4, 27, 84, 86, 130, 151, 165,
    181
capabilities, 38, 65, 67, 100, 103, 114–15,
    160, 214, 218, 249
capacity, 5-6, 9–11, 59–60, 62–66, 72-73,
    79, 81, 83, 94, 103, 126-27, 153, 169,
    173, 181, 203–5, 209, 214, 219, 233,
    263
Caprioli, Mary, 10, 194, 199, 208–9
cases, 11, 20, 40, 43, 47–48, 69, 75, 77,
    79, 83, 88–89, 98–99, 101, 107, 122,
    129–30, 142, 144–45, 150, 154, 161,
    163, 166, 169, 183, 186, 189, 193, 213,
    220, 222, 224, 234, 241, 245, 248, 262,
    268; difficult, 154, 259, 267; hard, 89,
    97; high-risk, 90, 265; individual, 151,
    167
Castro, Fidel, 115, 122, 266
casualties, 10, 23, 29, 35, 94, 105, 159,
    245; civilian, 119, 145, 147
causality, 223, 226–27, 242, 244

causal mechanisms, 27, 47, 68, 79, 106,
124, 131, 166–67, 192, 207, 212, 219,
232, 246
cease-fire agreements, 29, 142, 146
Cederman, Lars-Erik, 40, 44, 47, 51,
54, 80, 132, 149, 225–26, 244, 254,
263–64
Central Africa, 23, 77, 240
challenges, 9, 54–55, 60, 68-69, 122,
151, 186, 231, 241, 246, 255;
methodological, 81–82, 89, 234, 241
Chechnya, 23, 42, 45, 50–51, 240, 248
Chenoweth, Erica, 42, 56, 255–56
children, 157, 162–63, 165–66, 169, 172,
180, 200–202, 206
child soldiers, 162, 165, 169, 174, 206
China, 1, 20, 29, 70, 102, 261
CIA (Central Intelligence Agency), 164,
266
Cingranelli, David, 69, 269
CIRI (Cingranelli and Richards), 190, 269
citizens, 1, 36–38, 42, 54, 64, 98, 134–35,
165, 170, 173, 187
civil conflicts, 2, 7, 10–11, 16, 19, 22,
24, 27–29, 31, 34, 38–39, 61, 67–69,
71, 75–77, 79, 94–98, 103, 105–6,
108–9, 111–18, 120, 140–41, 144,
157–59, 161, 163, 165–66, 169, 171,
174–75, 203–4, 208–12, 216, 220,
226, 232–33, 235, 237, 240–43, 245,
247–49, 256–57, 259–60, 265–66,
268; actors, 112, 119, 240; armed,
232, 239, 241–42, 244–45, 270;
contagion, 82, 87; countries, 79, 158,
206, 265; data, 236, 241, 249–50,
252, 259, 261; duration, 95, 104;
dyads, 16, 84; dynamics, 225, 229,
231, 253; issues, 83, 87; locations, 18,
253; onset, 28, 223, 236, 241–43, 247,
251; outcomes, 143, 238; phases, 141,
147, 267; processes, 2, 4, 12, 40, 111,
118; recurrence, 132, 187; regions, 86,
97; renewal, 142–43, 148; resolution,
88, 111; risk, 235–36, 242
civilians, 3, 30–31, 52–53, 103, 116, 147,
157–61, 171–72, 185, 205–6, 256–57;
attack, 160, 185, 254; deaths, 160, 172,
268; targeting, 160, 254; victimization,
31, 51, 102–3, 161, 193, 257
civilizations, 25, 45, 264
civil peace, 198–99, 202, 209, 211–12;
democratic, 66, 73
civil society, 9, 136, 148, 152, 193
civil strife, 231, 234
civil violence, 10, 60, 68–70, 174
civil wars, 1–13, 15–18, 20, 22, 28–30,
32–45, 47–57, 59–73, 75–81, 83–91,
93–119, 121–25, 127–30, 132–37,
139–41, 143–53, 155–75, 179–81,
183–85, 187–90, 192–95, 197, 199,
201, 203, 205–21, 223–25, 227,
231–34, 236, 238–39, 242–43, 246–57,
259–64, 266–68, 270; adversaries, 125,
127, 131, 135, 137; civilians in, 160,
273; contexts, 141, 146, 148–49; data,
38, 119, 247, 249, 251, 253, 255, 257,
259, 270; duration, 4, 8, 54, 94, 102–3,
107; gendered nature of, 197, 203, 205,
212–14; internationalized, 87, 140;
longer, 7, 54, 70, 93, 254; mediation,
109–10, 112, 118, 266; neighbors, 79,
90; new, 30, 33, 36, 144; occurrence,
10, 195, 234; old, 30, 37; ongoing, 55,
119, 206, 255, 257; protracted, 5, 54,
100; risks, 235–36; settlements, 113,
116, 121, 123–25, 128–29, 131, 134–
35, 137; states, 7, 9, 134, 136, 139
cleavages, 37, 55–56, 225, 244; religious,
44, 56
climate, 11, 26, 235, 252; change, 11,
232, 235–36, 242, 245–46; variability,
235–37
clustering, 7, 11, 23, 26, 62, 75–78, 82, 89,
144, 264–65
coding, 12, 16, 35–36, 38, 72, 118, 222,
251–52, 257–58, 262, 269; rules, 72,
191, 258–59
coding decisions, 39, 69, 258, 262
coercion, 37, 59, 61, 70, 74, 186, 200
co-ethnics, 48–49, 51–53, 57, 98
Cohen, Bernard, 31, 53, 162, 182, 189,
201, 206
Cold War, 1, 5, 8, 15–20, 23, 25, 28–32,
34, 36, 39, 84, 90, 93–94, 97–99, 102,

106–9, 113, 124–25, 129, 137, 157, 215–16

Collier, Paul, 1, 38, 70, 101, 157–58, 166–67, 169–70, 173–74, 209, 215, 217, 219–20, 226, 228, 239–40, 253, 263

Collier and Hoeffler, 5, 32, 36–39, 50, 54, 85, 217–19, 221, 248–49, 253, 263

Colombia, 86, 109, 165, 172, 204, 224

combat, 100, 114, 137, 159, 162, 204–5, 228, 239, 243

combatants, 10, 22–23, 51, 53, 79, 85, 88, 94, 103, 113–17, 120, 142, 145, 160, 205–6, 239, 247; active, 204, 206, 213–14; female, 204, 214; male, 10, 211

commissions, 128, 184; trials and truth, 180, 185

commitment problems, 8, 12, 67, 69–70, 100, 105, 109, 114–16, 126–28, 131–33, 137, 143, 149–51, 188, 266

communal violence, 11–12, 236, 243

concessions, 50, 81, 87, 116, 129, 146, 160, 245

conditions, 4–5, 7–8, 36, 39, 44, 48, 51, 55, 69, 76–77, 80–81, 100, 110, 131, 137, 139, 141, 146, 149, 151, 155, 161, 170, 175, 189, 193–94, 202–3, 232, 234, 237, 242, 264–65, 268–69; economic, 238, 242; initial, 143, 155; scope, 181, 186, 189–91, 195

conflict events, 12, 56, 236, 241, 249, 251, 256–58

conflicts, 1–3, 5–8, 11–12, 16–23, 25–29, 32–45, 49–57, 65–68, 73, 75–90, 93–95, 97–102, 104–6, 108, 110–14, 116–22, 124–26, 129, 133–36, 139–41, 143–49, 157–60, 162–63, 165–72, 174–75, 185, 188, 192, 199, 201, 205, 213, 215–20, 222–24, 226–29, 231–54, 256, 258–59, 261, 263–66, 268–70; intercommunal, 29, 252, 257; international, 94, 105, 249, 256; new, 16, 19–20, 88, 94, 216, 261; non-state, 29–31, 241, 243, 245; ongoing, 16–18, 20, 93–94, 117, 193, 219, 255, 259; recurrent, 181, 183; religious, 43, 54, 57; renewed, 2, 9, 28, 180, 194–95; states, 79, 102, 106, 165, 169;

territorial, 16–17, 20, 27; zones, 22–24, 170, 240, 251

Congo, 84, 87, 98, 140, 144, 146, 165, 216, 221, 239, 248

contagion, 23, 75–76, 78, 80–83, 97, 264–65; effects, 76–78, 88–89, 170, 265

context, 31, 34, 39, 41, 53, 68, 95, 99, 108, 111, 125, 140, 143–45, 147, 149–51, 154, 179–81, 187, 189–95, 207, 209, 211, 213, 222, 236–37, 243, 248, 257, 260

control variables, 155, 197, 204, 208, 210, 223, 236

cooperation, 49, 52, 55, 88, 146, 152, 169, 202

Correlates of War (COW), 22, 26, 35, 118, 133, 147, 223, 247, 253

correlations, 54, 60, 68, 71–72, 82, 89, 120, 166, 212, 217, 221, 234, 238, 263

corruption, 60, 63, 65, 102, 134, 223, 228

costs, 22, 37–38, 50, 53, 61, 79, 103, 105, 111, 117, 123, 126–27, 129–30, 132, 137, 142, 149, 168–69, 171, 211, 217, 229

Côte d'Ivoire, 77, 110, 156, 165

counterinsurgency, 42, 52, 103, 238–40

coups, 17, 234

courts, 149, 181

COW. *See* Correlates of War

criminals, 35–36, 157, 229; crimes, 39, 180–83, 185, 187, 213; prosecutions, 180–84, 187, 189, 192

Croatia, 183, 269

Cuba, 27, 61, 102, 115, 122, 266

culture, 41, 46, 145–46, 201–3, 212, 266

Cunningham, David, 12, 41, 70, 76, 84–85, 87, 94–95, 102, 104, 112, 115, 118, 140, 146, 247–48, 250, 252, 254, 256, 258, 260, 263, 265

Cunningham, Kathleen, 6, 43–44, 46, 48, 50, 52, 54, 56, 118, 254–55

Cyprus, 146, 267

DALYs (Disability Adjusted Life Years), 22, 161

Darfur, 48, 150, 162

data, 22, 35, 40, 42, 56–57, 63–64, 69, 73, 76, 119, 153, 171, 190, 205, 216, 223–24, 226, 229, 234–35, 237, 241, 247, 249, 251–57, 259–60, 267, 270; availability, 147, 255; collection, 12, 47, 56, 88, 118–19, 121, 134, 190–92, 247, 249–50, 258–59, 263; cross-national, 53, 79; disaggregated, 53, 119, 249, 252, 266; fine-grained, 47, 119, 134, 223, 249; geocoded, 12, 56, 144; new, 38, 81, 191, 219, 249–50, 252–53; projects, 118, 248–50, 255, 258; quality, 224, 226, 228, 235, 241; quantitative, 230, 247; scarcity, 79, 85, 89; sources, 89, 118, 120, 247, 249, 259; spatial, 251–52; survey, 137, 252

datasets, 5, 12, 16–17, 20, 22, 46–47, 71, 89, 101, 104, 108, 112, 123, 125, 132–34, 191–92, 223, 247–48, 253, 255–57, 266–67, 269–70

Davenport, Christian, 40–41, 70, 258

Davis, David, 76, 98, 256

Daxecker, Ursula, 108, 268

DDR, 88, 143, 150–51, 154–55, 173

deaths, 1, 3, 19–20, 22, 29, 34–35, 94, 124, 146–47, 158–59, 161–62, 165, 169, 171, 227, 245, 248–49, 257, 268

decolonization, 16–18, 107

defense, 43, 52, 222

demands, 26, 50, 80, 87, 149, 254

DeMeritt, Jacqueline, 10, 179–80, 182, 184, 186, 188, 190, 192, 194–95, 209

demobilization, 39, 88, 100, 126, 143, 150, 173

democracy, 6, 31–32, 39, 55, 61–62, 64, 67–72, 77, 103, 107, 119, 130, 134, 139, 149–56, 180–81, 184, 187, 191–92, 208, 215, 249, 261, 264, 268; transitions, 189, 192

Democratic Republic of Congo (DRC), 84, 87, 90, 98, 104–5, 162, 206, 221, 239, 248

democratization, 60, 139–40, 148–56, 180, 192, 262, 267–69; efforts, 149–50, 152, 268; successful, 149, 151, 154–55

dependence, 64, 221-22, 229; commodity, 217, 237

deployment, 96, 101, 116, 125, 139–41, 144, 154, 181, 213

deprivation, 4, 36, 219–20, 234

DeRouen, Karl, 6, 59–66, 68, 70, 72, 109, 112–13, 117, 123, 129, 131, 264, 266–67

deterrence, 39, 107, 142, 200

development, 9, 11, 22, 34, 44, 64–66, 73, 75, 106, 108, 140, 171, 174, 186, 191, 210–11, 213, 217, 222, 225, 228, 243, 247, 252, 255, 259; capitalist, 68, 71

diamonds, 37, 86, 216–17, 224–25, 240, 263, 269

dictatorship, 6, 42

Diehl, Paul, 9, 26, 113, 117, 139–44, 146–48, 150, 152, 154, 156, 167, 181, 266–67

diffusion, 54, 78, 144, 241, 264–65

disarmament, 88, 126, 139, 143, 150, 155–56, 173

discrimination, 39, 45, 48, 129, 244

diseases, 9, 158, 161–63, 232

displacement, 156, 162, 185, 249; forced, 31, 262

disputants, 110, 143, 146–47, 267

disputes, 50–51, 54, 67–68, 110, 114, 120, 140, 147, 213, 236, 245, 253, 256; international, 84, 213

dissent, 34, 39–41, 74, 149, 179, 186, 256, 260

dissidents, 34, 36, 39–42, 59, 250, 253

distance, 26, 61, 100, 142, 250–51

Dixon, William, 69, 170

Downes, Alexander, 103, 239

Doyle, Michael, 66, 123, 143, 146, 152, 154, 253

DRC. *See* Democratic Republic of Congo

drought, 11, 231, 236, 242, 245

Druckman, Daniel, 140, 147, 156

drugs, 5, 11, 37, 86

Dugan, Laura, 36, 256

duration, 2, 4, 6–8, 11–12, 15, 48, 61, 64, 70, 86, 93–97, 99–103, 105–8, 124–25, 129, 131–37, 218–19, 228–29, 241, 243, 245, 247, 249, 253–55, 259, 261, 267

dynamics, 2, 6, 8, 11–12, 44, 48, 52, 57, 75–76, 79, 94, 144, 197, 224, 227–29,

241, 248, 253, 255–56, 259; escalatory, 245, 248; temporal, 40, 155

East Timor, 151, 182, 185
Eck, Kristine, 29, 157, 193, 238, 270
economic development, 9, 26, 31, 65, 68, 71, 148, 151, 153, 157–58, 166, 170, 173, 175, 210–11, 215, 236–38, 242, 268
economic growth, 9, 22, 79, 164, 166–75, 235–38, 243–44, 246, 268
economies, 4, 9–10, 32, 68, 71, 79, 156–58, 165–67, 169–71, 174, 181, 217, 221–22, 238, 242, 268
education, 11, 22, 63–64, 157–58, 164–66, 169, 171–75, 181–82, 268
effects, 61, 66, 68, 72–73, 80–81, 89, 119, 123, 131–34, 144, 147, 152, 155, 163, 167–70, 175, 183–84, 186–87, 190, 194-95, 208, 218, 222–23, 227–28, 232–33, 235–36, 263; deleterious, 170, 181; demonstration, 80–81, 87; direct, 153, 210; endogeneity, 228, 242; fixed, 222, 236; general, 112, 195; independent, 68, 71–72, 175, 218; opposite, 140, 229; pacifying, 143, 211; positive, 135, 153–55, 168, 172; selection, 97, 154; trickle-down, 157, 172
Egypt, 109, 142, 179–81
elections, 36, 65, 128, 130, 149–51, 153–55, 187; early, 153–54; monitor, 143, 267; supervision, 140, 143, 148, 151, 154; timing of, 149, 153
elites, 33, 43, 49, 55, 63, 133–36, 152, 234
Ellingsen, Tanja, 51, 69, 234
El Salvador, 4, 18, 33, 37, 77, 89, 185, 188, 204, 221
Elster, Jon, 181–82, 191, 268
emotions, 49, 172, 200, 213
empirical evidence, 11, 38, 135, 143, 152, 170, 203, 211, 237
empirical findings, 6, 36–37, 44, 55, 60, 70, 72, 134, 142, 150, 152, 154, 181, 187–90, 197, 203, 206–7, 222, 234, 236, 249, 264, 266
endogeneity, 52, 64, 135, 168, 213, 221, 223, 226–27, 237, 241–43

enemies, 9–10, 82, 132, 143, 146, 150–51, 188, 251
enforcement, 63, 65, 115, 145, 188, 194, 244
Enterline, Andrew, 7–8, 54, 84–85, 87, 93–98, 100–104, 106, 108, 114, 265
environment, 2, 150, 232–33, 238, 241–46, 270; conditions, 231–32, 234–35, 237–38, 241–43, 246; conflict, 231–35, 237, 239, 241, 243, 245; degradation, 231, 235, 240; factors, 232, 234, 237, 241–46; impacts, 237–38; post-conflict, 2, 127, 148, 154, 156, 186, 194; regional, 97–98, 107
Eritrea, 3, 20, 26–27, 141, 231
escalation, 12, 32, 48, 50, 78–79, 87, 117, 133, 142, 148, 179, 212, 241, 245, 260
estimates, 20–22, 40, 100, 117, 158–59, 161, 167, 172, 206, 228, 236-37, 242, 264, 266
Ethiopia, 3, 20, 27, 36, 141, 231, 233, 245
ethnic conflict, 44, 48–49, 51–53, 141, 234; ethnic cleansing, 52–53, 183; ethnic composition, 81, 149, 153; secession, 3, 98
ethnic fractionalization, 38, 54, 194, 248
ethnic groups, 3–4, 43, 47–48, 50–56, 69, 80–81, 128, 231, 234, 244, 251–52, 254; minorities, 3, 43, 224; polarization, 47, 51, 53–54, 238, 245
ethnicity, 4, 28, 38, 44–46, 48–50, 52–56, 79, 88, 98, 221, 263, 266, 268; divisions, 3, 6, 53, 55; identities, 44–48, 50–52
Ethnic Power Relations (EPR), 47, 56, 225, 254
ethnic violence, 43, 48–49, 52
European Union, 113, 145, 148
event data, 12, 104, 119, 250–51, 256–57, 266
exiles, 181–82, 184, 192
experiments, 49, 56, 213, 242, 268
external support, 76, 84–85, 89–90, 96, 101–2, 161

factions, 16, 52, 94, 103, 110–11, 118, 122, 124, 128, 135, 149, 266; warring, 94, 96, 100, 103, 105 famine, 11, 29, 231, 244–45

Farabundo Martí National Liberation Front, 33, 204

FARC (Fuerzas Armadas Revolucionarias de Colombia), 109

farmers, 171, 231, 244, 264

fatalities, 15, 22–23, 80, 144, 147, 256–57

Fearon, James, 43, 47, 50, 56, 62–65, 67, 70, 94, 99, 102, 114–15, 122, 126, 150, 234, 253, 262, 266

Fearon and Laitin, 5–6, 32, 35–40, 43, 50, 52, 60–61, 65, 68–69, 71, 94, 102, 107, 158, 218, 234, 248–49, 253, 262–63, 266

female participation in conflict, 194–95, 202–5, 209, 213

Fett, Patrick, 7, 94, 96, 100–102, 114, 253

fighters, 52, 79, 84, 203, 220, 224; foreign, 54, 102

fighting, 3, 8, 10, 16–17, 19, 21, 23, 41, 43, 51–53, 84, 86–87, 100, 110, 114–15, 118, 123–24, 133, 140–42, 146–47, 149, 159, 162, 166, 168, 172, 174, 203–6, 208, 235, 238, 244, 247–49, 252–54; capacity, 83, 85–86, 89

findings, 11, 22, 44, 61, 68–70, 72, 77, 80–82, 89–90, 94–95, 97–98, 100–101, 103–4, 106–8, 111, 117, 140, 143–44, 147, 149, 154, 161, 172, 184, 187, 197, 204, 210, 215, 217, 224, 226–27, 233–38, 241, 243, 246, 249, 261; consistent, 7–8, 71, 93; contradictory, 101, 220; counterintuitive, 7, 112

Findley, Michael, 34, 95, 98, 100, 104, 252, 257, 262

Fjelde, Hanne, 6, 39, 53, 63, 70, 75, 236, 264–65

food, 11, 61, 160, 171, 231–33, 237–40, 243–44; supply, 232–33, 239

forces, 19, 33, 62, 100, 109, 115, 122, 125, 127–29, 147, 150, 153–57, 161, 170, 172, 183, 186, 200, 202–3, 206, 213, 231, 239, 246, 261; armed, 15, 80, 112, 128, 179; project, 250–51

forests, 61, 115, 239–40, 270

Forsberg, Erika, 7, 54, 75–76, 78, 80–82, 84, 86, 88, 90, 170, 265

Fortna, Page, 96, 123, 125, 141–43, 145–46, 150, 152–55, 254, 257

fractionalization, 38, 46–47, 53

fragmentation, 17, 51–52, 205

framework, 2, 39, 99, 110, 118, 129, 151, 189, 245, 270; theoretical, 188, 208, 218, 223

Frank, Richard, 112–13, 117

Free Syrian Army (FSA), 29, 75, 84

FRELIMO, 160, 239

FSA (Free Syrian Army), 29, 75, 84

GAM Free Aceh Movement, 220, 225, 229

Gartner, Rosemary, 31, 116, 267

Gates, Scott, 22, 36, 50–51, 160–61, 183–85, 187, 191, 225, 231–32, 234, 236, 238–40, 242, 244, 246, 251–52, 262

GDP (gross domestic product), 6, 38, 40–41, 61–64, 90, 166–67, 217, 221–23, 228, 238, 248; per capita, 9, 38, 61–62, 264

GED (Geo-referenced Events Dataset), 119, 252, 256

Geddes, Barbara, 6, 70

gender, 45, 156, 197–200, 203–8, 210, 212–13, 261; equality, 194–95, 198–99, 202, 207–11; inequality, 208–9, 213; roles, 199–201, 205

genocide, 29, 31, 34, 44, 97–98, 100, 179, 182–83, 200, 204, 233, 262, 268–69

Gent, Stephen, 95, 101, 104, 110, 160–61

geography, 73, 129, 141, 191, 247, 250-53, 270; areas, 144, 147, 248

Germany, 17, 233

Ghobarah, Hazem, 9, 22, 76, 161–62, 206

Gibson, James, 192, 201, 269

Gilligan, Michael, 97, 143, 172

Gizelis, Ismene, 119, 195, 209, 235

Glaser, Sarah, 235, 238, 240

Gleditsch, Kristian, 1, 12, 15, 17, 19, 23, 34–35, 40, 51, 54, 76–77, 79–82, 84–85, 97–98, 112, 118, 132, 163, 170–71, 208, 236, 239, 244, 247–48, 250–52, 254, 256, 258, 260–61, 263, 265, 270

Gledistch, Nils Petter, 4–5, 15–16, 18, 20–22, 25–26, 28, 30, 32, 69, 72, 149, 234–36, 264

goals, 3–4, 6, 10, 35, 59, 72, 82, 93, 101, 122, 145–49, 151, 155–56, 174, 180–81, 189–91, 222, 243, 265
Goddard, Stacie, 50, 54
Goertz, Gary, 167, 262
gold, 128, 217, 240
Goldstein, Joshua, 20, 199, 201, 203, 207
Goldstone, Jack, 180, 182, 269
Goodwin, Jeff, 59, 64
governance, 4, 9, 60, 63–64, 66, 71–73, 132, 158, 169, 228
government, 3–4, 6–8, 12, 15–17, 19, 22, 26–29, 34–37, 43, 50, 54, 61–67, 80, 84, 93, 101–2, 104–5, 108–10, 112, 114–17, 124, 128–30, 136, 141, 144, 148, 150, 160–62, 165–66, 170–71, 173, 175, 179–81, 184, 188, 192, 206, 221, 224–25, 227–28, 238–39, 243, 245, 248, 251, 253–54, 257–58, 267, 269; armies, 59, 61, 64; authoritarian, 67, 70, 102; central, 5, 80, 126, 128, 220; effectiveness, 63, 134; expenditure, 63, 134, 165; forces, 101, 116, 252; national, 34, 127–28, 156, 226; new, 3, 182, 187; victory, 2, 7–8, 61, 93, 102, 123
Greece, 224, 256
greed hypothesis, 11, 38–39, 219, 264
Greig, Michael, 94, 113, 117, 155, 266
grid cells, 241, 253, 270
grievances, 4–5, 28, 33, 36–39, 41, 45, 48–51, 68–70, 74, 86–87, 95, 110, 188, 194, 209, 218–20, 231, 236, 262–63; ethnic, 48, 51; hypothesis, 38–39, 219–20
gross domestic product. *See* GDP
groups, 10, 16, 29, 33–34, 36–38, 45, 47–53, 55, 59, 67, 71, 76, 79–81, 87, 99, 113, 118, 122–23, 125–29, 132–33, 136–37, 140–41, 149–52, 160, 163, 172, 179, 185, 188, 194, 200, 202, 204, 207–8, 212, 219, 225, 231, 234, 243–45, 248, 252, 254–55, 257, 263–64, 270; armed, 30, 43, 52, 88, 204, 239; cohesion, 51–52; members, 48–49; militant, 248, 250; mobilized, 50, 132, 225; organized, 29, 55; religious, 47, 55; rival, 45, 48, 123, 126, 129

growth, 9, 68, 85, 166, 173, 175, 209, 217, 228, 233, 244, 255, 259
GTD (Global Terrorism Database), 252, 256–57, 270
Guatemala, 4, 77, 124, 165, 185
guerrilla warfare, 102, 160
Guevara, Ernesto, 102, 239
Guha-Sapir, Debbie, 159, 162
Guinea-Bissau, 77, 86
Gurr, Ted, 5, 36–37, 43–44, 48, 179, 248, 262
Gurses, Mehmet, 6, 39, 123, 131, 153

Habyarimana, James, 49, 56
Harff, Barbara, 29, 179
harm, 156–58, 162, 164–65, 167-68, 170, 172-74, 180, 239
Hartzell, Caroline, 8, 65, 121–26, 128, 130–32, 134, 136, 142, 194, 266–67
Hartzell and Hoddie, 8, 55, 123, 125, 129–31, 133–34, 149, 267
Hassner, Ron, 50, 54
Hayner, Priscilla, 182, 188, 192–94
Hazen, Jennifer, 84, 87, 89
health, 59, 76, 134, 157–59, 161–64, 166, 168–69, 171, 174–75, 181, 268; care, 64, 172, 182; civil wars effect on, 158, 161, 171, 173; psychological, 172, 277
Hegre, Håvard, 6, 32, 39, 68–69, 77, 95, 149, 234, 251, 261
Hegre and Sambanis, 32, 35, 50, 76–77, 79, 82, 261, 266
Heldt, Birger, 141, 145, 151, 153–55, 266
Hendrix, Cullen, 6, 11, 62, 218, 231–32, 234–40, 242, 244, 246, 258
Henshaw, Alexis, 197, 204
history, 12, 15, 48, 51–52, 56, 134, 182, 188, 203, 232, 241, 246
HIV/Aids, 156, 162–63
Hoddie, Matthew, 8, 55, 65, 123, 125, 129–34, 149, 267
Hoeffler, Anke, 1, 5, 11, 32, 36–39, 50, 54, 70, 85, 159–60, 167, 173–74, 209, 215, 217–21, 248–49, 253, 262–63
Högbladh, Stina, 84, 88, 113, 135
honor culture, 110, 150, 200–201, 203, 211–13

Horowitz, Donald, 44–45, 48, 55
hostilities, 95, 100–101, 111–12, 120, 143, 147, 241–42
Hudson, Valerie, 10, 199–200, 202
Hug, Simon, 79, 258
Hultman, Lisa, 29, 53, 103, 119, 145, 157, 160–61, 171, 193, 257
human capital, 9, 165–70, 172
humanitarian assistance, 97, 100, 124, 156, 239, 246
human rights, 97, 134, 179, 181, 183–87, 189–95, 268–69; abuses, 134, 180, 182–83, 185–87, 192–94; violations, 180, 185
Humphreys, Macartan, 56, 88, 167, 173, 175, 204, 215, 218, 222, 227, 229
Hungary, 99, 107
Huntington, Samuel, 25, 45, 180, 264
hurting stalemate, 8, 89, 100
Huth, Paul, 22, 53, 76, 160–62, 239
Hutus, 4, 100, 128, 149
hypotheses, 47, 61, 65, 123, 133, 186, 188–89, 192, 207, 209, 216, 218–19, 235, 247, 253, 264

ICTR (International Criminal Tribunal for Rwanda), 180–82
ICTY (International Criminal Tribunal for Former Yugoslavia), 180–81, 183, 269
identity, 4, 26, 30, 37, 43–57, 123, 191–92, 203–4, 220, 244–45, 263; cleavages, 47, 52–53; conflicts, 43–44, 53, 55; dimensions, 44, 52; groups, 46–47, 52, 54, 56; issues, 6, 43, 45, 47, 49, 51, 53, 55, 57, 263; organizational, 124, 266; particular, 45, 49–50; politics, 30, 44, 51, 54, 56; role of, 44, 50, 54, 57
ideological, 2, 4, 37, 82, 84, 86–87, 96, 216, 242
implementation, 65–66, 129, 132–33, 137, 142–43, 170, 180, 188, 193
implications, 2, 12, 36, 44, 65, 76, 78, 86, 99, 136, 174, 192, 215, 226, 218, 232, 235–36, 247, 259
incentives, 5, 8, 50, 52–54, 67–69, 83, 114–16, 133, 143, 150, 217, 239, 246, 258; economic, 215, 219; structures, 70, 246

incidence, 9, 11, 16, 18, 23, 140, 143, 208, 236, 261
incidents, 44, 53, 112, 142
inclusion, 41, 130, 132, 152, 207, 221
income, 4, 28, 38, 50, 61, 63–64, 128, 169, 222; per capita, 38, 63, 229
incompatibilities, 3, 27, 36, 52, 83, 87, 241; contested, 15, 112
independence, 3, 16–17, 23, 27, 51, 54, 63,.143, 183, 185, 217, 225, 231, 241, 262, 266
India, 20, 32, 36, 52, 251
indicators, 57, 61–64, 72, 113, 119, 127, 147, 156, 161, 188, 190, 194, 208, 221–22, 226, 229, 242, 248–49, 254, 269
individuals, 37, 42, 45–46, 55, 57, 113, 136–37, 160, 162–63, 168–69, 172, 180, 194, 199–201, 203, 205, 209, 211–12, 214, 225, 229–30
indivisible issues, 54, 266
Indonesia, 128, 185, 220, 225, 229
inequality, 4, 57, 207, 209, 211–12, 233, 263; economic, 3, 37; horizontal, 47, 244, 263
information, 22, 67–68, 70, 104, 111, 114–16, 118–19, 124, 135, 148, 151, 160, 172–73, 191–92, 205, 248–50, 253–59, 266, 269; asymmetries, 66–67, 69–70, 114–16, 169, 266
infrastructure, 9, 166, 168, 173–74, 194
insecurity, 149, 231
institutions, 9–10, 42, 54–55, 68, 71, 73, 104, 125, 127–31, 136, 145, 149, 180, 193–94, 227–28, 234, 237, 246, 264; democratic, 66, 139, 180, 191, 194, 242; legal, 237–38; strong, 153, 167; weak, 69, 227–28, 238
instrumental variables, 135, 242–43, 269
instruments, 10, 111, 131, 229, 235, 242, 245
insurgencies, 5, 28, 38, 48, 50, 60–62, 84, 102–3, 115, 234, 245, 256; groups, 5, 16, 45
insurgents, 53, 60, 80, 102–3, 114–15, 160, 193, 204, 206, 218, 239–40
intensity, 20, 33, 37, 46, 49, 127, 159, 262

interaction, 26, 33–34, 36, 39–42, 53,
69–70, 99, 106, 137, 199–200, 208–9,
213, 246, 249–50, 259–60; rebel-
government, 249–50; state-dissident,
40–41, 256
interests, 17, 36–37, 42, 44–45, 49, 55, 86,
98–100, 105–6, 108, 111, 124, 126,
128, 136–37, 165, 167, 189–90, 193,
195, 207, 209, 215, 223, 250, 252, 258,
265, 268
internal conflicts, 16, 29, 36, 44, 76, 78,
84, 95, 149, 167, 216–17, 228, 262
international community, 5, 9, 95, 97, 118,
124, 148, 151–53, 180, 193
International Criminal Tribunal (ICT), 10,
180, 182–83
International Criminal Tribunal for Rwanda
(ICTR), 180–82
international intervention, 8, 97, 101, 103,
international relations, 52, 75, 95–96, 99,
106–8, 250, 263
interstate conflicts, 15–16, 23, 26, 66, 73,
109, 115, 117, 140, 167, 208, 213, 238,
252, 263, 270; rivals, 98, 109
interstate wars, 1, 5, 7, 15–16, 20, 22, 39,
44, 67, 73, 78, 80, 94, 109–10, 115,
137, 159, 179, 190, 203, 207, 250,
252–53, 255, 264, 266
intervention, 7–8, 16, 20, 23, 48, 54, 84,
93–108, 111–12, 115, 119, 146, 148,
155, 171–72, 218, 220, 245; American,
106, 111; biased, 101–2; costs of, 97,
105; diplomatic, 96, 112; policy, 172,
174, 181; purpose of, 97, 288; strategy,
115–17; timing of, 101, 104
intrastate conflicts, 1, 16, 25–26, 29–30,
34–35, 47, 66, 99, 109, 121, 123–25,
137, 167, 217, 262
invasion, 19, 22, 250, 278
investments, 79, 157, 166, 170, 172–74,
202, 215, 217
IPCC (Intergovernmental Panel on Climate
Change), 235, 246
Iqbal, Zaryab, 76, 161, 206
Iran, 20, 23, 146
Iraq, ix, 15, 19–20, 22, 29, 32, 42–43, 45,
52, 56, 70, 79, 84, 103, 105–6, 108,
162–63, 250, 269

ISIL (Islamic State of Iraq and the Levant),
75
ISIS, 224
Islam, 25–26
Islamic State, 29, 43, 75–76
isolation, 62, 75, 83, 95, 106, 184, 191
Israel, 20, 109, 115–16, 141–42, 256, 266

Jarstad, Anna, 129, 131–32, 144, 149,
151–53, 267
Jenne, Erin, 54–55, 99
Jordan, 79, 163
justice, 10, 116, 180–82, 185, 192–93
Justino, Patricia, 168, 229

Kalyvas, Stathis, 30, 34, 37, 43, 52–53, 94,
99, 102–3, 107, 160, 179, 193, 216,
224, 256
Kathman, Jacob, 8, 88, 97, 109–10, 112,
114, 116, 118–20, 157, 160–61, 171,
257, 267
Kaufmann, Chaim, 52, 55, 63
Kenya, 29, 45, 171, 231, 236
Khmer Rouge, 27
killings, 10, 100, 179, 257, 269; mass, 31,
44, 49, 258
kin, 48–49, 80, 85, 202–3
Kocher, Matthew, 53, 94, 103, 108, 160
Korea, 19–20, 238
Kosovo, 80, 145, 181, 269
Koubi, Vally, 223, 235–36, 245
Krain, Matthew, 96, 179
Krane, Dale, 39, 41, 94, 103, 108, 160, 179
Kreutz, Joakim, 5, 28–29, 112–13, 123,
136, 261, 265
Kuwait, 62, 172
Kydd, Andrew, 34, 116

Lacina, Bethany, 21, 69, 84, 261
Lai, Brian, 164, 166, 172
Laitin, David, 5–6, 32, 35–40, 43, 50, 52,
60–62, 65, 68–69, 71, 94, 102, 107, 158,
218, 234, 248–49, 253, 262–63, 266
Lake, David, 76, 80–81, 87, 170
language, 45, 47, 268
Latin America, 1, 5, 189
law, 41, 63, 65, 106, 110, 127, 136, 139–
40, 148, 151, 156, 181–83, 268–69

Lea, Jenna, 129, 131, 267
leaders, 36, 41, 49, 53, 62–63, 67, 72, 97–99, 105–6, 127, 132–33, 136, 146, 149–50, 161, 186–87, 204, 208, 217, 225, 245, 254
learning, 80–81, 105, 145–46, 163, 182
Lebanon, 43, 79, 136, 141, 146
legacies, 9, 150, 157, 159, 161, 163, 165, 167, 169, 171, 173, 175, 180, 243, 268
legitimacy, 52, 63, 109, 117, 151–52, 180, 194
levels, 11–12, 18, 22, 25, 31, 39, 41, 52, 56, 64, 66, 71, 74, 98, 105, 107–9, 111, 118–20, 128, 143, 148, 150, 160, 164, 172, 174, 190, 197, 208, 211–13, 216, 221–25, 227–29, 232, 236, 249, 253, 256; domestic, 66, 73; high, 5, 37, 42, 50, 65, 81, 185, 231, 238, 259, 266; individual, 193, 197, 203, 211, 213, 224; low, 50, 79, 112, 127, 195; macro, 52, 68; national, 221, 223–24, 227; sub-national, 197, 219, 223–24, 250
Liberia, 38, 77, 86, 116, 146, 165, 206, 216
Libya, 56, 79, 104–5, 248
Lichbach, Mark, 39–40, 53, 160–61, 179, 262
Licklider, Roy, 3, 8, 94–95, 100, 122–23, 179
life expectancy, 161, 206
Linebarger, Christopher, 7, 93–94, 96, 98, 100, 102, 104, 106, 108, 264
links, 11, 38, 52, 57, 68, 73, 76, 86, 98, 103, 105–7, 160, 166, 173, 175, 186–87, 194, 215, 217, 220, 227–29, 232, 235–38, 243–46, 254
Lischer, Sarah, 76, 79, 171
locations, 1, 5, 7, 12, 15, 77–80, 82, 85, 88, 104, 119, 144, 151, 164, 216, 231, 243, 249–52, 259–60
Loescher, Gil, 76, 79
logic, 43, 54, 70, 94, 99–100, 108, 211, 217, 233, 244; causal, 186–87, 191, 233; theoretical, 154, 188, 212
lootable resources, 5, 11, 37–38, 40, 50, 168, 219, 224
Lord's Resistance Army (LRA), 109, 111
losses, 11, 22–23, 73, 105, 122, 150–51, 168, 239

lustrations, 10, 180–82, 187–88, 192
Luttwak, Edward, 95, 122
Lyall, Jason, 41, 53, 56, 102–3

Macedonia, 80, 144, 185, 269
Mack, Andrew, 94, 102, 125, 263
Malesky, Edmund, 55, 132, 134
Mali, 65, 79, 236
Mao, 102, 239
maps, 10, 12, 23–24, 26, 32, 181, 204, 251
Marineau, Josiah, 95, 98, 100
markets, 56, 156, 239–40
masculinity, 205, 208, 213
Mason, T. David, 1, 6–7, 10, 39, 41, 94, 96–97, 100–103, 108, 114, 123, 131–33, 142–43, 153, 160, 179, 204, 253, 264, 267
massacre, 34, 183
McDoom, Omar, 49, 52, 204
measurement, 35, 46, 62, 190, 211, 221, 223–24, 227, 229
measures, 47, 61, 64, 69, 72, 77, 113, 132, 137, 175, 207–8, 210, 216, 221–22, 226–27, 229, 235, 250–51, 261, 264
mechanisms, 10, 38, 42, 44, 49, 54, 68, 78–79, 89–90, 101, 114, 117, 127, 149, 152, 158, 160, 162–63, 165–67, 169–71, 181–82, 184–85, 187, 190, 192–94, 200, 203, 210, 216, 218–20, 226–29, 234, 237–38, 240, 243–45, 268; main, 165, 170, 232; multiple, 182, 184–85; retributive, 181, 183; theoretical, 158, 164
media, 22, 37, 48, 235, 249, 258
mediation, 8, 96, 109–21, 124, 265–67; definition of, 110, 112–13; effectiveness of, 110, 116–17, 119–20, 265; processes, 110, 118–19; success, 112, 116–17, 119–20; third party, 8, 88, 109, 262, 265
mediators, 8, 65, 88, 95, 110–14, 116, 120, 137, 265–66; biased, 116, 265
Meernik, James, 167, 183–84, 189–90, 269
Melander, Erik, 4–5, 10–12, 15–16, 18, 20, 22, 26–28, 30–32, 53, 112, 117–19, 184, 187, 194–95, 197–200, 202, 204, 206, 208, 210, 212, 214, 252, 254, 256, 264, 266

Melin, Molly, 117, 267
mental health, 157–58, 162, 171–72, 175;
    trauma, 158, 165–66, 172, 174
mercenaries, 79, 81–82, 86–87
Middle East, 23, 75, 108, 206, 242, 255
migration, 11, 85, 163, 234, 244–45
Miguel, Edward, 57, 66–67, 157, 167, 169,
    235–37, 242, 263
MILC dataset, 112–13
military, 6, 9, 15, 21, 23, 33, 44, 50–51, 61,
    64, 70, 75–76, 94, 98, 101, 104, 111,
    126–33, 137, 140–41, 145–46, 150,
    159, 161, 165, 170–71, 179, 206, 229,
    236, 240, 267; conflicts, 102, 183, 213;
    expenditures, 64, 166; force, 59, 95–96,
    98, 101–2, 108; intervention, 84–85,
    96, 99, 103, 105, 111–12, 117, 120;
    power, 103, 128–29, 132; regimes, 6, 70;
    spending, 165, 170; strength, 170, 252;
    support, 85, 87, 101; victory, 5, 7–8, 93,
    101, 121–25, 134–35, 194, 266, 268
militias, 29, 43, 150, 155, 185
minerals, 62, 104, 225, 269
mines, 86, 205
Mitchell, Sara, 1, 219, 240, 264, 267
MNLF (Moro National Liberation Front),
    16, 126
mobilization, 3–4, 37, 39, 41–43, 48–50,
    53–54, 88, 107, 131, 179, 188, 206,
    208, 212, 229, 245, 254
models, 12, 32, 38, 40–42, 60–61, 66,
    70, 82, 99, 106, 135, 150, 200, 208,
    218–19, 225, 233–34, 245, 262–63,
    269; complex, 220, 234; event history,
    133, 267; game theoretic, 69, 217;
    specification, 123, 236–37
Modelski, George, 95, 113
money, 63, 166, 170, 173
Moore, Will, 34, 40, 48, 53, 98, 174, 239,
    256
Moro National Liberation Front (MNLF),
    16, 126
mortality, 22, 158; infant, 61, 161, 201;
    rates, 206, 237–38
mothers, 49, 172, 200, 202
motivations, 6, 36–37, 41, 112, 188, 250,
    259

motives, 50, 53, 76, 97, 218–21, 229
mountains, 38, 61, 115, 157, 248
Mousseau, Michael, 68, 71
movement, 3, 42, 52, 88, 97, 102, 107,
    110, 171, 207, 225, 231, 233, 244–45;
    arms, 79, 81
Mozambique, 16, 84, 87, 89–90, 160, 165,
    239, 277, 295
Muller, Edward, 37, 69
Murdoch, James, 76, 79, 97, 167, 170
Muslims, 25, 46, 52, 76
Myanmar, 20, 54

Nalepa, Monika, 182, 192, 268–69
Namibia, 87, 143
nationalism, 44, 46–47, 54, 208, 272–73
nations, 1, 3–7, 9, 11, 27–28, 47, 60–61,
    93, 97, 107, 218, 223
nation-states, 2–6, 8–10, 26, 75
NATO (North Atlantic Treaty
    Organization), 21, 105
natural disasters, 11, 222
natural resources, 11, 38, 62, 64, 75, 77,
    85–86, 128, 215, 219, 221–23, 231,
    233, 240, 263
negotiated settlements, 5, 7–8, 50–51, 84,
    87–89, 93–94, 96–97, 100–102, 109,
    114–15, 121–25, 127, 129–31, 133–37,
    181, 194, 266–67
negotiations, 109–10, 117–18, 122–23,
    125, 131, 147, 199, 255
neighborhood, 11, 49, 51, 76, 82, 85,
    88–89, 163, 170; bad, 76–77, 90;
    countries, 7, 23, 78–79, 81, 87–88, 117,
    146, 163, 170–71, 264–65; effect, 76,
    89, 187, 265
Nepal, 4, 204
networks, 52, 61, 75, 84, 86, 88, 144
Neumayer, Eric, 22, 53, 206
NGOs, 117, 148, 155, 173, 234
Nicaragua, 4, 18, 27, 77, 89, 108, 128,
    151, 167, 173, 204
Nichols, Angela, 183–84, 194–95
Nigeria, 3, 27, 29, 45, 62, 136, 216–17,
    225, 244, 269
Nilsson, Desirée, 89, 129, 131–32, 267
Nitzschke, Heiko, 76, 85, 87

nondemocracies, 6, 67, 149

non-state actors, 54, 75, 84, 118, 193, 241, 243, 245, 254–56, 270

nonviolence, 34, 42, 183, 255, 260

Nooruddin, Irfan, 149, 167

Nordås, Ragnhild, 31, 53, 162, 206, 226, 235

norms, 10, 53, 68, 96–98, 169, 180, 192–93, 198–99, 203, 208–9, 246

Northern Ireland, 20, 193

Öberg, Magnus, 31, 112, 117, 264, 266

observers, 32, 42, 233, 268

office, 41, 105, 112, 127–28, 182, 254

oil, 11, 37, 62, 104, 126, 153, 215–18, 220–22, 224–25, 228, 233, 240, 264; dependence, 248–49; exports, 11, 222; fields, 216, 226, 229, 263; producers, 215, 221–22; reserves, 11, 222, 225; wealth, 216, 222, 227, 229

O'Loughlin, John, 77, 236

Olsen, Tricia, 185, 187, 190, 193, 268

Olson, Mancur, 68, 167

Oneal, John, 25, 249–50, 264

opponents, 21, 66–67, 125, 131, 160–61, 179, 188, 203

opportunity costs, 5, 37–38, 105, 170, 217, 264

opposition, 67, 102, 147, 179, 184, 186, 254; groups, 81, 110, 113, 253, 255

organizations, 12, 28, 52, 56, 122, 135, 145, 197, 206–7, 245, 247, 249, 253, 255–56, 259–60, 270; ethnopolitical, 206, 255; insurgent, 112, 114; intergovernmental, 97, 113; nongovernmental, 113, 151, 173; regional, 119, 148; structures, 35, 52, 124, 135, 249, 259

Østby, Gudrun, 226, 244

othering, 200–201, 203, 207–8, 212

Ottmann, Martin, 132–33, 144

outbreak, 2, 33, 39, 54, 144, 148, 194, 220, 248, 259

outcomes, 2, 4, 6–8, 11–12, 32, 36, 40, 50, 60, 70, 75–76, 83, 88, 93–95, 97, 99–109, 111–12, 117, 119, 122–25, 144, 147–48, 151, 153, 156, 158, 161, 163, 167, 173–74, 181, 189–90, 193–95, 198–99, 223, 228, 233, 242, 253–55, 263, 265

overthrow, 3–4, 27, 80, 141, 266

Pakistan, 3, 17, 25, 32, 46, 70, 159

Palestine, 20, 116, 141, 172, 266

Paris, Roland, 142, 153, 180

Parkinson, Sarah, 53, 56

participants, 37, 141, 203–4, 257, 264

participation, 5, 10, 50–51, 53, 187, 203–4, 207–9, 212–13, 221, 255; political, 69, 127, 136

parties, 15–16, 70, 85, 87, 89, 95, 110, 112–13, 121–24, 126–29, 131–32, 135, 137, 141, 143, 146, 151–52, 160, 241, 268; combatant, 110, 118; political, 29, 146, 149, 185; third, 66, 88, 95, 97–101, 104–5, 110–12, 115–17, 137, 143, 146–47

Patrinos, Harry, 166, 169

patrons, 99, 101, 107–8

patterns, 1–2, 4, 23, 47–48, 51, 53, 62, 73, 75, 89, 94, 114, 121, 182, 186, 197, 199, 201–3, 205, 211, 213, 224, 235, 237–38, 244

Payne, Leigh, 20, 185, 187, 190, 192–93, 268

peace, 3–4, 7–12, 18, 32, 34, 46, 55, 63, 67–68, 71, 77, 86–89, 91, 100, 108–9, 111, 113, 116, 119–27, 129–37, 139, 145–47, 152–55, 180, 187, 191–92, 194, 198–200, 203, 207–11, 213, 234, 246, 248–49, 262, 266–68; accords, 65, 119, 135; agreements, 2, 5, 8–9, 16, 18, 29, 60, 65–67, 88, 100, 109–10, 113–16, 118–21, 124, 126, 134–35, 137, 140, 143–44, 152, 154, 184, 187, 194, 265–66; democratic, 66, 68, 264; durability, 8, 10, 76, 117, 119, 121–23, 125, 131, 140, 142–44, 152, 156, 158, 181, 194, 267; duration, 123, 131, 133, 140, 147, 154, 194, 267; processes, 87, 104, 113, 115, 118, 136; settlements, 87, 110, 114, 116–17, 130, 132–35, 137; women, 199–200, 203, 207–8, 212 peacebuilding, 145, 148–53, 155, 267; missions, 139, 151, 153; operations, 140, 150, 156

peacekeepers, 95–97, 100, 140–47, 150–51, 153, 155–57, 183, 257, 268

peacekeeping, 19, 111, 117, 119, 139–48, 151–56, 209, 252, 257, 267–68; democratization, 140, 151, 156; efforts, 111, 119–20, 151; forces, 97, 116, 125–26, 139, 145, 148, 152–55, 209; impact of, 140, 148, 154, 267; missions, 88, 145–46, 150, 153, 155, 171, 181; operations, 9, 139–41, 143–48, 150–56, 194, 267; studies of, 139, 142, 154; success, 120, 147, 155

peacemaking, 19, 87, 120, 212

Peksen, Dursen, 63, 65

perceptions, 30, 51, 63, 107, 134, 137

perspectives, 36, 50, 53, 106, 108, 137, 202, 208–9, 246, 266; rationalist, 50, 114; theoretical, 60, 259

Peru, 4, 173, 181, 185, 256

Pettersson, Thérése, 16–17, 21, 24, 84

phases, 2, 4, 18, 108, 141–42, 147, 267

phenomena, 2, 11, 19, 34, 47, 56, 70, 75, 96, 98–99, 118, 140, 203, 210, 214, 235, 264

Philippines, 4, 16, 19, 23, 42, 86, 126, 165

Phillips, Brian, 167, 170

physical capital, 165–66, 168–69

Pickering, Jeffrey, 105, 152

Pinker, Steven, 20–22

PITF (Political Instability Task Force), 31, 234

Plümper, Thomas, 22, 53, 206

Poe, Steven, 179, 258, 268–69

Poland, 46, 233

polarization, 46–47, 53, 244–45

police, 50, 61, 64, 171–72, 179

policing, 52–53, 69, 218

policy makers, 38, 42, 95, 97, 99, 107–8, 156–58, 166, 171, 174, 193, 215, 228

political change, 56, 68, 180, 242

political institutions, 51, 65, 73, 184, 187, 194, 235, 237–38, 259, 268

political power, 4, 116, 128–29, 132–34, 226, 267

political process, 51, 60, 70, 110, 187

political systems, 11, 68, 77, 105–6

political violence, 34–36, 41, 43–44, 48, 69, 74, 139, 187–88, 193, 211–13, 233, 247–48, 256, 262

politicide, 29, 31, 34

politics, 30, 43, 175, 194, 227–29, 256, 258; contentious, 197, 206, 213; domestic, 54, 95, 98, 104–6; international, 96, 215, 223

population, 3, 11, 16, 25, 38–39, 41, 46–47, 61–64, 68–70, 73, 102–3, 132, 136, 145, 160–61, 171, 206, 232–33, 237–41, 244–45, 251–53; local, 146, 156, 237, 239

Portugal, 16, 160, 185

Posner, Daniel, 47, 56

Pospieszna, Paulina, 59–60, 63, 112–13, 117, 266

post-conflict, 2, 9–11, 55, 65, 88, 119, 121, 126, 136, 140–41, 143–44, 148–49, 151, 153, 156, 168, 180, 214, 240, 267; contexts, 139, 142–43, 147–50, 153–55, 267; justice, 188, 191; states, 131, 134, 136, 139, 181, 191

post-war, 9–10, 132, 149–50, 153, 157, 169, 172–75, 181, 183–84, 187, 190–91, 195, 206; countries, 2, 166, 174; peace, 9, 123, 147, 174, 180–81, 183, 186, 189–94, 268; recovery, 170, 174

poverty, 3, 5, 22–23, 38, 209, 251, 265

Powell, Robert, 50, 67, 100, 266

power, 1, 8–9, 23, 29, 34, 41, 49, 51–52, 55, 59–61, 63, 67, 73, 84, 87, 95–98, 100, 102, 106, 115, 121, 123–28, 130–37, 144, 146, 149, 160, 167, 179, 186–88, 199, 201, 208, 211–12, 248–50, 262, 264, 266–69; territorial, 9, 116, 128, 132–33, 267

power-sharing, 132–33, 136–37; institutions, 125–37; measures, 121, 128, 132–33, 136–37

predation, 33, 37–38, 85, 103, 236

preferences, 70, 98, 104–7, 114, 116, 141, 149, 153, 192–93, 219

presidents, 41, 106, 128, 179, 213, 235

primary commodities, 37, 217, 221, 240, 269

primordialist, 49, 55

PRIO (Peace Research Institute Oslo), 12, 17, 20–21, 25, 35, 248, 252

PRIO/Uppsala Armed Conflict Database, 190–91, 251

privilege, 37, 42, 200–201, 245; male, 200, 202, 213

problems, 42, 45, 50, 68, 72, 88, 105, 120, 135, 139, 141, 144, 146–47, 164, 166, 172, 174, 181, 189, 191, 205, 210, 213, 221–24, 226, 235, 237, 239, 241–43, 250, 253, 255, 258, 262, 264–65, 269; endogeneity, 222, 226, 242

processes, 5, 10, 12, 34, 36–37, 39–41, 57, 61, 64, 78, 80, 82–83, 87–88, 96–97, 100, 108–10, 115, 117, 123–26, 139–40, 142, 149–51, 155, 166, 170–71, 180–82, 188, 190, 192–95, 212, 227, 245, 258, 265; democratic, 149–50, 183; dynamic, 41, 248

production, 34, 36, 64, 66, 128, 166, 168, 210, 222–23, 226, 264, 269

profit, 86, 89, 133, 174, 219

promises, 51, 56, 132–33, 224, 227, 229

property, 45–47, 63, 239, 243–45; rights, 63, 238, 240, 244

Prorok, Alyssa, 1, 254

prosecutions, 181–84, 188–89

protection, 52, 61, 134, 144, 238

protests, 12, 47, 179, 207, 213, 242, 245, 248–49, 255, 257

provisions, 65–66, 123–24, 128, 131–32, 135, 137, 140, 143, 149, 184, 187, 218, 264

proxy wars, 84–85, 98–99, 103

psychology, 10, 56, 163, 169, 182, 199, 201–2, 205

PTS (Political Terror Scale), 190, 269

public opinion, 103, 105, 146

Pugh, Michael, 76, 85, 151

punishment, 62, 116, 182, 187

purges, 181–82, 184, 192

pursuit, 53, 127, 180–81, 195

puzzles, 2, 38–39, 101, 103–6, 108, 247

quality, 62–63, 120, 132, 134, 136, 147, 227, 230, 237; institutional, 106, 227, 237; regulatory, 63, 134

rainfall, 232, 235–37, 242–45

rape, 10, 53, 156–57, 162–63, 171, 183

Rasler, Karen, 40–41

rate, 28, 32, 65, 79, 93–94, 158, 163, 167–68, 171, 203, 206, 232, 240, 258–59

rebel groups, 4, 7, 12, 16, 23, 27, 29, 33, 35–37, 54, 67, 75–76, 81, 84–87, 99, 101–2, 104, 114–15, 118, 123, 141, 169, 193, 204, 219, 221, 225, 248, 253–57, 259, 270; characteristics of, 12, 252, 254; leaders, 4, 94, 194, 219, 225; military strength, 101, 104; military victory, 61, 102; multiple, 12, 175; troops, 126, 130; weak, 99, 115

rebellion, 3–4, 37–39, 47, 50–51, 53, 62, 69, 81, 85, 102, 170, 209, 217–18, 220, 224–25, 229–30, 246, 248, 262, 264; movements, 4, 6, 10, 26, 48, 99, 101–2, 117, 204, 225, 249

rebel organizations, 108, 110, 114–15, 118, 160, 209, 224–25, 250, 258; nascent, 7, 93, 102

rebels, 3–8, 12, 27, 34–35, 37–40, 44, 50–53, 61, 65, 67, 81, 84, 93, 98–101, 103, 105, 107, 109, 115–16, 130, 149, 160, 162, 165, 184, 188, 209, 217, 220, 224–26, 239, 249, 254–55, 258, 263–64; potential, 7, 61, 64, 170, 223; victories, 2, 7–8, 61, 93, 100, 123

reconciliation, 10, 55, 115, 180–82, 185, 188-89, 191-92, 195, 269

recruitment, 51, 53, 108, 165, 169, 224, 245

recruits, 38, 50, 61, 88, 160, 220, 224–25

recurrence, 4, 54–55, 60, 65, 115, 122, 136, 158, 174, 184–85, 188, 194–95, 197, 262; civil war, 183–85, 188, 192

reforms, 60, 63, 194, 244; institutional, 188, 193–94

refugees, 23, 34, 78–79, 142, 157, 163, 171–72, 206, 239, 265; camps, 79, 171; fleeing, 34, 170, 265; flows, 7, 76, 79, 87, 97, 161, 163, 171; host, 163, 171

Regan, Patrick, 7, 69, 88, 93–97, 100–101, 106, 111–13, 117, 119, 158, 263, 266–67

regimes, 3–4, 6, 17, 19, 27, 33, 39, 41–42, 68–70, 73, 75, 84, 87, 108, 182, 184, 186–87, 192, 245, 264; democratic, 64, 67; political, 9, 139; repressive, 33, 42, 108, 182, 187; type, 6, 39, 59–61, 63, 65–74, 81, 103, 184, 191, 221, 254, 264–65

regions, 3, 5, 11, 23, 25, 27, 41–42, 76–77, 82–83, 85, 99, 128, 136, 167, 170, 185, 216–17, 219, 224–26, 232, 238, 240–41, 255

reintegration, 88, 104, 143, 150, 173

relationship, 2, 11, 38, 46, 54, 65–66, 68–69, 71–72, 74, 108, 121, 131, 134, 162, 193, 195, 198–99, 208–10, 212, 215, 218, 222–23, 227–28, 232, 235–37, 240–43, 246, 250–52, 254, 256, 263; causal, 69, 210, 231–32, 238, 241, 243, 267; complex, 53, 231; endogenous, 158, 228, 246

religion, 25–26, 37–38, 45–49, 52, 54, 56–57, 99, 169, 203, 263–64, 266, 268; identities, 43–46, 51, 53, 209

remittances, 167, 171

RENAMO, 84, 239

reparations, 181–82, 184, 188, 192, 269

repatriation, 87, 142

representation, 52, 66, 127, 208–9, 223, 250–51, 259

repression, 5, 33–34, 36, 39–42, 44, 47, 51, 59, 61, 70, 108, 149, 179, 185–87, 204, 221, 256–57, 262–63, 270

reputation, 99, 111, 142

resolution, 8, 89, 109–11, 113, 115, 117, 119, 142, 197, 212, 246–47, 253, 259, 265

resource curse, 2, 11, 215–17, 220, 222–23, 226, 228, 261, 264

resources, 11, 38, 53, 64, 66–69, 73, 76, 83–87, 89, 96–97, 100, 126, 128, 144, 149, 152, 170, 172, 188, 202, 215–21, 223–25, 227–29, 233–34, 240, 244, 248, 258–59, 265, 269; abundance, 223, 229, 235, 244, 277; nonrenewable, 215, 235; renewable, 233, 242; scarcity, 231–32, 235, 242, 245–46; sectors, 217, 221, 228; wealth, 67, 216–18, 220–24, 226–29, 269

responsibility, 97, 108, 145, 152, 181, 226, 257

revenge, 37, 52, 188, 192, 232

revenues, 5, 11, 62–63, 126, 165–66, 170, 217–18, 221; commodity, 217, 221; extraction, 62–63; tax, 6, 64

revolution, 2–4, 6, 22, 27, 36, 47, 61, 64, 107–8, 216, 245, 262

Reynal-Querol, Marta, 47, 54, 159, 163, 167

Richardson, Lewis Fry, 80, 247, 250

rights, 113, 125, 188, 208–9, 211, 220, 264; human, 179, 183, 186, 190–91; physical integrity, 134, 194, 269; women's, 194–95, 264

riots, 12, 44, 244–45, 248, 257

risk, 1, 5–11, 17, 39–40, 47, 51, 63–64, 66, 68–70, 77, 81–82, 84, 87–88, 95, 103, 107, 127, 132, 139, 144–45, 149–50, 183–85, 187, 208–9, 217–20, 223, 225, 236, 241, 246, 249, 251, 264–65, 268; civil war, 107, 184–85, 188, 195

rivals, 8, 30, 45, 54, 98–99, 107, 110, 122, 125–27, 131, 144, 149, 216

Robinson, James, 67, 169, 237

Roeder, Philip, 47, 55, 133

Ross, Michael, 11, 37–38, 50, 100, 215–17, 219–23, 225, 227, 264

Rothchild, Donald, 55, 66, 76, 80–81, 87, 128, 133, 170

Rowlands, Dane, 96, 98, 100

Rudolfsen, Ida, 17–19, 21, 25–26

Ruggeri, Andrea, 69, 72, 119

Rummel, Rudolph, 29, 34

rural areas, 231, 239, 258

Russett, Bruce, 21–22, 25, 76, 161–62, 167, 170, 249, 264

Russia, 23, 32, 43, 50, 113, 240, 248

Rutter, Michael, 157, 163

Rwanda, 4, 29, 31, 44, 49–50, 84, 87, 97–98, 100, 149, 162–63, 165, 171, 182, 224, 233, 239, 248, 269

Rwandan Patriotic Front (RPF), 4, 100

Sachs, Jeffrey, 217, 221
safe havens, 7, 64, 76
Saideman, Stephen, 54, 80, 98–99, 106
Salehyan, Idean, 12, 34, 54, 76, 79–80, 82, 84–85, 96–99, 102–4, 118, 171, 236–39, 247–48, 250–52, 254, 256–58, 260
Sambanis, Nicholas, 32, 35, 38, 49–51, 55, 57, 66, 69, 76–77, 79, 82, 111, 123, 143, 146, 152, 154, 219–21, 226, 253, 261, 263, 266
sample, 41, 112, 117, 123, 189, 191, 204, 206, 213, 219, 227, 235–36, 238, 255
sanctions, 86, 89, 96, 119, 142; economic, 111–12, 120
sanctuaries, 23, 84, 96, 98, 103, 170
Sandler, Todd, 76, 79, 97, 167, 170, 270
Sarkees, Meredith, 1, 35, 118, 199, 248
Savun, Burcu, 119, 123, 131, 267
SCAD (Social Conflict in Africa Database), 12, 257
scarcity, 11, 79, 157, 231, 233, 235–36, 244; environmental, 234, 246
schools, 122, 157, 163–67, 169, 172, 174
Schrodt, Philip, 263, 270
secession, 2–3, 6, 17, 20, 26–27, 35, 55, 141, 174, 217, 221
security, 55, 60–61, 63, 85, 99–100, 106–7, 110, 115–16, 118, 123, 125–26, 131, 136, 161–62, 173, 236; dilemma, 51–52, 55, 131
self-determination, 52, 255
separatist groups, 27, 44, 51, 80
Serbia, 183
services, 62–64, 85, 156, 182, 240, 264
settlements, 33, 50, 52, 54, 67, 87–89, 101, 110, 113–14, 116–17, 121–26, 129–37, 140, 143, 146, 247, 252–53, 267
severity, 15, 20–21, 23, 31–32, 35, 81, 194, 241, 243, 245, 261
sexual violence, 10, 31–32, 53, 158, 185, 205–6, 213, 258; conflict-related, 205–6, 261
Seymour, Lee, 43–44, 46, 48, 50, 52, 54, 56
al-Shabaab, 231
Shannon, Megan, 8, 109–10, 112, 114, 116, 118–20, 157, 171, 257

Shayo, Moses, 49, 51, 57
Shellman, Stephen, 34, 40, 239, 253
Shemyakina, Olga, 165, 168
Sherman, Jake, 38, 85, 89
shocks, 108, 241, 244–45; economic, 168, 243–45; environmental, 241, 244
Sierra Leone, 38, 77, 86, 88, 128, 141, 163, 169, 181, 188, 216
Sikkink, Kathryn, 180, 184, 187, 189–90, 192, 269
Simmons, Beth, 80, 265
Singer, J. David, 35, 64, 248
Sisk, Timothy, 116, 151–52
Siverson, Randolph, 105, 163, 250
Skocpol, Theda, 59–60, 64, 262
Smith, Alastair, 69, 95, 97, 142
Smith, Benjamin, 11, 215–16, 218, 220–22, 224, 226–30, 237, 243, 263
Snyder, Jack, 38, 149–51, 153, 180
Sobek, David, 6, 54, 59–62, 64, 66, 68, 70, 72, 74, 94, 263
social capital, 149, 169, 171, 209
social networks, 46, 49, 53, 86
societies, 2, 9–11, 39, 43, 45, 47, 49–50, 56, 81, 96, 118, 132, 181, 194, 197–203, 207, 209, 212–13, 238, 241
soldiers, 23, 148, 162, 213, 267
Sollenberg, Margareta, 79, 83, 264
Somalia, 25, 36, 45–46, 56, 65, 152, 167, 231, 270
South Africa, 42, 85, 87, 107, 110, 182, 185
Southeast Asia, 159, 227
South Sudan, 3, 43, 65, 84, 88, 111, 128
sovereignty, 35, 98, 131–32
Soviet Union, 17, 20–21, 44, 46–47, 52, 84, 98–99, 105, 107–8, 111, 125, 216, 233
Spain, 20, 224, 256
spatial, 12, 41–42, 47, 77, 82, 241, 251–52, 265; clustering, 76–77, 264–65; distribution, 129, 144
spillover, 78–81, 87–88, 90
spoilers, 34, 83, 87, 141, 191
Sri Lanka, 159, 167, 204, 256
stability, 4, 19, 51, 55, 68, 70, 97–98, 111, 121–24, 127, 133, 139, 150, 152–53,

156, 170, 180–81, 193, 217, 266–67; political, 63, 215, 239

Staniland, Paul, 52–53, 56

Stanley, William, 33, 124, 167

Starr, Harvey, 39, 78, 163, 250

state capacity, 6, 38, 50, 59–67, 69–74, 81, 85, 108, 132, 137, 218–19, 227–28, 234, 238, 264; dimensions of, 6, 60; measuring, 6, 63–64, 66, 72; role of, 60, 65, 234, 249; weak, 39, 50, 62, 261

states, 2, 6–8, 10, 12, 15–16, 27, 29, 34–43, 47–48, 51–52, 54, 56, 59–67, 69, 71–75, 79–82, 84–86, 88, 94–100, 102–8, 110, 112, 119, 127–28, 139, 141, 144, 146, 149, 153, 155, 159, 161, 163, 165–67, 170, 172, 174, 179–82, 184–85, 187, 189, 192–95, 208–9, 213, 215, 217, 219, 223–26, 228, 232, 234, 237, 239, 241, 245–46, 248–50, 252–55, 261–65, 268, 270; authoritarian, 81, 107; democratic, 64, 68, 98, 107, 149, 187, 249, 264; postwar, 125, 127, 131, 173–74; strength, 127, 218, 244

status, 4, 47, 49, 87, 197, 200, 202–3, 207, 254

Stedman, Stephen, 79, 87, 97, 113, 116, 143, 172

Stromseth, Jane, 181, 269

Sub-Saharan Africa, 38, 216, 235

Sudan, 25, 84, 111, 126, 128, 141, 164–66

Sullivan, Patricia, 102–3, 105

Sundberg, Ralph, 12, 119, 213, 252, 256

Sunnis, 43, 46, 75

superpowers, 17, 21, 32, 107

Svensson, Isak, 26, 109, 116–17, 119, 137

Syria, 1, 20, 25, 34, 37, 41, 43, 45, 56, 75–76, 79, 115, 141, 146, 242, 245, 248

tactics, 40, 42, 86, 99, 102–3, 107, 116, 120, 160, 239; guerrilla, 114–15, 141, 239; nonviolent, 206–7, 255

Tajikistan, 130, 165

Tanzania, 163, 171, 244

targeting, 53, 96, 165, 171, 184, 239–40

taxation, 62–63, 65, 103, 173, 217, 240

Taydas, Zeynep, 63, 65

temperature, 232, 245

termination, 15, 28–29, 48, 174, 253–54

territory, 3, 6, 15–16, 18–19, 23, 26–28, 37, 50–51, 54, 59, 61–62, 73, 85–86, 98, 112, 115, 117, 131, 160, 179, 183, 206, 218, 220, 224–25, 233, 244, 250–52, 254

terrorism, 34, 44, 160, 254, 256–57, 262, 270

Thailand, 213

themes, 6, 32, 70, 72, 74, 131, 135, 157, 195, 220, 250

Themnér, Lotta, 34, 43, 79, 84, 88, 112, 159, 254, 270

theoretical arguments, 6, 9, 70, 139, 170, 187, 197–98, 207–8, 211–12, 249, 254, 267

Thies, Cameron, 64, 219, 223, 240

third party intervention, 7–8, 66, 88, 93, 95–97, 99–101, 103–8, 111–12, 117, 120, 249, 265, 267

Thoms, Oskar, 180, 186, 195

threats, 48–49, 70, 98, 131, 170, 187, 200

threshold, 16, 18, 20, 35, 40, 103, 112–13, 118, 134, 144, 147, 169, 190, 218, 227, 229, 256; battle-death, 34–36, 134, 243, 248

Thyne, Clayton, 9, 76, 88, 99, 102, 157–58, 160, 162, 164, 166, 168, 170, 172–74, 181, 263, 265

Tickner, Ann, 199, 201

Tilly, Charles, 35, 167, 179

Timor-Leste, 181, 185

Toft, Monica, 46, 50, 54, 103, 123, 125

tools, 42, 59, 81, 94, 108, 110, 112, 120, 165, 168, 245

topics, 2, 10, 70, 96, 105, 108, 135–37, 183, 219, 227, 247, 262

torture, 179, 185, 269

trade, 79, 83, 85–86, 216, 240; illicit, 86–87, 89; networks, 76, 86, 89

tradition, 40, 47, 75, 169, 211, 232, 263, 267

transition, 86, 107, 237, 265

transitional justice (TJ), 2, 10, 137, 179–81, 184–95, 262, 268; effects, 181, 183, 187, 189–90, 192, 194–95; institutions, 2, 10, 181–82, 185, 192,

195; mechanisms, 10, 181–86, 188–89, 193–94

transnational, 23, 51, 54, 80, 85, 98, 104, 248, 254, 265; dimensions of civil war, 7, 75–76, 78, 82–83, 85–86, 89–90, 254, 262

trials, 180–85, 187, 189–90, 192–94

tribunals, 10, 181, 189, 191

troops, 84, 90, 119–20, 143, 154, 165, 252

Trumbore, Peter, 98–99

trust, 67, 73, 143, 150–51, 169, 211

truth commissions, 180–82, 184–85, 187–94

Tunisia, 42, 179, 245

Turkey, 84, 224

Tutsis, 100, 128

UCDP (Uppsala Conflict Data Program), ix, 3, 12, 15–16, 18–20, 24–31, 35, 56, 84–85, 87–88, 112, 118–20, 134, 159, 241–43, 252, 254–57, 261, 270

Uganda, 49, 84, 87, 109 111, 163, 182, 231, 248

UNEP (UN Environmental Programme), 238, 240

UNESCO, 165, 172

UNHCR, 172, 206, 282

United Kingdom, 65, 113, 239

United Nations, 5, 63, 100, 113, 115–16, 119, 125, 148, 188

United States, 19–21, 33, 84, 99, 105, 107, 111, 113, 116, 125, 162, 240, 250–51, 270

units, 12, 41, 56, 75, 78, 82, 89, 104, 118–19, 141, 144, 223, 241, 248–50, 252–53, 268–69; geographic, 249, 253

Urdal, Henrik, 4–5, 15–16, 18, 20, 22, 26, 28, 30, 32, 206, 235, 264

Valentino, Benjamin, 49, 53, 103, 160, 179, 199

variables, 40, 63, 70, 72, 82, 99, 106, 134, 154, 175, 210–11, 213, 222, 226, 229, 232, 234–35, 237, 242–43, 245, 249, 253–54, 269–70; explanatory, 149, 222, 242, 269; independent, 158, 189, 208,

211, 228; instrumental, 135, 242–43, 269

Varshney, Ashutosh, 46, 52, 56, 262–63

Verwimp, Philip, 162, 165, 168, 204

victims, 10, 29, 144, 160, 165, 180–83, 187, 192, 205, 233

victory, 29, 65–66, 100–101, 103, 109, 122–23, 150, 161, 267; decisive, 8, 94, 143

Vietnam, 15, 20, 84, 99, 102–3, 105–7, 240

Vinjamuri, Leslie, 180, 184–85, 187, 190–91, 194

violence, 4, 11, 17, 20, 22, 29, 35, 38, 41, 43–44, 51, 53, 55, 69, 79, 83, 113, 119, 144, 147, 149, 153, 155, 163, 197, 204–5, 208–10, 243, 245, 248, 253, 255, 262, 267, 270; collective, 160, 209; one-sided, 29–31, 34, 241, 245; organized, 5, 30–31, 49, 110, 201, 270; preventing, 139, 142, 153; renewal of, 139, 143–48, 150–53, 156

violent, 20, 29, 34, 39, 44, 48, 51, 53, 56, 69, 80, 141, 144, 200–201, 206–7, 211, 216, 224, 232, 245, 250, 255–56, 259–60; behavior, 232, 245; challenges, 224, 234; conflict, 50, 52, 79, 141, 209, 216, 228, 236, 244, 262, 270; events, 22, 256, 258

voting, 3, 59, 151, 154, 185, 264

Vreeland, James, 69, 72, 153

vulnerability, 51, 60–61, 237

Wagner, Robert, 114, 122

Wallensteen, Peter, 16–17, 21, 24, 34–35, 43, 83, 87–89, 109, 112–13, 118, 129, 131, 159, 254, 267, 270

Walter, Barbara, 28, 34, 36, 43, 48, 50–51, 66, 81, 94, 100, 113, 115, 118, 122–23, 131, 142

war, 1, 4, 8–9, 12, 15, 18–23, 25–26, 29–37, 39–40, 43–46, 48, 50–51, 53–54, 56–57, 61, 65, 67, 70, 73, 75, 80, 83–84, 86–89, 94, 99–100, 102–9, 112–15, 117–18, 122–26, 129, 131–35, 141–42, 144–46, 148–50, 153, 157–58, 161–62, 167, 169–70, 173, 179–80, 183,

193–94, 200–203, 205–6, 211–14, 217, 219, 221, 223, 238, 242, 245, 247–49, 254, 258, 262, 266–68; actors, 89, 122, 131; duration, 54, 107–8; economies, 30, 76, 82, 84–87, 89; effort, 166, 170, 172; fighting, 23, 102–3, 105, 204–5; groups, 54–55, 85, 122, 129, 136–37; new, 30–31, 35–37, 93, 157; nuclear, 32, 84, 233; ongoing, 94, 112; onset, 5, 132, 222; outcomes, 7, 61, 64, 86, 103, 123–24, 153, 249, 256; parties, 8, 29, 83, 87, 89, 100, 110, 124–26, 153, 255; processes, 48, 51, 72, 95, 110, 259, 263, 266; renewal, 140, 143–45, 149–50, 155, 167, 185, 267; weariness, 80, 89
Ward, Michael, 17, 19, 40, 76–77, 82
warriors, 200, 203, 205, 211, 213
water, 11, 22, 211, 231, 233, 235, 239, 244–45, 269
Wayman, Frank, 1, 35, 118, 248
weak states, 5–6, 23, 26, 28, 38, 60, 62, 65, 102, 218–19, 228, 244
wealth, 4, 62–63, 66, 68–69, 71, 128, 195, 202, 222, 224, 227, 237, 239, 252–53, 268
weapons, 33, 79, 86, 88, 96, 109, 115, 126, 147, 150, 162, 166, 213
weather, 237, 245, 264
Weede, Erich, 37, 69
Weidmann, Nils, 50, 53, 251–52
Weinstein, Jeremy, 36, 38, 53, 56, 88, 173, 204, 224–25, 229–30
Werner, Suzanne, 113–14, 122, 124, 163
Whitaker, Beth, 79, 157, 171
Wiebelhaus-Brahm, Eric, 184, 190–91, 194

Wimmer, Andreas, 47, 51, 56, 219
winner, 66–67, 73, 121, 123, 142, 150–51, 161, 267
Wischnath, Gerdis, 26, 237, 245
women, 10, 53, 136, 194, 197–209, 211–12, 214; status of, 2, 10–11, 209
Wood, Elizabeth, 34, 37, 51, 53, 103, 160–61, 193, 206, 220, 229, 240, 269
Wood, Reed, 53, 103, 160–61, 193, 269
world, 1, 11, 23, 37, 43, 86, 94, 102, 107, 161, 163, 165, 180, 192, 207, 215–16, 221–22, 228, 247–48, 254, 258, 263, 270; developing, 59–60, 228
World Bank, 11, 38, 63, 151, 171, 215, 223, 226
World Health Organization (WHO), 22, 59, 161, 198
World War I, 17, 157
World War II, 1, 5, 7, 15–16, 18, 20–21, 23, 27–28, 32, 36, 93, 107, 121, 163, 167, 183, 239, 248, 261–62, 269
Wucherpfennig, Julian, 54, 135, 252, 254

Young, Joseph, 5, 33–34, 36, 38, 40, 42
youths, 41, 165, 169, 173
Yuen, Amy, 113, 122, 124
Yugoslavia, 17, 23, 25, 44, 49–50, 52, 180, 183, 185

Zaire, 87, 256
Zartman, William, 94, 100, 116
Zhukov, Yuri, 43, 103
Zimbabwe, 87, 98, 162, 193
zones, 175, 238, 242

About the Contributors

Halvard Buhaug is research professor at the Peace Research Institute Oslo (PRIO), professor of political science at the Norwegian University of Science and Technology (NTNU), and associate editor of *Journal of Peace Research*. Most of his recent work concerns security dimensions of climate change, funded by, for example, the European Union, the U.S. Department of Defense, UN OCHA, and the World Bank. Recent publications include the coauthored book *Inequality, Grievances, and Civil War* (Cambridge University Press 2013) and journal articles in, inter alia, *Global Environmental Change, International Security, Journal of Conflict Resolution, Political Geography*, and *PNAS*.

David E. Cunningham is associate professor in the Department of Government and Politics at the University of Maryland. He received his PhD in political science from the University of California, San Diego, and is an affiliate of the Peace Research Institute Oslo. He is the author of *Barriers to Peace in Civil Wars*, which was published by Cambridge University Press, as well as articles in the *American Journal of Political Science, International Organization, Journal of Conflict Resolution*, and *Journal of Peace Research*. His research focuses on civil war, conflict bargaining, conflict management, and international security.

Kathleen Gallagher Cunningham is associate professor at the University of Maryland, Department of Government and Politics, and senior researcher at the Peace Research Institute Oslo. Her work centers on civil conflict, nonviolence, self-determination and secession. Her book *Inside the Politics of Self-Determination* was published by Oxford University Press in 2014. Her work has appeared in the *American Political Science Review, American Journal of Political Science, International Studies Quarterly, Journal of Conflict Resolution, Perspectives on Politics*, and the *Journal of Peace Research*.

Jacqueline H. R. DeMeritt is associate professor of political science at the University of North Texas and the Castleberry Peace Institute. She earned her PhD from Florida State University in 2009. Her research centers on political violence, and particularly on reasons and remedies for human rights abuse. Other research interests include the application of quantitative methodology and formal theory to social scientific processes.

Karl DeRouen Jr. is professor of political science and director of the International Studies BA program at the University of Alabama. He has authored and coauthored numerous articles and chapters on civil war, mediation, diversionary use of force, foreign policy decision making, defense economics, and international political economy. His most recent books are the *Routledge Handbook of Civil Wars* (Routledge Press 2014, coedited with Edward Newman), *Introduction to Civil War* (CQ Press 2014), and *Understanding Foreign Policy Decision Making* (Cambridge University Press 2010, with Alex Mintz).

Paul F. Diehl is associate provost and Ashbel Smith Professor of Political Science at the University of Texas, Dallas. He was president of the International Studies Association for the 2015–2016 term.

Andrew Enterline is associate professor of international relations at the University of North Texas. His current research interests include externally promoted political regimes and national- and regional-level outcomes, forecasting political futures for Iraq and Afghanistan, the impact of civil war outcomes on third party domestic politics, origins of state systems and interstate behavior, and dynamic interstate conflicts. His research has appeared in such journals as *Journal of Politics*, *Foreign Policy Analysis*, *Conflict Management & Peace Science*, *Journal of Conflict Resolution*, *International Studies Perspectives*, *Journal of Peace Research*, *International Studies Quarterly*, *International Interactions*, *Political Research Quarterly*, *Foreign Policy*, and *International Security*.

Erika Forsberg (PhD 2009) is a researcher at the Department of Peace and Conflict Research, Uppsala University. Her dissertation explored different explanations for contagion effects in civil war, including transnational ethnic ties, refugee flows, and domino effects. Her research on contagion is also published in *International Interactions*, *International Studies Quarterly*, *International Studies Review*, and the *Journal of Peace Research*. Other current research interests include the determinants of external rebel support and the relationship between gender inequality and conflict.

Scott Gates is professor at the University of Oslo, Department of Political Science, and research professor at the Peace Research Institute Oslo. His research addresses issues concerning civil conflict, democratization, bureaucracy, and governance. He is the author of ten books, including *War and State-Building in Afghanistan*, Bloomsbury Press 2015. His work has appeared in the *American Political Science Review*,

American Journal of Political Science, Journal of Politics, World Development, Journal of Environmental Economics and Management, Journal of Conflict Resolution, and the *Journal of Peace Research.*

Kristian Skrede Gleditsch is professor in the Department of Government, University of Essex, and a research associate at the Peace Research Institute Oslo (PRIO). His research interests include conflict and cooperation, democratization, and spatial dimensions of social and political processes. Recent publications include *Inequality, Grievances, and Civil War* (2013, with Lars-Erik Cederman and Halvard Buhaug) and articles in the *American Political Science Review, International Organization, International Studies Quarterly, Journal of Peace Research,* and *World Politics.*

Nils Petter Gleditsch is research professor at the Peace Research Institute Oslo and professor emeritus at the Norwegian University of Science and Technology. He is former president of the International Studies Association and a member of the Royal Norwegian Society of Sciences and Letters and the Norwegian Academy of Science and Letters. He was awarded the Award for Outstanding Research of the Research Council of Norway in 2009 and the Lifetime Achievement Award of the Conflict Processes Section, American Political Science Association in 2011.

Caroline A. Hartzell is professor in the political science department at Gettysburg College and the editor of *Conflict Management and Peace Science.* Her research focuses on the termination of civil wars and the effects power-sharing institutions have had on the duration and quality of the peace. Her work has appeared in journals including the *American Journal of Political Science, International Organization, Journal of Conflict Resolution, Journal of Peace Research,* and *World Politics.*

Cullen Hendrix is associate professor at the Josef Korbel School of International Studies, University of Denver, and nonresident senior fellow at the Peterson Institute for International Economics. At Korbel, he leads the Environment, Food and Conflict (ENFOCO) Lab, which leverages collaborations between physical and social scientists and policy makers to produce scholarship on issues at the intersection of the environment, food security, and conflict. His work has been supported by the National Science Foundation, the U.S. Department of Defense Minerva Initiative, and the Smith-Richardson Foundation. His coauthored book, *Confronting the Curse: The Economics and Geopolitics of Natural Resource Governance,* was published in 2014.

Jacob D. Kathman is associate professor in the Department of Political Science at State University of New York, Buffalo. He studies issues of civil war, third party intervention, United Nations peacekeeping, and violence against civilians. He has published research in numerous journals including the *American Political Science Review, American Journal of Political Science,* and the *Journal of Politics.*

Christopher Linebarger is visiting assistant professor at the National Security Studies Institute (NSSI) at the University of Texas, El Paso. His work is on the international dynamics of civil conflict, third party intervention, social unrest, and African political violence. His work has appeared in *International Interactions, Studies in Comparative International Development,* and *Foreign Policy Analysis.*

T. David Mason is the Johnie Christian Family Professor of Peace Studies and Regents Professor of Political Science at the University of North Texas. He directs UNT's Peace Studies Program and cofounded UNT's Castleberry Peace Institute, which he directed from its inception in 2009 until 2014. He served as associate editor of *International Studies Quarterly* (2004–2007) and then editor-in-chief (2007–2008) of that journal. Mason served on the American Political Science Association's Task Force on Political Violence. He is the author of *Caught in the Crossfire: Revolution, Repression and the Rational Peasant* (Rowman & Littlefield 2004), *Sustaining the Peace after Civil War* (Strategic Studies Institute 2007) and coeditor *of Conflict Prevention and Peace-Building in Post-War Societies: Sustaining the Peace* (with James Meernik, Routledge 2006). His research on the politics of reform, repression, and civil conflict has appeared in a number of journals.

Erik Melander is professor at the Department of Peace and Conflict Research and director of the Uppsala Conflict Data Program, Uppsala University. He is also adjunct research professor at the Joan B. Kroc Institute for International Peace Studies, Notre Dame University. His articles have been published in journals such as *European Journal of International Relations, International Interactions, International Studies Quarterly, Journal of Cold War Studies, Journal of Conflict Resolution, Journal of Gender Studies,* and *Journal of Peace Research.*

Sara McLaughlin Mitchell is professor of political science and department chair at the University of Iowa. She received her PhD in political science at Michigan State University in 1997 and her BS degree in economics and political science at Iowa State University in 1991. She is author of *Domestic Law Goes Global: Legal Traditions and International Courts* (Cambridge University Press 2011), *Guide to the Scientific Study of International Processes* (Wiley-Blackwell 2012), *The Triumph of Democracy and the Eclipse of the West* (Palgrave Macmillan 2013), and *Conflict, War, and Peace: An Introduction to Scientific Research* (CQ Press/Sage 2013); she has edited several special journal issues, and she has published more than thirty journal articles and book chapters. She is the recipient of several major research awards from the Department of Defense, National Science Foundation, and the United States Agency for International Development. Her areas of expertise include international conflict and political methodology. Professor Mitchell is cofounder of the Journeys in World Politics workshop, a mentoring workshop for junior women studying international relations. She received the Faculty Scholar Award (2007–2010), the Collegiate Scholar

Award (2011), and the Graduate College Outstanding Faculty Mentor Award (2012) from the University of Iowa. She is currently president of the Peace Science Society.

Alyssa K. Prorok is assistant professor of political science at the University of Iowa. She received her PhD from the University of Maryland in 2013 and was a predoctoral fellow at the Brookings Institution during the 2012–2013 academic year. Her current research examines leadership in civil conflict processes, the treatment of civilian populations during war, territorial conflict and disputes, and the role of international law in both civil and interstate conflict. She has published on these topics in the *American Journal of Political Science*, the *Journal of Politics*, and the *Journal of Conflict Resolution*.

Idean Salehyan is associate professor of political science at the University of Texas, Dallas. He is also the codirector of the Social Conflict Analysis Database, which tracks social and political unrest in Africa and Latin America. His research focuses on civil conflict, international migration, protest movements, and environmental security. He is the author of *Rebels without Borders: Transnational Insurgencies in World Politics* (Cornell University Press 2009), and his articles appear in journals such as the *American Journal of Political Science*, *World Politics*, *International Organization*, and the *Journal of Peace Research*. Dr. Salehyan received his PhD from the University of California, San Diego, in 2006.

Lee J. M. Seymour is assistant professor of political science at the University of Amsterdam. His research interests include the politics of self-determination and separatism, and the behavior of armed groups, particularly in the Horn of Africa. His work has appeared in the *Journal of Conflict Resolution*, *Journal of Peace Research*, *Perspectives on Politics*, the *European Journal of International Relations*, and *International Security*.

Megan Shannon is assistant professor of political science at the University of Colorado, Boulder. Her research explores how international institutions mitigate violence between and within countries. She has published work in the *American Political Science Review*, *American Journal of Political Science*, and *Journal of Politics*. Her research has been supported by the Folke Bernadotte Academy of Sweden and the Kroc Institute for International Peace Studies at Notre Dame.

Benjamin Smith is research foundation professor and associate professor of political science at the University of Florida. From 2002 to 2004 he was Academy Scholar at the Harvard Academy for International and Area Studies. His first book, *Hard Times in the Lands of Plenty*, was published in 2007 by Cornell University Press. Smith's research focuses on ethnic conflicts and on the politics of resource wealth and has been published, among other venues, in *World Politics*, the *American Journal of Political Science*, *Perspectives on Politics*, *World Development*, and *Conflict Management* *and Peace Science.* It has been funded by the National Science Foundation, the Social Science Research Council, the Harry Frank Guggenheim Foundation, and the Ford Foundation.

David Sobek is associate professor of political science at Louisiana State University. He has been at LSU since 2004 and received a BA from the College of William and Mary and his MA and PhD from Pennsylvania State University. His research has appeared in the *Journal of Politics, International Studies Quarterly, Journal of Conflict Resolution, Journal of Peace Research, International Interactions,* and *Conflict Management and Peace Science,* among others. In addition, he published *The Causes of War* with Polity Press.

Clayton L. Thyne is associate professor of political science at the University of Kentucky. His research focuses on domestic conflict and instability. Specific topics include work on coups d'état, democratization, and international education policy. His most recent work has been published in the *British Journal of Political Science, Journal of Politics,* and *International Studies Quarterly.*

Henrik Urdal is research professor at the Peace Research Institute Oslo (PRIO), editor of the international bimonthly *Journal of Peace Research,* and director of the PRIO Conflict Trends project. Urdal's work on demography, environment, and conflict has appeared in journal such as *Global Environmental Change, International Studies Quarterly, Journal of Conflict Resolution, Journal of Development Studies, Journal of Peace Research,* and *Political Geography.*

Joseph K. Young is associate professor at American University with a joint appointment in the School of Public Affairs and the School of International Service. His research seeks to understand the cross-national causes and consequences of political violence. Recent work appears in *Perspectives on Politics, International Studies Quarterly, Security Studies,* and other journals.